Lecture Notes in Computer Science   8839

Commenced Publication in 1973
Founding and Former Series Editors:
Gerhard Goos, Juris Hartmanis, and Jan van Leeuwen

Kulthida Tuamsuk   Adam Jatowt
Edie Rasmussen (Eds.)

The Emergence of Digital Libraries – Research and Practices

16th International Conference
on Asia-Pacific Digital Libraries, ICADL 2014
Chiang Mai, Thailand, November 5-7, 2014
Proceedings

 Springer

Volume Editors

Kulthida Tuamsuk
Khon Kaen University
Information and Communication Department
Khon Kaen 40002, Thailand
E-mail: kultua@kku.ac.th

Adam Jatowt
Kyoto University
Graduate School of Informatics
Yoshida-Honmachi, Sakyo-ku, Kyoto 606-8501, Japan
E-mail: adam@dl.kuis.kyoto-u.ac.jp

Edie Rasmussen
The University of British Columbia
School of Library, Archive and Information Studies
Vancouver, BC, V6T 1Z1 Canada
E-mail: edie.rasmussen@ubc.ca

ISSN 0302-9743   e-ISSN 1611-3349
ISBN 978-3-319-12822-1   e-ISBN 978-3-319-12823-8
DOI 10.1007/978-3-319-12823-8
Springer Cham Heidelberg New York Dordrecht London

Library of Congress Control Number: 2014952466

LNCS Sublibrary: SL 3 – Information Systems and Application, incl. Internet/Web
and HCI

Typesetting: Camera-ready by author, data conversion by Scientific Publishing Services, Chennai, India

Printed on acid-free paper

Springer is part of Springer Science+Business Media (www.springer.com)

Preface

This volume contains the papers presented at ICADL 2014, the 16th International Conference on Asia-Pacific Digital Libraries, held during November 5–7, 2014 in Chiang Mai, Thailand. The International Conference on Asia-Pacific Digital Libraries (ICADL) constitutes a forum that brings together researchers, developers, content providers, and users in the field of digital libraries to share their research and practice. The organizers were Chiang Mai University with Khon Kaen University, Suranaree University of Technology, and Thammasat University in Thailand.

ICADL welcomes submissions in any area related to aspects of digital libraries. This year the conference theme was "The Emergence of Digital Libraries Research and Practices." The topics of the conference were divided into five areas, of which "Digital Humanities" was specifically highlighted as it is an emerging issue and the aspect of Asia-Pacific's digital humanities is quite unique and exclusive. The other topic areas included: "Services," "Contents," "Infrastructures," and "Foundations."

We were delighted to present a strong technical program at the conference as a result of the hard work by authors, reviewers, and conference organizers. We received 114 submissions of which 79 qualified for review. During the review process, each paper was evaluated by at least three different Program Committee (PC) members. On average each paper had 3.73 reviews. After careful evaluation we accepted 20 full-length papers (23.5% acceptance rate), 19 short papers, and 12 poster papers.

This year the conference included two pre-conference workshops: the Digital Meets Cultural Workshop and the Doctoral Consortium and International Workshop on Global Collaboration of Information Schools (DC-WIS2014). We are also pleased to have invited Dr. Jieh Hsiang and Dr. Akihiro Shibayama to give exciting keynote talks.

We would like to thank the authors of submitted papers and presenters as well as the conference participants for making this conference a success. We express our gratitude to the PC members and reviewers for their hard and dedicated work. We also thank the workshop and tutorial chairs and the local Organizing Committee for managing the workshops and tutorials. Lastly, this conference would not be possible without the generous help of our sponsors and supporters and the efforts of the financial chairs.

We hope that you will find these proceedings interesting and thought-provoking.

August 2014

Kulthida Tuamsuk
Adam Jatowt
Edie Rasmussen

Organization

Organizers

Department of Computer Science, Faculty of Science, Chiang Mai University
The Central Library, Chiang Mai University
Information and Communication Department, Faculty of Humanities and Social
Sciences, Khon Kaen University
School of Information Technology, Suranaree University of Technology
The Central Library, Thammasat University

General Chair

Vilas Wuwongse   Eastern Asia University, Thailand

Program Chairs

Adam Jatowt   Kyoto University, Japan
Edie Rasmussen   University of British Columbia, Canada
Kulthida Tuamsuk   Khon Kaen University, Thailand

Local Organizing Advisor

Sampan Singharajwarapan   Chiang Mai University, Thailand

Local Organizing Chairs

Churee Techawut   Chiang Mai University, Thailand
Jeerayut Chaijaruwanich   Chiang Mai University, Thailand
Wararak Pattanakiatpong   Chiang Mai University, Thailand

Publicity Chairs

Atsuyuki Morishima   University of Tsukuba, Japan
Wararak Pattanakiatpong   Chiang Mai University, Thailand

Workshop Chairs

Joseph Tennis   University of Washington, USA
Nisachol Chamnongsri   Suranaree University of Technology, Thailand

Tutorial Chairs

Hao-ren Ke   National Taiwan Normal University, Taiwan
Srichan Chancheewa   Thammasat University, Thailand
Wararak Pattanakiatpong   Chiang Mai University, Thailand

DC-WIS Chairs

Chern Li Liew   Victoria University of Wellington, New Zealand
Gobinda Chowdhury   Northumbria University, UK
Kanyarat Kwiecien   Khon Kaen University, Thailand
Kulthida Tuamsuk   Khon Kaen University, Thailand
Malee Kabmala   Khon Kaen University, Thailand
Shigeo Sugimoto   University of Tsukuba, Japan

Poster and Exhibition Chair

Chumpol Boonkhumpornpat   Chiang Mai University, Thailand

Financial Chairs

Srichan Chancheewa   Thammasat University, Thailand
Wararak Pattanakiatpong   Chiang Mai University, Thailand

Program Committee

Adam Jatowt   Kyoto University, Japan
Akira Maeda   Ritsumeikan University, Japan
Andreas Rauber   Vienna University of Technology, Austria
Antoine Doucet   Normandy University - Unicaen, France
Areerat Trongratsameethong   Chiang Mai University, Thailand
Benjamas Panyangam   Chiang Mai University, Thailand
Bhuva Narayan   Queensland University of Technology, Australia
Chao-chen Chen   National Taiwan Normal University, Taiwan
Chen Hsin-Liang   Indiana University, USA
Chern Li Liew   Victoria University of Wellington, New Zealand
Chumphol Bunknumpornpat   Chiang Mai University, Thailand
Dana Mckay   Swinburne University of Technology Library,
                                      Australia
Dion Goh   Nanyang Technological University, Singapore
Donatella Castelli   Italian National Research Council, Italy
Dong-Geun Oh   Keimyung University, South Korea
E. Rama Reddy   University of Hyderabad, India
Edie Rasmussen   University of British Columbia, Canada
Ekawit Nantajeewarawat   Thammasat University, Thailand

Namtip Wipawin	Sukhothai Thammathirat Open University, Thailand
Nei-Ching Yeh	National Taiwan University, Taiwan
Nicola Ferro	University of Padua, Italy
Nopphadol Chalortham	Silpakorn University, Thailand
P. Nieuwenhuysen	Vrije Universiteit Brussel, Belgium
Patitta Garcia	Prince of Songkhla University, Thailand
Pavel Braslavski	Ural Federal University, Russia
Ratsameetip Wita	Chiang Mai University, Thailand
Richard Furuta	Texas A&M University, USA
Sakorn Mekruksavanich	University of Phayao, Thailand
Sally Jo Cunningham	Waikato University, New Zealand
Schubert Foo	Nanyang Technological University, Singapore
Shaheen Majid	Nanyang Technological University, Singapore
Shigeo Sugimoto	University of Tsukuba, Japan
Simone Marinai	University of Florence, Italy
Sujin Butdisuwan	Mahasarakham University, Thailand
Takashi Nagatsuka	Tsurumi University, Japan
Therdsak Maitaouthong	Srinakharinwirot University, Thailand
Tipawan Silwattananusarn	Prince of Songkhla University, Thailand
Trond Aalberg	Norwegian University of Science and Technology, Norway
Tru Cao	Ho Chi Minh City University of Technology, Vietnam
Unmil Karadkar	The University of Texas at Austin, USA
Varin Chouvatat	Chiang Mai University, Thailand
Wanida Kanarkard	Khon Kaen University, Thailand
Wei-Jane Lin	National Taiwan University, Taiwan
Weining Qian	East China Normal University, China
Yan Quan Liu	Connecticut State University, USA
Yun-Ke Chang	Nanyang Technological University, Singapore

Table of Contents

Digital Preservation and Archiving

Digital Repositories and Tools

Scholarly Document Repositories

Metadata and Ontologies

Linked Data and Knowledge Sharing

Digital Books and eBooks

Digital Libraries Usage and Applications

Data Management and Classification

Information Retrieval and Search Methods

User Skills and Experiences

Poster Papers

Content Profiling for Preservation: Improving Scale, Depth and Quality

Artur Kulmukhametov[1] and Christoph Becker[1,2]

[1] Information and Software Engineering Group
Vienna University of Technology, Austria
http://www.ifs.tuwien.ac.at/dp
[2] Faculty of Information
University of Toronto, Canada
http://ischool.utoronto.ca/christoph-becker

Abstract. Content profiling in digital preservation is a crucial step that enables controlled management of content over time. However, large-scale profiling is facing a set of challenges. As data grows and gets more diverse, the only option to control it is to combine outputs of multiple characterization tools to cover the varieties of formats and extract features of interest. This cooperation of tools introduces conflicting measures and poses challenges on data quality. Sparsity and labeling conflicts make it difficult or impossible to partition, sample and analyze large metadata sets of a content profile. Without this, however, it is virtually impossible to manage heterogeneous collections reliably over time.

In this paper, we present the content profiling tool C3PO, which includes rule-based techniques and heuristics designed for conflict reduction. We conduct a set of experiments in which we assess the effect of creating such a mechanisms and rule set on the quality and effectiveness of content profiling. The results show the potential of simple conflict reduction rules to strongly improve data quality of content profiling for analysis and decision support.

Keywords: Digital Preservation, Characterization, Content Profiling, Conflict Reduction.

1 Introduction

A crucial starting point for any digital curation process is a full awareness of the set of objects at hand and an assessment of their alignment with the needs of the users, the capabilities of the organization and the evolving context of the digital ecosystem. For digital preservation, such an assessment strongly relies on mechanisms such as characterization and property extraction tools and leverages content profiling to achieve a comprehensive overview on the data held in a repository. A full awareness of data is achievable through running rich in-depth characterization which provides a nuanced view on the diversity of collections, identify risks or help understanding evolution of features. In particular, characterization enables focused preservation planning.

K. Tuamsuk et al. (Eds.): ICADL 2014, LNCS 8839, pp. 1–11, 2014.

Despite a variety of characterization tools available nowadays, there is no single tool that would cover all data types and their properties [13]. In such situations, combining several tools is the only practical approach to cover the heterogeneity of digital artefacts. This raises a new set of challenges:

Depth. Which tools can we use to address this heterogeneity, and how can we combine their output?

Quality. How do we deal with conflicting values? How can we leverage additional tools to improve the quality rather than report conflicts?

Scale. How can we effectively analyze the substantial amount of metadata that is produced when combining multiple tool results?

This paper addresses these challenges and in particular focuses on the improvement of data quality to enable in-depth profiling at scale. We describe the scalable content profiling tool C3PO and introduce a set of improvements, including a mechanism for extensible pre-processing based on a stateless rule engine as part of the gathering process that populates the database of the profiling tool. We describe an experiment on a publicly available large data set, present the resulting rule set, and assess the effect of creating such mechanisms and rule set on the quality and effectiveness of content profiling. The results demonstrate that this is a very cost-effective and robust mechanism for improving the quality of content profiles, which in turn can improve the quality of curation and preservation decisions substantially.

The remainder of this paper is organized as follows: Section 2 gives an overview of related work in characterization and content profiling. Section 3 discusses challenges during content analysis and describes the contribution to address these. Experimentation and results are presented in Section 4. Finally, Section 5 provides conclusions and a short outlook on future work.

2   Characterization and Content Profiling

Characterization is a complex process of taking measures that result in characteristics describing the properties of the content in focus. More specifically, according to [1] we can distinguish 3 aspects of characterization: *identification* of a data structure of a content by file format name and file format version, *format validation* by checking a data structure of a digital object against its format specification and *feature extraction* from characteristics of interest of the content. There is no need to consider all 3 modes of characterization only to obtain general knowledge such as the format name or version. However, deeper characterization will reveal much more detailed insight into the features and risks of a given set of digital objects.

The question arises how many properties should be considered for characterization. There are different view points on this question. From one side, it is possible to select a minimum of properties, a lowest common denominator that can be applied across any type of content. An example of such an approach may be to restrict characterization to producing format profiles [4], which are created by characterization of 2 features - a file format name and a format version.

Format profiles are used in the Registry of Open Access Repositories (ROAR), a list of open access repositories of research material. In contrast, it is also possible to purposefully consider the set of properties necessary to describe some aspects of the content.

Decision makers consider data from different aspects, depending on the context and the task at hand. While some may be interested only in volume and number of objects, others are interested in provenance or authenticity. Each aspect requires its own set of properties. For example, Hedstrom et al. [9] introduced 'significant properties' that *"affect their quality, functionality, and look-and-feel so that custodians can select appropriate methods which preserve those significant properties of digital objects that are deemed important by designated user communities"*. The significance of properties may vary in each case, depending on the context and stakeholders [6]. To define which properties are significant, a practitioner must hence possess prior knowledge derived from business goals, policies or planning. C3PO supports a variety of characterization tools and thus enable analysis of different aspects, leaving it up to the decision maker to choose the appropriate set of properties and perspective.

To expand the coverage of properties practically, the straightforward solution is to use several tools that partially characterize the content from different perspectives and provide corresponding metadata. However, combining characterization tools results may be not trivial due to differences in their output schemas, namings, encodings etc. FITS (File Information Tool Set)[1] is an example of the approach. At its core, FITS is a wrapper for other characterization tools such as Apache Tika, DROID, Exiftool, FFIdent, File Utility, Jhove and others. Based on configuration settings, FITS can have different tools run on specific file formats. Extension of tool support for FITS is possible by creating a mapping from a target tool to the FITS XML schema.

When considering data quality, the results from existing tools are far from perfect, and better tools are clearly needed [14]. There is little common understanding of how to test tools in a systematic and rigorous way. A recent experiment in the SCAPE project[2] evaluated several characterization tools [13]. Hutchins [10] describes his activity on testing file characterization tools by comparing results of the tools against each other on the publicly available Govdocs1[3]. The author also raises the issue of lacking standard ground-truth and methods, which made it impossible to check whether a single standalone tool produces correct results. The BenchmarkDP project[4] is developing an approach to generate benchmark datasets for objective, trustworthy validation of properties of characterization tools such as functional correctness [2].

Aggregation and analysis of characterization results is called **content profiling** [12]. Aggregation techniques provide an overview of the content and allow the user to access new knowledge and help explain phenomena surfacing in the

---

[1] http://www.fitstool.org
[2] http://www.scape-project.eu/
[3] http://digitalcorpora.org/corpora/files
[4] http://benchmark-dp.org/

data. Content profiling tools should support the exploration of the content by extraction and analysis of as many characteristics as desired. Rich metadata helps to better describe the content, which may bring additional benefits to preservation processes, such as a more detailed analysis of the content, better requirements specification etc.

C3PO (Clever, Crafty, Content Profiling Tool) [12] is a software tool that enables large-scale content analysis of data collections. Figure 1 describe a general content profiling workflow used in C3PO. The tool uses results from characterization of digital collection as input, aggregates them, generates a profile of a content set in an automated manner. It produces a detailed content profile describing the key properties of the collection.

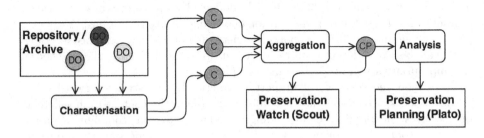

Fig. 1. Content profiling workflow adopted in C3PO

As shown in Figure 1, the workflow starts with running characterization tools on the content. The results are collected and stored by C3PO. Currently, C3PO supports the metadata schema of FITS. C3PO uses MongoDB[5], a scale-out NoSQL solution with sharded cluster calculations and map-reduce support. The content profile generated by C3PO is used in digital preservation tools such as Scout[6] [7] and Plato[7]. Built with an easily extensible architecture, C3PO may be enriched with support for new tools, processing and storing metadata through implementing well-documented APIs. C3PO runs analytical queries to calculate a range of statistics from the size of a collection to distributions of different properties in the collection. The combination of such statistics form a content profile. Basic interactive analytics features are accessible through a web-application. C3PO provides facilities for data export and further analysis of the content, such as helpful visualizations and querying the content characterization results, partitioning the metadata into homogeneous sets based on any captured characteristic selected, and generating representative samples.

The results of content profiling will differ depending on properties chosen for aggregation. For example, we may have a distribution of the MIME-type property values of the collection as in Figure 2. Sometimes it is also necessary to

---

[5] http://www.mongodb.org/
[6] http://openplanets.github.io/scout/
[7] http://ifs.tuwien.ac.at/dp/plato/

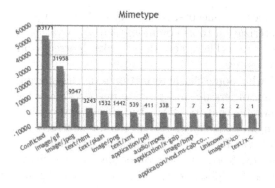

Fig. 2. MIME type property value distribution of the collection

for specific characteristics, for example to classify PDF 1.2 documents according to the applications which created them to identify documents at risk.

A crucial task within content profiling is generating representative samples. Sampling is a process of picking digital objects which represent the whole collection based on certain criteria. For example, sampling may help describe file format name distribution of a collection by picking samples from the 4 most popular format names. Sampling enables controlled experimentation without the need to use the entire collection. Representative samples, the metadata and the digital objects themselves can be used for further experiments without dealing with the collection. This is extremely important in case the collection is of a huge size and you have to run planning process, where preservation workflows should be evaluated on the dataset. Having representative samples, it is possible to test workflows on these samples and have reasonable confidence in their behavior on the entire set without expensive experimentation setup. However, without tool support, criteria have often been based on intuition, prone to individual bias and not based on an understanding of the technical variety of content [3].

Limitations of combining characterization and content profiling emerge from their nature. Most importantly, the overall data quality is dependent on the quality of characterization. If characterization tools do not return correct results, it is not possible for content profiling to provide correct data analysis and insight. However, combining multiple tools should allow us to improve the quality provided the right mechanisms are in place.

3   Challenges and Contribution

While combining metadata from the tools, conflicts will arise in identifying a correct value for a property. This may happen due to several reasons. We group them in 3 overall categories:

No Common Vocabulary. A common problem among tools in the absence of agreed terminology has been the introduction of proprietary vocabulary, giving new names to concepts, properties and their possible values. For example, characterization tools commonly supply a variety of different labels for the TIFF format. These can all be called 'correct', but pose challenges for further processing.

Specificity of Tools. Some characterization tools may perform on specific content better then others do and provide deeper knowledge. For example, 2 tools report on a file that its MIME type is either "application/xhtml+xml" or "application/xml". Such two results could be deemed completely different, when, in reality, the former is a refinement of the latter.

Conflicting Results. Tools provide competing characterization results, i.e. tool A says a file is a PDF document, while tool B says the file is a TIFF image.

This list is not exhaustive. A deeper classification of reasons of conflicts can be found in [5]. The authors run a case study to analyze the nature of digital object properties that were captured in different preservation institutions.

Apart from these peculiarities, a challenge arises regarding scalable data processing. As the sizes of collections in institutions are increasingly measured in petabytes, traditional methods and database systems are hardly applicable. Doing analytics on such collections becomes more complex, takes more time and requires scalable approaches.

It is also important to note that representative sampling is a challenging task. In order to capture the technical variation in the set of objects, samples should be representative according to more than one dimension. Current tool support for this is scarce, and the quality of input data will limit the sampling accuracy.

To address the given challenges we used and extended the functionality of C3PO by adding the following features:

Rule-Based Engine. As part of the gathering step, once a characterisation result is read by C3PO, the metadata is processed by a plug-in based on the Drools framework before storing in a database. Drools[8] is a business rule management system with a rule engine based on the Rete algorithm[8]. It allows to create an extensible set of human written rules to solve a broad range of business tasks including conflict reduction. Further, this section describes the rules created for conflict reduction.

Vocabulary. Properties stored in C3PO are mapped to the existing vocabulary, PW Ontology[9] [11]. It defines a common list of measures that may help to describe digital preservation context and is used in preservation tools Plato and Scout.

Characterisation Tool Support. Apache Tika[10] was added to the list of supported tools. This allows running fast format identification before doing

---

[8] http://www.jboss.org/drools/
[9] http://purl.org/dp/quality/measures
[10] http://tika.apache.org/

fully featured and time-consuming characterisation with FITS. Having results from different tools, C3PO is capable to consolidate them to provide more details.

Aggregation Mode. Although MongoDB is a well-recommended database solution for working with large-scale data, it requires some technical background in order to setup a cluster with appropriate data sharding settings. As an alternative we have added a new processing mode, called *DirectProfile* and available in C3PO starting from version 0.5. In this mode, data is processed on the fly without entering a database. C3PO iteratively reads characterisation outputs and accumulates metadata statistics in memory. This allows incremental content profiling with small footprint. Interactive querying and filtering is not applicable in this mode.

When creating a new rule, it must contain 4 elements: name, priority (a number from 0 to 1000), when- and then- clauses. The last 2 elements define correspondingly a list of conditions when a rule should be triggered and actions occurred on a trigger event. Within this work, we have created a list of rules, presented in Table 1. These rules address conflicts in govdocs1 processed by FITS version 0.6.2 and are available in C3PO starting from version 0.5.

Table 1. Identified conflicts per property

Rule ID	Treated property	Target tool	Rule description
1	mimetype, format	Droid	if Droid will report a file format is "Microsoft Powerpoint Presentation", but Exiftool will not report a MIME-type "PPT/S", ignore this identification (Droid alone has false positives on "Microsoft Powerpoint Presentation"). This is a pre-cleaning step to remove wrong mimetypes or formats
2	mimetype	Exiftool, Droid, all	if Exiftool and Droid will both report a file format "Microsoft Powerpoint Presentation", ignore others (format and mimetype), because if the first two tools agree, then the identification is correct
3	format	Exiftool, Droid, all	if Exiftool and Droid will both report a file format "Microsoft Powerpoint Presentation", ignore others (format and mimetype), because if the first two tools agree, then the identification is correct
4	mimetype, format	Jhove, Droid, all	If Jhove and Droid will both report a file mimetype "application/xhmtl", ignore others, because if the first two tools agree, then the identification is correct
5	mimetype, format	Jhove, all	If Jhove will report a file mimetype "text/html" and some other tools will report the file mimetype "application/xhtml+xml", ignore the "text/html" mimetype and the corresponding format
6	format	Jhove, all	If Jhove will report a file format "HTML Transitional" and other tools will claim it to be "Hypertext Markup Language" at least 2 times, "Hypertext Markup Language" is used
7	author	Exiftool, all	If Exiftool will mention file author, ignore others, because Exiftool is correct

4 Experiments

C3PO conflict resolution capabilities were tested on a publicly available data set, govdocs1, which contains approximately 1 million files. For the experiment, we obtain characterization results from running FITS version 0.6.2 on the corpus.

Next, we split the data in 2 parts: first part with 100000 files and second part with 900000 files. The first part is used as a training set, for which conflict resolution rules are created and verified. Testing of the rules is done on the second part of the data. This will shed light on how wide and general the rules can be applied in real world cases.

Firstly, the training set was analysed using C3PO. C3PO reported less amount of processed data, which may happen due to imperfection and bugs in code base of C3PO and FITS. The analysis revealed conflicts in properties identified and reported by FITS. For the experiment, we selected 4 properties with statistics on conflicts, presented in Table 2.

Secondly, a set of rules (see Table 1) was created to address the mentioned conflicts. They were obtained by empirically studying reasons of the conflicts in every case. The most common reasons are addressed in the rules.

Thirdly, we iteratively applied the rules 1-7 from Table 1 to the training set in accumulated fashion: in the first iteration, we applied the rule 1, in the second - the rules 1 and 2 and so on. In total, there are 7 iterations. After each iteration we calculated the amount of conflicts remained after reduction process. The results are presented in Figure 3.

Figure 3 contains a stacked area chart, each area of which corresponds to one of the properties of interest: "Author", "Mimetype", "Format version" and "Format". Statistics are presented in Table 2. Before running experiments, the training set contains 72572 conflicts in characterisation results of 65929 digital objects. After applying the 7 rules, there are 45988 conflicts left, which is 63% of the total amount of conflicts. With respect to the selected properties, 40665 conflicts were reduced down to 11483 conflicts, which is 28% of the initial amount. The chart demonstrates that the rules affect mostly "Format" and "Mimetype" properties, as the amount of conflicts of theirs reduces in every iteration. Conflicts in "Author" property are reduced by the rules 1 and 7. The "Format version" property is affected only by the rule 1.

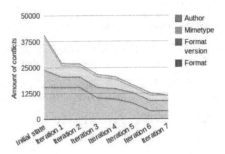

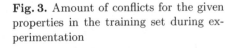

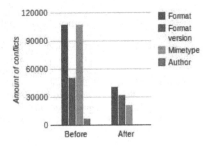

Fig. 3. Amount of conflicts for the given properties in the training set during experimentation

Fig. 4. Amount of conflicts for the given properties in the test set before and after experimentation

Finally, we also want to know how generally the rules 1-7 may be applied on the test set. To check this, we run C3PO with the 7 rules created for the training set on the test set. Figure 4 contains the chart with the results of this experiment. Before running experiments, the test set contains 656412 conflicts in characterisation results of 579587 digital objects. After applying the 7 rules, there are 473022 conflicts left, which is 72% of the total amount of conflicts. With respect to the selected properties, 273723 conflicts were reduced down to 95642 conflicts, which is 35% of the initial amount.

The most effective rule is the rule 7, which resolves 99,8% of conflicts of the "Author" property in the test set. The least amount of conflicts reduced are of the "Format version" property, which is 36% of the total amount of conflict of that property. This is an interesting discovery since there is no single rule that addresses this property directly. The conflicts are mostly covered by the rule 1.

Characterization measures are generally not independent from each other. This can be seen also in the fact that the amount of conflicts in format and mime type is identical: Where multiple tools were able to characterize one file, they generally disagree on how to label it, even if they classify it identically.

From the last experiment we can conclude that the rules created for the training set performed effectively in the test set. It is important to note that this judgment is done based on an expert analysis. The expert studied the content and selected the list of rules that solve certain conflicts. The rules created by experts can be easily shared and assessed in comparative experiments. The heuristics thus enable analysis with much improved data quality.

The test set contains similar proportion of conflicted objects that were identified in the training set: 69% and 70% - before experiments, 40% and 35% - after experiments, correspondingly. The conflicted objects and conflicts are evenly distributed in the FITS characterization results of govdocs1.

Table 2. Conflicts in training and test sets

Set	Total amount of objects	Measurement done wrt experiments	Objects with conclicts	Amount of conflicts				
				in a set	in Format	in Format version	in MIME type	in Author
Training Set	96207	Before	65929	72572	15529	8332	15529	1275
		After	34245	45988	3838	5018	2603	24
Test Set	849539	Before	579587	656412	107546	50969	107546	7662
		After	336451	473022	41024	32236	22225	157

5 Summary

In this paper, we discussed and addressed challenges that concern quality, depth and scale of content profiling and presented an approach to improve data quality efficiently by extending the content profiling tool C3PO. We introduced a mechanism for extensible post-processing of metadata based on stateless rule processing engine Drools in C3PO. This engine was adapted to provide conflict reduction capabilities which improves gathered metadata quality. The resulting rule set is presented during the series of experiments on a publicly available large data set. The results demonstrate that this is a very cost-effective and robust mechanism for improving the quality of content profiles, which in turn can improve the quality of curation and preservation decisions substantially. The rule mechanism and the set of rules are part of the publicly accessible c3po, which is freely accessible on github[11].

As a next step, we will evaluate the rule creation mechanism on large real-world datasets. Besides potential further scalability challenges, it is an opportunity to deepen and share the community's knowledge about reasons of characterization conflicts and heuristics to treat them, evaluate how rules from different content collections may improve conflict reduction, and thus contribute to the evidence base of digital preservation. We will also address challenges in representative sample generation, evaluating and selecting appropriate sampling heuristics.

Acknowledgements. Part of this work was supported by the Vienna Science and Technology Fund (WWTF) through the project *BenchmarkDP* (ICT12-046), and by the EU in the 7th Framework Program, IST, through the *SCAPE* project, Contract 270137. The authors would like to thank Petar Petrov for his technical support.

References

1. Abrams, S., Morrissey, S., Cramer, T.: What? So What.: The next-generation JHOVE2 architecture for format-aware characterization. IJDC 4(3) (2009)
2. Becker, C., Duretec, K.: Free benchmark corpora for preservation experiments: using model-driven engineering to generate data sets. In: Proc. JCDL. ACM (2013)
3. Becker, C., Rauber, A.: Preservation decisions: Terms and conditions apply. In: Proc. JCDL. ACM (2011)
4. Brody, T., Carr, L., Hey, J., Brown, A., Hitchcock, S.: PRONOM-ROAR: Adding format profiles to a repository registry to inform preservation services. IJDC 2(2) (2008)
5. Dappert, A.: Deal with conflict, capture the relationship: The case of digital object properties. In: Proc. IPRES, pp. 21–29 (2010)
6. Dappert, A., Farquhar, A.: Significance is in the eye of the stakeholder. In: Agosti, M., Borbinha, J., Kapidakis, S., Papatheodorou, C., Tsakonas, G. (eds.) ECDL 2009. LNCS, vol. 5714, pp. 297–308. Springer, Heidelberg (2009)
7. Faria, L., Petrov, P., Duretec, K., Becker, C., Ferreira, M., Ramalho, J.: Design and architecture of a novel preservation watch system. In: Chen, H.-H., Chowdhury, G. (eds.) ICADL 2012. LNCS, vol. 7634, pp. 168–178. Springer, Heidelberg (2012)
8. Forgy, C.L.: Rete: A fast algorithm for the many pattern/many object pattern match problem. Artificial Intelligence 19(1), 17–37 (1982)
9. Hedstrom, M., Lee, C.A.: Significant properties of digital objects: definitions, applications, implications. In: DLM-Forum, vol. 200, pp. 218–27 (2002)
10. Hutchins, M.: Testing software tools of potential interest for digital preservation activities at the national library of australia. NLA Australia Staff Papers (2012)

---

[11] https://github.com/openplanets/c3po

11. Kulovits, H., Kraxner, M., Plangg, M., Becker, C., Bechhofer, S.: Open preservation data: Controlled vocabularies and ontologies for preservation ecosystems. In: Proc. IPRES, pp. 63–72
12. Petrov, P., Becker, C.: Large-scale content profiling for preservation analysis. In: 9th International Conference on Preservation of Digital Objects (IPRES 2012) (2012)
13. van der Knijff, J., Wilson, C.: Evaluation of characterisation tools. part 1: Identification. Technical report, National Library of the Netherlands (2011)
14. Wheatley, P.: The practitioners have spoken: "we need better characterisation!". Blog post (2012),
http://www.openplanetsfoundation.org/blogs/2012-10-19-practitioners-have-spoken-we-need-better-characterisation (accessed June 2014)

Digital Preservation of Palm-Leaf Manuscripts in Thailand

Prasittichai Lertratanakehakarn

Librarian, Professional Level, National Library of Thailand
Ph.D.Candidate, Program in Information Scienzce, Department of Information Science,
School of Liberal Arts, SukhothaiThammathirat Open University
eak.pras@hotmail.com

Abstract. This paper is to study the digital preservation of palm-leaf manuscripts and the organizations that are responsible for creating, storing and digitizing palm-leaf manuscripts in Thailand. Palm-leaf manuscripts are the cultural heritage and wisdom records of the local ancestors. It appears to be cultural heritage of South East Asia. In Thailand, this kind of cultural heritage is found in many areas of the country. Palm-leaf manuscripts should be preserved in the digital form for both knowledge and the manuscripts themselves, for long term use throughout its lifecycle, for the purpose of education, preservation and research for future generations. This paper also suggests a digital preservation plan of Palm-leaf manuscripts to be easily accessed by researchers and scholars.

Keywords: Digital Preservation, Palm-Leaf Manuscripts, Digitization, Manuscript digitization, Manuscript preservation.

1 Introduction

The palm leaf manuscripts (PLMs) are valuable cultural heritage, recording history, knowledge, and wisdom of ancestors. The PLMs are proved in regions throughout the country. These manuscripts are archaic records which present development of the country, local community structure, tradition, belief, politics, economics, traditional medicine, arts, etc. Significantly, most of contents of PLMs are Buddhist stories. Therefore, especially in Thai community, the PLMs are regarded as an important cultural heritage of Southeast Asia Region and as monographs beneficial to study and research in various fields in order to develop the country in the future. (Kongkaew Veeraprajak,1987; National Library, 2005)

With recognition of importance and benefit of the PLMs, several institutions in Thailand both in public and private sectors comprising local level, national level and educational institutions, that are responsible for preservation of the PLMs and dissemination of knowledge recorded on the PLMs, realize a problem that possibly occurs and influences on the original PLMs.

As the PLMs were made from palm tree leaves which are natural material easy to be in a stage of decomposition due to the passage of time, natural disasters (fire or flood), sunlight, temperature, inappropriate humidity in storage place, insects, and

K. Tuamsuk et al. (Eds.): ICADL 2014, LNCS 8839, pp. 12–21, 2014.

human's act both in an unintentional and intentional way, and in order to preserve the original PLMs and extend knowledge recorded on the PLMs to be more accessible, all institutions involved as mentioned above consider information technology as a useful tool, in accordance with evolving environment at the present and in the future, for preservation and dissemination of knowledge on the PLMs, without destroying the original ones. So, Digitization means of preservation of manuscripts that acquiring, converting, storing and providing information in a computer. In this paper, the author will summarize a current digitization state of PLMs, process to digitize the PLMs of the institutions in Thailand, and suggestion on appropriate digitization of PLMs. (Kongkaew Veeraprajak & Neeyada Phasugond, 1994; National Library, 2009; Sineenad Somboonanek, 2012; UNSCO, 2011).

2   Methodology

The current digitization state of PLMs was studied and collected by interview and review literatures from 16 institutions in Thailand that intended to preserve the PLMs and then only institutions with digitization of PLMs for preservation were selected and studied.

Table 1. List of 16 Institutions Supporting on Palm Leaf Manuscript Management

National Level	Local Level	Educational Level
1. National Library	1. Wat Tha Muang, Roi Et Province	1. Social Research Institute, Chiang Mai University
2. "Survey, Study, and Digitize Local Manuscripts from Western Thailand" Project, Princess Maha Chakri Sirindhorn Anthropology Centre	2. Wat Mahachai Museum, Maha Sarakham Province	2. Chiang Mai University Library
	3. Wat Khian Bang Kaeo Museum	3. Palm Leaf Manuscript Centre, Institute of Languages, Arts, and Culture, Chiang Mai Rajabhat University
	4. Cultural Centre of Phatthalung Province, Satri Phatthalung School	4. Institute for Research in Culture and the Arts, Burapha University
	5. Wat Lai Hin, Lampang Province	5. Office of Arts and Culture, Nakhon Ratchasima Rajabhat University

Table 1. *(Continued)*

National Level	Local Level	Educational Level
		6. Institute for Southern Thai Studies, Thaksin University
		7. Office of Arts and Culture, Songkhla Rajabhat University
		8. Project for Palm Leaf Manuscript Preservation in Northeastern Thailand, Mahasarakham University
		9. Local Information and Archives, Office of Academic Services, Ubon Ratchathaini Unniversity

From table 1, list of 16 institutions supporting on palm leaf manuscript management, there are 2 institutions in national level, 5 institutions in local level and 9 institutions in educational level.

3   Results of the Study

After reviewing related literatures and research papers including in-depth interview from 16 institutions both in public and private sectors comprising local level, national level and educational institutions responsible for preservation of the PLMs and dissemination of knowledge recorded on the PLMs, it was indicated that 10 out of 16 institutions had only one format available, the original manuscript, and 6 institutions had digitized the PLMs, as follows: 1) National Library; 2) "Survey, Study, and Digitize Local Manuscripts from Western Thailand" Project, Princess Maha Chakri Sirindhorn Anthropology Centre; 3) Social Research Institute, Chiang Mai University; 4) Chiang Mai University Library; 5) Palm Leaf Manuscript Centre, Institute of Languages, Arts, and Culture, Chiang Mai Rajabhat University; and 6) Project for Palm Leaf Manuscript Preservation in Northeastern Thailand, Mahasarakham University. All the current digitization states of PLMs were summarized and analyzed as below.

An analysis of current digitization state of PLMs in Thailand from 6 institutions were summarize as the following.

3.1   National Library

National Library is an institution that is directly responsible for preservation of PLMs, with three formats: 1) the original PLMs; 2) the microfilms; and 3) the copy of PLMs in TIFF format on CD-ROM. There are 30 fascicles of PLMs to be digitized. The PLM services are provided to users in three formats: 1) the original PLMs; 2) the microfilms; and 3) the digitized files. At first, the users can be accessed applying search tools through bibliography. In the near future, National Library plans to develop database for storing and searching the digitized files for the users.

However, the digitization is conducted only for some PLMs, not all of them. National Library currently has no clear policy on this kind of management and preservation of PLMs.

Fig. 1. The Process of digitized microfilms to Images in National Library

3.2   "Survey, Study, and Digitize Local Manuscripts from Western Thailand" Project, Princess Maha Chakri Sirindhorn Anthropology Centre

"Survey, Study, and Digitize Local Manuscripts from Western Thailand" Project is one of the projects of Princess Maha Chakri Sirindhorn Anthropology Centre that is intended to survey, collect and preserve the archaic records such as PLMs and Thai traditional books at temples in western Thailand. This section is responsible for surveying, registering, categorizing, and preserving archaic documents for temples. For preservation, the archaic documents amounting to 19 fascicles and 374 photos are digitized by photography and stored in TIFF format similar to Palm Leaf Manuscript Centre, Institute of Languages, Arts, and Culture, Chiang Mai Rajabhat University. The project also provides the database service for users.

3.3   Social Research Institute of Chiang Mai University

In the same way like Chiang Mai University Library and Palm Leaf Manuscript Centre, Institute of Languages, Arts, and Culture, Chiang Mai Rajabhat University,

Social Research Institute of Chiang Mai University is also responsible for preservation and dissemination of knowledge on PLMs, especially regarding Lanna language and culture, and northern Thai language and literature. It contains 17,257 fascicles and 220 roles of microfilms of PLMs in TIFF format on CD-ROM, so they all are digitized. In the future, it is planned to develop an electronic storage space for archaic Lanna documents and rare books and provide PLMs in digitized files.

3.4   Chiang Mai University Library

As Chiang Mai University Library realizes an importance of preservation with digitization of the PLMs, a project named Digitization Initiative for Traditional Manuscripts of Northern Thailand is arranged. Main objective of project is to preserve the archaic records such as PLMs and Thai traditional books with 1,063 titles for storing and providing service in the library, including 489 roles of the microfilms from the Centre for the Promotion of Arts and Culture, Chiang Mai University. The copy of archaic records is made in JPEG format on CD-ROM and DVD — digitization. Chiang Mai University Library plans to develop the database (tools for access of the archaic records) and create metadata for storing and giving detail of each document. The searching service is provided for users with the database "CMUL Digital Heritage Collection".

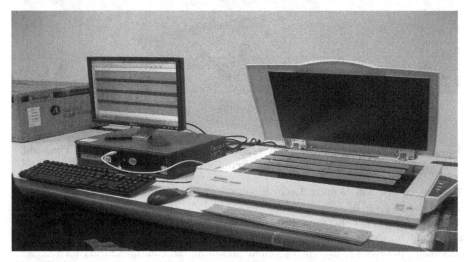

Fig. 2. Digitization of Palm Leaf Manuscripts with Scanner of Chiang Mai University Library

3.5   Palm Leaf Manuscript Centre, Institute of Languages, Arts, and Culture, Chiang Mai Rajabhat University

Due to Chiang Mai Rajabhat University stresses an importance of preservation of the cultural heritage, Palm Leaf Manuscript Centre, Institute of Languages, Arts, and Culture, Chiang Mai Rajabhat University is established in order to store, collect, preserve, and disseminate the archaic documents (concerning language, tradition and literature in Northern Thailand and its neighborhood) such as palm leafs, Thai traditional books. Two methods of preservation are as follows: 1) to provide copy of the PLMs in JPEG format on CD-ROM; and 2) to digitize the PLMs. At the present, 3,284 items are digitized. During survey, if PLMs aged over 200 years are found, they will be copied in JPEG format on CD-ROM or DVD — digitization. Then, these CD-ROM or DVD will be given to the temples for storage and dissemination.

Fig. 3. Digitization of Palm Leaf Manuscripts with digital camera of Chiang Mai University Library

3.6 Project for Palm Leaf Manuscript Preservation in Northeastern Thailand, Mahasarakham University

This project is established to survey, preserve, transform, and research PLMs in Northeastern Thailand. It consists of five missions: 1) to survey, categorize, and preserve the PLMs as learning resources for people in 19 provinces in northeastern part of Thailand; 2) to transliterate PLMs in the categories and disseminate to others; 3) to train and give knowledge about traditional scripts and writings on PLMs; 4) to study and research about PLMs with basic and applied researches, focusing on interdisciplinary method; and 5) to apply modern technology in recording and managing the records of PLMs and provide service for general both inside and outside the country.

In total, 40 fascicles and 1,882 pages of long PLMs and 930 pages of short PLMs are digitized. The digitization of PLMs is made for the users by organizing and scanning photo files, JPEG format. The service of PLMs in digitized files is provided for users on database. This project currently has no clear policy on this kind of management and preservation of PLMs.

Fig. 4. Digitization of Palm Leaf Manuscripts with digital camera of The Project for Palm Leaf Manuscript Preservation in Northeastern Thailand, Mahasarakham University

In summary, for preservation of the PLMs by digitization in Thailand, many institutions use information technology for preserving the original copies are as follows in the table 2.

Table 2. Current digitization state of PLMs in Thailand

Institutions	Digitization Equipment	Format		Storage	Availability
		Master Image	Access Image		
1. National Library	Microfilm, Scanner	TIFF	JPEG	CD-ROM	CD-ROM
2. The Princess Maha Chakri Sirindhorn Anthropology' s Western local literature Survey, Collects and studies project	Digital camera	TIFF	JPEG	CD-ROM	Database
3. Chiang Mai University's Institute of Social Research	Microfilm, Scanner	TIFF	JPEG	CD-ROM	Database and CD-ROM

Table 2. *(Continued)*

4. Chiang Mai University Library	Scanner, Microfilm and Digital camera	TIFF	JPEG	CD-ROM, DVD	Database
5. Center Palm-Leaf Manuscript, Institute of Language, Art and Culture of Chiang Mai Rajabhat University	Digital camera	TIFF	JPEG	DVD	Database
6. Project for Palm Leaf Manuscript Preservation in Northeastern Thailand, Mahasarakham University	Scanner, Digital camera	TIFF	JPEG	CD-ROM	Database

Methods of preservation available in the study are to photograph and scan the original copies, scan from the PLMs' microfilms, make the PLMs' files in TIFF for the original files and JPEG for the display on the database for disseminating and providing service for all users, and record the information to make a copy in JPEG format on CD-ROM and computer. Some institutions give them to the temples for storage and dissemination. The selection criterion for PLMs to be digitized is to consider PLMs aged over 200 years with a lot of loss or damage prior to digitization. Before doing digitization, content classification of PLMs and preservation of the original copies are conducted. In some institutions, the service of PLMs is provided for users in form of CD-ROM. Some institutions develop offline and online database for users; they require the metadata elements to determine its ability to support main tasks of the document storage and retrieval systems in describing document for search and access. However, several institutions have no clear process on the management of digitized PLMs or any manual with clear standard for cataloging of PLMs and developing search tools for them.

4   Problems of Preservation of the PLMs by Digitization

Five problems of preservation of the PLMs by digitization were found as below.

1. The management of the PLMs in digital form: There is no clear policy on the management of digitized PLMs, both the selection criteria for PLMs to be digitized and the techniques to be used in order to achieve the best quality possible for digitized PLMs. Negative effects on preservation and dissemination of PLMs may be occurred in the future.

2. The classification of the PLMs: There is no manual with clear standard for cataloging of PLMs and developing search tools for them.

3. The staff member to work on the PLMs: It is lack of expertise to work on the PLMs in digital form.

4. The budget of the PLMs: A lot of budget is needed in order to digitize PLMs, used to provide the materials, information technology tools, and develop the database.

5. The collaborative networks of the PLMs: Institutions in local level, national level, and educational institution have less collaborative networks of PLMs in digital form.

So, a number of current problems of digitization preservation of the PLMs in these institutes were summarized, including lack of clear policy on the PLM selection criteria, lack of standardized digitization and access methodologies, lack of experienced staffs, lack of sufficient findings, and lack of inter-institutional collaborations.

5   The Guidelines of Preservation of the PLMs by Digitization

As there are problems of preservation of the PLMs by digitization, the author would like to suggest the guidelines to provide solutions. Any institutions doing digitization must plan the clear policy on the management of digitized PLMs and propose the project to other institutions both in public and private sectors in Thailand including local level and national level that have recognition of the importance and benefits of preservation of the PLMs in digital form, in order to support on budget, personnel, and information technology tools. The institutions must determine the manual with clear standard for cataloging of PLMs and disseminating them. In addition, the collaborative networks of the PLMs in the public and private sectors including local level, national level, and educational institutions must be created more, so the selection criteria for PLMs to be digitized and the techniques to be used in order to achieve the best quality possible for digitized PLMs can be made by learning, sharing, helping each other, and supporting the digitization to be the national policy to reach the standard in the preservation and dissemination of the PLMs.

Moreover, the author concludes and suggests that these institutions must collaborate for the management of digitized PLMs, find and use the open source software for digitization, be willing to shared the information in an open access and develop the technical standards for the preservation and dissemination of PLMs in order to achieve the best quality possible for digitized PLMs.

6   Conclusion

It is indicated that the preservation of the PLMs in digital form in Thailand is very important and necessary to operate because the digitization (by using information technology tools) of the PLMs can preserve the original copies and it is easy to retrieve the PLMs for utilization according to current situation. Moreover, not many institutions being responsible for the digitization of the PLMs; some institutions are still in the beginning stage. The digitization is conducted in a small number of PLMs in Thailand. If there are not more preservation of the original PLMs and digitization of them, these PLMs, as a cultural heritage (the manuscripts and knowledge), will be lost or damaged soon. In addition, five problems are encountered in the preservation of the

PLMs: no clear policy on the management of digitized PLMs; less support on budget; lack of expertise; no manual with clear standard for the digitization of the PLMs; and less collaborative networks. Thus, institutions both in public and private sectors in Thailand including local level and national level having recognition of importance and benefits of the digitization of the PLMs must collaborate in planning, setting clear policy on the management of digitized PLMs, and developing the database requiring the standard for the preservation and dissemination of PLMs in order to achieve the best quality possible for digitized PLMs. Moreover, to find other tools which the open source software that be willing to share and use the information in an open access.

References

1. Alahakoon, C.N.K.: Management, Conservation AND Preservation of Palm-Leaf Manuscripts: A Research Study Based on Selected Collections in Srilanka. Master's thesis, University of Colombo Sri Lanka (2003)
2. Center Palm-Leaf Manuscript, Institute of Language, Art and Culture of Chiang Mai Rajabhat University, Management and corporation for the Cultural Heritage documents. Chiang Mai Rajabhat (2012)
3. Veeraprajak, K.: Ancient documents. Library 38(3), 1–22 (1987)
4. Veeraprajak, K., Phasugond, N.: Preparation of Sa-mut-khoi and Plam leaves Manuscripts. National Library, Bangkok (1994)
5. Northeast Palm Leaf Manuscripts Preservation Project MSU (2004), Preservation Project, http://www.bl.msu.ac.th/2554/bailan.htm (retrieved May 20, 2014)
6. National Library, Manual working for the manuscripts. National Library, Bangkok (2005)
7. National Library, Manual of the Survey, acquisition and collection for the manuscripts. National Library, Bangkok (2009)
8. Princess Maha Chakri Sirindhorn Anthropology Centre. Annual Report 2012: Princess Maha Chakri Sirindhorn Anthropology Centre (2013), http://www.sac.or.th/main/uploads/aboutus/sac-report-2555.pdf (retrieved May 20, 2014)
9. Somboonanek, S.: Chiang Mai University Library digitization of Palm leaf manuscripts. T.L.A. Bulletin 56(1), 22–32 (2012)
10. UNSCO, Preserving and sharing access to our documentary heritage (2011), http://www.unesco.org/new/fileadmin/MULTIMEDIA/HQ/CI/CI/pdf/mow/Memory%20of%20the%20World%20%20Preserving%20and%20sharing%20access%20to%20our%20documentary%20heritage.pdf (retrieved May 20, 2014)

A Distributed Platform for Archiving
and Viewing Cultural Artifacts in 3D

Weeraphan Chanhom[1], Chutiporn Anutariya[2], and Sumanta Guha[1]

[1] Computer Science and Information Management Program,
AIT Asian Institute of Technology. P.O. Box 4, Klong Luang,
Pathumthani 12120, Thailand
weeraphan@mediaartsdesign.org, guha@ait.ac.th
[2] Asian University
89 Moo 12, Highway 331, Huay Yai, Banglamung,
Chonburi 20260, Thailand
chutiporna@asianust.ac.th

Abstract. In this paper we describe an architecture for the digital museum and propose the suitable museum data model for distributed digital contents, especially in 3D cultural objects. The development of a data model is viewing interoperability, standards, museum data model and feedback from two museums in Chiang Mai pilot sites under the Museum Thailand project. We analyzed the notable metadata enabling and supporting all of museum content management processes. In addition we also described a system that will integrate data from different museums. Finally, the museums can use this model to implement their system for providing services to cultural content experts and public entities.

Keywords: Metadata, Digital Museum, Artifacts, Works of Art, 3D Cultural Objects, Thailand, Local Museum.

1 Introduction

Cultural heritage is important for each society since history is defined by and studied through. People may improve quality of life by using economic development of the surrounding population. UNESCO defines the cultural heritage of world value as architectural works, works of monumental sculpture and painting, elements or structures of an archaeological nature, inscriptions, cave dwellings and combinations of features, which are of outstanding universal value from the point of view of history, art or science[1]. The cultural heritage has involved with human beings from the past to present. In order to preserve and take care of it, museums play an important role to manage and share knowledge with the community. Currently, physical museums are facing with many problems such as insufficient spaces for collecting and displaying the cultural artifacts, researchers doing too many documents for preserving the world's heritage resources and conserving their own digital products. Moreover, the museums are now facing new demands of audiences while technological pushes can facilitate achieving data via the Internet networking. Another important problem is that several museums cannot share data among each other.

K. Tuamsuk et al. (Eds.): ICADL 2014, LNCS 8839, pp. 22–29, 2014.

3D digital is used by many cultural heritage institutions as preservation techniques to preserve delicate museum artifacts and to develop online collections. Such 3D illustrations improve access to physical collections and provide accurate digital surrogates for scholar analysis. As 3D data digitization tools become more reasonable and obtainable, the amount of 3D data required for storage, indexing and search services will grow dramatically. Because high quality metadata are extremely expensive, museums deeply explore how they can provide their collections to exchange with other museums, as well as to serve the cultural knowledge to their members or visitors.

While the digital world have been growing and changing rapidly over the past few years, there are various technologies that are able to convert analogue information to digital format. These technologies are good tools for digitizing cultural artifact from real objects to 3D objects. Therefore, digitizing the huge collection of cultural artifacts around the globe is real challenging. This is because the 3D cultural artifact modeling can avoid direct damages caused by natural disasters or even human behaviors.

For the situation of cultural heritage areas in Thailand, we now have many cultural sources, such as national and local museums and art galleries, spreading around the country. The museums need the platform to distribute their collections with mapping and linking data in an open environment, especially the 3D objects, as information technology continues to evolve.

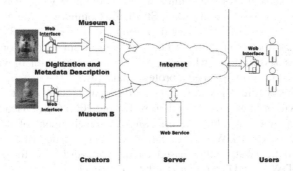

Fig. 1. The proposed distributed digital museum platform for preserving, searching and visualizing 3D cultural collections

Fig.1 shows the broad picture of the museums data exchanged to solve the problems above. There are three parts involved creator side, server side, and user side. In this paper we focus on the data model of the cultural objects in the part of the creator side. The data model that we proposed provides platform for museums to develop their system for collection, reviewing, updating, preservation, and sharing their cultural information to other museums via the Internet. Additionally, the museums are able to offer a wide range of high quality scientific 3D digital models of cultural artifacts usable for further study.

The paper is organized as follows. Section 2 reviews related works. Section 3 presents the proposed data model. Section 4 demonstrates the Museum Thailand project which has been developed based on the constructed platform and data model. Section 5 draws conclusions and future research direction.

2   Related Works

2.1   Metadata Standard in Cultural Heritage Area

Today there are many discussions about the metadata standards in cultural domain when we planned to select them for implementing in Cultural Artifacts and Works of Art areas. Amongst these, some of the most outstanding and involving with our project are: the Dublin Core (DC), the SPECTRUM, the Visual Resources Association's Data Standards Committee (VRA), the Categories for the Description of Works of Art (CDWA), and the SEPIA Data Element Set (SEPIADES).

DC is one of the most widely used schemas and illustrates many of the issues. Although the Dublin Core Metadata Initiative (DCMI) does not deal specifically with cultural heritage archives, the Dublin Core Metadata Element Set (DCMES) is of importance for resource discovery across domains and hence of great relevance to any system proposing information retrieval over the Internet. It is also pertinent to issues of interoperability and information exchange [2].

SPECTRUM is a procedural and data standard for museums, archives, and cultural heritage institutions primarily in the UK. SPECTRUM is more than a metadata schema. It is a guide to documenting all the procedures a museum might need to undertake in managing its collections [3].

VRA is a data standard for the cultural heritage community that was developed by the Visual Resources Association's Data Standards Committee. The element set provides a categorical organization for the description of works of visual culture as well as the images that document them. It takes its name from its developing body: the Visual Resources Association, which is a US based association of visual resource librarians and associated image media professionals. [4].

CDWA and DWA Lite: CDWA is a standard for cataloguing cultural objects, such as those found within museums and galleries. During 2005-6 a revised version of the CDWA was prepared and released, reflecting the development of the Cataloguing Cultural Objects (CCO). CDWA Lite is an XML schema to describe core records for works of art and material culture based on the Categories for the Description of Works of Art (CDWA) and Cataloging Cultural Objects [5].

SEPIADES is a metadata for describing photographic collections. At the Single Item level, SEPIADES makes a distinction between a Visual Image and its Physical Description. Physical Description is further divided up into Photographs and Digital Photo File [6].

A metadata analysis assumed by this project showed that no single existing metadata element set was suitable for the range of processes envisioned in the system. More specifically, there are no metadata standards which provide the digitization, storage and management, and dynamic creation of intelligent search of cultural heritage objects.

In developing the metadata element set, the advantages described above were taken into account and in fact, our project draws on elements from a number of these, in particular the DCMES and SPECTRUM using the concept of application profiles. An application profile is a metadata schema which draws on existing metadata element sets, adapting and customizing specific elements for a particular local application.

2.2   Real World Projects

In this section, we have studied the notable project on cultural heritage domain that are related with our project as follows.

Augmented Representation of Cultural Objects (ARCO) project has developed technology to create, manipulate, manage and present digitized cultural objects in virtual exhibitions accessible both inside and outside museums. The ARCO system consists of three main architectural components: content production, content management, and visualization [7].

MUSEUMFINLAND project has developed a semantic web portal. The system contains an inter-museum exhibition of over 4,000 cultural artifacts, such as textiles, pieces of furniture, and tools. Also metadata concerning some 260 historical sites in Finland were incorporated in the system [8].

Science and Technology in Archaeology Research Centre (STARC) project has developed the metadata schema for the documentation of archaeological assets. The goal of the project is to enable data interoperability and access to the digital resources stored in the local repository. Its structure allows retrieving models, activities, decision and answers the research question on how data can be used for data interpretation. The datasets stored in STARC repository refer to 2D and 3D archaeological data as museum objects [9].

3DSA project is created under the cultural heritage institutions aimed to develop simple, semantic annotation services for 3D digital objects that will facilitate the discovery, capture, inference and exchange of valuable cultural heritage knowledge. The focusing is annotations of 3D models for efficient indexing, search and retrieval of 3D artefacts from large-scale museum digital libraries [10].

3   Proposed Data Model

In this project we are focusing on the data model of data exchange for the digital museums. Before developing the data model, we should know how museums work with data collections—the process from digitization to visualization.

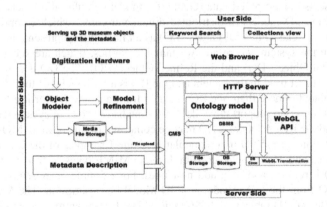

Fig. 2. The architecture of the museum content management system

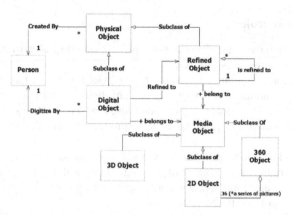

Fig. 3. The proposed data model for distributed digital museums

Fig.2 shows the museum content management system architecture improving from the architecture of the ARCO system [11]. It is divided into three conceptual areas according to the interaction of the user with the data. (1) The creator side, which is responsible for the creation of the multimedia content. The process of digitizing 3D objects is done using 3D scanners, and the refinement of the object is performed with 3D software, which is then exported to the object format file. After completing the digitization of the 3D objects, the object file is uploaded to the system along with the database and the associated metadata.

(2) The server side, which is responsible for storing and organizing data model to Database Management System (DBMS), authoring with PHP and MySQL. The WebGL middle API is provided for transforming the 3D object to the user side section, which is given in the next step. Additionally, this part includes Content Management System (CMS) to manage content for front end and backend such as user account, file categories, etc. (3) The user side, which is responsible for preparing dynamic presentations to be displayed on the Web browser. The features include advanced search, WebGL renderer functions. Visitors can use the former to simply search and browse the database contents.

Fig.3 presents our proposed data schema for modeling cultural artifacts, digitization process, 2D and 3D models in distributed digital museums, which comprises various related classes. A class Physical Object (PO) as an intangible representation of a tangible artifact in the system. There are two tangible entities, which are subclasses of the PO, the Digital Object (DO) and the Refined Object (RO). The DO is a digitization of the physical artifact used in the system and the RO is a refinement of the DO or another ROs. There may be more than one ROs created from a single DO or itself. The Media Object (MO) is used to support the collection of media files on our system which belong to the DO and the RO. A DO or a RO may be composed of one or more MOs. The MOs are representations of the PO in a particular medium. Examples of the MO are 3D Object, 2D Object, and 360 object each with different MIME types. A RO inherits all MOs from the PO it refines, and may add new ones. For example, a museum curator may create the RO from the DO by adding a 3D Model or Description. The MO has three entries: 2D Object, 3D Object, and 360 Object. The Person entity refers to people who make cultural objects.

Table 1. The element of vocabulary terms associated with ontology model entities

Class	Metadata Elements		
Physical Object	spectrum:ObjectTitle,	spectrum:History,	sp:ctrum.Dimension,
	vra:Title,	dc:Rights,	spectrum:Unit,
	dc:Creator,	spectrum:Condition,	spectrum:Artstyle,
	dc:Contributor,	vra:style-period,	spectrum:AcquisitionNote,
	dc:Date(dc:date),	spectrum:period,	vra:Location,
	vra:ArtworkType,	vra:Material,	vra:Subject,
	spectrum:ObjectType,	vra:Techniques,	vra:Relation,
	dc:Description,	vra.Measurements,	vra:Source.
Digital Object	dc:Identifier,	dc:Publisher,	dc:Format,
	dc:Title,	dc:DateCreated(dc:date),	dc:Source.
	dc:Creator,	dc:Description,	
	dc:Contributor,	dc:Rights,	
Refined Object	Same as Digital Object elecment. + Relation is version of		
Media file Object	sepides:Title, sepides:Description,	sepides:Date,	sepides:DateOfCreation,
	sepides:Names,	sepides:Descriptors,	sepides:Subject
		sepides:Status,	
3D Object	mt:Digitization Process,	mt:Digital Information,	mt:VRML Version,
	mt:Software version,	mt:Unit,	mt:Number of Textures,
	mt:Data Object,	mt:Number,	mt:Composite
2D Object	sepides:CaptureDevice,	sepides:Resolution,	sepides.Compression,
	sepides:CaptureSoftware,	sepides:ColorSpaceDepth,	sepides.Correction,
	sepides:ColourManagement,	sepides:FileFormat,	sepides.Purpose
	sepides:Dimensions,	sepides:FileSize,	
360 Object	mt:Number of Images,	mt:Step Angle	
Person	spectrum:Name,	spectrum:Date,	pectrum:Gender,
	spectrum:Address,	spectrum:Place,	spectrum:Group
	spectrum:BiographicalNote,	spectrum:Death,	
Remark:			
dc=Dublin Core Metadata Initiative, specturm= The UK Museum Collections Management Standard,vra=Visual Resources Association Core, sepides=SEPIA Data Element Set,mt=The Museum Thailand schema.			

Table 1. shows elements of each entity used in our system; element sets represent their origin. For each element set, it comes from several metadata standards that involve our process of content management system architecture and requirement from users. The following table shows a list of element sets.

4   Prototype System

The Museum Thailand project uses this data Model End-Users. The web interfaces allow access to both 2D and 3D virtual collections containing virtual representations of cultural artifacts and works of art. These collections are visualized in virtual collection through the Web. Fig. 4 illustrates the interface design of the home page.

Fig. 5 shows visualization of the metadata of the same cultural object within the museum and over the Web. The visualization of metadata information in a 3D object is also presented. The metadata are related to the object in a 2D window in front of the user's viewpoint.

Fig. 4. Sample Web interface of the Museum Thailand project

Fig. 5. A cultural artifact with its 3D model and annotated metadata

In order to evaluate the effectiveness of the approach, we evaluated three key criteria: (1) improvements to the search and discovery services; (2) usability of the system from an end-user point of view; (3) system design, efficiency and deployment from an administrative point of view. Feedback from users searching the collection from suitable categories (type, period, art style, title, and material) and on relevance of search results indicated that the data models and metadata elements are suitable for the digital museum that can explain the meaning of data collection, ready to exchange information with other museums especially in 3D format. End-users of the system comprise of two types: the creator who can produce and edit the contents and the general public who search the collection. Users attaching the website found the user interfaces, easy to access and the data presented demonstrate that 3D cultural artifacts on the web browser to get attention, important to prepare and publish information collections with museums in the digital age as well.

5   Conclusions and Future Work

We have described the development of data model according the process of museum content management system from digitization of cultural artifacts and works of art object to the Web interface. The metadata requirements of each entity are different because a great deal of technical information is required to maintain and preserve them. The data model described on section 3 works well with cultural artifacts and works of art collected in museums or galleries. Furthermore, this data model will be extended to the ontology in the cultural heritage areas as CIDOC CRM [12], which are beyond the standard cataloguing of museum collections, and to multimedia Internet publishing and exchanging, as well as dynamic virtual reality systems. Additional works in this area involve further study and implementation of the ontology for data exchange on web service application including the consideration of web service technology.

Reference

1. The United Nations Organization for Education Science and Culture (UNESCO), http://whc.unesco.org/en/convention
2. The Dublin Core Metadata Initiative, http://dublincore.org/documents/dces/
3. SPECTRUM: the UK Museum Collections Management Standard, http://www.collectionslink.org.uk/spectrum
4. Visual Resources Association Core, http://www.vraweb.org/projects/vracore4/index.html
5. Categories for the Description of Works of Arts, http://www.getty.edu/
6. SEPIA Data Element Set, http://www.ica.org/lid=7363
7. Mourkoussis, N., White, M., Patel, M., Chmielewski, J., Walczak, K.: AMS–Metadata for Cultural Exhibitions using Virtual Reality. In: International Conference on Dublin Core and Metadata Applications, p. 193 (2003)
8. Hyvönen, E., Mäkelä, E., Salminen, M., Valo, A., Viljanen, K., Saarela, S., Kettula, S.: MuseumFinland Finnish museums on the semantic web. Web Semantics: Science, Services and Agents on the World Wide Web 3(2), 224–241 (2005)
9. Athanasiou, E., Faka, M., Hermon, S., Vassallo, V., Yiakoupi, K.: 3D documentation pipeline of Cultural Heritage artifacts: a cross-disciplinary implementation
10. 3DSA Portal project, http://3dsa.metadata.net/3dsa/
11. White, M., Mourkoussis, N., Darcy, J., Petridis, P., Liarokapis, F., Lister, P., Gaspard, F.: ARCO-an architecture for digitization, management and presentation of virtual exhibitions. In: Computer Graphics International, pp. 622–625. IEEE Press (2004)
12. The CIDOC Conceptual Reference Model, http://www.cidoc-crm.org/

Comparative Study of Digital Repositories: A Case Study of *DESIDOC Journal of Library & Information Technology*

Alka Bansal and Dipti Arora[*]

Defence Scientific Information & Documentation Centre (DESIDOC), DRDO,
Ministry of Defence, Metcalfe House, Delhi-110054, India
{alkabansal777,dipti30arora}@gmail.com

Abstract. *DESIDOC Journal of Library & Information Technology (DJLIT),* is an international, peer-reviewed, open access journal. In early 2002, to provide metadata and full-text of each article of *DJLIT*, a digital repository was created using GSDL software. It was named '*DJLIT* Digital Library' which covered all volumes and was made available at intranet for its users spread all over the country but not on internet. In early 2007, *DJLIT* automated its publishing process by using OJS software and a repository was created with metadata and full-text of articles as well as archive of all issues and was made available at internet. As same articles were available at two platforms, an attempt is made to study key features of both repositories, building-up process; search and retrieval; etc., to understand if *repository* available on OJS can replace *DJLIT* Digital Library without compromising any features and what modifications will be required in OJS *repository*.

Keywords: Open journal system, digital library, digital repository, *DESIDOC Journal of Library & Information Technology.*

1   Introduction

Digital repository is a mechanism for managing and storing digital content which can have subject or institutional focus and for a variety of purposes and users. A repository supports research, learning, and administrative processes. Repositories enable open standards to ensure that the content they contain is accessible, searchable and retrievable for later use. A policy decision is made by respective institution or administrator regarding the technology used, software, and contents, etc. Typically content can include research outputs, e-theses, articles, and teaching materials, etc [1]. Defence Scientific Information & Documentation Centre (DESIDOC) brings out number of scientific and technical publications such as *Defence Science Journal, Technology Focus, DRDO Newsletter, Monographs*, etc. It started digitising its collection in early 2000 and built digital repositories. *DESIDOC Journal of Library & Information Technology (DJLIT)* [2] is one of the premier publications of DRDO, published by DESIDOC. It is an international,

---

[*] Corresponding author.

K. Tuamsuk et al. (Eds.): ICADL 2014, LNCS 8839, pp. 30–38, 2014.
© Springer International Publishing Switzerland 2014

peer-reviewed, open access, bimonthly journal that endeavours to bring recent developments in IT applicable to LIS. It is meant for librarians, documentation and information professionals, researchers, students and others interested in the field. It is being published since 1981 and was formerly known as *'DESIDOC Bulletin of Information Technology (DBIT)'*. The articles published in the Journal are covered in Scopus, LISA, LISTA, EBSCO Abstracts/Full-text, Informed Librarian Online, DOAJ, Open J-Gate, Indian Science Abstracts, Indian Citation Index, Full text Sources Online, WorldCat, Proquest, Index Copernicus, and OCLC.

In 2002, DESIDOC came up with pdf versions of articles of *DJLIT* for its intranet users under its digital repository building project. All the back issues of *DJLIT* were scanned and pdf were created. At that time Corel Ventura 8 software was being used as publishing software so current issues were created directly as pdf. All these volumes were maintained under its digital library *'DJLIT* Digital Library' built using. Greenstone Digital Library (GSDL), an open source software (OSS). The *DJLIT* Digital Library was made available on local intranet (Fig. 1(a)) and still continuing. When open access boomed, DESIDOC came up with open access of *DJLIT* in early 2007. Open Journal System (OJS), one of the premier open access journal management and publishing software was chosen and implemented to expand and improve access to research and free access was given to its users on internet at publications.drdo.gov.in/ojs/index.php/djlit (Fig. 1(b)). The metadata and full-text were made available under 'Archives'. Since then, two digital repositories of *DJLIT* are maintained using two open source software *i.e.,* on local intranet using GSDL and on internet using OJS. Users can search, retrieve, download, print, etc., from both these repositories.

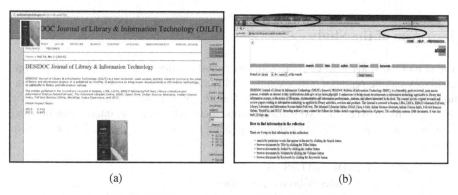

(a)   (b)

Fig. 1. *DJLIT* repositories: (a) GSDL and (b) OJS

Though OJS itself is not digital library software, but many of the features such as uploading of articles, browsing, search, downloading, printing, that are mandatory for a digital library are available in OJS. As the same data and information was being presented through two different modes, so, there was a need to do a comparative study to understand the features of both for repositories and their differences using various parameters such as search facility, indexing, availability and depth of information available, communication facility, customization and interoperability, etc. There was a need to understand if with some modifications/variations, the *DJLIT* repository on OJS can replace the *DJLIT* digital library created using GSDL.

2   Literature Survey

Several studies have been undertaken by various researchers across the globe to understand the features, function, and usability of open source software for building of digital repositories. The study by Patil & Kanamadi [3] makes out the comparison, features, function and usability of OSS like DSpace, GSDL, and EPrints. According to them, GSDL and EPrints are widely used and also low cost option for a repository primarily aimed at open access to article pre-prints and post-prints including digital theses. A range of object types can be uploaded, including video, audio, images and zip files. Edgar & Willinsky [4] carried out a survey of 998 scholarly journals and highlighted that use of OJS can alter a field of communication, for OJS appears to have created a third path, dedicated to maximizing access to research and scholarship, as an alternative to traditional scholarly society and commercial publishing routes. According to Willinsky [5], OJS has been designed to reduce the time and energy devoted to the clerical and managerial tasks associated with editing a journal, while improving the record keeping and efficiency of editorial processes. It seeks to improve the scholarly and public quality of journal publishing through a number of innovations, from making journal policies more transparent to improving indexing. Maxwell [6] explored the possibilities of using OJS to run small, independent magazines and concluded that there can be additional requirements of an open–ended repertoire of content types; content repurposing; content granularity, collaborative editing and annotation; audience interaction; single–source/multi–mode production; and flexible configuration to use it as magazine publishing software.

3   Aim of the Study

The aim of the study is to verify if with some modifications/variations, the *DJLIT* digital library can be replaced with existing OJS repository. To carry out such transmutation, it was imperious to understand the features of the two digital repositories, the heterogeneity between the two software tools, their customization, interoperability, and ease in creation, passivity, and tranquillity to the end-users. Hence, the following were studied:

(1) Features of GSDL and OJS
(2) Prevailing attributes of both repositories
(3) Process to build up the repositories
(4) Analogous comparison of both repositories
(5) Full-text retrieval in both repositories

4   Methodology

In this paper 'digital library' and 'repository' carry the same meaning. The features of both the software were studied from their respective sites at www.greenstone.org/ and http://pkp.sfu.ca/ojs/. Both *DJLIT* repositories available respectively at DRDO intranet and on internet (http://publications.drdo.gov.in/ojs/index.php/djlit/) were studied.

The process of building up the repositories and comparative characteristics were studied in administrator mode. To analyse and understand the retrieval, a search was performed using the keyword 'Digital Reference' on both the repositories.

5   Analysis and Findings

5.1   Software Features

The GSDL software [7] is developed by University of Waikoto and further distributed in association with UNESCO and the Human Info NGO. It is cross platform, multi lingual software to empower users, particularly in universities, libraries, etc., to build their own digital libraries. It is readily extensible, and with the support of GNU-licensed modules, it helps in full-text retrieval, database management, and text extraction from proprietary document formats and runs on all versions of Windows, Unix/Linux, and Mac OS-X. Its main library runs on main web server, where it inter-operates with standard web server software (e.g. Apache). It is also interoperable with Open Archives Protocol for Metadata Harvesting (OAI-PMH), and can harvest documents over OAI-PMH and include them in a collection. Open Journal System [8] (OJS) is developed under Public Knowledge Project and released under GNU general public license. OJS facilitates the development of open access, peer-reviewed publishing, technical infrastructure for the online presentation of journal articles, and entire editorial management workflow, including article submission, multiple rounds of peer-review, and indexing. The OJS is built on PHP platform and it is available in more than 30 languages. It was originally released in 2001, and now it is running in version 2.4.2.

5.2   Prevailing Attributes of Both Repositories

Presently, *DJLIT* digital library is running in version 2.8 of GSDL at intranet. It is cross platform and English language has been used for publishing. Windows platform is being used for building up. Its main library runs with its main web server on Linux, where it interoperates with Apache as standard web server software. The repository of *DJLIT* is available on OJS on internet and currently running in version 2.3.8.0. It facilitates the development of open access, article submission, peer-reviewed publishing, online availability of articles, and indexing. DESIDOC also maintains a mirror server at backend to ensure data security in case of exigency. On both the repositories, the metadata, cover of each issue, contents page, and full-text of articles are available.

5.3   Building Up of *DJLIT* Digital Library Using GSDL and OJS

DJLIT follows the standard publishing process of journal publishing. The manuscripts are received, initially scrutinised, peer-reviewed, and the selected manuscripts are edited, DTP processed. Then pdfs for individual articles for the issues are created.

Each pdf file is stored in the GSDL repository using its five standards steps as: (a) Download; (b) Gather; (c) Enrich; (d) Design; (e) Create. Once the library is created, it is transferred to *DJLIT* server using FTP.

GSDL has two separate interactive interfaces, the Reader interface and the Librarian interface. End users access the *DJLIT* digital library through the Reader interface, which operates within a web browser. The Librarian interface is a Java-based graphical user interface through which it gathers material for a collection, which is then enriched with metadata. GSDL was customised for the searching and browsing facilities that the collection will offer the end user. Though the prede-fined metadata sets are Dublin Core, RFC 1807, NZGLS, AGLS, but *DJLIT* uses DC metadata structure. New metadata sets can always be defined using Green-stone's Metadata Set Editor. Plug-ins can also be used to ingest documents in the formats like PDF, PostScript, Word, RTF, HTML, Plain text, Latex, ZIP archives, Excel, PPT, Email (various formats), source code. There are two ways of building up the repository on OJS

(a) Fetching the metadata directly from the author submission--It only requires the full-text pdf files to be uploaded. With this way, each paper is scheduled separately for the table of contents for a single issue (Fig. 2 a).
(b) Manually generating the metadata like author name, affiliation, title, abstract, keywords, etc., and then uploading the pdf. (Fig. 2 b).

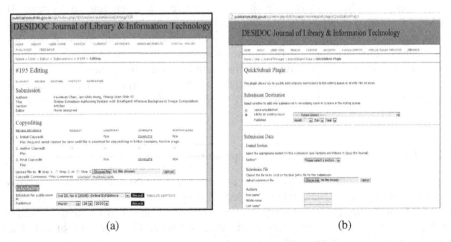

(a)   (b)

Fig. 2. Metadata creation on OJS digital repository: (a) Fetching metadata (b) creating metadata

Users register on OJS website (http://publications.drdo.gov.in/ojs/index.php/djlit/user/register) and submit paper. Though no registration is required if someone wants to read or download metadata including abstract or full-text of the current contents (issue) or any back issue, though administrator has the option to alter it anytime. Willinsky [5] in his paper on OJS, described the use of DC metadata structure for indexing on OJS with the fields: Title, Creator; Subject, description, publisher, contributor, type, format, identi-fier, source, language, relation, coverage and rights. *DJLIT* also uses same metadata structure for its full-text searching on internet. The *DJLIT* (OJS) also provides the policies, submission, and any other information.

5.4   Comparative Characteristics

Both the repositories carry similarities such as both carry plugin architecture; have indexing facility; search facility; and open access support. They are dissimilar in certain ways: The OJS is LOCKSS-compliant, which ensures permanent archiving for ongoing access to content of journal. There is availability of active features and provision to feed general information like policies, guidelines, subscription information, announcements, etc., as part of OJS, whereas GSDL needs an interface at front end (such as web page) to feed such information. OJS also supports Web 2.0 feature like RSS feed which enables reader to know the current changes in the websites. Notification can be automatically sent to the registered users. OJS offers more extensive plugin architecture than GSDL to add new features, applets, and also for creating dynamism to the repository. By activating plugin at administrative end, the articles on repository can be indexed through any search engine on internet. The Counter plugin on OJS allows recording and Counter reporting on site activity. One can use Report Plugins to implement various types of reports and data extracts such as article readership, articles information, etc. There are many plugins available on developer's website at *https://pkp.sfu.ca/ojs/docs/userguide/2.3.3/systemInstallingPlugins.html*

5.5   Browsing and Search Results

DJLIT digital library on GSDL has various fields available through which browsing can be done such as (a) Title (a-z listing); (b) Author (a-z listing); (c) Volume; (d) Keyword (a-z listing) and in repository on OJS the indexes available are: (a) Title (alphabetically), (b) Author (a-z listing) and (c) Volume and Issue wise.

Both the repositories provide full access to articles and provide inbuilt search tools. Users can access, search, retrieve, download, save, and print the desired article. One can search in *DJLIT* Digital Library (GSDL on intranet) using any of the tools like title, author, keywords, abstract, year, volume, etc. Search is also available in full-text mode and Allfields mode. Repository on OJS offers search tools such as author, title, full-text, date, index term, etc. Advanced searching can be done at author, title, full-text, supplementary fields, date of publishing, discipline, keywords, type (method/approach), and coverage. It also uses Boolean operators, wildcard, removal of common words, etc. Search terms are case-insensitive (Fig. 3).

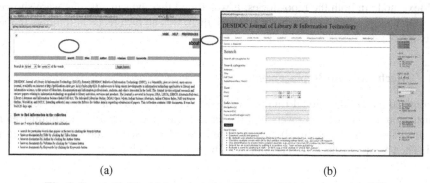

(a)   (b)

Fig. 3. Search facility (a) intranet using GSDL and (b) internet using OJS

Before replacing one repository with another, it was important to understand if the search results were same for both the repository or not. A search was performed with keyword 'digital reference' on both the repositories. The *DJLIT* Digital Library considered 'digital' as a single keyword and 'reference' as another keyword. Apart from showing the related results, it also showed the word count (the no. of times the keyword searched appeared in the retrieved results) and the no. of documents matched the query (Fig 4). Since *DJLIT* used only pdf format for full-text for uploading so only pdf format was retrieved.

In OJS, search can be performed index-term-wise, in abstract only, title only, author only and advanced searching. In index-term, the search will be done only in index term assigned to the article. A keyword 'digital reference' was searched through index-term. The result showed that OJS repository considered the two terms 'digital' and 'reference' separately and showed results regarding papers where both the terms were included in the index terms (assigned earlier in the index field while loading the articles) but either as combined or separately (Fig. 4).

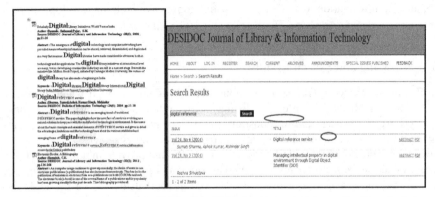

Fig. 4. Keyword search on GSDL and OJS with *'Digital Reference'* as keyword

When same term 'digital reference' was searched through abstract field in OJS, it considered the two terms 'digital' and 'reference' separately and showed results containing articles where both the terms were included in the abstract but either as combined or separately. When the searching was done for the 'Digital Reference' in full-text mode in both the repositories, it was found that the same results were shown by both the repositories (Figs. 5 & 6). Hence there was no difference in findings in the outcome.

5.6   Mechanism for Replacement

To replace the *DJLIT* Digital Library with OJS repository, one has to cease new user registration as authors, reviewers and readers keeping the rights of the administrator to enroll any user at any time.It can be done by disabling this feature at administrator end. Then a copy of the OJS repository can be uploaded on intranet.

Fig. 5. Search in *DJLIT* Digital library with 'Digital Reference' as keyword in full-text

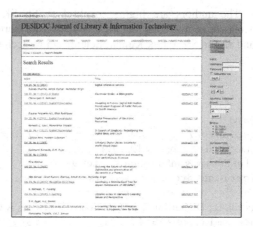

Fig. 6. Search in *DJLIT* repository (OJS) with 'Digital Reference' as keyword in full-text

6   Discussions and Conclusions

Both repositories of *DJLIT* carry wide hit counter of accessing its contents. Both provide scholarly information storage, search and retrieval through title, author, volume (issue in OJS), etc. GSDL offers searching through title, author, keywords, abstract, year, volume, full-text mode and allfields mode. OJS offers three search categories—(a) author, title, full-text, and supplementary fields; (b) Date; and (c) Index terms—Disciplines, keywords, type (method/approach), and coverage. It also uses Boolean operators, wildcard, removal of common words, etc. It is noted that OJS offers more search features than GSDL. OJS has built-in active additional features such as provision for information regarding policies, guidelines, subscription information, etc. about the repository.

While GSDL needs an interface at front end to feed such information such as a web page. There is no need for separately creating any webpage for OJS to give such additional information. OJS also supports Web 2.0 feature like RSS feed which enables reader to know the current changes in the website contents. It also supports active tabs like notifications, announcements, etc., for updating its users for any new development or plans regarding future issues. To replace the GSDL only as a repository (only search and retrieval) on intranet, one has to cease new user registration by disabling it as administrator end. Using OJS repository, the readers will be facilitated more with active control of contents and time saving. With the analysis, it was found that there is no need for maintaining two different repositories for same data. It is not only the duplication of efforts rather dispersal of resources, storage space and extra time consumed for building two separate repositories using different software tools. With modifications in the Administrator mode, one can disable the registration of users as authors, reviewers and readers still maintaining the rights of the administrator to enroll any user at any time. The features of OJS can be tailored to convert it to a digital repository for archiving and preserving scholarly data anytime without the use of any external hardware and interoperability support system.

Acknowledgements. The authors are highly thankful to Sh SK Jindal, Director, DESIDOC for his encouragement to carry out the analysis of the journal and permission to publish the work and also to Sh Ashok Kumar, Scientist G for technical advice.

References

1. What-is-a-repository,
   http://www.rsp.ac.uk/start/before-you-start/what-is-a-repository/ (accessed on February 10, 2014)
2. DESIDOC Journal of Library & Information Technology,
   http://publications.drdo.gov.in/ojs/index.php/djlit (accessed on February 10, 2014)
3. Patil, M.S., Kanamadi, S.: Digital Library Open Source Software: A Comparative Study,
   http://www.academia.edu/250425/Digital_Library_Open_Source_S
   oftware_A_Comparative_Study
4. Edgar, B.D., Willinsky, J.: A Survey of Scholarly Journals Using Open Journal Systems. Scholarly and Research Communication 1(2) (2010)
5. Willinsky, J.: Open Journal Systems: An example of open source software for journal management and publishing. Library Hi Tech 23(4), 504–519 (2005)
6. Maxwell, J.W.: Extending OJS into small magazines: The OMMM Project. First Monday 12(10) (2007),
   http://journals.uic.edu/ojs/index.php/fm/article/view/1962/
   1839#author
7. GSDL software, http://www.greenstone.org/ (accessed on February 10, 2014)
8. Open Journal systems, http://pkp.sfu.ca/ojs/ (accessed on February 10, 2014)

Personal Digital Libraries: Keeping Track of Academic Reading Material

Mohammed Al-Anazi, Annika Hinze, Nicholas Vanderschantz,
Claire Timpany, and Sally Jo Cunningham

Dept. of Computer Science, University of Waikato,
Private Bag 3105, Hamilton New Zealand
msma1@students.waikato.ac.nz,
{hinze,vtwoz,ctimapny,sallyjo}@waikato.ac.nz

Abstract. This paper discusses optionsfor tracking academic reading material and introduces a personal digital library solution. We combined and extended the open source projects Zotero and Greenstone such that material can be easily downloaded and ingested into the combined system. Our prototype system has been explored in a small user study.

1   Introduction

Researchers have to keep track of an increasing number of electronic publications. Not all articles and papers are read immediately, and keeping track of one's reading list is not straightforward[4]. Once a text has been evaluated, read or identified to be read later, many researcher instigate their own routine for managing the process of recording and remembering the context, location and identified need for that book or article. This paper is our first investigation into how to manage this problem for eReading environments. We report on a project that aimed to identify the issues academics encounter as they keep track of their reading material, and a software solution to support this process. We explored popular citation management software systems and rather than devising a completely new system, we instead re-use and extend available systems (the two open source projects Zotero and Greenstone) to form a personal digital library system for tracking digital reading material. The resulting prototype was evaluated in a small-scale user study.

2   User Study

The study investigated the kinds of reading materials that students and academicskeep track of, as well as thesoftware or methods they use for tracking. Each participant answered questions in a questionnaire and an interview. Twenty people participated (14 male/6 female; 2 under 29, 10 under 39, 5 under 48 and three 48 and over; 14 students/6 academics; 13 from IT and 7 from other academic fields). All were highly experienced with computers (>10 years) and 18 used computers more than 4 hours each day. In our evaluation here we focus on academic reading.

K. Tuamsuk et al. (Eds.): ICADL 2014, LNCS 8839, pp. 39–47, 2014.
© Springer International Publishing Switzerland 2014

Reading Material. 14 participants indicated that academic reading occupies about 66% to 85% of their reading materials, for two it is more and for the other four it is less. For 15 participants, more than 60% of their reading is articles and conference papers (>80% for 9 of these), and all 20 rea about 20% are books and theses. 18 of 20 read articles and papers wholly or predominantly in electronic form, and 14 read books predominantly as hardcopies. The remainder of academic reading is largely done electronically.

Tracking Intention. None of the participants were interested in tracking which non-academicreading they had done or were currently engaged in, but only the reading they wished to do in future. For academic reading, all participants were interested in tracking what they *will* read and what they *had read*; 10 wish to track their current reading. All participants keep copies of electronic materials on their computers, and 10 print the materials in various circumstances. All participants noted that they tend to track theiracademic digital materials only when they do a project, research, or write a paper.

Tracking Have-Read Material. Participants use three main methods to track materials they have read (some use several): folders and subfolders (19 of 20), a list (4), and software (7). No-one keeps only a list, and only one uses only software. Within folders and subfolders, documents may be sorted according to the structure of the document to be written; sometimes with a further structure according to importance. Participantsindicated that not all the materials they place in their folders need be read or used – for this distinction they rely on their memory based on title or abstract.The software used is: Endnote (2), Mendeley (2), Zotero (1), NVivo (1) and Safari bookmarks (1). Each of the four participants who kept lists had their own method of what to record.

Tracking Current Reading. Only half of the participants keep track of current reading, of which four use software tools. Five participants leave the materials open on screen, two leave sticky notes in the office/on screen, one uses the Safari reading list, another Excel sheets and Endnote, and another one uses PDFreader software on a phone/tablet.

Tracking Future-Read Material. Five different methods are used for keeping track of future reading material: software tools (5), download of documents (9), email with material/title or link (2), sticky notes (3), and print-outs (1). The software tools used were the online system for to-do lists Remember-the-Milk (named twice), a referencing system, reading lists in Safari, and bookmarks.Two participants also wished to track future reading but did not currently have any method for doing so. None of the participants who download documents had a specific location on their computers for storing these documents, but some reported maintaining a folder called 'Want to read' or similar.

Tracking Problems Encountered. A number of problems were reported about the methods used to track electronic reading materials. 10 participants mentioned that they spend quite some time looking for specific papers, and that often very little of the stored information is used. Four people reported reading a paper more than once because they do not know if it has been read or not. Papers that need to be used in two or three different projects are hard to place, replicating folders and applying different highlights (4 participants). Two participants mentioned saving a hyperlink, and the paper being gone when they returned to the link later. Two participants talked of the difficulty in identifying downloaded files by file names containing just numbers and letters. They also mentioned not finding files again, or downloading papers more than once.

Referencing Material. 14 of 20 participants used software for referencing, e.g., Endnote (8), MS Word (2), and Bibtex, Jabref, Mendeley, and Zotero (1 each). 6 of 20 do their referencing manually. The participant using Bibtex was the only one writing papers in LaTex; all others write using MS Word.

We observe a discontinuity in the processing/tracking of reading materials as the participants use different methods for each stage. For previously read material most use folders and subfolders, which is not used at all for 'currently reading' and 'planning to read'. It seems as if participants try different methods, but have no effective common strategy. As a consequence, several participants observed spending too much time looking for a specific paper, that often very little of the information is used, and that duplication of material and information is problematic.Further time is wasted by re-reading material unintentionally. Most participants use software tools to format references when writing, often those that integratewith the users chosen word processing software.

3   Requirements

We now define the requirements for a system for tracking academic reading, based on the user study results.The system needs to provide software features to

— R1) Download the reading material and its metadata
— R2) Store the material itself as well as its metadata
— R3) Browse the reading material
— R4) Search within the material and the metadata
— R5) Indicate the reading status of materials
— R6) Reference material when writing papers/articles
— R7) Annotate material

We will use these requirements to analyse the related work, andto design our own system (the prototype supports R1 to R5, leaving R6and R7 for future work).

4   Related Work

We reviewed four popular citation management systems (Endnote, RefWorks, Zotero and Mendeley), two social networking systems (LibraryThing and Goodreads), and one digital library (Greenstone).[1] Endnote is a commercial tool for managing references that can manage large libraries in a desktop system. Trinoskey et al. [5] concluded that it was particularly suitable for academic writing. Endnote fully supports R2, R3 and R7; it partially supports the R1 (download metadata only) and R4 (search in metadata only). RefWorks is a web-based system with features similar to those of Endnote. RefWorks supports R2 and R7; it partially supports R4 through search in metadata only. While RefWorks and Endnote were designed to manage citations, Zotero and Mendeley were developed to manage publications [3].Zotero is a free open-source system that can be used as desktop software (for citations during writing) and as a Firefox browser extension (for import/download of documents). Zotero automatically recognises the records types (e.g., 'conference papers and books'), and its collections can be synchronized over multiple computers. Zotero fully supports R1, R2, R4 and R7. It partially supports R3, although one cannot browse the document through Zotero itself.

Mendeley is a free web-based system with a synchronising desktop component. Mendeley imports and organises PDFs and bibliographic citations via manual upload or metadata import from web-sources. It organises material into a folder structure. Mendeley fully supports R2, R3, R4, and R7. It partially supports R1 (metadata download) and R7 (indicating read/unread). Barsky (2010)statesthat Zotero and Mendeley are easier to use than Endnote and RefWorks[2]. LibraryThing is a social online service for cataloguing books. Users can add books to the collection by searching through the Library of Congress and over 695 world libraries. Any item in the collection can be tagged, reviewed, annotated, and rated, and can be shared with friends. Users can organise their collections in folders and sub folders, such as 'To read' and 'Currently reading'. LibraryThing supports R5 and R7; it partially supports R1, R2, R4 (only for metadata). Goodreads is a social online service for book recommendations and private library catalogues. Users can add books to their bookshelves by searching online or adding them manually. Users may organise the books into shelves such as 'Read', 'Currently reading', or 'Want to read'. Because Goodreads is a social network digital library like LibraryThing, it supports similar features: R5 and R7 fully and R1, R2, and R4 partially for metadata. Greenstone is an open source system for building one's own digital library, which may contain books, images, audio, video and PDFs. It is able to gather, organise, and build those items automatically [6], and provides functions for accessing items (browse, search, and index). Greenstone fully supports R2, R3, and R4. The other requirements are not supported.

Summary. We identified seven requirements for software that tracks reading materials. Seven systems were reviewed according to these requirements. Our findings are summarised in Table 1, and it is apparent that none of the systems support all our requirements. The next section introduces our system design that combines and extends a combination of two of these systems.

---

[1] The systems are available at http://endnote.com, www.refworks.com, www.zotero.org, www.mendeley.com, www.librarything.com, www.loc.gov/index.html, www.goodreads.com

Table 1. Summary of requirements comparisons (x=fulfils requirement, o=partially fulfils requirement, empty = system does not fulfil the requirements)

	R1 Download	R2 Store	R3 Browse	R4 Search	R5 Reading status	R6 Reference	R7 Annotate
Endnote	o	x	x	o			x
RefWorks		x	o	o			x
Zotero	x	x	o	x			x
Mendeley	o	x	x	x	o		x
LibraryThing	o	o		o	x		x
GoodReads	o	o		o	x		x
Greenstone		x	x	x			

5   System Design and Prototype Implementation

Here we introduce our system design from initial decisions to final prototype.

5.1   Conceptual Design

We decided to create a system that is a combination of Zotero and Greenstone, extended by additional functionalities. Both these systems are open source and freely available, and from our initial investigation it is clear that together they already fulfil a number of our requirements. In our design, we focus on requirements R1 to R5 (options for how to incorporate R6 and R7 will be discussed in Section 7). Although Greenstone and Zotero fulfil similar requirements, they follow very differently philosophies and provide different user experience:

- **R1:** Users can download metadata and documents through the Zotero browser add-on. Greenstone can incorporate metadata and documents through the librarian interface, but does not support easy online incorporation.
- **R2:** In both Zotero and Greenstone, material and metadata can be stored long-term.
- **R3:** Users can browse the material full-texts as well as the metadata in greenstone. Zotero keeps the full-texts but does not support browsing through its software.
- **R4:** Both systems support search in metadata. Greenstone provides search in full-texts and indicates results within the full-texts.
- **R5:** Neither system directly supports indication of the reading status, but Greenstone can hold additional indexes and folders that can be extended for this purpose.

Zotero provides easy incorporation into web-search and automatic meta-data analysis, while Greenstone provides support for browsing, full-text search and easy extension for indexes. In our combined system, we use Greenstone as the document management system and Zotero as the metadata and document provider. We designed additional data transfer modules from Zotero into Greenstone, and extended Greenstone to capture information about the current reading status of documents. The PDF full-texts and its metadata usually reside on a website, and users capture these using Zotero. The system then imports this data into the Greenstone collection, and tracks the reading status.

5.2   Implementation

Our system has several modules as shown in Figure 2. Electronic articles and papers located on websites often have two components, i.e., PDFs and metadata (grey and yellow elements in Figure 2).Elements of Zotero are indicated in red, parts of Greenstone are shown in green and our system extensions are shown in blue.

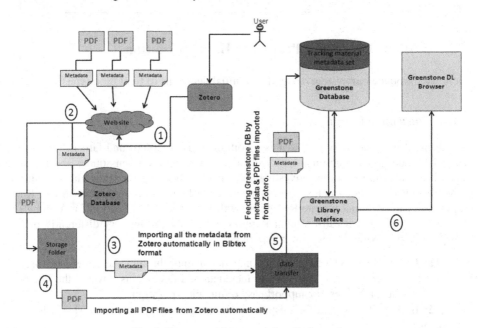

Fig. 1. System architecture and walk-through

We now explain the working of the system architecture using a walk-through (numbers in steps are also shown in the architecture).

(1) Using the Zotero tool, the user adds records from websites.
(2) Zotero stores the metadata of the records added (type of source, title, author...), and available source files (e.g., PDFs or Web pages)in a 'Storage Folder'.
(3) Our system imports the metadata automatically in Bibtex format from Zotero.
(4) Our system imports the metadata files automatically from Zotero.
(5) Our system exports the metadata and PDFs to Greenstone database.
(6) Greenstone builds the library by organising the metadata and its files, which will be shown in the browser.

The system is now ready to track reading information. Initially all reading material is classified as "to read", later to be changed into "reading" or "have read". Indexes hold the information for each of the three types.Figure 3 shows the interface for the reading phase. The example shows one document each in "to read" and in "have read". Changing the reading phase of a document can be done for each document separately (see Figure 4). Further details about the system implementation can be found in [1].

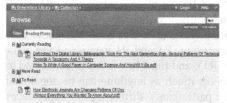

Fig. 2. Reading phase overview

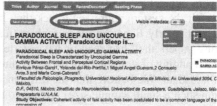

Fig. 3. Changing the reading phase

6   Evaluation: Exploratory User Study

Our exploratory user study consisted of three phases: an interview before using the software, a diary study while using the software, and an interview after using it. We recruited four participants and installed our software on their computers, encouraging them to use the software andto fill in a diary about their experiences. All participants were from Computer Science(three faculty members and one Master's student).

Participant Background. Even though three participants had previously used the Greenstone interface, none of them had any experience with building collections in Greenstone (i.e., the librarian interface). Two participants had previously used Zotero for a long time (P1 and P2), while the other two had never used it. All participants were experienced in downloading papers for their research. For tracking reading material, P1 and P2 use a folder structure (to read/have read), while P3 accumulates electronic papers for writing articles but does not have any specific structure. P4 uses a folder structure that assigns topics once a paper has been read. None of the participants tracked their current reading. P3 and P4 do not track papers that they wish to read in the future.

Observations While Using the System. ll four participants added material to the system: three participants encountered no problems but P2 felt that there were too many steps involved in successfully adding an item.   P2 and P4 also added items that did not come with PDF full-texts. For other items, they observed that reading a PDF in Greenstone is not always convenient, and they instead opted to use an external PDF viewer. Three participants (P1, P2 and P3) wished to not need to click the "add item" button for each item.P1 suggested that the system should detect the reading of material automatically, and adjust the reading phase information. P3 wished to group items in the way they are structured in Zotero and asked for this feature to be added to the system. P1 wanted to be able to mark the reading place in the electronic document so they could come back to it later on and finish reading; similarly P4 wanted to bookmark places in the documents. Missing PDFs or inconvenient display of PDFs was commented on by all participants. Additionally, they wished to convert the webpages into PDF (P1), and reformat the way that Greenstone displays the PDF (P2). P1 also suggested connectingthe system with Google scholar to download items more easily.

Discussion: P1 andP2, who were familiar with Zotero, organized their downloaded papers into folders and used tags, while P3 and P4 put all items into one folder. All fourfelt the system addressed a lack they had noticed in their own strategies. P1 and P2 particularly liked the reading phase feature (R5), as it was useful to know how many papers they had read or have started reading. P3 and P4 mentioned the automated adding of items and metadata feature (R1), and liked how a file is connected to its metadata. We believe that the differences (as much as anything can be concluded from such a small sample size) are due to the participants' different prior experiences in using a referencing system. This needs to be explored further.

7   Discussion and Conclusion

This paper explored ways keeping track of electronic reading materials. We analysed popular citation management systems as related work, and used a combination of Zotero and Greenstone to createa personal digital library system for tracking electronic reading material. The resulting prototype was evaluated in a small-scale user study. There are a number of necessary improvements that became apparent even from our very small exploratory study. For example, the downloading of metadata and material should support ingest of several documents at one time, instead of a one-by-one approach. Within the system, better organization should be supported by tags and folders. The formatting of articles needs to be more comfortable for reading, and the metadata needs to be displayed alongside the text. We conclude that our system fulfilled its basic requirements, but better user support and more elaborate methods for organizing content are needed. Future work in this project is manifold: once some of the elementary difficulties have been addressed, the system needs to be explored in a larger user study. More complex extensions may include an automated document ingest with transparent apparent internal workings, automaticdetection of"current readings", and noting the last accessed position within documents. Finally, we wish to explore requirements R6 (citing from collections while writing), and R7 (full-text annotations of documents).

References

1. Al-Anazi, M.S.: Keeping Track of Electronic Reading Material, Master's Thesis, Computer Science Department, University of Waikato (2014)
2. Barsky, E.: Electronic Resources Reviews and Reports. Issues in Science and Technology Libraries 62 (2010)

3. Butros, A., Taylor, S.: Managing information: evaluating and selecting citation management software. In: Proceedings of the 36th IAMSLIC Annual Conference, pp. 1–27 (2010)
4. Hinze, A., McKay, D., et al.: Book selection behavior in the physical library: implications
   for ebook collections. In: Proceedings of the JCDL, pp. 305–314 (2012)
5. Trinoskey, J., Brahmi, F.A., Gall, C.: Zotero: A Product Review. Journal of Electronic
   Resources in Medical Libraries 6(3), 224–229 (2009)
6. Witten, I., Bainbridge, D., Boddie, S.J.: Greenstone: open-source digital library software
   with end-user collection building. Online Information Review 25(5), 288–298 (2001)

Quality Assurance Tool Suite for Error Detection in Digital Repositories*

Roman Graf and Ross King

Research Area Future Networks and Services
Department Safety & Security
Austrian Institute of Technology, Vienna, Austria
{roman.graf,ross.king}@ait.ac.at

Abstract. Digitization workflows for automatic acquisition of image collections are susceptible to errors and require quality assurance. This paper presents the automated quality assurance tools aiming at detection of possible quality issues that supports decision making for document image collections. The main contribution of this research is the implementation of various image processing tools for different error detection scenarios and their combination in to a single tool suite. The tool suite includes: (1) The *matchbox* tool for accurate near-duplicate detection in document image collections, based on SIFT feature extraction. (2) The finger detection tool aims at automatic detection of fingers that mistakenly appear in scans from digitized image collections, which uses processing techniques for edge detection, local image information extraction and its analysis for reasoning on scan quality. (3) The cropping error detection tool supports the detection of common cropping problems such as text shifted to the edge of the image, unwanted page borders, or unwanted text from a previous page on the image. Another important contribution of this work is a definition of the quality assurance workflow and its automatic execution for error detection in digital document collections. The presented tool suite detects described errors and presents them for additional manual analysis and collection cleaning. A statistical overview of evaluated data and characteristics like performance and accuracy is delivered. The results of the analysis confirm our hypothesis that an automated approach is able to detect errors with reliable quality, thus making quality control for large digitisation projects a feasible and affordable process.

Keywords: digital library, digital preservation, quality assurance, image processing.

1 Introduction

Many large-scale digitization projects are currently running in digital libraries, archives and other cultural heritage institutions. These institutions are facing the challenge of assuring adequate quality of document image collections that may comprise millions of books, newspapers and journals with hundreds of pages in each document. Thus, the

---

* This work was partially supported by the SCAPE Project. The SCAPE project is co-funded by the European Union under FP7 ICT-2009.4.1 (Grant Agreement number 270137).

K. Tuamsuk et al. (Eds.): ICADL 2014, LNCS 8839, pp. 48–58, 2014.

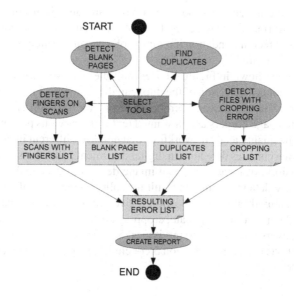

Fig. 1. The workflow for the DIGLIB QA suite that comprises different QA tools

overall volume in these projects has reached a level where a comprehensive manual audit of image quality of all digitized material would be neither feasible nor afford-able. Statistical methods would also require the manual review of tens of thousands of documents, assuming that the errors were uncorrelated, which is usually not the case. Therefore, automated quality assurance tools aiming at detection of possible quality is-sues are required. We apply various image processing tools for error detection scenarios and their combination in to a single tool suite.

In a typical book digitisation workflow, the ability to update a digital copy is a frequent requirement. Either a new digital copy is created by scanning the original analogue resource again, or a new digital derivative based on the raw digital object is produced. The new derivatives are either created to obtain an improved representation of the digital image by removing page borders or skew, or to enrich the digital object by adding related information like full text, layout or semantic representations, etc. In this context, image analysis and comparison technology can help to align any document changes that occur from one version to another.

The selection between the old and the new version of the associated documents are basic operations in this regard. The *matchbox* tool is used for accurate near-duplicate detection in document image collections. This tool is based on Bag of Words and SIFT feature extraction techniques. The finger detection tool (see Figure 4) supports auto-matic detection of fingers that mistakenly appear in scans from digitized image col-lections. This tool makes use of processing techniques for edge detection, local image information extraction and its analysis for reasoning on scan quality. The cropping error detection tool (see Figure 3) supports the detection of common cropping problems such as text shifted to the edge of the image, unwanted page borders, or unwanted text from a previous page on the image. This tool is based on luminance projection. By making use of the various information provided by the tool suite, a decision support system can automatically make a recommendation if a digital object can be safely overwritten or if human inspection is required.

The presented tools shown in Figure 1 cover multiple error scenarios. The main use case for *matchbox* tool is a detection of the duplicated documents. Finger should not be visible on the scans. The use cases for cropping errors are: text shifted to the edge of the image; unwanted page borders and unwanted text from previous page on the image. Figure 1 presents the quality analysis workflow that employs different image processing tool for error and inaccuracies detection in digital document collections. This workflow includes the acquisition of local and global image descriptors, its analysis and an aggregation of resulting data in a common result for collection in form of a report.

The paper is structured as follows: Section 2 gives an overview of related work and concepts. Section 3 explains the duplicate, cropping error and finger on scans detection process and also covers image processing issues. Section 4 presents the experimental setup, applied methods and results. Section 5 concludes the paper and gives outlook on planned future work.

2   Related Work

One of the possible tools for duplicate detection is a *matchbox* tool [7], which is a modern quality analysis tool based on SIFT [11] feature extraction. In contrast to SIFT descriptor matching, the matchbox tool makes use of a bag of visual words (BoW) [2] algorithm. Typically, approaches in the area of image retrieval and comparison in large image collections make use of local image descriptors to match or index visual information. Near duplicate detection of key frames using one-to-one matching of local descriptors was described for video data [16]. A BoW derived from local descriptors was described as an efficient approach to near-duplicate video key frame retrieval [15]. Local descriptors were employed for the detection of near-duplicates [9].

The CROPDET (cropping detection) approach for cropping error detection employs computation of average luminance values for X axis. The [13] algorithm uses a colour profile in form of its three component profiles for image segmentation based on the watershed transform method. Our approach does not use the RGB image directly but transforms it into a greyscale image and subsequently creates a luminance projection.

In the context of digital preservation computer vision techniques are employed in different scenarios. The challenges of finger detection are caused by varying image quality, different finger sizes, direction, shape, colour and light conditions. Currently employed related techniques are trained-model, vision-, or colour-based. None of them completely address the given challenge. Finger masking using closest similar zones of the background images based on a model was described in [10]. However, this method appears to be applicable only for finger detected in the near from border and the image processing method is not further specified. In many real life cases fingers cannot be modeled due to large variations in shape, size and illumination. Sometimes a finger only appears in an image as a light spot or as a blurred shape. This is one reason why the Support Vector Machine method described in [3] cannot be effectively applied to finger detection.

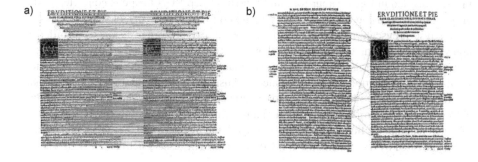

Fig. 2. Evaluation results samples from book identifier 151694702 for duplicate detection with *matchbox* approach: (a) similar pages with 419 matches, (b) different pages with 19 matches

3 Duplicate, Cropping Error and Finger Detection Process

Due to huge number of images and text documents in modern digital collections the quality assurance plays an increasingly important role. Decision making process for quality assurance in digital preservation requires deep knowledge about image processing, file formats and regular library processes. The manual search for such knowledge is very time consuming, requires an expertise in the domain of digital preservation and image processing skills. Therefore we aim at providing automatic error identification and verification methods in order to support decision making regarding the collection cleaning.

3.1 Duplicate Detection Workflow

Collection analysis for duplicates [8], [14] is conducted according the quality assurance workflow. The user triggers a complete collection analysis, the results of which are stored in a text file. In order to detect duplicates we aggregate collection specific knowledge and analyze collections using SIFT feature extraction demonstrated in Figure 2, filtering and matching, as well as the structural similarity analysis. Local feature descriptors are extracted from SIFT keypoints. Robust descriptor matching employs the RANSAC [4] algorithm which is conditioned on an affine transformation between keypoints locations. In the next step we compare images by matching consistent local features with each other. Finally human expert should validate the list of duplicate candidates. Additionally, duplicate candidates contained in a shortlist can be validated by structural similarity comparison, which requires additional computation time and also is limited for documents with printed text written in supported language.

3.2 Cropping Error Detection Workflow

In order to detect documents with cropping error we aggregate specic expert knowledge and analyse images using luminance projection technique. In the first workflow step the image is loaded in RGB colour format. In the next step RGB image is converted to the greyscale format using the perceptually weighted formula (see [6]). In subsequent steps we analyse greyscale image and calculate left and right border distances in order to apply different parameters like minimal and maximal border distance, left to right border relation and average luminance for the image. Additionally the average luminance for the whole collection can be calculated and used as a parameter in the analysis. The evaluated average luminance values for X axis demonstrate calculated values visually. This supports the human expert to infer an informed evaluation of the cropping quality of image candidates that could be mis-cropped and evaluate whether these images are in fact affected by the indicated error and to perform necessary actions.

3.3　Finger Detection Workflow

The finger detection algorithm [5] starts with loading of data from given file. Since the point- and edge-based features are regarded to be robust against lighting variants [12], the Canny edge detection algorithm is employed [1] in order to retrieve edges of a RGB image. Additionally at this stage we flatten the bands of the original image, using the average value of the pixels at each location, in order to obtain a new single-band image. We filter the flattened single-band image pixels by applying a threshold parameter P for pixel value, where P is a coefficient with value in the range from 0.0 to 1.0. We analyze a given scan image in order to detect finger candidates with associated pixel coordinates. To do so we evaluate the next existing pixel on the right from the given position on the X axis and examine its coordinates regarding association with current finger candidate. Given a preliminary finger candidates list, we apply the parameters evaluated from expert knowledge like finger size, points count, variance and distance to border to evaluate the extent to which the candidate matches the requirements. In the final step we draw green rectangle around the detected finger areas and display the resulting image for user reasoning.

4　Evaluation

The goal of our evaluation was the application of different methods for collection analysis for duplicates, cropping error and finger on scans detection resulting in its cleaning, i.e. a collection with no duplicates, cropping error pages and without wrongly cropped scans. Additionally, a statistical overview of evaluated data and characteristics like performance and accuracy is delivered.

4.1　Hypothesis and Evaluation Methods of the Collection Analysis

The presented three evaluation use cases find duplicate pairs, pages with cropping error and finger on scans and present them for additional manual analysis and collection cleaning. Our hypothesis is that automatic approach should be able to detect mentioned corrupted pages with reliable quality and to ignore unattended scans. We consider three use cases. First one is a duplicate detection. The *matchbox* analysis should provide the results of image processing methods and structural similarity scores for similar files should have similar values. The second use case is a cropping error detection. For this scenario we use luminance projection with specified expert parameters for expected collection. The third scenario is about finger on scans detection. For this use case we apply expert parameters, which should match to the analyzed digital collection. We also aim to evaluate whether ground truth files for another quality assurance use case will impact the current use case scenario. If described hypothesis is true then this methods would be a significant improvement over a manual analysis. The considered collection is a mix from different sources.

The collection for duplicate detection use case has identifier Z151694702 and is provided by then Austrian National Library. This collection contains 730 documents corresponding to a single book. Manually created ground truth was available. The cropping detection collection comprises 42 real life sample files and is provided by expert of Austrian National Library. For finger detection files we use collection of 186 files aggregated from different sources in Internet. This collection also comprises two duplicate pairs. All this collections are mixed in one common collection of 958 documents.

We assume that employing of described quality assurance tool suite should correctly detect errors associated with the particular tool and should not detect too many false positive results from other use cases. We also expect that image processing tools *matchbox* [1], cropping detection tool [2] and finger detection tool [3] with an OpenCV 2.4.3 based python workflow and subsequent analysis will demonstrate good performance by sufficient good accuracy. Evaluation takes place on an Intel Core i73520M 2.66GHz computer using Java 6.0 and Python 2.7 languages on Windows OS. We evaluate duplicate candidate pairs, documents with cropping error, documents with finger on scan, calculation time and calculation accuracy for each evaluation method.

4.2 Experimental Results and Its Interpretation

For the first scenario the threshold value 0.9 was determined using statistical approach and robust estimators. The threshold can be adapted dependent from the content. In the first instance we find points of interest in each document and calculate associated SIFT descriptors. In conjunction with similarity threshold we are able to isolate most of the duplicate pairs. The number of pages between the original and the new version of the duplicated documents in the collection is an additional help to find duplicates, since duplicates often appear in a sequence. Some of the detected duplicates have a dominating color and relative high similarity score like documents 2 - 9. These documents should be verified manually and independent from the average similarity score and offsets.

The manual analysis of the test collection shows ten duplicate pairs. The automatic approach of duplicate search did not find three duplicated pages (3, 5 and 6) which were identified as duplicates by manual analysis. The reason for that is the computed average similarity score was higher than the scores of pages 3, 5 and 6. In this specific case we have to deal with nearly empty pages with dominating white color, which makes it difficult to identify these pages as a pair of duplicates. The pages in the range 108 to 115

---

[1] http://openplanets.github.io/matchbox/

[2] http://openplanets.github.io/crop-detection-tool/

[3] http://openplanets.github.io/finger-detection-tool/

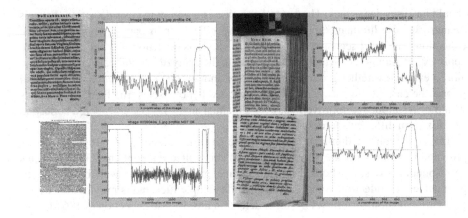

Fig. 3. The correct (left upper side) and corrupted (remaining scans) documents from the test collection with associated average luminance values for X axis

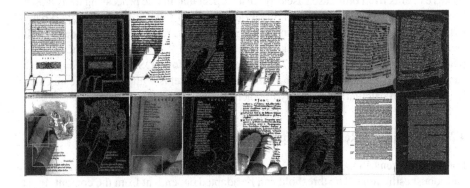

Fig. 4. Positive (first six columns) and negative (last two columns) detections of fingers on scans with associated edges where suspected areas are marked by green rectangles

and pages 117, 124 are detected as false positives by the automatic analysis. In contrast to the dominating color case similarity scores are in range here. Manual checking of mentioned pages reveals that there are no duplicates. The reason for detecting false positive is a high structural similarity of digital image data. But this high similarity does not always mean semantically text similarity that can be validated only by human expert. The calculation time of the *matchbox* tool is about four hours.

Applying cropping error detection tool we evaluated images with corrupted cropping and calculated accuracy for each image. Images were analysed for previously defined cropping use cases like text shifted to the edge of the image, unwanted page borders, or unwanted text from previous page on the image. Figure 3 in the left upper corner presents the average luminance values for X axis for document 00000145.jpg. This document has correct cropping for both borders. The left border distance from border to text edge is about 60 pixels and the larger right border distance is about 270 pixels from the total image width of 900 pixels. The average luminance for this document is 160 on an axis from 0 to 255, where 0 is completely black and 255 is completely white. Figure 3 demonstrates that both borders are white and have correct border relation significant for text document. The text space from 60 to 730 on the X axis is dark what is correct and expected for pages printed in black font. Remaining documents presented in this figure shows documents samples with cropping error. The document 00000496.jpg would match to the expert definitions as a correct document but the black stripe on the lower right side spoils the right border calculation and the whole document is marked as having cropping error. The calculation time of the cropping error detection tool was 7672 seconds. The average luminance values for X axis have corroborated our initial hypothesis that calculation of average luminance values for X axis could be a useful method for detecting cropping errors in document collections.

The result of the finger on scans analysis is a set of documents with finger candidates marked with a green rectangle (see Figure 4). The greyscale image beneath of the colored scan is a computation step in finger detection workflow and demonstrates detected edges. The proposed method has been tested with a variety of images from different origins using a default set of parameters. Mis-classifications (see last two columns) coming along with correct results (see first six columns) are few and happen with shapes similar to finger shape definition. The calculation time of the finger detection on scans tool is 901 seconds. The reason for false detections is that shapes of the text, warping shadow, and cover surface inconsistencies create a structure that looks similar to the finger form. Such cases are difficult to avoid and manual expertise is required to eliminate these false positives.

Therefore all three examined tools present reliable results for digital documents analysis and can be applied for quality assurance of digital collections. All of these approaches help to automatically find out corrupted document candidates in a huge collection. Following this, manual analysis of error page candidates separates real corrupted pages from structural similar documents and evaluates resulting error page list. Presented methods save time and therefore costs associated with human expert involvement in quality assurance process. Only few false positive detections were made despite the low homogeneity of experimental digital collection. Therefore our initial hypothesis is true. But further research is required to improve performance and accuracy metrics of mentioned methods.

The search effectiveness for duplicates, cropping error and finger on scans detection can be determined in terms of a Relative Operating Characteristic (ROC). Similarity analysis divided the given document collection in two groups "error pages and "correct pages by associated expert parameters and thresholds. The tool suite detected seven true positive TP duplicates, 940 true negative TN documents, ten false positive FP duplicates and three false negative FN documents. The cropping detection process evaluated 86 TP document candidates with wrong cropping, 821 true negative TN documents, eight false positive FP images and 43 false negative FN documents. Finally, the finger on scans detection process sorted out 157 TP document candidates with wrong cropping, 772 true negative TN documents, 32 false positive FP images and 29 false

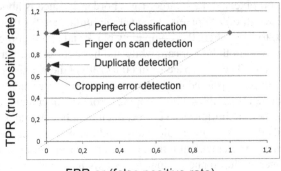

FPR or (false positive rate)

Fig. 5. ROC space plot

negative FN documents. The main statistical performance metrics for ROC evaluation are sensitivity or true positive rate TPR and false positive rate FPR (see Equation 1).

$$TPR = \frac{TP}{(TP + FN)}, FPR = \frac{FP}{(FP + TN)}. \tag{1}$$

Therefore the sensitivity TPR of the presented approach for duplicate detection is 0.7, the FPR is 0.013. For cropping error and finger on scans tools TPR values are 0.666 and 0.844 and FPR values are 0.0096 and 0.0398. The associated ROC values for duplicate detection, cropping error and finger on scans detection are represented by $(0.013, 0.7)$, $(0.001, 0.666)$ and $(0.04, 0.844)$ points respectively. The ROC space (see Figure 5) demonstrates that the calculated FPR and TPR values form all these points are located very close to the so called perfect classification point $(0, 1)$. These results demonstrate that an automatic approach for error page detection of mentioned methods is very effective and it is a significant improvement compared to manual analysis. The distribution of collection points above the red diagonal demonstrates quite good classification results that could be improved by refining of expert settings. Therefore, analysis methods based on image processing techniques can be suggested as an effective method for duplicate page, cropping error and finger on scans detection and as a verification step for quality assurance of digital collections. The results of the analysis confirm our hypothesis that an automated approach is able to detect errors with reliable quality, thus making quality control for large digitisation projects a feasible and affordable process.

5   Conclusion

We have presented an automated quality assurance tools that support decision making for accurate duplicates, cropping error and finger on scans detection in document image collections. This tool suite uses automatic information extraction from the image processing tools, performs analysis and aggregates knowledge that supports quality assurance process for preservation planning.

An important contribution of this research is the implementation of various image processing tools for different error detection scenarios and their combination in to a single tool suite. The tool suite includes tool for accurate near-duplicate detection in document image collections, the finger detection tool and the cropping error detection tool. The presented tool suite detects different quality errors and presents them for additional manual analysis and collection cleaning.

Another important contribution of this work is a definition of the quality assurance workflow and its automatic execution.

The experimental evaluation presented in this paper demonstrates the effectiveness of employing the of different methods for collection analysis for duplicates, cropping error and finger on scans detection resulting in its cleaning. The tool suite reliably detects quality errors like duplicates, cropping error pages and without wrongly cropped scans. An automatic approach delivers a significant improvement when compared to manual analysis.

The tool suite for document image collections presented in this paper ensures quality of the digitized content and supports managers of libraries and archives with regard to long term digital preservation.

As future work we plan to extend an automatic quality assurance approach of image analysis to other digital preservation scenarios. The rules could be combined with different subject categories in order to meet requirements for different use cases.

References

1. Canny, J.: A computational approach to edge detection. IEEE Trans. Pat. Anal. Mach. Intell., 679–698 (1986)
2. Csurka, G., Dance, C.R., Fan, L., Willamowski, J.: Visual categorization with bags of keypoints. In: Workshop on SLCV, ECCV, pp. 1–22 (2004)
3. Felzenszwalb, P.F., Girshick, R.B., McAllester, D., Ramanan, D.: Object detection with discriminatively trained part-based models. Pattern Analysis and Machine Intelligence, IEEE Transactions on Pattern Analysis and Machine Intelligence 32, 1627–1645 (2010)
4. Fischler, M.A., Bolles, R.C.: Random sample consensus: a paradigm for model fitting with applications to image analysis and automated cartography. Commun. ACM 24(6), 381–395 (1981)
5. Graf, R., King, R.: Finger detection for quality assurance of digitized image collections. In: Archiving Conference (2013)
6. Lu, G., Phillips, J.: Using perceptually weighted histograms for colour-based image retrieval. In: Fourth International Conference on Signal Processing, vol. 2 (1998)
7. Huber-Mörk, R., Schindler, A.: Quality assurance for document image collections in digital preservation. In: Blanc-Talon, J., Philips, W., Popescu, D., Scheunders, P., Zemčík, P. (eds.) ACIVS 2012. LNCS, vol. 7517, pp. 108–119. Springer, Heidelberg (2012)
8. Huber-Mörk, R., Schindler, A.: Quality assurance for document image collections in digital preservation. In: Blanc-Talon, J., Philips, W., Popescu, D., Scheunders, P., Zemčík, P. (eds.) ACIVS 2012. LNCS, vol. 7517, pp. 108–119. Springer, Heidelberg (2012)
9. Ke, Y., Sukthankar, R., Huston, L.: An efficient parts-based near-duplicate and sub-image retrieval system. In: Proceedings of the 12th Annual ACM International Conference on Multimedia, MULTIMEDIA 2004, pp. 869–876. ACM, New York (2004)

10. Le Bourgeois, F., Trinh, E., Allier, B., Eglin, V., Emptoz, H.: Document images analysis solutions for digital libraries, document image analysis for libraries. In: Proceedings of the First International Workshop on Document Image Analysis for Libraries (DIAL 2004), pp. 2–24 (2004)
11. Lowe, D.G.: Distinctive image features from scale-invariant keypoints. Int. J. of Comput. Vision 60(2), 91–110 (2004)
12. Marr, D., Hildreth, E.: Theory of edge detection. In: Proc. of the Royal Soc. London, pp. 187–217 (1980)
13. Meyer, F.: Color image segmentation. In: Image Processing and its Applications, pp. 303–306 (1992)
14. Graf, R., King, R., Schlarb, S.: Blank page and duplicate detection for quality assurance of document image collections. In: APA CDAC 2014 (2014)
15. Wu, X., Zhao, W.-L., Ngo, C.-W.: Near-duplicate keyframe retrieval with visual keywords and semantic context. In: Proc. of the 6th ACM ICIVR, pp. 162–169. ACM, New York (2007)
16. Zhao, W.-L., Ngo, C.-W., Tan, H.-K., Wu, X.: Near-duplicate keyframe identification with interest point matching and pattern learning. IEEE Transactions on Multimedia 9(5), 1037–1048 (2007)

Altmetrics for Country-Level Research Assessment

Hamed Alhoori[1], Richard Furuta[1], Myrna Tabet[2], Mohammed Samaka[3],
and Edward A. Fox[4]

[1] Dept. of Computer Science and Engineering, Texas A&M University,
College Station, USA
{alhoori,furuta}@tamu.edu
[2] Qatar University Library, Qatar University, Doha, Qatar
myrna.tabet@qu.edu.qa
[3] Dept. of Computer Science, Qatar University, Doha, Qatar
samaka.m@qu.edu.qa
[4] Dept. of Computer Science, Virginia Tech, Blacksburg, VA, USA
fox@vt.edu

Abstract. Changes are occurring in scholarly communication and the geography of science.Policymakersand research funding agencies are looking for ways to measure the comprehensive impact of research and benefit from the research experiences of other nations. Recently, altmetrics have been used to measure broader impact of research activities.In this paper, we study altmetrics based on the country-levelimpact andfind that altmetrics can support research evaluation for all countries studied. We compare altmetrics with several traditional metrics and findsignificant relationshipsbetween country-level altmetrics and the number of publications, citations, h-index, and gross domestic expenditure on research and development (GERD). We also find a significant yearly increase in the number of articles published between 2010 and 2014 that received altmetrics.

Keywords: Altmetrics, Research Evaluation, R&D, GDP, H-index.

1 Introduction

Countries collaborate, compete, and compare their scientific production with other countries[1]. The scholarly standing of a country plays a vital role in preparing young researchers, attracting top scientists from around the world, promoting that country's creativity and business, opening doors for international collaboration, creating new jobs, and improving the quality of life for citizens and residents.

Research in general has a range of outcomes including articles, patents, software, data, products, and services. Governments require that their dedicated GERD be utilized effectively and transformed into desirable outcomes [2]. Articles and citations have remained the dominant indicatorsof scholarly performance for researchers, journals, universities, and countries [3][4].While citations can help measure research impact, they reveal only part of the impact story, as they may not exist for newly published articles, or articles that have local or limited regional benefit.

K. Tuamsuk et al. (Eds.): ICADL 2014, LNCS 8839, pp. 59–64, 2014.

An increasing number of researchers are sharing articles on social media sites and discussing their results online. The increase in use of social media for research, is estimated at 5–10% per month [5]. Social-based metrics, known as altmetrics [6][7], have been proposed as a complement to citations. Few studies have examinedthe relationship between scholarly productivity and altmetrics at the country-level[8]. Moreover, it is not clear whether altmetrics can be considered as a universal measurement tool since Internet access and usage of social media tools vary from one country or region to another. In this paper, we address two research questions:

1. Can altmetrics support research assessment for various countries?
2. How do altmetrics differ at article and country levels?

This paper is structured as follows.In Section 2, we discuss related work. We describe the data collection and methodology in Section 3. In Section 4, we present and discuss our results. In Section 5, we highlight some planned future work.

2   Related Work

Researchers have investigated several factors when measuring and comparing different countries' scholarly outcomes, such as the number of publications, citations, GERD, and gross domestic product (GDP), to evaluate the return on investment and assist with science policy [9]. Moya-Anegónet al.[10] found a correlation ($R^2 = 0.687$) between the GDP of Latin American countries in 1995 and the number of indexed articles from those countries in 1996. They also found a higher correlation between GERD and the number of articles ($R^2 = 0.865$).Tasli et al. [11] found that the number of articles in dermatology journals from 1999–2008 correlated with the GDP, population and h-index of OECD countries. Meo et al.[12] found that GERD, number of universities, and number of scientific-indexed journals correlated with publications, citations, and h-index in different science and social science fields.

Research communities are looking for additional approaches to measure both the scientific and social impacts of research [13][14].A number of studies [15][16] found a moderate correlation between citations and Mendeley readerships in various disciplines and journals. Haustein et al. [17] found a low correlation between citations and tweets on the article-level.Zahedi et al.[18] used a sample of 20,000 publications from WoSwith altmetrics from impactstory.org. They found that Mendeley's coverage was the highest among all altmetric sources.Holmberg and Thelwall[19] analyzed tweets from selected researchers across ten disciplines and found some disciplinary differences in how researchers used Twitter, such as type of tweets, retweets, sharing links,or conversations.In [20] we investigated a new social-based journal measure and found several significant correlations with traditional citation-based metrics. We also found that usage and coverage of social media for research activities is high within a few platforms such as Mendeley and Twitter. Most of the previous studies attempted to understand altmetrics using only a few measures and focused on article-level but not on the country-level, which this study has explored.

3   Data and Methods

We selected 35 developed and developing countriesthat have published 2,000 or fewer indexed articlesper yearfromJanuary 1, 2010 to June 5, 2014.We included articles that were co-authored by researchers from different countries. We downloaded the bibliometric data of those articles from Scopus, including the DOI, citation, and year published. We used only the articles that included a DOI, resulting in a total of 76,517 bibliometric records. For each country studied, we obtaineditsh-index from SCIMago[1]. We matched Scopus DOIs with data from altmetric.com for each article.We thencompared citation-based data with fivetypes of altmetrics data sources: Twitter, Facebook, mainstream news outlets, blogs, and Google Plus.

We downloaded the GDP, GDP per capita, number of Internet users, number of mobile users, and number of researchers per countryfrom the World Bank'sDataBank[2] for the years 2011 and 2012, since publications in 2012 could be fundedin 2011 or prior. For the few countries that did not have a GDP documented at the World Bank, we used data from the United Nation's National Accounts Main Aggregates Database[3].We used the latest GERD available for 2011 for each country from the World Bank. Similarly, some countries did not have a GERD, so we used data from *R&D Magazine*[4]. We obtainedthe data on usage of social networksfor countries from the World Economic Forum's Global Information Technology Report[5].We used Spearman's rank correlation coefficient, ρ(rho), to compare different metrics.

4   Results and Discussion

4.1   Article-Level Altmetrics

At the article-level, we found weak correlations between citations and various altmetrics. The highest correlations were between blogs and news ($\rho = 0.32$) and between blogs and citations ($\rho = 0.28$). This shows that article-level altmetrics measure a social impact that is different from scholarly impact.The total number of articles that were cited (citations coverage) washigher than the number of articles that received any type of altmetrics (altmetrics coverage) with significant difference.

However, by considering individual years, we found that altmetrics are increasing significantly as shown in Figure 1. Moreover, articles published in 2014 have more altmetrics (27%) than citations (10%) with significant difference. Among these articles, 22% have only altmetrics and 6% have only citations, whichshows that altmetrics can work as an early social impact indicator. Fifteen percent of the articles were shared via Twitter, 4% were posted to Facebook, 2% were blogged, 1% were posted to Google Plus, and 1% reached the mainstream news.

---

[1] http://www.scimagojr.com/countryrank.php
[2] http://databank.worldbank.org/data/home.aspx
[3] http://unstats.un.org/unsd/snaama/introduction.asp
[4] http://www.rdmag.com/
[5] http://www.weforum.org/reports/global-information-technology-report-2014

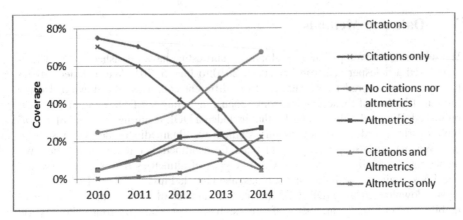

Fig. 1. Coverage of citations and altmetrics from 2010 to 2014

The articles that received citations and altmetrics did not exceed 20% per year, which creates challenges when evaluatingor validating the scholarly impact using both types of metrics. Moreover, a huge proportion of the published articlesremain without anycitation or altmetrics, even years after publication. For example, articles that have neither citations nor altmetrics are 25% in 2010 and 53% in 2013.

4.2   Country-Level Altmetrics

At the country-level, we found that metrics from 2012 had similar correlationstometrics from2011, so we chose to report correlations based on metrics from 2011 only, as shown in Table 1.

Table 1. Correlations between country-level altmetrics and traditional metrics

	GERD	Total articles	Total citations	H-index	Citations coverage	Altmetrics coverage	Internet users
GERD	1.00	0.75	0.67	0.63	0.72	0.61	0.47
Total articles	0.75	1.00	0.91	0.70	0.98	0.84	0.49
Total citations	0.67	0.91	1.00	0.79	0.95	0.94	0.42
H-index	0.63	0.70	0.79	1.00	0.75	0.83	0.33
Citations coverage	0.72	0.98	0.95	0.75	1.00	0.89	0.49
Altmetrics coverage	0.61	0.84	0.94	0.83	0.89	1.00	0.44
Internet users	0.47	0.49	0.42	0.33	0.49	0.44	1.00

The GERD had higher correlations than the GDP. The GDP per capita and citations per article had low correlations with other metrics; however, the h-index had strong correlations. The number of Internet users, the number of mobile users, and usage of social networks have low-moderate correlations, which shows that altmetrics are not strongly related to the number of general users.

Individual altmetrics counts (e.g., scholarly tweets count) and altmetrics coverage were strongly correlated with citations and citations coverage. The numbers of researchers were not available for ten countries; however, comparing the available 25 countries showed low correlations between the number of researchers with other metrics. All correlations were significant at ($p < 0.05$).

Figure 2 shows a significant high level of correlation ($\rho = 0.92$) between citations coverage and altmetrics coveragebased on normalized datafor all articles and years, which can help in predicting and validating the scholarly and social impacts.

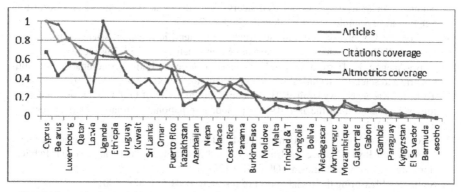

Fig. 2. Countries' scholarly production impact and social impactbased on normalized data

5   Future Work

In the future, we plan to extend the study with more countries and explore if altmetrics can help determine the local social impact of research and emerging research interests across nations. We will investigate why the altmetrics coverage was high for some countries such as Uganda, and whether social attention measures new findings, public interest, gaming of the altmetrics system, or even spam that would target scholarly communities. We also intend to investigate how altmetrics can be used when major social media tools are blocked in some countries.

Acknowledgements. This publication was made possible by NPRP grant # 4–029–1–007 from the Qatar National Research Fund (a member of Qatar Foundation). The statements made herein are solely the responsibility of the authors.

References

1. Zhou, P.: The growth momentum of China in producing international scientific publications seems to have slowed down. Information Processing & Management 49, 1049–1051 (2013)
2. Leydesdorff, L., Wagner, C.: Macro-level indicators of the relations between research funding and research output. Journal of Informetrics 3, 353–362 (2009)

3. Bornmann, L., Leydesdorff, L.: Macro-indicators of citation impacts of six prolific countries: InCites data and the statistical significance of trends. PLOS ONE. 8, e56768 (2013)
4. King, D.A.: The scientific impact of nations. Nature 430, 311–316 (2004)
5. Adie, E., Roe, W.: Altmetric: enriching scholarly content with article-level discussion and metrics. Learned Publishing 26, 11–17 (2013)
6. Priem, J., Piwowar, H.A., Hemminger, B.M.: Altmetrics in the wild: Using social media to explore scholarly impact. arXiv:1203.4745 (2012)
7. Alhoori, H., Furuta, R.: Can social reference management systems predict a ranking of scholarly venues? In: Aalberg, T., Papatheodorou, C., Dobreva, M., Tsakonas, G., Farrugia, C.J. (eds.) TPDL 2013. LNCS, vol. 8092, pp. 138–143. Springer, Heidelberg (2013)
8. Thelwall, M., Maflahi, N.: Are scholarly articles disproportionately read in their own country? An analysis of Mendeley readers. Journal of the Association for Information Science and Technology (2014), doi: 10.1002/asi.23252
9. Vinkler, P.: Correlation between the structure of scientific research, scientometric indicators and GDP in EU and non-EU countries. Scientometrics 74, 237–254 (2008)
10. Moya-Anegón, F., Herrero-Solana, V.: Science in America Latina: A comparison of bibliometric and scientific-technical indicators. Scientometrics 46, 299–320 (1999)
11. Tasli, L., Kacar, N., Aydemir, E.H.: Scientific productivity of OECD countries in dermatology journals within the last 10-year period. International Journal of Dermatology 51, 665–671 (2012)
12. Meo, S.A., Al Masri, A.A., Usmani, A.M., Memon, A.N., Zaidi, S.Z.: Impact of GDP, Spending on R&D, Number of Universities and Scientific Journals on Research Publications among Asian Countries. PLOS ONE 8 (2013)
13. Smith, R.: Measuring the social impact of research. BMJ 323, 528 (2001)
14. Alhoori, H., Furuta, R.: Understanding the Dynamic Scholarly Research Needs and Behavior as Applied to Social Reference Management. In: Proceedings of the 15th International Conference on Theory and Practice of Digital Libraries, pp. 169–178 (2011)
15. Bar-Ilan, J., Haustein, S., Peters, I., Priem, J., Shema, H., Terliesner, J.: Beyond citations: Scholars ' visibility on the social Web. In: Proceedings of the 17th International Conference on Science and Technology Indicators, Montréal, Canada, pp. 98–109 (2012)
16. Mohammadi, E., Thelwall, M.: Mendeley readership altmetrics for the social sciences and humanities: Research evaluation and knowledge flows. Journal of the Association for Information Science and Technology 65, 1627–1638 (2014)
17. Haustein, S., Peters, I., Sugimoto, C.R., Thelwall, M., Larivière, V.: Tweeting biomedicine: An analysis of tweets and citations in the biomedical literature. Journal of the Association for Information Science and Technology 65, 656–669 (2014)
18. Zahedi, Z., Costas, R., Wouters, P.: How well developed are altmetrics? A cross-disciplinary analysis of the presence of 'alternative metrics' in scientific publications. Scientometrics (2014), doi:10.1007/s11192-014-1264-0
19. Holmberg, K., Thelwall, M.: Disciplinary differences in Twitter scholarly communication. Scientometrics (2014), doi:10.1007/s11192-014-1229-3
20. Alhoori, H., Furuta, R.: Do Altmetrics Follow the Crowd or Does the Crowd Follow Altmetrics? In: 2014 IEEE/ACM Joint Conference on Digital Libraries (JCDL) (2014)

OA Policies and the Sustainability of Digital Libraries of Scholarly Information

Gobinda G. Chowdhury

iSchool@northumbria, Department of Mathematics & Information Sciences,
Northumbria University, Newcastle NE1 8ST,UK
gobinda.chowdhury@northumbria.ac.uk

Abstract. Beginning with an introduction to scholarly communications and recently introduced OA (open access) policies of various government agencies and research funding bodies, this paper discusses the sustainability of digital libraries. It discusses how the specific OA policies and their implementation can influence the economic, social and environmental sustainability of digital libraries of scholarly information.

Keywords: Digital libraries, open access, sustainable digital libraries, social sustainability, economic sustainability, environmental sustainability.

1   Introduction

Scholarly communication is a process through which research and scholarly outputs are created, peer-reviewed, disseminated, and preserved for future use [1]. Traditionally scholarly communications have been publicly funded both for the creation of scholarly output through various research and scholarly activities, and also for managing scholarly output through library and information services. Various international, regional, national, and local bodies as well as a number of regulations, funding models, technologies and governance policies support and control the activities associated with scholarly communication processes.

The open access movement emerged in the early 1990s with the establishment of the open archive known as arXiv.org (formerly xxx.lanl.gov) in order to provide free access to research and scholarly information in high-energy physics. The Santa Fe Convention in 1999, in which the Open Archives Initiative was launched, and subsequently the Budapest Open Access Initiative (BOAI) in 2001, brought a new era in scholarly communications promising free access to scholarly information. Over the years, two models for OA emerged: (1) the Gold OA model where the cost of publications is recovered from authors and in return the resulting publications are made available to everyone free ofcost, and (2) the Green OA model where the published papers are made available to everyone free of cost after a certain period of time is elapsed since the first publication of the paper (called the embargo period) through the process of self-archiving where the authors are required to submit a final copy of their papers to a repository that can be accessed by everyone free of cost.

K. Tuamsuk et al. (Eds.): ICADL 2014, LNCS 8839, pp. 65–75, 2014.
© Springer International Publishing Switzerland 2014

The overall goal of both the OA modelsis to facilitate free access to scholarly information. However, thespecific aspects of these policies and their implementation can have some significant implications for the sustainability of digital libraries of scholarly information [2]. While the different aspects of economic, social and environmental sustainability of digital libraries and information services have been discussed in the recent literature ([3-5]), this paper discusses these sustainability issues in the context of open access content and institutional repositories. By drawing on data from some research projects on open access and institutional repositories, and the recently introduced OA policies of various international and national research funding bodies, this paper for the first time discusses the economic, social and environmental sustainability of open access digital libraries.

2   Sustainability of Digital Libraries

There are three forms, often called the three pillars, of sustainability, viz. economic sustainability, social sustainability and environmental sustainability [2].A digital library is an evolving organisation. It comprises three distinct systems – viz. a *Digital Library* that provides digital content to its users through a series of functionalities that are controlled by some quality and policy measures; a*Digital Library System* which is a software system that supports the functionalities of a *Digital Library;* and *Digital Library Management System* which is a generic software system that provides the appropriate infrastructure for the functionalities of the *Digital Library System* [6].

In order to study the sustainability of digital libraries, it is necessary to identify the challenges that are associated with all the three systems that form a digital library, as well as the activities and functions of all the actors. Chowdhury proposes that [3-5]:

- The target for the economic sustainability of digital libraries is to provide cheaper, easier and better access to digital information through a sustainable business model;
- the target for the social sustainability of digital libraries is to ensure equitable access to information in order to build a better, well informed, and healthy society; and
- the target for environmental sustainability of digital libraries is to ensure reductions in the environmental impact of digital information systems and services.

However, often the factors responsible for ensuring one form of sustainability can affect the other form of sustainability of digital libraries. For example, while the open access policies can ensure the social sustainability of digital libraries by ensuring better and more equitable access to information, unless appropriate measures are taken they may affect the economic sustainability of digital libraries because of the increased costs of building and managing a number of institutional repositories. This paper discusses how the recently introduced of OA policies of various research funding agencies at the national and international level can influence the economic, social and environmental sustainability of open access digital libraries. It points out that more research is needed in order to ensure all the three forms of sustainability of open access digital libraries.

3   Recently Introduced OA Policies

Research and funding bodies and institutions in many countries support the motto of OA, and accordingly they have come up with specific OA policies.The European Commission recommends the following two options for open access [7]:

- Gold OA where research papers will be made immediately accessible online by the publisher and the researchers will be eligible for reimbursement of the APCs from the Commission; or
- Green OA where researchers will make their research papers available through an open access repository no later than six months after publication (or 12 months for articles in the fields of social sciences and humanities).

UNESCO introduced an OA policy from 1st June 2013 that "would grant an irrevocable worldwide right of access to copy, use, distribute, transmit, and make derivative works in any format within certain constraints" [8]. The World Bank also introduced a similar OA policy that covers both content and data sets:

- "For work carried out by Bank staff, the policy applies to manuscripts and all accompanying data sets (a) that result from research, analysis, economic and sector work, or development practice; (b) that have undergone peer review or have been otherwise vetted and approved for release to the public; and (c) for which internal approval for release is given on or after July 1, 2012.
- For external research funded by the Bank, for which funding was approved on or after July 1, 2012, the policy applies to the final report provided by the researchers to the funding unit within the Bank." [9].

The Australian Research Council (ARC) has also introduced an OA policy from 1st January 2013. It requires that any publications arising from an ARC supported research project must be deposited into an open access institutional repository within a 12 period from the date of publication [10].The OA access policy of the US National Institute of Health (NIH) states that:

> "all investigators funded by the NIH submit or have submitted for them to the National Library of Medicine's PubMed Central an electronic version of their final, peer-reviewed manuscripts upon acceptance for publication, to be made publicly available no later than 12 months after the official date of publication." [11]

The Wellcome Trust OA policy requires"electronic copies of any research papers that have been accepted for publication in a peer-reviewed journal, and are supported in whole or in part by Wellcome Trust funding, to be made available through PubMed Central (PMC) and Europe PubMed Central (Europe PMC) as soon as possible and in any event within six months of the journal publisher's official date of final publication" [12].

The Research Councils in UK (RCUK) have gone a step further in that they have not only shown a preference for the Gold OA, but also proposed a funding mechanism to support that. The policy document states that:

- "The RCUK Policy on Open Access aims to achieve immediate, unrestricted, on-line access to peer-reviewed and published scholarly research papers, free of any access charge." [13, p.2]
- "The Research Councils UK (RCUK) policy supports both 'Gold' and 'Green' routes to Open Access, though RCUK has a preference for immediate Open Access with the maximum opportunity for re-use." [13, p.1]

With regard to access the RCUK policy states that:

"RCUK recognises a journal as being compliant with this policy if:
The journal provides, via its own website, immediate and unrestricted access to the final published version of the paper, which should be made available using the Creative Commons Attribution (CC BY) licence. This may involve payment of an 'Article Processing Charge' (APC) to the publisher.

    Or,

The journal consents to deposit of the final Accepted Manuscript in any repository, without restriction on non-commercial re-use and within a defined period. No APC will be payable to the publisher. In this latter case, RCUK will accept a delay of no more than six months between on-line publication and the final Accepted Manuscript becoming Open Access. In the case of papers in the arts, humanities and social sciences (which will mainly be funded by the AHRC and the ESRC), the maximum embargo period will be twelve months. In some circumstances, where funding for APCs is unavailable during the transition period, longer embargo periods may be allowable." [13, P.2].

In a policy memorandum released on February 22, 2013, the Office of Science and Technology Policy (OSTP) of the US government directed all US Federal agencies with more than $100M in R&D expenditures to develop plans to make the published results of federally funded research freely available to the public within one year of publication and requiring researchers to better account for and manage the digital data resulting from federally funded scientific research [14].

4   OA Policies and the Economic Sustainability of Scholarly Digital Libraries

Both the Green and Gold OA models have some implications for the economic sustainability of digital libraries of scholarly communications. One of the most significant outcomes of the Green route to OA has been the establishment of several specialized open access digital libraries like PubMed Central, and thousands of institutional repositories. The first institutional repository in the UK was set up in Southampton in 2001 [15], and the first institutional repository in the US was set up in 2002 at MIT "as a new strategy that allows universities to apply serious, systematic leverage to accelerate changes taking place in scholarship and scholarly communication"[16].

Over the past decade several new technology, software and standards have emerged facilitating the creation and management of institutional repositories. Details of these are available in Open Archives Initiative website (http://www.openarchives.org/) and in numerous publications.

While the Green OA policies introduced by different research funding bodies (discussed above) will promote the mission of institutional repositories and therefore open access to scholarly information, it should be noted that there are costs associated with building and running the institutional repositories. A study by the Joint Information Systems Committee (Jisc) in the UK noted that [17]:

- Annual operating costs for the institutional repository, including the cost of depositing items, range from around £26,000 to almost £210,000; and
- The cost of depositing a single article varies from around £6.5 to £15.4, with the annual cost of depositing into the repository all articles produced by each university ranging from just over £4,000 GBP to over £75,000.

Even at an average cost of £135,000 per annum for running an institutional repository, the total costs for the institutional repositories in 166 HEIs (higher education institutions) in Britain would be £22.4 million per year which is nearly 15% of the annual journal subscription budget of UK universities which is estimated to be £150 million [19]. It may be noted that the costs of institutional repositories vary quite significantly depending on the size and nature of the universities, their research income and activities, number of research papers produced per year, and so on. Table 1 shows the cost figures for some institutional repositories in the US.

Table 1. Typical Cost figures of Institutional Repositories in the US [18]

Costs	Study sample	Minimum	Median	Mean	Maximum
Implementation	17	$1,200	$25,000	$52,100	$300,000
Annual	20	$500	$31,500	$77,300	$275,000
Personnel, Annual	17	$100	$70,000	$86,186	$235,200
Software, Annual	10	$2,500	$23,000	$22,350	$40,000
Hardware, Annual	6	$500	$5,500	$13,250	$50,000

Thus, if every author and institution chooses the Green OA route, there will be a significant amount of cost associated with the implementation and management of the local institutional repositories.

There is also a huge cost associated with the preservation of scholarly information in institutional repositories. Most of the specific institutional repositories today do not have a long-term preservation plan. Only about 8% of the 2553 institutional repositories in the OpenDOARdatabase have a clear preservation policy. This indeed is a cause for concern for the economic and social sustainability of the institutional repositories. The costs can be significantly reduced if preservation tasks are performed by a central agency. In fact, a Bill, called FASTR, introduced in the US Congress in March 2013, makes a specific recommendation for preservation [20]. It states that the federal funding agency should ensure that the electronic copy of the submitted manuscript is preserved in a stable digital repository maintained by the agency or in another suitable repository that ensures free long term access, interoperability and long-term preservation [20,21].

The essence of the Gold route to OA is that the cost of publication of journal articles is recovered from some sources other than the user subscriptions, and thus users don't pay any fees for accessing scholarly content. Over the past few years APCs have become the most common route for gold access to OA. A Jisc funded study in the UK modelled the OA options for publication of scholarly papers in the UK and noted that if universities switch from the current subscription-based system to publishing all their articles in OA journals that charge APCs[17]:

- there would be savings for all universities, compared to their current spends on journal subscriptions, when the APC fee is £700 per article or less;
- where APCs are £500 per article, the largest university would save around £1.53 million per annum; and the maximum savings could be achieved, @ £1.7 million per annum, for medium-sized universities;
- If the APCs are £1000 per article, all but the largest universities would save and it could range from £ 0.17 to 1.4 million per annum; and large universities would face extra costs of around at about £1.86 million per annum;
- When APCs are more than £2000 GBP per article, it is likely that most universities would spend more money than the current subscription-based system.

However, APCs vary from discipline to discipline, and from journal to journal within a discipline. Studies show that the specific amount of fees charged to authors varies from US$ 1,000-3,000 [22], or even up to US$3,900 [23]. Bjork [24] notes that the number of hybrid journals – those that follow the commercial as well as the gold OA model through APCs -- has doubled in the past couple of years rising to 4,300; and about 12,000 open access articles were published through APCs in 2011.

The above discussions clearly indicate that APCs and the corresponding Gold OA policies will have a significant implication for the overall the scholarly communication process. For example, depending on how research active the peopleare, and where they publish their research, a University may end up spending more money than their current spend on journal subscriptions. Furthermore, the RCUK policy states that a block grant for APCs will be provided and it should be managed at the institution level. These local policies, and moreover, the overall affordability of authors and their institutions in terms of APCs will be an important factor for selection of the appropriate journals for research publications. In other words, in future scholarly communications will not only be decided by the quality of a research paper, but also the affordability of the researcher to pay the APCs of the target journals.

5   OA Policies and the Social Sustainability of Scholarly Digital Libraries

The social benefits of both the OA policy are enormous because they promote free and equitable access to scholarly information which are currently restricted by the subscription-only model. However, depending on how these policies are implemented, there may be some implications for the social sustainability of digital libraries of scholarly information.

Green OA policies of research funding and regulatory bodies vary in terms of the embargo period – the period of time between the publication of a paper and its availability on the OA repository. Some OA regulations go for a 12 month embargo period. For example, the Australian Research Council requires free public access to research papers within a 12 month period from the date of publication [10], and the US National Institute of Health requires open access within a 12 month period from the date of publication [13]. Many OA regulations require free access within six months or within a year, but they do not distinguish between disciplines. The RCUK regulations have proposed different embargo period for different modes of OA and also for different disciplines that may range from 6-12 months, and up to 24 months depending on the disciplines and the journal policies and authors' choice (in fact, capability) for a specific route to OA. In other words, depending on the discipline, and the option that a researcher chooses to publish their papers, users may have to wait for a reasonably long period before they can get free access to the content.

Institutional repositories use a number of different, largely open source, software. There are also a number of duplications in the institutional repositories. This can be avoided by building national repositories that can reduce the management costs, and improve access. The White House directive for OA policies in the US, discussed earlier in this chapter, recommends repositories at the large funding agency level rather than specific institutional level. As a result, funding bodies like NSF (National Science Foundation) propose specific measures for developing a national infrastructure for access to OA publications. It is reported that during the financial year 2014 NSF will "design and test system architecture to manage a subset of NSF-supported research products (at a minimum, journal articles, conference proceedings, and book chapters)" (http://www.nsf.gov/about/budget/fy2014/pdf/45_fy2014.pdf). NSF also proposes to develop capabilities for seamless access to other OA repositories like PubMed.Such efforts will result in a few national repositories created by national funding bodies which will be more economically sustainable because it will not require repositories to be created and managed at the specific institution level, and socially sustainable because they will have uniform search and access facilities offered by the central repository service provider.

In order to truly meet the objective of the OA initiatives and guidelines, the OA content should be made accessible to everyone in society. This will pose a significant challenge in terms of the design and usability of user interfaces and information access systems as a whole. Currently institutional repositories are designed for the academic and scholarly communities, and hence extending them to the general public, may require a substantial re-design of the search and retrieval features and facilities of the repository services. Furthermore, the intention of OA, as stated specifically in the RCUK OA guidelines, is to facilitate data and text mining and various data analytics that would facilitate access to, and use of, research content and data for different purposes. This will require more research in linking of research content and data.

In order to maximise the opportunities for access to, and re-use of repository content, the Research Councils would like research papers in repositories to be made available using the most liberal and enabling licences, ideally CC BY. While in principle this will promote better use of research content and data, and will promote sustainable development in a knowledge economy, there are some concerns here. From the point of view of the economic sustainability of scholarly communications, this may disadvantage some authors and researchers in that their work could be re-used for commercial benefits without requiring the users to pay a share of the benefits to the original creators of the idea or knowledge. From social sustainability point of view, there may be concerns related to research ethics and data protection. Currently the research ethics and data protection guidelines require that a researcher or a team get specific permissions for creation and use of research data sets under specific circumstances for a specific research purpose. How the research findings and the corresponding research data sets could be used by others for a different purpose, and more so for commercial purposes, is not quite clear. More research needs to be done and specific guidelines are to be formulated in this area.

Gold OA policies and APCs may restrict the researchers' choice of appropriate journals which in turn will have implication for the scholarly communication process. This will also have implications for the collaborative research and publication activities. It may affect collaborative publication decisions where several authors from different universities and institutions are involved; and all of them may not have the same amount of resources available to pay for the APCs. The situation will be worse when international collaboration is involved, and especially when authors from the developing countries are involved in research and publications with authors in those countries where APCs are provided by the research funding councils or government.

6   OA Policies and the Environmental Sustainability of Scholarly Digital Libraries

The way in which institutional repositories are implemented now is not environmentally sustainable. For example, even if each of the 166 HEIs in the UK has one server running an institutional repository on a 24x7 basis, overall the energy consumption and the corresponding GHG (greenhouse gas) emissions will be quite substantial. The total energy costs for a computing equipment may be estimated by combining the embodied energy costs, sometimes also called emergy costs, and the actual socket energy costs [4]. Emergy costs of a device can be obtained by considering the total energy used during the manufacturing of the devices, and then taking a fraction of that depending on what proportion of the devices' full life has been used in a specific operation. It can be estimated by taking the following three factors into account: (1) the manufacturing energy costs, (2) the lifetime, i.e. the replacement cycle of that device, for example a laptop may be replaced every three years, and (3) the fraction of its life used in an operation which may be based on the actual time used and the capacity in which it is used, for example in 25% capacity or in 100% capacity. Assuming that the total embodied energy cost of a server is 5 GJ (Gigajoules), it works at 50% capacity and is replaced every three years, the embodied energy cost of a server will be $((5/2) \times 10^9) / (3 \times 365 \times 24 \times 60 \times 60) = 26$ W. The socket energy cost can be estimated by the required power to run the device and the amount of time the device is used for an operation or for a specific activity. The socket energy cost of a server is 300 Watts (http://www.susteit.org.uk/files/category.php?catID=4). So, the total annual energy costs for each server will be ((326 W) x (4380 hours)) or 1.4 MW (assuming that the server works at 50% capacity). At this rate the total annual energy costs for all the institutional repositories in the UK will be quite substantial.However, this is just one aspect of the energy and environmental cost of the institutional repositories. A number of other factors need to be considered for estimation of the overall energy costs of institutional repositories. For example, the actual number of servers and other devices used to host and manage the repositories, i.e. the server-side costs, plus the amount of time, and number and type of computing devices used by the users, and also an estimation of the fraction of the Internet time and energy used for self-archiving as well as for access and use of the repositories.

7   Conclusion

While both the Green and Gold OA access policies aim to facilitate free and wider access to scholarly information, how these policies are implemented can significantly influence the economic, social and environmental sustainability of open access digital libraries and information services. So far, little research has been undertaken to compare the various models of OA in the context of the sustainability of digital libraries of scholarly information and data [2,4]. This paper provides an idea of the various issues and challenges, and points out that more research is needed for the design and management of economically, socially and environmentally sustainable digital libraries. It is also important to study how the various OA policies impact on the user behavior and institutional policies both in the context of digital information creation as well as information access, use and management.

References

1. ACRL. Principles and strategies for the reform of scholarly communication 1,
   http://www.ala.org/acrl/publications/whitepapers/principless trategies (accessed May 15, 2013)
2. Chowdhury, G.: Sustainability of digital information services. Journal of Documentation 69(5), 602–622 (2013)
3. Chowdhury, G.: Sustainable digital libraries: a conceptual model and a research framework. International Journal on Digital Libraries (accepted for publication)
4. Chowdhury, G.: Sustainability of digital libraries: a conceptual model. In: Aalberg, T., Papatheodorou, C., Dobreva, M., Tsakonas, G., Farrugia, C.J. (eds.) TPDL 2013. LNCS, vol. 8092, pp. 1–12. Springer, Heidelberg (2013)
5. Chowdhury, G.G.: Social sustainability of digital libraries: A research framework. In: Urs, S.R., Na, J.-C., Buchanan, G. (eds.) ICADL 2013. LNCS, vol. 8279, pp. 25–34. Springer, Heidelberg (2013)
6. The Digital Library reference Model (2010),
   http://bscw.research-infrastructures.eu/pub/bscw.cgi/ d222816/D3.2b%20Digital%20Library%20Reference%20Model.pdf
7. Europa, Scientific data: open access to research results will boost Europe's innova-tion capacity (2012),
   http://europa.eu/rapid/press-release_IP-12-790_en.htm (retrieved)

8. UNESCO, Open Access policy concerning UNESCO publications (2013),
   `http://www.unesco.org/new/fileadmin/MULTIMEDIA/HQ/ERI/pdf/`
   `oa_policy_en_2.pdf`
9. World Bank, World Bank open access policy for formal publications (April 2012),
   `http://www-wds.worldbank.org/external/default/`
   `WDSContentServer/WDSP/IB/2012/04/03/000406484_`
   `20120403130112/Rendered/PDF/6783000PP00OFF0icy0Approved0Apri`
   `12.pdf`
10. Australian Research Council, ARC open access policy (2013),
    `http://www.arc.gov.au/applicants/open_access.htm` (retrieved)
11. National Institutes of Health, National Institutes of Health public access. NIH public
    access policy details (2013), `http://publicaccess.nih.gov/policy.htm`
    (retrieved)
12. Wellcome Trust, Open access policy: position statement in support of open and un-
    restricted access to published research (2013),
    `http://www.wellcome.ac.uk/About-us/Policy/Policy-and-`
    `position-statements/WTD002766.htm` (retrieved)
13. Research Councils, UK. RCUK policy with open access and guidance (2013),
    `http://www.rcuk.ac.uk/documents/documents/RCUKOpenAccessPoli`
    `cy.pdf` (retrieved)
14. The White House, Office of Science and Technology Policy (2013),
    `http://www.whitehouse.gov/blog/2013/02/22/expanding-public-`
    `access-results-federally-funded-research`
15. Cullen, R., Chawner, B.: Institutional repositories, open access and scholarly communica-
    tion: a study of conflicting paradigms. The Journal of Academic Librarianship 37(6),
    460–470 (2011)
16. Lynch. C.: Institutional repositories: essential infrastructure for scholarship in the digital
    age. Association of Research Libraries. ARL Bimonthly report no. 226 (2003),
    `http://www.arl.org/resources/pubs/br/br226/br226ir.shtml`
17. Swan, A.: Modelling scholarly communication options: costs and benefits for uni-versities.
    Report to the JISC (February 2010),
    `http://repository.jisc.ac.uk/442/2/Modelling_scholarly_`
    `communication_report_final1.pdf` (retreived)
18. Burns, C.S., Lana, A., Budd, J.J.: Institutional repositories: exploration of costs and value.
    D-Lib Magazine 19(1/2) (2013),
    `http://www.dlib.org/dlib/january13/burns/01burns.html#appendix`
19. Finch, J.: Accessibility, sustainability, excellence: how to expand access to research publi-
    cations. Report of the Working Group on Expanding Access to Published Research Find-
    ings (2012), `http://www.researchinfonet.org/wp-content/uploads/`
    `2012/06/Finch-Group-report-FINAL-VERSION.pdf`
20. Fair Access to Science and Technology Research Act of 2013 (2013),
    `http://doyle.house.gov/sites/doyle.house.gov/files/documents/`
    `2013%2002%2014%20DOYLE%20FASTR%20FINAL.pdf`
21. Price, G.: OA: Fair Access to Science and Technology Research Act (FASTR) Leg-
    islation Introduced in U.S. Congress, InfoDocket, Library Journal (February 14, 2013),
    `http://www.infodocket.com/2013/02/14/fair-access-to-science-`
    `and-technology-research-act-fastr-legislation-introduced-in-`
    `u-s-congress/`

22. Bird, C.: Continued Adventures in Open Access: perspective. Learned Publishing 23(2), 107–116 (2010)
23. Zoubir, A.: Open access publications: more than a Business Model? IEEE Signal Processing 29(6), 2–6 (2012)
24. Bjork, B.C.: The hybrid model for open access publication of scholarly articles: A failed experiment? Journal of the American Society for Information Science and Technology 63(8), 1496–1504 (2012)

Evaluating the Academic Performance of Institutions within Scholarly Communities

Lili Lin, Zhuoming Xu[*], Yuanhang Zhuang, and Jie Wei

College of Computer and Information, Hohai University, Nanjing,
China, Postcode 210098
{linlili,zmxu}@hhu.edu.cn,
{yhzhuang90,weijie9209}@gmail.com

Abstract. Most state-of-the-art studies either conduct peer assessment or adopt bibliometric indicators for institution evaluation. However, peer assessments are labor intensive and time consuming, and existing bibliometric methods may produce a biased evaluation result because they do not synthetically model many crucial factors that reflect the academic performance of institutions in a unified way. Thus, we propose a factor graph-based institution ranking model to leverage institutions' individual information (i.e., quantitative and qualitative information) and scholarly network information (i.e., collaborative intensity) in this paper. We choose the peer assessment result from the best-known U.S. News & World Report as the ground truth and conduct a case study on the U.S. institution ranking in the library and information science (LIS) research field. The experimental results indicate that our approach can be a better alternative for the manual peer assessment for institution evaluation when compared with existing bibliometrics methods.

Keywords: Institution evaluation, academic performance, scholarly network, factor graph.

1 Introduction

Evaluating the academic performance of institutions in scholarly communities has attracted wide attention in the last few years [1-4]. Reasonable evaluations of the institutional excellence in a given discipline or research field serve a variety of practical purposes. For example, the assessments can reveal outstanding institutions, allowing researchers to seek a better employment or to assist students to decide where they want to study. In addition, the evaluations also offer valuable insights for both internal and external administrators to set goals in recruiting the most qualified potential employees or to make decisions in helping allocate funding rationally. Aside from these purposes, it would be of great utility to help institutions in internal self-evaluations and improvements in order to stimulate competitions among institutions by providing academic performance evaluations.

---

[*] Corresponding author.

K. Tuamsuk et al. (Eds.): ICADL 2014, LNCS 8839, pp. 76–86, 2014.

As far as we know, such performance evaluations usually take the form of rankings. Generally speaking, peer assessments and bibliometric indicators are two main approaches to rank the academic performance of institutions. An expert assessment method is a form of peer assessment. It has been criticized for its subjectivity because of the difficulty for a handful of domain experts to trace and assess research performance at the institutional level [3]. Moreover, manual assessments by experts are obviously labor intensive and time consuming. In order to tackle the peer assessment problems, bibliometric methods are widely used in research evaluation for objectivity and operability [3]. Currently, most bibliometric indicators for institution rankings can be divided into two main categories including quantitative indicators and qualitative indicators. The quantitative methods evaluate the institutional performance based on the quantity of the research achievements, while the qualitative methods concentrate on the quality of the research achievements. However, there are some issues in existing bibliometric ranking studies. Many existing bibliometric studies cannot provide an overall performance because they adopt multiple single indicators to get different rankings of the institutions. In addition, these methods do not take into account many crucial factors that reflect the academic performance of institutions from different perspectives in a unified way for more precise institution evaluation. Therefore, it is meaningful to study how to combine different kinds of scholarly information, including institutions' individual information and network information, in order to get a more reasonable overview of institutional performance.

With comprehensive observations, we adopt five classical bibliometric indicators including paper counts, citation counts, h-index, average citation counts and ratio of high-quality papers to represent institutions' individual information. In addition, we use published papers to generate an institution collaboration network which contains scholarly network information. As factor graphs have the potential to unify modeling complicated problems in the real world with great generality and flexibility [5], we propose a factor graph-based institution ranking model (*FGIRM*) to model all of the above information in a unified way in order to get a global performance ranking of institutions. To the best of our knowledge, so far, our method is the first one to evaluate the academic performance of institutions by leveraging institutions' quantitative information, qualitative information and scholarly network information.

In order to validate the proposed approach, a case study on the U.S. institution ranking in the library and information science (LIS) research field is conducted based on the data collected from the Information Science & Library Science category of Web of Science covering the period from 2008 to 2012. We choose the peer assessment result of the Library and Information Studies Rankings in the United States from the best-known U.S. News & World Report as the ground truth. The comparisons between the proposed approach and baseline methods demonstrate that the proposed approach can be a better alternative for the manual peer assessment for institution evaluation when compared with existing bibliometrics methods. The remainder of this paper is organized as follows: Section 2 reviews related work on various methods for evaluating the academic performance of institutions. Section 3 explicates the proposed approach. Section 4 presents the experimental results that validate the efficiency of the proposed approach. Finally, we conclude our work and propose future work in Section 5.

2   Related Work

Until now, there are many organizations and researchers conducting studies on ranking institutions by adopting objective indicators or subjective assessments/surveys.

As a well-known news magazine, U.S. News & World Report [6] publishes annual print and e-book versions of its authoritative rankings of Best Colleges, Best Graduate Schools and Best Hospitals by adopting a number of indicators including academic peer review, employer review survey, citations per faculty member, international student and international faculty factors and student-to-faculty ratio. However, this ranking system relies on highly subjective data obtained from reputational surveys which are obviously labor intensive and time consuming.

The Academic Ranking of World Universities (ARWU) [7], also known as the Shanghai Ranking, is a publication that was founded and compiled by the Shanghai Jiao Tong University to rank universities globally. ARWU provides a series of bibliometric ranking metrics containing Nobel- and Fields-winning alumni/faculty, the number of highly cited researchers, number of articles published in *Nature* and *Science*, the number of articles indexed in *Science Citation Index Expanded* and the *Social Science Citation Index* and a weighted average of all the scores obtained from the previous metrics. But the vast majority of institutions have no Nobel- or Fields-winning alumni/faculty. Besides, few institutions have highly cited researchers in many disciplines or research fields.

Different from the above ranking systems, the CWTS Leiden Ranking [8] offers advanced indicators of the scientific impact and collaboration based on Web of Science indexed publications. Among the indicators, the impact indicators include mean citation score, average number of citations and proportion of top 10% publications, while the collaboration indicators contains proportion of inter-institutional collaborative publications, proportion of international collaborative publications, proportion of collaborative publications with industry and proportion of long distance collaborative publications. Similarly, the SCImago Institutions Rankings (SIR) project [9], developed by SCImago Research Group, offers a wealthy of analytical tools to analyze research outputs of universities and research-focused institutions. Based upon the Scopus database, SIR provides world and iberoamerican institutions rankings using different bibliometric indicators such as the number of published publications indexed in Scopus, the ratio of high quality publications, the ratio of publications collaborated with foreign institutions and normalized citation impact. Besides the Leiden Ranking and SIR, other researchers also adopt different single bibliometric indicators to evaluate the performance of institutions. For example, Grant et al. [2] employed the number of publications, the total number of times those publications were cited and Hirsch's h-index to conduct rankings of U.S. and Canadian academic institutions based on their relative contribution to the field of conservation biology. Acuña et al. [1] evaluated the productivity of the research institutions in forestry by analyzing the number of publications indexed in Web of Science and Scopus, frequency of citations, impact indexes, self-citation, h-index and international collaboration. However, those studies offer a number of different rankings instead of a global ranking for institutions due to the adoption of different single indicators. A notable exception is the study conducted by Torres-Salinas et al. [4]. They presented an Institution-Field Quantitative and Qualitative Analysis index (IFQ2A index) by combing three quantitative indicators and three qualitative indicators to compare the research output of a group of institutions in a given research field. However, in their study, institutions' mutual influences hidden in scholarly networks were neglected when evaluating the institutions' performance, making the evaluation result biased.

3   Proposed Approach

In this section, we detail the way by which we solve the institution evaluation problem in scholarly communities. First, we describe our data collection. Second, two main modules of the proposed approach are presented in detail, including the construction of a weighted institution collaboration network from the raw data and the establishment of a factor graph-based institution ranking model based on the constructed institution collaboration network.

3.1   Data Collection

The goal of our case study is to provide a ranking of U.S. institutions in the library and information science research field. Thus, the full records and cited references of 25,657 papers were collected from the Web of Science (WOS) through Advanced Search '(WC=Information Science & Library Science AND CU=USA) AND LANGUAGE: (English) Indexes=SSCI Timespan=2008-2012'. Each downloaded paper contains related author(s), title, source, published year, abstract, author address/ affiliation, reference, citation counts, and soforth.

The raw data was preprocessed in two steps in order to construct a local institution collaboration network. The first step is to filter out papers without affiliations since no institution information can be extracted from such records to construct an institution collaboration network. The second step involves institution name disambiguation because one institution may have several different affiliation names in the downloaded dataset. Forty-four prestigious U.S. institutions owning master's degree programs in library and information studies were chosen as the candidate institutions based on Library and Information Studies Rankings from U.S. News & World Report[1]. In this case, name disambiguation for all the candidate institutions is implemented semi-automatically. For example, "UNIV ILLINOIS", "UNIV ILLINOIS LIBS", "UNIV ILLINOIS LIB" and "UNIV ILLINOIS URBANA LIB" were all firstly identified manually as "UNIV ILLINOIS URBANA CHAMPAIGN". Then all the papers whose affiliation name is "UNIV ILLINOIS" or "UNIV ILLINOIS LIBS" or "UNIV ILLINOIS LIB" or "UNIV ILLINOIS URBANA LIB" and whose city name is "Champaign" or "Urbana" were merged automatically into papers that have been published by UNIV ILLINOIS URBANA CHAMPAIGN.

---

[1] http://grad-schools.usnews.rankingsandreviews.com/
best-graduate-schools/top-library-information-science-
programs/library-information-science-rankings

3.2   Weighted Institution Collaboration Network

Yan et al. pointed out that the collaboration relation is one of the most representative social relationships in scholarship [10].Thus, in this paper, we construct an institution collaboration network based on the downloaded dataset in order to explore social interactions between institutions. Note that institution self-collaboration is not considered in this paper. Fig. 1 shows the procedure for constructing an initial institution collaboration network based on the preprocessed data. An *institution-paper network* (IPN), containing candidate institutions and their published papers, is firstly generated from the preprocessed data, especially from its author affiliation information. Second, an *initial institution collaboration network* (IICN) is constructed based on the institution-paper network. In IICN, each node represents one institution, and each edge represents a collaboration relation between each institution pair. It should be noted that the collaborative times on the edges of IICN is also defined as the *collaborative intensity* in this paper.

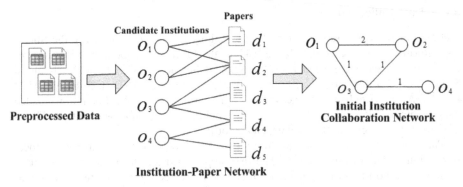

Fig. 1. The procedure of constructing an initial institution collaboration network

The performance of institutions is not only related with their productivity but also depends on the degree that their research achievements are valued, accepted or cited. Thus, based on the consideration of research "quality" and "quantity", we use five quantitative and qualitative indicators to reflect the performance of institutions in terms of their individual information. These indicators are as follows:

— *Paper Counts (PC)*: one institution tends to be more influential in academic research fields if it has published more papers. The values of this indicator can be acquired from the institution-paper network by simply calculating the number of papers published by each institution.
— *Citation Counts (CC)*: one institution tends to be more popular in academic research fields if its research achievements have been cited more times. The values of this indicator can be acquired from the institution-paper network together with "Times Cited" information in the preprocessed data by simply calculating the sum of "Times Cited" values of all papers published by each institution.
— *H-Index (HI)*: it is used to assess the quality of institutions' published papers and the overall productivity of institutions. The values of this indicator can be acquired from the institution-paper network together with "Times Cited" information in the

preprocessed data according to one rule that "an institution has index h, if the h of its N_p papers have at least h citations each, and the other (N_p-h) papers have at most h citations each".

— *Average Citation Counts (ACC):* it indicates the quality of institutions' research output and can avoid an unfair advantage to bigger institutions by taking into account the relative size of the institutions. The values of this indicator can be acquired by simply calculating the value of *paper counts* divided by that of *citation counts* for each institution.

— *Ratio of High-Quality Papers (R-HQP):* one institution will be more significant in academic research fields if it has published more papers in high-quality journals. The values of this indicator can be acquired by calculating the ratio of papers that an institution publishes in the most influential academic journals which ranked in the first quartile (25%) in the category for one particular discipline or research direction. For example, the top 25% journals used in the case study of this paper are indexed in the 2012 version of the Journal Citation Reports (JCR) Social Science Edition in the Information Science & Library Science category.

Note that the values of the above five indicators are all normalized within the range of [0.01, 1] to avoid bias. The normalized five indicators are put as the weight of each node in the initial institution collaboration network. And thus a *weighted institution collaboration network*(WICN) is finally generated.

3.3   Factor Graph-Based Institution Ranking Model

In order to synthetically model all the information encoded in the generated weighted institution collaboration network, we develop a factor graph-based institution ranking model to leverage quantitative indicators, qualitative indicators and collaborative intensity. As shown in Fig. 2, the bottom part is the weighted institution collaboration network $G = (O, E, W_O, W_E)$ where $O = \{o_m\}_{m=1}^M$ is the set of institutions, $E = \{e_{mn}\}_{1 \leq m,n \leq M}$ is the set of edges representing collaboration relationships between institutions o_m and o_n, $W_O = \{W_{o_m}\}_{m=1}^M$ is the weight vectors for the set of institutions O, and $W_E = \{W_{e_{mn}}\}_{1 \leq m,n \leq M}$ is the weight vectors for the set of edges E representing collaboration relationships between institution pair. Among of those, $W_{o_m} = [s_m, c_m, h_m, a_m, q_m]$ is the weight vector for institution o_m, where s_m, c_m, h_m, a_m , q_m indicate the normalized value of paper counts, citation counts, h-index, average citation counts and ratio of high-quality papers of institution o_m, respectively. And $W_{e_{mn}} = [r_{mn}]$ is the weight vector for the edge between institutions o_m and o_n, where r_{mn} indicates the collaborative intensity between institutions o_m and o_n. The top part of Fig. 2 is the factor graph where $Y = \{y_m\}_{m=1}^M$ is a set of hidden variables corresponds to the set of institutions $O = \{o_m\}_{m=1}^M$, $f(y_m)$ is a node function defined with the quantitative indicators and qualitative indicators, and $g_{mn}(y_m, y_n)$ is an edge function defined with collaborative intensity.

Here, in order to define the node function, we need to divide the five indicators into two groups representing quantitative and qualitative information, respectively. We perform a Principal Component Analysis (PCA) analysis over the normalized

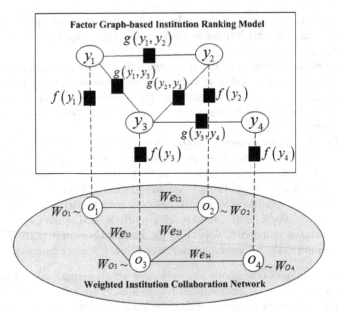

Fig. 2. Graphical representation of the proposed factor graph-based institution ranking model

values for the five indicators. The results of the PCA analysis are shown in Table 1. It demonstrates that the five indicators can be reduced into two components where the first component, representing the quantitative information, is composed of the normalized value of paper counts, citation counts, h-index, and the second component, representing the quantitative information, is composed of the normalized value of average citation counts and ratio of high-quality papers.

Table 1. PCA analysis of the five bibliometrics indicators

Indicators	Component 1	Component 2
PC	0.39409	
CC	0.51819	
HI	0.51141	
ACC		0.43028
R-HQP		0.64601

Thus, we define the **node function** as equation (1) to indicate that institutions with higher values of quantitative indicators and qualitative indicators are more likely to get higher performance.

$$f(y_m) = \exp\left(\sqrt[3]{s_m c_m h_m} * \sqrt[2]{a_m q_m} * y_m\right) \qquad (1)$$

where $m \in \{1, \cdots M\}$ and $y_m \in \{0,1\}$ reflects the performance of an institution, $y_m = 1$ indicates institution o_m has high performance and $y_m = 0$ indicates institution o_m has low performance; s_m, c_m, h_m, a_m , q_m indicate the normalized value of paper counts, citation counts, h-index, average citation counts and ratio of high-quality papers of institution o_m, respectively.

Intuitively, an institution o_m with high performance will have more influence on one of its neighboring institutions o_n if their collaborative intensity is higher. In this case, institution o_n has higher probability to become an institution with high performance. In order to capture this scholarly network information, we define the **edge function** as equation (2).

$$g_{mn}(y_m, y_n) = \exp(y_m * y_n * r_{mn}) \tag{2}$$

where $e_{mn} \in E$ and $m, n \in \{1, \cdots M\}$; and r_{mn} indicates the collaborative intensity between institutions o_m and o_n.

Based on above, we finally define the **joint distribution** by considering all the functions according to factor graph theory [5, 11] as in equation (3).

$$p(Y) = p(y_1, y_2 \cdots, y_M) = \frac{1}{\Delta} \prod_{m=1}^{M} f(y_m) * \prod_{e_{mn} \in E, \ m, n \in \{1, \cdots M\}} g_{mn}(y_m, y_n) \tag{3}$$

where $Y = \{y_1, y_2 \cdots y_M\}$ corresponds to all hidden variables; $f(y_m)$ is the node function and $g_{mn}(y_m, y_n)$ is the edge function; and Δ is a normalizing factor.

Until now, we have built the factor graph-based institution ranking model. Next, our task is to perform inference against $p(Y)$ in order to find a configuration for $Y = \{y_1, y_2 \cdots y_M\}$ to maximize the joint probability $p(Y)$. Because the constructed factor graph model contains cycles, we adopt the Max-Product algorithm [11] to find a configuration Y^{max} that maximizes the objective function $p(Y)$ so that $Y^{max} = \arg\max_Y p(Y)$. Finally, marginal probability for each institution can be calculated accordingly.

4   Experimental Results and Discussion

As the U.S. News & World Report provides America's oldest and best-known ranking of academic institutions, it is reasonable to use the peer assessment result from this magazine as the ground truth for evaluation. In addition, we choose paper counts (PC), citation counts (CC), h-index (HI), average citation counts (ACC), ratio of high-quality papers (R-HQP), and $IFQ2A$index [4] as the baseline methods to validate our approach ($FGIRM$). As our goal is to evaluate the performance of U.S. institutions within the research field of library and information science, we adopt the peer assessment result of the Library and Information Studies Rankings in the United States from U.S. News & World Report as the ground truth to conduct comparisons between the baseline methods and our approach. Ranks of the six baseline methods and our approach were calculated accordingly. The results are shown in Table 2. Because of the limited space, we only list the ranks for five prestigious institutions based on the peer assessment, the six baseline methods and our approach. It is not surprising to see that ranks of these methods are all different from each other, and our approach tends to make the more prestigious institutions to be ranked in the top.

Table 2. Ranks for five prestigiousinstitutionsbased the peer assessment, the six baseline methods and our approach

Institution Name	PA	PC	CC	ACC	HI	R-HQP	IFQ2A	FGIRM
UNIV ILLINOIS URBANA CHAMPAIGN	1	2	14	36	13	33	20	7
UNIV N CAROLINA CHAPEL HILL	2	9	11	16	7	25	12	1
UNIV WASHINGTON	3	4	3	13	2	17	4	5
SYRACUSE UNIV	4	15	25	32	23	24	24	6
UNIV MICHIGAN ANN ARBOR	4	1	6	28	5	35	15	11

In order to conduct an overall comparison of the correlations among the above eight methods, a spearman correlation (two-tailed) test of different ranks for 44 candidate U.S. institutions is calculated. As shown in Table 3, it is interesting to see that the rank of our approach has a relative higher correlation with that of *PA, PC, CC, HI* or *IFQ2A* than that of *ACC* or *R-HQP* at a confidence level of 0.05, indicating that the evaluation result produced from of our approach tends to be more similar to that of mainstream institution evaluation methods. Relatively speaking, only the rank of our approach is neither dramatically different from that of the six baseline methods nor highly correlated with that of the six baseline methods. Thus, we can draw a conclusion that the evaluation result generated by our approach is a good tradeoff between that of existing bibliometrics methods for institution evaluation because the proposed approach takes into account different perspectives of scholarly information in a global way.

Table 3. The spearman correlation test of different ranksfor 44 candidate institutions based on the peer assessment, the six baseline methods and our approach

	PA	PC	CC	ACC	HI	R-HQP	IFQ2A	FGIRM
PA	1.0000							
PC	0.7699	1.0000						
CC	0.6300	0.8522	1.0000					
ACC	0.1821*	0.3665	0.7302	1.0000				
HI	0.6138	0.8608	0.9846	0.6896	1.0000			
R-HQP	0.1053*	0.2266*	0.4873	0.7160	0.4408	1.0000		
IFQ2A	0.5588	0.7834	0.9749	0.7918	0.9553	0.6296	1,0000	
FGIRM	0.6938	0.7924	0.7966	0.4440	0.7672	0.3218	0.7570	1.0000

Note: * means that they are not significantly correlated at the 0.05 confidence level

As the Normalized Discounted Cumulated Gain (NDCG) [12] is an important measure of the average performance of a ranking algorithm, achieved by comparing the ranking results with a given "standard" ranking list, we then use the NDCG as the metric to compare different ranks of institutions based on our approach and the baseline methods at the top 10, 30 and all ranks. As shown in Table 4, our approach achieves the best performance, while *R-HQP* performs the worst with respect to

NDCG scores. Thus, we can conclude that our approach, aimed at efficiently evaluating the academic performance of institutions, can provide a more reasonable evaluation of the institution excellence. That is to say, our approach can be regarded as a better alternative for the manual peer assessment for the academic institution evaluation when compared with existing bibliometrics evaluation methods.

Table 4. Comparison of NDCG scores of different ranks of institutions based on our approach and the six baseline methods

Methods	NDCG@10	NDCG@30	NDCG@all
PC	0.4322	0.4931	0.4931
CC	0.0927	0.3058	0.3062
ACC	0.0053	0.1146	0.2235
HI	0.1912	0.34	0.3404
R-HQP	0.0057	0.1049	0.2158
IFQ2A	0.062	0.2746	0.275
FGIRM	0.5124	0.5311	0.5311

5   Conclusion and Future Work

With the emergence and rapid proliferation of social applications, the problem of evaluating the academic performance of institutions in scholarly communities has attracted increasingly more attention. In order to tackle the problem, we propose a factor graph-based institution ranking model to leverage institutions' individual information (i.e., quantitative and qualitative information) and scholarly network information (i.e., collaborative intensity) in this paper. Furthermore, we compare our approach with six baseline methods by choosing the peer assessment from the best-known U.S. News & World Report as the ground truth. The experimental results indicate that the proposed approach tends to make the more prestigious institutions to be ranked in the top. In addition, comparison of the NDCG scores of our approach and six baseline methods indicates that our approach achieves the best performance and thus can be regarded as a better alternative for the manual peer assessment for the academic institution evaluation when compared with existing bibliometrics evaluation methods.

Our future work includes how to incorporate temporal information into our model in order to conduct systematical analysis of institutions' performance over time. We also plan to conduct more case studies on institution evaluations with our approach for examining its applicability to various disciplines or research fields.

Acknowledgments. This work was supported by the following grants: grant No. BK20141420 and No.BK20140857 from the Natural Science Foundation of Jiangsu Province of China.

References

1. Acuña, E., Espinosa, M., Cancino, J.: Paper-based Productivity Ranking of Chilean Forestry Institutions. Bosqu 34(2), 211–219 (2013)
2. Grant, J.B., Olden, J.D., Lawler, J.J., et al.: Academic Institutions in the United States and Canada Ranked according to Research Productivity in the Field of Conservation Biology. Conservation Biology 21(5), 1139–1144 (2007)
3. Huang, M.: Exploring the H-index at the Institutional Level - A Practical Application in World University Rankings. Online Information Review 36(4), 534–547 (2012)
4. Torres-Salinas, D., Moreno-Torres, J.G., Delgado-López-Cózar, E., et al.: A Methodology for Institution-Field Ranking based on a Bidimensional Analysis: the IFQ 2 A Index. Scientometrics 88(3), 771–786 (2011)
5. Kschischang, F.R., Frey, B.J., Loeliger, H.: Factor Graphs and the Sum-Product Algorithm. Institute of Electrical and Electronics Engineers Transactions on Information Theory 47(2), 498–519 (2001)
6. U.S. News & World Report - Best Rankings, http://www.usnews.com/rankings
7. Academic Ranking of World Universities, http://www.shanghairanking.cn/
8. CWTS Leiden Ranking, http://www.leidenranking.com/
9. SCImago Institutions Rankings, http://www.scimagoir.com/
10. Yan, E., Sugimoto, C.R.: Institutional Interactions: Exploring Social, Cognitive, and Geographic Relationships between Institutions as Demonstrated through Citation Networks. Journal of the American Society for Information Science and Technology 62(8), 1498–1514 (2011)
11. Bishop, C.M.: Pattern Recognition and Machine Learning, pp. 359–419. Springer Publications, New York (2006)
12. Jarvelin, K., Kekalainen, J.: Cumulated Gain-based Evaluation of IR Techniques. Association for Computing Machinery Transactions on Information Systems 20(4), 422–446 (2002)

Axis-Based Alignment of Scholarly Papers and Its Presentation Slides Considering Document Structure

Yuhei Kawakami, Atsuto Nishida, Toshiyuki Shimizu,
and Masatoshi Yoshikawa

Kyoto University, Yoshida-Honmachi, Sakyo, Kyoto 606-8501, Japan
{kawakami,a.nishida}@db.soc.i.kyoto-u.ac.jp
{tshimizu,yoshikawa}@i.kyoto-u.ac.jp

Abstract. Recently, most researchers make a presentation with presentation slides to introduce a paper in academic conferences. We can often retrieve and browse papers and presentation slides through websites. We consider that we can obtain information efficiently by using both of them, and we propose a method to align papers and its presentation slides at the fine granularity. Though there are some existing works on this alignment, our system tried to achieve better accuracy for this problem by proposing the two approaches: 1) the adjustment by *axis alignments*; and 2) two-step alignment. The content similarity between each slide and paragraph is unstable due to the small amount of texts in the slides. Therefore we also calculate the content similarity in section-level and consider the ancillary alignment in section-level. Also, we succeed to obtain better alignments by adjusting the alignment score or narrowing down the alignment candidates. Finally, for each slide, we calculate the scores of each paragraph, and determine the alignment according to the scores by associating the slide to a sequence of paragraphs. We created a small dataset manually and conducted an experiment to confirm the effectiveness of the proposed method.

Keywords: Alignment, scholarly paper, presentation slide, axis slide.

1   Introduction

Recently, most researchers make a presentation with presentation slides to introduce a paper in academic conferences. We can often retrieve and browse papers and presentation slides through websites such as the author's home page or the conference website. Also, we can use search systems, for example Google Scholar[1], Microsoft Academic Search[2], and SlideShare[3]. Papers have a lot of texts and give us more detailed information about the methods, the experiments, and the related research. On the other hand, presentation slides tend to have many figures and tables, and a

---

[1] http://scholar.google.com/
[2] http://academic.research.microsoft.com/
[3] http://www.slideshare.net/

K. Tuamsuk et al. (Eds.): ICADL 2014, LNCS 8839, pp. 87–97, 2014.

small amount of text. As they have different features, we use them selectively depending on the purpose. For example, we make use of papers in the case that we need to grasp the contents in detail, and presentation slides in the case that we would like to get the overview in a short time.

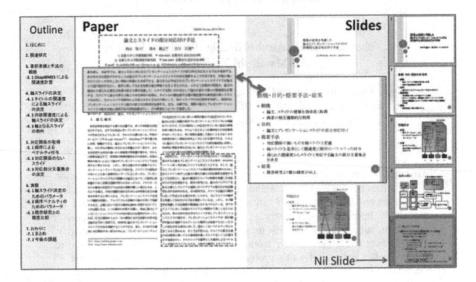

Fig. 1. System image

We considered that we can obtain information efficiently by combining them and integrating the information of both. In this study, we propose a method to align papers and its presentation slides at the fine granularity. Fig. 1 shows the overview image of our system.

The alignment is especially useful for the beginner of the research or people unaccustomed to reading the paper. For example, this system helps them to understand the research by presenting the related paragraphs secondarily when they skim through the slides. Also, they can use this system when they attend a seminar of paper introduction and want to grasp the detailed content in a short time. Another scene is the case that they see the animation or the figure on the slides when they peruse the paper.

The content similarity between each slide and paragraph is unstable because the amount of the texts in slides is small. In this paper, we propose the *axis alignment* for aligning them. The *axis alignments* are the confident relation pairs of the slide and the section. We adjust the alignment score by using them and obtain the more proper alignments. We call the slides having the *axis alignments* the *axis slides*. Also, we propose the two-step alignment which narrows down the candidates of the alignments by utilizing the document structure. We expect the improvement of accuracy by applying the above methods.

The rest of the paper is organized as follows. In Section 2, we refer the related works. In Section 3, we elucidate the problem setting and explain our baseline method. In Section 4 and 5, we introduce axis-based adjustment by *axis alignment* and the two-step alignment. In Section 6, we evaluate our proposed method and show its effectiveness. In Section 7, we state the conclusion of this paper.

2   Related Work

Kan[1] proposed a digital library of aligned document and presentation pairs and the method of alignment. For each slide in the presentation, they retrieve the top n most similar paragraphs (n set to 10) and examine all possible spans constructed by choosing one paragraph to be the start of the span, another to be the end. The best method of this paper was the one that calculate the score using bigram-based Jaccard similarity and simply align the span having the highest score to the slide. Kan's method give the score the penalty considering the order of the target slide and before and after that to calculate final score, but our method use *axis slides*to give order penalty.

Bahrani *et al.*[2] proposed the method to align paper and presentation slide in section-level. They calculated similarities by tf-idf and give them the order penalty considering the position for the entire document. They treated the slides as image files and used the machine learning with a linear support vector machine by the histogram. The slides are classified as Text, Outline, Drawing, Result, and Result is aligned the section of "Experiment" or "Results". Others are aligned considering the weights of the text similarity and the linear ordering. Our system align in paragraph-level unlike this research. And the order penalty is different from our proposed method.

Hayama *et al.*[3] align papers and presentation slide by using Hidden Markov Model aiming for making the Corpus which is used for generating the presentation slide from a paper automatically. This is the method to improve the Jing's research[4] to adapt academic paper and its presentation slide. This method align in section-level but our method align in finer granularity of paragraph.

3   Problem Setting and Outline of the Proposed Method

3.1   Problem Setting

In this paper, we call the whole document of the presentation slide made by such an application as PowerPoint "presentation slide" and a sheet of slides "slide".

We convert the paper and its presentation slide to XML documents and use them as input. We regard papers as semi-structured documents which have sections, subsections and paragraphs, and presentation slides as the sequence of slides. The input of our system is a pair of the paper and its presentation slide, and the output is the corresponding relationships between them, which is the alignment of a sequence set of paragraphs and a slide. We used not section but a sequence of paragraphs for the granularity of paper because the slides aligned more properly in paragraph-level than in section-level are seen in plenty.

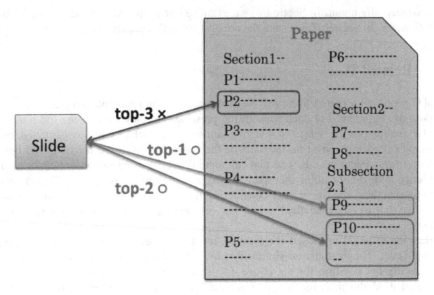

Fig. 2. Determination of a paragraph sequence

3.2   Baseline Method

In this section, we explain the baseline method, which is the basis of this study. We write $s_i (0 \leq i \leq L)$ as the ith slide of the presentation slide and "p_j" $(0 \leq j \leq M)$ as the jth paragraph. L is the number of the slides in the presentation slide. M is the number of the paragraphs in the paper.

First, we calculate the content similarity of each slide and each paragraph of the paper by using the words of slides as query. We used the formula in Kikori-KS[5], which is the tf-idf based formula improved for XML documents. And we rank top k_i paragraphs per each slide s_i according to the score. They are the candidates for alignments. We determine k_i based on the following criteria.

$$S(s_i, p_j) > \frac{MaxSimAvg}{\delta} \tag{1}$$

$S(s_i, p_j)$ is the content similarity between s_i and p_j. We regard p_j which meets above formula as the candidate and the number of them are k_i. $MaxSimAvg$ is the average of the largest content similarities between each slide and paragraph. δ is parameter which meets $\delta > 0$. The trend of the content similarity differs according to the pair of the paper and its presentation slide, and we can estimate the appropriate threshold value by using $MaxSimAvg$.

Then, we determine the sequence of paragraphs which should be aligned to a slide (Fig. 2). First, we align top 1 paragraph (the best match paragraph) of the score for each slide. Next, we check the paragraph in descending order of score, and align it if it is continuous with the sequence aligned already. We repeatedly carry out this operation and complete for the slide if it is not continuous or all of top k_i are checked. We determine the alignments for all slides in this way.

The slides written "Outline", "Question", "Thank you" should be regarded as nil slide, which explain the flow of the presentation and have no alignments and relation with the contents of paper. So we need to set the appropriate parameter δ and eliminate candidates of alignment by the formula (1).

3.3   Outline of the Proposed Method

In this section, we briefly explain the outline of our method which is the improvement of the baseline method. We calculated the content similarities between each slide and sections in the paper, and considered rough alignment in section-level. By considering document structure (hierarchy of sections and paragraphs), we propose 1) axis-based adjustment and 2) two step alignment. The details are described in Section 4 and 5 respectively.

In 1), we utilized the observation that presentation slides are generally made based on the corresponding paper and their orders are similar. We define *axis alignments* as the pairs of the slide and the section of the papers which are considered to be in a corresponding relation with high probability, and adjust the content similarity of the pairs deviating the order by giving the penalty. We also call the slides which are in *axis alignments* *axis slides*. *Axis slides* are determined by calculating the title similarity (the degree of similarity between the titles of slides and the sections of papers) and the relative content similarity. In 2), we first align each slide and a section, then in finer granularity of the paragraphs again.

In this paper, we apply 1) and 2) on the baseline method as shown in Fig. 3, and evaluate each method by the experiment.

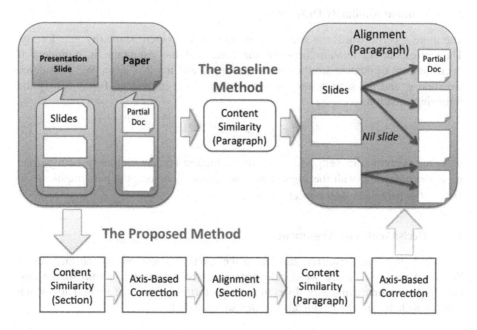

Fig. 3. Outline of our method

4   Axis-Based Adjustment

The order of content description in the presentation slide is similar to the paper. This is because it is made for the purpose of the presentation of the paper. We considered *axis alignment* in section-level because the order of sections is more stable. We expect to improve the accuracy by giving the order penalty based on the *axis alignments*. We first get candidates of the *axis slides* from the perspective of the title similarity and the content similarity, then select consistent *axis slides* from the candidates.

4.1   Title Similarity

Sometimes, slide titles and section titles share the same words. Such words include "INTRODUCTION, "CONCLUSION", and so on. They are thought to have a corresponding relation if their titles are the same phrase.

We considered the pairs of s_i and sec_k is a candidates of *axis alignment* if they satisfy the following equation. sec_k is the kth section ($0 \leq k \leq N$). N is the total number of the sections (including subsections) in the paper.

$$cos(x, y) > \alpha \tag{2}$$

x is the vector of the word set in the title of slide s_i, y is that in the title of sec_k, and cos is a function that computes the cosine similarity. α is the threshold which meets $0 \leq \alpha \leq 1$.

4.2   Content Similarity Difference

The more specific words the slide has, the higher the content similarity gets locally. The corresponding relation between the slide and the paragraph is confident if the difference of content similarity between top 1 and top 2 is large. We considered the slide s_i and the section sec_k is a candidate of *axis alignment* if they satisfy the following equation.

$$S(s_i, p_j) > \frac{MaxSimAvg}{\beta} \tag{3}$$

p_x is the paragraph in $sec_{x\prime}$, which have the highest content similarity with s_i, and p_y is the paragraph with the highest content similarity among the paragraphs not in $sec_{x\prime}$. β is parameter which meets $\beta > 0$.

4.3   Decision of Axis Alignments

We decide the conclusive *axis slides* from the candidates selected by the methods in Section 4.1 and 4.2. First, we decide them in descending order of title similarities. Next is the content similarity difference. In performing them, the candidates which conflict with the already decided *axis slides* are excluded.

4.4   Order Penalty

We explain about how to give the order penalty in this section. We assume that the order of the paper and its presentation slide is basically similar. So we adjust the content similarity calculated in the baseline method by using the *axis alignments*.

s_i and s_j are the *axis slides* and s_x is the target slide. Assuming the order of $s_i s_x s_j$, s_x is likely aligned the paragraph in the sections between $sec_{i'}$ and $sec_{j'}$. $sec_{i'}$ and $sec_{j'}$ is the sections aligned with the *axis slides$_i$* and s_j (Fig. 4). Therefore, we give the order penalty to the paragraphs before section $sec_{s_{i'}}$ and after section $sec_{s_{j'}}$ (Fig. 5).

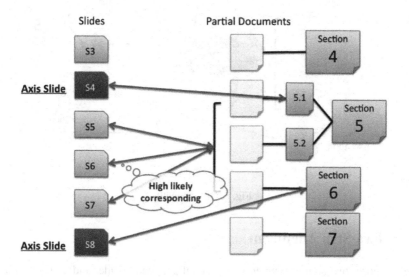

Fig. 4. Order penalty 1

We give the penalty by multiplying the content similarity and the following equation.

$$\{1 - \gamma \cdot \frac{log(1+SectionDistance)}{log(1+N)}\} \tag{4}$$

N is the total number of the sections (including subsections) in the paper. *SectionDistance* is calculated by the following formula.

$SectionDistance =$

$$\max\left(\left((am\_sec\,(s_i) - anc\_sec\,(p_k)\right),\left(anc\_sec\,(p_k) - am\_sec\,(s_j)\right)\right) \tag{5}$$

s_i and s_j are the *axis slides*. p_k is the target paragraph. $am\_sec(s_i)$ (access match section) is the function which outputs the number of the section s_i aligns with.

$anc\_sec(p_k)$ (ancestor section) is the function which outputs the number of the section p_k belongs to. We define $SectionDistance = 0$ if $SectionDistance < 0$. γ is the parameter which meets $0 \leq \gamma \leq 1$.

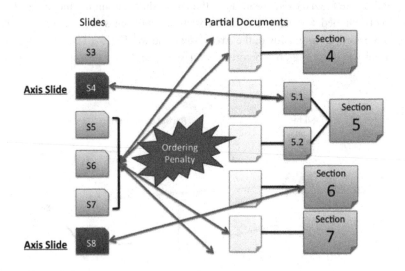

Fig. 5. Order penalty 2

5   Two-Step Alignment

We propose *two-step alignments*, which aligns each slide and the section as a beginning, then in paragraph-level again. (Fig. 3)

We perform the baseline method by replacing "paragraph" with "section" as the first step. We calculate the content similarity between the slides and the section, and align the pair having the highest similarity. Next, we perform the baseline again. We calculate it between the slides and the paragraph contained in the section which aligned in the first step, and decide the final alignment as the second step.

By the *two-step alignment*, we think we can correct some alignments of the pair having highest score per slide. We expand the set from the top 1 of the paragraph when we determine the aligned sequence set of paragraphs in the baseline method. Therefore top 1 is very important in our method. For example, we consider the case that top 1 of paragraph belongs to the section 5 and the paragraphs between top 2 and top 10 belong to the section 3. This slide is likely to be aligned with the section 3 but our baseline method actually aligns it with the section 5. We expect to be able to correct this by the two-step alignment.

Also, the computational cost is reduced by the two-step alignment because we can narrow down the paragraphs to calculate the content similarity or the axis-based adjustment.

6   Experiment

First, We need to set the parameters α, β, γ, and δ in our proposed method. α and β are the parameters which used to determine the *axis slides* in equation (2) and (3), and meet $0 \leq \alpha \leq 1$ and $\beta > 0$. γ is the parameter to determine the weight of the order penalty in equation (4), and meets $0 \leq \gamma \leq 1$. δ is the parameter to determine top k in equation (1), which are the candidates of the paragraphs to align. δ meets $\delta > 0$. We conducted the preliminary experiments for setting them, and used the following values in this experiment; $\alpha = 0.75$, $\beta = 2.50$, $\gamma = 0.75$, $\delta = 2.0$. These are thought to be appropriate for the our data set.

6.1   Evaluation of Proposed Method

We evaluate the accuracy of the alignment by our method. We manually aligned 11 pairs of papers and presentation slides and conducted an experiment to confirm the effectiveness of the proposed method. The paper is treated as semi-structured XML document in our corpus, which has section, paragraph, title, figure, table, and so on. The presentation slide also has body, title, and number. And we manually created the gold standard data of these pairs.

We evaluated the four methods, (1) the baseline method, (2) the baseline method + the axis-based adjustment, (3) the baseline method + the two-step alignment (4) the baseline method + the axis-based adjustment + the two-step alignment. We calculated the precision, the recall, and F-measure in the granularity of paragraph and their averages.

The results of the experiments are shown in the Table 1.The method (2) is the better than the method (1) in the precision and the recall. The precision decline slightly but the others are improved in the method (3). This is because the sequence set of the paragraphs become large by applying the two-step alignment and the continuous paragraphs being likely gathered. The method (4) results the best accuracy in the all method. From the results above, we can say the axis-based adjustment and the two-step alignment are effective and we obtain further effects by their combination.

6.2   Comparison with Existing Method

In this section, we show the comparison with the existing method.

SlideSeer[1] give the ordering penalty considering the order of the front and rear slides, and determine the alignments from the candidates of the paragraph spans. It sets a high value on the paragraph span having the larger size of the same degree of the scores. The method by Bahrani*et al.*[2] align in section-level and its problem setting is different from our work. We referred SlideSeer for the comparison as it aligns with a focus on the text parts and we can compare the order penalty and the determination algorithm of the spans of paragraphs.

We adopt the SlideSeer and compare with the alignment accuracy in the paper of SlideSeer. We used the evaluation corpus of 20 presentation document pairs used in his paper as the data set, to which the minimum required tags "section", "paragraph" and "title" are added. Other tags are not used, for example, "figure", "table" and so on.

We observed the Weighted Jaccard Accuracy same as his paper, which penalizes false positive by 1/5th the penalty of false negative.

Table 1. Accuracy comparison in paragraph unit

Method	Avg. Precision	Avg. Recall	Avg. F-measure
(1)Baseline method	0.535	0.264	0.350
(2) 1 + axis-based adjustment	0.549	0.288	0.374
(3) 1 + two-step alignment	0.531	0.292	0.373
(4) Proposed method (1 + both)	0.566	0.314	0.400

Table 2. Accuracy comparison with SlideSeer

Method	Weighted Jaccard Acc.
Proposed Method	47.5%
SlideSeer[1]	41.2%

The result is shown in Table 2. The accuracy of the proposed method is 6.2% higher thanSlideSeer. The corpus has the drawback of the paragraph split accuracy. Therefore, the proposed method has the small range of alignments by the algorithm. On the other hand, SlideSeer is unlikely to be affected by the drawback, and has the large range by considering the paragraph spans. Nevertheless, we can see the proposed method works pretty well. We think SlideSeer tends to align with the large range of paragraphs and the proposed method align with the narrow and properly range.

From this result, we can see the effectiveness of the axis-based adjustment and the algorithm to determine the sequence of the paragraphs by comparing the existing method. Also we find that the two-step alignment works well.

7   Conclusion

In this paper, we proposed the method to align scholarly papers and its presentation slides. Because we have small amount of texts in slides, it is difficult to align them correctly. We considered the baseline method and two improvement plan and evaluate them. The first is the axis-based adjustment, which adjusts the content similarities on the basis of the *axis alignments* and attempts to obtain the correct alignments from the point of view that the order of content in slides made for the purpose of the presentation of the paper is similar to the paper. The second is the two-step alignment, which corrects some alignments of the pair having highest score per slide by aligning each slide and the section as a beginning, then the sequence of the paragraphs again.

We conducted the experiment and found that we succeeded to improve the baseline method by them. Also, the performance of the proposed method exceeded the method motivated by SlideSeer. This is because our method aligns the suitable range of paragraphs.

In future work, we will consider and discuss the other algorithms for determining the sequence set of the paragraphs properly. Also, we would like to develop the application for this system. Besides, we should consider not only the structural information of the papers but also the structures of the presentation slides, and make use of them.

References

1. Kan, M.-Y.: SlideSeer: A digital library of aligned document and presentation pairs. JCDL, 81–90 (2007)
2. Bahrani, B., Kan, M.-Y.: Multimodal alignment of scholarly documents and their presentations. JCDL, 281–284 (2013)
3. Tessai, H., Hidetsugu, N., Susumu, K.: Alignment between a technical paper and presentation sheets using a hidden markov model. AMT, 102–106 (2005)
4. Jing, H.: Using Hidden Markov Modeling to Decompose Human-written Summaries. Comput. Linguist. 28(4), 527–543 (2002)
5. Shimizu, T., Terada, N., Yoshikawa, M.: Kikori-KS: An effective and efficient keyword search system for digital libraries in XML. In: Sugimoto, S., Hunter, J., Rauber, A., Morishima, A. (eds.) ICADL 2006. LNCS, vol. 4312, pp. 390–399. Springer, Heidelberg (2006)

An Evaluation Study of the Automating Metadata Interoperability Model at Schema Level: A Case Study of the Digital Thai Lanna Archive

Churee Techawut[1,*], Lalita Tepweerapong[1], and Choochart Haruechaiyasak[2]

[1]Computer Science Department, Faculty of Science,
Chiang Mai University, Thailand
churee.t@cmu.ac.th
[2]National Electronics and Computer Technology Center,
National Science and Technology Development Agency, Thailand
choochart.haruechaiyasak@nectec.or.th

Abstract. In digital library, large digital information is collected with some deviations of metadata structures. Various types of metadata standards and application profiles containing different sets of metadata elements are primarily concerned for information sharing and accessing among several digital collections. To allow information interoperability, librarians and domain experts traditionally take in a part of matching those metadata elements, which is a time consuming task. To alleviate the problem, a basic automating metadata interoperability model (AMI Model) is proposed for matching between two sets of simple level metadata elements by implementing a Crosswalk method based on the estimation of the semantic similarity values. The proposed model is evaluated on a case study of the Digital Thai Lanna archive based on the Mean Reciprocal Rank (MRR) performance measures. The result shows the proposed model accuracy is higher than the average accuracy at high acceptance level.

Keywords: Automating Metadata Interoperability, Crosswalk, Semantic Similarity, Digital Thai Lanna Archive, Filtering, Basic Global Thresholding.

1 Introduction

The digital Thai Lanna archives in northern part of Thailand have been collected and dispersedly stored in several conserving organizations. Chiang Mai University (CMU) has three institutions, CMU Library, Faculty of Humanities, and The Center for the Promotion of Arts and Culture, taking care of digital preservation and data management of Thai Lanna archives. They manage the digital information in their own ways with different metadata element sets. This resultings in some problems of data integration, accessing, and maintaining that our research has focused on.

Most digital information has been described by various types of metadata standards and application profiles. An application profile is a set of metadata elements, policies

---

*Corresponding author.

K. Tuamsuk et al. (Eds.): ICADL 2014, LNCS 8839, pp. 98–106, 2014.

and guidelines defined for particular applications [1]. In order to access those digital information whether via a single point of access or cross-domain searching, metadata interoperability is needed to create a connectivity at schema level that is the basic level of metadata mapping. Crosswalk is a mapping of the elements, semantics, and syntax from one metadata scheme to those of another [2]. Interoperability at schema level is the first gate to achieve through the mappings in record level and repository level. The results usually appear in one table displaying a set of common elements or application profiles from different metadata schemas. Efforts, task complexity and semantic quality of matching up several metadata elements must take in to account.

An example of automatic metadata mapping is VAMP [3]. It is approached for expressing the semantics explicitly by formalizing the constraints of various multimedia profiles using ontologies and logical rules, thus enabling interoperability and automatic use for MPEG-7 based applications. It can also detect any inconsistencies of the semantic constraints formalized. However, the metadata mapping is scoped within a group of multimedia metadata standards and lacks of flexibility to map with non-metadata standards.

Metadata mapping requires a semantic similarity for maintaining the semantic of metadata structures. Some semantic similarity techniques are presented and compared by [4]. However, Wu-Palmer's semantic similarity [5] is the most interesting based on edge counting in a taxonomy like Word Net [6], and defined as formula (1).

$$Sim_{Wup} = max \left[\frac{2 \times depth(LCS(a, b))}{length(a, b) + 2 \times depth(LCS(a, b))} \right] \tag{1}$$

a and b are two words used for calculating a semantic similarity value. The depth (LCS (a, b)) is a depth of the lowest node in hierarchy that is a hypernym of the two words. The length (a, b) is a number of edges in the shortest path between two words in hierarchy. The semantic similarity value from this formula is normalized in [0, 1] giving us to easily compare within range and is affected by the common characteristics of the concepts that are compared. The value decreases with differences of words and is affected by the position of words in the taxonomy. Hence, we focus on mapping two sets of application profile elements using Wu-Palmer's semantic similarity.

We proposed a conceptual framework of a basic automating model supporting metadata interoperability which can reduce efforts and task complexity of the domain expert. We also ran an experimental study to observe the accuracy of semantic metadata mapping based on metadata element sets of the digital Thai Lanna archive. The automating metadata interoperability model (shortened to AMI Model) matches two sets of simple level metadata elements based on Crosswalk method and the estimation of semantic similarity values.

This paper is mainly divided into 5 parts. We start to present a conceptual framework of our case study. We describe our proposed AMI Model. Then, we show the evaluation details of AMI Model and discuss our analysis of result. Finally, we give the conclusion and point out some recommendation.

2   Conceptual Framework

Fig. 1 shows the conceptual framework of metadata mapping and evaluation of the matching result. Our approach considers the basic mapping of both metadata standard and non-metadata standard. AMI model handles metadata extraction and matching application profile elements. The matching result will be evaluated for the accuracy. Details will be explained as follows.

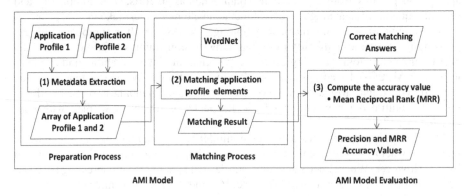

Fig. 1. Conceptual framework

3   AMI Model

AMI Model has the methodology to match two application profiles containing metadata elements at simple level. The model can be divided into two major parts, preparation process and matching process.

3.1   Preparation Process

Two application profiles are originally in a RDF/XML format [7]. They are extracted for two sets of metadata elements or terms. Only metadata terms are loaded into an array.

3.2   Matching Process

Based on our previous work [8], the matching is done in one-way direction. For example, if we have two application profiles such as A and B, the matching will be done twice with different two directions (A→B and B→A). This matching process of AMI Model (Fig. 2) proposed in this paper has been extended by adding a filtering of some semantic similarity values. There are six processing steps as follows:

Step 1

The model considers and compares synonym sets or synsets (sets of words with the same or similar meanings) of each metadata elements in both application profiles. Wu-Palmer's semantic similarity [5] calculation based on a lexical database (WordNet) is used to detect the similar meaning. The semantic similarity value ranges from zero to 1. For example, we want to find semantic similarity values of two words, "Author" and "Creator". The word "Author" has three synsets and The word "Creator" has two synsets then there are six pairs of synset calculation. The semantic similarity values in each synset pairs are 0.133, 0.706, 0.125, 0.667, 0.0 and 0.0 which means both words are most similar in synset pair 2 and 4, but synset pair 5 and 6 are not similar.

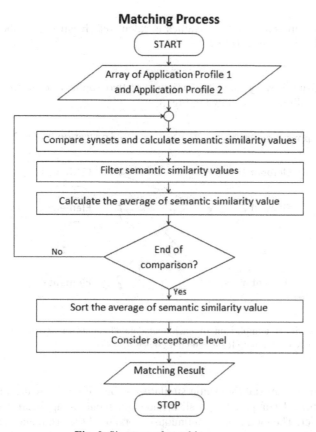

Fig. 2. Six steps of matching process

Step 2
We added the filtering method to remove the metadata elements that has small semantic similarity value indicating low implications. The filtering number ranges from 0.1 to 0.9. Two filtering methods are selected, fixed filtering method and non-fixed filtering method.

Fixed Filtering Method
This method previously selects the exact filtering numbers start from 0.1 to 0.9 respectively. If the filtering number 0.3 is specified, it means to filter out some metadata elements having semantic similarity values below 0.3.

Non-fixed Filtering Method
The filtering number is calculated from Basic Global Thresholding method [9]. This method is used for automatically determining an appropriate filtering number, and filter out some metadata elements having the semantic similarity values below the filtering number. If the filtering number is 0.5 then the remained semantic similarity values after finishing step 2 are 0.706 and 0.667.

Step 3
The average of semantic similarity values is calculated. From step 2, the average of semantic similarity values is 0.687.

Step 4
Do step 1 to 3 until every metadata elements of two application profiles have been compared inone direction as shown in Fig. 3.

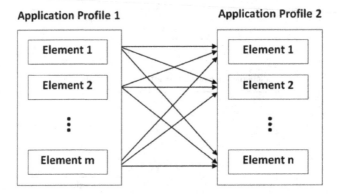

Fig. 3. One directional comparison of each metadata elements in two application profiles (Source: The 3rd CMU Graduate Research Conference, p. 199)

Step 5
The model sorts the average semantic similarity values of the 1st metadata element in application profile 1 compared with all metadata elements in application profiles 2in descending order. The model also continuously sorts until the last metadata element in application profile 1 compared with all metadata elements in application profiles 2.

Step 6
The model considers every rank of matching with acceptance level ranging from 0.1 to 0.9. If the average semantic similarity value is less than acceptance level, the matching will not be considered.

4   AMI Model Evaluation

In this evaluation study, we performed a Crosswalk method with our case study. Three application profiles of Thai Lanna archive are used as the input of the AMI Model. They are compared in directions as shown in Fig. 4.

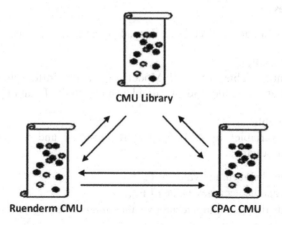

Fig. 4. Comparison of three application profiles

The input application profiles for AMI Model evaluation are the followings:

1. Digital Thai Lanna archive application profile of Chiang Mai University Library [10] (CMU Library)
2. Digital Thai Lanna archive application profile of Ruenderm Building, Faculty of Humanities, Chiang Mai University [11] (Ruenderm CMU)
3. Digital Thai Lanna archive application profile of The Center for the Promotion of Arts and Culture, Chiang Mai University (CPAC CMU)

Two application profiles from CMU Library and Ruenderm CMU are both defined by using metadata standard in their own ways, and CPAC CMU is individually defined using non-metadata standard. These three application profiles contain some elements with 35 percentages of similarity.

First, we set the evaluation objectives, defined a hypothesis and then designed the evaluation tasks. Finally, we discussed the evaluation results.

4.1   Objective

We expect to use a non-fixed filtering method in our model to gain more automatically and precisely in AMI model. A non-fixed filtering method can automatically select the suitable filtering number based on a considering group of semantic similarity values. Therefore, the evaluation study is conducted with the following objective.

To study the accuracy values computed by non-fixed filtering method (F_g) and the accuracy value computed by averaging of fixed filtering value (F_{avg}) at each acceptance level. We defined three levels of acceptance as followings:

- High acceptance level = 0.7 – 0.9
- Medium acceptance level = 0.4 – 0.6
- Low acceptance level = 0.1 – 0.3

4.2   Variables

We studied two evaluation variables, independent variable and dependent variable.

Independent Variable
The independent variables of AMI Model are factors influencing the dependent variables. There are two independent variables in this study, F_g and F_{avg}.

Dependent Variable
The dependent variables of AMI Model are observed and analyzed. We mainly focused on the followings:

- AF_g represents the accuracy value of F_g.
- AF_{avg} represents the accuracy value of F_{avg}.
- AF_x represents the maximum accuracy value of any filtering number.

4.3   Hypothesis

Our hypothesis is that at high acceptance level, the accuracy value of F_g (or AF_g) is higher than the accuracy value of F_{avg} (or AF_{avg}).

4.4   Task

There are four tasks to perform in this evaluation.

1. Prepare the matching results. Every application profile input is processed by AMI Model in directions as shown in Fig. 4.
2. Prepare the correct matching answers.
3. Compute the accuracy value by comparing the matching results from the first task and the correct matching answers from the second task. Mean Reciprocal Rank (MRR) [12] is selected as a performance measure considering the accuracy value of all ranks of matching results.
4. Create the comparison graph presenting AF_g, AF_{avg} and AF_x of MRR performance measure.

5   Result Analysis

Fig. 5 shows the accuracy value of MRR performance measure. The horizontal axis represents acceptance levels and the vertical axis represents MRR values. The value trend of the graph shows the correctness trend of overall matching. At high acceptance level 0.7 to 0.9, the MRR value increases, because AMI Model provides the increasing of correct matching by reducing a number of insignificant matching. It implies that AMI model can match metadata elements correctly with high accuracy at high acceptance level. The graph line of AMI model in Fig. 5 shows the overall progressive trends with the accuracy increasing closes to the maximum accuracy value. It can imply that AMI model can increasingly produce the accuracy while the acceptance level is higher.

At acceptance level 0.5 to 0.7, the MRR value decrease, because some correct matching results are canceled and then remained no match. For example, element a and element b are correct match but the semantic similarity value is less than the acceptance level so that the matching is canceled.

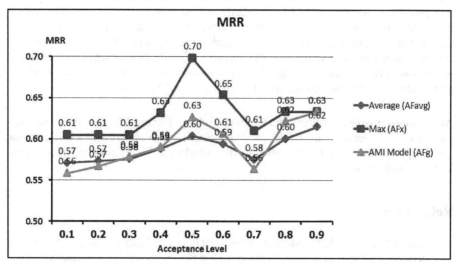

Fig. 5. MRR performance measure of AMI Model at each acceptance level

Moreover, table 1 shows AF_g, AF_{avg} and AF_x of MRR at each acceptance level. At acceptance level 0.9, AF_g equals to AF_x and then AF_g is a maximum value for MRR performance measures. It shows that the acceptance level 0.9 has the best accuracy values (AF_g=0.63). We can see from table 1 that most accuracy values of AF_g is higher than AF_{avg} at high acceptance level. Therefore, our hypothesis is accepted. We can conclude that AMI Model with non-fixed filtering method has effectiveness and high accuracy at high acceptance level.

Table 1. AFg, AF_{avg} and AF_x of MRR performance measure

Acceptance	MRR		
Level	AF_g	AF_{avg}	AF_x
0.1	0.56	0.57	0.61
0.2	0.57	0.57	0.61
0.3	0.58	0.58	0.61
0.4	0.59	0.59	0.63
0.5	0.63	0.60	0.70
0.6	0.61	0.59	0.65
0.7	0.56	0.58	0.61
0.8	0.62	0.60	0.63
0.9	0.63	0.62	0.63

6   Conclusion and Recommendation

At high acceptance level, the accuracy of AMI Model with non-fixed filtering method is higher than the average of fixed filtering method based on MRR performance measures. Hence, AMI Model can be used for matching metadata elements in application profiles containing metadata standards or non-metadata standards. We recommend that AMI Model can be further developed by semantically considering the description of metadata elements in the matching processing. The future experiment can be conducted to examine the effectiveness of AMI Model when matching between some diverse application profiles from other domains. Further study of ontology technique would also be considered to improve the AMI Model.

Acknowledgements. We thank the Graduate School, Chiang Mai University for supporting us the research grants. We also thank Krerk Akkarachinores, PichaiSangboon and Chappana Pinngoen for providing us the metadata of Thai Lanna archives to evaluate our AMI Model.

References

1. Chan, L.M., Zeng, M.L.: Metadata Interoperability and Standardization - A Study of Methodology Part I: Achieving Interoperability at Schema Level. D-Lib Magazine (2006)
2. NISO (National Information Standards Organization).: Understanding Metadata. NISO Press (2004)
3. Troncy, R., Bailer, W., Hausenblas, M., Hoffernig, M.: VAMP: Semantic Validation for MPEG-7 Profile Descriptions. Technical Report INS-E0705 (2007)
4. Hliaoutakis, A., Varelas, G., Voutsakis, E., Petrakis, G.E., Milios, E.: Information Retrieval by Semantic Similarity. Journal on Semantic Web and Information Systems 55–73 (2006)
5. Warin, M., Volk, H.: Using WordNet and Semantic Similarity to Disambiguate an Ontology. Stockholms University (2004)
6. WordNet: A Lexical Database for English, http://wordnet.princeton.edu
7. RDF/XML Syntax Specification (Revised),
   http://www.w3.org/TR/REC-rdf-syntax
8. Tepweerapong, L.,Techawut, C.:Experimental Study on Automating Metadata Interoperability Model Among Application Profilesat Simple Level. In: The 3rd CMU Graduate Re-search Conference, pp. 195–202 (2012) (in Thai)
9. Thresholding: Digital Image Analysis, http://www.cpe.eng.cmu.ac.th
10. Trakarnpan, A.: Prototype of Metadata for Heritage Manuscripts Digitisation Initiative for Traditional Manuscripts of Northern Thailand, pp. 121–125. Pulinet (2010) (in Thai)
11. Techawut, C.: Metadata Creation: Application for Thai Lanna Historical and Traditional Archives. In: Chowdhury, G., Koo, C., Hunter, J. (eds.) ICADL 2010. LNCS, vol. 6102, pp. 144–147. Springer, Heidelberg (2010)
12. Christopher, D.M., Prabhakar, R., Hinrich, S.: Introduction to Information Retrieval. Cambridge University Press, New York (2008)

The Construction of an Ontologies Using Recommender Management System for Tourism Website of Northeast Thailand

Issara Chuenta

Faculty of Informatics, Mahasarakham University, Mahasarakham 44150, Thailand
issara.chuenta@gmail.com

Abstract. The Northeast of Thailand had high potentiality to earn revenue from eco-tourism in this region. The existing websites in northeastern Thailand had few ontologies, which helped users to retrieve easily relevant information. The development of ontology was a challenge, as it required identifying appropriate concept and relationship, irrespective of top-down, down-top and combination approaches. The objectives of this study ware to developed ontology by using Recommender Management System for tourism websites. The results showed that using ontologies had better than other websites (not using ontology) which was indicated with the F-measure (95.98 %).

Keywords: Ontology, Semantic web, Owl, Information retrieval, Recommender management system.

1   Introduction

The majority of the search engines were working with key-word based technology, through it was getting improved, it was not very effective as semantic web, which depended on heavily ontology. Tom R. Gruber [1] defined ontology as a specification of a conceptualization. With this background, the present was undertaken to develop an ontology application of Northeast Thailand, where ontology was difficulty to find out under large growth of information and data. The ontology had not only retrieved the relevant information, it also could guide the users decision to search the process.

The ontology technology could help to present the structured content. Ontology was widely used in areas such as Geographic [2], Bio-medical Informatics [3], Information Processing system [4], Integration System [5], Information Retrieval System[6], Tourism Information Retrieval [7], Rule-based Systems [8], Recommend Systems [9] Ontology development could be classified into three approaches: top-down, bottom-up and combination [10]. Each of these approach had it's own problems in determining the initial concept, which affected the ontology structure, ultimately impact on performance of information retrieval.

Top-down approach was general–to-specific approach of the concepts in a domain. For example, concept 'wine' start a broader concept and then to sub class, include red

K. Tuamsuk et al. (Eds.): ICADL 2014, LNCS 8839, pp. 107–121, 2014.
© Springer International Publishing Switzerland 2014

wine, white wine and rose wine, further specified with the names of red wine as cabernet, syrah and red burgundy.

Bottom-up approach was specific–to- general approach from a set of concepts in a domain. For example, start from specific name of wine such as, pauillac and margaux. Then create the super class.

Combination approach (top-down and bottom-up), first defined a salient concept, and then generalize and specify it's appropriately. This start with a general concept such as wine and a specific concept and relate it's to local concepts and names which were not usually available in established ontology. Therefore the concept of other relevant consideration were related to a middle level concept, with region specific meanings to local terms or names or popular places in development of ontology.

Many researchers had adopted different approaches in development of ontology. Paul and Nicolaas [11] had been proposed an bottom-up approach for the development of ontology for chemical purity analysis. Since the data of pure substances were complex, it start with the lowest level or a very small one. The results showed that the bottom-up approach was suitable for basic physical chemical data rather than top-down approach. For example Sadasivam and Saravana [12] had presented the development of ontology and retrieval technology for tourism in India. The study showed both the development of ontology and its updating. The approach used in this study showed both top-down and bottom-up independently not as a combination methods. The retrieval results showed that top-down approach was much more versatile than bottom-up approach. Moreover, Tang and Cai [13] described a framework of ontology development methodology called TOCM (Tourism Ontology Construction Method), integrating knowledge using FCA, while Kathrin and colleagues [7] used a harmony based Adaptive Ontology Mapping in it's Semantic Web Information Retrieval System for e-Tourism. Shu-Hsien Liao et al. [14] proposed association rules to find Adidas brand, as a purchase behavior of customers in Taiwan through the Web Application. Association rules were used for grouping of Data Mining with the Apriori algorithm from brand Adidas. Association rules resulted in the conversion of the ontology to be used in conjunction with a web application language ontology. In addition, Tanatorn Tanantong and colleagues [15] proposed ontology to help in the analysis of the patient's heart signal from the Electrocardiogram (ECG). The ECG signals were captured in form of ontology. The analysis of ontology was undertaken using Semantic Web Rule Language (SWRL). The rules were created by medical experts, which were used for automatic analysis of patients using ECG signals, and to help doctors in diagnosis of heart disease and to minimize the delay in diagnosis.

Therefore, in this paper, ontologies had been developed and measure the performance of each approach, which includes top-down bottom-up and combination.

2   Literature Review

2.1   Ontology

Ontology was a technology used to store and to deliver content using structured description of the idea with the specifications. To conceptualization of the various existing concepts in a domain describe the extent of interest. The requirement was to create an understanding about the structure of knowledge-base, and to share information among the people in the domain. The ontology was a logical theory that determined the meaning of the lexical scope of interest, which was scheduled to explain the meaning of it's with formal explicit description of structural and hierarchical relationships. Ontology enabling technology had the ability of Inheritance [16].

There are three possible approaches in developing a class hierarchy, namely [17]

A top-down is to develop process starts with the definition of the most general concepts in the domain and subsequent specialization of the concepts.

A bottom-up is to develop process starts with the definition of the most specific classes, the leaves of the hierarchy, with subsequent grouping of these classes into more general concepts.

A combination development process is a combination of the top-down and bottom-up approaches: We define the more salient concepts first and then generalize and specialize them appropriately.

Requirements ontology was one that stakeholders understand the scope of knowledge in the domain who worked in the same direction. In this context, model of the node or relation, properties, and slot had a hierarchical relationship, with the form and structure, in describing the ontology language used in the semantic web languages such as XML, RDF, RDFS and OWL [18].

2.2   Semantic Web

Semantic Web technology was used to store and deliver structured content. Including the ability to analyze or to classified, it appeared that the data were correlated with each other, or were collected and presented in a hierarchy.

Currently, the website development had grown rapidly cause problems of information overload, resulting ineffective search or navigation to find relevant information. Keyword-based search, which was common and a basic tools used for searching information, which cannot understand and process the meaning of words or relationships. The keyword-based searches were using word matching and it's hyperlinks without semantics. Semantic web was a program-based search, where it was able to understand the data elements, it's relations to search easier and guide users to search.

2.3   Ontology Information Retrieval System

Ontology-based Information Retrieval System could also handle documents in various formats such as books, journal articles, etc. including recordkeeping document [19]. Fig. 1 showed ontology-based information retrieval system that provided the functionality of a working on concepts which was divided into 6 parts. Part 1 Local-Source Layer was part of the source repository system. Part 2 Wrapper Layer was for conversion of data from each system in to the XML-based and then using DB2XML.

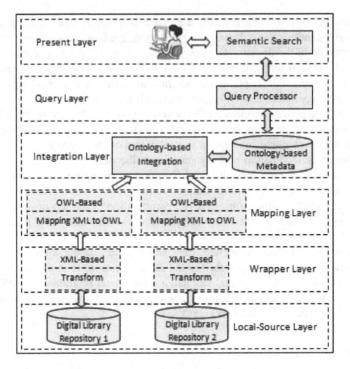

Fig. 1. The process of information retrieval

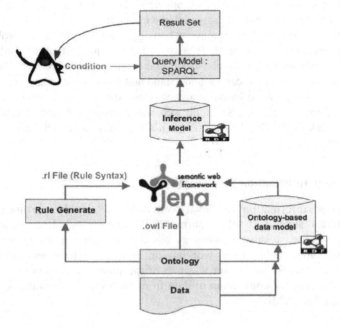

Fig. 2. Recommendation System Framework

Part 3 Mapping Layer was a data conversion from XML to OWL format to improve semantics of data. Part 4 Integration Layer helped to align and define. Ontology-based Metadata, Part 5 Query Layer was for searching process and using language SPARQL (The SPARQL Protocol and RDF Query Language). Part 6 Presentation Layer was the user interface for the retrieval and display.

2.4   Recommender Management System (RMS)

RMS was a user interface to determine various settings of Recommender Configuration. It can be used to discover and learn rules to provide the user with personal recommendations. It helped selections, type, recommend or matching, list of properties to show in the results of recommender.

Fig. 2.provided an overview of Recommendation System. The main components included data contained in the database, or may be in the form of RDF, ontology and rule. Users can add, update and edit rules in the form of IF-THEN as needed [20].

3   Methodology

The research methodology had five stages 1) Analyze the compiled information and the definition 2) Design and development ontology 3) Mapping ontology 4) Information retrieval and recommend and 5) Evaluation.

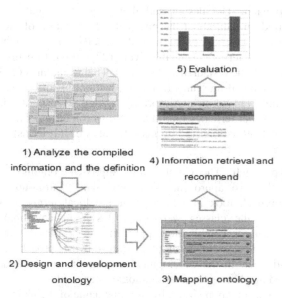

Fig. 3. The research methodology

3.1   Compilation of Concepts and Terms

The concepts considered for the tourism website in the Northeast were accommodation, restaurants, attractions, travel, etc. These concepts were compiled by considering a set of words that generate keywords (concepts), which derived the scope of tourism in the Northeast of Thailand. The concepts were compiled using the database from Department of Tourism (Http://www.tblthailand.com) The study had compiled 1104 terms to define the concept, and to design and develop ontologies.

3.2   Design and Development Ontology

Design and development of an ontology in this study was based (third approach) i.e. combination of both top-down and bottom-up. It was already established from the studies that the structure of the ontology, even within the same domain, depended on the approach (bottom-up or top-down), due to the starting concept of the ontology. The ontology in this study was designed and developed using Protégé 4.1 in the form of OWL.

Top-Down Approach. The design ontology, in this study, was based on relationship of object property, Data property and instance tourism. It consist of 6 main classes Annualfestival (27 terms), Accommodation (273 terms), Restaurants (267 terms), Attractions (267 terms), Locations (239 terms), and Transportations (31 terms) as shown in Fig. 4.

Bottom-Up Approach. The design and development of ontology in bottom-up approach was based on data about the physical infrastructure of the tourism. There were 21 main classes, Districts (94 terms), Ratings (6 terms), Provinces (19 terms), Accommodations (124 terms), Annualfestivals (27 terms), Sub district (24 terms), Hotels (143 terms), Ethnic restaurants (29 terms), Thai restaurants (203 terms), Coffee shops (35 terms), National museums (8 terms), Natural history museums (19 terms), University museums (14 terms), Airport (8 terms), TransportCo.Ltd (23 terms), Manmade attractions (41 terms), Cultural attractions (68 terms), Historical attractions (63 terms), Natural attractions (57 terms), Rural area (1 terms) and Urban area (1 terms) as shown in Fig. 5.

Combination Approach. The Combination approach combined the design and development of the two approaches (top-down and bottom-up). The design in combinational approach took into account of the local terms in Thai Language. Therefore, some of the classes were core classes in developing a bottom-up development. Museum on combination approach was combined with the attractions. Some classes were subclass of developing a top-down approach such as province, district and sub-district. In the development of combination approach, it's became master classes, and in addition local terminologies were added.

The combination as mention above, because the name of the main class represented the concept of broader domain. The name of a class may change in different terminology. But the class was still the same concept to reflect the existing reality. The important was to distinguish between the hierarchy of the class and the class name. Which reflected the narrow definition in order to digest it. The class name consists of the same general principle. Some classes can be merged. And resulted in reducing number of core classes and sub-classes increased.

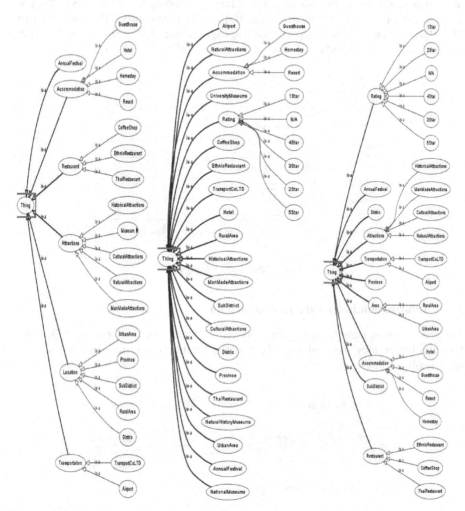

Fig. 4. Top-Down Approach   **Fig. 5.** Bottom-Up Approach   **Fig. 6.** Combination Approach

The design and development in the combination approach had 10 main classes: ratings (6 more terms) annualfestivals (27 terms) districts (94 terms) attractions (67 terms), transportations (31 terms) provinces (19 terms) areas (2 terms) accommodations (267 terms) Sub districts (124 terms) and restaurants (267 terms) as shown in Fig. 6.

3.3   Mapping Ontology

In order to retrieve data in Thai language, ontology mapping technique was employed to facilitate of tourist information searching in Thai language. This may due to SPARQL language did not support Thai language statement. Hence the configuration was undertaken for property and vocabulary mapping (Fig. 7).

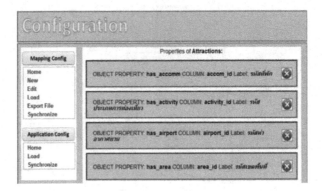

Fig. 7. Mapping Ontology

3.4   Information Retrieval and Recommend

The present recommender management System (RMS), was developed by NECTEC: National Electronics and Computer Technology Center. The results retrieval screens wais displayed in Fig. 8.

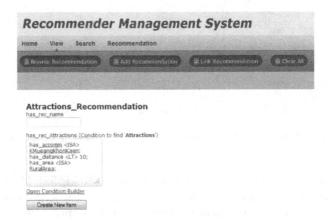

Fig. 8. The results retrieval screens

Retrieved Results from Top-Down Approach. The query about "Suk San Hotel" with the property 'attraction' search results from 1 to 7 items (Fig. 9.), were selected from the standards ontology. Because the list did not includes local facilities in the standards ontology. Where RMS in the class 'attractions' did not recognize as nearby accommodation. The development of an ontology for top-down in relations of class 'Attractions', included the local names and poplar terminologies.

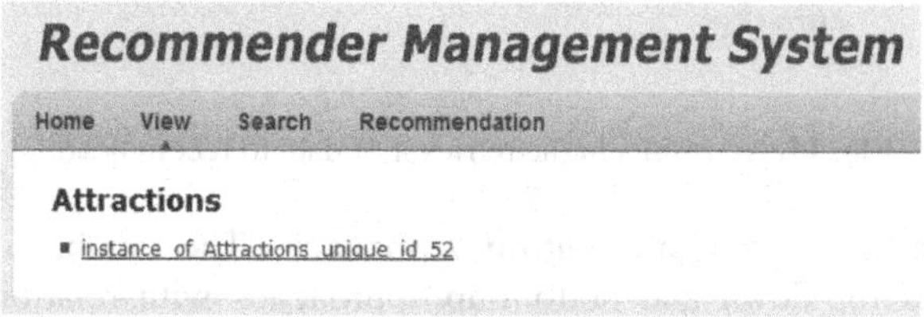

Fig. 9. The results of the recommend retrieval

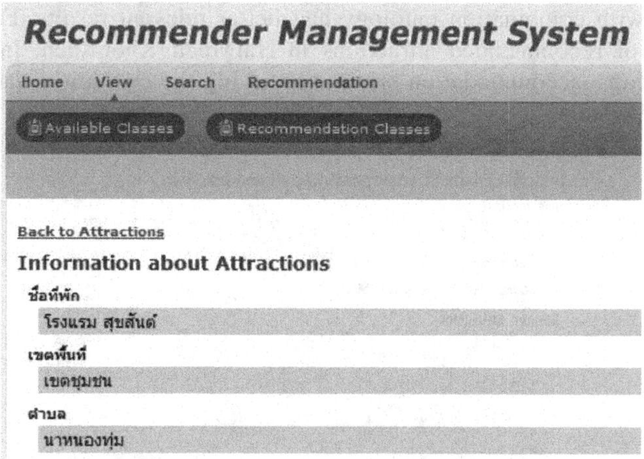

Fig. 10. Results suggest attractions ("PhaNokKhao")

After the retrieving in the RMS with the conditions of destination, showed the first item of an introduced the "PhaNokKhao" in Fig. 10.due to lack of combination with the local facilities and terminologies, developed of an ontology for top-down relationship object property. Data property, of class 'accommodation' and 'attractions' did not comply with the conditions.

Retrieved Results from Bottom-Up Approach. No results for some cases were retrieved. For example, search criteria to guide right sights nearby accommodation known as "highway hotel" will most likely not to be retrievable. Due to the relationship between ontology and bottom-up class development "attraction" was the main class named object property accommodation. Relating class "accommodation", one of the attractions set near the hotel accommodation. "Highway Hotel" will be chosen as the nearest accommodation right from the process of designing and developing ontology. Therefore, this case did not show result in the retrieval, as shown in Fig. 11.

Fig. 11. No results in the retrieval of data to recommend.

Retrieved Results from Combination Approach. The combination approach, which combines top-down and bottom-up approaches with relationship between 'object property' and 'data property' with local terms and class would show better results than other two approach. Example, the relevant information which retrieved to class 'attraction'would be better combination approach. Therefore, class 'attractions' with combination ontology had better relevant results. For example, added terms of recommended attractions in NaiMuangKhonKaen. Including the transport stations, accommodation prices, specifying the cost lower than 500 baht, there were 12 results.

Information about Attractions_Recommendation

has_rec_id

uid_9

has_rec_name

Recomment Price <LT> 500

has_rec_Attractions

instance_of_Attractions_unique_id_44

instance_of_Attractions_unique_id_43

instance_of_Attractions_unique_id_42

instance_of_Attractions_unique_id_41

instance_of_Attractions_unique_id_40

instance_of_Attractions_unique_id_46

instance_of_Attractions_unique_id_45

instance_of_Attractions_unique_id_36

instance_of_Attractions_unique_id_35

instance_of_Attractions_unique_id_38

instance_of_Attractions_unique_id_37

instance_of_Attractions_unique_id_39

Recommended To:

Accommodation, which have this condition (Remove This Recommendation Link) has_once <LT> 500;.

Fig. 12. Retrieval results to a recommend after entering the complex

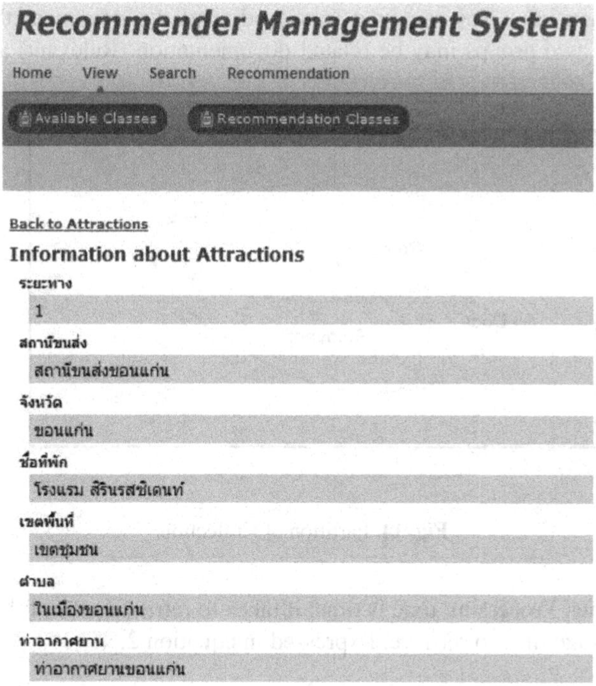

Recommender Management System

Home   View   Search   Recommendation

🗎 Available Classes   🗎 Recommendation Classes

Back to Attractions

Information about Attractions

ระยะทาง

> 1

สถานีขนส่ง

> สถานีขนส่งขอนแก่น

จังหวัด

> ขอนแก่น

ชื่อที่พัก

> โรงแรม สิรินรสชิเดนท์

เขตพื้นที่

> เขตชุมชน

ตำบล

> ในเมืองขอนแก่น

ท่าอากาศยาน

> ท่าอากาศยานขอนแก่น

Fig. 13. Results suggest attractions "Hong MunMangMeungKhonkaen"

Fig. 12 showed the results, Hong MunMangMeungKhonkaen, San Lag MeangKhonkean, WatNong Wang, Artand Culture, Khonkaen National Museum, Thung Sang Health Park, BuengKaenNakhon, Wat Pa SaengArun, KohSamet, HupTaem Sin Si, Wat Chai Sri and Huean Lao Museum If it access to the result list it will display recommend on Fig. 13.

3.5   Evaluation

This research was measured the effectiveness of an ontology design by F-measure and Processing Time.

F-measure. F-measure was used to measure the relationship between precision and recall for retrieval system performance as shown from equation 1.

$$F-measure = \frac{2 \times \text{Precision} \times \text{Recall}}{\text{Precision} + \text{Recall}} \times 100 \tag{1}$$

Precision is a Measure of Eliminate Irrelevant Documents. Recall is a measure of system to retrieve relevant documents. Due to retrieve documents based on the questions. When users enter a query system, they will divide the document into two parts: a document that was removed (retrieved) and the document that cannot be pulled out. The two groups may be related documentation (Relevant) and. Irrelevant Fig. 14.

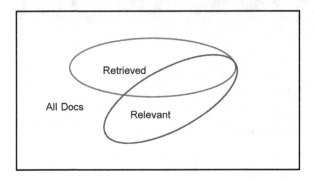

Fig. 14. Partition of Collection

Processing Time. Processing time is time, it takes to retrieve each of the keywords to find out an average time to retrieve. Expressed in equation 2.

$$\text{Processing Time} = \frac{\sum_{i=1}^{N} elapsedTimeMin}{N} \qquad (2)$$

When elapsedTimeMin is the episode time to retrieve and N is the number of times to retrieve. The retrieval information in each category will take on retrieval difference. Log file from the SOS program is to retrieve each time when it appears in Fig. 15, the retrieval time. (elapsedTimeMin) 0.014933334 Sec

```
rt_name              key 74
2557-05-26 19:57:36   INFO ModelInteraction:202 -
transport>>has_transport_name
2557-05-26 19:57:36   INFO ModelInteraction:204 -
le is : ¹⁴ÂÊ¦¦¹ó¦¦ᵘþº
2557-05-26 19:57:36   INFO GetResult:139 -  label
2557-05-26 19:57:36   INFO GetResult:185 - s Time
1401109056108
2557-05-26 19:57:36   INFO GetResult:187 - Total
hod callMethod() is :0.014933334 elapsedTimeMin
```

Fig. 15. Log file of time spent in each retrieval

4   Results

In this paper had developed ontologies. An evaluation of information retrieval systems used the f-measure, which is the relationship between the precision and the recall as well as the processing time. All in all classes from 1104 data used keywords, 50 keywords and tested 50 times.

4.1   F-measure

Measuring the performance of retrieval had been used the F-measure, which was the most widely used in statistics. To measure the performance of the developed ontologies in 3 approach of top-down bottom up, and combination of which can be shown as Fig. 15.

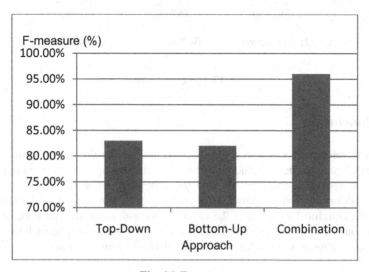

Fig. 16. F-measure

Fig. 15 The comparison of each technology and ontologies, the results showed that the retrieval of information from the combination approach was maximum with an F-measure (95.98 %), followed by retrieval top-down F-measure (83 %), and from bottom-up approach had the lowest F-measure (81.99 %).

4.2   Processing Time

The researchers used computer CPU Intel (R) Core (TM) 2 Speed 1.87 GHz Memory 2.0 GB. The average time to retrieve the information from the ontology development of the three approaches was shown in Fig. 16.

Fig. 16 showed the average time to retrieve data from a top-down ontology development (0.0796 seconds). Bottom-up took an average less than (0.1209 seconds) and the combination average took (0.1122 seconds).

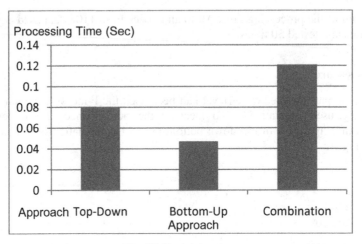

Fig. 17. Processing time

5   Conclusion

Ontology development was a new approach in developing the semantic web. There were several approaches, including top-down, bottom-up and combination. The combination approach ontology allowed the efficiency retrieval of up to 82.26%, while the bottom-up was the lowest effective retrieval. But at least retrieval may be due to the hierarchical structure of the ontology without combination of the localized concepts. Further research needed to develop ontology with dynamic inclusion of the local names and terms in local language particularly for tourism field.

Acknowledgement. The authors are grateful to the Mahasarakham University for funding this research.

References

1. What is an Ontology?,
   http://wwwksl.stanford.edu/kst/what-is-an-ontology.html
2. Liu, C.-H., Chen, K.-L., Ca, J.J.-Y., Hung, S.-C.: Ontology-Based Context Representation and Reasoning Using OWL and SWRL. In: 8th Annual Communication Networks and Services Research Conference, pp. 215–220. IEEE (2010)
3. Hendler, J., Musen, M. (eds.): Making Biomedical Ontologies and Ontology Repositories Work, pp. 78–81. IEEE Computer Society (2004)
4. Park, C., Shon, J.: A Study on the Web Ontology Processing System. Knowledge & Inference Research Team: ETRI, pp.1035 – 1038 (2005)
5. Zhu, H., Tian, Q., Liang, Y., Ji1, S.: Domain Ontology Component-based Semantic Information Integration. In: First International Workshop on Education Technology and Computer Science, pp. 101–103. IEEE (2009)
6. Hwang, M., Kong, H., Kim, P.: The Design of the Ontology Retrieval System on the Web. In: ICA0T 2006, pp. 1815–1818 (2006)

7. Prantner, K., Ding, Y., Luger, M., Yan, Z.: Tourism ontology and semantic management system. In: IADIS International Conference: IADIS, pp. 111–114 (2007)
8. Zhao, Y., Pan, J., Ren, Y.: Implementing and Evaluating A Rule-based Approach to Querying Regular EL+ Ontologies. In: Ninth International Conference on Hybrid Intelligent Systems, pp. 493–497. IEEE (2009)
9. Choi, C., Cho, M., Kang, E.-Y., Kim, P.: Travel Ontology for Recommendation System based on Semantic Web. In: ICA0T 2006, pp. 624–627. IEEE (2006)
10. Why develop an ontology?,
    http://protege.stanford.edu/publications/ontology_developmen
    t/ontology101-noy-mcguinness.html
11. van der Vet, P.E., Mars, N.J.I.: Bottom-Up Construction of Ontologies. IEEE Transactions on Knowledge and Data Engineering 513–524 (1998)
12. Sudha Sadasivam, G., Kavitha, C., SaravanaPriya, M.: Ontology Based Information Retrieval for E-Tourism (IJCSIS) International Journal of Computer Science and Information Security, 78–82 (2010)
13. Tang, S., Cai, Z.: Tourism Domain Ontology Construction from the Unstructured Text Documents. In: Cognitive Informatics (ICCI 2010), pp. 297–300. IEEE (2010)
14. Liao, S.-H., Chen, J.-L.: Hsu. T-Y.: Ontology-based data mining approach implemented for sport marketing, pp. 11045–1156 (2009)
15. Tanantong, S.: Towards Continuous Electrocardiogram Monitoring Based on Rules and Ontologies. Bioinformatics and Bioengineering (BIBE), 327–330 (2011)
16. Zhang, S.-M., Guo, J.-Y., Yu, T., Lei, C.-Y.: An Approach of Domain Ontology Construction Based on Resource Model and Jena Information Processing (ISIP), pp. 311–315 (2010)
17. Ontology Development,
    http://protege.stanford.edu/publications/ontology_development/
    ontology101-noy-mcguinness.html
18. Guarino, N.: Formal Ontology and Information Systems. In: Proceedings of the 1st International Conference on Formal Ontologies in Information Systems, pp. 3–15 (1998)
19. Electronic And DigitalLibrary Using Ontology BaseMetadata,
    http://wiki.nectec.or.th/ru-
    newwiki/bin/view/IT630_13_Assignment/MSIT06Gr06ElectronicAnd
    DigitalLibraryUsingOntologyBaseMetadata
20. Rule Management System and Recommender Application Management System,
    http://text.hlt.nectec.or.th/ontology/

Learning Object Metadata Mapping
for Linked Open Data

Noppol Thangsupachai[*], Suphakit Niwattanakul,
and Nisachol Chamnongsri

Information Technology, Social technology,
Suranaree University of Technology, Thailand
zoliblade@hotmail.com, {suphakit,nisachol}@sut.ac.th

Abstract. Database is a great part of data store on the Internet. However, the transition to web of data and shareable contents to open standard like LOD requires new structuring of traditional data. In order to achieve this interoperability of information systems, RDF is important file format in resolving semantic heterogeneity. This paper proposes the metadata mapping processes to convert database to RDF. DB2RDF is a tool that automatically generates RDF from database by mapping from LO ontology and stored in TDB. The mapping process start by extract database schema and restructuring in form of RDF using Jena API make them available to query. The created model modification query uses SPARQL queries. We proceed set of class and properties from database attributes and redefine with specific domain control vocabulary to populate RDF. Finally, we test the query results that can preserved the database semantic by validated the resulting by SPARQL queries with RDB on SQL queries.

Keywords: Linked Open Data, Learning Object, Metadata Mapping, RDF.

1 Introduction

The changes of technology in education and learning objects: LO creation become a primary problems of teachers, who use only contents from textbooks there are not enough. Teachers have to provide valuable contents in electronic form that can reusable [1]. Teachers have to learn a lot of tools to create lessons in electronic format, and there are many raw data out there to manage and search from multiple data sources to find the information that they need is only for the simply courses [2].

However, a lots of learning objects stored in a traditional CMS and database in several website are have many a problems in search and reuse. Teachers need to take a long time to search huge contents because (1) the huge of results stored in various databases with redundancy and duplicated contents in multiple websites, (2) the contents are not relate to title or topic of an article, and (3) hard to find suitable reuse data from scattered databases. From the survey teachers need some portal web or have a

---

[*] Corresponding author.

K. Tuamsuk et al. (Eds.): ICADL 2014, LNCS 8839, pp. 122–129, 2014.

central database to store the learning contents that can access and search from a single point directly. And may be linked to other relevant databases.

Fromthese problems, the researchers have used the concept of storing data in an open standard based on the concept of Berners Lee [3] is the link Open Data: LOD. Users can store the database of their own learning objects or convert data from other databases that has various schema to semantic web on RDF file. LOD maintains semantic of data which can search learning objects from a single site and also link to other node with applied search term in simultaneously.

This paper will presents in 6 sections include introduction. We have developed a tool call DB2RDF to covert relational database to RDF file for semantic data and open standard to Linked Open Data in particular case of Thai mathematics courses. Section 2 reviews about mapping theories approaches from literature reviews and we give general architecture in section 3. Then in section 4, we will introduce DB2RDF tool an illustrated in case study data tables and attributes in case study and present mapping process. Section 5 present in evaluation of query from database and from RDF file. And Section 6, we conclude the mapping processes remark and future work.

2 Mapping Background

Mapping is an important operation for data migration from legacy systems, a database model system, to other modern web technology or semantic system that computers can understand meaning of data. These are in many application domains, such as semantic web, schema or ontology integration, data integration etc. The methodology of mapping can distinguish three ways are: (1) database schema mapping, (2) Ontology mapping, and (3) database to RDF mapping, on which we focus only pre-ontology development is database to RDF file format mapping.

1. Database Schema Mapping: Mappings are established between the schemas of the individual databases in specific domain. This process takes two database schemas as input and produces a mapping between elements of the two schemas that correspond to each other. Some interesting works in this area are the works of Fuxman et al. [4] and Miller et al. [5]. That is old school data migration in legacy system.

2. Ontology Mapping: The main purpose of this process is to relate in integrate the set of class and properties of two ontologies or more that share the same domain or collapse domain. Kalfoglou et al. gives in [6] an excellent survey on ontology mapping and case study of Ontology Schema mapping from Bountouri et al. [7] that show applied metadata mapping to ontology. Majula et al. [8] show some secured ontology mapping for ensure semantic of data are maintain and provide more accuracy of mapping experiment in specific domain.

3. Database to RDF Mapping: This is the process whereby a database and an ontology are semantically or RDF file that related at a conceptual and schema level, i.e. correspondences are established between the database components and the ontology components [9], [10]. The database to semantically file on RDF and ontology approaches may be classified into two main categories as follows fig 1.

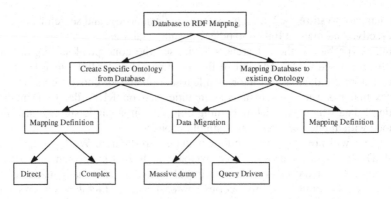

Fig. 1. Classification of data mapping approaches (Ghawi, et al. [11])

3   System Architecture

In this section, we give an overview of DB2RDF architecture and its main components. It is an integrated system between several data storage from database and retrieval system that shows results for user queries on this data source. User queries are submit through query service that transforms keyword or search phases to SPARQL syntax. Queries analyzed and modified keyword via Keyword Reference and redefine module to bridge the gap of user's keyword and control vocabulary. In Data source provider service is main module to convert database and backup file in SQL file to RDF. This module has specified LO ontology are used to mapping and describe the semantic of information source with database schema, in a mapping result provides RDF file and store in triple store ready for queries from query service. Query results will presented through Visualization web service module in UI on web platform that shows in fig. 2.

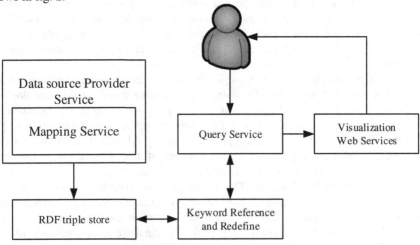

Fig. 2. Architecture of DB2RDF system

3.1 Data Source Provider Service

This services prepare data from source from internal database or database backup files in SQL format and convert to RDF. In addition to the information source, the data source provider service contains a learning object (LO) ontology that develops from other exiting LO ontologies representing the semantics of the information source. In this paper, we will only deal with information source based on internal relational database and external SQL file backup in domain of Mathematic courses. The automatic mapping of models to other domain of learning object is beyond the scope of this paper.

The LO ontology is manually generated from major LO ontologies (ALOCOM, SCROM, CISCO) using the Protégé tool which free software for manipulate semantic web and ontology that will be presented in details in the rest of this paper. Mapping process uses D2RQ mapping tool that also generates a description file (.ttl) of the mapping between database and the LO ontology for creates RDF file. Our objective is to keep the instances integrated in the structure in their RDF format.

3.2 Mapping Service

This service is used to connect the reference LO ontology. It compares the two schema of database schema and ontology schema using the methods defined in mapping rule in description file (.ttl file), and produces RDF file mappings which will be stored in the appropriate data provider service, as well as an up-to-date version of the mappings directory in the triple store.

In general, a mapping web service estimates similarity between the components of ontology and database, using structural and semantic (graph based and information value based) methods. We use metadata schema matching and mapping with controlled vocabulary in SKOS and user pre-define keyword.

3.3 Keyword Reference and Redefine

This is component contains the reference vocabulary and mapping directory. The reference vocabulary describes a specified knowledge domain. It represents the database topics model for LO ontology models and is supposed to cover all the local domains, i.e. each concept, role and attribute in any LO ontology has a corresponding concept, role and attribute in the reference ontology. The mapping directory contains information about the mappings between the LO ontology and the local database. The D2RQ mapping tool are used by the Mapping service to estimate the similarity between ontology and database components.

3.4 Query Service

When a queries is submitted, and analyzed by this service they will decomposed into a set of modular queries. Then using the modified keyword with control vocabulary in Keyword Reference and redefine. The query service redirects the single queries to the suitable data provider services via RDF triple store.

In fact, queries are expressed in SPARQL language [12], therefore, a query is composed of a set of triple patterns. Each triple pattern corresponds to a class and a properties in RDF in triple store. In other words, in data source provider service will provide RDF in triple patterns which are covered by LO ontology.

When an SPARQL query is received by RDF triple store. The query will executed and return its result is encapsulated as an SPARQL response and returned to the query service. The web service collects the responses returned from RDF triple store and recomposes them in a response which sent to the visualization web service.

3.5   Visualization Service

The final result will be redirected to the visualization service which is responsible for presenting the query results in a website interface but the visualization in deep processes is out of the scope of this paper. The following section introduces our approach DB2RDF as well as the mapping process which it uses.

4   Data Mapping Module

Propose of the DB2RDF system is to automatically create a new RDF file from a relational databases. In our architecture, DB2RDF is exploited by the data source provider service to generate a backup of database for each RDB. Currently, DB2RDF design to map specific domain of databases to one schema. Also, mapping different database schema is performed by mapping their specific ontologies to create RDF file in same domain.

The created RDF is described in RDF/XML language, a W3C recommendation for publishing and sharing ontologies on the web. RDF/XML is based on Description Logics [13], which is characterized by its expressiveness and reasoning rule are valuable to web services. The mapping process starts by detecting some particular cases for tables in the database schema. According to these cases, each database component is then converted to a corresponding LO ontology components. The set of correspondences between database components and LO ontology components is conserved as the mapping result to be used later. In the following subsections, we introduce the explanation of table relationship cases which must be detected in the usual databases in order to exploit them throughout in all of our mapping process.

4.1   Define Database Table Cases

The mapping process used in our approach on learning object domain that taken in account during the ontology creation. These cases will be showed using the following case study databases, which represents a learning object database in mathematic.

Case 1 Many to Many relationship: When a table T is used only to relate two other tables Ti, Tj in a many-to-many relationship, it can be divided into two disjoint subsets of columns attribute Ai, Aj, each participating in a referential constraint with Ti and Tj respectively. Therefore all T columns are foreign keys:F and primary key:P as well because their combination uniquely defines the rows of T, so: col(T) = PF(T).

Thus, the necessary and sufficient condition for a table T to be in case 1 is not occurs in this schema tables.

Case 2 One to Many relationship: This case occurs when a table T is related to another table Ti by a referential integrity constraint whose local attributes are also primary keys. In this case all the primary keys of T are foreign keys because they participate in a referential integrity constraint: $P\_(T) = \emptyset$. Thus, the necessary and sufficient condition for a table T to be in case 2 are between table Contributor and other learning object tables (Course, Lesson, ContentObject and Asset).

Case 3 This case is the default case, it occurs when none of previous cases occur.

When these different cases are detected in the database, the mapping process can use them to appropriately map database components to suitable ontology components as follows.

4.2   Database Convert Process

The mapping process is done as follows. It starts by mapping the tables to concepts and then mapping the columns to properties. Thus, the table cases mentioned above are used twice: one time for table-to-class mapping and the other time for column-to-property mapping. The mapping process consists therefore of the following steps:

1. The database tables that are in case 3 are mapped to ontology classes.

2. The tables in case 2 are mapped to subclasses of those classes corresponding to their related tables, so T is mapped to a subclass of the class corresponding to Ti. For example, the tables Course, Lesson and Content object and Asset are mapped to subclasses of the class corresponding to the table Contributor.

3. For tables that are in case 3, we map their referential constraints to object properties whose ranges are classes corresponding to their related tables, we set the object property as functional. So it will have at most one value for the same instance. This characteristic is obvious because it comes from the uniqueness of key.

4. The tables that are in case 2 and have other referential constraints than the one used to create the subclass, we map them to object properties as in the previous step. For example, the table Lesson is in case 2 and has a referential integrity constraint with the table Contributor, so we assign to Lesson an object property Lesson.lessonID which is functional and whose range is Contributor, and we assign to Contributor an object property isCreate whose range is Lesson.

5. Finally, for all tables we map their columns that are not foreign keys to datatype properties. The range of a datatype property is the XML schema data type [14] equivalent to the data type of its original column. The column NAME in the table Contributor is mapped to a datatype property Contributor.Name whose range is XSD string datatype.

4.3   Mapping Generation

During the mapping process, a DB2RDF [14] document is automatically generated to record the relationships between generated ontology components and the original database components. It includes (1) a full description of the database schema, (2) a set of concept map definitions consisting of the name of concepts with their identifying column(s), and (3) a set of relation and attribute map definitions. This document can be used by the query web service to translate ontological queries into SQL queries and retrieve corresponding instances [11]. Figure 3 shows an example of a class mapping definition from the mapping document.

```
# Table asset
map:asset a d2rq:ClassMap;
        d2rq:dataStorage map:database;
        d2rq:uriPattern "asset/@@asset.AssetId|urlify@@";
        d2rq:class vocab:asset;
        d2rq:classDefinitionLabel "asset";
        .
map:asset__label a d2rq:PropertyBridge;
        d2rq:belongsToClassMap map:asset;
        d2rq:property rdfs:label;
        d2rq:pattern "asset #@@asset.AssetId@@";
```

Fig. 3. Mapping document for Lesson class and properties

5   Result Validation

5.1   Case Study

Our implementation are approach in Learning Object database in Mathematical developed a Java application using the classes and interfaces provided by the Jena API [10], [15] from convert RDB in the MySQL database.

5.2   Verifying the Preservation of Semantic with SPARQL

The last step is to give some examples of query of database via SQL statements and SPARQL queries to interrogate the resulting RDF by analogy to the interrogation of the RDB by the SQL queries. For example, to retrieve the names of all lessons of mathematic in grade 7 that the lessons having the grade "ม.1"in Thai educational level In RDB, we must pass through the "Lessons" table. In RDF file, it is sufficient to apply an assertion of the "Lessons.Level" property.

We used JenaARQ which is a SPARQL query engine for querying generated ontologies, thus, for theprevious query, the result give 100% accurate. That they are the same values of result.

6   Conclusion

The results that we obtained by passing several RDB to our prototype show the accuracy and performance of our approach. Indeed we have shown throughout this paper that this approach preserves the data of different records of the RDB, and represents explicitly the semantics implicit presented by foreign keys. We have also shown through an example, the possibility to find for a SQL query its corresponding SPARQL query. One can therefore say that we are proposing a feasible and effective approach. Our future work will address the storage of ontologies in the RDB; indeed, ontologies, increasingly voluminous, begin to appear, calling into question their storage ways based, so far, on documents XML in his majority. The objective of this work is to improve the existing proposals or suggest others in order to ensure an ontologies storing in RDB while keeping their specificities, exploiting storage performance offered by the DBMS.

References

1. Office of the National Education Commission.: National Education Plan (2009-2016) (2011)
2. Prangprasopchok, S., Boonprajak, S., Phuaudom, J.: Innovation to improve the quality of-Thai children in math: Thailand's weak mathematics education causes and solutions. Phanakorn Rajabhat University (2006)
3. Berners Lee, T.: Linked Data –Design Issue, http://www.w3c.org/Designissue/linkedData.html
4. Fuxman, A., Hernández, M.A., Ho, H., Miller, R., Papotti, P., Popa, L.: Nested Mappings: Schema Mapping Reloaded. In: Proc. VLDB 2006 Conf., Seoul, Korea, pp. 67–78 (2006)
5. Miller, R., Haas, L., Hernandez, M.A.: Schema Mapping as Query Discovery. In: Proc. VLDB 2000 Conf., Cairo, Egypt, pp. 77–88 (2000)
6. Kalfoglou, Y., Schorlemmer, M.: Ontology mapping: the state of the art. Knowledge Engineering Review 18(1), 1–31 (2003)
7. Bountouri, L., Gergatsoulis, M.: The semantic Mapping of Archival Metadata to CIDOC CRM Ontology. Journal of Archival Organization 9, 174–207 (2011)
8. Manjula, S.K., Dinesh, A.U.: Secured Ontology Mapping. International Journal of Web & Semantic Technology (IJWesT) 3(4), 83–91 (2012)
9. Rodriguez, J.B., Gómez-Pérez, A.: Upgrading relational legacy data to the semantic web. In: Proceedings of the 15th International Conference on World Wide Web, WWW 2006, Edinburgh, Scotland, May 23 - 26, pp. 1069–1070. ACM Press, New York (2006)
10. Bakkas, J., Bahaj, M.: Generating of RDF graph from a relational database using JENA API. International Journal of Engineering and Technology (IJET) 5(2), 1970–19875 (2013)
11. Ghawi, R., Cullot, N.: Database-to-Ontology Mapping Generation for Semantic Interoperaability. In: VLDB (2007)
12. Prud'Hommeaux, E., Seaborne, A.: SPARQL Query Language for RDF. World Wide Web Consortium, Working Draft WD-rdf-sparql-query-2006 (2006)
13. Baader, F., Horrocks, I., Sattler, U.: Description logics as ontology languages for the semantic web. In: Hutter, D., Stephan, W. (eds.) Mechanizing Mathematical Reasoning. LNCS (LNAI), vol. 2605, pp. 228–248. Springer, Heidelberg (2005)
14. Barrasa, J., Corcho, O., Gómez-Pérez, A.: R2O, an Extensible and Semantically Based Database-to-Ontology Mapping Language. In: Second Workshop on Semantic Web and Databases (SWDB 2004), Toronto, Canada (August 2004)
15. The Jena website, http://jena.apache.org/index.html

Transformation of DSpace Database into Ontology

Humaira Farid[1], Sharifullah Khan[2], and Muhammad Younus Javed[1]

[1] College of EME
[2] School of EECS
National University of Sciences and Technology, Islamabad, Pakistan
humaira.farid@gmail.com, sharifullah.khan@seecs.edu.pk,
myjaved@ceme.nust.edu.pk

Abstract. Ontologies enable controlled sharing and exchange of information among autonomous data sources. DSpace is an open source software for institutional repositories. It employs a traditional database to store the metadata that provides detailed description about digital documents. We need to transform the DSpace database into an ontology in order to share and reuse its information. However, the existing transformation systems are not able to transform the DSpace database accurately into an ontology because its schema is meta-schema. The proposed system first creates a normalized relational database for the data model of an institute from DSpace database and then transforms it into an ontology. The system has been implemented and its results demonstrate that transformation is correct.

Keywords: Digital libraries, metadata, semantic web, ontology.

1   Introduction

Semantic web applications have enabled sharing and reusing of existing information and can create an integrated view of multidisciplinary information [10]. An ontology can represent a data source at a higher level of abstraction and manifest the semantics of a source that are required for the sharing and exchange of information among autonomous data sources [16]. For example, VIVO[1] is an open source ontology (i.e., semantic web application) which has been developed to enable discovery of research and scholarship across disciplines [10,11]. On the other hand, institutional repositories (IRs) are often built to organize and manage the intellectual output of an institute. Mostly existing IR systems, e.g., DSpace[2], EPrints[3] and Archimede[4] are using relational database for maintaining the metadata of their digital contents. The metadata provides detailed description about digital documents, for example, author, publication data, document

---

[1] http://vivoweb.org/
[2] http://www.dspace.org/
[3] http://www.eprints.org/
[4] http://www.bibl.ulaval.ca/archimede/index.en.html

K. Tuamsuk et al. (Eds.): ICADL 2014, LNCS 8839, pp. 130–137, 2014.

type (i.e. thesis, article, report) and publisher. In order to enable users from the outside world to discover and explore the full range of research and scholarship available in an institute, we need to transform an IR relational database into an ontology. The ontology helps in integrating IR data with other ontologies, such as, VIVO, for sharing information with other information systems to discover new knowledge.

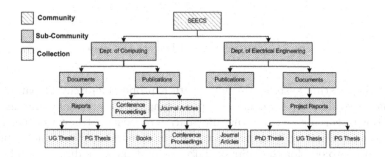

Fig. 1. DSpace data model of an institute

DSpace is an open source software for institutional digital repositories, developed by MIT and HP Labs, USA, and it has been deployed by institutions worldwide for building institutional repositories [14,15]. The main promising feature of DSpace is its flexible data model that arranges the digital documents in a repository according to the organizational structure of an institute [15]. An example data model is shown in Figure 1. The data model is divided into *communities*, which can be further divided into *sub-communities* reflecting a typical organizational structure of an institute. For example, communities and sub-communities are defined to be the schools, departments and centers of an institute. Communities contain *collections*, which are groupings of related contents. Each collection is composed of *items*, which are the basic archival elements of a repository. DSpace has defined a comprehensive database schema for its flexible data model, as shown in Figure 2. The DSpace database handles the many different data models that institutes have without the need for changes to its internal schema. The data model of an institute is not directly transformed into DSpace database schema, but it is stored in the DSpace database. DSpace schema is *meta-schema* i.e., a schema to describe schema. In other words, DSpace schema is not a normalized schema (i.e., relation normal form) with respect to a data model of an institute.

The existing relation to ontology transformation systems, such as [1,2,3,5,6,7,13] are when applied on DSpace database, they generate ontology classes for the relations e.g., *Community, sub-community, collection, community2_ community* and *community2_ collection;* included in the DSpace database schema. These classes are odd because they do not represent the entities e.g., *Project Reports* and *Books;* of DSpace data model of an institute. Moreover,

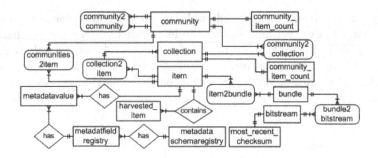

Fig. 2. Major relations of DSpace Database

most of the existing systems do not create a proper hierarchy of parent and child classes so they are not capable of preserving the data model hierarchy. The goal of this research is to share the information of existing IRs with other information systems. However the existing transformation techniques cannot generate an accurate ontology for the DSpace data model if they are directly applied on the database. We observed that it is essential to extract the data model from the IR database schema prior to transforming it into an ontology in order to generate an accurate ontology for DSpace database. It makes the transformation complicated and different from the typical transformation tasks.

Our proposed system first of all identifies the data model of an institute from DSpace database and builds a typical normalized relational schema for the data model of an institute. The normalized relational database is created for the identified data model and metadata of the repository is extracted to populate this database. Following this a relational to ontology transformation technique is applied on this normalized database to transform it accurately into an ontology. Experimental results demonstrate that the transformation is correct. The rest of this paper is organized as follows. Section 2 provides the related work. Sections 3 describes the proposed system. Section 4 describes evaluation results and finally section 5 concludes the paper.

2   Related Work

We divide the related work into two parts: (a) extracting metadata from IRs and (b) transforming metadata into an ontology. The existing extraction techniques [8,9,12] extract metadata from deep web, static web and legacy databases using reverse engineering techniques. The technique proposed by [9] builds a conceptual model (i.e., extended entity-relationship diagram) from database tables. The technique is suitable for data sources with little descriptions for the fields in their tables and no description for keys. The authors in [12] presented a method for extraction of data from tables and transformation of tables into a relational database accessible by formal languages, like SQL, for relational tables or SPARQL for RDF triple stores. This system primarily focused on large statistical information sites which are generated dynamically from databases and often no direct public access is provided to the databases themselves. The authors in [8] proposed a process which semi-automatically lifts meta-models into ontologies for the semantic integration of modeling languages. This allows to transform a meta-model into an ontology representing the concepts covered by these modeling languages. Existing metadata extraction techniques are domain and application oriented and apply reverse engineering techniques for extracting data. They cannot be applied in different domains and applications.

On the other hand, most of the existing transformation systems [1,2,5,6,9] use the basic transformation rules. Relational.OWL [7] is the most popular and dominant work in the generation of a database schema ontology. However, it causes a lack of separation among classes, properties and individuals. The novelty of DataMaster [13] is to offer two alternative modeling versions of Relational.OWL that manage to stay within the syntactic bounds of OWL DL (i.e., Description Logic) by providing the separation among classes, properties and individuals. D2RQ [4] is one of the most prominent tools which generates a domain-specific RDFS ontology. It exports the contents of a relational database to an RDF graph. The mapping is specified in a custom mapping language and a user can also modify the generated mapping. The engine that uses D2RQ mapping to translate requests from external applications to SQL queries on the relational database is called D2R Server [3]. Moreover, DataMaster and D2R server do not create a proper hierarchy of parent and child classes so they are not capable of preserving the data model hierarchy. The existing transformation systems are only capable to transform a normalized relational database.

3   Proposed Transformation System

The proposed system extracts metadata, creates a normalized intermediate database and transforms it into an ontology. The system is divided into two main modules: (i) metadata extraction and (ii) relation to ontology transformation.

3.1   Metadata Extraction

Metadata is extracted from the meta-schema of a DSpace database. This module further comprises three sub-components as discussed below.

Identification of Data Model (IDM). In this sub-component, entities of the data model (DM) and its relationship are identified in order to build an intermediate database and subsequently an ontology's classes. The entities of a data model $E\,(DM)$ are categorized into communities CM and collections CL; and communities are further categorized into main communities CM_m and sub communities CM_s. In the process of IDM, entities of DM are identified by extracting identifiers (IDs) of an item and its corresponding collection CL_i from *item* table of DSpace schema. Collection name is then extracted from *collection* table. An identifier of the community, containing CL_i, is extracted from *community2collection* table and subsequently its name is extracted from *community* table. This process of identifying communities is continued till the main community is identified.

The hierarchy of entities are identified for all items maintained in the *item* table. In the end, a list of hierarchy of entities is produced.

Building of Schema (BS). In building of the schema, the extracted data model (DM) is used for creating the schema of an intermediate database. First of all, an item identifier is selected from DSpace database table *Items* for obtaining its main community. If a table exists in the intermediate database (IDB) in a main community then its sub-communities are identified, otherwise the process is repeated for the remaining main communities. The same process is repeated for sub-communities until a table is created for their respective collection. Attributes of IDB relations are then extracted from *metadatafieldregistry* table of DSpace database and respective table is updated accordingly.

Population of Intermediate Database (PID). In populating the intermediate database, the first step is getting all items and their corresponding communities and collections from the identified data model. The tables of intermediate database which were created for communities are searched and item identifiers are inserted. Then the table, created for corresponding collection, is searched and metadata values of respective attributes are inserted in this table. These metadata values are extracted from *metadatavalue* table of the DSpace database. Before inserting values, we check whether an attribute is multivalued/complex attribute. If it is found to contain such an attribute, a new table is created. This process is repeated for all items.

3.2   Relation to Ontology Transformation

The intermediate database is transformed into an ontology by using the proposed transformation rules. The rules are as follows: (1) An OWL class C_i is created for a relation R_i, if one of the following conditions is satisfied (i) R_i does not contain any foreign key, and (ii) the primary key of the relation does not contain key of any other relation. (2) If two relations R_i and R_j have their primary keys linked with a foreign key constraint, they are mapped to two OWL classes C_i and C_j respectively, the one is a super-class of the other. (3) An OWL class C_i is created for a relation R_i and *rdfs:subClassOf* is added, if it fulfills the following criteria (i) R_i has a composite primary key; and (ii) R_i has non-key attributes. (4) An OWL class is not created for R_i, if it fulfills the following criteria (i) R_i has a composite primary key; and (ii) R_i does not have any non-key attribute. A *DataTypeProperty* is created for the primary key attribute which is not a foreign key and added to the class which has been created for its parent relation. The attribute which is both primary key and foreign key is discarded because it has already been converted to the functional datatype property in the parent relation. (5) For each non key attribute of a relation R_i, an OWL *DatatypeProperty* is created. (6) For each primary key attribute of a relation R_i, a *functional DatatypeProperty* is created with *minCardinality* restriction of 1 as a primary key is UNIQUE and NOT NULL. (7) For each foreign key of a relation R_i, an *ObjectProperty* is created. The domain and range of the *ObjectProperty* are specified. (8) For every tuple, the value of an attribute maps to a value of the property.

4 Evaluation and Results

We have implemented the transformation system in Java and generated an OWL ontology using the Jena-2.6.4 Ontology API for the DSpace data model. For evaluation of the proposed system, a subset of DSpace data of Massachusetts Institute of Technology (MIT), USA, was harvested in the proposed system. This data set includes 3 main communities, 10 sub-communities, 18 collections consist of 3 collections which were empty as they do not have any item. A total 2,242 items have been harvested from 15 collections. These items contain 11 non-multivalued, 5 multivalued and 3 complex metadata fields, and these contain 37,032 metadata values.

In transformation systems, the main emphasis is on the correctness of transformation. A correct and loss-less transformation ensures that all data in a source model is represented in the target model. The evaluation criteria for the proposed system is loss-less and correct transformation. This criteria finds out whether the source model (i.e., relational database) is completely transformed into the target model (i.e., ontology). In this evaluation, ontology classes, properties and instances were compared with (i) the intermediate relations, attributes and tuples respectively; and (ii) the DSpace data model entities (i.e., communities, sub-communities and collections), items' metadata fields and items' metadata values respectively.

In Table 1, column 1 represents the attributes of the DSpace data model, column 2 represents the attributes of the intermediate database and column

Table 1. Summary of Results - Ontology Creation

DSpace Data Model (Source Model)		Intermediate Database		OWL Ontology (Target Model)	
Main Communities	3	Primary Entities	3	Primary Classes	3
Sub-communities (with non-empty collection(s))	10	Sub-entities	10	Sub-classes	10
Non-empty Collections	15	Sub-entities	15	Sub-classes	15
Metadata Fields (complex)	3	Weak Primary entities	3	Sub-classes	3
Metadata Fields (multivalued)	5	Weak Secondary Entities	5	Datatype Property	5
Metadata Fields (not multivalued)	11	Non Key Attributes	14	Datatype Property	14
		Primary Keys (not foreign key)	11	Functional Datatype Property with minCardinality=1	6
		Primary Keys (foreign keys)	33	Functional Object Property with minCardinality=1	28
Total items in 15 collections	2,242	Total tuples of R_{CL} (relations corresponding to collections)	2,242	Total instances of C_{CL} (classes corresponding to R_{CL})	2,242

3 shows the attributes of the target OWL ontology. Three main OWL classes have been created for main communities and 28 sub-classes have been created for sub-communities, collections and complex attributes. 19 Datatype Properties have been created for non-multivalued, multivalued and non-key attributes. Six functional Datatype properties with a min-cardinality 1 were created for primary key attributes which are not foreign keys. 28 functional object properties with min-cardinality 1 were created for those primary key attributes which are also foreign keys. In this transformation all the communities, sub-communities, collections and all metadata fields of DSpace data model are preserved. However there are a few properties which have not been appropriately assigned to metadata fields. We can conclude on the basis of this result that information is preserved in transformation and there is minimum semantic loss. Hence the result reflects that the transformation is correct.

5   Conclusion

Institutional digital repositories are built to serve a specific institution's community of users. Existing institutional repositories (IRs) use relational database schema for maintaining the metadata of their digital contents. We transform DSpace database into an ontology, so that its metadata can be easily shared with other information system for knowledge discovery. We found in this research that the existing transformation techniques cannot generate an accurate ontology for the DSpace database. The distinguishing features of the proposed system are (i) identifying the data model of an IR; (ii) extracting metadata of the repository; (iii) creating a proper hierarchy of parent-child classes of the ontology to preserve the data model hierarchy. The evaluation results show that information is preserved in transformation and hence it is correct.

In this research, the proposed system was also tested on multiple data sets having different sizes which have not been included in this paper due to space limit, however they do not affect the accuracy of the system. Moreover the focus of the proposed transformation system was on DSpace and it has not been applied on other existing institutional repositories systems. It may not be equally applicable in them due to their specific database schemas. The first future step of this research is to match and translate the data of the produced ontology with other existing ontologies, such as, the VIVO and integrate them, so that their information can be shared and used for knowledge discovery. The next step of this research is to extract RDF triples from the text of digital documents of an institutional repository and upload them into the VIVO ontology for knowledge discovery.

References

1. Albarrak, K.M., Sibley, E.H.: Translating relational & object-relational database models into owl models. In: Proceedings of the IEEE International Conference on Information Reuse and Integration, IRI 2009, Las Vegas,Nevada, USA, pp. 336–341 (August 2009)

2. Astrova, I., Korda, N., Kalja, A.: Rules for mapping sql relational databases to owl ontologies. In: Proceedings of the 2nd International Conference on Metadata & Semantics Research, Corfu Island in Greece, pp. 415–424 (October 2007)

3. Bizer, C., Cyganiak, R.: D2r server-publishing relational databases on the semantic web (poster). In: 5th International Semantic Web Conference (ISWC 2006), Athens, USA, p. 26 (November 2006)

4. Bizer, C., Seaborne, A.: D2rq-treating non-rdf databases as virtual rdf graphs (poster). In: 3rd International Semantic Web Conference (ISWC 2004),Hiroshima, Japan, p. 26 (November 2004)

5. Cerbah, F.: Mining the content of relational databases to learn ontologies with deeper taxonomies. In: Proceedings of 2008 IEEE/WIC/ACM International Conference on Web Intelligence and Intelligent Agent Technology Workshops (WI-IAT 2008), Sydney, NSW, Australia, pp. 553–557 (December 2008)

6. Cullot, N., Ghawi, R., Yétongnon, K.: Db2owl: A tool for automatic database-to-ontology mapping. In: Proceedings of the Fifteenth Italian Symposium on Advanced Database Systems, SEBD 2007, Torre Canne, Fasano, BR, Italy, pp. 491–494 (June 2007)

7. de Laborda, C.P., Conrad, S.: Relational. owl: a data and schema representation format based on owl. In: Proceedings of the 2nd Asia-Pacific Conference on Conceptual Modelling, Newcastle, Australia, vol. 43, pp. 89–96 (January/February 2005)

8. Kappel, G., Kapsammer, E., Kargl, H., Kramler, G., Reiter, T., Retschitzegger, W., Schwinger, W., Wimmer, M.: Lifting Metamodels to Ontologies: A Step to the Semantic Integration of Modeling Languages. In: Wang, J., Whittle, J., Harel, D., Reggio, G. (eds.) MoDELS 2006. LNCS, vol. 4199, pp. 528–542. Springer, Heidelberg (2006)

9. Khan, S., Sonia, K.: R2o: Relation to ontology transformation system. Journal of Information & Knowledge Management (JIKM) 10(01), 71–89 (2011)

10. Krafftt, D.B., Cappadona, N.A., Caruso, B., et al.: Vivo: Enabling national networking of scientists. In: Proceedings of Web Science Conference 2010 (WebSci 2010), Raleigh, NC, pp. 1310–1313 (April 2010)

11. McCue, J., Chiang, K., Lowe, B., et al.: Vivo: connecting people, creating a virtual life sciences community. D-Lib Magazine 13(7/8), 1–16 (2007)

12. Nagy, G., Seth, S.C., et al.: Data extraction from web tables: The devil is in the details. In: Proceedings of 11th International Conference on Document Analysis and Recognition (ICDAR 2011), Beijing, China, pp. 242–246 (September 2011)

13. Nyulas, C., OConnor, M., Tu, S.: Datamaster a plug-in for importing schemas and data from relational databases into protege. In: Proceedings of the 10th International Protege Conference, Budapest, Hungary (July 2007), http://protege.stanford.edu/conference/2007

14. Tansley, R., Smith, M., Walker, J.H.: The dSpace open source digital asset management system: Challenges and opportunities. In: Rauber, A., Christodoulakis, S., Tjoa, A.M. (eds.) ECDL 2005. LNCS, vol. 3652, pp. 242–253. Springer, Heidelberg (2005)

15. Thakuria, J.: Building an institutional repository with dspace. In: Proceedings of 6th Convention Planner, Nagaland, India, pp. 102–114 (November 2008)

16. Wache, H., Voegele, T., Visser, U., et al.: Ontology-based integration of informationasurvey of existing approaches. In: Proceedings of IJCAI 2001 Workshop: Ontologies and Information Sharing, Washington, USA, pp. 108–117 (August 2001)

An Application Profile for Linked Teacher Profiles and Teaching Resources

Chariya Nonthakarn[1], Rathachai Chawuthai[2], Vilas Wuwongse[3]

[1]Computer Science and Information Management, Asian Institute of Technology,
Pathumthani, Thailand
st109925@ait.ac.th
[2]The Graduate University for Advanced Studies, Japan
and National Institute of Informatics, Tokyo, Japan
rathachai@nii.ac.jp
[3]Asian University, Chonburi, Thailand
vilasw@asianust.ac.th

Abstract. This paper designs and develops an application profile for teaching resources management systems that emphasize how to link information of teacher profiles and teaching resources. The design and development are based on the Singapore Framework for a Dublin Core Application Profile, which is a framework for designing metadata schemas for maximum interoperability. The designed application profile integrates five entities – teacher profiles, course materials, academic works, events, and awards, all of which are considered to be important information about teachers, their academic contributions and achievements. By employing the Linked Open Data (LOD) principle to represent the application profile, teachers are able to share their teaching resources, and to cooperate with among themselves. The application profile has been implemented and evaluated against requirements collected from teachers. It has been found that the application profile is practically useful and the employment of application profile is an efficient means for the design of metadata schemas.

Keywords: Application Profile, Linked Open Data, Metadata, Teacher Profile, Teaching Resource.

1 Introduction

Education, which is the cornerstone of development in every country, receives a relatively large portion of the national budget. Especially in the period of rapid technological change, a lot of resources and efforts have been spent in order to improve the quality of education, resulting in a remarkable change in teaching and learning processes. In addition, it has become easier for teachers and students to access learning resources via the Internet as well as to create their own educational materials. It has also become a challenge for teachers to take advantage of the Internet technology to improve their quality of teaching, learning resources, and self-development. Moreover, teachers, who are experts in particular fields of study, have the opportunity to learn from others by sharing their professional skills. However, most of their

K. Tuamsuk et al. (Eds.): ICADL 2014, LNCS 8839, pp. 138–148, 2014.

professional profiles are not well-organized. It is difficult to find and link some similar expert teachers. As a result, the collaboration among them is hardly developed. For these reasons, a teaching resources management system should be designed and developed with the following properties.

- A well-organized information model that describes teaching resources in order to support teaching and learning as well as other academic applications.
- A process that supports collaboration and sharing of educational resources and teacher's self-development experience.

To accomplish these challenges, this paper introduces an approach to the design of a standard data model for exchanging and linking information about teacher profiles and teaching resources. The data model is a crucial part of teaching resources information management system. It provides a foundational framework for the improvement of the quality of information management and the development of collaboration. It is well known that the metadata principle is a world-wide selected approach for developing data schemas for interoperability and standardization [3] and [8], and there are many works that use metadata and the application profile approach to develop data models for educational resources such as [7], [12], [13]. As a consequence, this paper aims to develop a data model based on the Singapore Framework for a Dublin Core Application Profile (SF for DCAP) [15], which is a framework for designing metadata schemas for maximum interoperability. This paper also represents metadata by means of the Resource Description Framework (RDF) [6] and the Linked Open Data (LOD) principle [2]. LOD has become a useful concept in educational context [5] and is used in many works for supporting education such as [11] and [14]. LOD enables the enhancement of information access, search, share and link of teaching resources and also link to the LOD cloud[1]. The designed application profile integrates five types of information for teaching resources management system, i.e., teacher profiles, course materials, academic works, awards or certificates, and academic events. Furthermore, to have maximum interoperability, the application profile also integrates some metadata from well-known schemas, such as Dublin Core Metadata Element Set (DC), Friend of a Friend (FOAF), VIVO Ontology, Bibliographic Ontology (BIBO), Event Ontology, and Learning Object Metadata (LOM). In this case, the application profile contributes to the sharing of teaching resources and cooperation among teachers. When their professional data is linked through the LOD cloud, teachers could improve their cooperation. A teaching resources management system, therefore, increases the overall value of the collaboration and efficiency of teaching and academic administration.

Section 2 presents related works on some previous data models and systems for teacher profiles and teaching resources information management. Section 3 proposes the overall idea of our application profile design approach and some details of application profile development. Section 4 describes an evaluation of the designed application profile. Finally, Section 5 draws conclusions and suggests possible future works.

---

[1] Linked Open Data Cloud, `http://datahub.io/group/about/lodcloud`

2   Related Works

There has been a number of research works carried out in order to improve educational content and learning/teaching methods. The use of appropriate technology can facilitate and improve the quality of teaching and learning as well as the equity in access to quality education. For example, e-learning, could provide students with more opportunities to access learning materials. In addition, sharing educational resources is a significant issue that should be paid attention because it allows learners to access materials more easily and encourages teachers to share their materials and know-how to develop better teaching and collaboration.

The well-known concept, which develops a support system for sharing educational resources, is Open Educational Resource (OER) [1]. With the OER, more learning and teaching materials are freely available online. Teachers, learners and other consumers can create, access and share open educational resources regardless of location or affiliation. There are many OER systems, such as MIT OpenCourseWare[2], a set of free web-based course materials provided by MIT faculty.

Despite the concept and the development of support systems for sharing teaching/learning resources, data models are also fundamentally important to the success of the development of those systems. Therefore, there are several data models developed to support sharing educational resources.

LOM (Learning Object Metadata)[3], a well-known data model, describes a learning object and similar digital resources. This metadata supports reusability of learning objects to increase discoverability, and facilitates interoperability in the context of online learning management systems (LMS). Moreover, LOM becomes a fundamental component for the development of other data models, such as Learning Resources Exchange Metadata Application Profile [9], MIT OCW Metadata [10], and the LOM application profile for agricultural learning resources of the CGIAR [16].

MELT[4] (A Metadata Ecology for Learning and Teaching), a LOM-based application profile, is a Content Enrichment Project supported by the European Commission. It aims to develop some useful types of metadata for learning content and to harvest metadata from schools for learners. This work focuses on developing collaboration among teachers and learners. The data model however covers only learning resources.

XCRI-CAP[5] (eXchanging Course Related Information, Course Advertising Profile) is a standard which aims to develop formats for sharing and integrating information about courses and other learning opportunities among learning information systems across all educational sectors in the UK. This data model also supports how to describe course information and share information between knowledge providers.

---

[2] MIT OpenCourseWare, `http://ocw.mit.edu/about/our-history/`
[3] IEEE Learning Object Metadata,
   `http://www.cen-ltso.net/main.aspx?put=211`
[4] MELT,
   `http://info.melt-project.eu/ww/en/pub/melt_project/welcome.htm`
[5] XCRI Knowledge base, `http://www.xcri.co.uk/`

mEducator[6] data model helps to share educational resources in the medical science field. The model enables medical educational content to be discovered, retrieved, shared, and reused across European higher academic institutions. Although mEducator schema is represented in RDF, its data can be linked, but the data model still focuses on course materials only.

In Thailand, there exist many efforts to support the sharing of teaching and learning resources and to develop collaboration among teachers, e.g., vchakarn.com[7] and thaischool.net[8]. However, they do not employ any standardized data models to support these types of systems.

In short, most of previous works focus on sharing teaching/learning resources, especially on class materials rather than focusing on building collaborative networks for teachers. In practice, teachers have many other kinds of materials that could benefit learning and teaching activities. Therefore, it could be good if there is a standardized data model that covers the link discovery of teaching resources for supporting teaching resources management systems, and improves collaboration among teachers.

3   The Proposed Approach

This paper proposes an approach to the development of a system for teaching resources information management and for the collaboration among teachers. The system should have the following components:

- A data model that can support data sharing among schools. Each school can enhance the data model to meet their local requirements while preserving interoperability and collaboration among them. Teaching resources can be kept separately in different schools for self-management purposes. A user can use any type of application for managing and preserving their data.
- A data representation scheme that can lead to data exchange, sharing and linking among diverse schools and other academic communities.
- A method that can support data sharing among schools via the LOD cloud.

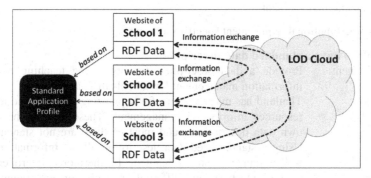

Fig. 1. Overall of the proposed teaching resources information management system

---

[6] mEducator, http://www.meducator.net/

[7] http://www.vcharkarn.com/

[8] http://www.thai-school.net/

The first component as in Fig. 1, i.e., data model, is fundamental and important. Therefore, this article proposes an approach to the development of a data model that will serve as a crucial component of a teacher resources management system. The approach employs the SF for DCAP which is a framework for designing metadata applications for maximum interoperability and for documenting such applications for reusability. A DCAP defines metadata records which meet specific application needs while providing semantic interoperability with other applications. It can use any terms that are defined on the basis of RDF; combining terms from multiple namespaces as needed which results in interoperability. Based on the SF for DCAP, an application profile consists of:

- Functional requirements for describing what a community of teachers wants to accomplish with its application.
- The domain model for characterizing the types of things described by the metadata and their relationships.
- The Description Set Profile (DSP) for enumerating the metadata term to be used.
- Usage guidelines for describing how to apply the application profile and how the designed metadata terms are intended to be used in the application context. This element is optional.
- Encoding syntax guidelines define syntax that will be used to encode the data. This element is optional.

3.1   Functional Requirements Gathering

The requirements for this application profile are gathered by studying documents from primary and elementary schools and interviewing teachers. Interviewees comprise:

- Teachers who would use the system to manage their profiles and teaching resources along with other academic works. They could utilize the system to manage information for upgrading academic standing and search for information and collaboration for further self-development.
- Academic administrators who would use the system to retrieve related information for academic management.

The principle functional requirement specifications are:

- **Be able to have a standard data description**
  Requirement: Provide a data description for organizing teaching resources information management for schools in Thailand.
  Scenario: Thailand has many systems for supporting teaching and learning resources information management. These systems have their own data descriptions, and most of them are not standardized. Using a standardized data description allows information to be well-organized and exchanged. Furthermore, interoperability among teachers in different schools or communities is required.

- **Be able to have complete description set for academic activities**

Requirement:	Provide a richer data description for describing teaching resources information in Thailand.
Scenario:	Currently, data description is not a comprehensive explanation of all relevant teaching resources information, but it focuses on course materials that are not sufficient for teaching resources management and collaboration. Having a data description that covers other relevant teaching resources information can make teaching resources management decision-making more efficient.

- **Be able to develop collaboration among teachers or schools**

Requirement:	Facilitate the development of collaboration among teachers or schools.
Scenario:	All available systems were developed using different data descriptions, so a lack of standardization that makes it difficult to establish collaboration between teachers and schools.

- **Be able to discover more teaching resources**

Requirement:	Build the discovery of teaching resources information across different schools and other academic communities.
Scenario:	Using dissimilar data descriptions and data representation results in the difficulty of sharing teaching resources among schools. The standard formats should support the discovery of relevant teaching resources among communities easier. However, it does not need the centralized data center. In other words, teaching resources should be collected in local sites of each school, but their metadata sets are only harvested by each site.

3.2   Domain Model Development

After specifying the functional requirements, the next step is to develop a domain model for the description of the things to be described by the metadata and the relationships among them. Therefore, given the requirement specifications, the domain model for this work consists of the fives following entities, and the relationships between them are defined by properties that are illustrated in Fig. 2.

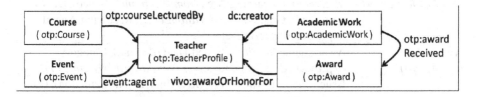

Fig. 2. The Domain model of Application Profile

- **Teacher Profile** for describing some necessary details of a teacher
- **Course** for informing courses taught by teachers

- **Academic Work** for introducing some academic works produced by teachers
- **Event** for recording some academic activities participated by teachers
- **Award** for showing awards or certificates received by teachers

3.3   The Metadata and Description Set Profile Modeling

After the domain model is defined, all metadata used to describe things in the domain model will be defined in this step. Because the application profile proposed in this work is developed by integrating related metadata schemas, this step scans for available RDF standard vocabularies corresponding to the metadata designed to meet all stakeholder requirements and cover the domain models. The remaining metadata that has not been defined in any namespaces will be created for local requirements. This study uses the following namespaces: DC *(http://purl.org/dc/elements/1.1/)*, FOAF *(http://xmlns.com/foaf/0.1/)*, VIVO *(http://vivoweb.org/ontology/core#)*, BIBO *(http://purl.org/ontology/bibo/)*, Event *(http://purl.org/NET/c4dm/event.owl#)*, Timeline (TL) *(http://www.w3.org/2006/time#)*, LOM *(http://ltsc.ieee.org/xsd/LOM)*. Moreover, some properties that do not exist in the according namespaces are newly defined by a new namespace for Online Teachers' Portfolio named OTP *(http://ipst.ac.th/ns/2014/01/otp/)*. An example of schema crosswalks for teacher profile is available in Table 1.

Table 1. Application profile comprising terms and equivalence URIs in round brackets

Entities	Included Significant Properties
Teacher *(otp:TeacherProfile)*	Identifier *(vivo:identifier)*, Prefered Title *(vivo:preferredTitle)*, First name *(foaf:firstName)*, Last name *(foaf:lastName)*, Academic Standing *(vivo:hasTeacherRole)*, Academic Degree *(otp:hasAcademicDegree)*, Email *(foaf:mbox)*, Website *(foaf:homepage)*, Field of Expertise *(otp:expertIn)*, Learning Area *(lom:discipline), etc.*
Course *(otp:Class)*	Course Code *(dc:identifier)*, Course Name *(dc:title)*, Lecturer *(otp:courseLecturedBy)*, Begin Date *(tl:beginAtDateTime)*, End date *(tl:endAtDateTime)*, Learning Area *(lom:discipline)*, Grade *(lom:educationLevel), etc.*
Academic Work *(otp:AcademicWork)*	Title *(dc:title)*, Category *(lom:learningResourceType)*, Author *(dc:creator)*, Learning Area *(lom:discipline)*, Issued Date *(bibo:issued)*, Grade *(lom:educationLevel)*, Receiving Award *(otp:awardReceived), etc.*
Award *(otp:Award)*	Award name *(dc:title)*, Issued Date *(dc:date)*, Category *(otp:awardCategory)*, Receiver *(vivo:awardOrHonorFor)*, Issuer *(vivo:awardConferredBy)*, Image *(foaf:depiction)*, Outcome *(vivo:outcome), etc.*
Event *(otp:Event)*	Event name *(dc:title)*, Attendance *(event:agent)*, Place *(dc:coverage.spatial)*, Begin Date *(tl:beginAtDateTime)*, End date *(tl:endAtDateTime)*, Image *(foaf:depiction), etc.*

To have a better understanding of the application profile, an example of a primary school teacher is expressed in RDF as below:

```
ex:Prayut        rdf:type               otp:TeacherProfile
                 vivo:identifier        "1976072189" ;
                 foaf:firstName         "Prayut" ;
                 vivo:hasTeacherRole    otp:ExpertTeacher ;
                 lom:discipline         otp:Art, otp:Math ;
                 otp:expertIn           otp:WaterColor .

ex:art101        rdf:type               otp:Course
                 dc:title               "Fundamentals of Art 1" ;
                 dc:identifier          "ART-101" ;
                 otp:courseLecturedBy ex:Prayut ;
                 lom:discipline         otp:Art ;
                 lom:educationLevel     otp:Grade1 .

ex:video063      rdf:type               otp:AcademicWork ;
                 dc:title               "Water Color for Beginner" ;
                 dc:creator             ex:Prayut ;
                 lom:learningResourceType   otp:InstructionMedia ;
                 lom:discipline         otp:Art ;
                 bibo:issued      "1995-06-11T00:00:00Z"^^xsd:DateTime;
                 otp:awardReceived      ex:award9503 .

ex:award9503     rdf:type               otp:Award ;
                 dc:title               "Art Teaching Award 1995" ;
                 otp:awardCategory      opt:Contest ;
                 vivo:awardOrHonorFor ex:Prayut ;
                 vivo:awardConferredByex:EducationOffice1 ;
                 vivo:outcome           otp:FirstPrize .

ex:event201      rdf:type               opt:Event ;
                 dc:title               "Teaching Camp 2005" ;
                 event:agent            ex:Prayut, ex:Buhnga ;
                 dc:coverage.spatial  ex:SuphanburiEduOffice1 ;
                 foaf:depiction <http://ex.org/img/DC03248.jpg> .
```

4   Evaluation

The proposed data model has been evaluated by implementing a prototype system based on it and receiving feedback from teachers. The prototype for online teachers' portfolio named OpenTeacher has been developed by integrating OpenScholar[9] with RDF SPARQL endpoint module[10], taking into account the designed application profile. It has been found that the designed application profile is realizable and suitable

---

[9] An open source web application of academic, http://openscholar.harvard.edu/
[10] A Drupal module for SPARQL Endpoint,
    https://drupal.org/project/sparql_ep

for the real implementation. Data about teachers and their teaching as well as other materials among testing sites can be linked as well. The prototype system has also been demonstrated to some school teachers and administrators. It has been found that the end users appreciate the prototype in the sense that it will support and enhance their activities as a teacher. Table 2 illustrates the evaluation of the proposed application profile against all functional requirements specified in Section 3.1.

Table 2. The evaluation of the proposed application profile against functional requirements

Functional Requirements	Solutions by the proposed application profile
Be able to have a standard data description	The designed application profile reused existing vocabularies from well-known ontology such as DC, FOAF, VIVO, BIBO, Event Ontology, and LOM.
Be able to have complete data description set of academic activities	The designed application profile consists of teacher profiles, course descriptions, academic works, awards/certificates, and academic events. All of this information covers teaching resources, information, teaching processes, and self-development of teachers.
Be able to develop collaboration among teachers	Regarding the power of LOD, the application profile expressing in RDF makes teaching resources be accessible, reused, and shared among schools. Thus, all users can share their professional skills and develop further collaboration easily.
Be able to discover more teaching resources	When all resources are described by the common application profile, common and implicit metadata allows teaching resources be linked. Thus, users can browse much more relevant teaching resources conveniently under the precise context.

5   Conclusion and Future Works

The main contribution of this paper is the design of a metadata schema for connecting teacher profiles and teaching resources. This paper began with requirement gathering that was carried out by discussing with potential users such as school teachers and administrators in Thailand. We found that the collaboration among teachers and teaching resources becomes a key player. Therefore, the data describing teachers and teaching resources must be designed based on standard metadata. The application profile approach has been utilized to design a common metadata schema or data model for any teaching resources management systems. The designed data model consists of five elements – teacher profile, course, academic work, award, and event. In order to link all data via the LOD cloud, some properties from the well-known ontology, such as DC, BIBO, EVENT, FOAF, LOM, and VIVO, are employed, and our namespace named OTP was originated. The data model was evaluated by developing a web-based Online Teachers' Portfolio, called OpenTeacher, as a prototype and tested by end users. The result demonstrated that proposed application profile is possible and suitable in the real development, and the users gave positive feedback. It shows that the model satisfies all requirements and can be carried out in the real-world situation.

Since the OpenTeacher is an ongoing project, one of the future works is to continue its development, implementation, and on-site deployment. A great user experience design for both web and mobile applications should be considered as well. Such a design would help attract many teachers who are not familiar with computers to realize the importance of linked data and to use the system. Moreover, the system should be integrated with a digital preservation system in order to make all materials be long-term accessible.

Acknowledgements. We would like to thank Dr.Pongtawat Chippimolchai, Ms. Neelawat Intaraksa, and other staffs from Punsarn Asia Co., Ltd. for their assistance and guidance in getting metadata scheme and technical support. We are also grateful for valuable requirements and comments from academic officers from The Institute for the Promotion of Teaching Science and Technology; and teachers from Wat Pathum Kongka school, Prathomsuksa Thammasat school, Wat Paprajao school, Ban Klongchaom school, and Wat Supparostes school.

References

1. A guide to open educational resources (2013),
   http://www.jisc.ac.uk/publications/programmerelated/2013/
   Openeducationalresources.aspx
2. Bizer, T., Heath, T., Berners-Lee, T.: Linked data—the story so far. IJSWIS 5(3), 1–22 (2009)
3. Duval, E., Hodgins, W., Sutton, S., Weibel, S.: Metadata Principles and Practicalities. D-Lib Magazine 8(4) (2002)
4. Heery, R., Patel, M.: Application Profiles: mixing and matching metadata schemas. Ariadne 25, 27–31 (2002)
5. Keßler, C., Aquin, M., Dietze, S.: Linked Data for Science and Education. Journal of Semantic Web 4(1), 1–5 (2013)
6. Klyne, G., Carroll, J.: Resource Description Framework (RDF): Concepts and Abstract Syntax - W3C Recommendation (2004), http://www.w3.org/TR/rdf-concepts/
7. Koutsomittropoulos, D.A., et al.: The use of Metadata for Educational Resources in Digital Repositories: Practices and Perspectives. D-Lib Magazine 16 (2010)
8. Chan, L.M., Zeng, M.L.: Metadata Interoperability and Standardization – A Study of Methodology: Achieving Interoperability at the Schema Level. D-Lib Magazine 12(6) (2006)
9. Massart, D., Shuman, E.: Learning Resource Exchange Metadata Application Profile version 4.7. European Schoolnet (2011)
10. Metadata Specification, M.O. (Version 1.0),
    http://cwspace.mit.edu/files/9OCW_Metadata_Spec_10.pdf
11. Ruiz-Calleja, A., Vega-Gorgojo, G., et al.: A Linked Data approach for the discovery of educational ICT tools in the Web of Data. JCE 59, 952–962 (2012)
12. Sampson, D.: The Evolution of Educational Metadata: From Standards to Application Profiles. In: ICALT 2004. IEEE, Joensuu (2004)

13. Sutton, S.A., Mason, J.: The Dublin Core and Metadata for Educational Resources. In: DC 2001, pp. 25–31. NII, Tokyo (2001)
14. Taibim, D., Fulantelli, G., et al.: A Linked Data Approach to evaluate Open Educational Resources. In: ICEduTech 2013, Venice, Italy, pp. 154–157 (2013)
15. The Singapore Framework for Dublin Core Application Profile (2008),
    http://dublincore.org/documents/singapore-framework/
16. Zschocke, T., Beniest, J., et al.: The LOM application profile for agricultural learning resources of the CGIAR. IJMSO 4, 13–23 (2009)

Knowledge Sharing by Students: Preference for Online Discussion Board vs Face-to-Face Class Participation

Shaheen Majid[*], Pan Yang, Huang Lei, and Guo Haoran

Nanyang Technological University, Singapore
asmajid@ntu.edu.sg,
{PANY0007,LHUANG008}@e.ntu.edu.sg,
guohaoran8@hotmail.com

Abstract. The purpose of this study was to investigate students' preference for participation in face-to-face and online discussions, and the factors that can either motivate or pose barriers to knowledge sharing. A questionnaire was used for data collection and 149 post-graduate students from two public universities in Singapore participated in this study. It was found that a majority (82.5%) of the students preferred in-class face-to-face discussions for knowledge sharing and a majority of them agreed that the factors such as encouragement by instructors, challenging discussion topics, and thought provoking questions from instructors and classmates were likely to motivate them to participate. The motivating factors for participation in online discussions were: more time to refine ideas, less nervousness, and flexible access to online discussion boards. The major barriers to face-to-face participation were shyness and uninteresting topics. On the other hand, the major hurdles to online discussions were unfriendly interface and time constraints.

Keywords: Online Discussion Boards, Face-to-Face Sharing, Knowledge Sharing, Post-graduate Students, Singapore.

1 Introduction

Emergence of educational technologies has revolutionized the education sector by opening new and innovative ways for teaching, learning and knowledge sharing. Many tertiary educational institutions have also been making concerted efforts to smartly integrate the instructor-centric method with certain other learning approaches such as problem-oriented learning, interactive learning and collaborative learning. Collaborative learning, also known as peer learning, is considered one of the established, popular and effective learning approaches (Ratsoy, 2011). Knowledge sharing, through online discussion boards and face-to-face class participation, is considered an essential element of this type of learning.

Collaborative learning approach can also make the learning process more interactive, interesting, and engaging (Majid & Tina, 2009). It can also result in higher student motivation and achievements, greater comprehension and retention of

---

[*] Corresponding author.

K. Tuamsuk et al. (Eds.): ICADL 2014, LNCS 8839, pp. 149–159, 2014.

knowledge, development of critical thinking skills, and improved communication skills (Steel, Laurens, & Huggins, 2013). Through in-class face-to-face knowledge sharing, students are usually motivated to learn from their classmates as well as share their own real-life experiences (O'connor, 2013). Students can present their thoughts and viewpoints, and in return, receive feedback from their instructors and classmates (Augustsson, 2010). Dallimore, Hertenstein & Platt (2010) examined the relationship between class participation and student learning. The survey, participated by 323 business students, reported that class preparation was positively related to frequency of participation as well as to students' comfort in knowledge sharing. It was also found that students' comfort in participating in class discussion was in turn positively related to their learning process.

In spite of many benefits of class participation, some studies suggest that Asian students less actively participate in class discussions (Tani, 2008). Lee (2009) studied class participation of Korean students in graduate seminars in the United States. It was found that multilayered factors, including the students' English proficiency, differences in socio-cultural values and educational practices between two cultures, individual differences, and classroom environment were intertwined, and each factor singly and collectively influenced students' participation in class discussions. Some reasons given for limited class participation by Korean students were: respect for hierarchy and authority, perception of humility, low English language proficiency, cultural barriers, shyness, and lack of confidence. Majid, et al. (2010) reported that the knowledge sharing barriers faced by local and overseas students in Singapore were: low English language proficiency, cultural barriers, shyness, and lack of confidence.

Now-a-days online learning systems, in addition to advanced content creation and delivery features, provide many sophisticated collaboration tools for knowledge sharing by students and instructors. Artino (2010) believed that online learning and knowledge sharing can play an important role in promoting life-long learning. Innovations in ICT and Web 2.0 are continually transforming the traditional instructions into asynchronous learning with many powerful online collaboration tools (Sulisworo, 2012). Qiu & Mcdougall (2013) reported that, from students' perspective, online discussion can provide more avenues for socialization and meaningful interactions. Campbell et al., (2008) claimed that students actively participating in online discussions are more likely to obtained higher marks than those only engaged in face-to-face discussions. In a more recent study, Green et al. (2014) found that the total number of posts by students have a significant direct relationship with their final marks.

There are several factors that contribute positively to students' participation in online discussion boards. A study by Kim (2013) found that encouragement by instructors can result in high number of posts by students. In addition, it was also revealed that, as compared to discussion forums of large classes, students more actively participate in small-group discussion forums. Yukselturk (2010) collected responses from 196 Turkish students through an online survey and semi-structured interviews. The results of her study showed that student characteristics such as academic achievements, gender, and weekly hours on the Internet contributed significantly towards students' participation in online discussion forums.

Appreciating the importance of face-to-face instruction and potential of e-learning tools for content delivery and collaboration, many universities are now using a hybrid approach for enhancing their students' learning experience. Online education discussion boards are an exciting addition to the learning environment which can effectively supplement in-class face-to-face discussions (Meyer, 2008). Online collaboration tools can bring students and lecturers together to discuss ideas and share their opinions on a 24/7 basis. It can also be an effective communication medium for students with limited language proficiency as they can get more time to gather and express their thoughts. Similarly, less confident, introvert and shy students are likely to feel more comfortable in expressing their opinions through online discussion boards (Majid, et al., 2010).

There is no doubt that both face-to-face and online discussion boards have their own unique strengths and advantages. It would be interesting to explore students' perceptions and use of these communication channels for knowledge sharing. A majority of the studies on this topic have been undertaken either in North America or Europe. Only a limited number of studies have been done in Southeast Asia which has its own unique culture and learning environment. The main objective of this study was to investigate students' preference for participation in face-to-face and online discussions, and the factors that were likely to either motivate or create barriers to their knowledge sharing.

2   Methodology

A pre-tested questionnaire was used for data collection and a total of 149 post-graduate students from two public universities in Singapore, i.e. National University of Singapore (NUS) and Nanyang Technological University (NTU), participated in this study. Post-graduate students were chosen for this study because at the graduate level students are usually more matured and likely to actively involved in class discussions, case study analyses, group projects, and other collaborative activities. Students with some work experience can also share their experiences with other students. A convenience sampling technique was used and students were approached during their class breaks, in graduate lounges and in their study rooms. Some areas covered in the questionnaire were demographics, respondents' understanding of various knowledge sharing activities, their preference and frequency of participation in face-to-face and online discussion forums, and students' perceptions, motivations and barriers to using different knowledge sharing channels. Data were collected from different schools of the participating universities to have adequate diversity in responses. The survey was conducted in March/April 2013.

3   Findings

A comparable number of students from both the universities (NUS=51.7% and NTU (48.3%) participated in the questionnaire survey. The proportion of male and female participant was 54.8% and 45.2% respectively. The majority (60.3%) of the respondents were less than 25 years old while another 27.6% were in the age group of

25-29 years. The remaining 12.1% of the participants were more than 30 years old. Some 49.3% of the participants were from Singapore, 28.2% from China, 7.4% from India and the remaining 15.1% students from other countries. The respondents came from different subject areas: engineering (33.6%); arts, humanities and social sciences (24.8%); IT and computer science (21.5%); sciences (9.4%); business (7.4%) and other disciplines (3.3%).

3.1   Perceptions of Knowledge Sharing Activities

The students were asked what learning activities, in their opinion, are considered as knowledge sharing activities. The purpose was to investigate students' perceptions of various educational activities that can be used for knowledge sharing. For the convenience of discussion, in this as well as in the subsequent sections, the categories 'strongly agree' and 'agree' are merged. Similarly, the responses for 'strongly disagree' and 'disagree' are also merged.

Over 80% of the students agreed that answering instructors' queries, asking questions from instructors, and making comments on the topic under discussion are considered important knowledge sharing activities (Table 1). Another 74% of the students concurred with the suggestion that sharing personal experiences is part of knowledge sharing. However, one-half of the responded disagreed that whispering in the ear of nearby students is knowledge sharing.

Table 1. Perception of knowledge sharing activities

S. No.	Activity	Strongly Agree/Agree	Neither Agree Nor Disagree	Strongly Disagree/ Disagree
1	Answering instructor's questions	88.6%	8..0%	3.4%
2	Asking questions	86.3%	8.2%	5.5%
3	Making comments on topic under discussion	80.3%	13.4%	6.3%
4	Sharing personal experiences	74.0%	19.6%	6.4%
5	Asking questions about examination	54.6%	28.3%	17.1%
6	Whispering to nearby students	25.3%	24.7%	50.0%

3.2   Preferred Knowledge Sharing Modes

The students were asked if they prefer face-to-face or online discussion board for sharing education related knowledge and ideas. An overwhelming majority (82.5%) of the students expressed their preference for face-to-face mode of communication. Only 17.5% of the respondents preferred using online discussion board for their class contributions. The students were further asked that, on average, how many times they have contributed through face-to-face and online discussion boards for each subject module during the last one semester. About one-third of the respondents each reported using both face-to-face and online discussion board once or twice for sharing their ideas (Table 2). On the contrary, 25.2% of the students used the face-to-face mode for more than 6 times while only 5.6% of the students reported putting the same number of comments on their online discussion boards. A more surprising finding was where 39% of the students revealed that they have never participated in course-based online discussion boards.

Table 2. Use frequency of different communication modes

Communication Modes	Participation Frequency				
	1-2 times	3-4 times	5-6 times	> 6 times	Never
Face-to-Face in-class discussion	32.8%	27.7%	11.4%	25.2%	2.9%
Online discussion board	32.2%	19.8%	3.4%	5.6%	39.0%

It was also found that, on the whole, Singaporean and Indian students were more actively involved in knowledge sharing using both the communication modes. Probably students from other countries were comparatively less frequently participating in discussions due to their limited English language proficiency and certain other factors which will be discussed in the following sections 3.5 and 3.8. It was also revealed that over 35 years old students with more than 5 years' work experience were more frequently using the face-to-face mode for sharing their knowledge and experiences than younger students with no work experience. It appeared that older and experienced students are more likely to actively participate in face-to face discussions.

It was further revealed that a majority of the students from the subjects of arts, humanities and social science as well as from business were more frequently using the face-to-face mode for knowledge sharing compared to the students from IT, computer science and engineering disciplines.

3.3   Perceived Benefits of Face-to-Face Class Discussions

The students were asked about the potential benefits of face-to-face in-class discussions. As can be seen in Table 3, all the benefits listed in the questionnaire received good support from the respondents. However, the top three benefits of class participation were: improvement in communication skills, immediate feedback on ideas and suggestions, and rigorous discussions can trigger critical thinking. These benefits were also previously reported by Steel, Laurens, & Huggins (2013) and O'connor (2013).

3.4   Motivating Factors for Face-to-Face Class Participation

A list of possible motivating factors was given to the students and asked if they agree or disagree that these factors can encourage students' class participation. The top three motivating factors for face-to-face in-class participation were: encouragement from instructors, interesting and challenging topics, and that class discussion is essential for students' learning process (Table 4). Kim (2013) also argued that encouragement from instructors can motivate students to actively take part in class discussions. It was also interesting to note that the students felt that interesting and challenging topics are likely to stimulate their class participation. It appeared, as also reported by Majid, et al. (2011), graduate students are usually less inclined to answer routine, fixed-answer questions as well as questions based on concepts discussed during the previous class sessions. Instead graduate students usually prefer expressing their thoughts on topics involving critical thinking, in-depth analysis, and their personal opinion and ideas.

Table 3. Perceived benefits of face-to-face class participation

S. No.	Activity	Strongly Agree/Agree	Neither Agree Nor Disagree	Strongly Disagree/ Disagree
1	Improves communication skills	88.7%	10.0%	1.3%
2	Students can get immediate feedback	88.0%	8.3%	3.7%
3	Rigorous discussion triggers thinking	88.0%	8.7%	3.3%
4	Improves independent thinking	78.6%	16.7%	4.7%
5	Eye contact and body language can improve communication	76.6%	19.0%	4.4%
6	Improves reasoning skills	76.0%	21.3%	2.7%
7	Class discussions can bring students and instructors closer	70.6%	24.7%	4.0%
8	Class discussions can bring classmates closer	63.3%	26.0%	10.7%

Table 4. Motivating factors for face-to-face class participation

S. No.	Motivating Factor	Strongly Agree/Agree	Neither Agree Nor Disagree	Strongly Disagree/ Disagree
1	Encouragement by passionate and friendly instructor	91.7%	4.7%	3.6%
2	Interesting and challenging topics	86.0%	10.3%	3.7%
3	Discussion is an essential part of learning	82.3%	12.0%	5.7%
4	Provoking questions from instructors	78.7%	15.6%	5.7%
5	Related work experience	76.3%	19.0%	4.7%
6	Good communication skills	74.6%	21.7%	3.7%
7	Pre-class preparation / readings	66.5%	26.1%	7.4%
8	Adequate time for class discussion	66.5%	29.2%	5.3%
9	Marks reserved for class participation	58.7%	28.0%	13.3%
10	Urge to make a good impression on instructors or classmates	44.0%	38.7%	17.3%

Comparatively less number of the students agreed that marks reserved for class participation (58.7% students) and the urge to impress instructors and classmates (44.0% students) were important factors in motivating them to participate in class discussions. Once again, it can be seen that students were more inclined to participate in meaningful and thought provoking discussions rather than to impress instructors or obtain marks reserved for class participation.

3.5   Barriers to Face-to-Face Class Participation

As shown in Table 5, the top barrier to in-class participation was uninteresting discussion topics. This finding supports a previous finding of this study which highlighted that interesting and challenging topics are likely to motivate robust class discussions. It is, therefore, necessary for instructors to come-up with interesting and stimulating topics which can inspire students to get involved in class discussions. Another barrier with which 84.2% of the students either agreed or strongly agreed was shyness to express personal thoughts in the class. The problems of shyness and introvert personality were also reported by Lee (2009) and Majid, et al. (2010).

Table 5. Barriers to face-to-face class participation

S. No.	Barriers	Strongly Agree/Agree	Neither Agree Nor Disagree	Strongly Disagree/ Disagree
1	Uninteresting discussion topics	84.6%	12.7%	2.7%
2	Too shy to express my opinion in public	84.2%	13.6%	2.2%
3	Unnecessary comments and ideas can prolong class duration	81.3%	10.4%	8.3%
4	Fear of making wrong comments	80.7%	13.6%	5.7%
5	Unfamiliar or difficult to understand instructors' pronunciation	63.3%	24.5%	12.2%
6	Limited English language proficiency	62.7%	26.7%	10.0%
7	Some instructors prefer monologue rather than dialogue	60.5%	27.3%	12.2%

Two other barriers agreed/strongly agreed by more than 80% of the students were unnecessary and irrelevant comments made by some students which can prolong class duration, and fear of making wrong comments. A considerable number of the graduate students pursue their studies on part-time basis by taking evening classes and probably that is why they do not want their classes to go beyond the scheduled class time. It is understandable as these working students might be feeling tired due to a very heavy work-study schedule and obviously looking for time to relax.

However, it was interesting to note that among the listed barriers, limited English language proficiency appeared at the second last position. It appeared students did not think that English language was the major hurdle in their class participation. It was probably because most of them, including international students, have finished their undergraduate studies in English language programs and now feeling comfortable with it.

3.6   Perceived Benefits of Online Discussion Boards

Like face-to-face in-class discussion, the students were also asked about the potential benefits of using online discussion boards for knowledge sharing. It was found that the top two perceived benefits of online discussion board were: online content can easily be reviewed before examinations, and access to the content is convenient due to user-friendly interface (Table 6). However, it was worth noting that the percentage of students agreeing with the listed benefits of online discussion boards was much lower than face-to-face in-class participation. This confirms a previous finding of this study (section 3.2) where an overwhelming majority of the students preferred using face-to-face mode for knowledge sharing.

Table 6. Perceived benefits of online discussion board

S. No.	Activity	Strongly Agree/Agree	Neither Agree Nor Disagree	Strongly Disagree/ Disagree
1	Online content can easily be reviewed before exams	77.0%	15.7%	7.3%
2	Convenient and user-friendly access	70.7%	23.6%	5.7%
3	Students can avoid asking similar questions repeatedly since answers may be already available online	67.7%	18.0%	14.3%
4	Knowledge sharing in a harmonious environment of freedom and equality	66.4%	26.7%	6.9%
5	More time to understand online content than spoken content in class	55.6%	29.7%	14.7%

3.7   Motivating Factors for Participation in Online Discussion Board

The top motivating factor for participation in online discussion board was less nervousness while expressing opinions online (Table 7). Shy and introvert students are likely to feel more comfortable expressing their opinions over online discussion boards. Three other motivating factors receiving endorsement from more than 76% of the students were: opportunity to ask additional questions after the class, more time to refine ideas before posting, and availability of online discussion board on 24/7 basis. Support for the remaining motivating factors was also quite good, except for the factor *'urge to leave a better impression on instructors and classmates'*. This finding is in line with another finding of this study (section 3.4) where this motivation factor was also at the bottom of the list for face-to-face class participation.

3.8   Barriers to Participation in Online Discussion Boards

Finally, the students were asked about the possible barriers to their participation in online discussion boards. It was found that the top barrier was limited or no response for certain discussion topics (Table 8). This finding is understandable as previously

39% of the students (section 3.2) said that they have never participated in any online discussions. Two other barriers endorsed by over 62% of the students were '*some online discussion systems are not well-designed*' and '*long waiting time to get answers or feedback from classmates*'. On the contrary, only 39.4% of the students agreed that poor network connection was a barrier to their participation in online discussions.

Table 7. Motivating factors for online discussion boards

S. No.	Motivating Factor	Strongly Agree/Agree	Neither Agree Nor Disagree	Strongly Disagree/ Disagree
1	Feeling of less nervousness while expressing opinions online	79.7%	13.6%	6.7%
2	Students can ask additional questions online after the class	78.5%	14.8%	6.7%
3	Students get more time to refine ideas before putting them online	76.6%	17.3%	5.4%
4	Online discussion board can be used anytime anywhere	76.0%	15.4%	8.6%
5	Students with limited language competence can focus on their sentence structure and grammar	72.7%	20.7%	6.6%
6	Enough marks allocated for online discussion	71.4%	14.3%	14.3%
7	Urge to leave a better impression on instructors and classmates	47.7%	33.3%	18.30%

Table 8. Barriers to participation in online discussion boards

S. No.	Barriers	Strongly Agree/Agree	Neither Agree Nor Disagree	Strongly Disagree/ Disagree
1	Some topics may not be responded by anyone at all	80.7%	16.4%	2.9%
2	Some online discussion systems are not well-designed	64.2%	26.2%	9.6%
3	Long waiting time to get answers or feedback from classmates	62.0%	26.7%	10.6%
4	Lack of adequate free time	58.5%	20.9%	20.6%
5	Limited familiarity with the features of online discussion broad	50.4%	26.2%	23.4%
6	Hard to understand some slangs or abbreviations used by some students	49.5%	33.3%	17.2%
7	Poor network or Wi-Fi connections	39.4%	26.2%	34.4%

4   Conclusion

It is an established fact that active knowledge sharing contributes considerably to students' learning process. Instructors often use various academic activities to encourage knowledge sharing among students. Access to online discussion boards is an exciting addition to in-class discussions. This study revealed that an overwhelming majority of the students preferred participating in face-to-face in-class discussions. The main reasons given for this preference were: likely improvement in communication skills, immediate feedback from others, and improvement in critical thinking skills. Similarly, there was also a good support for participation in online discussions, reflecting students' awareness of the benefits of online discussion forums. It is obvious that the scope and mechanics of face-to-face and online discussions are considerably different. It is, therefore, desirable that instructors should take full advantage of both communication channels and come up with an appropriate strategy to effectively use face-to-face and online discussions for knowledge sharing. Such a strategy is likely to make the learning process more interactive, interesting and engaging.

This study was limited in scope as it investigated only perceptions and preferences of students for face-to-face in-class discussions (synchronous communication mode) and course-based online discussion boards (asynchronous communication mode). In recent years online learning systems have started offering certain synchronous collaborative tools such as instant messaging, live chat, whiteboard drawings, video conferencing, etc., for real-time communication. Though Skype and other similar platforms are not part of many e-learning systems, they can also be used for study-related knowledge sharing. Depending on the need and situation, both asynchronous and synchronous modes of communication have their own strengths and weaknesses. It would be interesting to compare in future the effectiveness of face-to-face in-class knowledge sharing with different synchronous communication platforms.

References

1. Artino, A.R.: Online or face-to-face learning? Exploring the personal factors that predict students' choice of instructional format. The Internet and Higher Education 13(4), 272–276 (2010), doi:10.1016/j.iheduc.2010.07.005
2. Augustsson, G.: Web 2.0, pedagogical support for reflexive and emotional social interaction among Swedish students. Internet & Higher Education 13(4), 197–205 (2010)
3. Campbell, M., Gibson, W., Hall, A., Richards, D., Callery, P.: Online vs. face-to-face discussion in a Web-based research methods course for postgraduate nursing students: a quasi-experimental study. International Journal of Nursing Studies 45(5), 750–759 (2008), doi:10.1016/j.ijnurstu.2006.12.011
4. Dallimore, E.J., Hertenstein, J.H., Platt, M.B.: Class participation in accounting courses: Factors that affect student comfort and learning. Issues in Accounting Education 25(4), 613–629 (2010), doi:10.2308/iace.2010.25.4.613
5. Green, R.A., Farchione, D., Hughes, D.L., Chan, S.: Participation in asynchronous online discussion forums does improve student learning of gross anatomy. Anatomical Sciences Education 7(1), 71–76 (2014), doi:10.1002/ase.1376

6. Kim, J.: Influence of group size on students' participation in online discussion forums. Computers & Education, 62123–62129 (2013)
7. Lee, G.: Speaking up: Six Korean students' oral participation in class discussions in US graduate seminars. English for Specific Purposes 28(3), 142–156 (2009)
8. Majid, S., Tina, R.R.: Perceptions of LIS graduate students of peer learning. In: Asia-Pacific Conference on Library & Information Education and Practice (A-LIEP), Japan, March 6-8 (2009)
9. Majid, S., Yeow, C.W., Audrey, C.S.Y., Shyong, L.R.: Enriching learning experience through class participation: A students' perspective. In: 76th IFLA General Conference and Assembly: Satellite Meeting on Cooperation and Collaboration in Teaching and Research, Gothenburg, Sweden, August 8-9 (2010)
10. Majid, S., Mon, A.A., Soe, C.M., Htut, S.M.: Students' perceptions of knowledge sharing through class participation. In: International Conference on Knowledge Management and Information Sharing, Paris, France, October 26-29 (2011)
11. Meyer, K.A.: Student perceptions of face-to-face and online discussions: The advantage goes To... Journal of Asynchronous Learning Networks 11(4), 55–69 (2008)
12. O'connor, K.J.: Class participation: Promoting in-class student engagement. Education 133(3), 340–344 (2013)
13. Qiu, M., McDougall, D.: Foster strengths and circumvent weaknesses: Advantages and disadvantages of online versus face-to-face subgroup discourse. Computers & Education 67, 1–11 (2013)
14. Ratsoy, G.R.: Class participation in an aboriginal theatre project: An exemplar of undergraduate student engagement. Canadian Journal for the Scholarship of Teaching and Learning 2(1), 13 (2011),
    http://dx.doi.org.ezlibproxy1.ntu.edu.sg/10.5206/cjsotl-rcacea.2011.1.3
15. Steel, A., Laurens, J., Huggins, A.: Class participation as a learning and assessment strategy. Law: Facilitating Students' Engagement, Skills Development and Deep Learning. University of New South Wales Law Journal 36(1), 30–55 (2013)
16. Sulisworo, D.: Designing the online collaborative learning using the Wikispaces. International Journal of Emerging Technology and Learning 7(1), 58–61 (2012)
17. Tani, M.: Raising the in-class participation of Asian students through a writing tool. Higher Education Research and Development 27(4), 345–356 (2008)
18. Yukselturk, E.: An investigation of factors affecting student participation level in an online discussion forum. Turkish Online Journal of Educational Technology - TOJET 9(2), 24–32 (2010)

A Comparative Analysis of Children's Reading Activity for Digital Picture Books in Local Public Libraries

Keizo Sato, Chihiro Arakane, and Makoto Nakashima

Dept. of Computer Science and Intelligent Systems, Oita University
700 Dannoharu, Oita-shi, 870-1192, Japan
{k-sato,v12e3002,nakasima}@oita-u.ac.jp

Abstract. Children's rooms in local public libraries are important places for children's reading activity. Although the locational conditions of local public libraries affect children's reading activity, there is no detailed analysis considering their correlation. In this paper we clarify this correlation by comparatively analyzing page flipping for digital picture books in the children's room. We conducted a field study in 6 local public libraries in Oita prefecture, Japan. The page flipping data was collected automatically over the course of 5 months. Through the field study, we found that children's population and the number of parking lots strongly affect the ratio of actually read digital picture books to opened ones. Another finding was that the convenience of private/public transportation strongly affects the page flipping patterns for digital picture books. The results of the study suggest that recording children's page flipping data is a promising approach worth developing further.

Keywords: locational conditions of public library, digital picture books, children's room.

1 Introduction

Reading picture books together with family members and/or friends is important for children to experience a range of emotions or to acquire literacy skills [13]. Children's rooms in local public libraries are one of the best places for children to read picture books in a group. The recent dissemination of digital picture books published on the Web, has provided the opportunity to easily enrich collections within children's rooms. Although the diversity of the collection is important in attracting children to the library, it can be easily surmised that the locational conditions of the library are also important in attracting children. It is important to clarify the factors pertaining to locational conditions affecting children's reading activity.

In this paper, we clarify a correlation between locational conditions of public libraries and children's reading activity by comparatively analyzing page flipping [1] for digital picture books in the children's rooms in local public libraries. For the analysis we use the four factors within the area surrounding these local public libraries: (i) children's population, (ii) the number of educational facilities, (iii) the convenience of public transportation usage, and (iv) the convenience of private transportation usage.

K. Tuamsuk et al. (Eds.): ICADL 2014, LNCS 8839, pp. 160–170, 2014.

The data for these factors are usually public information and can be easily gathered from official websites of the libraries and municipalities, online maps, etc. On the other hand, for collecting data on children's reading activity, we need a field study in the same period at multiple local public libraries for comparison purpose. There are various approaches [3], [11], [14] to analyzing children's reading activity, such as through observing, questioning, and/or interviewing a child in the experimental or physical children's reading rooms. However, these researches involve the creation of special plans valid for a limited period of time. The data on children's reading activity should be automatically collected since we are not allowed to directly observe, question, and interview a child in a public library. We here employ a free-style field study of allowing children to freely read the digital picture books without control or direction from the researchers.

In our free-style field study the BrowsReader [8,9,10] on which children could find and read various picture books, was used as a book reader. We also used the method of deciding if children have not only opened the digital picture book but have also in fact read it, by analyzing page flipping for digital picture books, based on the extraction of the page-specific data and on the identification of the flipped pages [1]. This method requires no human effort in observing, nor questioning or interviewing of a child. To study how children spent their time at each public library using the BrowsReader, we analyzed the ratio of read digital picture books to opened ones. We can assume that the higher the ratio is, the more suitable the environment of the library is for picture book reading.

The field study lasted over a period of 5 months in the children's rooms of 6 local public libraries in Oita prefecture, Japan. The same 1,740 digital picture books could be read on the BrowsReader. By analyzing the logged data, we found that the children's population and the number of parking lots of a library strongly correlate with the ratio of read digital picture books to opened ones. The children being driven to visit the library could read the picture books thoroughly, where the children flipped some pages backwards. In one city library built downtown, which has the highest number of nearby educational facilities, the average flipping time per page was statistically lower than that in the prefectural library built on the outskirts of the city. Using public transportation did not allow the children in that city library to stay long enough to read the books thoroughly when on their way home from school.

The rest of this paper is organized as follows: Section 2 surveys related work. Section 3 describes the detail of our methodology for a field study. In Section 4 we detail the field study that was conducted in 6 local public libraries. Finally, Section 5 summarizes the methodology and discusses a future research direction.

2   Related Work

We describe here previous researches in terms of analyzing children's reading activity and analyzing accessibility of libraries. The former is for clarifying how children read picture books or the children's comprehension level after having read them. The latter is for understanding potential library users by using the locational conditions of a library.

Begeny et al. [3], Hamilton et al. [5], and Paris et al. [11] have focused on checking the children's comprehension levels in reading. Also the digital formats have been compared to the paper formats [14] and an AR (augmented reality) picture book [4] in the comprehension level of children. To check the comprehension level, the children who read designated books were interviewed or asked to answer the quizzes related to the stories of read books. In these researches, the children's behavior was controlled or directed. Additionally children's reading activity has barely been analyzed over a long period of time and in multiple libraries.

As the researches about locational conditions of a library, Hertel et al. [6], Kinikin [7], and Park [12] have focused on analyzing accessibility through measuring the distance between users' homes and the public library which they must often use. They have examined the physical accessibility of public libraries by using geographic information systems (GIS). Although accessibility is important to attract children to the library, the addresses of the children's homes are usually restricted information and the relationships between the accessibility of public libraries and children's reading activity have been not considered. Baeg et al. [2] have investigated the correlation between the location of a public library and the development of children's reading skills. They concluded that the location is an important factor related to visiting the library and achieving better reading skills in children.

The above researches have required human effort to collect the data or restricted information in order to perform their analysis. We install a system in multiple children's digital reading rooms to automatically collect the information about how many digital picture books are read and how each digital picture book is read. Then a comparative analysis can be performed to clarify the relationship between children's reading activity and the locational conditions of multiple public libraries, which are open information, on a long term basis.

3   Methodology

Our focus is, through a comparative analysis, to clarify the factors in locational conditions of the local public library, which are affecting children's reading activity. For the analysis we decided upon the following four factors within the area surrounding these local public libraries based on our hypothesis: If a number of children live in the area and they can easily visit the library, then the children visit it frequently and read many picture books.

- *The factors regarding the children in the local public library's surroundings*
    (F11) The ratio of children aged 3-9 years to the total population in the local area
    (F12) The number of nearby educational facilities, i.e., nursery schools, kindergartens, and elementary schools
- *The factors regarding the convenience of public/private transportation usage*
    (F21) The proximity to a bus stop and a train station
    (F22) The number of parking lots

We selected the population of children aged 3-9 years due to the fact that they comprise the major age group who visit children's rooms with their families/friends [10]. Since most of these children are kindergarteners or lower graders in elementary schools, the number of nearby educational facilities within the vicinity of the library is a mandatory factor. The convenience of public transportation usage is important for many lower graders aged 6-9 years who can take the bus/train when visiting the library as well as when going to their schools. The number of parking lots is for the preschool children aged 3-6 years who cannot use public transportation alone and are being driven to visit the library with their family.

The BrowsReader [8,9,10], shown in the left in Figure 1, which is a system assisting children together with their families and/or friends, is installed in the children's rooms in multiple libraries. The BrowsReader allows children to easily browse a large number of digital picture books as if they are browsing in the physical bookshelves of the children's room, to read a wide variety of digital picture books as if they are reading ordinary printed picture books on a table. Any digital picture book can be enlarged by finger touching or character input as shown in the right in Figure 1. The BrowsReader can be sufficiently operated even by younger children without instruction.

(a)   (b)

Fig. 1. The BrowsReader in a children's room

To analyze how children read the digital picture books on the BrowsReader, we use the method of graphing the curves of page flipping for digital picture books [1]. By analyzing the page flipping data, this method figures out (a) if the children have spent appropriate time for flipping many of the pages, and (b) how the pages are flipped; forwards and/or backwards. The result in (a) can be used to decide whether the children have actually read the digital picture books, and that in (b) can help to find how children read the digital picture books. This method can classify the page flipping curves for read digital picture books into 3 patterns. These patterns are for: (I) flipping all the pages in the forward direction, (II) suspending the flipping for some pages and (III) flipping some pages backwards.

The ratio of read digital picture books to opened digital picture books is calculated by dividing the number of read digital picture books by the number of opened digital picture books to study how children spent their time at each library. How children read the digital picture books is available according to the above 3 patterns I, II, and III.

4   Field Study

We conducted a free-style field study in the children's rooms of the following 6 local public libraries in Oita prefecture, Japan: Oita Prefectural Library (OPL)[1], Beppu Municipal Library (BML)[2], Oita Citizens Library (OCL)[3], Yufu City Library (YCL)[4], Usa Public Library (UPL)[5], and Yufuin Branch of Yufu City Library (YBL)[4]. We set the BrowsReader up as a book reader in each of the children's rooms and installed a logging system in each BrowsReader for collecting the page flipping data. The PCs for the BrowsReader were basically the same in all the libraries. A 30-inch touch-display was utilized to encourage the children together to operate the BrowsReader by gathering around it.

4.1   Setting

Table 1 shows the statistics of the local public libraries for the field study. Table 2 shows the data for the four factors of each library, which were gathered according to the official websites of the libraries and municipalities, and online maps[6]. Although the locational conditions of those libraries differ, the same 1,740 digital picture books could be read on the BrowsReader. These digital picture books were found on various websites and certified by the librarians of two university libraries in Japan (Beppu University and Oita University) [10]. The page-specific data for identifying each page were collected priori to setting the BrowsReader to the libraries. These digital picture books are in a variety of genres, length and difficulty. Note that every child was allowed to freely use the BrowsReader for reading these digital picture books without control or direction from the researchers. We did not observe the children's behavior in the libraries and also did not record their personal data.

4.2   Results and Considerations

Correlation between Locational Conditions and Children's Reading Activity. In the study period, the children opened cumulatively 6,128 digital picture books. Among them 303 were decided to have been read according to the method mentioned in Section 3. Figure 2 shows the number of opened digital picture books and the ratio of read digital picture books to opened digital picture books. There were no statistical differences in the ratio of read digital picture books among the libraries (chi-square test with the Bonferroni correction, $p=0.05$). The ratio was below 10% in each library. It can be said that the children tended to carefully select digital picture books.

---

[1] http://library.pref.oita.jp/

[2] https://www.city.beppu.oita.jp/tosho/

[3] http://www.library.city.oita.oita.jp/index.html

[4] http://library.yufu-city.jp/

[5] http://www.usa-public-library.jp/

[6] The distance was measured by the websites Mapion (http://www.mapion.co.jp/) and NAVITIME (http://www.navitime.co.jp/).

Table 1. Statistics of the local public libraries for the field study

		OPL	BML	OCL	YCL	UPL	YBL
The number of printed picture books		9,088	8,951	8,352	7,916	5,378	1,009
The number of digital picture books		1,740					
The average number of pages per digital picture book		14.2±10.6					
The study period		September 12, 2013 to February 26, 2014 (September 12, 2012 to February 26, 2013[†])					
Open days	School days	90	44[‡]	86	81	75	80
	Holidays	47	24[‡]	52	41	53	41

[†]For OCL (Oita Citizens Library), we could only collect the data from 2012 through 2013 with the moving to its new building.
[‡]Due to the system malfunction, we could not collect the data for some days.

Table 2. The locational conditions of the local public libraries for the field study

Factors	OPL	BML	OCL	YCL	UPL	YBL
F11: The ratio of children aged 3-9 years to the total population in the local area (the number of children aged 3-9 years in the local area)	0.066 (31,328)	0.051 (6,490)	0.066 (31,328)	0.058 (2,020)	0.056 (3,325)	0.058 (2,020)
F12: The number of nearby educational facilities[*]	11	14	20	3	2	2
F21: The proximity to a bus stop and a train station[**]	long	short	short	short	long	short
F22: The number of parking lots	196	10	175	60	40	20

[*] We counted the number of nursery schools, kindergartens or elementary schools within 1 km or less of the library.
[**]If there are both of a bus stop and a train station within 1 km or less of the library, then "short", else "long."

In order to identify which factor affects children's reading activity, we used the correlation analysis for the ratio of read digital picture books to opened digital picture books and each of the four factors in locational conditions. As shown in Figure 3 we plotted two scatter diagrams between the ratio of read digital picture books to opened digital picture books and each of two factors, F11 and F22, which were strongly correlated with this ratio. Figure 3(a) and (b) are for F11 and F22, respectively. The correlation coefficients in the cases of F11 and F22 were 0.94 and 0.89, respectively. The correlation coefficients for the other factors, F12 and F21, were 0.33 and 0.14, respectively. This result reveals that F12 and F21 are seemingly unrelated to children's reading activity.

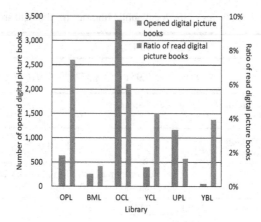

Fig. 2. The numbers of opened digital picture books and the ratios of read digital picture books to opened digital picture books

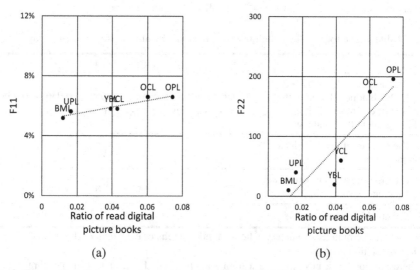

Fig. 3. The scatter diagrams between the ratio of read digital picture books and each of two factors, F11 and F22

To analyze the details of children's reading activity on a daily basis, we carefully checked the logged data of 3 libraries, OPL, OCL, and UPL, where their numbers of opened digital picture books were statistically larger than that of the other 3 libraries (chi-square test with the Bonferroni correction, p=0.05). We can surmise that the larger the number is, the larger the number of children who visited the library is throughout the study period. Figure 4 shows the number of opened digital picture books on school days and holidays. For each of OPL and UPL, the number of opened digital picture books on holidays was statistically larger than the number on school days (chi-square test, p=0.05). Since the factor of the proximity to a bus stop and a train station is "long" for both of OPL and UPL, many children could not easily visit the libraries on their way home from school on school days. On holidays, it can be said that the children visited OPL or UPL by cars with their families. On the other hand, the number of opened digital picture books in OCL, which has the highest number of nearby educational facilities, on school days was larger than the number on holidays. It can be easily surmised that many children visited OCL nearby their schools on foot after school and then went home on public transportation. Although we could not find out exactly how each child came to the library, the logged data in a period of over5 months could reveal the children's travelling mode to the library.

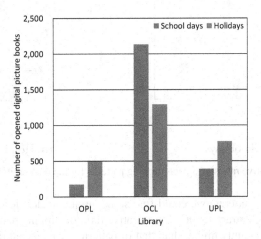

Fig. 4. The number of opened digital picture books on school days and holidays in OPL, OCL, and UPL

According to the above results, the factors about the children in the local public library's surroundings had a different effect on children's reading activity. As the ratio of children aged 3-9 years to the total population in the local area (F11) increases, the ratio of read digital picture books to opened picture books increases as well. In Japan, the larger the population of a city, the greater the number of education-minded parents there tend to be. It is easy to imagine that many of these parents visited OPL and OCL, the libraries in the biggest city in Oita prefecture, and then read the picture books with their children. Although we could not clarify a similar correlation between the number of nearby educational facilities (F12) and children's reading activity, the convenience of public (F21) and private (F22) transportation usage had a positive effect in attracting the children to visit the library on school days and holidays, respectively. Even if a bus stop or train station is far from the library, children visit it on holidays with their families if the library has ample parking lots.

Correlation between Locational Conditions and Page Flipping Patterns. The question that remains now is how children read the digital picture books. We analyzed the page flipping data in the 3 libraries, OPL, OCL, and UPL, and classified the children's page flipping patterns into the 3 types previously mentioned in Section 3. Figure 5 shows the relative ratios of the 3 patterns in reading the digital picture books in each of the libraries on school days and holidays.

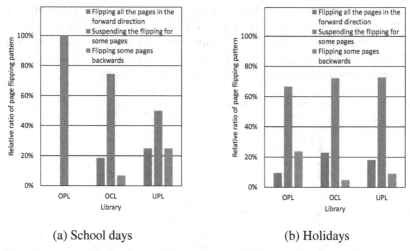

(a) School days   (b) Holidays

Fig. 5. The relative ratios of 3 page flipping patterns for the read digital picture books

In flipping page patterns, we could find some unique tendencies related to the factors F21 and F22. Contrary to OCL, the relative ratio of flipping pattern III in OPL on holidays was significantly higher than that of pattern I. This meant that many children being driven to visit the library, which has a large number of parking lots, had sufficient time to thoroughly read the picture books. Also, those who used public transportation were unable to stay long enough to flip some pages backwards even if on holidays because they had to be on time to catch the bus or train home. These differences in flipping page patterns caused by the factors F21 and F22 were evident in children's average flipped time per page as shown in Table 3. The time in OCL was statistically shorter than that in OPL (unpaired t-test with the Bonferroni correction, p=0.05). The relative ratio of flipping pattern III in UPL on school days was statistically higher than that on holidays. Since UPL is built in a small city in a rural part of Oita prefecture, some students who attend the local elementary school nearby UPL visited this library on foot on their way home from school and could stay for a long period of time.

Table 3. The average flipped time per page

Library	Av. (sec.) ±SD
OPL	12.9±9.5
OCL	8.9±4.2
UPL	10.8±9.5

About 88% of the read digital picture books in the 3 libraries were read only once in the study period. However, the average numbers of total pages of the read digital picture books in the libraries were not statistically different (unpaired t-test with the Bonferroni correction, p=0.05)from each other. Table 4 shows these average numbers. Note that regardless of differences within the libraries, the relative ratio of read digital picture books with flipping pattern II, in which the children suspended the flipping for some pages, was significantly higher than that of flipping patterns I and III (chi-square test with the Bonferroni correction, p=0.05). These results reveal that, even when there is a major flipping page pattern to read digital picture books and a pre-ferred number of pages, the children have varied interests in read digital picture books. It can be said that a large number and wide variety of digital picture books is important in attracting children to libraries.

Table 4. The average number of pages per read digital picture book

Library	Av. ±SD
OPL	9.4±6.6
OCL	9.7±7.6
UPL	9.9±6.2

When attracting children to the library, our study indicated that the convenience of transportation usage is an important factor. Although children can read digital picture books both ways, fast and slow, especially for younger children, preparing enough space for parking lots so as to encourage the children visit the library with their fami-lies is of great importance. From the result of analyzing the read digital picture books, it has been shown that a wide variety of digital picture books is preferable in order to satisfy the children's interests.

5   Conclusions

We conducted a field study which lasted over a period of 5 months in the local public libraries in Japan to clarify the factors of locational conditions correlated with child-ren's reading activity. The factors were mainly the ratios of children in the population and the number of parking lots. The results of our study suggest that recording child-ren's page flipping data in multiple local public libraries, as the basis of analyzing children's reading activity, is a promising approach when a children's room intends to attract as many children as possible.

Our field study allowed the children to freely select the digital picture books and read them themselves. Severalcharacteristics of the read digital picture books, e.g., genre, length, and difficulty, should be analyzed to clarify the preferences of children in reading picture books. Our comparative analysis is also able to be applied to reveal the factors correlated with children's reading activity, which stem from seasons, cultures, etc. In our future work, we will analyze the other factors and details to obtain knowledge in order to enrich the collections of the digital picture books and/or to improve the reading environments.

References

1. Arakane, C., Liu, J., Sato, K., Nakashima, M., Ito, T.: Figuring out if Children Actually Read Digital Picture Books and Which ones should be Collected. In: Chen, H.-H., Chowdhury, G. (eds.) ICADL 2012. LNCS, vol. 7634, pp. 249–258. Springer, Heidelberg (2012)
2. Baeg, J.H., Choi, W., Lee, D.J., Lee, J.: The Impact of the Public Library on Early Reading Achievement: Using the Early Childhood Longitudinal Study (ECLS) 1st Grade Student. In: Proceedings of iConference 2012, pp. 538–540 (2012)
3. Begeny, J.C., Krouse, H.E., Brown, K.G., Mann, C.M.: Teacher Judgments of Students' Reading Abilities Across a Continuum of Rating Methods and Achievement Measures. School Psychology Review 40(1), 23–38 (2011)
4. Cheng, K.H., Tsai, C.C.: Children and Parents' Reading of an Augmented Reality Picture Book: Analyses of Behavioral Patterns and Cognitive Attainment. Journal of Computers & Education 72, 302–312 (2014)
5. Hamilton, C., Shinn, M.R.: Characteristics of Word Callers: An Investigation of the Accuracy of Teachers' Judgments of Reading Comprehension and Oral Reading Skills. School Psychology Review 32(2), 228–240 (2003)
6. Hertel, K., Sprague, N.: GIS and Census Data: Tools for Library Planning. Library Hi Tech 25(2), 246–259 (2007)
7. Kinikin, J.: Applying Geographic Information Systems to the Weber County Library System. Information Technology and Libraries 23(3), 102–107 (2004)
8. Liu, J., Nakashima, M., Ito, T.: BrowsReader: A System for Realizing a New Children's Reading Environment in a Library. In: Goh, D.H.-L., Cao, T.H., Sølvberg, I.T., Rasmussen, E. (eds.) ICADL 2007. LNCS, vol. 4822, pp. 361–371. Springer, Heidelberg (2007)
9. Liu, J., Sato, K., Nakashima, M., Ito, T.: Browse&Read Picture Books in a Group on a Digital Table. In: Buchanan, G., Masoodian, M., Cunningham, S.J. (eds.) ICADL 2008. LNCS, vol. 5362, pp. 309–312. Springer, Heidelberg (2008)
10. Liu, J., Ito, T., Toyokuni, N., Sato, K., Nakashima, M.: Enhancing Children's Activity in Browsing/reading Together by the Installation of the BrowsReader in the Children's Room of a Library. Information Processing and Management 48(6), 1094–1115 (2012)
11. Paris, A.H., Paris, S.G.: Children's Comprehension of Narrative Picture books. Report #3-012, CIERA, Ann Arbor (2001),
http://www.ciera.org/library/reports/inquiry-3/3-012/3-012.html (accessed on February 3, 2014)
12. Park, S.J.: Measuring Public Library Accessibility: A Case Study using GIS. Library & Information Science Research 34(1), 13–21 (2012)
13. Taira, M.: Reading-to-children Strikes Through the Heart in a Brain (in Japanese). Kumon Shuppan, Tokyo (2009)
14. Wright, S., Fugett, A., Caputa, F.: Using E-readers and Internet Resources to Support Comprehension. Educational Technology & Society 16(1), 367–379 (2013)

A Log Analysis Study of 10 Years of eBook Consumption in Academic Library Collections

Haley Littlewood, Annika Hinze, Nicholas Vanderschantz,
Claire Timpany, and Sally Jo Cunningham

Dept. of Computer Science, University of Waikato,
Private Bag 3105, Hamilton New Zealand
hml15@students.waikato.ac.nz,
{hinze,vtwoz,ctimapny,sallyjo}@waikato.ac.nz

Abstract. Even though libraries have been offering eBooks for more than a decade, very little is known about eBook access and consumption in academic library collections. This paper addresses this gap with a log analysis study of eBook access at the library of the University of Waikato. This in-depth analysis covers a period spanning 10 years of eBook use at this university. We draw conclusions about the use of eBooks at this institution and compare the results with other published studies of eBook usage at tertiary institutes.

1   Introduction

Mostacademic libraries are now offering eBooks and eJournals in addition to paper books and paper journals for today's researchers. For the purpose of this paper, an eBook is understood to be an electronic book rather than any electronic text. eBooks are usually viewed and accessed via specialist software or hardware such as eReaders and eCollections. The eCollections surveyed in this study are Ebrary and EBL. While the selection and consumption of physical books has been comprehensively studied (e.g, [14,30,31]), the library patrons' habits in accessing eBooks have been less well explored (e.g., [22] studied how patrons make relevancy decisions when selecting eBooks). In the current paper, we explore the consumption of eBooks, in particular the use of patron-driven acquisition, eBook acceptance and usage, and the handling of eBooks in an academic library. In a log-analysis study, we explored the use of eBooks at the library of the University of Waikato since 2003 when digital documents and eBooks began to be offered to students and staff.

2   Related Work

Understanding usage patterns of physical libraries, digital libraries and eBook systems can be of benefit to Librarians and researchers in Digital Libraries. Even though a number of studies on eBook collections have been reported [1,27,21,22], Tucker observes that due to the rapidly and constantly evolving nature of this field, the conclusions from works published as recently as five years previously may or may not be

K. Tuamsuk et al. (Eds.): ICADL 2014, LNCS 8839, pp. 171–181, 2014.

applicable to the current environment [32]. Furthermore, the variation in data made available complicates comparative analyses [8,9,26,29]. Studies looking at book use in libraries and eBook collections seem to approach the issue from one of two directions. Observations and interviews have been conducted to better understand the decision-making process in the selection and consumption of eBooks (e.g., [30,31]). Transaction log analysis is also commonly used in studies to understand user behaviour and information seeking in online library catalogues [5,4] and digital libraries [19,24]. Using transaction log analysis can help to provide insight into aspects of the reading process that may not be easily observed otherwise [25, 22]. Previous studies using the Ebrary system have looked into user penetration as a tool for librarians improving their services, e.g., [26]. It was observed that managing multiple eCollections from different publishers can be problematic for librarians. Other studies have looked into subject-related acceptance of eBooks, and publisher market share, e.g., finding that eBooks in health sciences and hotel had highest usage [32].Overall, the lack of recent data on eBook selection is widely acknowledged [28, 22, 14], and an awareness for the frequency with which patrons abandon their search [23] indicates a need for further research. The patrons' difficulties with digital systems for eBook search and selection likely result in lost sales (in online bookshops) or unwarranted paid use (in libraries, where readers perceive books as "free" [13]).

3   Methodology

We used data from the academic library of the University of Waikato, a small institution with about 12,550 undergraduates, 2800 postgraduates, and 628 academic staff.

3.1   The eBook Collections

The University of Waikato (UoW) Library offers a variety of eBook platforms, access to which depends on the Library's licence agreements with individual providers. The eBooks studied here are provided by Ebrary. From 2003 to 2008, Ebrary was the only provider of eBooks to Waikato, with offerings increasing from an initial 30,000 titles in 2003, to 110,000 in 2008. Since 2008, the Ebrary offerings have remained at this level while other providers have been gradually included in the UoW catalogue, which provides access to 180,657 eBooks as of March 2014. Some eBooks are acquired as part of whole collections and others as single titles, according to need. The Ebrary offering, while static in overall numbers, remains dynamic with new titles being included, while older, unused eBooks are discontinued. All eBooks on offer are available via the library catalogue; most are owned by the library, with an increasing minority becoming available on an ad-hoc basis (patron-driven acquisition [22,12]). The difference between owned and un-owned eBooks is invisible to readers.

The Ebrary eBook holdings comprise a general academia-oriented collection, with a small number of supporting or recreational titles; eBooks are mainly categorized as Business & Economics, Social Sciences, Science, Education, Technological Science and Medicine, while the least populated categories are specific, such as Gardening, Pets, and Bibles. The library also owns a large number of small, specialised collections aimed at specific subjects, and a small number of larger, more generalised collections that mostly contain journals, but may also contain eBooks. Librarians may buy single books and access to small specialised collections. They may also maintain access to the "Academic Complete" collection within Ebrary, which changes periodically and titles are added and removed as a consequence. Within the academic collection, books may get deleted both individually and in groups by the publisher, independently of librarians. Librarians can change single-use into multi-use books, some of which may still be subject to restrictions on the number of simultaneous accesses. Some collections are removed as they are shut down, or merged into another collection.

3.2   eBook Log Analysis

The data on which this study was based was collected over the period of 1 August 2003 to 31 December 2013, covering 11 out of the almost 12 years that eBooks have been available at the UoW library. The data thus represents a range of academic users including students, academic staff and research students. The Ebrary logs are available in a form that is anonymised by individual readers. Unlike previous studies [23], we did not have access to data that would allow us to track user sessions. eBooks that were deleted at some point from the catalogue only appear in the statistics if the book was previously accessed. There are no statistics available about how many books have been deleted and when. The statistics for accessed books are complete, including deleted books. All statistics used for this paper concern Ebrary books only, on data from both the main library and the specialist Education library. Statistics for the numbers of eBook on offer are taken from the University's annual reports covering all eBook resources.

4   Log Analysis of eBook Accesses

We explored six aspects of eBook usage through the Waikato University logs: access over time, popular eBooks, the number of pages accessed or printed, single vs multiple access schemes, queuing for access and patron-driven acquisition.

4.1   eBook Access Over Time

When analysing the eBook access over time (both number of user sessions and number of pages accessed) a clear pattern can be seen that correlates with the timing of semesters A (March to June), B (July to November), and summer school (January).

Figure 1 shows the number of pages viewed (blue bars) and the number of user sessions (red line). Pages viewed including all pages that were turned to, regardless of how long the user spent on the page. Since 2011, eBook usage has steadily increased for both A and B semesters as well as during down-times (such as between semesters and during summer breaks). A comparison of yearly user sessions confirmed an increase from 1431 in 2003, 19252 in 2008, to 42,225 in 2013.

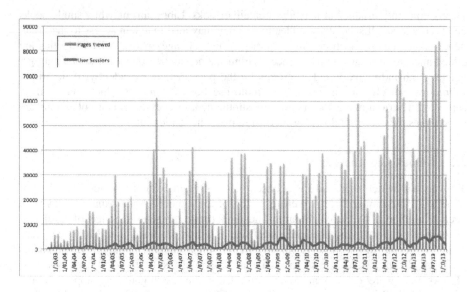

Fig. 1. Number of user sessions and pages viewed over time

We next explored whether this increased usage was caused by an increase in the number of eBooks available or by changes in staff and student numbers. The average pages viewed per accessed book and month was found to remain relatively stable at between 10 and 20 pages. While the number of staff and students remained relatively stable between 16,000 (2003) and 14,000 (since 2005), the average number of accessed books per person was increasing from 0.5 (2005) to 1.4 (2009) and 2.2 (2013). We observe that over the years, an increasing proportion of books were accessed, from about 2% (2003) to about 10% (2005), falling to 7% over 4 years (2011), and steadily increasing since then to 14% in 2013. The observed dip was caused by disparity between stability in the numbers of accessed books while the overall number of books grew. Overall, there were 44,001 unique book accesses between 2003 and 2013. We note that between 2006 and 2011, the increasing numbers of books available did not seem to influence the number of books accessed. We conclude that the increase in number of pages and eBooks accessed is not caused by an increase in patrons or available eBooks, but by an increased use of eBooks over time. Of the books available at UoW library via Ebrary (13,899), about 39% have been accessed since 2003.

4.2   Popular eBooks

Of the most frequently accessed books, only five were found to be eReserve books, i.e., eBooks that had been used as the recommended text in a course. All of the eReserve books can be found among the top 38 of most accessed. While, on average, each accessed book was involved in 5.2 user sessions, the top 49 books have been accessed 180 to 1,300 times. The top category was Social Science, from which 10 eBooks were accessed overall 3,720 times. The areas with the second highest

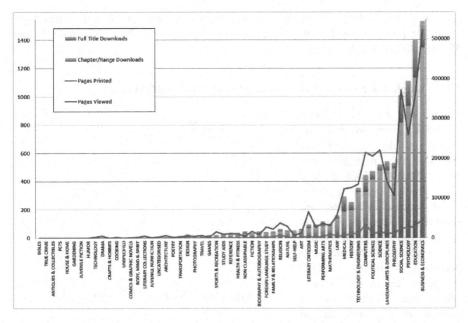

Fig. 2. Pages accessed and pages printed downloads (range vs whole books)

usage were Education, and Business & Economics (8 books each). The areas with the highest average access per book were Philosophy (667 on 1 book) and Psychology (480.5 on 4 books).

4.3   Pages Accessed/Read/Printed

Figure 2 shows the number of pages that were accessed online or printed out, ordered by subject area. Though 10 of the 49 top accessed books were from Social Science, this area comes second in the number of pages accessed (370,000 pages). Business & Economics (8 books in the top 49) is first with more than 500,000 accessed pages. The explanation for this seeming anomaly might be either that business books contain more pages than social science books or that business students and researchers read more pages of the eBooks they access. In comparison to books available in each field (Fig.2), we note that for most subjects the number of pages viewed rises with the number of books available (e.g., most available books are from Business & Economics, and so are most pages viewed). Exceptions are Political Science (proportionately fewer pages viewed), and Education (proportionately more pages viewed). This might be due to either different patron behaviour or different book lengths in different fields. There are a number of areas in which large proportions of eBook pages are printed for reading (orange in Fig. 2). The classifications that show the largest proportion of printed to viewed pages are: Antiques & Collectibles (162% -- more pages printed than viewed), Bibles (70%), and Humour (45%). These most likely refer to private interests rather than study and research purposes. Fields with more than 20% printed pages are Mathematics (35%), Transportation (28%), Gardening (26%) and Religion (22%). It appears that Computer Science (18%) and Mathematics (35%) are the two subjects where patrons print significant proportions of accessed pages. Downloads of eBooks in part or in full has only been available since January 2012; it varied between 35 and 120 per month in Ebrary.

4.4   Single User vs Multiple User Books: Queues and Turnaways

The eBooks available through the UoW library are predominantly single user books (SUPO) and multiple user books (MUPO). Both of these hold perpetual access licenses. Other access schemes are short-term *loans* for one day or for seven days, and patron-driven acquisition (leading to perpetual licenses). Attempting to access a single user eBook that is already in use may mean a patron has to

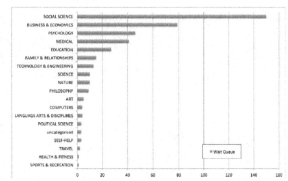

Fig. 3. Wait Queues per Primary Category

wait. *Queues* refer to users waiting for access to an eBook with single-user access rights that some other patron is currently using. If a user accepts to join a wait queue to access a book, they are shown a window giving their position in the queue. Once the user reaches the front of the queue they are prompted again. They are then given 5 minutes to access the document before access is revoked and given to the next person. If they choose to open the document within those 5 minutes then they have unlimited access (until they close the document), unless there are other users queued. Figure 3 shows the number of users that had to wait for a book to become available before they could access it, sorted by category. The data refers to all users that chose to join a wait queue, regardless of whether they reached the book or left early. *Turnaways* refer to users who, when asked in a session to wait for an eBook to become available, decided not to enter a queue. Since August 2010, there were 508 turn aways in total for eBooks at the UoW library.

4.5   Patron-Driven Acquisition

In 2010, the UoW library started offering patron-driven acquisition (PDA) of eBooks, in which a patron selecting an eBook from the catalogue triggers the acquisition of this eBook. Statistics for PDAs were available from April 2012 onwards, and detailed acquisition data since July 2010. Figure 4 shows a comparison between sessions accessing librarian-acquired books (blue) and sessions on patron-driven acquisitions (red). We observe that few PDAs are accessed/acquired each month, and moreover, that they do not follow the semester structure, i.e., PDA peaks are seen in January and August. One aspect of these anomalies can be explained by the funding structure: there is only a small budget set aside for pre-paid PDAs. This budget is typically exhausted relatively quickly and is not always renewed. This may account for the months with very few PDAs and also for the absence of PDAs between September and December 2013 (as there was most likely no budget left). From 04/2012 to 08/2013 (the period for which statistics are available), on average 150 to 250 pages were accessed per PDA book (outlier: 08/2013: 970 per book, 16 books). There are no wait queues associated with PDAs as these eBooks are bought immediately when requested. When there is no budget for PDAs these eBooks are not shown as being available. Overall, since July 2010 1,449 PDAs were triggered (during 179 sessions, no information about distribution). As users are not prompted to confirm PDAs, it is possible that through research in areas that are poorly served by available eBooks, a small group of patrons inadvertently triggered a large number of PDAs.

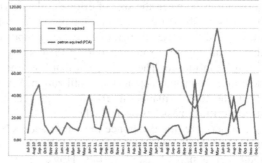

Fig. 4. Access of eBooks acquired by librarians vs patron-driven acquisition

5   Discussion

Comparison with Similar Studies. Other academic studies also observed that eBook usage follows the semester structure [2,3,27]. The British national eBook project [17] found that text-book usage varied by more than 50% depending on the teaching and assessment calendar. For the University of Waikato, these fluctuations are much more pronounced with differences of up to 600% recorded between the summer break and the height of B semester in 2013. The additional mid-summer peak observed in the Waikato data (December/January) was not found in other studies and might indicate the beginning of a greater use of eBooks during summer school or for research and class preparation. Further investigation of course offerings and reading assignments for that period would be necessary for clarification.   Similarly, an increase of eBook usage was widely observed [3,22,27,32]. Tucker et al report a 54% increase over 3 years, with a 26% increase in pages viewed [32]. The UoW data from a similar time period shows an even higher increase (both eBook and page access between 2010 and 2013 increased more than 200%). Again, because of the large degree of uncertainty caused by different recording mechanisms, it is hard to draw clear conclusions from this data beyond identifying an increased use of eBooks. The British national survey found that eBooks were predominantly used for quick look-up of facts and brief viewing at Universities [17]. While we also found these same usage patterns (i.e., accessing a few pages only), the average page access per book was 10 to 20 pages and quite a number of books were downloaded or printed in their entirety. The highest numbers of printed pages were found in Mathematics and Computer Science, the reasons for which could not be determined from this log analysis, but would warrant further exploration. The percentage of all accessed eBooks out of all the collections on offer seems to vary greatly between universities: Waikato patrons have accessed in total about 39% since 2003 (approximately 10% each year), while Sprague and Hunter reported that 16% of Ebrary titles were assessed at least once for the University of Idaho [29], at Australia's Edith Cowan university, 8% of eBooks were browsed and 5% were read (over a three year study period) [1,2], and Swinburne patrons accessed about 48% and created loans for approximately 19% in one month alone(these percentages are calculated from the usage data presented in [22]).Lamothe found strong correlations between the size of eBook collections and the level of eBook usage [20]. We were unable to confirm this for the UoW collections, as the number of eBooks available did not seem to influence the number of eBook sessions. Lamothe found that of all factors examined during their study the size of the collection had the strongest influence. They suggested that both the size and the content of a collection determines patron acceptance and utilization. We would argue that certainly the quality of the content matters in eBook acceptance, but the size may not matter as much once a critical mass has been reached.

Furthermore, the difference in ease of access between the various types of eBooks may also heavily influence their usage. At UoW the eBooks that the library owns are indicated as part of search results. However, eBooks that are available to UoW patrons via PDA do not automatically appear in search results. The patron has to explicitly ask for these to be included.

While Sprague and Hunter found that fewer than 2% of their eBooks have had repeated usage [29], we observed that over half of the eBooks accessed each year had been accessed in a previous year. Even with slightly inflated usage results (due to multiple accesses by the same user being counted as separate sessions), this is a significant difference. We found that course reserve books are only partially responsible for this high degree of re-use. Further analysis is needed about re-use of eBooks.

Statistics and Comparability. A noticeable hurdle in the evaluation of eBook usage is the data availability. For example, we were unable to evaluate Waikato usage for titles from publishers other than Ebrary. Even if data is available, it is often not directly comparable. This has repeatedly been mentioned in other publications about eBook usage analysis. Cox compared the statistical data available for different eBook vendors with those in COUNTER [6] and SUSHI [8,9]. Counter is an international, extendible Code of Practice for e-Resources that allows the usage of online information products and services to be measured in a consistent and compatible way. SUSHI is a SOAP web services "wrapper" for the XML version of Counter reports. Counter lists 130 publishers as being compliant for journals and databases with only 34 compliant for eBooks, although there are more than 100 unique eBook publishers [8,9]. Furthermore, EBook publishers typically use hosting companies and aggregators as their route to market. We wish to record our agreement with both their observation that eBook usage data is essential for libraries and their opinion that standardisation efforts are "prizes well worth fighting for" [9]. The main finding of our study is that it is very difficult to draw reliable conclusions from the data currently available. Because previous studies used different statistics (as there was no standard available) and covered shorter time spans, we can detect usage patterns, but find it hard to verify if these are typical for this type of institution (e.g., much higher fluctuation between semester and break times than in other studies, greater increase in eBook usage over the last few years, etc.) Similar to Sprague and Hunter [32], we appreciate the data and patterns we found, but feel stymied in making sense of it in the wider context. Furthermore, the data available makes it almost impossible to identify the reasons for some of the observed patterns. There are no clear records kept as to what activities took place over the last 10 years to promote eBook usage. Thus it is impossible to say which of these activities might be responsible for the high uptake of eBooks in some areas. Because the data is anonymised, the true benefits of a longitudinal study (e.g., changes in the patrons' usage patterns) are not as conclusive and specific as they might be had this data been available. At present, reuse and revisits cannot be identified. Furthermore, by using log analysis we are restricted to the observable patterns without external verification. It would be interesting to compare our findings with insights from patron observations and interviews.

6   Conclusions

This paper provides a log analysis study that covers the 10 years since the University of Waikato library started offering access to eBooks. Our study covers a longer period of time than is typically reported in other similar studies and gives insights into the trends of eBook usage at an academic institution. We found that our log analysis almost raises more questions than it answers. For example, neither the reasons for printing so many books or pages, nor the level of eBook usage during the summer months can be explained satisfactorily. When analysing the data for the university, we may conclude that the library has been successful in promoting eBook use as we found a much higher uptake and usage than in other studies. However, we are unable to identify the exact activities that contributed to their successful introduction. We conclude that libraries need to keep clear records of their efforts to promote eBook usage as a retrospective analysis based on eBook numbers alone is not sufficient. From the data available it is also not clear whether the results from Waikato are in fact significantly different from those of other institutions (as the statistics are difficult to compare). We encountered a number of obstacles when comparing the data to other studies available. In order to eliminate these, we recommend the use of standardised log keeping for eBook access that provides for identification of user patterns (while anonymising patron-specific data).

References

1. Ahmad, P.: E-book Adoption in Academic & Research Libraries: Self-Reported Information Behaviour (2013)
2. Ahmad, P., Brogan, M.: Scholarly use of e-books in a virtual academic environment: A case study. Australian Academic & Research Libraries 43(3), 189–213 (2012)
3. Christianson, M., Aucoin, M.: Electronic or print books: Which are used? Libr. Collect. Acquis. 29(1), 71–81 (2005)
4. Cooper, M.D.: Usage patterns of a web-based library catalog. Journal of the American Society for Information Science and Technology 52(2), 137–148 (2001)
5. Cousins, S.A.: In: their own words: An examination of catalogue users' subject queries. J. Inf. Sci. 18(5), 329–341 (1992)
6. Counter, COUNTER: Counting Online Usage of NeTworked Electronic Resources (2007), http://www.projectcounter.org

7. Cummings, I.: Kansas libraries lead way in e-book access. Kansas, USA (2011), http://Kansan.com

8. Cox, J.: Making sense of e-book usage data. The Acquisitions Librarian 19(3-4), 193–212 (2008)

9. Cox, L.: Librarians' use of usage statistics for journals and e-books. Learned Publishing 24(2), 115–121 (2011)

10. Gibson, C., Gibb, F.: An evaluation of second-generation eBook readers. The Electronic Library 29(3), 303–319 (2011)

11. Hamblen, M.: Amazon: E-books now outsell print books. Computerworld (2011), http://www.computerworld.com/s/article/9216869/Amazon_E_book s_now_outsell_print_books2011 (last accessed April 11, 2012)

12. Hardy, G., Davies, T.: Letting the patrons choose: using EBL as a method for unmediated acquisition of ebook materials. In: Information Online, ALIA, Sydney (2007)

13. Hernon, P., Hopper, R., Leach, M.R., Saunders, L.L., Zhang, J.: E-book use by students. The Journal of Academic Librarianship 33(1), 3–13 (2007)

14. Hinze, A., McKay, D., Timpany, C., Vanderschantz, N., Cunningham, S.J.: Book selection behaviour in the physical library. In: JCDL, Baltimore, MD (2012)

15. Holt, K.: E-book sales statistics from BISG survey. In: Publishing Perspectives (2010, 2011)

16. Jantz, R.C.: E-Books and New Library Service Models: An Analysis of the Impact of EBook Technology on Academic Libraries (2001)

17. Jamali, H.R., Nicholas, D., Rowlands, I.: Scholarly e-books: the views of 16,000 academics. Aslib Proceedings 61(1), 33–47 (2009)

18. Jansen, B.J., Spink, A.: How are we searching the WWW? A comparison of nine search engine transaction logs. Information Processing & Management 42(1), 248–263 (2006)

19. Jones, S., Cunningham, S.J., McNab, R.: An analysis of usage of a digital library. In: Nikolaou, C., Stephanidis, C. (eds.) ECDL 1998. LNCS, vol. 1513, pp. 261–277. Springer, Heidelberg (1998)

20. Lamothe, A.R.: Factors influencing the usage of an electronic book collection: size of the e-book collection, the student population, and the faculty population. College & Research Libraries 74(1), 39–59 (2013)

21. Littman, J., Connaway, L.S.: A Circulation Analysis of Print Books and E-Books in an Academic Research Library. Library Resources & Technical Services 48(4), 256–262 (2004)

22. McKay, D., Hinze, A., Heese, R., Vanderschantz, N., Timpany, C., Cunningham, S.J.: An Exploration of ebook Selection Behavior in Academic Library Collections. In: Zaphiris, P., Buchanan, G., Rasmussen, E., Loizides, F. (eds.) TPDL 2012. LNCS, vol. 7489, pp. 13–24. Springer, Heidelberg (2012)

23. McKay, D., Buchanan, G., Vanderschantz, N., Timpany, C., Cunningham, S.J., Hinze, A.: Judging a book by its cover: interface elements that affect reader selection of ebooks. In: 24th Australian Computer-Human Interaction Conference, pp. 381–390. ACM (2012)

24. Mahoui, M., Cunningham, S.J.: Search behavior in a research-oriented digital library. In: Constantopoulos, P., Sølvberg, I.T. (eds.) ECDL 2001. LNCS, vol. 2163, pp. 13–24. Springer, Heidelberg (2001)

25. Marshall, C.C.: Reading and Writing the Electronic Book. Morgan & Claypool, Chapel Hill (2010)

26. McLuckie, A.: E-books in an academic library: Implementation at the ETH Library, Zurich. Electronic Library 23(1), 92–102 (2005)

27. Obradovic, K.: Intrepid Traveller: the University of Auckland Library on the E-Book Journey. In: VALA - Victorian Library Association Conference, Melbourne Australia (2006)
28. Rowlands, I., Nicholas, D., et al.: What do faculty and students really think about e-books? Aslib. Proc. 59(6), 489–511 (2007)
29. Sprague, N., Hunter, B.: Assessing eBooks: taking a closer look at eBook statistics. Library Collections, Acquisitions & Technical Services 32(3-4), 150–157 (2009)
30. Stelmaszewska, H., Blandford, A.: From physical to digital: a case study of computer scientists' behaviour in physical libraries. JoDL 4(2), 82–92 (2004)
31. Stieve, T., Schoen, D.: Undergraduate Students' Book Selection: A Study of Factors in the Decision-Making Process. J. Acad. Libr. 32(6), 599–608 (2006)
32. Tucker, J.C.: Ebook collection analysis: subject and publisher trends. Collection Building 31(2), 40–47 (2012)

Family Visits to Libraries and Bookshops: Observations and Implications for Digital Libraries

Nicholas Vanderschantz, Claire Timpany, Annika Hinze,
and Sally Jo Cunningham

Dept. of Computer Science, University of Waikato,
Private Bag 3105, Hamilton New Zealand
{vtwoz,ctimpany,hinze,sallyjo}@waikato.ac.nz

Abstract. This paper explores how families select books for leisure reading. We recruited 17 families (adults and children) for this study, and spent time with each in both bookshops and public libraries. Our research aims to add to understanding of how families interact with books and bookshelves in these places, and how digital libraries might best support the shared needs of these inter-generational users. Much of our understanding of how an eBook should look and feel comes from generalizations about books and assumptions about the needs of those *individuals* who read them. We explore how children *and* adults search and browse for books *together*, with specific focus on the type of information seeking tasks that families undertake and on the families' shared search and browsing strategies. We further explore the implications of this study for the development of digital libraries for children and families.

Keywords: participant observation, social space, collaborative information behaviour, families.

1 Introduction

We report here on an observational study exploring how family groups interacted with books in both library and bookshop environments. We aim for an added understanding of families' book selection strategies in these places, to provide insight into how digital libraries could be designed to support the collaborative family behaviour observed in physical environments.

We conducted interviews and observations with 17 family groups who each visitied both a public library and a bookshop. Previous investigations of children's information behaviour have rarely focussed on recreational reading and family groups. Similarly, most digital libraries for children focus on supporting the needs of an individual child searching for a book on their own. We see in this present study and in an earlier study [1] that for children, the practice of searching for a book is often far more social than individual. The process of search, interaction and decision making is often completed in collaboration with, or, alongside a parent or sibling.

The remainder of the paper is structured as follows: Section 2 discusses related work on children and book/ebook selection in physical and digital libraries. Section 3

K. Tuamsuk et al. (Eds.): ICADL 2014, LNCS 8839, pp. 182–195, 2014.

describes our study methodology and Section 4 presents the results of our study. We analyse our findings in Section 5, and discuss implications for DL in Section 6.

2 Related Work

Large et al. [2] observe that the childhood years have a strong impact on both the reading levels of children and their ability to navigate a library. As children mature they form strategies for selecting books collaboratively and individually. Family information needs can broadly be divided into two categories: education books and leisure books [2, 3]. Search for and selection of education books is usually initiated by a third party such as a teacher wanting students to respond to an assignment [4]. Leisure books are typically self-selected by the child or family and selection is motivated by personal interests. Reading books not directly associated with homework has been found to encourage families to enjoy reading and to read more for both pleasure and learning [5].

2.1 Book Search and Selection Strategies

Cunningham [1] found that younger children clearly selected books on the basis of serendipitous encounters that match a preference, rather than actively employing a strategy to search for books of a particular genre, theme, author, or other characteristic. Similarly, Raqi and Zainab [6] observe that the strategy most frequently employed by children was browsing the (physical) library shelves. Books of interest are then usually identified based on the cover, genre, author, series, print size, number of pictures and pages, and colourful cover illustrations. Information seeking in printed resources typically follows the two stages of selecting an appropriate source and finding the information within it [2]. Children were observed to follow two methods to evaluate a non-fiction book: the 'sequential access' of flipping through the pages to find information and 'selective access' using the content page or the index [7]. Sequential access was used when the book was short, the child was interested in the entire book or even when a younger child was seeking particular information. Selective access was used for thicker books, or to find particular items of information.

2.2 Social Aspects of Book Finding

Another strategy used by children is to request assistance to locate desired book topics, authors and series [6]. This was observed especially in children who are still developing their reading skills. Fogget [8] noted that children would request help from friends, family or librarians once they had exhausted their own information resource of browsing the shelves. In an anonymous observation study Hinze et al.[9] noted that many family visitors to a public library seemed to be "spending time". In 24 of the 56 family groups observed by Hinze et al., children were observed playing, sometimes with items from the library (including pillows, a rocking horse, puzzles, books, and paper and scissors), or with items they brought along (such as mobile phones and iPads). Hinze et al. also described the library as seemingly providing a place for parents to meet with other adults in an environment that offered distraction or entertainment for their children. Cunningham[1] observed that for children finding a book is very rarely a solitary activity; instead, they visit bookshops and libraries with parents, siblings, and friends. She noticed how young children bring books back to adults for reading and approval; friends and siblings give advice to each other (both encouragement and warnings); and parents offer recommendations and guidance. Retrospective studies often comment on the strong influence of recommendations by others, but largely do not capture the rich behaviour, as observed by Cunningham. Our study aims to add to the insights gained from her observational study.

2.3   Digital Libraries for Children

The work on the International Children's DL (ICDL) focusses on providing interfaces for searching and browsing the Digital Library in a manner appropriate for children. Reuter and Druin [10] found that children were able to navigate hierarchies in browsing, but that visual Boolean search, which had been developed to avoid the need for correctly-spelled keywords, remained generally underused. Visual/graphical DL interfaces have also been successfully employed for an Indian village DL aimed at user groups with low textual literacy [11]. The social aspect of book finding has begun to be explored for inter-generational co-design in digital libraries [12], though the collaborative aspects are still ill-supported in existing DL.

3   Method

We invited 17 families to visit both a library and a bookshop, to observe how they interacted with the physical space, bookshelves and books. The focus for this study was on the book selection process of the family group.

We interviewed families pre- and post- observation, and members of the family groups at times interacted directly with the researcher in an informal talk-aloud style. The pre-interview involved meeting with the parent and child/ren at their home or at a location chosen by the family. The aim of the first meeting was twofold: researchers would be involved in the whole process of planning the visit and the visit itself, and the child/ren could build confidence and familiarity with the researcher and therefore would be more likely to have natural interactions during the observations. This meeting also gave the opportunity for the researcher to conduct an interview with the parent covering basic demographic information as well as the types of books they have in their home and the reading behaviours of the family.

The observations occurred at both libraries and bookshops located in Hamilton and Tauranga, New Zealand. Each family chose the bookshop and library that they would visit during the study. The researcher encouraged each familiy to choose a bookshop and library to visit based on familiarity of the envirionments to the family. Three different libraries were visited, two in Hamilton (Garden Place Library – F1 & F3, and Chartwell Library – F2) and one library in Tauranga (Tauranga City Library – F4 – F17). All families chose to visit the children's sections of the library except for group F4 with an 11 year old boy who chose to visit the Teen Section of the Tauranga City Library. Five different book shops were chosen by the families, Whitcoulls, Center Place Hamilton (F1), Books for Kids, Hamilton (F2, F3), Books a Plenty, Tauranga

(F4, F5, F12), Whitcoulls, Davenport Rd, Tauranga (F6, F7, F10, F11, F13, F14, F17), and Paper Plus, Grey St, Tauranga (F8, F9, F15, F16). Whitcoulls and Paper Plus are both nationwide chain book stores in New Zealand, while Books a Plenty is a Tauranga based independent book seller and Books for Kids is Hamilton based independent bookshop speacialising in books for children. All book shops were single-storey buildings; the chain stores were considerably bigger than the independent bookshops.

The observations involved the researcher following the family group during the process of selecting books and noting the interactions that occur in the book selection process.It was explained to participants that they were in no way obliged to purchase or loan a book at any stage. The researcher followed the parent and child/ren for the complete duration of their visit to the library or bookshop. Our researcher noted how the participants moved around the physical space, which shelves they looked at, what features of the books they used to help them with selecting, and their interactions with each other.

The researcher was a silent participant during the visits, unless directly engaged by a family member. Sometimes the children interacted with the researcher, usually in a 'stream-of-consciousness' type of explanation of their activities, about their selection decisions and book preferences. One child in group F13 read the blurb of a book to the researcher and the child in F2 asked the researcher to read him a book he had selected.

Finally, a short semi-structured interview followed the observation to gain further understanding of the interactions that had been observed.

3.1   Participant Sample

Seventeen family groups participated in the study, each of which completed an observational session in a public library and a bookshop. Participant families were recruited through personal invitation, via word of mouth and through a general participant call. No selection criteria was applied to the participant families that responded to the recruitment invitations. It is likely that only active readers agreed or self selected to participate in the study. Discussion of the reading habits of the participants is outlined in Section 4.1 of our paper.

In the 17 family groups there were a total of 35 children; 22 male and 13 female. Six of the children were alone with the parent, seven were in pairs and 4 were in groups of 3 or 4 children (see Table 1). The children's ages ranged from 2 years to 11 years, with most children between 5 and 11 years. All accompanying adults except two were mothers (F1 was a female Au Pair and F12 was the father in this family). The observations were scheduled at the convenience of the families who volanteered to participate without remuneration. For this reason, the families nominated the parent(s) or guardian(s) who would participate in the study with their children. While we did not sitpulate when observations should be conducted, all families chose to participate in the observations before 5pm on a week day and this may be indicative of the choice of which guardian or parent participated.

Table 1. Overview of all participant groups

Family	F1	F2	F3	F4	F5	F6	F7	F8	F9	F10	F11	F12	F13	F14	F15	F16	F17
Parent	P(F)	P(F)	P(F)	P(F)	P(F)	P(F)	P(F)	P(F)	P(F)	P(F)	P(F)	P(M)	P(F)	P(F)	P(F)	P(F)	P(F)
Children	A(M,2) B(M,5)	A(M,3)	A(M,4)	A(M,11)	A(F,5) B(F,9)	A(F,7) B(M,9) C(M,11)	A(M,5) B(F,9) C(F,11)	A(M,9)	A(M,6) B(M,9)	A(M,2) B(F,9)	A(F,5) B(M,9)	A(M,5) B(F,7) C(M,10a) D(M,10b)	A(F,9) B(F,11)	A(M,6) B(M,7) C(M,8) D(F,9)	A(M10)	A(M,7) B(F,8)	A(M,9)

4   Results

Here we present the results of our interviews and observations.

4.1   Interviews

In the initial interview, families with children of up to nine years old reported to read with their child either daily or every second day. Most of the 10 and 11 year olds still read frequently, but independently of their parents. Nine families read with at least one of the children daily, one family twice a week, five families 3 or 4 times a week and 2 families had children who were now independent readers only. Five of the 15 families who read with their youngest children also described their older children as independent readers who did not participate in the shared reading with the parents. 11 parents stated they personally read daily, four parents stated they read two to three times a week, one parent stated twice a week and one parent stated they read once a week.

The frequency of visits to the library varied greatly across the 17 families (see Fig.1). Over half of the families would visit the library once or more during a month. Some commented that while as a family they may only visit once a month, or less frequently throughout the year, over school holidays they would visit every week as part of a school holiday programme. Three of the families responded that they would visit the mobile library as a family once a fortnight, but their child would visit the school library with their class every week. Overall, participants reported on visiting a bookshop less frequently than a library. One participant described that the family would visit a bookshop together only when they had a voucher (no frequency was given). One mother said she would only visit a bookshop without her children.

4.2   Observations

The researcher went together with the families to the bookshops and libraries. From the pre-observation interviews we learned that only two families (F2 & F4) indicated that they were not looking for anything in particular this day, either in the library or the bookshop, and just wanted to browse. Nine families (F1, F5, F6, F7, F8, F12, F13, F16) had a particular series in mind to look for. Six families were interested in books by a specific author(F9, F10, F12, F13, F14, F17).Eight families were intending to look for books on a particular subject(F3, F6, F7, F10, F11, F12, F15, F17), and only 2 had a specific title in mind that they wanted to search for(F8 & F14).

The length of time for the observations in a library ranged from 15 to 60 minutes with a mean length of 40.8 minutes. Most observations lasted approximately 45 minutes. The length of time for the observations in a bookshop ranged from 10 to 45 minutes with a mean length of 18.8 minutes. Most observations lasted approximately 15 minutes.

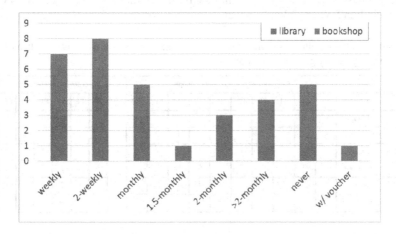

Fig. 1. Frequency of family visits to library and bookshops

There was no correlation between age of children and the length of time they spent in the bookshop or library. F1 with a 2 and a 5 year old spent 45 minutes in the library, while F2 with a 2 year old spent only 20 minutes. Neither did the number of children determine the length of the stay, nor their habit of regularly visiting the library (F3 went every week and F4 went never though both groups stayed for 45 minutes in the library).

Collaborative vs Individual Search. The observed searching for, interacting with, and decision about books were considered to be collaborative if the child/ren interacted with the parent or asked the librarian or bookshop person for assistance. We analysed the predominant interaction pattern of each family group for bookshop and library, resulting in the overview shown in Table 2. 61 of 102 possible interaction types were collaborative or used a mixture of collaborative and individual searching, interacting or decision making.

Table 2. Individual (I, blue) vs collaborative (C, orange) interaction patterns (* indicates mix)

	Family	F1	F2	F3	F4	F5	F6	F7	F8	F9	F10	F11	F12	F13	F14	F15	F16	F17
Search	Library	C	I	C	I	I	I	I	C	I	C	I	C	C	I	C	I	C
	Bookshop	C	C	I	I	I	C	C	I	C	C	I	C	I	I	C	I	C
Interaction	Library	C	C	C	C	C	I	I	*	I	I	I	I	I	C	C	I	C
	Bookshop	C	C	C	I	*	I	C	I	C	C	C	C	*	C	I	I	I
Decisions	Library	C	C	C	I	*	I	C	*	C	I	I	C	*	I	I	I	C
	Bookshop	C	C	C	I	*	*	*	C	*	*	*	C	*	*	I	*	C

When we consider the reading ability of young children, it is perhaps unsurprising that for the children who were 5 years and younger, collaborative search was the prominent method of identifying books. In our study 9 of the children were 5 years old or younger. Therefore when we re-contextualize Table 2 we see in Table 3 that while collaborative decision making decreases substantially in both bookshops and libraries, collaborative search in the library is still common for families who do not include children 5 years old or younger.

Table 3. Individual (I, blue) vs collaborative (C, orange) interaction patterns (* indicates mix) broken down by family groups with younger members

		Families with 5 year olds and younger										Families all members 5 years old+						
	Family	F1	F2	F3	F5	F7	F9	F10	F11	F12	F14	F4	F6	F8	F13	F15	F16	F17
Search	Library	C	I	C	I	I	I	C	I	C	I	I	I	C	C	C	I	C
	Bookshop	C	C	I	I	C	C	C	I	C	I	I	C	I	I	C	I	C
Interaction	Library	C	C	C	C	I	I	I	I	I	C	C	I	*	I	C	I	C
	Bookshop	C	C	C	*	C	C	C	C	C	C	I	I	I	*	I	I	I
Decisions	Library	C	C	C	*	C	C	I	I	C	I	I	I	*	*	I	I	C
	Bookshop	C	C	C	*	*	*	*	*	C	*	I	*	C	*	I	*	C

Observed Behaviour Patterns. The level of involvement of parents with the children in both the library and bookshop visits varied greatly. At younger ages parents were generally highly involved with the child's book search, and also spent time to read with them or discuss the content of books (e.g., F1, F2, F4). Above a certain age the parental involvement went one of two ways: parents were either still highly involved, or left their children to be largely independent while they conducted their own search in the library or bookshop, or relaxed on a couch. Several parents (5 of 17) assisted their children in the library with their search for books by teaching them or introducing them to a library facility or book features that they had not previously used. Two of the parents (F13 and F15) showed their children of 9 & 11 years and 10 years, respectively, how to use the Dewey decimal system to help them find non-fiction books in a particular subject area they were interested. Another adult (F1) showed a 5 year old how to use the catalogue to find books in a series by a particular author, and helped him write down the reference and find to books on the shelf. One parent (F10) showed her children, 7 and 9 years, where the "Recent Returns" shelf was and suggested that this was a way to find books that were popular. A fifth parent explained to a 6 and 7 year old that reading the blurb on the back of a book can help with trying to decide if the book will be of interest (F14). Perhaps an effect of the self selection of the participants in our study, many of the parents appeared to be confident library users who supported their children in searching and showed knowledge in library and bookshop layout and use.

Overall, a wider range of actions were conducted in libraries (see Fig.2) and many more reading-related activities were likely to occur in a library. The library is also used as a place to read books. Both more reading-related activities and more play was happening in the bookshops.

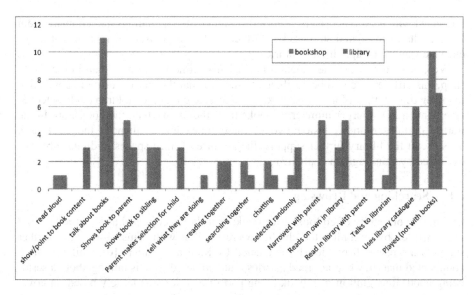

Fig. 2. Actions of children

Book Sampling Behaviour. The observed book sampling behaviours (in both libraries and bookshops) did not seem to be age specific. The main exception was the reading of the back cover (13 instances), which was mostly done by older children (aged 8-11 years). The youngest children in the study who were observed reading a book's back cover were 6 and 7 years old. They had just learned about it from their mother (F14) who encouraged them to read the blurb on the back of the book. The front cover was used by children across all ages (34 instances), with many children using the cover not just for initially deciding to look at the book (and taking the book off the shelf), but also as the sole means for assessing the content of the book. The mother of a 5 year girl stated that "[the girl] usually picks books with "girly covers" like animals or babies" (F11). The back cover was also used (13 instances) and use of the spine (6 instances) during book sampling. We also noted page-by-page flipping (16 instances), full book page flipping (7 instances) and use of the title or author (13 instances) during decision making by children. Illustrations found within the book were also observed to be used as a regular feature (12 instances) to help children determine if they would like to read a book. Comments made by the two children who noted the number of pages in a book (2 instances) seemed to indicate that it was a way for them to assess how appropriate that book would be for their reading level or age. All of these sampling behaviours were conducted by the children, at times independently, or encouraged by the parent or older children in the group and at times as a method for sharing a decision or seeking guidance.

5   Discussion

We analysed the observation and interview data to determine how participants looked for books, how they interacted with books, how they made decisions, and how they interacted with each other. Here we briefly summarise our findings and compare them with results from related studies. We further explore how these insights might influence the way we design digital libraries.

We observed that families spent a much longer time in libraries than in the bookshop; this difference could be attributed to the fact that the space was more conducive to taking time with exploring and making choices, and that the children could select to take home a much larger number of books from the library than the bookshop. In the library our observations lasted two to three times longer than in the bookshop. This use of the library further supports the premise of third spaces in digital libraries discussed by Cunningham et al. [13].

5.1   Searching and Browsing

Children in our study often looked for books that they recognised as being a part of a series written by an author the children were familiar with. This observation further supports the research previously conducted by Raqi and Zainab [6]. Children often commented that they had not read a series, but had heard friends talking about a series being good. Recognition of a book being part of a series was largely based on cover images or spine. Older children also knew that more information about a series could be available inside a book, where they looked for a list of other books in the series. Younger children also seemed to be drawn to books that were a part of a series, these books were commonly associated with a character with which they were familiar.

Collaborative search for books involved a parent and child walking along the shelves together, or two siblings looking for books in the same series, or an older sibling helping a younger sibling to find the book they want, or a parent showing a child/ren how to look for books in the library in a certain way. For most of the observed family groups, the search process appeared generally more collaborative in libraries than in bookshops. Our study provides here additional data, and confirms the findings from Cunningham [1].

Different from Raqi and Zainab [6] we also observed group members that were asking for help in using a library catalogue or a book feature. Only a very small number of children used the catalogue search in the library (6 groups) or asked for assistance from a staff member to search for books (6 in the library and 1 in the bookshop), preferring to browse the shelves to find what they are looking for. The child in family group F7 illustrated this behaviour when searching the shelves for a specific author without success and stated, "It will turn up". This preference for browsing and trust in visual serendipity may indicate that either children or parents find the catalogue keyword search (as also typically used in digital libraries) not to be an effective tool. Equally, it might mean that they had never tried or are unaware of the catalogue search. While we did not probe the reasons for this lack of catalogue use or interaction with staff, investigation into this will be of further interest to researchers in developing solutions for digital libraries.

5.2   Interactions with Books

Front covers, back covers and illustrations were all book features used by participants when interacting with the books and deciding which books they were interested in issuing or purchasing. Large et al. [2] suggested that in a family situation either the 'sequential access' of flipping through the pages to find information or the 'selective access' of using the content or the index of a book to look for information are most commonly used to determine if a book will be good to read. In our observations both of these methods were used, however, 'sequential access' was predominant. Only one participant used a table of contents and none were observed to use an index. The most common type of 'selective access' was used by the older children in our study who were looking at the list of books in a series, printed at either the front or back of the book. Many children also read books aloud, or asked their parents to read to them. This was not necessarily for decision making, but rather a form of book consumption.

5.3   Decision Making

The age of the child seemed be the biggest factor when making decisions about which books to select. Age was used as an indicator of 'appropriateness'. For older children the decision making process was generally done individually, whereas for younger children this was more often done in collaboration with a parent. Children seemed very aware of which age section they should be looking in. Some of the younger children did look at chapter books and picture books but only the older children (10-11 years) went to the teenage section, others walked past it straight to the non-fiction books. Cunningham [1] observed visual cues in libraries and bookshops to indicate the age for which the books are suitable. We similarly observed that libraries and shops conveyed a geography that related to age and classification groupings.

5.4   Social Interactions

In the library the majority of interactions revolved around selecting books or sitting down to read a chosen book. In the bookshops, many interactions revolved around either sharing funny parts of a book or reading a passage out loud. It also seemed that families were more likely to share a snippet from a book if they were not going to leave the library or store with the book. Some families stayed in the bookshop or library to read together: four families read in the library, and only one family read in the bookshop. The family reading in the bookshop did so in an area that provided beanbags for customers. Typical of New Zealand libraries, spaces for casual reading were supplied in all libraries that the families visited. Seating is not often found in New Zealand bookshops and this was also the case in those visited by families in our study, only one of the bookshops had a seating area for casual reading. For seven-family groups, the behaviour patterns observed seemed to vary between the library and the bookshop, such as family group F10 who went from partaking in collaborative search, individual interaction and individual decisions in the library to being in the bookshop where they were searching individually, interacting collaboratively and then making individual decisions.

5.5   Limitations and Further Work

The nature of the participant recruitment may be a factor influencing the type of participants that formed the sample of this study. It was likely that families who were active readers, and inevitably active users of libraries and bookshops would opt to participate in such a study. This may have resulted in a narrow view of shared use of these spaces. Arguably, however, these regular users of physical libraries and book-shops may also be, or become, the regular users of DL's in the future because of their typical reading practices.

The single visit to each environment with each family may also have given only a small sample of how a family typically uses these spaces. The impact of being observed may too have influenced interactions. A longitudinal study with a smaller sample of families is warranted in the extension of this work.

Our study focused on family wide interactions and does not follow individual members of the group. How individuals, specifically individual children, use these spaces would be of interest and benefit to the development of Digital Libraries. Equally, our recruitment did not attempt to ensure a spread of male and female guardians. Future studies may benefit from analysis of how, or if, different use of these spaces by different role models exists. Indeed, also of interest is if different role models interact with the children in these spaces differently.

It has been suggested by a reviewer of this paper that future work in this area may include interviewing librarians and bookshop personnel as experts to gain insight into our findings. We see this as sound advice and agree that such a comparison of experts' observations to our own will garner further implications for the development of future systems. We expect that there is also a need to further probe families about the use of digital or expert knowledge that is available in these environments and when and why these systems or experts are or are not used.

6   Conclusions: Implications for Digital Libraries

This paper reports on a study in which we explored how 17 families select books for leisure reading in both bookshops and public libraries. Currently, much of our understanding of how an eBook should look and feel comes from generalizations about books and assumptions about the needs of those individuals who read them. Our paper explored how children and adults search and browse for books together.

We now analyse the implications of our observations on the design of eBooks and Digital Libraries. Our interviews revealed the need for inter-generational reading environments for children up to the age of 10, who still read daily with their parents. We found that 10 and 11 year olds still read frequently, but more independently of their parents and may not need regular inter-generational support in a DL. This was also supported by our observations which showed that these young children were supported by their parents in their searches, while the older children were either supported or allowed to independently search. When a child conducted independent searches, adults often conducted their own searches, thus suggesting the need to facilitate parents' use of the DL even as the child becomes an independent searcher.

1. Strong Visual References. The lack of catalogue search and the predominance of visual browsing as well as decision making based on cover images and illustrations, suggest that a digital library that caters for families needs to have very strong visual references to support decision making by young and old family members. We agree with the suggestion by Large et al. [2] that searches in digital libraries for children should not rely on linguistic methods but rather use visual indicators such as cover images. We would suggest designers of digital libraries for inter-generational use to go further and include other visual cues. These additional visual cues may include example illustrations and indication of the number of illustrations contained in a book and the size of a book, all of which might help families generate conversation around book content. Colour seems to have been understood by several children as an indicator for interesting books, and a digital library could support browsing based on colour.

2. Clear Geography. Children seem to take their cues about the appropriateness or suitability of books not just from cover images and illustrations (addressed in 1. above), but also from the spatial layout of the physical library. A digital library similarly might incorporate spatial areas for different ages, and sections for non-fiction and fiction books that are clearly visually marked. Similarly areas of related topics might be indicated visually. The ability to present information in a number of ways in a digital environment allows for overlapping geographies that serve the needs of family members of different age groups. Cunningham [1] previously noted that these spatial or geographical areas need to be consistent to support recognition.

3. Physicality of eBooks. Children in our study noted the length of books by either checking the number of pages or by estimating their length from the thickness of the spine. This is common in studies of both children and adults. A digital library needs to have a clear visual encoding of the length of a book to serve family members in making selection decisions.

4. Series and Recurring Characters. Children were very keen on identifying books in a series. In a digital library, these connections between books should be identifiable and be visually clear. Because authors of books for children and youth often write for a number of age and interest levels, the ability to identify other books by an author, within a series or with a relationship to a family members interests would likely also serve other family members. Again, groups of books with similar bibliographic metadata should be presented spatially close.

5. Social Interaction and Recommendations. Many children selected books based on recommendations from friends, teachers or parents. In a DL, this would require some means of awareness of other people so that one could have information about books others read, or feedback on known or similar books. These might be restricted to a selected group such as family or school class, or open, similar to social, or commercial systems. Other social interaction observed in both library and bookshops were children exploring individually and returning to parents to show their finds or to receive help with selecting. Supporting these actions in a digital library means going beyond the concept of a child as the isolated user. The digital equivalent might not be restricted to synchronous interactions, so that, for example, grandparents could participate with their grandchildren in selecting books when not physically co-located.

6. Reading Together. A number of family groups were observed reading together in the library or bookshops.Shared reading of interactive books enhance the ability for adults and children to engage in meaningful shared reading experiences that draw on both physical and intellectual enhancements in the stories to encourage discussion about the story and illustrations and the asking of questions[14]. Reading out loud or shared reading could be easily supported and would be of interest to small children who cannot read themselves. The support for the social interaction of being read to by a parent is harder to incorporate. Being able to record readings for a child might open new opportunities for relatives who live far away. As an extension of (5.) above, synchronous but remote interaction in which a child selects a book and a, say, grandparent may record a reading or that book, may open up new opportunities for social interaction involving books.

We suggest here design extensions to digital libraries that go beyond designing for children only, but rather embrace the concept of a library as a third place for shared family use. We noted previously that bookshops are predominantly social spaces / third places with the social uses of these spaces addressing more than just book search or book purchasing needs [13]. Our suggestions address how to incorporate this aspect of libraries and bookshops for families using digital libraries.

Acknowledgements. We would like to thank the Tauranga and Hamilton libraries and bookshops for their support for this study along with Mrs Phillips for her invaluable assistance recruiting participant families. We acknowledge the support of the University of Waikato and our summer student research scholar, Laura Phillips, who admirably and capably conducted all observations.

References

1. Cunningham, S.J.: Children in the physical collection: Implications for the digital library. Proc. Am. Soc. Inf. Sci. Technol. 48, 1–10 (2011)
2. Large, A., Nesset, V., Beheshti, J.: Children as information seekers: what researchers tell us. New Rev. Child. Lit. Librariansh. 14, 121–140 (2008)
3. Nadelson, S.G., Nadelson, L.S.: In Search of the Right Book: Considerations in Common Read Book Selection. J. Coll. Read. Learn. 43, 60–66 (2012)
4. Gross, M.: Children's information seeking at school: Findings from a qualitative study. Youth Inf.-Seek. Behav. Theor. Models Issues, 211–240 (2004)
5. Environics Research Group: Young Canadians in a wired world: Phase I. Ott. Media Aware. Netw. MNet (2001) (retrieved September 29, 2002)
6. Raqi, S.A., Zainab, A.N.: Observing Strategies Used by Children When Selecting Books to Browse, Read or Borrow. J. Educ. Media Libr. Sci. 45 (2008)
7. Shenton, A.K., Dixon, P.: Sequential or selective access? Young people's strategies for finding information in non-fiction books. New Rev. Child. Lit. Librariansh. 9, 57–69 (2003)
8. Foggett, T.: Information literacy at the primary school level? Aust. Libr. J. 52, 55–63 (2003)
9. Hinze, A., Alqurashi, H., Vanderschantz, N., Timpany, C., Alzahrani, S.: Social Information Behaviour in Physical Libraries: Implications for the design of digital libraries. In: 2014 IEEE/ACM Joint Conference on Digital Libraries (JCDL), London, 10p. IEEE (in press, 2014)

10. Reuter, K., Druin, A.: Bringing together children and books: An initial descriptive study of children's book searching and selection behavior in a digital library. Proc. Am. Soc. Inf. Sci. Technol. 41, 339–348 (2004)

11. Jones, M., Harwood, W., Buchanan, G., Lalmas, M.: Storybank: an indian village community digital library. In: Proceedings of the 7th ACM/IEEE Joint Conference on Digital Libraries (JCLD), pp. 257–258. ACM (2007)

12. Guha, M.L., Druin, A., Fails, J.A.: Cooperative inquiry revisited: Reflections of the past and guidelines for the future of intergenerational co-design. Int. J. Child-Comput. Interact. 1, 14–23 (2013)

13. Cunningham, S.J., Vanderschantz, N., Timpany, C., Hinze, A., Buchanan, G.: Social Information Behaviour in Bookshops: Implications for Digital Libraries. In: Aalberg, T., Papatheodorou, C., Dobreva, M., Tsakonas, G., Farrugia, C.J. (eds.) TPDL 2013. LNCS, vol. 8092, pp. 84–95. Springer, Heidelberg (2013)

14. Timpany, C., Vanderschantz, N., Hinze, A., Cunningham, S.J., Wright, K.: Shared Reading of Interactive Children's Books. In: Tuamsuk, K., Jatowt, A., Rasmussen, E. (eds.) ICADL 2014. LNCS, vol. 8839, Springer, Heidelberg (2014)

Shared Reading of Children's Interactive Picture Books

Claire Timpany, Nicholas Vanderschantz, Annika Hinze,
Sally Jo Cunningham, and Kristy Wright

Dept. of Computer Science, University of Waikato,
Private Bag 3105, Hamilton New Zealand
{ctimpany,vtwoz,hinze,sallyjo}@waikato.ac.nz,
kaw37@students.waikato.ac.nz

Abstract. We report on a study of children and parents shared reading of interactive printed books. We investigated the differences between books with interactive features and books with expressive typography in order to evaluate which features within a book encouraged interaction between the reading participants and the book. 11 parent and child groups took part in the study that involved three observed reading sessions. From our observations we offer suggestions for the development of books and eBooks to encourage shared reading practices.

1   Introduction

The purpose of our study was to observe and subsequently evaluate shared reading between children and parents. By focusing on differences between books with interactive features and books with expressive typography, the aim of our study was to evaluate which features within a book aided interaction both between the shared reading participants and with the physical book. Children's books are an important learning device for young readers. In a picture book the words and illustrations are equally important to the story. Both pictures and words work together to create one unified story [1]. Picture books are not simply limited to supporting literacy, but instead promote wider-learning through aspects of problem solving, socialization, hand eye coordination, creativity and an understanding of the world [2]. Interactive eBooks and digital libraries provide opportunities for developing books and collections that enhance the interactive reading experience and could further enhance the shared reading experience.

2   Related Work

The significant related work to our study includes the literature around shared reading, interactive books and pictures, and expressive typography.

2.1   Shared Reading

We here consider shared reading to be the activity of a child and adult reading together. This practice is recommended "to promote students' understanding and engagement

K. Tuamsuk et al. (Eds.): ICADL 2014, LNCS 8839, pp. 196–207, 2014.

with a text" [3]. Shared reading builds on the act of reading aloud which is beneficial for enabling children to hear language fluency, broaden their vocabulary and improve their knowledge of the world [4], in reading aloud situations the child is more passive than in a shared reading experience.In shared reading adults act as mediators and helping in the transition between the child not being able to read, and the child reading independently. Shared reading, consequently, is an important learning tool, promoting discussion, questions and a fun learning environment.

Participating in shared reading extends traditional schooling practices, teaching the child that they become a partner in communication when interacting with text [5]. This means that shared print experiences do not only enhance literacy development, but the communication skills of the child in general. Certain features and criteria enable shared-reading to be more productive. A book chosen for shared reading should invite involvement from both the child and the parent[2]. The language within the book should be age appropriate, and should support the child in reading and understanding the book. This means that the child is not required to know or understand all of the words and meanings within the book to gain from the reading experience. Reutzel and Cooter discuss how "shared reading books should have literary merit, engaging content, (both fiction and non-fiction) and high interest" [7].The act of shared reading can be undertaken in a variety of ways, with the general consensus being that any form of shared reading is better than none at all. However, Girolametto & Weitzman discuss three key behaviours and their associated techniques designed to gain responses from young readers and promote further learning and engagement: child-oriented behaviours, interaction-promoting behaviours, and language-modelling behaviours [8]. These responsive behaviours rely on parents reacting to situations and taking action accordingly and are expanded on by Ezell and Justice [8] in the context of shared reading.

- *Child Oriented Behaviours* "follow the child's lead, pace and topic" [8]. In a shared reading environment, this means responding to the child's engagement and encouraging them to take the lead. This is important for promoting independent questions and observations from the child. The potential interactions of the child vary greatly according to the child, ability, understanding and willingness to engage.
- *Interaction-Promoting Behaviours* "are used by responsive adults to engage children in conversation" [8]. This behaviour is utilised to encourage interaction and engagement from children who are somewhat reserved from the reading session. By asking the child thought-provoking questions, specifically who, what, when, where, why and how [8], the child will become more involved in the shared reading session. Interaction-promoting behaviours have the potential to encourage children to initiate interactions with books. Utilizing interaction-promoting behaviours effectively can therefore lead to child-oriented behaviours as the child instigates the discussion, resulting in a wider range of shared reading techniques and therefore greater potential for learning.
- *Language Modelling Behaviours* are "used by responsive adults to extend children's language and literacy involvement to provide models of more advanced forms and features of oral and written language" [6]. This is seen most commonly through pointing to and identifying features of the story and book – whether it is objects,

characters, letters or other features within the picture book. This labelling provides clarity and understanding in the context of the picture book, as applied to concepts in the child's environment [8].

2.2   Importance of Pictures

Bloom [9] states that children think and learn through both the words and pictures. Including imagery within a children's book enables a child to grasp concrete ideas through the "cross over and discovery of meaning in nonverbal representations" [10]. Pictures are a representation of the story, allowing children to grasp meaning even when the literature itself is above their reading ability. Within picture books, "art contributes so much to the emotional and cognitive impact of a story" [11]. The images help to convey emotions, reactions, and body language to children. These are important social and behavioural skills to learn from a young age. Consequently, the appropriate design and composition of images on the page is essential to a successful, engaging children's picture book.

2.3   Interactive Books

At the most basic level, interactivity within books can be understood as becoming aware of "a book's unique physical structure, [bringing attention] to the momentous moment: the turning of the page" [12]. However, 'interactive' is a broad term that encompasses a wide range of variables. Bongers & van der Veer discuss how "an interaction can be described in several layers, taking the user from a goal and intention, formulating a task and subtasks, carrying out these actions whilst receiving feedback on the physical level, and evaluating the result" [13]. 'Interaction' varies greatly between children and other age groups[14]. From a previous survey of children's interactive books, we observed that interactivity is a continuum with books demanding different types of interaction so that the content can be consumed by the reader. Interactive books include features that engage the reader in either physical of intellectual interactions with the books and its content [15]. Physical interactions can occur at different levels, from pop-ups and opening additional pages to lifting flaps, tactile content or creating or re-arranging content. Intellectual interaction can guide the reader in a non-linear course through content, get them to solve puzzles or make decisions to effect the outcome of the story. How we understand which books engage a child in either physical or intellectual interactive experiences is discussed by Timpany and Vanderschantz [16] where they explain thatmost interactive books only appeal to just one area or the other.

Digital interactive books offer new opportunities for added interactive value not available in printed books. The level of interaction in different types of digital books ranges from basic interactions in eBooks, video, audio and interactive elemnts in enhanced books and interactive eBooks where engagement with the storyline is increased beyond the experience available in printed media[17]. Itzkovitch[17] explain that in digital books there is the opportunity to create meaningful interaciotns which enhance the engagement with the storyline in ways that printed books cannot, but the value of this interactive ability is yet to be fully explored.

From current understanding of what interactive books are in both printed and digital environments, we can broadly define them as books which use physical or intellectual enhancements to engage the reader in activities that enhance the storyline.

2.4   Expressive Typography

Expressive typography refers to typography that differs in some form from the typical, typed text. Phinney and Colabucci discuss the varying types of expressive typography, listing variations of typeface or the size, style (weight or italics), colour, or position of the type [16]. They stress that expressive typography is not limited to plain text, and that it can be a substitute for illustrations or literary devices to advance the story [16]. They found that the inclusion of expressive typography within children's books is often used to emphasise specific elements of the story [16], and is used as both a literary device and to provide a point of interest. Thus the typography itself may mimic the illustrative style of the book, may relate to the message of the story, or may provide the reader context for further understanding of the word or story in general. Therefore we can define expressive typography in books as being the elaboration or variation of typography to enhance the meaning of the words and the story reading experience.

3   Study Methodology

For this study, 11 families were invited to participate in a total of three, half hour shared-reading observation sessions. The participants were recruited through the personal contacts of the researchers. The citieria for selection was that child was aged between 4 and 7, and the family were comfortable angaging in shared reading for the purpose of this study.

The Sessions. These sessions were video recorded and manual field notes were made by the researcher. Each session included an observation of shared reading and a post-observation semi-structured interview. An initial interview was conducted by the researcher before the first observation session. This interview recorded demographic information and sought an understanding of the child and parents' reading habits. Interviews and observations were conducted with all 11 families by the same researcher in the homes at times that were selected by the families.

After the initial interview, the child and parent then took part in the first observation, a shared reading of the control book, 'Edward the Emu' by Sheena Knowles. After the parent and child had read the book they were asked questions about interactions they had engaged in while reading and what each of them liked most about the book they had just read. Information about the reading environment, duration of the session and the time of day were noted by the researcher after each observation.

The second session involved the researcher observing the parent and child participating in shared reading with three interactive books. Two of these books were chosen by the child and parent from the child's current collection. The researcher asked the participants to select books that the participants believed to contain interactive elements. The third book – 'Blue 2' by David Carter - was provided by the researcher as a control book. Observations focused on how the interactive elements of the book affected the way the readers used the book and read the story. After each book, the researcher conducted a short semi-structured interview asking them about how they used the features of the book and what they liked most about it.

The third observation was run in the same way as the second, but with three books that contained expressive typography. The participants selected two books from their own collection which they deemed to contain expressive typography. The third book was provided by the researcher – '*Beautiful Oops*' by Barney Saltzberg. The observations of the shared reading conducted using these books again focused on recording details about the interactions the parent and child had with the book as well as with each other and how the use of expressive typography within the book influenced these interactions. Again a semi-structured interview followed the observations.

In all interviews, questions considered interactions driven by physical enhancement or intellectual enhancement in the book, as well as non-book driven interactions.

The Books. We describe here the books used for the observations. *Edward the Emu* was chosen as the control book for its appealing illustration and story. This children's picture book provides no features that encourage interaction, meaning that interaction must be driven purely by the parent and child within the shared reading environment. *Blue 2* is an interactive children's book that features pop-ups, and requires the reader to search for the blue '2' on each page by following the written clues. These written clues are somewhat abstract, and do not read with the same flow or story structure as a typical children's book. The interactive books chosen by the parents from their personal collections included search-and-find books, pop-up or lift-the-flap books, and books that included toys, puppets and different textures. The expressive typography within *Beautiful Oops* is based on a hand-drawn approach that attempts to mimic a child's writing and drawing. In contrast, the books chosen by parents from their personal collections included more typical examples of expressive typography: changes in font, size, colour, and placement of text.

The Participants. Our participant sample included 11 parents and their children who were aged between 3 and 6 years old. Table 1 details our participant sample. When asked in a pre-interview about their current reading practices all participants stated that they take part in shared reading with their children on a daily basis. Nine of the 11 children look at books independently every day, and the remaining two would use books independently once a week (E & K).

Table 1. Participant Sample

ID	A	B	C	D	E	F	G	H	I	J	K
Age	4	3	4	5	4	3	6	4	6	5	6
Child	F	M	M	M	F	F	F	M	F	F	M
Parent	F	F	F	M	F	F	F	F	F	F	M

4   Results

We discuss here the results of our three interview and observation sessions.

4.1   Control Picture Book - *Edward the Emu*

Even though the control book included no elements of book-driven interaction, ten of the parents asked children questions throughout the shared reading. In addition, eight of the eleven children asked their parents questions throughout the observation session. Nine of the children also interacted with the book by physically touching the pages, whilst seven of the children pointed out elements within the book throughout the shared reading sessions. When asked what their favourite part of the book was, all of the children participants chose the illustrations. Five of the children also stated that they enjoyed the message of the book, and were able to easily identify the message as 'the importance of being true to yourself'. When parents were asked the same question, they mentioned that they enjoyed the illustrations (eight parents), the rhyming and rhythm of the text (six), the overall message or moral of the story (four) and the overall level of the book and easy readability (three).

4.2   Interactive Books

Each family was observed with *Blue 2* and twoadditional interactive books from their personal collection. Written clues used in *Blue 2* are somewhat abstract and are grouped in threes, and do not read with the same flow or story structure as typical children's books. Consequently, when reading through the book, one parent did not even realise that the book contained text until almost half way through. A total of four of the eleven parents found the story difficult to read due to vocabulary and flow of text, and consequently the physical interaction rather than the shared reading was the focus. All participants, both children and parents, physically interacted with *Blue 2* throughout the observed reading sessions.

Five of the parents were concerned by the delicate and intricate nature of *Blue 2*, these included the parents of two three-year-olds, two four-year-olds and one five-year-old. Parent B stated that the book was "maybe too delicate for the age" (3years) and parent D said they were "worried about it breaking". All five parents stated that they changed their interactions due to the delicate nature of the book. This was observed as the parent undertaking the interactions rather than the child and the parent encouraging the child just to watch, which was not observed with other interactive books.

Two of the eleven parents enjoyed the fact that *Blue 2* could be read differently each time, by reading it out of order or by finding different features to talk about each time, including both the physical aspects of the book and the story line. Parent D stated that the book enabled you to "re-read it without getting bored", and Parent J stated that you "could read it differently every time".

Two of the parents stated that the interactive books that they owned (lift the flaps) were no longer read or fully utilised by the child because the interactive features are superficial to the story and tend to have little or no impact on the way the story is read. Parent D stated about his child that "when he was younger and looking at pictures he would flip them to be involved, but now he focuses just on the story. If the flaps were more important to the story they would be more effective". It is relevant to note that Parent D commented on the ability to read *Blue 2* differently each time and the importance of this within the shared reading environment. Parent G believed that 'lift the flap' features are "only good if they can't read on their own" as they often only include added illustrated content, rather than adding to the story.

Six of the children stated that finding the *Blue 2* was their favourite part of the book, whilst the remaining five children pointed to specific pages that they believed were the best. Similarly, when asked why the pop-up features were in the book, six of the children said that they were included to increase the complexity or difficulty of the book. Child I stated that the pop ups "make it hard to find and makes it fun" (I), whilst Child D stated that the pop up features "make [the book] more exciting … cool things to touch … I liked it because it was hard".

In six of the 22 observations involving the personal collection of interactive books, the children stated that the illustrations were their favourite aspects, while eleven of the children stated that the interactive elements were their favourite features.

4.3   Expressive Typography Books

Each family was observed with *Beautiful Oops* and two expressive typography books from their own collection. Only one parent stated that the expressive typography within *Beautiful Oops* changed the vocal expression they used when reading. In contrast, all parents noted that the expressive typography present in books from their personal collections affected the way that they read the text. For example, when observing the books from the personal collections, Parent F stated that the expressive typography made her "[place] emphasis on those specific words" and Parent B stated that the use of different sized typography changed the voice that she used when reading, "with big writing you read it louder, more impressive. With little text you use a little voice".

Three of the parents noted that *Beautiful Oops* had the potential to be read differently - both in subsequent reading sessions and as the child got older. Parent E stated that the expressive typography within the book would enable her to "talk about the text as she got older", allowing for a further explanation of the meaning of words and the relation between text and image. Only one parent (B) noted the potential for this within an expressive typography book that was from their collection.

Six of the parents were observed asking questions when reading *Beautiful Oops*, these included "what's that?" and "what does it look like?". Whilst the text of the book itself did not promote questions, the parents clearly believed that the nature of the imagery and layout lent itself to a question and answer interaction.

Within 14 of the 22 personal expressive typography books, the children stated that the illustrations were the favourite aspect of their books. Two of the children stated that they liked the story content, and five children that they enjoyed the rhythm of text and typography. Whilst the children could not identify the feature as 'typography' they were able to understand the basic concept. For example, child D made a "hissssssssssss" noise and stated that she liked how the 'sound' was "written on the page" in a shape that mimicked that of the snake illustration.

Beautiful Oops also included aspects of physical interactivity. Within *Beautiful Oops*, 7 of the children stated that the interactive features were their favourite, and the remaining 4 stated that the illustrations were their favourite features.

When asked what they believed the purpose of expressive typography was, all eleven children understood that it was designed to help you read as well as to change the way specific words were read. These comments ranged from aspects of shape and colour to verbal cues. "Makes you whisper and be loud", "The letters look the same as the dog". Parent D stated that the "text [was] too cramped" within one of their own personal collection expressive typography books. This made it confusing for his child to read. The researcher noted that the child (who was reading) was unsure which word or group of text was next in sequence due to the scattered nature of the text.

5   Discussion

We acknowledge the effect of having a third party observing the reading sessions may have had on the reading experience. This may be seen through the parent or child being engaged more or less, or in a different way to how they would usually interact because of the researchers presence or the video camera. The researcher endeavoured to be as unobtrusive as possible throughout the session.

Our study has shown that the fundamental elements of the children's book such as effective illustrations and clear typography continue to be successful if implemented, and the interactive elements and expressive typography will aslo be successful if implemented in ways suitable for children.

Illustrations remain an important aspect within children's books, as discussed by Gibbons [19], Bloom [9] and Piro [10]. The illustrative content is engaging and memorable, and in turn aids the child in understanding and enjoying the text. Over the 22 observations of personal expressive typography books 14 children stated that the illustrations were their favourite aspects, whilst similarly 6 children from the 22 observations of personal interactive books made the same claim about illustrations. 4 children also identified the illustrations as their favourite features within *Beautiful Oops*. All children stated that the illustrations were their favourite aspect of *Edward the Emu* - the control Picture Book. Consequently, when designing children's books, effective illustrations can be applied to a wide range of books, including those with elements of expressive typography and interactivity. It would also be recommended to implement physical and intellectual enhancements within these illustrations.

The three 'responsiveness' behaviours [8] (child-oriented behaviours, interaction-promoting behaviours and language-modelling behaviours) as discussed in Section 2.1 help to engage both parent and child in the process. However, unless a parent is taught how to engage their child in this way, these behaviours will not occur. When designing a children's picture book it is consequently important to consider how the aspects of the book itself can promote these behaviours. Goodwin's discussion of shared reading promotes the idea that the practice should "invite involvement", giving the child a chance to push their level of understanding to a new level in an environment that encourages the child to take a chance [6]. The importance of this was observed within Blue 2, with six of the eleven children commenting on the difficulty of the interactive task adding to the overall enjoyment of the book. Consequently, the level of difficulty helps to encourage further learning from the child as well as have a direct impact on the level of engagement and enjoyment.

From our observations, we conclude that the interactive features within the children's picture book must have an impact on the story itself. Whilst 'lift-the-flap' features are effective with younger readers, the novelty wears off with older children. Even though *Blue 2* is an interactive book that requires physical engagement (through touching and moving the book) and intellectual engagement (by searching for the hidden '2'), the story itself is not engaging. Consequently the book is more of an 'activity' book than a 'reading' book for the age group observed. An effective children's interactive book must include an appropriate and engaging story that can be read within the shared reading environment, and must include interactive features that promote further engagement or have an impact on the outcome or reading of the story.

Expressive typography needs to be simple in order to be effective. Many of the children participants found the typography within *Beautiful Oops* hard to read, and there were further comments about the 'confusing' aspects of some books from personal collections. These included comments of using script, which was hard for young readers to read, as well as text in shapes being placed in different places on the page, meaning that young readers found it difficult to follow the flow of the story. This highlights the importance of readability over interactive features.

All parents within the study commented on the effect of expressive typography on their reading style - ranging from utilising voices as well as expression and tone. Whilst this is key within the shared reading environment, it is important to note that children's picture books tend to transition with the child as the young reader moves from listener to reader. Consequently when utilising expressive typography it is important to consider readability first and foremost. Even though this study included a wide age range of children, all were able to identify the purpose of expressive typography. If children are able to understand that this design feature is implemented to aide understanding and to imply emphasis, it is important that the typography itself is designed in such a way that the children can undertake this act. *Beautiful Oops* was perhaps the wrong choice for testing the control of expressive typography, as the typography itself was more difficult to read than a standard typed font. However this allows a further understanding of how important it is to consider not just aesthetics, but the practicality of typography used when designing children's books.

6   Recommendations for Children's Interactive Book Design

This paper reported on a study of shared reading between parents and children, including a wide range of books with varying levels of interaction from parent and child. Based on successful elements observed in our study, we now explore what implications for successful interactive electronic books (eBooks) that encourage shared reading.

Age-Appropriate Story and Illustrations. Our observations confirm that successful children's picture books need to firstly include an engaging story that is appropriate for the age and reading level of the child. The story must have a rhythm that drives the story, and a message that relates to the real world and reaches the child at their emotional level. The illustrations must be appropriate for the text and be equally as engaging as the story itself, allowing younger children to 'read' the images and understand the combination of pictures and words. These illustrations must be designed and utilised in such a way that they support the story as well as the other features within the book. These observations hold for both conventional books and eBooks.It is also important that when creating interactive books that the interaction is age appropriate as well as appropriate for the story. In observations it was noted that the interactive features of *Blue 2* were not engaging for readers at all age levels. This shows that the interaction and story level needs to both be carefully considered alongside eachother for age-appropriateness.

Engaging Interactive Features. Parents that engage in effective shared reading practices will find aspects within all children's books that can draw on a range of interactions, both physical and intellectual. All of the parents within the study participated in this way, however it is the parents that are not participating in effective shared reading practices that need to be catered for. Whilst it is understood that the asking of questions, from both parents and children, promotes wider learning and understanding, books must be designed to encourage this practice. This can be implemented by the inclusion of questions within the text of the book itself, or through the inclusion of imagery and elements that lend themselves to inquisitiveness from the child within the shared reading environment. Also, the book itself must encourage comments to be made by parents and children. Many comments noted throughout the study were centred on the interaction of characters - both in the story and the imagery - and the identification of elements. By designing a children's book that encourages the readers to 'look closer' - both figuratively and literally - shared reading practices including comments and questions will be encouraged of shared reading partners.Many of the interactive features currently seen in digital interactive books seem to be included for entertainment purposes, rather than to encourage shared reading and engage the child with the story. Interactive features included in digital books (sound, games, video, etc.), must tie very closely to the story. Presently many of the digital interactions seem distracting (particularly in-book games or puzzles that are rooted to a single page, unlike the *Blue 2* puzzle that spans the book). It can also be argued that many eBooks today are designed for a single user, rather than for shared reading. Further research needs to be conducted to investigate how eBooks are used in shared reading and how their interactive elements influence the shared reading process.

In a digital library engaging interactive features could be included either within individual books or created in a way that creates connections between stories or ideas from stories to facilitate the shared reading experience beyond individual books. This may include having questions that fascilitate discussion between the adult and child or may be activities that bring together the ideas from several storylines. The possibilites of creating meta-interactive features in digitial libraries is an area that requires further investigation.

Adaptivity. As is often seen with young children's reading practices, the repetitive reading of a text lends itself to a child memorising the story and elements. Several of the parents within the observations noted the importance of being able to read the story differently each time or for there to be several levels or layers of interaction within a book that will appeal to readers of different ages. Consequently children's picture books need to include a level of adaptivity to allow the child and parent to interact with the book differently each time they read it. This adaptivity may be easier to include in electronic books. When designing children's books in the future it will be imperative to consider how one book can be adapted to provide new learning possibilities as the child grows. These adaptive qualities could relate to different storylines, different interactive activities, or different learning outcomes. We strongly believe that the features of interactivity that encourage shared learning will be applicable to books in both print and in electronic form (ebooks) and the design of these features needs to be explore.

When applying the idea of adaptivity to interactive books in digital libraries we need to consider that this may mean that the entire collection could be given different contexts as the age of the child increases or the library could be used as a way toadjust or refine the books that are offered based on the types of interaction that appeal to the child at present. Digital libraries could also manage changes in storylines or interactive features across a collection to adapt to the changing needs of the reader. The adaptivity of interactive books and their integration into digital libraries and how they can best support adaptive features is an area where the possibilities need to be explored further.

Digital Interactive Books. While this study only observed children and parents engaging in shared reading with printed books, we can still draw some recommendations from this study for the design of digital interactive books and their incorporation into digital libraries, which can be investigated further in future studies.This study explored the physical and intellectual interactions of shared reading with physical books, it is clear that similar interactions will be present in shared reading of eBooks on mobile devices.Interactivity in a book, whether printed or digital, falls into 2 areas depending on the types of interaction that it uses. Meaningful interaction is that which engages the reader and enhances the storyline, reading or learning experience through the interactive experience. Inconsequential interactivity is often seen in the form of a game, or activities that are "for the sake of it", which are frequently adaptations of print books into eBooks[17]and add nothing to the storyline and can often distract from the story itself or hinder the learning experince. Digital interactions should create a value that is not available in printed books[17]. When designing interactive books for children it is important to remember that the interaction should enhance the reading exerience for the child.

References

1. Galda, L.: Literature and the child. Wadsworth Cengage Learning, Australia (2014)
2. Freedman-De Vito, B.: Why reading is so important for children (2004),
   http://www.familyresource.com/parenting/child-development/
   why-reading-is-so-important-for-children (retrieved January 6, 2010)
3. Worthy, J., Chamberlain, K., Peterson, K., Sharp, C., Shih, P.-Y.: The Importance of Read-Aloud and Dialogue in an Era of Narrowed Curriculum: An Examination of Literature Discussions in a Second-Grade Classroom. Lit. Res. Instr. 51, 308–322 (2012)

4. Rog, L.J.: Read, Write, Play, Learn: Literacy Instruction in Today's Kindergarten. International Reading Association, Newark (2011)
5. Rose, D.: Meaning beyond the Margins: Learning to Interact with Books. Semiot. Margins Mean. Multimodalites. 177 (2011)
6. Goodwin, P. (ed.): Understanding children's books: a guide for education professionals. Sage, Los Angeles (2008)
7. Reutzel, D.R., Cooter, R.B.: Teaching children to read: the teacher makes the difference. Pearson, Boston (2012)
8. Ezell, H.K., Justice, L.M.: Shared storybook reading: building young children's language & emergent literacy skills. Paul H. Brookes Pub., Baltimore (2005)
9. Bloom, P.: How Children Learn the Meanings of Words. MIT Press, Cambridge (2002)
10. Piro, J.M.: The picture of reading: Deriving meaning in literacy through image. Read. Teach. 56 (2002)
11. Hall, S., Hall, S.: Using picture storybooks to teach literary devices: recommended books for children and young adults. Oryx Press, Phoenix (1990)
12. Selznick, B.: Caldecott Medal Acceptance. Horn Book Mag. 84, 393–406 (2008)
13. Bongers, B., Veer, G.C.: Towards a Multimodal Interaction Space: categorisation and applications. Pers. Ubiquitous Comput. 11, 609–619 (2007)
14. Lander, D.: Online learning: Ways to make tasks interactive. Ultibase R. Melb. Inst. Technol. (1999)
15. Timpany, C., Vanderschantz, N.: A Categorisation Structure for Interactive Children's Books. Int. J. Book. 9, 97–110 (2012)
16. Timpany, C., Vanderschantz, N.: Using a Categorisation Structure to Understand Interaction in Children's Books. Int. J. Book. 10, 29–44 (2013)
17. Itzkovitch, A.: Interactive eBook Apps: The Reinvention of Reading and Interactivity (2012), http://uxmag.com/articles/interactive-ebook-apps-the-reinvention- of-reading-and-interactivity
18. Phinney, T., Colabucci, L.: The Best Font for the Job. Child. Libr. J. Assoc. Libr. Serv. Child. 8, 17–26 (2010)
19. Gibbons, J.: Visual Literacy and Picture Books. Teach. Curric. 3 (1999)

Cross Media Recommendation in Digital Library

Jia Zhang[1,2], Zhenming Yuan[2,*], and Kai Yu[2]

[1] State Key Laboratory of Digital Publishing Technology
100871, Beijing, China
[2] School of Information Science and Engineering, Hangzhou Normal University
311121, Hangzhou, China
{zhangjia,zmyuan,yk}@hznu.edu.cn

Abstract. Rapidly increasing volumes of heterogeneous media digital contents are produced into the digital library by the forms of the digital books, videos, images, etc. However, traditional recommendation approaches in the digital library cannot support the potential semantic connections across different types of media data. In this paper, a cross-media recommendation algorithm for the digital library is proposed, in which the retrieved items may come from different data sources, and the results do not need to be of the same media type the user ever read or tagged. Firstly, a fused user-item-feature tensor is used to represent the cross-media data set. Then the item-context latent space and item-user rating latent space are reconstructed by TUCKER based tensor decomposition. And the structural grouping sparsity approach is used to select the feature groups and the subset of homogeneous features in one group, which can deal with the difficulty of sparse and high dimension of the big feature matrix. Finally, the Top-n items are recommended according to the prediction probability estimated. Experiments conducted on a cross-media dataset based on China Academic Digital Associative Library (CADAL). The performances evaluation is based on the recall precision and diversity score. The experiment results show that our approach has good recommendation accuracy as well as good diversity.

Keywords: Cross-media Recommendation, Feature Selection, Sparse Representation, CADAL.

1 Introduction

The retrieval and recommendation methods in most of the digital library only provide single modal search, such as the text keyword search. Nowadays, rapidly increasing volumes of heterogeneous media digital contents are feed into the digital library by the forms of the digital books, videos, images, which involve multimodal data. Single modal keywords based query do not have the ability to make personalized retrieval according to not only the personal reading habits, but also the potential semantic connections across different types of media data. Under such circumstances, cross-media retrieval or recommendation is imperative to many applications of practical interest, such as finding

---

* Corresponding author.

K. Tuamsuk et al. (Eds.): ICADL 2014, LNCS 8839, pp. 208–217, 2014.

relevant textual documents of a tourist spot that best match a given image of the spot or finding a set of images that visually best illustrate a given text description [1,2].

However, cross-media recommendation in the digital library faces two main challenges. One is the heterogeneity-gap between multi-modal data, which has been widely understood as a fundamental barrier to successful cross-media retrieval and recommendation. For example, the user once read the book "Facebook: The Missing Manual", then the system may return not only the book "Facebook guide" but also the movie "The social network". To reduce this gap, one way is to map the multi-modal data into a common feature space. In these methods, the keywords-based or content-based [3,4] retrieval systems only consider the digital contents as the homogenous ones, which lack of the query ability across different media sources. The other challenge is to find the potential structure information between multi-modal data. On one hand, the data in digital library have the structural characteristics, that is, different modal of data (such as text, images, video, sound, etc.) and labeled information have strong or weak association, which contain rich relationships with cross-media features. On the other hand, these cross-media data would be rated, labeled, shared or distributed by users with certain social network relations, which introduce the social network context attributes into the digital content to derive rich structural information in the multi-modal data.

In order to utilize the social information, the retrieval systems in digital library increasingly provide personalized recommendation services, which use collaborative filtering based [5], content-based or hybrid-based algorithms. The dataset in such approaches assemble not only the user reading behavior but also the heterogeneous digital contents, which are always high dimension and sparse. Traditional tensor factorization based context-aware approaches [6] consider the context as homogeneous ones, which uses Latent Factor Model (LFM) factorization to decomposed dataset into a sum of rank-1 matrices by SVD or Funk-SVD [7] as the single context version. Different from such systems, in this paper a cross-media recommendation algorithm is proposed to recommend the items coming from different data sources by balancing the high retrieval accuracy and good diversity. We collect the cross-media data, such as the books, the movies, the tags, and the user reading habits, as a high dimensional tensor. A TUCKER based tensor factorization is used to get the cross-media item model and user model simultaneously. Then the structural grouping sparsity approach [8] is conducted to select the optimal structural sparse-based heterogeneous features, and finally the probability prediction is learned by multi-label boosting approach.

The remainder of the paper is organized as follows. In section 2, we introduce the related works about the recommendation system and the cross-media analysis. The proposed recommendation algorithm is detailed in section 3, which includes the representation of cross-media data in digital library, the structural sparse-based feature selection and the kNN probability prediction based retrieval. In section 4, some experiment results in early stage are given to validate the effectiveness and the diversity of the cross-media retrieval. Finally some concludes and future works are proposed in section 5.

2   Related Works

Along with more and more cross media and socialization data is stored in the digital library, many web-based digital libraries support not only the data resources retrieval but also the recommendation for users. Recommender system produces the list of personalized digital resources, which can be the books, the paintings, the images, and the videos, etc. Such system models the user preferences by collecting and mining explicit user feedback (such as history score record) and implicit feedback (such as renting, browsing, reading and other behaviors). Generally speaking, the technology used in recommender system can be divided into four main categories [15]: collaborative filtering based recommendation, content-based recommendation, knowledge-based recommendation, and hybrid recommender system.

The basic idea of collaborative filtering based recommendation is a simple and effective strategy base on the credit and social policy [16], which produces personalized recommendation for target users based on the similar users' suggestions [17]. In most cases, the system produces the recommended results calculated by explicit recommendation score from the online user. Resnik *et al.* [18] firstly introduced the collaborative filtering into the news recommendation system, the goal of which is to adapt the mean score rated by the most similar users as the unread news. Collaborative filtering based recommendation has been further extended to the neighborhood based and model based recommendation algorithms [19]. As both the neighborhood based recommendations, the item based similarity query time would be better than user-based similarity query. In contrast, model based recommendation builds a prediction model using the user-score matrix as the training dataset and predicts the unknown rating score using matrix factorization and reconstruction. In the last decades, model based technology has got great success, which achieved the more accuracy than that of the neighbor based algorithm in Netflix contest [20]. However, the neighborhood-based approach and the model-based approaches both face the sparse matrix and the cold start problems [21]. In practice, the rating density may be 1% or less achieved from the recommender system. The fact is that it is difficult to find the similar user using only the neighborhood based approach, because there are too many items not rated by any users and few pairs of users with enough ratings on public items, which lead to fail in calculating the Pearson correlation coefficient or cosine distance similarity metrics.

Content-based recommendation is another main recommender approach. It's realized by analyzing the goods' content or description to infer the target user's favorites [4]. Generally, the content-based recommender system not only studies users' preference, but also analyses the item's characteristics, which were rated by the users. Because content-based recommendation can partly overcome the cold start problem, it has already been an important approach, especially to handle the high sparsity data. However, how to understand the items' content or description is still an unresolved problem in the domain of graphics comprehension and knowledge comprehension. Therefore, the content-based recommendation would be limited to use in certain aspect.

Knowledge-based recommendation infers the user's demands using the decision support model. It gets the recommended results by some recommender rules or mining user's history interaction data [22]. The main advantage of knowledge-based recommendation is to combine flexible rules from different domains or categories. For instance, the cold start problem wouldn't be occurred if the business rules were merged into the recommender algorithm. But it would be very hard to get the accuracy rules, so the pure knowledge-based recommender system is limited to use, and usually should be merged into other technology mentioned earlier.

Hybrid recommender system integrates several recommender technologies to prevent a single technology limit [23]. Thus it would get more accurate results than ones using only single recommender technology intuitively [24]. In fact, most context based post-filtering approaches belong to the hierarchical hybrid approaches. That is, we would predict the rating score using collaborative filtering approach, and adapt different predicted system using context information.

Along with the spread of Web 2.0, the associated attributes between the users in the social network and the socialized labels would become the abundant context information, and have been introduced into the recommender system research gradually. In addition to the context properties of the association between users and the recommender items' description would require to be considered together, the research of modern cognitive science indicates that people's perception of the outside world showing cross-media properties. Similarly, the recommended items also show the cross-media properties. Different with the traditional single type of media data research, cross-media recommendation is not only attention to the single modal media data, but also concern about the links between heterogeneous data. Most of the current researches associated with cross-media data recommendation are focused on the cross-media retrieval mainly. The purpose of cross-media retrieval is to achieve different types of media data correlation analysis, providing efficient retrieval approach for the different types of data.

Furthermore, due to the existence of those reasons, the cross-media recommender system outputs the diverse recommended results according to different users' needs, and those ones should have a structural semantic relevance and good interpretability. However, traditional recommender system built on the user-item-rate triplet structure is difficult to deal with these massive socialized cross-media data and also is difficult to cope with the diverse needs from different users.

3   Proposed Approach

Considering the cross-media data in digital libraries may have common and distinctive context, which can be used to discover the latent structural grouping semantics and cross-media relations to improve the diversity of recommendation results. In this paper, we propose a structural cross-media content recommend algorithm, which was used to recommend social media [9] before. Firstly, the TUCKER based tensor factorization is conducted on the N-dimensional fused user-item-content tensor. We consider there are two types of media data set in the retrieval system, which are two feature matrixes for two homogeneous media data. A fused feature matrix concatenates such two feature sets into one big feature set to construct the bridge for cross-media data by preserving the heterogeneous features while finding the common homogeneous features. In addition to the big item-feature matrix, we present the user model as a user-feature matrix. Then a 3-order tensor representation of the cross-media data is built, which has the characteristics of sparsity and high-dimension. The cross-media tensor is factorized by TUCKER model into some latent spaces with structured sparsity to be unified as a consensus representation for the cross-media semantics. Then the hidden structural representation is defined as the solution of the structural sparse coding with the loss function by regularizing the terms according to some principal context components. The structural grouping sparsity(MtBGS) learning approach is used to select the optimal components hidden in the similar users to improve the performance of retrieval. Finally, the items with the highest n prediction probabilities are returned by means of a k-nearest-neighborhood approach.

3.1 Representation of Cross-Media Data

Suppose there are two types of cross-media data set in the digital library, $\mathbf{X}_A=\{\mathbf{x}_i, i=1,\ldots,n\}$ and $\mathbf{X}_B=\{\mathbf{x}_j, j=1,\ldots,m\}$, which are two feature matrixes for two homogeneous media data, where $\mathbf{x}_i=\{x_{i1},\ldots,x_{it_A}\}$ and $\mathbf{x}_j=\{x_{j1},\ldots,x_{jt_B}\}$. Here n is the number of items in $\mathbf{X}_A$, $\mathbf{x}_i$ is the ith item in $\mathbf{X}_A$ and t_A is the number of features of each item $\mathbf{x}_i$. For example, $\mathbf{x}_i$ and $\mathbf{x}_j$ are the tags of $\mathbf{X}_A$ and $\mathbf{X}_B$, which are extracted from different tags corpus respectively. It is reasonably that there are many common features (tags) between two features sets. Therefore, a big fused feature matrix $\mathbf{X}$ is build from $\mathbf{X}_A$ and $\mathbf{X}_B$ by preserving the heterogeneous features while extracting the homogeneous features.

In addition to the feature matrix, the jth feature of the ith item is associated with K-dimensional rating vector, $y_i = \{y_{ij1}, \ldots, y_{ijK}\}^T \in \{0,1\}^K$, where $y_{ijk} = 1$ if the jth feature in the ith item has been rated by the kth user and $y_{ijk} = 0$ otherwise. Then we can build a 3-order tensor representation, $\mathcal{A}$, of the cross-media data, which is a very sparse tensor because of the little user ratings and the large tag sets. Here, we use TUCKER model[9] to factorize the cross-media tensor into some latent spaces with structured sparsity that can be exploited to simultaneously learn a low-dimensional latent space [10].Given the $I \times J \times K$ cross-media tensor $\mathcal{A}$, the approximate of the original tensor can be expressed as the n-mode multiplication of the *core tensor* $\mathcal{S}$ with three orthogonal matrices $\mathbf{U}, \mathbf{V}, \mathbf{W}$:

$$\mathcal{A} = \mathcal{S} \times_1 \mathbf{U} \times_2 \mathbf{V} \times_3 \mathbf{W} \tag{1}$$

where $\mathcal{S} \in \mathbb{R}^{I \times J \times K}$, $\mathbf{U} \in \mathbb{R}^{I \times I}$, $\mathbf{V} \in \mathbb{R}^{J \times J}$, $\mathbf{W} \in \mathbb{R}^{K \times K}$, and $\times_n$ operation is n-mode product. Such tensor algebra defines multi-linear operators over the set of latent spaces, which is composed of the item space, $\mathbf{U}$, the feature space, $\mathbf{V}$, and the user space $\mathbf{W}$.

3.2 Learning Structural Sparse-Based Feature Selection

Considering the sparse and high dimension of the cross-media feature matrix, a sparse-based feature selection should be developed to find a good latent interaction along with the subset of corresponding latent preference modeling features. Different with traditional feature selection algorithms [8], such as *lasso* [11] or *group lasso* [12], we use a framework of multi-label boosting by the selection of heterogeneous features with structural grouping sparsity [13] to satisfy the interpretability of the model, which utilize the structure priors between heterogeneous and homogeneous features for latent cross-media modeling. In order to find the latent relationships among the user preferences $\mathbf{U}$, the item preferences $\mathbf{V}$ and the context features $\mathbf{W}$, the item-context feature matrix, $\mathbf{X}$, and the user-item rating indicator matrix, $\mathbf{Y}$, are reconstructed by the sum of the core tensor $\mathcal{S}$ multiplied by $\mathbf{V}$ and $\mathbf{W}$.

$$\mathbf{X} = \sum_{i=1}^{R_1} \sum_{j=1}^{R_2} \delta_{ijk}(u_i{}^{\circ}v_j) \tag{2}$$

$$\mathbf{Y} = \sum_{i=1}^{R_1} \sum_{k=1}^{R_3} \delta_{ijk}(u_i{}^{\circ}w_k) \tag{3}$$

where $\mathbf{X} \in \mathbb{R}^{I \times J}$, $\mathbf{Y} \in \mathbb{R}^{I \times K}$. Given the kth user and his corresponding rating vector $\mathbf{Y}(:,k)$, the regression model of MtBGS is defined as follows:

$$\min_{\hat{\beta}_k} \left\| \mathbf{Y}(:,k) - \sum_{l=1}^{L} \mathbf{x}_l \hat{\beta}_{kl} \right\|_2^2 + \lambda_1 \sum_{l=1}^{L} \left\| \hat{\beta}_{kl} \right\|_2 + \lambda_2 \left\| \hat{\beta}_k \right\|_1 \tag{4}$$

where L is the number of disjoint groups of homogeneous features, $\mathbf{x}_l$ is the features of the training data corresponding to the lth group, $\hat{\beta}_{kl}$ is the estimation of the corresponding coefficient vector for the kth user, $\beta_k = (\beta_{k1}^T, \dots, \beta_{kL}^T)^T$ is the entire coefficient vector for the kth user.

Suppose that the extracted J-dimensional heterogeneous features are divided into L disjoint groups of homogeneous features, with J_l the number of features in the lth group, $\sum_{l=1}^{L} J_l = J$. We use a matrix $\mathbf{X}_l \in R^{I \times J_l}$ to represent the features of the training data corresponding to the lth group, with corresponding coefficient vector $\beta_{kl} \in R^{J_l}$ $(l = 1, \dots, L)$ for the kth user, and $\lambda_1 \sum_{l=1}^{L} \left\| \hat{\beta}_{kl} \right\|_2 + \lambda_2 \left\| \hat{\beta}_k \right\|_1$ is the regularizer term, and is called the structural grouping penalty [11]. Then the selection of the lth group of homogeneous features for the kth user is determined by minimizing

$$J(t) = \sum_{m=1}^{p_l} \left(\frac{\theta_m}{\|\theta_{kl}\|}\right)^2 \tag{5}$$

where $t_m = sign(\theta_m) \in [-1,1]$, and θ_{kl} is the coefficients. Finally, the subgroup within each selected group is identified by

$$\min_{\theta_m} \left\| r_{kl} - \sum_{m=1}^{p_l} X_m^l \theta_m \right\|_2^2 + \lambda_1 \left\| \theta_{jl} \right\|_2 + \lambda_2 \sum_{m=1}^{p_l} \|\theta_m\|_1 \tag{6}$$

where X_m^l is the corresponding p_l-dimensional homogeneous features of kth user, $r_{kl} = Y(:,k) - \sum_{i \neq l} X_i \beta_{ki}$ is the partial residual when the lth group is removed. This regression model with the structural grouping sparsity can be optimized by the Gauss-Seidel Coordinate Descent approach [14].

3.3   Personalized Recommendation of Top n Cross-Media Data

Suppose the selected structure sparse feature for user k is $\hat{\beta}_k$, the predicted rating of the unlabeled item $\mathbf{X}^u$ by the kth user is computed by projecting the item feature on the structure sparse feature space:

$$\hat{y}_u = \mathbf{X}^u \hat{\beta}_k \tag{7}$$

Finally, for the kth user, the personalized Top-n results are retrieved by k-nearest-neighborhood approach. We defined an experienced threshold to control the diversity of the homogeneous features. The top n items with the biggest estimated ratings, as well as whose rating are larger than the threshold, are recommended to a specific user.

4   Experiments

Experiments are conducted on a cross-media dataset in China Academic Digital Associative Library (CADAL), which was co-constructed by Chinese and American institutes and researchers and has more than 1.5 million digital volumes. CADAL also provides a personalized service to users, such as the personalized comments, social networks and recommendations.

4.1   Dataset

We selected four types of digital collections from CADAL as the cross-media dataset, which are the digital books, videos, calligraphy copybooks and Chinese paintings. The features of the items are defined according to the meta data and the users' comments. Users commit the ratings and comments during the reading history. We divide the features into several categories manually. The whole dataset has 11,000 users, 180,000 books, 35,000 videos clips, 4500 calligraphy copybooks and 15,000 Chinese paintings. There are totally 3,524 tags and 147,369 rates in the dataset.

4.2   Evaluation Metrics

The performances evaluation is based on the recall precision and diversity score. We use cross-validation to get the evaluation, which randomly select about 25% of the data in the dataset as training data each time. This process was repeated ten times to generate 10 random training and test groups. The average performances in terms of recall and diversity score are evaluated. The recall metric and the diversity metric are defined to measure the performance of our algorithm.

$$recall = \frac{\sum_{u=1}^{k} \text{hit-ratio-recall}(u)}{k} \times 100\% \tag{8}$$

where $hit\text{-}ratio\text{-}recall(u) = \frac{|Test_u \cap TopN_u|}{|Test_u|}$, and $Test_u$ is the recommended items tagged by user u in the test set.

Diversity is an important metric to represent how widely the system can recommend across the different types of media data. However, there are somewhat subjective about diversity. So we invited the volunteers to evaluate the diversity.

$$diversity = \frac{\sum_{i=1}^{m} recall_i * num\_chosen_i}{\sum_{i=1}^{m} num\_chosen_i} \tag{9}$$

where m is the number of types of cross-media data, and num_chosen_i is the number of items chosen by the volunteers which are rated with the highest n ratings.

4.3   Experiment Results

We compared recall and diversity under different k of kNN and different algorithms as in Fig. 1. As in the left figure of Fig. 1, the diversity and the recall are inversely proportional, and there are turning points on the curves, which can be used to guide the selection of the best k. We also compare our approach with the traditional collaborative filtering based recommendation. And It is obviously our approach has better diversity ability as well as better retrieval accuracy than that of CF based approach.

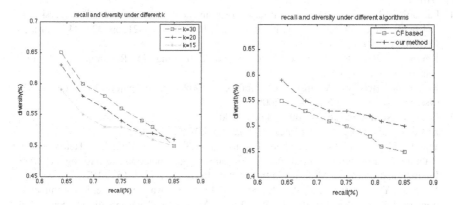

Fig. 1. Recall and diversity plots under different k (left figure) and different algorithms (right figure)

5   Conclusion and Future Work

In this paper, we propose a structural cross-media content recommend algorithm. A fused user-item-feature tensor is used to represent the cross-media data set. The item-context matrix and item-user rating matrix are factorized by TUCKER based tensor decomposition. And the multi-label boosting by structural grouping sparsity is used to select the feature groups and the subset of homogeneous features in one group. Finally, the Top-n items are recommended according to the prediction probability estimated. The results show that our algorithm has good recommendation accuracy as well as good diversity in our experiments on the cross-media dataset from CADAL.

In our research, we only use the users' ratings and tags as the labels of the multi-modal digital resources, which is still a kind of method to map the multi-modal data into a common feature space. Although we can use the meta data as the initial labels, they are not enough to represent the semantic of digital resources completely, especially for the image, painting or video. Therefore, one of the future works can be the extension of the algorithm based on the sematic networks or the knowledge graph of the cross-media digital resources.

Acknowledgement. This research is supported by the Opening Project of State Key Laboratory of Digital Publishing Technology and Zhejiang Provincial Natural Science Foundation of China (Grant No. Z12F020027).

References

1. Wu, F., Lu, X., Zhang, Z., Yan, S., Rui, Y., Zhuang, Y.: Cross-media semantic representation via bi-directional learning to rank. In: Proceedings of the 21st ACM International Conference on Multimedia (MM 2013), pp. 877–886. ACM, New York (2013)
2. Zhuang, Y., Yang, Y., Wu, F.: Mining semantic correlation of heterogeneous multimedia data for cross-media retrieval. IEEE Transactions on Multimedia 10(2), 221–229 (2008)
3. Ricci, F., Rokach, L., Shapira, B., Kantor, P.: Recommender Systems Handbook. Springer (2010)
4. Pazzani, M.J., Billsus, D.: Content-based recommendation systems. In: Brusilovsky, P., Kobsa, A., Nejdl, W. (eds.) Adaptive Web 2007. LNCS, vol. 4321, pp. 325–341. Springer, Heidelberg (2007)
5. Koren, Y., Bell, R.: Advances in collaborative filtering. In: Recommender Systems Handbook. Springer (2010)
6. Koren, Y., Bell, R., Volinsky, C.: Matrix factorization techniques for recommender systems. Computer 42(8), 30–37 (2009)
7. Funk, S.: Netflix update: Try this at home (2006), http://sifter.org/?simon/journal/20061211.html
8. Wu, F., Han, Y.H., Liu, X., Shao, J., Zhuang, Y.T., Zhang, Z.F.: The Heterogeneous feature selection with structural sparsity for multimedia annotation and hashing: A survey. International Journal of Multimedia Information Retrieval 1(1), 3–15 (2012)
9. Yuan, Z., Yu, K., Zhang, J., Pan, H.: Structural context-aware cross media recommendation. In: Lin, W., Xu, D., Ho, A., Wu, J., He, Y., Cai, J., Kankanhalli, M., Sun, M.-T. (eds.) PCM 2012. LNCS, vol. 7674, pp. 790–800. Springer, Heidelberg (2012)
10. Tucker, L.R.: Some mathematical notes on three-mode factor analysis. Psychometrika 31(3), 279–311 (1996)
11. Harshman, R.A.: Foundations of the PARAFAC procedure: models and conditions for an "explanatory" multimodal factor analysis. University of California at Los Angeles (1970)
12. Tibshirani, R.: Regression shrinkage and selection via the lasso. J. R. Stat. Soc. Ser. B (Statistical Approachology) 58(1), 267–288 (1996)
13. Yuan, M., Lin, Y.: Model selection and estimation in regression with grouped variables. J. R. Stat. Soc. Ser. B (Approachological) 68(1), 49–67 (2006)
14. Wu, F., Han, Y., Tian, Q., Zhuang, Y.: Multi-label boosting for image annotation by structural grouping sparsity. In: Proceedings of the 2010 ACM International Conference on Multimedia (ACMMM), New York, NY, USA, pp. 15–24 (2010)
15. Ricci, F., Rokach, L., Shapira, B., Kantor, P.B. (eds.): Recommender Systems Handbook, 1st edn. Springer (2011)
16. Hill, W., Stead, L., Rosenstein, M., Furnas, G.: Recommending and evaluating choices in a virtual community of use. In: Proc. of the SIGCHI Conference on Human Factors in Computing Systems (CHI 1995), pp. 194–201 (1995)
17. Goldberg, D., Nichols, D., Oki, B.M., Terry, D.: Using collaborative filtering to weave an information tapestry. Communications of the ACM 35(12), 61–70 (1992)
18. Resnick, P., Iacovou, N., Suchak, M., Bergstorm, P., Riedl, J.: An open architecture for collaborative filtering of netnews. In: Proc. of the ACM Conference on Computer Supported Cooperative Work (CSCW 1994), pp. 175–186 (1994)
19. Adomavicius, G., Kwon, Y.O.: New recommendation techniques for multi-criteria rating systems. IEEE Intelligent Systems 22(3), 48–55 (2007)
20. Bell, R., Bennett, J., Koren, Y., Volinsky, C.: The million dollar programming prize. IEEE Spectrum 46(5), 28–33 (2009)

21. Schein, A.I., Popescul, A., Ungar, L.H., Pennock, D.M.: Methods and metrics for cold-start recommendations. In: Proc. of the 25th Annual International ACM SIGIR Conference on Research and Development in Information Retrieval (SIGIR 2002), pp. 253-260 (2002)
22. Lops, P., de Gemmis, M., Semeraro, G.: Content based recommender systems: state of the art and trends. In: Recommender Systems Handbook. Springer (2010)
23. Burke, R.: Interactive critiquing for catalog navigation in e-commerce. Artificial Intelligence Review 18(3-4), 245–267 (2002)
24. Schclar, A., Tsikinovsky, A., Rokach, L., Meisels, A., Antwarg, L.: Ensemble methods for improving the performance of neighborhood-based collaborative filtering. In: Proc. of the 3th ACM Conference on Recommender Systems, pp. 261–264 (2009)

Towards a Full-Text Historical Digital Library

Robert B. Allen and Yoonmi Chu

Yonsei University, Seoul, Korea
rba@boballen.info, yoonmichu@gmail.com

Abstract. A new generation of digital libraries is now possible based on the large amount of open-access full-text and other rich-media materials available. Such content can be more richly modeled and cross-linked than is possible for traditional document-level digital libraries. For collections which include details of events such as collections of newspapers, structured descriptions could be developed to focus on events. For higher-level historical analysis a combination of content and discourse descriptions is needed. Prior work on composite hypertexts has focused almost exclusively on the relationship of the discourse terms without considering the semantics of the content. Here, we describe a framework and interface widgets that support interaction with a historical text which incorporates both discourse and content descriptions. Further, we consider broader issues of interaction based on rich description of content.

Keywords: Adversarial Argumentation, Community Model, Claims Browser, Digital History, Discourse, Footnotes, Historiography, Human-Information Interaction, Long-form Historical Analysis, Model-based Argumentation, Semantic Microworlds, Tables of Contents, Widgets.

1 Introduction

A great many full-text repositories of digitized historical texts from archives, libraries, historical societies, and publishers are now available online. [4] has called for rich linking of full-text scientific research reports. Here we consider the potential for full-text and rich-media collections of historical materials.

Historical collections are composed of many types of content. There are primary sources such as letters and oral histories but also historical analyses which evaluate the credibility of these primary sources as well as interpreting them. The analyses vary greatly in complexity including book-length long-form arguments. We examine how the layers of content in a historical digital library can be coordinated in a structured way. Ultimately, such structures should be useful in developing services for casual readers, students, and historians.

2 Information Organization for Historical Materials

As with traditional document-level libraries, structured descriptions are a central concern for full-text libraries. Indeed, determining the organizational structure which is

K. Tuamsuk et al. (Eds.): ICADL 2014, LNCS 8839, pp. 218–226, 2014.
© Springer International Publishing Switzerland 2014

needed should precede indexing, text extraction, development of interactive services, and personalization for complex material.

The value of semantic description is increasingly recognized with projects such as schema.org and dbpedia.org along with broader work on ontologies and linked open data. Our approach is related to these projects in seeking rich description but we view them as occupying different points in a space with dimensions of scope, completeness, and formality. In this paper, we consider the coordination of semantics with discourse while other forthcoming work explores semantic microworlds for relatively detailed representations for historical Community Models. In terms of semantics, our approach follows "realist" ontologies such as the Basic Formal Ontology (BFO) which is an upper ontology that is widely used in biomedicine. Beyond ontologies, we also argue that modeling should include an explicit representation of states [3, 4, 6].

Discourse is interpretation about entities and events. For historical analysis, we attempt to separate descriptions of entities and events from discourse about them [5]. However, there are many ambiguous cases; for instance, there is a vigorous debate about whether causation is fact or interpretation. We do not resolve that here.

Rhetorical Structure Theory (RST) [14] provides a framework for describing rhetorical relationships in texts. Rhetoric is related to discourse. It is an approach to the systematic and persuasive presentation of a position. In addition to relationship labels, RST proposes that there is an overall pattern for connecting discourse elements. Specifically, it proposes that some elements are part of a "nucleus" while secondary elements (those which amplify the nuclei) form "satellites". For carefully authored text the nuclei structures are claimed to be hierarchical [14].

Issue-based information systems (IBIS) interconnect concepts related to policy. Composite hypertext systems[1] have applied that approach in a variety of other domains by implementing sets of discourse relationships as labels for the links between concepts. Some of those composite hypertexts focus on supporting argumentation and, thus, are termed argumentation systems. However, these argumentation systems have consistently emphasized discourse relationships without also structuring the semantics of the content. By comparison, we consider ways that discourse and semantics can be combined. For instance, we propose a model-based argumentation approach in which models of the content are integral to argumentation.

Shum (e.g., [17]) made an early proposal for applying discourse tags in the context of a scholarly digital library. Notable as that work is, it did not provide end-user widgets. Moreover, like the argumentation systems described above it did not link the discourse labels to the semantic content in a general way.

3   Long-Form Historical Analysis

Historical analyses differs from simple recounting of historical entities and events and such analyses are often extended. Indeed, they are often long-form book-length texts. Such complex integrated works have only rarely been considered by hypertext or digital object researchers. Yet, such texts are very important in the humanities.

---

[1] Halasz, F. "Seven issues": Revisited (closing keynote address). ACM Hypertext' 91 Conference, San Antonio, TX.

As an example, consider Gibbon's *History of the Decline and Fall of the Roman Empire* [9]. This classic study argues that a decrease in civic virtue led to the decline and fall of the Empire. The book makes its case by describing a broad range of trends including, somewhat controversially, the growth of early Christianity. Temporal structure is often used as an organizing strategy in historical analysis. In some cases, there is also organization of the discussion by sectors of the society (e.g., military, governance).

For historical analysis, claims of causation replace logical inference which is usually considered in an argumentation system. However, the nature of causation is controversial. For broad sweeps of history, causation is often claimed for trends and generalizations rather than for specific events (see [3]). Those trends and generalizations are themselves the subject of argumentation.

4   Widgets

Techniques to support interaction and navigation in traditional paper books have evolved through hundreds of years. Given new interface technologies and the wide availability of rich digital content, [2] has proposed a new focus on "widgets" that can support interaction with digital content. Such widgets are also related to the psychological notion of "cognitive organizers" and should benefit students, lay readers, and scholars. There are many types of widgets. The Preface to a volume often helps to put the creation of the content in a historical context. A Colophon helps to embed the production of a volume within a historical context. Following work in the hypertext community, Timpany [20] discusses linking within parts of a book though she did not appear to consider tables of contents. Widgets can also be applied across works in a collection. An example is the "meta-dex" project [11] which developed a unified index for items in a collection.

Widgets require structure but no general framework has been developed. The Open Annotation framework has recently been proposed as a framework for single annotations [22]. However, annotations almost never appear in isolation so examining sets of annotations is necessary. Thus, annotation macros will have to be developed. Alternatively, perhaps "named graphs" could be structured more systematically to cover scholarly widgets.

5   Enhanced Table of Contents Interaction Widget

5.1   TOC Interaction Widget

While the features of document abstracts have been studied extensively [12], remarkably there is no theory or general model for TOCs. There can be many different types of mapping between a set of short descriptors and sections of the body of the text.

Traditional tables of contents are ad hoc but they could be more explicitly structured. They vary in resolution (e.g., chapter, section, paragraph, sentence), in the content type of the label, and in the type of user interaction they support. One common approach is a "fish-eye" or "focus+context" TOC which allow viewing of multiple levels of resolution. Further, fish-eye TOCs may allow single or multiple foci and selected sections of the text may be highlighted. Taken together, these attributes can define a TOC structure which could also include TOC metadata attributes such as author and date of creation.

Timelines which map to text segments might also be considered a type of TOC, or perhaps a type of index, for organizing events described in a text (cf. [1]). Claim browsers, which can also be considered a kind of TOC, provide an overview of specific issues or claims and may not follow the linear structure of a document. Because that evidence may be spread across sections of the work, the claim browser could include bridging material to explain how the parts fit together.

5.2   Discourse and Semantic Descriptions in a TOC

As noted earlier many composite hypertext frameworks have focused on discourse relationships. We suggest that the semantics should also be included. As an illustration, we developed a prototype TOC with two-part labels. For our low-level TOC, we applied RST-style discourse labels and concepts which could plausibly be derived from a semantic ontology for the passage.

We developed and applied the prototype browser to a selection from Volume 1 of Gibbon's History of the Decline and Fall of the Roman Empire obtained from Project Gutenberg.[2] This volume of the "Decline and Fall" describes the Roman Empire in the 2nd and 3th centuries AD. The selection started with:

> Till the privileges of Romans had been progressively extended to all the inhabitants of the empire, an important distinction was preserved between Italy and the provinces.

Gibbon is simultaneously framing his approach and also defending it. Gibbon contrasts the status quo between Italy and the provinces. He then lists specific examples. In the following paragraphs, he examines the ways in which that convergence occurred. The first of these was by expansion of settlements; the second by extending language; and the third, by extending language and arts. Finally, there is a paragraph about the status of slaves which does not directly support the claim but completes the description of the structure of the society.

Although Gibbon does not provide a TOC at this resolution, we can create one in an electronic edition to help orient readers. As described above, indicating both the semantics and discourse should help a reader in several ways. First, knowing that this is a comparison of the two types of political units within the Roman Empire (i.e., Italy and the Provinces) suggests some of the attributes on which that comparison will be made. In addition, knowledge of the semantics helps orient the reader to the parallelism in some of the points that are made about the two different types of political units. Figure 1 shows the implementation of this TOC widget with a prototype Java applet. There are two independently scrollable panels. The left panel has the text while the right panel has the interactive discourse-semantics outline.

---

[2] http://www.gutenberg.org/files/731/731-h/731-h.htm#link22HCH0002

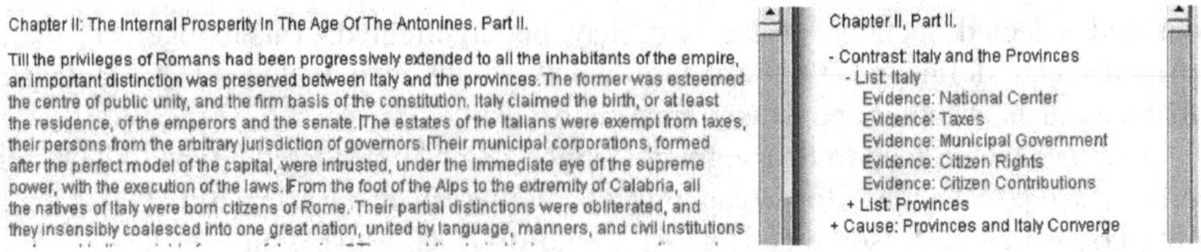

Chapter II: The Internal Prosperity In The Age Of The Antonines. Part II.

Till the privileges of Romans had been progressively extended to all the inhabitants of the empire, an important distinction was preserved between Italy and the provinces. The former was esteemed the centre of public unity, and the firm basis of the constitution. Italy claimed the birth, or at least the residence, of the emperors and the senate. The estates of the Italians were exempt from taxes, their persons from the arbitrary jurisdiction of governors. Their municipal corporations, formed after the perfect model of the capital, were intrusted, under the immediate eye of the supreme power, with the execution of the laws. From the foot of the Alps to the extremity of Calabria, all the natives of Italy were born citizens of Rome. Their partial distinctions were obliterated, and they insensibly coalesced into one great nation, united by language, manners, and civil institutions

Chapter II, Part II.

- Contrast: Italy and the Provinces
  - List: Italy
    Evidence: National Center
    Evidence: Taxes
    Evidence: Municipal Government
    Evidence: Citizen Rights
    Evidence: Citizen Contributions
  + List: Provinces
+ Cause: Provinces and Italy Converge

Fig. 1. Prototype semantics-discourse TOC applet for the first paragraph

In addition to the two-part TOC labels, we have added several features to enhance the usability of the TOC: (a) The TOC does not map to defined section boundaries but to conceptual units (b) The selected conceptual unit is highlighted in red (gray in the reproduction) (c) low-level subsections within the conceptual unit are indicated with vertical black tick marks rather than with still lower level TOC labels which would probably be distracting for the reader.

This interface should be especially useful for people who are not familiar with the topic. Just as interaction with a search engine teaches users about the relevant dimensions of what they are searching for even if they do not enter any of the documents, this browser can help people better understand the text.

There are several limitations to the prototype interface. First, the enhanced labels are highly abbreviated and may be cryptic for readers who are not familiar with the topic. Second, it may be difficult for readers to understand the role of this passage in the context of the entire work. Both of these issues could be addressed with additional widgets. For instance, tooltips or even audio descriptions could be used to provide richer, more complete descriptions. In addition, a graphical argumentation template could lead the reader through the narrative [7] and support more complex reasoning (cf. [15]). Finally, additional commentary could be provided about the relationship between the discourse and semantics as well as about the strategy of the author in relating the two.

6   Footnotes

There has been an evolution of humanities footnotes through time [10]. Gibbon is renowned for his extensive use of footnotes and is often considered one of the first modern historians in this regard. Footnotes which include citations and the discussion of the work of other authors go beyond basic rhetorical structures in which one author is trying to make a case for a position. Indeed, citations require that a work is embedded in broader literature. While citation linking in scientific research articles has been extensively studied (e.g., [19]), footnotes in humanities have not.[3] Footnotes in humanities are often different from those in science including sometimes lengthy analysis that is not directly relevant to the main thesis of the text.

6.1   Gibbon's Footnotes

We examined the footnotes in Chapter 2, Part II of the "Decline and Fall". Gibbon's footnotes ranged from 1 to 15 lines. More than 90% included reference links to

---

[3] Though, see [13] for a description of the use of footnotes in fiction.

other works; there were frequently several links in a given footnote. However, one of the editors who contributed annotations mentioned the work of others but did not always provide specific citations. The majority of the footnotes was for clarification or extension of a point in the text; only about 20% of them were simple citations with no other text.

Importantly, for our ultimate goal of developing a full-text digital library the full-texts for almost all of the numerous sources mentioned in Gibbon's footnotes which we checked are available online. In many cases these were open-access clean-text English translations. However, in other cases, there was no translation, they were poor quality OCR from digitized copies, or they required a password to access.

6.2   Footnote Widget

Consider footnote #26 from Chapter 2, Part 2 of "The Decline and Fall":

> 26 The senators were obliged to have one third of their own landed property in Italy. See Plin. l. vi. ep. 19. The qualification was reduced by Marcus to one fourth. Since the reign of Trajan, Italy had sunk nearer to the level of the provinces.]

Although it is not part of the main document, this footnote provides support not just for a specific claim but also for the broader shift which may be viewed as Gibbon's main claim in this section about the spread of the rights of Citizens across the empire.

Gibbon rarely expresses direct disagreement with others; however, the Project Gutenberg edition also included annotations by H. Milman, the editor of the 1845 print edition, as well as by editors of the Project Gutenberg editions. These editors made wide ranging comments including mentioning Gibbon's support of abolitionism when commenting on his discussion of Roman slaves. In Footnote #261, Milman (identified as "M") cites the work of the German jurist Savigny who published his research several years after Gibbon wrote "The Decline and Fall".

> 261 It may be doubted whether the municipal government of the cities was not the old Italian constitution rather than a transcript from that of Rome. The free government of the cities, observes Savigny, was the leading characteristic of Italy. Geschichte des Romischen Rechts, i. p. G.—M.]

Footnotes can be considered as widgets. When encountering a footnote a reader with an enhanced interface could be given a description of the contents of a footnote with a tooltip. If the reader clicked through and found a source to follow, a browser, similar to the one in Figure 1, could be launched to organize both the discourse and the issues of the target article (cf., [4]). In other words, with a concept-based full-text digital library citations can be de-emphasized in favor of linking concepts. Footnote 261 cited above might apply extended RST terms to show adversarial argumentation. Some of the ontologies which have been proposed for characterizing citations might be a place to find such terms. Then, an interaction widget could summarize the two positions and highlight the differences.

7   Standards for a Full-Text Digital Library of Historical Materials

There are some relatively small full-text collections such as the Perseus project which collected ancient Greek writings [8]. Here, we consider developing standards which could be applied to the much larger set of Roman-era writings and, ultimately, across all of history. Because resources are spread across the web, we need a registry of definitive versions of these works to identify permissions on their use for different purposes. In addition, those repositories, as well as archives and historical collections, should adopt standard formats and a standard way of identifying anchor points[4].

Information organization is key to coordinating the contents. The upper ontology for semantics needs to be complemented by lower-level domain ontologies. Our analysis of the "Decline and Fall" could incorporate ontologies of terms relating to the Roman government, regional boundaries[5], religion, and military organization. For the work we have done with 1900's Norfolk, Nebraska, we need ontologies of Protestant traditions, small-town Midwest US government organization, and 19th century railroads. In addition, it will be helpful to have structured collections of mundane, but ubiquitous, cultural knowledge such as organizational by-laws, rosters of popular entertainers, job descriptions, lists of cities hosting sports teams, and national holidays.

We also need a comprehensive discourse ontology suitable for history and standards for widgets such as those described above. Finally, we need standards to incorporate non-textual materials such as data sets and videos.

8   Discussion

The development of the full-text and rich-media digital libraries we propose here and in [5] is a grand challenge. While some of that challenge is coordinating publishers and collections, the bigger challenge is developing a broad range of interoperable information organization structures to support user services. Consider an interface to support interaction with a collection of digitized historical newspapers. Such an interface should be based on a rich model of the community which evolves through time. Communities as described in newspapers are very complex but they are also highly structured and we should be able to capture that structure. In addition, the interface could be personalized for the background and interests of the reader and and description could be presented as a narrative.

We have focused on discourse in this paper but we should note the relationship between discourse and logic. While discourse can be simply a style of presentation, generalization and inference are related to logic. Generalizations can be seen as induction or as a weak form of predicate-logic. The role of logic in human argumentation is widely debated especially with respect to inference in science. In sciences such as biology, the goal is to identify universals through research and theory. In humanities and social science finding universals is much more difficult, if it is possible at all. In history,

---

[4] See http://en.wikipedia.org/wiki/Fragment_identifier
[5] See http://orbis.stanford.edu

the notion of "covering laws" is no longer widely accepted (see [16]); rather, history is much more likely to be based on generalizations.

There is also a vigorous debate about the upper ontologies for social activities (e.g., [18]). Nonetheless, it is worthwhile to explore the development of Community Models such as might be applied to an interactive digitized newspaper interface described above. Cultural frames and a variety of sociological structures may help define aspects of the community within a given perspective.

In the approach to historical information organization we propose, all of history could be part of a single "fabric". Events, evidence, authors, editors, and collection management policies can all be represented within that fabric. This broad overview of history with links from all types of events can be viewed as an implementation of the archival Continuum Model [21]. In a different research tradition, there have been attempts to link the BFO with information resources[6].

While semantic support tools which could automate the task of creating the widgets we discuss here are likely to be developed, the implementation of these proposals will require considerable human effort. We believe such effort would be forthcoming for works such as "The Decline and Fall". After all, the editors of Project Gutenberg have already proven willing to do substantial work and it seems likely that others would be willing to further enrich such classics.

Although we have focused on the specification of information structures for historical materials and end-user services which could be applied to them, tools could be developed to support working with the structured content. Once a substantial body of structured descriptions is available, tools could check for consistency in an author's arguments.

In addition, while this paper has focused on re-mapping existing texts, these structures should also be useful for developing models of and widgets for entities and events which are not anchored in text. Rather, the structure itself could organize all of the evidence and argumentation and services could be developed to support such model-based authoring.

Overall, there are opportunities for a new generation of digital libraries of historical materials which integrate and support access to full text and other types of rich media. Indeed, perhaps texts and other materials from all fields could be unified with rich linking.

Acknowledgment. We thank Yonghwan Kim for his assistance.

References

1. Allen, R.B.: Timelines as Information System Interfaces. In: Proceedings International Symposium on Digital Libraries, pp. 175–180 (1995), http://boballen.info/RBA/PAPERS/TL/isdl.pdf
2. Allen, R.B.: Weaving Content with Coordination Widgets. D-Lib Magazine (2011), doi: 10.1045/november2011-allen
3. Allen, R.B.: Visualization, Causation, and History. In: iConference (2011), doi:10.1145/1940761.1940835

---

[6] That work has not yet considered collections and standards for organizing information resources such as OAIS and FRBR could be also be applied.

4. Allen, R.B.: Model-Oriented Information Organization: Part 1, The Entity-Event Fabric. D-Lib Magazine (July 2013), doi: 10.1045/july2013-allen-pt1
5. Allen, R.B.: Rich Linking in a Digital Library of Full-Text Scientific Research Reports. In: Columbia Research Data Symposium (2013), http://hdl.handle.net/10022/AC:P:19171
6. Allen, R.B.: Frame-based Models of Communities and their History. In: Nadamoto, A., Jatowt, A., Wierzbicki, A., Leidner, J.L. (eds.) SocInfo 2013. LNCS, vol. 8359, pp. 110–119. Springer, Heidelberg (2014)
7. Allen, R.B., Acheson, J.A.: Browsing the Structure of Multimedia Stories. ACM Digital Libraries, 11–18 (2000), doi:10.1145/336597.336615
8. Crane, G.: The Perseus Project and Beyond. How Building a Digital Library Challenges the Humanities and Technology. D-Lib Magazine, doi:10.1045/january98/01crane.html
9. Gibbon, E: The Decline and Fall of the Roman Empire. Harper, New York (1782/1845), http://www.gutenberg.org/files/731/731-h/731-h.htm with production notes for the electronic edition at http://www.gutenberg.org/files/25717/25717-h/25717-h.htm
10. Grafton, A.: The Footnote: A Curious History. Harvard University Press, Cambridge (1999)
11. Hugget, M., Rasmussen, E.: The Meta-Dex Suite: Generating and Analyzing Indexes and Meta-Indexes. ACM SIGIR, 1285–1286 (2011), doi:10.1145/2009916.2010162
12. Lancaster, F.W.: Indexing and Abstracting in Theory and Practice, 3rd edn. University of Illinois Press, Champaign (2003)
13. Maloney, E.: Footnotes in Fiction: A Rhetorical Approach. Dissertation, Ohio State University (2005), https://etd.ohiolink.edu/!etd.send_file?accession=osu1125378621
14. Mann, W.C., Thompson, S.A.: Rhetorical Structure Theory: Toward a Function Theory of Text Organization. Text 8(3), 243–281 (1987)
15. Reed, C.: Wigmore, Toulmin, Walton: The Diagramming Trinity and their Application in Legal Practice. In: Cardozo Conference on Graphic and Visual Representations of Evidence and Inference in Legal Settings (2007), http://tillers.net/reed%20diagramming%20trinity.pdf
16. Roberts, C.: The Logic of Historical Explanation. Pennsylvania State University Press, State College (1995)
17. Shum, S.B., Motta, D., Dominguez, J.: ScholOnto: An Ontology-based Digital Library Server for Research Documents and Discourse. International Journal of Digital Libraries (2000), http://oro.open.ac.uk/23353/
18. Smith, B., Searle, J.: The Construction of Social Reality: An Exchange. American Journal of Economics and Sociology 62, 285–309 (2003)
19. Teufel, S., Siddharthan, A., Tidhar, D.: An annotation Scheme for Citation Function. In: ACL SIGdial Workshop on Discourse and Dialogue, pp. 80–87 (2006), doi:1654595.1654612
20. Timpany, C.: Designing the Printed Book as an Interactive Environment. The International Journal of the Book 7(1), 11–28 (2012), http://hdl.handle.net/10289/6592
21. Upward, F.: Structuring the Records Continuum, Part One: Postcustodial Principles and Properties. Archives and Manuscripts 25(1) (1997), http://www.infotech.monash.edu.au/research/groups/rcrg/publications/recordscontinuum-fupp1.html
22. W3C: Open Annotation Data Model (2013), http://www.openannotation.org/spec/core/20130208/oa.owl

Information Package Development of Alternative Primary Foods on 3D E-book Media

Abdurrakhman Prasetyadi, D.W. Ari Nugroho, and Fitria Laksmi Pratiwi

Technical Implementation Unit-Information Technology Division,
Indonesian Institutes of Sciences, Bandung 40135, Indonesia
{abdu060,dwi001,fitr002}@lipi.go.id

Abstract. The empowerment of information resources with more innovative technique is absolutely necessary by a library in the digital age now a days, and 3D e-book information package is one way that can be done, as in this research. The alternative primary food theme is taken since it is one of the national priority programs that have been declared by the government of the Republic of Indonesia. Alternative primary food in this study focused on rhizomes, such as cassava, sweet potatoes, and canna. The method used in this study is information repackaging through stages such as information gathering, analysis and synthesis makimg, design templates packaging, and information packaging in printed and electronic media (3-dimensional e-book). The result and benefit of this research is the creation of attractive, innovative, and appealing information packaging that can be used as a guide for the public insight knowledge about the importance of primary food sources other than rice which have high potential to be developed.

Keywords: Information Package, Library, Alternative Primary Food, 3D e-book.

1   Introduction

Don Tapscott refers the millennial generation to net generation who has eight specific norms namely: freedom, customization, a careful researcher (scrunity), integrity, collaboration, entertainment, velocity (speed), and innovation [1]. The emergence of millennial generation or net generation is characterized by high awareness of telecommunication technology. Therefore, from a variety of characteristics noted above, it can be underlined that this generation does have special characteristics, especially in accessing information.

Library users of millennial generation are those who crave information access that connected to the Internet for 24 hours, the availability of interactive and virtual information, as well as information that fit their needs. Therefore, Libraries as the information providers have to move fast to compensate for this generation phenomenon [2]. On the other hand, the librarians/library managers are already aware of the shift in the provision of information and services that replaced by digital devices, where it is the biggest challenge for libraries today and in the future. Therefore, in the implementation of its activities, Information Technology Division-LIPI Library employs and attaches the resources of both hardware and software that aims to provide excellent service for users.

K. Tuamsuk et al. (Eds.): ICADL 2014, LNCS 8839, pp. 227–232, 2014.

In addition to digitizing collection and developing library automation system and database, Information Technology Division-LIPI library has also made anticipatory and other innovative steps related to information repackaging services. Information repackaging provides insight to the library managers in providing information services, and the activities that match are repackage information, and present that information according to the will of users. Information repackaging can be done by:

- Formatting and synthesizing raw information,
- Combining the information of the subject as a source of relevant information, and
- Providing assistance (hint) for users in accessing the information [3,4]

Package done in this study is using the method of information repackaging as mentioned above with the systematic making process that combines text with graphics to match the needs of users. In addition, there will be images or illustrations of data observation process and the process of this information repackaging. The title of this information package is **"The Variety of Rhizomes As Alternative Primary Foods"**.

The alternative primary food theme is taken since food issue is one of national priority programs in Indonesia. Indonesian people are used to eating rice and they do not feel full before eating rice, because rice is the main source of carbohydrates. This traditional eating habit can threaten the availability of rice in Indonesia. Rice can actually be replaced by local foods as potential alternative primary foods. The replacement is extensible to support food security [5].

Focuses of this information package are selection, acquisition, processing and dissemination of various sources of information on the types of alternative food crops of rhizomes, among others, cassava, sweet potato, and canna. This is necessary so that the development of information package can be focus and be effective in a particular theme. The goal is to provide solutions to the community including students to obtain information like the nutrient content information, rhizomes cultivation, and food diversification,in the form of information package published by 3D e-book media [6].

2   Methods

According to [3,4] of information repackaging is used as the basis of the method in this study, in which every resources obtained from the print and electronic literature that have relevance to the topic of the research were collected, studied, and analyzed. Hence, data collections done using literature study, observation, and do interviews with the researcher/expert of rhizome plants from the Farm Ministry.

The scope of the information package classified into 7 reviews of each rhizome plant. Each category will review:

- Alternative primary food
- Potential map of rhizomes
- Potential nutrition of rhizomes
- Rhizomes cultivation
- Rural area of food diversification
- Various processed foods from rhizomes
- Supreme varieties

3   Repackaging Process Stages

Information Packaging at Information Technology Division-LIPI library consists of 1 outputs on 3D e-book media. The process of information repackaging is carried through several stages as follows:

- Collect and synthesize raw information about rhizome plants which will be concentrated into 7 categories of information package review,
- Design 3D e-book templates using graphic design software (Adobe In Design), which is then converted into .PDF document, and
- Finalize information package using 3D e-book publishing software.

4   Benefits

This study is aim at enhancing the skills of librarians in providing information repackaging services, as well as stimulating the librarians in terms of collecting credit score. The results of this study is hoped for contributing economically valuable knowledge for library, so it can be fully utilized for information seekers who came from the academia, researchers, and industrial communities.

Other benefits of information package, namely:

- Being attractive and informative guidebook for public and library users in particular [7],
- Increasing as well as fostering the stakeholders knowledge and awareness about the importance of alternative primary food information,
- Strengthening technological information database on Information Technology Division-LIPI library website about alternative primary food.

5   Results and Discussion

5.1   Information Collected and Synthesis

Collecting information begins with the literature study from the library of agriculture ministry in Bogor, Indonesia. Researchers obtain various kinds information from books and scientific journals. The information obtained is still raw information about the entire range of rhizome plants. Secondly, researchers collected information by observation to rhizomes plantation in Yogyakarta and Malang. In addition, researchers also obtain information regarding the various processed rhizomes of Small and Micro Business in Bantul, Yogyakarta. Researchers also doing interviews with researcher from the ministry of agriculture. Information obtained from the meeting not only about the characteristics of rhizomes it self but also about the Indonesian government's policy and implementation in the field associated with primary food sources that have been and will continue to do.

Data field also obtained from observation to Sidoarjo village of Progo (D.I.Yogyakarta) subdistrict government. This data is then used as the information regarding the village development as rice diversification village. Information collected then synthesized and classified into seven (7) reviews as follows: alternative primary food; potential map of rhizomes; potential nutrition of rhizomes; rhizomes cultivation; rural area of food diversification; various processed foods from rhizomes; and supreme varieties.

5.2   Information Package Template Design

Once the information collected process and synthesis is completed, the next stage is to design standardized template of information package. Standardized template consists of 2 parts, the cover and content template. Researchers using graphic design software to create more interesting and attractive information package design than an ordinary reading book. Graphics software used is Adobe InDesign, produced by Adobe System which can be used to create posters, magazines, brochures and even books. The use of Adobe InDesign application facilitate researchers in designinge-book because it has features that are fairly complete and easy. Following is display of 3D e-book using Adobe Indesign software, see figure 1 and 2 below

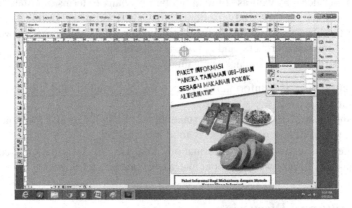

Fig. 1. Book cover design template process

Fig. 2. .PDF files import process on Flippingbook Publisher

5.3   Publish The Information Package on 3D E-book Media

After all the design and creation of cover and content template is completed, the next process is to export graphics into Portable Document Format (.PDF). Once the conversion process is completed, the next process is to design information package using Flippingbook Publisher software. Flippingbook Publisher or 3D software is an e-book application that allows users to import .PDF, MS. Office, Image, SWF files and others into 3D e-book. This application allows us to create 3D e-book online publications for websites and 3D off-line book publication on CD/DVD. Following are stages of 3D e-book packaging using Flippingbook Publisher applications:

Stage 1: Running FlippingBook Publisher, after the application is performing. Enter .PDF files that have been made to FlippingBook Publisher, as follows:

- Click the Import menu, and then click Import .PDF
- Click the file you want to use, then click the Open button
- Go ahead and start the process of importing .PDF document, click on the Start menu, see figure 2 below

Stage 2: After the above process is completed, we modify the appearance of 3D e-book with creating hardcover and eliminate some tools like download, print, make contents list, bookmarks, etc.

Stage 3: Files that have been saved will be published with Flippingbook Publisher in Html or .Exe format. The stages are:

- In the Publish menu there are two (2) options menu, To Html and Exe.
- We store the publications in .Exe format, whereas if it is stored on the internet should save it in Html format. Once completed the results can be seen by pressing the view result.

Next is the final layout of information package in flash mode which can be saved into CD/DVD, see figure 3 below

Fig. 3. Pages layout of alternative primary food review on Flash

6   Conclusions

Information repackaging in ways that are more varied and modern required by a library in which it is one of the answers to the challenges in this millennial era. Each information package generated by Information Technology Division-LIPI library carries superior information value because it has visual and attractive graphics. This is done solely for the sake of library's users needs of qualified information.

With the creation Information Package of Various Alternative Primary Food in 3D E-book Media will not only strengthen the insight and knowledge about the potential of alternative non-rice food in Indonesia, but also will encourage the development of similar studies with different themes according to users needs.

References

1. Tapscott, D.: Grown Up Digital: How the Net Generation is Changing Your World. McGraw-Hill, United States (2009)
2. Safitri, D.: University Library Welcomes the Millennial Generation, http://edukasi.kompasiana.com/2010/03/09/perpustakaan-perguran-tinggi-menyambut-asa-generasi-millenial-90116.html (acessed on June 3, 2014)
3. Saracevic, T., Woods, J.A.: Consolidation of Information: A Handbook on Evaluation, Restructuring, and Repackaging of Scientific and Technical Information. General Information programme and UNISIST of UNESCO, Paris (1981)
4. Bunch, A.: The basics of information work. Bingley, London (1984)
5. Djaafar, T.F., Sarjiman, Pustika, A.B.: Development Of Arrow root Cultivation And Processing Technology To Support Food Security. Jurnal Litbang Pertanian 29(1), 25–26 (2010)
6. Prasetyadi, A., Ari Nugroho, D.W.: Information Repackaging of Renewable Energy Technologies on E-book 3D. In: The 6 Indonesian Digital Libraries Conference, pp. 64–65. Perpusnas Republik Indonesia, Malang (2013)
7. Perdananugraha, G.M.: Analysis and Development of Food and Health Information Package Through the Utilization of Information Technology and Multimedia. INKOM 3(1-2) (2009)

Player Acceptance of Human Computation Games: An Aesthetic Perspective

Xiaohui Wang[1], Dion Hoe-Lian Goh[1], Ee-Peng Lim[2],
and Adrian Wei Liang Vu[2]

[1] Wee Kim Wee School of Communication and Information
Nanyang Technological University, Singapore
{Wang0870,ashlgoh}@ntu.edu.sg
[2] School of Information Systems
Singapore Management University, Singapore
{eplim,adrianvu}@smu.edu.sg

Abstract. Human computation games (HCGs) are applications that use games to harness human intelligence to perform computations that cannot be effectively done by software systems alone. Despite their increasing popularity, insufficient research has been conducted to examine the predictors of player acceptance for HCGs. In particular, prior work underlined the important role of game enjoyment in predicting acceptance of entertainment technology without specifying its driving factors. This study views game enjoyment through a taxonomy of aesthetic experiences and examines the effect of aesthetic experience, usability and information quality on player acceptance of HCGs. Results showed that aesthetic experience and usability were important contributors of player acceptance. Implications of our study are discussed.

Keywords: Human computation games, aesthetic experience, usability, information quality, acceptance.

1   Introduction

Human Computation Games (HCGs) are applications that utilize human intelligence to perform computations that cannot be effectively done by software systems alone [1]. Specifically, game elements in HCGs can serve as motivators to accomplish tasks or solve problems in various domains [2]. In the context of digital libraries, HCGs may be harnessed to involve users in contributing content or metadata such as tags for images and music [e.g. 1, 3]. One example is *Herdit* [4] in which players listen to a music clip and are then quizzed about its content. These short text-based answers describe various aspects of the music clip which can be used as annotations for it. *Herdit* makes this game format attractive by utilizing visually pleasing design, intuitive interfaces, and by fostering a sense of community.

Previous HCG research has found that usability, quality of generated outputs, and enjoyable game experience are significant predictors of player acceptance [e.g. 5, 6]. These studies are useful to understand why players are motivated to complete

K. Tuamsuk et al. (Eds.): ICADL 2014, LNCS 8839, pp. 233–242, 2014.

computation tasks in a game environment but they do not clarify the concept of terms such as "fun" and "game enjoyment", which are central issues in entertainment technologies [7]. Put differently, although previous studies have demonstrated that HCGs can provide enjoyable experiences [e.g. 1, 4], empirical research on what exactly makes these games enjoyable has been lacking. This is of considerable value since an understanding of these factors will be beneficial for HCG development [8].

In particular, games for pure entertainment delve into the notion of the aesthetic experience as critical for enjoyment. Game aesthetics deals with the general pleasures that players feel as a result of interacting with a game [9]. Here, the mechanics-dynamics-aesthetics (MDA) model defines the aesthetic experience as the emotional responses evoked in players during gameplay [10]. This model specifies a taxonomy of aesthetic elements, providing a concrete way of examining game enjoyment, thus facilitating the design and evaluation of game enjoyment [11]. In many ways, aesthetics is fundamental to good game design. Yet it has been overlooked in HCGs, and the MDA model has not been applied in this context, thus representing a research gap.

In the light of this, the present study investigates players' perceptions of HCGs through an aesthetic perspective. Two objectives will be addressed. First, we develop a HCG based on the MDA model. Secondly, we examine the effect of perceived aesthetic experience on player acceptance of HCGs. We compare the strength of the effects of perceived aesthetic experience against perceived usability and the perceived information quality, which have been previously examined in the context of HCGs.

2 Acceptance of Human Computation Games

Acceptance research seeks to examine the contributing factors that affect user's willingness to use a system or product [12]. It has attracted attention from both practitioners and researchers since the understanding of user acceptance can imply better methods for evaluating and predicting users' response to a system [12]. User acceptance has thus been an important topic in information systems research [13].

Although influential, research on player acceptance towards HCGs is still in its infancy. The limited work available has shown that the perception of enjoyment in terms of leisure and control is positively associated with the intention to play HCGs [6]. However, enjoyment as a state of positive emotional experience is an elusive and vague term related to perceptions such as pleasure, fun, immersion and flow [7]. It is unclear what constitutes game enjoyment [8]. This study thus extends previous work by examining the factors related to game enjoyment in HCGs and their effect on player acceptance. This can lead to a better understanding of HCGs and provide guidance for effective integration of game elements into computation tasks.

2.1 Aesthetic Experience

Game aesthetics is one of the various terms adopted to characterize the experience of gameplay [7]. One of the more specific definitions of game aesthetics comes from the MDA framework which describes three interconnected layers in games: Mechanics-Dynamics-Aesthetics. This framework explains how the different mechanics of a game are needed so that a player's experiences can be formed during his/her real-time interactions (dynamics) with the game. Aesthetics describes designed emotional responses evoked through gameplay [10], and includes but is not limited to happiness, anxiety and relaxation [7]. Importantly, the MDA model proposes a taxonomy of game aesthetics, which includes eight categories: sensation, fantasy, narrative, challenge, fellowship, discovery, expression, and submission. This taxonomy goes beyond obscure items such as "fun" and "game enjoyment" and provides designers and researchers with a concrete means to analyze the game experience [10].

Previous studies have confirmed the assumption that the aesthetics taxonomy of the MDA framework can be applied to describe the emotional responses of a game and act as guidance for game design [e.g. 11, 14]. Here, [11] utilized the MDA model to create a general framework for educational game design and evaluation. In the context of HCGs, [14] measured perceived aesthetic experience in a HCG based on the MDA taxonomy. Results indicated that the taxonomy could characterize aesthetic game experiences in different HCGs [14]. However, that study did not test the effect of perceived aesthetic experience on player acceptance of HCGs. We deem that the taxonomy of aesthetic experiences can be applied to describe a player's emotional responses, and that a player's perceived aesthetic experience may have a positive effect on acceptance of HCGs. Thus, we propose the following hypothesis:

H1: *Perceived aesthetic experience has a positive effect on acceptance of HCGs.*

2.2   Usability and Information Quality

Usability concerns the mechanics layer of a game. Besides aesthetics, a successful game should provide players with immediate feedback, natural mapping of controls, error prevention, and ease of learning [15]. Failure to address usability issues may lead to a negative effect on the overall quality of the game and diminish a player's preference for it. Research has shown that usability in HCGs was important for players' sustained usage [5]. Thus we propose the following hypothesis:

H2: *Perceived usability has a positive effect on acceptance of HCGs.*

Next, information quality has always been considered as a vital factor for user acceptance of an information system [16]. Individuals may be motivated to use a HCG because it provides useful information or helps in collecting quality information [2]. Previous research indicated that perceived quality of computation outputs was positively related with the intention to play HCGs [6, 17]. Hence, we propose that:

H3: *Perceived information quality has a positive effect on acceptance of HCGs.*

Perceived enjoyment plays a more important role in predicting user behavior than technical factors in hedonic information systems [18]. Since HCGs are entertainment-oriented, users could be motivated by benefits from interaction with the system [19]. Research has also found that seeking for leisure was a more prominent factor than perceived ease of use in HCGs [5]. We thus expect that perceived aesthetic experience is a more dominant predictor of player acceptance than perceived usability and information quality in HCGs, and propose:

H4: *For HCGs, perceived aesthetic experience plays a more important role in predicting acceptance than perceived usability and perceived information quality.*

3   Kpoprally: The HCG Used in This Study

Annotating music videos with tags is the initial step that enables such videos to be retrieved. However, both the huge amount of music videos and the vocabulary of useful tags make this work difficult and time-consuming [4]. Besides, music videos are described by many subjective tag categories such as theme and mood, the lack of objectivity in those categories makes it difficult to train automatic annotation systems. Thus human computation has been harnessed for the collection of data spanning an excerpt of music videos [20]. *Kpoprally* (Figure 1a) is a HCG based on a guessing game genre for collecting tags of videos to facilitate their retrieval. Specifically, players contribute tags through answering questions related to K-pop (a genre of popular music originating in Korea) music videos to obtain points as well as reputation as incentives. The contributed answers are utilized to index the music videos presented in the game. We chose K-pop music videos as our computation target because of its popularity in Asian countries.

During a gaming session, a video clip will be played for 30 seconds, followed by a question about the video (see Figure 1b). The questions come in two categories. First, objective questions refer to those that have known, unambiguous answers, such as name of the artist in the video and title of the song. Next, subjective questions are those that have no fixed answers and may vary according to individual opinion such as the mood of the video or the color of the video. Points for objective questions are awarded based on accuracy. For subjective questions, points awarded equal to the percentage of other players in agreement. In this way, answers with the highest percentage of agreement can be utilized as tags for the corresponding music videos.

Kpoprally was developed based on the MDA framework. Aesthetic elements in terms of sensation, narrative, challenge, fellowship and submission were accounted for [10]. Specifically, sensation represents the extent to which players feel sensory pleasure due to the audiovisual and tactile impressions of the game. This is provided by an appealing interface design in *Kpoprally*. Narrative represents a sense of dramatics in games, operationalized as an avatar and a backstory to provide a setting and goals of the game (Figure 1c). Challenge means an appropriate level of difficulty that matches players' skills. This is achieved with questions of varying difficulty. Fellowship pertains to support for social interaction. Here, *Kpoprally* is deployed on *Facebook*, and players can invite friends and share their in-game achievements, creating a sense of community. Moreover, players can socialize with others through leaving messages in the game's message board. Submission means that games act as a tool for leisure and passing time and players may feel detached from the real world and feel an altered sense of time during gameplay [15]. *Kpoprally* engages players with attractive tasks and multiple goals, such as earning scores for the avatar and fighting for higher rankings in the leaderboard (Figure 1d). However, because *Kpoprally* is a casual game, three categories of aesthetics (fantasy, discovery, and expression) were not included as they typically are not found in such games.

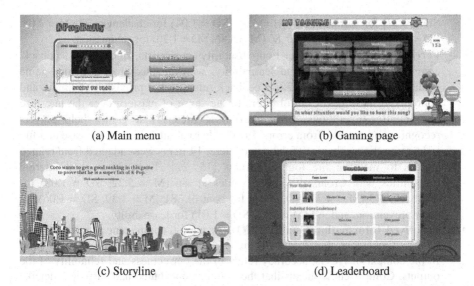

(a) Main menu   (b) Gaming page

(c) Storyline   (d) Leaderboard

Fig. 1. Screen shots of *Kpoprally*

4   Methodology

An evaluation of *Kpoprally* was conducted to address the study's hypotheses. We recruited 122 participants from local universities, comprising undergraduate and graduate students. Fifty were male and 72 were female, with ages ranging from 19 to 41 and an average of 23 years. In addition, 82 (67.2%) participants watched music videos online on a regular basis (more than once a month). Further, 62 (50.8%) participants played casual games frequently, and the majority of the participants (more than 52.5%) played games on social networking applications such as Facebook.

The study began with a researcher providing information about HCGs and their potential for collecting useful data. Participants were also briefed on the purpose, structure and usage of *Kpoprally*. Next, each participant was handed out a card with gameplay instructions, ensuring that participants consistently experienced all elements of *Kpoprally*. The study then commenced with participants playing the game. Once concluded, participants were asked to complete a questionnaire that captured perception and acceptance of *Kpoprally,* as well as demographic data. The entire study took about 40 minutes to complete.

Three aspects were covered in the questionnaire related to the perception of *Kpoprally*. Items were adapted from previous work [e.g. 14, 21] and were all rated on a 7-point scale ranging from 1 (strongly disagree) to 7 (strongly agree).

- **Perceived Aesthetic Experience (PAE).** This was assessed with five constructs (sensation, narrative, challenge, fellowship, and submission) adopted from the MDA model. Here, 19 items were adapted from past studies related to the evaluation of game aesthetics [6, 8, 14], Tests show good internal reliabilities with Cronbach's alpha values at .93 (M = 4.97, SD = 1.13) for sensation, .90 (M = 3.73,

SD = 1.27) for narrative, .64 (M = 4.34, SD = 1.04) for challenge, .77 (M = 4.08, SD = 1.39) for fellowship, and .86 (M = 3.86, SD = 1.20) for submission.

- **Perceived Usability (PU).** Four usability constructs, including feedback, control, error prevention, and learnability, were adapted from previous game evaluation studies [e.g. 15, 22]. Feedback refers to the provision of timely and appropriate messages. Control refers to the sense of mastery over the interface and intuitive operations. Error prevention means that games help players recognize and recover from errors. Finally, learnability refers to the ease and fun in learning the mechanics of the game. Here, 14 items were adapted from related studies to measure the four constructs [15, 22]. Tests show good internal reliabilities with Cronbach's alpha values at .86 (M = 5.22, SD = 1.08) for feedback, .75 (M = 4.77, SD = .87) for control, .81 (M = 4.39, SD = 1.06) for error prevention, and .69 (M = 4.77, SD = 1.01) for learnability.
- **Perceived Information Quality (PIQ).** Accuracy, completeness, relevancy are quality dimensions that frequently appear in information quality studies [16]. In the context of HCGs, accuracy refers to the correctness and reliability of the outputs. Completeness means that the outputs contributed had sufficient details. Relevancy refers to the appropriateness of the outputs in relation to the computation purpose [17]. PIQ was assessed with three constructs and 7 items from prior work [16, 17]. Tests also show good internal reliabilities with the Cronbach's alpha values at .79 (M = 5.01, SD = .93) for relevancy, .80 (M = 4.41, SD = 1.15) for completeness, and .79 (M = 4.87, SD = .92) for relevancy.

Finally, acceptance of *Kpoprally* was operationalized as attitude, intention to play, and intention to recommend. As indicated in prior work, attitude, representing the affective evaluation to a set of behaviors [12], is a strong predictor of actual usage; intention to use and intention to recommend reflects the user's satisfaction with the system and their willingness to use and recommend it to others [23]. Those three constructs were measured in the questionnaire with 10 items adapted from previous studies [2, 23]. Again, tests show good internal reliabilities with Cronbach's alpha values at .93 (M = 4.41, SD = 1.36) for attitude, .94 (M = 3.94, SD = 1.43) for intention to play, and .91 (M = 4.10, SD = 1.30) for intention to recommend.

5   Results

To test the proposed hypotheses, a hierarchical regression analysis was conducted. The independent variables were the components of PU, PAE and PIQ. The dependent variables were attitude, intention to use and intention to recommend.

The multiple regression results are shown in Table 1, For attitude towards this game, 55.8% of the variance was accounted for and the model was statistically significant [F(5, 109) = 11.54, p < .001]. Only narrative (β = .25, p < .05) and submission (β = .48, p < .001) were significant predictors. With regards to intention to play, 54.4% of its variance was accounted by this model [F(5, 109) = 12.49, p < .001]. Among the antecedent variables, learnability (β = .19, p < .05), sensation (β = .21, p < .05), narrative (β = .25, p < .05), and submission (β = .37, p < .01) were significant predictors. Feedback was also a significant predictor of intention to play (β = -.17,

$p < .05$), but interestingly, the association was negative: More timely and informative feedback resulted in a smaller inclination to play. As for intention to recommend, our model was significant $[F(5, 109) = 8.44, p < .001]$ and explained 50.9% of the variance. Sensation ($\beta = .20, p < .05$), narrative ($\beta = .24, p < .05$), and submission ($\beta = .31, p < .01$) were significant predictors.

Table 1. Hierarchical regression analysis with PU, PIQ, and PAE as predictors of player acceptance of HCGs, N = 122

Independent Variables	Dependent Variables					
	Attitude (N = 122)		Intention to play (N = 122)		Intention to recommend (N = 122)	
	β	t	B	t	β	T
First Block						
Feedback	-.02	-.26	-.17	-2.08*	-.04	-.42
Control	.06	.56	-.03	-.23	.02	.21
Error Prevention	.03	.30	.02	.22	.06	.72
Learnability	.09	.97	.19	2.12*	.17	1.80
R^2 Change (%)	.25***		.23***		.26***	
Second Block						
Completeness	.09	.98	.05	.53	.05	.49
Accuracy	.05	.49	-.02	-.18	.15	1.28
Relevancy	-.08	-.74	-.04	-.36	-.19	-1.69
R^2 Change (%)	.08**		.05*		.06*	
Third Block						
Sensation	.14	1.57	.21	2.32*	.20	2.20*
Narrative	.23	2.11*	.25	2.27*	.24	2.12*
Challenge	-.05	-.60	-.04	-.38	-.11	-1.12
Fellowship	-.06	-.75	-.04	-.48	-.03	-.39
Submission	.42	3.98***	.37	3.50**	.31	2.77**
R^2 Change (%)	.23***		.26***		.19***	
Total R^2	.56		.54		.51	

$*p < .05, ** p < .01, *** p < .001$

We summarize our results below:

- Hypothesis 1 was partially supported. Participants who rated higher for narrative and submission elements of this game were more likely to have a positive attitude and adopted it than those who rated these elements lower. Further, participants who rated the sensory element of this game more positively were more likely to have a behavioral intention to play and recommend it.
- Hypothesis 2 was partially supported. The block of PU variables was significant in explaining player's attitude and behavioral intention. However, only learnability was positively related to intention to play.
- Hypothesis 3 was not supported in this study. Although the PIQ block was statistically significant in influencing player acceptance of HCGs, no variables in this block were significant predictors.

- Hypothesis 4 was partially supported. Comparing the variance of player acceptance explained by PU and PAE, PAE was a stronger predictor than PU regarding intention to play *Kpoprally*, while weaker comparing to PU in predicting player's attitude and intention to recommend. In addition, PAE was stronger in explaining the variance of player acceptance than PIQ.

6   Discussion and Conclusion

We developed a HCG using the MDA framework and examined the factors that influenced player acceptance. The evaluation suggested that *Kpoprally,* our developed HCG, provided players with a positive aesthetic experience. Further, perceived aesthetic experience and perceived usability were significant predictors of attitude towards, intention to play and intention to recommend HCGs. As HCGs have increasingly attracted the attention of both researchers and practitioners, as well as have the potential to be deployed in the digital libraries context, we expect that this study will help in the development of this game genre.

Our results showed that PAE was a significant predictor of player acceptance, highlighting the importance of fostering an aesthetic experience in HCGs. Results showed that submission was a dominant factor influencing acceptance of *Kpoprally*. This demonstrates the importance of helping players ease boredom and pass time in HCGs, such as providing multiple tasks and goals to induce players to linger. Sensation and narrative also affected player acceptance, suggesting that developing HCGs with attractive interface designs and engaging storyline should be pursued. Aesthetic elements such as challenge and fellowship did not show a significant effect in this study, contrary to prior work [e.g. 15]. One plausible explanation could be that the participants could not match the difficulty level of the questions. Participants also did not have time to socialize due to the duration of the study. This suggests more explicit support for fostering a sense of challenge and fellowship in future iterations of the game. For instance, game tasks need to be properly evaluated for difficulty so that they can be better matched with players' abilities.

Second, the significance of PU suggests that usability issues can be a strong catalyst in facilitating acceptance of a HCG. Here, we found that PU was a more prominent factor in explaining players' attitude and intention to recommend HCGs compared to PAE, which is inconsistent with findings in entertainment technologies [e.g. 18]. We hypothesize that although emotional responses play a vital role in predicting acceptance of HCGs in general, usability problems may hinder this effect, as these could immediately turn potential players away. However, more investigation needs to be done to support this. The significant positive effect of learnability on intention to play HCGs suggests that interface design of HCGs should be intuitive and easy to learn. The negative effect of feedback on players' intention to play is surprising [e.g. 22]. One possible explanation could be the questions in *Kpoprally* were more difficult than players expected. More incorrect answers would lead to more negative feedback, thus frustrating players and contributing to the negative relationship. Further, the non-significant results for the other variables suggest that players pay less attention to those issues in HCGs. However, this could be due to short period of the study, and future work could focus on longer-term usage.

We found it interesting that PIQ only accounted for a small amount of variance for player acceptance, and none of the components of PIQ showed a significant influence on player acceptance of *Kpoprally*. This nonetheless does not indicate the unimportance of information quality. Rather, one possible explanation could be that collecting quality tags is a latent function of *Kpoprally*. Players of *Kpoprally* focused on gaming and did not perceive it as an information system that could generate useful information. This implies that in order to engender enjoyment from computation contribution, HCGs developers should consider making the task overt to players. For instance, applications can deploy a dashboard to indicate the amount of contributions that a player has been made.

Our findings yield the following contributions. One, we add to the understanding of the predictors of HCG acceptance. While the main objective of our HCG is collecting useful computations, interestingly, PIQ may not always be a significant contributor for its acceptance. Instead, players may be more concerned about aesthetic elements and usability issues. This suggests that developing such applications is challenging because of the need to adhere to design principles of both games and information systems [6]. Two, significant factors behind acceptance covered in our study provide guidance for developers to allocate their limited resources in HCG development. For instance, the importance of sensation, narrative and submission in influencing player acceptance underlines the need to develop HCGs with interesting backstories, high quality graphics, and to help players pass time.

There are some limitations in this study that could be addressed in future work. First, our findings were generated from one study based on a single genre of HCG in the area of video tagging. Thus, testing the findings with different game genres and computation tasks would increase the generalizability. Second, players' individual differences, such as age, gender, prior experience, and personalities could have effect on their perception of aesthetic experience in HCGs. Further, our data was collected in a single study for a short period of time. A longitudinal study involving sustained usage of our game would provide more robust data on players' perceptions.

Acknowledgment. We would like to express our gratitude to Ziqian Wang, Kangli Ma, and Siva Kumar for assisting in the data collection.

References

1. Von Ahn, L., Dabbish, L.: Designing games with a purpose. Communications of the ACM 51(8), 58–67 (2008)
2. Goh, D.H., Lee, C.S.: Perceptions, quality and motivational needs in image tagging human computation games. Journal of Information Science 37(5), 515–531 (2011)
3. Morton, B.G., Speck, J.A., Schmidt, E.M., Kim, Y.E.: Improving music emotion labeling using human computation. In: Proceedings of the ACM SIGKDD Workshop on Human Computation, pp. 45–48. ACM (2010)
4. Barrington, L., O'Malley, D., Turnbull, D., Lanckriet, G.: User-centered design of a social game to tag music. In: Proceedings of the ACM SIGKDD Workshop on Human Computation, pp. 7–10 (2009)
5. Kothandapani, S., Goh, D.H.L., Razikin, K.: Influence of playability and usability in a mobile human computation game. In: 2012 32nd International Conference on ICDCSW, pp. 75–78. IEEE (2012)

6. Goh, D., Razikin, K., Lee, C.S., Chua, A.: Investigating user perceptions of engagement and information quality in mobile human computation games. In: Proceedings of the 12th ACM/IEEE-CS Joint Conference on Digital Libraries, pp. 391–392 (2012)

7. Calvillo-Gámez, E.H., Cairns, P., Cox, A.L.: Assessing the core elements of the gaming experience. In: Evaluating User Experience in Games, pp. 47–71. Springer, London (2010)

8. Wu, J., Li, P., Rao, S.: Why they enjoy virtual game worlds? An empirical investigation. Journal of Electronic Commerce Research 9(3) (2008)

9. Fencott, C., Clay, J., Lockyer, M., Massey, P.: Game invaders: The theory and understanding of computer games. John Wiley & Sons (2012)

10. Hunicke, R., LeBlanc, M., Zubek, R.: MDA: A formal approach to game design and game research. In Proceedings of the AAAI Workshop on Challenges in Game AI, p. 04 (2004)

11. Aleven, V., Myers, E., Easterday, M., Ogan, A.: Toward a framework for the analysis and design of educational games. In: 2010 Third IEEE International Conference on Digital Game and Intelligent Toy Enhanced Learning (DIGITEL), pp. 69–76. IEEE (2010)

12. Dillon, A., Morris, M.: User acceptance of new information technology: theories and models. In: Williams, M. (ed.) Annual Review of Information Science and Technology, vol. 31, pp. 3–32. Information Today, Medford (1996)

13. Lee, M.K.O., Cheung, C.M.K., Chen, Z.: Acceptance of internet-based learning medium: the role of extrinsic and intrinsic motivation. Information & Management 42(8), 1095–1104 (2005)

14. Carranza, J., Krause, M.: Evaluation of game designs for human computation. In: Eighth Artificial Intelligence and Interactive Digital Entertainment Conference, Stanford, Palo Alto, CA (2012)

15. Sweetser, P., Wyeth, P.: GameFlow: a model for evaluating player enjoyment in games. Computers in Entertainment (CIE) 3(3), 3 (2005)

16. Lee, Y.W., Strong, D.M., Kahn, B.K., Wang, R.Y.: AIMQ: a methodology for information quality assessment. Information & Management 40(2), 133–146 (2002)

17. Pe-Than, E.P.P., Goh, D.H.-L., Lee, C.S.: Enjoyment of a mobile information sharing game: Perspectives from needs satisfaction and information quality. In: Chen, H.-H., Chowdhury, G. (eds.) ICADL 2012. LNCS, vol. 7634, pp. 126–135. Springer, Heidelberg (2012)

18. Ha, I., Yoon, Y., Choi, M.: Determinants of adoption of mobile games under mobile broadband wireless access environment. Information & Management 44(3), 276–286 (2007)

19. Van der Heijden, H.: User acceptance of hedonic information systems. MIS Quarterly, 695–704 (2004)

20. Morton, B.G., Speck, J.A., Schmidt, E.M., Kim, Y.E.: Improving music emotion labeling using human computation. In: Proceedings of the ACM SIGKDD Workshop on Human Computation, pp. 45–48. ACM (2010)

21. Desurvire, H., Caplan, M., Toth, J.A.: Using heuristics to evaluate the playability of games. In: CHI 2004 Extended Abstracts on Human Factors in Computing Systems, pp. 1509–1512. ACM (2004)

22. Pinelle, D., Wong, N., Stach, T.: Heuristic evaluation for games: usability principles for video game design. In: Proceedings of the SIGCHI Conference on Human Factors in Computing Systems, pp. 1453–1462. ACM (2008)

23. Hamari, J., Koivisto, J.: Social motivations to use gamification: an empirical study of gamifying exercise. In: Proc. of ECIS, pp. 1–12 (2013)

Uses of Online Survey: A Case Study in Thailand

Thitima Srivatanakul[1] and Nuwee Wiwatwattana[2]

[1] Information Science Program, School of Liberal Arts
SukhothaiThammathirat Open University, Thailand
thitima.sri@stou.ac.th
[2] Department of Mathematics, Faculty of Science
Srinakharinwirot University, Thailand
nuwee@swu.ac.th

Abstract. Online survey is now being more widely considered as an effective tool to conduct surveys. The uses of online survey have been applied in extensive areas, for example, in academic research, marketing research, and in companies seeking to provide better services to customers and to improve HR management performance. The purpose of this paper is to identify the current usage of online surveys in Thailand created on an online survey software platform 'SurveyCan' in 2013. Using a more systematic approach, we classified surveys based on survey questions' measurement objects, sponsoring bodies and their relations to the respondents. A combination of key-phrases was used to determine the measurement objects that the surveys represent. The surveys were categorized into survey types and the concepts of interest. The finding of the paper shows that online survey provides massive applications potential for a variety of research topics. Several uses of online survey in Thailand are highlighted in the paper.

Keywords: online questionnaire, survey classification, survey usage, online research tool, survey type, data-driven online marketing.

1 Introduction

Over the years, there have been an increased number of companies, researchers and individuals who have switched from paper-based surveys to web-based surveys. If conducted properly, online surveys have advantages over other formats due to low-delivery cost, timeliness and instant feedback mechanisms. Conducting surveys on the World Wide Web also provides the ability to carry out large scale data collection from a wider audience. This is useful when the target respondents reside in different places and regions. One popular example of such is the presidential election poll in 2012 in the USA [1]. The collection of data from large and diverse segments of the population with traditional paper-and-pencil interviews or mail surveys has major drawback of being costly, tedious and time-consuming.

In Thailand, with the proliferation of smartphones and increasing availability of broadband, the number of internet users has reached26 million people or about 40.3% of the total population in 2013 [2]. The use of online survey has gained increasing interest from academic and industry researchers in Thailand. An article search on

K. Tuamsuk et al. (Eds.): ICADL 2014, LNCS 8839, pp. 243–251, 2014.
© Springer International Publishing Switzerland 2014

google scholar shows that the number of research articles(within the context of 'Thailand') conducted using or related to online survey has increased more than 4 times from 2009 to 2013. However, there is very limited systematic research on the uses of online survey in different sectors of Thailand. One of which is by [3], but the focus was on web-based survey design principles based on a Thai language background. This paper analyzes 1,311 surveys created on a cloud-based application software named 'SurveyCan' in year 2013 [4]. SurveyCan is chosen as the scope of our study due to its user-friendly interface design and local service provided by a Thai-owned company. It also provides both free and paid plans, which are suitable for both individual and enterprise users in Thailand. The objectives of this paper are to determine the different survey categories of online surveys that were predominantly conducted via a low-cost and freely accessible online tool and to analyze the types of surveys that are prevalent in different sectors (e.g. government, business and academic). By accomplishing this, we propose a systematic approach to help categorize the surveys, our main contribution. Content analysis was used to conduct the research. Our approach categorizes surveys using key-phrases identified from the survey questions and choices, survey titles and additional information appeared in the surveys.

2   The Past and Present of Online Survey

Online surveys have been around for more than three decades with e-mail as the first survey mode in late 1980s followed by initial web-based surveys in the 1990s [5]. At the beginning, conducting an online survey[1] would require programming skills or IT resources to implement one. The technology and tools nowadays have facilitated individuals, organizations and communities to conduct their own surveys for their own purposes. Barriers to creating own web surveys have much reduced with the introduction of friendly-interface web-based software applications which allows users to easily create surveys and deploy them at their own discretion. Researchers in small-scale or resource-limited environments are able to carry out large-scale empirical research that would not otherwise be possible to conduct. Online survey is usually in web-formed, accessible by internet protocols. Surveys created and accessible on the web is not limited to self-administering, they can too be used by phone or face-to-face interviewers as a media to fill in the responses.

3   Our Approach

Survey data, including survey titles, survey questions and choices, and other supporting information such as survey creation dates and number of responses were used as inputs in the analysis process. Responses of each survey were not made available by 'SurveyCan' as this would infringe the terms and conditions of the service. Only surveys which are publicly accessible (not password-enabled)with fifty or more number of responses are

---

[1] In the literature, 'web survey', 'Internet survey' and 'online survey' tend to be used rather interchangeably.

included in the study. The surveys created in 2013 meeting the above criteria totaled to 1,311.

The survey title, survey questions and choices and other supporting information on the survey itself were manually analyzed. The aim is to determine the application areas of the surveys and the survey sponsoring bodies. The following sections describe the analysis approach used in our study.

3.1   Survey Categorization

Classification of surveys can be viewed from many perspectives. If the focus and scope of target population are concerned, surveys can be roughly classified as census and sample surveys. On the other hand, longitudinal and cross-sectional surveys are the types of surveys when the time frame for data collection is considered. If survey mode is being considered, surveys can be referred to as interview surveys (face-to-face and telephone) and self-administered surveys (mail and online) [6]. The survey topics and the concepts of interest that the survey topics represent are the focal point for this work. Surveys can be designed to capture information requirements from as simple as voting for your favorite idols or to a very complex ones as behavior, life style pattern of consumers. Survey topics can be anything from households to business partners, from a neighborhood coffee shop to a large e-commerce website, from commuting with bike to school to traveling abroad. In this paper, we refer to these types as *"concepts of interest"*. Survey topics are also often referred to as categories such as customer satisfaction survey, employee engagement survey, marketing survey and business survey. Commercial survey sites such as [7, 8] offer category-specific surveys templates based on this perspective. In this paper, we used the term *"survey types"* for this view.

It is however challenging to identify which *survey types* the survey falls into. Without a systematic approach, the analysis would be subjective to a limited content found on the survey. Reading only a few questions would not be sufficient to precisely determine the *survey types* or even the *concepts of interest*. In [9], survey topics were automatically extracted and categorized using machine learning algorithms such as topic modeling and fuzzy clustering. However, the judgment criteria to define *survey types* were not discussed in the paper. In this paper, we take a different approach which is to determine how *survey types* can be systematically defined. [10] explained eight basic topic categories that are often measured by survey questions. They are attributes, images, decisions, needs, behavior, lifestyle, affiliations, and demographics. We made use of these measurement objectives to identify whether survey questions contain such elements of measurement or not. During the analysis process, we had decided to exclude some and introduce additional measurement objectives. These are summarized briefly as follows:

- Attitudes (AT) – subjectively measure a respondent's feeling and the likelihood of intention to behave.

- Behavior (B) – subjectively measure what the respondent did, where and when the action takes place, and how often was the action.

- Decisions Making (DM) – subjectively measures decision process of respondent to choose actions or impact on choices/actions.
- Need-related concepts (N) – subjectively measures the respondent's needs, preferences, desires or motives that underpin his/her behavior.
- Profile/Configuration (C) – objectively captures what respondent does or owns.
- Images (I) – subjectively measures how a subject is described, this can reflect positive/negative attitudes towards attributes/characteristics.
- Literacy & Skills (LS) - subjectively measures the literacy and skills of the respondents towards the subject of interest.

3.2   The Analysis Process

The approach taken in this work to determine different topic-based categories is as follows:

1. Identification of measurement objects and the related concept of interest: each survey question was carefully analyzed for its purpose. Key-phrases as illustrated in Table 1 are used to map the questions to the measurement objectives. One survey can contain one or more measurement objectives. For example, a typical customer satisfaction survey would ask respondent's attitudes towards a service (AT), and how the respondent has used the service (B). Measurement objectives that are applicable to the surveys were then recorded together with *the concept of interest*.

2. Identification of survey sponsoring bodies and the relations to the respondents: sponsoring bodies were derived from the text available on the survey. This includes survey titles, survey questions and choices, or from additional text provided on the survey. This may be explicitly stated or implicitly derived. The surveys are categorized into broad group of (1) government, (2) business, (3) academic, (4) bank and (5) individuals and communities. Surveys with insufficient information to determine the sponsoring organizations were grouped into 'Unknown'. For government and business sectors, the respondents in relation to the sponsoring bodies were also identified. This can be viewed as business-to-business (B2B), business-to-consumer (B2C), business-to-employee (B2E), government-to-government (G2G), government-to-citizen (G2C), government-to-employee (G2E) and government-to-business (G2B) relationships.

3. Identification of survey types: survey types were derived by considering the measurement objectives of the concepts of interest. Table 2 shows a few examples of survey types against main measurement objectives. Sponsoring bodies and their relations to the respondents were also used to narrow down the survey types to a specific domain. For example, a satisfaction survey from a company's customer would be 'customer satisfaction survey' while from an employee would be 'employee satisfaction survey'. To illustrate how this is used, consider the first record in Table 2: a consumer's attitudes (AT) of a product used from a business sector would be referred to as a 'customer satisfaction survey'

Table 1. Mapping of translated key-phrases (from Thai) to measurement objectives

Measurement Objectives	Key-phrases	
Attitudes (AT)	what do you think	you believe/trust/would like
	do you agree with	attitudes towards
	what is your opinion	perceptions of/about
	what will you decide	you will tend to
	you want to (intention)	
Behavior (B)	have you ever	what are the reasons that you
	how often have you	most of the time, you will
	how long have you	what are your experiences on
Decisions Making (DM)	what are the factors (that affect your decision on)	
	who influences (your choice to)	
	how likely would the following factors affect your decision	
	you would [action] only if [condition/factor]	
Need-related concepts (N)	you would like to	you want (needs/desires)
	you are expecting	
Profile/Configuration (C)	your hobbies/usual activities include	
	you have in your possessions	
	how many [belongings] do you have	
Images (I)	how is this [product/service] different from other	
	when you hear/ of [product/service], you would think of [attributes/characteristics]	
Literacy & Skills (LS)	do you understand/know about (with choices of 'yes' and 'no')	
	how would you rate your knowledge/skill on	

Table 2. Example of how survey types are defined based on different elements

Main Measurement Objectives	Sponsoring Bodies	Concepts of Interest (at general-level)	Audience Group	Resulting Survey Types
AT	Business	Product	Consumer	Customer Satisfaction Survey
AT	Business	Work climate	Employee	Employee Engagement Survey
DM/AT/B	Business or Government	Service	general	Market Research Survey
AT	Government	Organizational process/management	Employee	Organization Development Survey
AT	Academic	Upcoming event	Faculty & Student	Event Planning Survey

4   Results

All occurrences of surveys created were studied. This would show how frequent the use of one particular type occurred over another, which means that the surveys, as the subject of our study, could be from the same survey creators. We highlight here our findings from the analysis of 1,311 surveys. Academic sector was predominantly users of software tool which totaled to 51.9% of surveys created. Academic sector includes researchers, students, universities and other education institutions. About 79.4% of the surveys from the academic sector are conducted to find out answers to research questions by researchers and graduate-level students. Other uses within the academic sector include event evaluation & planning surveys (6.5%), faculty & student feedback and satisfaction surveys (5.3%) and training survey (4.0%). Event evaluation surveys gather insight from attendees to improve future events, while event planning surveys seek to get attendees' feedback to plan the upcoming events. Faculty & student surveys acquire faculty members and students' satisfaction level or feedback on products and services offered to them by the institutions. Training surveys are reported separately from event-related surveys since they focus mainly on satisfaction of the members of the schools or universities towards trainings and courses offered to them. Another small portion (4.8%) of uses include school survey, fun survey, graduates follow-up surveys, course selection surveys, auditing and satisfaction surveys from external users of the institutions' websites or services.

Business sector accumulated to 23.6% of the total surveys created. Most of the surveys (79.9%) are created to acquire information from the consumers (B2C). Uses as B2E and B2B surveys resulted to 11.0% and 3.6% respectively. Business sector also seeks general target audience (4.9%) to participate in the surveys, mostly to understand market needs. B2G's event evaluation survey and external audit surveys (0.6%) are also identified in the analysis. Fun surveys (44.1%) and customer experience related surveys (32.4%), including satisfaction surveys, feedback surveys and perception surveys, were the majority of the surveys conducted in the B2C area. In B2E area, the importance has been given to get insight from employees and hear their opinions about work/job climate, environment, facilities, management, and their engagement towards their work and company, totaling 61.8%. Other B2E surveys include event evaluation and planning surveys (23.5%) and training surveys (14.7%).

10.8% of the survey sponsoring bodies was identified to be from the government sector.A little more than half of the surveys from the government sector are G2C surveys (54.9%), followed by G2E surveys (33.1%), G2G surveys (6.3%), G2B surveys (2.1%) and another 3.5% was conducted for the general target population. Customer satisfaction and feedback surveys (75.6%) are the main type identified from the G2C surveys. G2E was predominantly used to understand its employees' needs and satisfaction level (51.1%) and to evaluate training courses (36.2%).Official statistics surveys are used to conduct surveys between other government units (77.8% of G2G surveys).

Other sponsoring bodies identified are from individuals and communities (4.0%), banks (0.8%). Some surveys (9.0%), however, lack of sufficient information for us to identify their sponsoring bodies. Surveys created by individuals and communities includes but not limited to fun surveys, voting, event planning surveys, opinion polls, satisfaction surveys, feedback surveys and membership forms. Table 3 shows the proportion of concepts of interest of the surveys conducted.

Table 3. Proportion of concepts of interest of the surveys conducted

Concepts of interest	%	Concepts of interest	%	Concepts of interest	%
Advertising & Marketing	1.4%	Finance	2.2%	Organizational Management/HR	8.1%
Agriculture & Forestry	0.5%	Food & Drink	8.8%	People & Society	3.7%
Arts & Entertainment	6.0%	Games	9.9%	Pets & Animals	1.5%
Autos & Vehicles	1.4%	Green Living & Clean Energy	1.6%	Politics	0.6%
Baby & Children	0.7%	Health & Wellness	3.4%	Real Estate	0.7%
Beauty & Fitness	4.7%	Hobbies & Leisure	1.4%	Retail Trade	1.5%
Books & Literature	1.4%	Home & Garden	1.3%	Shopping	2.0%
Business & Industry	1.4%	Internet & Telecom	2.8%	Sports	1.9%
Business Service	1.9%	Jobs & Education	9.2%	Transportation & Logistics	2.2%
Computers & Electronics	3.4%	Law & Government	0.4%	Travel	3.1%
Event & Listing	5.6%	Online Communities	5.2%		

We grouped concepts of interest into a bigger cluster of interest. The concepts of interest identified are very diverse, especially from the academic sector. The main topics of interest for the government sector are on online communities and organizational management/human resource management. In the business domain, organizational management/human resource management, event & listing, jobs & education and games are among the popular ones. It is worthy to note that almost all (97.87%) of the surveys under study was carried out in Thai language.

5   Discussion

The result shows that some particular application areas are more convenient and preferable for online surveys. In terms of number of responses, fun surveys and entertainment-related topics are probable to receive high attention from the respondents. Online satisfaction surveys towards organizations' websites and IT services can be found in both business and government sectors. Interestingly, our work shows that individuals and small communities are able to conduct online surveys with medium to large samples, ranging up to around 70,000 samples. As mentioned earlier, not only commercial companies care about their consumers' satisfaction, but governments too are interested in and use surveys also to evaluate the need for public services. Government surveys tend to seek respondents' attitudes towards concept of interest, while both academic and business sectors are interested in consumers' behaviors and factors that determine decision-making.

One of the best uses of online survey is when survey research is conducted often [11]. We found that event evaluation surveys, fun surveys, and customer satisfaction surveys are the areas of application that occurred often (i.e. more than ten times) by the same sponsoring body. Survey research interests are tightly related to our daily activities. Especially in academic surveys, questions were asked about the taste of your favorite coffee, eating habit of your family members or how you travel to school.

Based on the results and from our observation during the analysis process, we see several prospects for the use of online surveys as follows:

Digital Marketing

In recent years, digital marketing has received vast attentions from as small as on an individual-owned shop to as large as a state-owned enterprise. Facebook ads and Google Ad Words are one of the popular advertising tools currently sought by many types of business. These allow companies to target consumers based on their demographic, interests or behavioral data. All digital marketers can benefit from a clear understanding of their potential consumers. As online surveys have close ties to digital marketing, we see this as a growing opportunity for business owners to carry out online surveys in order to better develop their online/digital marketing strategy.

B2B, G2B and G2G Areas

Online surveys can be seen to be applicable not only to business-to-consumer (B2C) but also business-to-business (B2B). However, B2B online surveys had received much less attention in the research [11] and the focus was more on B2C. Although, the use of B2B is not yet popular in the business sectors based on our findings, but there are strong opportunities in this area as customer relationship management (CRM) in B2B market continues to grow. Government surveys may not be prevalent among the G2B and G2G surveys in comparison to G2C, however, there are great potential that the use of online survey could help government and other non business organizations in Thailand understand the needs of their partners more.

Service-Integrated Surveys

Nowadays, we can see that survey is tightly integrated with delivery of service. A survey form maybe presented on a table after being served in a restaurant, or after checking out from a hotel, you may be asked to fill in your suggestions and complaints. When a traditional pen-and-paper survey is used, negative feedbacks can be easily filtered out by those who are affected. Online surveys provide a better solution to allow managerial positions to receive instant feedbacks once the responses get submitted.

Our results, however, contradict with the statement in [12] which states that "the replacement process of internet surveys over other survey modes are faster and most visible in the commercial surveys than within the academic, public and government bodies". This is our work limitation. We only made use of one local online software tool as our case study. There are many other similar tools and software available, especially for commercial surveys, this may be carried out by large consulting companies or marketing and research firms.

6   Conclusion

We used a more systematic approach to define survey types, which can therefore be used to categorize surveys in the scope of our study. Online surveys provide a massive application potential for a variety of research topics. Research conducted by individuals or resource-limited organizations had benefited from the use of online surveys. In Thailand, we can see the potential usage of online surveys most visibly to those bound with growing online communities. There are several prospects on the uses of online surveys, not only to the Thai communities but elsewhere. The limitation of this work is the evaluation of the approach we used to categorize the surveys. As the current existing approach found in the literature in [9] does not provide the criteria on how the survey types are defined, it is unattainable for us to compare results. However, the results of this work can be used as a basis to develop and to evaluate future system development to automatically extract and categorize survey topics. Other areas of future work include: topic modelling on Thai survey questions, generations of question banks and templates for Thai users. To our best knowledge, this has not yet existed.

Acknowledgement. We would like to acknowledge the support from SurveyCan for providing input materials for this research work.

References

1. Garland, P., Goldberg, D., Epstein, L., Suh, A.: 2012 Presidential Election Poll (2012), http://www.slideshare.net/SurveyMonkey/ surveymonkey-2012-presidential-election-poll-final-models (retrieved June 5, 2014)
2. Nectec. Internet User and Statistics in Thailand, http://internet.nectec.or.th/webstats/internetuser.iir?Sec=i nternetuser (retrieved June 5, 2014)
3. Vate-U-Lan, P.: Internet-based Survey Design: Principles from a Thai Experimental Study. In: 7th IEEE International Conference on Advanced Learning Technologies(ICALT), pp. 525–529. IEEE Computer Society, Los Alamitos (2007)
4. SurveyCan, http://www.surveycan.com
5. Schonlau, M., Fricker Jr., R.D., Elliott, M.N.: Conducting Research Surveys via E-Mail and the Web. Rand Publishing, Santa Monica (2001)
6. Stoop, I., Harrison, E.: Classification of Surveys. In: Handbook of Survey Methodology for the Social Sciences, pp. 7–21. Springer, New York (2012)
7. Surveymonkey, http://www.surveymonkey.com
8. Questionpro, http://www.questionpro.com
9. George, C.P., Wang, D.Z., Wilson, J.N., Epstein, L.M., Garland, P., Suh, A.: A Machine Learning Based Topic Exploration and Categorization on Surveys. In: 11th International Conference on Machine Learning and Applications (ICMLA), vol. 2, pp. 7–12. IEEEComputer Society, Washington (2012)
10. Alreck, P.L., Settle, R.B.: The survey research handbook, 3rd edn. McGraw-Hill/Irwin, New York (2004)
11. Evans, J.R., Mathur, A.: The value of online surveys. Internet Research 15(2), 195–219 (2005)
12. Vehovar, V., Manfreda, K.L.: Overview: online surveys. In: The SAGE Handbook of Online Research Methods, pp. 177–194. Sage Publications, Thousand Oaks (2008)

Finding Co-occurring Topics in Wikipedia Article Segments

Renzhi Wang, Jianmin Wu, and Mizuho Iwaihara

Graduate School of Information, Production and Systems, Waseda University
Fukuoka 808-0135, Japan
ouninnyuki.ips@asagi.waseda.jp,
jianmin.wu@moegi.waseda.jp, iwaihara@waseda.jp

Abstract. Wikipedia is the largest online encyclopedia, in which articles form knowledgeable and semantic resources. Identical topics in different articles indicate that the articles are related to each other about topics. Finding such co-occurring topics is useful to improve the accuracy of querying and clustering, and also to contrast related articles. Existing topic alignment work and topic relevance detection are based on term occurrence. In our research, we discuss incorporating latent topics existing in article segments by utilizing Latent Dirichlet Allocation (LDA), to detect topic relevance. We also study how segment proximities, arising from segment ordering and hyperlinks, shall be incorporated into topic detection and alignment. Experimental data show our method can find and distinguish three types of co-occurrence.

Keywords: LDA, MLE, Link, Wikipedia.

1 Introduction

Wikipedia articles are edited by different volunteers with different thoughts and styles. Same entities or events are often mentioned in multiple articles, so detecting co-occurring topics among articles is important for comparing descriptions in different articles and reorganizing overlapping descriptions. In Wikipedia, the concept name where a link is from and the article name of the link destination do not need to completely match. Thus topic co-occurrence cannot be found only by links when the same topic is expressed in a different way. Using only link information cannot find whether topics are co-occurring between portions of articles.

Current methods about comparing similarities between texts are largely relying on text features and topic generative models. TF-IDF is a measure to evaluate how important a word is to a document in a static corpus. Latent Dirichlet Allocation (LDA) is often used to cluster articles into topics by latent meaning [1] [2]. Explicit Semantic Analysis (ESA) [7] is a method to use Wikipedia links to assess the relatedness of articles. The Wikipedia Link-based Measure (WLM) [8] is another method to obtain semantic relatedness from Wikipedia links.

In this paper, we propose an LDA-based algorithm to find co-occurring topics in Wikipedia articles, at the level of logical segments such as paragraphs. To improve

K. Tuamsuk et al. (Eds.): ICADL 2014, LNCS 8839, pp. 252–259, 2014.
© Springer International Publishing Switzerland 2014

the results, our algorithm combines LDA with Maximum Likelihood Estimation (MLE) to smooth the LDA result. Considering the effect of neighboring articles, we also utilize Wikipedia links to reflect the network influence. Our experimental results show combinations of smoothing parameters where F1-score becomes highest.

2   Related Work

2.1   ESA and WLM

Explicit Semantic Analysis (ESA) [7] is a vector-space model, in which not only term weight vectors are compared, but also link weight vectors are compared to evaluate relatedness, such as linked documents like Wikipedia. The vector elements in ESA are Wikipedia-based concepts which are constructed by human, so it is costly. The method compares the text vectors which reflect concept space and calculate their similarity. WLM [8] utilizes the vector-space model and normalized Google distance to measure relatedness. Their link vectors are similar to TF-IDF vectors. They use link counts weighted by the probability of each link occurrence, and reasonable results can be easily calculated.

2.2   LDA

LDA is a generative topic model that each document is viewed as a mixture of various topics and the topic distribution is assumed to have a Dirichlet prior. The LDA model can provide us semantic topic by training the corpus. The LDA model is already proved to work well as a topic tracking and classification tool in many fields such as Facebook, newspaper, academic literature [2]. We can expect the LDA model will work well in the Wikipedia corpus, but there are issues that need to be resolved. If the corpus consists of the complete articles in Wikipedia, the result will not be good enough, because the articles are long in average and most of them having not only one topic. However, due to the corpus size, the result of LDA training becomes a sparse matrix, where a sparse matrix means that each article is only mapped to one or few main topics. The minor topic will not be obvious enough to be extracted. Another deviation is that all the articles in the corpus are seen as independent during training. But as we know, Wikipedia has a network structure of articles, where articles are connected by interlinks. If we just see the articles as independent, such structure information will not be reflected.

3   Proposed Algorithm

3.1   Link-Weighed Corpus

As the world largest encyclopedia, Wikipedia creates a large, complex network, where articles are connected by interlinks. The link distance between two article nodes and other graph-theoretic information can be utilized for topic detection. We assume that the links from a central article to neighboring articles assist complementing the content of the central article by incorporating the neighboring articles. In order to use this structure information, we propose to create a suitable corpus for target articles.

Definition (distance-based sphere): Given a central article A and a distance $k>0$ which is measured by the number of links between two article nodes, a k-*sphere* $SP_k(A)$ is the set of article nodes that are connected to A by k or less links and A itself, where link directions are ignored.

We define the union of the terms in $SP_k(A)$ as the corpus. Thus, all the articles in the corpus are directly or indirectly connected to the central article.

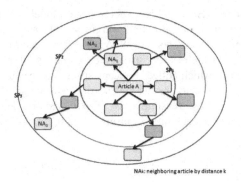

Fig. 1. The distance-based sphere of the article

Wikipedia articles are edited by many different online volunteers. Articles are usually long with multiple topics. The LDA model proved to work well when the articles in the corpus are relatively short like online news articles. But Wikipedia articles often have long, detailed texts, and additional contents can be found from its neighbor articles. So we divide one whole article into several segments based on its logical structure. The best situation is that each segment is short and contains only a few topics. As articles are paragraphed by editors when it was edited, we can just divide the whole article into segments by paragraphs. We regard each segment as a document in the corpus. These documents (segments) fit the LDA model better than directly applying onto whole articles.

3.2   Two Types of Co-occurrence

In our model, there are two types of co-occurrence. The first type of co-occurrence is that two segments describe one common entity or one common event. The event or entity is represented as a set of words which contain one key word or one key phrase. All the other words are supplementing the keyword or key phrase. This set of words is a subset of one topic. For example: "He began his presidential campaign in 2007 and, after a close primary campaign against Hillary Rodham Clinton in 2008, he won sufficient delegates in the Democratic Party primaries to receive the presidential nomination." from the article "*Barack Obama*". Also, "Running in the 2008 Democratic presidential primaries, Hillary Clinton won far more primaries and delegates than any other female candidate in American history, but narrowly lost the nomination to U.S.

Senator Barack Obama, who went on to win the national election." from the article *"Hillary Rodham Clinton"*. The two segment pair belongs to Type-1. The second type of co-occurrence is that two segments belong to one category. Here we consider that one category contains more than one topic, and a category is the summary of several similar topics. In our experiment, we examine the categories in the bottom part of Wikipedia articles to acquire new categories. As an example: the 4th segment of article Barack Obama and the 4th segment of article Hillary Rodham Clinton describe the two people's work after graduating from law school. Even though the word "lawyer" does not appear in the segment pair, both segments belong to the category of lawyer. The segment pair belongs to Type-2. If neither Type-1 nor Type-2 co-occurrence is found, then the two segments are not related. In this case, their major topics are dissimilar, and they belong to no common category.

We utilize an existing category hierarchy to test Type-1 and Type-2 co-occurrences. The ODP website [9] is the largest, most comprehensive manually-edited directory of the Web. It is constructed and maintained by a passionate, global community of volunteer editors. We do not choose the category hierarchy in Wikipedia because the category structure in Wikipedia is not a tree, but a network. There is also an ambiguity in the Wikipedia category structure, that is, there are articles under a category, but its sub category is also under the same category. Sometimes it leads to the confusion of category layer. Conversely, the ODP category structure has 16 obvious roots, each node depth is comparable, and node layers are aligned. Using the ODP category tree as our standard of judgment, a segment pair is categorized into three types as follows: If the category two segments describe is in the leaf node of ODP, then we judge the two segments asType-1. If the common category of two segments, if any, is at a height less than or equal to 3, we judge these two segments asType-2. Otherwise, the two segments are judged as having no relation.

3.3   Algorithm

We argue that linked articles bring additional information to the central article and affect the topic of the central article. We discover topics of articles by three approaches: the first is the obvious part, which can be observed by simple term occurrence. The second part is the latent part, where a latent topic model is employed to extract the latent part. The third part is the link structure information from the sub graph based of k-sphere. We construct the corpus as the union of $SP_k(A)$ with given article A. Then we divide all the articles into segments by paragraphs and regard each segment as a document in the training data. We find what topics each segment has and calculate their segment-wise similarities. We use term probabilities as the feature vector elements of the similarities. In the LDA model, a topic is seen as a distribution on all the words, so one of method is to set all the words in the corpus as our vector elements.

After training an LDA model, we can obtain the probability of a term in a document by the following formula:

$$P_{LDA}(w \mid d, \hat{\theta}, \hat{\phi}) = \sum_{z=1}^{K} P(w|z, \hat{\phi}) \, P(z|\hat{\theta}, d) \tag{1}$$

Where $\hat{\theta}$ and $\hat{\phi}$ are the posterior estimates of θ and ϕ respectively. The probability of terms can be specified by the document language model [3] [4]. We refer to the first and second item in brackets for the obvious part of the probability, which is a linear combination of the document-level probability and collection-level probability:

$$P_o(w|D) = \lambda \left[\frac{N_d}{N_d+\mu} P_{ML}(w|D) + \left(1 - \frac{N_d}{N_d+\mu}\right) P_{ML}(w|Coll) \right] + (1 - \lambda) P_{LDA}(w|D) \quad (2)$$

Here N_d is the number of terms appearing in the segment, $P_o(w|D)$ is the probability of word w in document D without link information [5] [6]. We adjust the value of μ to optimize the obvious part. The third part is the potential part consisting of the probability of the word appeared in the segment estimated by LDA. Smoothing parameter λ is to adjust the ratio of the obvious part and potential part. By the formulae (1) and (2) we can obtain the probabilities of all the words in the corpus being generated by the segment itself. We describe the structure part as follows:

$$\sum_{i=1}^{N_D} u(D, D_i) P_o(w|D_i) \quad (3)$$

Here, Di is an article which has a link from D, $u(D, D_i)$ is the weight of the link from D to Di, $P_o(w|D_i)$ is the probability by LDA of word w appearing in D_i. N_D is the number of links from the source segment. So our overall word probability is given as follows:

$$P(w|D) = \alpha P_o(w|D) + (1 - \alpha) \sum_{i=1}^{N_D} u(D, D_i) P_o(w|D_i) \quad (4)$$

In (4), α is the parameter to adjust the ratio of the weight of the segment itself and the structural information from links. Let s and t be the source article and target article about a link, respectively. We calculate the link weight (normalized LF-ICF) in a TF-IDF fashion as below. The link frequency represents how important a link in one segment and the inverse corpus frequency represents how important a link in the corpus. The function $u(s, t)$ is the weight of the link from s to t, calculated as the normalized *link frequency* (LF) multiplied by the *inverse corpus frequency* (ICF) defined as below:

$$LF(s, t) = \frac{N(s,t)}{N(s,*)} \quad (5)$$

$$ICF(t) = \log \frac{N(all)}{N(*,t)} \quad (6)$$

Where $N(s, t)$ is the number of links from s to t. $N(s,*)$ is the number of links from s to any target. $N(*,t)$ is the number of links from any source to t. $N(all)$ in the total number of all links in the corpus. The normalizing function is $\sum_{i=1}^{N_S} LF \cdot ICF(s, i)$, and we define $u(s, t) = \frac{LFICF(s,t)}{\sum_{i=1}^{N_S} LFICF(s,i)}$, where $\sum_{i=1}^{N_S} u(s, i) = 1$. Here N_S is the number of links from source segment s.

The words having the top-T highest probability in the segment are expected to explain the segment. It is expected that if there are co-occurring topics in two segments, the vectors of two segments have a high cosine similarity. So we set a threshold on similarities to determine whether segments have co-occurring topics.

4   Experimental Evaluation

4.1   Corpus Data

Our experimental corpus is obtained from the latest revision of pairs of articles in Wikipedia shown in Table 1. The corpus includes 14 pairs (pair-1 and pair-2) of articles, we set sphere distance is 1.The average of segment counts in each article is 30.In our experiment, we set topic number K as 100, and λ is varied from 0.0 to 1.0. α is varied from 0.0 to 1.0. We set μ as 1000.

Table 1. Experimental data

Article pair-1 title	Word count	Segment count	Article pair-2 title	Word count	Segment count	Article counts in sphere
CSharp (programming language)	5376	21	Java (programming language)	6771	31	158
Google	8081	21	Yahoo!	5075	31	297
Facebook	10959	46	Twitter	9835	41	363
Tencent QQ	2294	23	Windows Live Messenger	5278	20	96
Buddhism	16717	59	Christianity	12190	37	565
Apple Inc	12328	31	Samsung	6937	82	411
DirectX	4438	11	OpenGL	5794	26	134
League of Legends	4185	4	Defense of the Ancients	2196	14	55
Linux	6717	20	Microsoft Windows	5752	19	350
Barack Obama	11970	36	HillaryRodham Clinton	14389	32	515
Shaquille O'Neal	12166	25	Kobe Bryant	13150	35	383
Winfield Scott	5293	25	RobertE.Lee	11921	23	275
AvrilLavigne	8473	24	Yui(singer)	3357	17	183
Lionel Messi	14054	46	CristianoRonaldo	16171	43	299

4.2   Result

We mark co-occurring topics by human, and compare them with the co-occurring topics extracted by our method. We track the three different types of pairs of segments which are separately marked as Type-1, Type-2, and no-relation. We observe how the similarity changes with λ in each type of pairs. In the case that two segments having co-occurring topics of Type-1, as λ becomes larger, the similarity between the two segments constantly decreases. The similarity is highest when λ is 0. In the case of two segments having co-occurring topics of Type-2, the similarity between two segments is not monotonically decreasing. There is a peak point. In our experimental data, when λ is 0.5, the similarity between the two segments is highest. For segment pairs that are not related, the similarity increases slowly with λ. The proportion of the structure part is controlled by α. We observed a trend such that as α increases, namely the structural part is having less influence, the similarity decreases.

Now we discuss thresholds on similarities to determine co-occurrence types of segment pairs. The similarity should be more than a threshold if two segments are determined as sharing co-occurring topics. In our experiment, the range of the threshold on which pairs are assigned as Type-1 is more than0.9. For segments which are not related, the range is set as less than0.6. For segment pairs which belong to Type-2, we set the threshold range as [0.6, 0.9]. Even though in our experiment data, segment pairs having similarities in range of [0.6, 0.7] and [0.8, 0.9] are rare, and their similarities are mostly in the range of [0.7, 0.8]. Overall, we set the threshold range as [0.6, 0.9] to determine the segment pair belongs to Type-2.

4.3   Evaluation

We measure the precision, recall and F1-score to evaluate our method. The reference relationship of the two segments is judged by human. The parameters are described above. As shown in Figure 2, F1-Score for correctly finding Type-1co-occurrence reaches 0.5 when λ is 0.5 and α is 0.9.

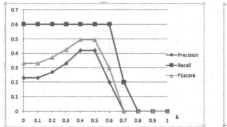 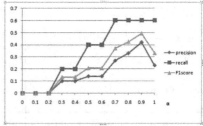

Fig. 2. Evaluation on correctly finding Type-1co-occurrence with λ and α

The F1-score is highest in our experiment data when the potential part and structure part are suitable. When the proportion of one part is too large, the similarity of segment pair usually cannot reach the threshold value. It leads to low F1-score as the figure shows. We can observe that the F1-score is highest when α is 0.9. It means that adding surrounding articles has positive improvement on finding occurring topics.

5   Conclusion and Future Work

In this paper, we proposed an LDA-based algorithm to find co-occurring topics in different segments of Wikipedia's articles, and evaluated the method. We make several improvements on developing corpus by incorporating neighboring articles via interlinks. Our approach is combining the LDA model with MLE and the link information. We defined three types of relationships between segments based on different abstract levels of topics. We examined weights to measure impact of the link information. In our experiment, we confirmed that adding link information was actually improving the performance of finding segment-pairs having Type-1 co-occurring topics.

In future work, the weight of the structure information should be further optimized, and the function of calculating the weight of each link should be improved. For explaining the co-occurring topics, top-T words are not appropriate, since they are hard to comprehend. Our method of finding co-occurring topics between Wikipedia articles should help illuminate overlapping topics between long articles, so that users can discover multiple articles dealing with the same topic, and compare viewpoints of these articles.

References

1. Blei, D.M., Ng, A.Y., Jordan, M.J.: Latent Dirichlet allocation. Journal of Machine Learning Research 3, 993–1022 (2003)
2. Blei, D.M., Moreno, P.J.: Topic segmentation with an aspect hidden markov model. In: Proceedings of SIGIR (2001)
3. Lavrenko, V., Croft, W.B.: Relevance-based language models. In: SIGIR 2001, pp. 120–127 (2001)
4. Liu, X., Croft, W.B.: Cluster-based retrieval using language models. In: Proc. 27th International ACM SIGIRConf. Research and Development Information Retrieval, pp. 186–193 (2004)
5. Xing, W., Croft, W.B.: LDA-Based Document Models for Ad-hoc Retrieval. In: Proc. 29thACM SIGIR Conf., pp. 178–185 (2006)
6. Zhai, C., Lafferty, J.: A study of smoothing methods for language models applied to ad hoc information retrieval. In: Proc. 24th ACM SIGIR 2001, pp. 334–34 (2001)
7. Evgeniy, G., Shaul, M.: Computing semantic relatedness using Wikipedia-based explicit semantic analysis. In: Proc. IJCAI 2007 Proceedings of the 20th International Joint Conference on Artifical Intelligence, San Francisco, pp. 1606–1611 (2007)
8. David, M., Ian, H.W.: An Effective, Low-Cost Measure of Semantic Relatedness Obtained from Wikipedia Links. In: Proc. AAAI Workshop on Wikipedia and Artificial Intelligence: an Evolving Synergy, Chicago, pp. 25–30 (2008)
9. http://www.dmoz.org

Parameter-Free Imputation for Imbalance Datasets

Jintana Takum and Chumphol Bunkhumpornpat

Theoretical and Empirical Research Group,
Department of Computer Science, Faculty of Science,
Chiang Mai University, Chiang Mai 50200, Thailand
jintana_t@cmu.ac.th, chumphol@chiangmai.ac.th

Abstract. Class imbalance is a problem that aims to improve the accuracy of a minority class, while imputation is a process to replace missing values. Traditionally, class imbalance and imputation problems are considered independently. In addition, filled-in minority-class values that are substituted by traditional methods are not sufficient for imbalance datasets. In this paper, we provide a new parameter-free imputation to operate on imbalance datasets by estimating a random value between the mean of the missing value attribute and a value in this attribute of the closet record instance from the missing value record. Our proposed algorithm ignores mean of instances to avoid an over-fitting problem. Consequently, experimental results on imbalance datasets reveal that our imputation outperforms other techniques, when class imbalance measures are used.

Keywords: Imputation, Parameter-Free, Class Imbalance, Classification, K-Nearest Neighbours.

1   Introduction

Classification [12] is an important process in data mining and knowledge discovery. The process learns known instances to build a model called a classifier, and then identifies the class label of unknown instances by defining a decision boundary among classes. A classifier is evaluated by the number of correctly classified instances in a dataset.

A classification with distributions of classes that are significantly different is called a class imbalance problem [9]. In this situation, a classifier seldom detects a minority class (positive class), because it is too small compared with a very big majority class (negative class). The goal of this problem is to improve the accuracy of detecting a minority class. F-measure [6] and AUC [5] are appropriate for this specific problem.

There are several strategies to solve class imbalance problems, such as over- samplings and under-samplings [7]. Over-sampling increases synthetic or duplicate positive instances in a dataset to upsize a minority class. Under-sampling deducts negative instances from a dataset to downsize a majority class. However, the two techniques encounter different disadvantages. With over-sampling, synthetic instances are not actual instances and duplicate instances increase computational costs. With under-sampling, removal instances might be useful information.

K. Tuamsuk et al. (Eds.): ICADL 2014, LNCS 8839, pp. 260–267, 2014.
© Springer International Publishing Switzerland 2014

The objective of imputation is to fill in a missing value by an estimated value. This paper aims to apply imputation for classification tasks, especially class imbalance problems. To do so, we design a new imputation based on 1-nearest neighbour with the advantage of parameter-free property for handling imbalance datasets. We evaluate the method's performance by its predictive performance on a minority class, because we perform imputation and class imbalance problems simultaneously.

The structure of this paper is as follows: Section 2 summarizes the K-N based imputation of our related work; Section 3 presents our new imputation for class imbalance problems; Section 4 shows the experimental results and Section 5 concludes.

2 Related Work

Imputation is a preprocessing step before feeding a modified dataset into machine learning algorithms. The technique is used to fill in estimated values in missing-values attributes. Imputations can be divided into four groups [13]:

- Case deletion [8], the easiest, removes records that obtain incomplete data, such as missing values, outliers or noise. Only the remaining complete record in a smaller dataset is used.
- More complex method estimates missing values based on statistical analysis or a machine learning approach, such as mean computing or k-nearest neighbours (K-NN) concept.
- Model-based imputation applies the maximum likelihood with expectation–maximization (EM) algorithms.
- Machine learning imputation uses classifiers, such as decision trees, fuzzy methods and support vector machines, to learn training instances before imputing missing values.

In this paper, we focus on the second category that applies the concept of mean computation or K-NN. K-NN imputation has two strategies: 1NN and KNN. The methods in this group include:

- Mean imputation [1]. This is the most frequently used method for imputing the missing values of observations of variables. This process replaces missing values by mean, which is calculated from the average of values in a missing values attribute.
- 1-nearest neighbour algorithm [11]. This is the simplest imputation that applies the concept of K-NN. In a record that contains a missing value, 1-NN imputation replaces the missing value by a value in a missing value attribute of the most similar instance.
- K-nearest neighbours algorithm [3]. This looks for the most k similar instances, instead of the closest one. In contrast to 1-NN imputation, K-NN imputation substitutes a missing value by mean of values in a missing value attribute from k nearest instances.

3　Parameter-Free Imputation

We propose a new parameter-free imputation called PFI for handling class imbalance problems. Our purpose is to fill in missing values in minority instances, before feeding an imputation dataset to any classification algorithms in order to improve the predictive performance on a minority class. The steps of PFI are as follows:

Step 1: For each minority instance, we detect and mark each missing value to be used in the next step. Table 1 shows minority instances in an imbalance dataset. The symbol '1' in the last attributes represents a minority label and '?' represents a missing value.

Table 1. An instance R3 with a missing value at attribute A2

	A1	A2	A3	Class
R1	38	69	21	1
R2	42	59	0	1
R3	50	?	13	1
R4	59	62	35	1
R5	66	58	1	1

Step 2: For each minority instance R at attribute A with a missing value, we determine the nearest neighbour of R by temporally ignoring A, so $R3$ is (50, 13, 1). For example, the nearest neighbour of $R3$ is $R1$ (38, 21, 1), when deleting $A2$. In this paper, we use normalized Euclidean distance. However, any types of distances can be applied to this step.

Step 3: We determine the average of all values in A, called *mean*. We denote *nn* as a value at A of the nearest neighbour of R. For example, *mean* of A2 is computed as 62; and *nn* is equal to 69. Then we impute a value in the range between *mean* and *nn*. The imputation value can be a value from 62 to 69. This procedure is illustrated in Figure 1.

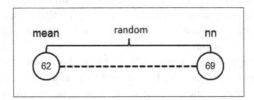

Fig. 1. Random imputation range

After completing all steps, a dataset is fulfilled by complete records of minority instances. All imputation values are varied to improve minority class prediction, because a minority decision region would be larger and less specific.

4   Experiment

Our experiment is designed as follows. We use several imbalance datasets from UC Irvine Machine Learning Repository, as shown in Table 2. We choose various types of classifiers: a rule-based classifier (RIPPER), a probabilistic-based classifier (Naive Bayes) and a distance-based classifier (K-NN) using a software Weka [10] with default settings. We apply performance measures for class imbalance: F-measure and AUC. PFI is compared with four methods: case deletion (Remove), mean Imputation (Mean) and k-nearest neighbours imputations by setting k as 1 and 5 (1NN and 5NN).

Table 2. Description of experimental datasets

Dataset	Instances	Attributes	Minority Instances	Minority Class	Percentage of Minority Class
Pima	768	8	268	Tested positive for diabetes	34.90
Haberman	306	3	81	The patient died within 5 years	26.47
Ecoli	336	7	35	Inner membrane, uncleavable signal sequence	10.42
Satimage	6,435	36	415	Damp grey soil	9.36
Glass	214	10	17	Vehicle windows	7.94
Yeast	1,484	8	30	VAC	2.02

In Table 2, each dataset contains complete records. However, we create missing values in the datasets by randomly removing 40% of the values of minority instances. We transform each multiple-class dataset into a two-class dataset with minority and majority classes. Each dataset is split into a training set (2/3) and a test set (1/3), except Satimage, in which UCI already provides both sets.

F-measures are shown in Table 3 and Figure 2. Results of PFI and 1-nearest neighbour imputation are not obviously different. Case deletion has the lowest result. The overall average of PFI is the highest value. All results of the Yeast dataset are 0, which means that each minority instance is misclassified.

AUCs are shown in Table 4 and Figure 3. PFI has the best overall average compared to all comparable imputation techniques. The average of case deletion is the worst.

Table 5 shows paired t-tests of our imputation against other comparable techniques. We set significance level (α) as 0.1. For positive accuracy, PFI is comparable to all experimental imputations (higher, but not significantly different). For F-measure, PFI is significantly better than case deletion and 5-nearest neighbours imputation. For AUC, only 1-nearest neighbour imputation is comparable to PFI.

Table 3. Comparison of F-measures

Classifier	Dataset	Remove	Mean	1NN	5NN	PFI
RIPPER	Haberman	0.133	0.364	0.350	0.350	0.350
	Glass	0.000	0.000	0.000	0.000	0.000
	Pima	0.843	0.835	0.844	0.856	0.841
	Ecoli	0.471	0.476	0.538	0.500	0.538
	Satimage	0.543	0.597	0.579	0.580	0.609
	Yeast	0.000	0.000	0.000	0.000	0.000
Naive Bayes	Haberman	0.229	0.270	0.270	0.270	0.270
	Glass	0.222	0.208	0.208	0.204	0.208
	Pima	0.845	0.845	0.848	0.851	0.851
	Ecoli	0.483	0.485	0.485	0.485	0.485
	Satimage	0.513	0.505	0.507	0.504	0.507
	Yeast	0.000	0.000	0.000	0.000	0.000
K-NN	Haberman	0.216	0.279	0.304	0.244	0.286
	Glass	0.000	0.000	0.000	0.000	0.000
	Pima	0.819	0.829	0.820	0.820	0.833
	Ecoli	0.667	0.720	0.720	0.692	0.720
	Satimage	0.646	0.711	0.698	0.698	0.698
	Yeast	0.000	0.000	0.000	0.000	0.000

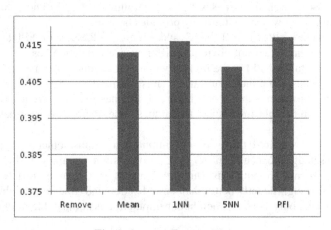

Fig. 2. Average F-measures

Table 4. Comparison of AUCs

Classifier	Dataset	Remove	Mean	1NN	5NN	PFI
RIPPER	Haberman	0.530	0.588	<u>0.590</u>	<u>0.590</u>	<u>0.590</u>
	Glass	0.500	0.500	0.500	0.500	0.500
	Pima	0.744	0.711	0.768	0.755	<u>0.770</u>
	Ecoli	0.672	0.703	<u>0.775</u>	0.707	<u>0.775</u>
	Satimage	0.707	0.747	<u>0.769</u>	0.741	0.763
	Yeast	0.500	0.500	0.500	0.500	0.500
Naive Bayes	Haberman	<u>0.715</u>	0.689	0.694	0.690	0.699
	Glass	0.732	<u>0.751</u>	0.738	0.735	0.735
	Pima	0.848	0.853	<u>0.856</u>	0.854	0.854
	Ecoli	0.914	<u>0.920</u>	0.919	0.918	<u>0.920</u>
	Satimage	0.927	0.929	<u>0.930</u>	<u>0.930</u>	<u>0.930</u>
	Yeast	0.724	0.721	0.711	0.711	0.712
K-NN	Haberman	0.536	0.615	0.571	0.604	<u>0.616</u>
	Glass	0.660	<u>0.749</u>	0.737	0.742	0.742
	Pima	0.779	0.792	0.788	0.789	<u>0.854</u>
	Ecoli	0.921	0.925	<u>0.927</u>	0.921	0.925
	Satimage	0.910	0.931	0.933	<u>0.935</u>	0.933
	Yeast	0.530	0.518	0.515	0.511	0.515

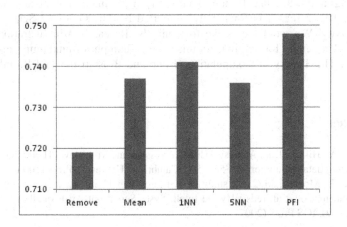

Fig. 3. Average AUCs

Table 5. Paired t-tests for PFI and other techniques

Measure	Method	Variable Tested			
		Mean Difference	Variance Difference	t-statistic	p-value
F-measure	Remove	0.368333	0.099695	2.442813	0.025787
	Mean	0.395778	0.100155	1.078912	0.295698
	1-NN	0.398389	0.100037	0.654900	0.521295
	5-NN	0.391889	0.100189	2.146882	0.046523
AUC	Remove	0.713833	0.022697	2.973901	0.008515
	Mean	0.730111	0.021246	1.750475	0.098061
	1-NN	0.734500	0.022252	1.430047	0.170826
	5-NN	0.729611	0.021491	2.229259	0.039575

5   Concusion

In this research, we present a PFI method to solve imputation problems in imbalance datasets. The experimental results show that PFI outperforms other techniques when evaluating based on imbalance measures. PFI reduces the over-fitting effect, since PFI generates varied values rather than repeating mean values in the same attribute, so the outcome is an expanded decision region of a minority class. In contrast to K-NN imputation that needs k tuning, PFI does not require any parameters due to the approach of 1-NN. The experimental results support PFI's ability. For future work, we are modifying PFI to consider values in a missing value attribute of majority instances before imputing. This will prevent the over-lapping problem.

Acknowledgments. Jintana Takum is currently a graduate student at Chiang Mai University. This research is financially supported by The Graduate School, Chiang Mai University. We would also like to thank the Research Administration Center, Chiang Mai University for helping edit this paper. Chumphol Bunkhumpornpat is also members of The Theory of Computation Group and Biostatistics and Bioinformatics Cluster.

References

1. Gelman, A., Hill, J.: Data Analysis Using Regression and Multi-level/Hierarchical Models. In: Missing-data Imputation, pp. 529–544. Cambridge University Press (2006)
2. Batista, G., Monard, M.C.: A study of K-nearest neighbour as an imputation method. In: Abraham, A., et al. (eds.) Hybrid Intell. Syst., Ser. Front Artif. Intell. Appl., vol. 87, pp. 251–260. IOS Press (2002)

3. Batista, G., Monard, M.C.: Experimental comparison of K-nearest neighbour and mean or mode imputation methods with the internal strategies used by C4.5 and CN2 to treat missing data. Tech. Rep., University of Sao Paulo (2003)
4. Blake, C.L., Merz, C.J.: UCI Repository of Machine Learning Databases. Department of Information and Computer Sci-ences, University of California, Irvine, California, USA (2009), http://archive.ics.uci.edu/ml/
5. Bradley, A.P.: The Use of the Area Under the ROC Curve in the Evaluation of Machine Learning Algorithms. Pattern Recognition 30(6), 1145–1159 (1997)
6. Buckland, M., Gey, F.: The Relationship between Recall and Precision. Journal of the American Society for Information Science 45(1), 12–19 (1994)
7. Bunkhumpornpat, C., Subpaiboonkit, S.: Safe Level Graph for Synthetic Minority Oversampling Techniques. In: The 13th International Symposium on Communications and Information Technologies (ISCIT) indexed in IEEE Xplore, Samui Island, Thailand, pp. 570–575 (2013)
8. Zhu, H., Lee, S.-Y., Wei, B.-C., Zhou, J.: Case-deletion meas-ures for models with incomplete data. Biometrika, 727–737 (2001)
9. Japkowicz, N.: Class imbalance Problem: Significance and Strategies. In: The 2000 International Conference on Artificial Intelligence (IC-AI 2000), Las Vegas, NV, USA, pp. 111–117 (2000)
10. Hall, M.A., Frank, E., Witten, I.H.: Data Mining: Practical Machine Learning Tools and Techniques, 3rd edn. The Kaufmann Series in Data Management Systems (2011)
11. Solomon, N., Oatley, G., McGarry, K.: A Fast Multivariate Nearest Neighbour Imputation Algorithm (2007) (manuscript received March 9)
12. Pazzani, M., Merz, C., Murphy, P., Ali, K., Hume, T., Brunk, C.: Reducing Mis-classification Costs. In: The 11th International Conference on Machine Learning, ICML 1994, pp. 217–225. Morgan Kaufmann, San Francisco (1994)
13. Garcıa-Laencina, P.J., Sancho-Gomez, J.-L., Figueiras-Vidal, A.R.: Pattern classification with missing data: a review. Neural Computing and Applications (2009)
14. Randall Wilson, D., Martinez, T.R.: Improved Heterogeneous Distance Functions. AI Access Foundation and Morgan Kaufmann Publishers. Journal of Artificial Intelligence Research 6, 1–34 (1997)

Cost Evaluation of CRF-Based Bibliography Extraction from Reference Strings

Naomichi Kawakami[1], Manabu Ohta[1], Atsuhiro Takasu[2],
and Jun Adachi[2]

[1] Okayama University, Okayama 700-8530, Japan
{kawakami,ohta}@de.cs.okayama-u.ac.jp
[2] National Instituteof Informatics, Tokyo 101-8430, Japan
{takasu,adachi}@nii.ac.jp

Abstract. The effective use of digital libraries demands maintenance of bibliographic databases. Especially, the reference fields of academic papers are full of useful bibliographic information such as authors' names and paper titles. We, therefore, propose a method of automatically extracting bibliographic information from reference strings using a conditional random field (CRF). However, at least a few hundred reference strings are necessary for training the CRF to achieve high extraction accuracies. As described herein, we propose the use of active sampling and pseudo-training data to reduce the amount of training data. Then we evaluate the associated training costs by experimentation.

Keywords: Information extraction, CRF, Reference string, Active sampling, Pseudo-training data.

1 Introduction

Research papers usually provide references listed at the end. Using them provides users of digital libraries with efficient access to large amounts of information. For example, identifying cited papers using existing bibliographic databases can provide links that enable direct access to the cited papers. To identify the cited papers accurately, a reasonable approach is that of first extracting the bibliographic elements from reference strings and then identifying the reference entities by matching the individual bibliographic elements against databases. Accurate and inexpensive bibliography extraction from reference strings is therefore a prerequisite for this task.

Most studies of bibliography extraction from reference strings, however, specifically examine the improvement of extraction accuracy to the greatest extent possible. To provide users with extracted bibliographies, however, human intervention must be regarded as assuring the quality of extracted bibliographies. There are two kinds of human intervention for bibliography extraction: post-editing the results after automatic bibliography extraction and preparing a large amount of training data for a reference string parser that uses some machine-learning techniques. For reducing the former human cost, we developed a bibliography extraction model that assures the accuracy of extracted bibliographies by detecting less-confident samples to check

K. Tuamsuk et al. (Eds.): ICADL 2014, LNCS 8839, pp. 268–278, 2014.
© Springer International Publishing Switzerland 2014

them manually during post-editing [1]. For reducing the latter human cost, a reference string parser must learn with as few training data as possible because the preparation of human-labeled data for training is expensive. As described in this paper, we evaluate the cost for learning our CRF-based reference string parser that we developed to extract bibliographic elements from reference strings with high accuracy.

For accurate information extraction from reference strings, rule-based methods might be applicable to some extent. Digital libraries for research papers, however, usually include journals of various kinds. The rules should be tailored to each kind of journal for accurate extraction because different journals usually have different formats for reference strings. It becomes increasingly difficult and expensive for us to formulate and manage such rules as a digital library grows and comes to contain greater varieties of journals. Therefore, many methods that use machine learning have been proposed for bibliography extraction. Peng et al. proposed a CRF-based method of extracting bibliographies from the title pages and reference sections of research papers presented in PDF format [2]. More recently, Councill et al. released an open-source implementation of a reference string parsing package, ParsCit [3]. However, no report in the literature, with the exception of our proposal, describes an attempt to evaluate the relation of learning costs and extraction accuracy when methods using machine learning are applied to bibliography extraction from the reference strings of research papers. We evaluated the relation when our CRF-based method was applied to bibliography extraction from the *title pages* of research papers [4].

We first briefly describe our CRF-based bibliography extraction. We then propose two methods for reducing the amount of training data: active sampling and pseudo-training data, both of which use three confidence measures calculated using a CRF. Although some of these measures were applied to active sampling for bibliography extraction from title pages of research papers in [4], we empirically examine the effectiveness of the three measures for active sampling and pseudo-training data generation for bibliography extraction from reference strings.

2   CRF-Based Bibliography Extraction

2.1   Problem Definition

This paper specifically examines a reference string parser for research papers, by which we extract all major bibliographic elements such as a title, authors, and a journal name from a reference string. Fig. 1 depicts an example of a reference string and its parsed and labeled result. As the figure shows the result of bibliographic information extraction from a reference string is its sequence of tokens labeled either as a bibliographic element such as "Author" and "Title" or as a delimiter such as DC (comma + space) and DS (double quotation). Here <D*> tags stand for individual kinds of delimiters that we defined.

Our CRF-based parser for reference strings is two-tiered: first it segments each reference string into a sequence of tokens $x = x_1, \cdots, x_n$; then it assigns the tokens in a token sequence the appropriate label from a set of class labels $L = \{l_1, l_2, \cdots, l_m\}$ representing either bibliographies or delimiters. In parsing reference strings, we first tokenize them using predefined delimiters as shown in Fig. 1(a). Next, we learn a

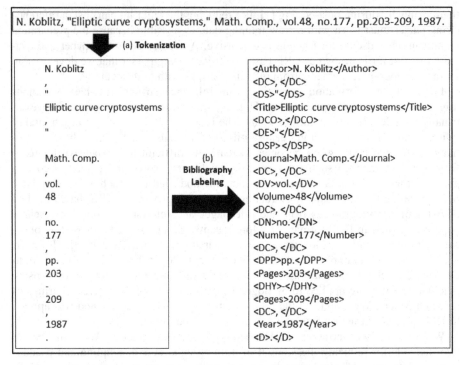

Fig. 1. Example of reference string parsing for bibliography extraction

CRF and make it label the tokens in the token sequence generated from a reference string, either as bibliographies or as delimiters as presented in Fig. 1(b). In our previous work [5], we proposed a tokenization method using delimiters and evaluated the accuracy. As described in this paper, however, we use manually tokenized reference strings as input for experiments because we particularly examine the cost evaluation of learning a CRF for bibliography labeling.

We define a set of bibliographic elements to be extracted from reference strings in papers of three academic journals used for the experiments. The bibliographies consist of an "Author", "Editor", "Translator", "Other author", "Title", "Book title", "Journal", "Conference", "Volume", "Number", "Page", "Publisher", "Day", "Month", "Year", "Location", "URL", and "Other".

2.2 CRF

In this study, we apply a common linear-chain CRF to labeling tokens constituting a reference string. We define the conditional probability of a label sequence, $y = y_1, \cdots, y_n$, given an input-token sequence, $x = x_1, \cdots, x_n$, as

$$P(y|x) = \frac{1}{Z(x)} \exp \left\{ \sum_{i=1}^{n} \sum_{k=1}^{K} \lambda_k f_k(y_{i-1}, y_i, x) \right\}, \tag{1}$$

where $Z(x)$ is the partition constant. The feature function $f_k(y_{i-1}, y_i, x)$ is defined over consecutive labels y_{i-1} and y_i, and the input sequence x. The feature function f_k is also associated with its learned weight λ_k.

A CRF assigns the label sequence y^* to the given sequence x that maximizes Eq. (1), i.e.,

$$y^* := \underset{y}{\operatorname{argmax}} P(y|x). \tag{2}$$

The input-token sequence x is the sequence of tokens acquired by segmenting a reference string by delimiters, whereas the label sequence y is the sequence of names of bibliographic elements or delimiters.

2.3   Features of the CRF

We use the CRF++ 0.58 package[1] [6], which is an open source implementation of CRFs, for labeling token sequences. Features of 48 kinds were adopted for token labeling. Among them, 47 are unigram features. The remaining one is a bigram feature. Table 1 summarizes the set of feature templates we used. Their instances are generated automatically from training token sequences. The unigram features include the position of a token in a token sequence, the number of characters, words, and periods that are contained in a token, the ratio of characters grouped by character type such as kanji, hiragana, katakana, alphabet, and digit that constitute a token, up to four first and last characters of a token, the token string as is, the presence of capitals, digits, and several symbols, and the matching against keywords and entries of dictionaries. We prepared dictionaries for person names[2], journal names[3], conference names[4], publisher names[5], place names[6], and months. In Table 1, the last numbers in column *Feature* indicate those of kinds of the individual feature templates. For example, <keyword(i)> comprises two feature templates. Additionally, the numbers in parentheses such as 0 and i in column *Feature* indicate the relative position of the token from which features are extracted where 0 is the position of the current token to be labeled and $i \in \{-4, -3, -2, -1, 0, 1, 2, 3, 4\}$. We also took into account a label bigram that reflects the syntactic constraints of reference strings.

3   Cost Reduction Strategies for Learning a CRF

3.1   Confidence Measure

In active sampling, less-confident samples are more informative for learning [7]. We, therefore, use three measures to evaluate the confidence of the CRF-based

---

[1] http://crfpp.googlecode.com/svn/trunk/doc/index.html
[2] http://www.census.gov/genealogy/names/, etc.
[3] http://science.thomsonreuters.com, etc.
[4] http://www.allconferences.com/, etc.
[5] http://www.narosa.com/nbd/PublisherDistributed.asp, etc.
[6] http://www.fallingrain.com/world/index.html, etc.

Table 1. Feature template

Type	Feature	Description
Unigram	<token_ab_pos(0)>:1	Absolute position of the current token in a token sequence
	<token_re_pos(0)> :1	Relative position of the current token in a token sequence
	<num_char(0)>:1	Number of characters in the current token
	<num_word(0)>:4	Number of words in the current token
	<num_period(0)>:4	Number of periods in the current token
	<f_kanji(0)>:1	Ratio of full-width kanji that constitute the current token
	<f_hiragana(0)> :1	Ratio of full-width hiragana that constitute the current token
	<f_katakana(0)> :1	Ratio of full-width katakana that constitute the current token
	<f_alphabet(0)> :1	Ratio of full-width alphabets that constitute the current token
	<f_digit(0)> :1	Ratio of full-width digits that constitute the current token
	<h_alphabet(0)> :1	Ratio of half-width alphabets that constitute the current token
	<h_digit(0)> :1	Ratio of half-width digits that constitute the current token
	<h_symbol(0)> :1	Ratio of symbols that constitute the current token
	<first_1-4_string(0)> :4	Up to four first characters of the current token
	<last_1-4_string(0)> :4	Up to four last characters of the current token
	<token(0)> :1	Token itself
	<last_char(i)> :1	Character type of the last character of the i-th token
	<token_lc(i)> :1	Lowercase character string of the i-th token
	<capital(i)> :1	Presence of capitals in the i-th token
	<digit(i)> :1	Presence of digits in the i-th token
	<symbol(i)> :2	Presence of full-width or half-width symbols in the i-th token
	<dictionary(i)> :8	Presence of entries of dictionaries in the i-th token
	<keyword(i)>:2	Presence of keywords in the i-th token
	<num_token(0)> :1	Number of tokens in a token sequence
	<editor(0)>:1	Presence of keywords suggesting editor in a token sequence
	<URL(0)>:1	Presence of keywords suggesting URL in a token sequence
Bigram	<y(-1), y(0)> :1	Previous and current labels

bibliographic labeling. We can select less-confident samples according to the measures to use the selected samples for learning our CRF-based parser. We earlier proposed similar confidence measures for CRF-based bibliography extraction from reference strings [1]. In [1], however, we used measures for evaluating the difficulty of the CRF-based bibliographic labeling to detect extraction errors while we use measures for selecting informative samples in this paper. Additionally, the definition of confidence measures themselves was different. We empirically examine how much these measures correlate with the informativeness of samples by evaluating the tradeoff between the extraction accuracies and the amount of training data.

Normalized Likelihood. The first measure uses the conditional probability given by Eq. (1). The CRF calculates the hidden label sequence y^*, that maximizes the conditional probability of the token sequence x given by Eq. (1). Higher $P(y^*|x)$ signifies more confident assignment of labels, whereas lower $P(y^*|x)$ means that the token sequence makes it difficult for the current CRF to assign labels. The conditional probability is affected by the length of the token sequence x. Therefore, we use the following normalized conditional probability as a confidence measure:

$$c_{NLH}(x) = \frac{\log(P(y^*|x))}{|x|}. \tag{3}$$

In that equation, $|x|$ is the length of the token sequence x. We denote the normalized likelihood as NLH.

Minimum Probability of Token Assignment. The second measure uses the marginal probability of the assigned label. More formally, let Y_i denote a random variable for assigning a label to the i-th token in x, i.e. x_i. Let L be a set of class labels. For label $l \in L$, $P(Y_i = l)$ denotes the marginal probability that label l is assigned to the i-th token x_i. We can then infer that the maximum probability $\max_{l \in L} P(Y_i = l)$ represents confidence in labeling x_i. Therefore, we use the following minimum probability of an assigned label in the reference string as a confidence measure:

$$c_{MP}(x) = \min_{i \leq |x|} \max_{l \in L} P(Y_i = l). \tag{4}$$

We denote the minimum probability of token assignment as MP.

Average Token Entropy. The third measure uses the entropy of marginal probabilities of all candidate class labels. The NLH and MP use probabilities only of the most likely label sequence (NLH) and of the most likely, i.e., assigned, labels (MP). However, we consider that the distribution of label assignment probabilities over all the class labels also reflects confidence in labeling. Therefore, we propose using entropy of labeling as described below.

The CRF is regarded as less confident in labeling and so is in the assigned label sequence if there are many class labels with almost identical probability as the most likely one has. The CRF is regarded as confident in its labeling when it assigns one label to a token with probability of nearly one and the other labels have a probability of nearly zero. Therefore, we use the following average token entropy as a confidence measure:

$$c_{ATE}(x) = -\frac{\sum_{i \leq |x|} \sum_{l \in L} -P(Y_i = l) \log P(Y_i = l)}{|x|}. \tag{5}$$

Therein, $\sum_{l \in L} -P(Y_i = l) \log P(Y_i = l)$ is the entropy of label assignment of i-th token x_i. The minus sign in front of the right side of Eq. (5) ensures that $c_{ATE}(x)$ acts as a confidence measure just like $c_{NLH}(x)$ and $c_{MP}(x)$ because higher entropy signifies less confidence in labeling. We denote the average token entropy as ATE.

3.2   Active Sampling

The training samples in active learning are given incrementally. A model is modified using the given training samples [8]. The key to active sampling is how to choose samples to modify the model. We can learn a CRF more efficiently, i.e., with fewer training data, by active sampling than, say, by random sampling when choosing informative samples based on confidence measures.

We apply the following active sampling strategy to this task.

1. Gather a large number of reference strings S without labeling.
2. Choose an initial small number of reference strings S_0 from S, label them, and learn initial CRF M_0 using the labeled reference strings S_0.
3. Repeat until convergence.
   (a) Calculate any one of the three confidence measures $c.(x)$ of reference strings in $S - \bigcup_{i=0}^{t-1} S_i$ using Eqs. (3), (4), or (5) using the CRF M_{t-1} we obtained in the previous loop.
   (b) Rank the reference strings in ascending order in accordance with the individual measures.
   (c) Choose few reference strings S_t from the top n ranked strings in the pool $S - \bigcup_{i=0}^{t-1} S_i$.
   (d) Label the reference strings S_t manually.
   (e) Learn CRF M_t using the labeled reference strings $\bigcup_{i=0}^{t} S_i$.

Therefore, the number of samples used for t-th training is

$$\text{\# of training data} = n_0 + nt, \tag{6}$$

where $n_0 = |S_0|$ and $n = |S_t|$.

3.3   Pseudo-training Data

We propose augmentation of the training data by adding pseudo-training data generated from the original training data by randomly substituting individual bibliographic element entities in the training reference strings with those found in existing bibliographic databases. The pseudo-training data are generated automatically without human intervention.

We learn CRF M_t using training samples $\bigcup_{i=0}^{t} S_i$ in active sampling, as explained in the preceding section, where the increment in samples of t-th iteration is S_t. When using pseudo-training data, we also generate pseudo-training data P_t at the t-th iteration by bibliography-wise substitution of S_t and learn CRF M_t using training samples $\bigcup_{i=0}^{t} S_i \cup P_i$ where $P_0 = \emptyset$. Both S_t and P_t for $t > 0$ consist of manually labeled reference strings having identical delimiters but having different entities for individual bibliographic elements because bibliographic element entities in the sequences of P_t are substituted from those of S_t.

In the experiment, we vary the number of pseudo-training samples by multiplying $n = |S_t|$ by m. Therefore, $|P_t| = m|S_t|$ holds. The number of samples used for t-th training with addition of pseudo-training data is

$$\text{\# of training data} = n_0 + n(1 + m)t. \tag{7}$$

4   Empirical Evaluation

4.1   Experimental Setup

We tested the CRF-based reference string parser to evaluate the effectiveness of confidence measures used for cost reduction strategies on the following three academic journals:

— Japanese papers published by the Institute of Electronics, Information and Communication Engineers in Japan (IEICE-J). We used papers published in 2000, which included 4,787 reference strings.
— English language papers published by the Institute of Electronics, Information and Communication Engineers in Japan (IEICE-E). We used papers published in 2000, which included 4,497 reference strings.
— Japanese papers published by the Information Processing Society of Japan (IPSJ). We used papers published in 2000, which included 4,574 reference strings.

Japanese language papers have both Japanese and English reference strings. Moreover, these reference strings were tokenized manually for the experiments.

We used the following accuracy as the evaluation metric:

$$\frac{\text{\# of successfully labeled sequences}}{\text{\# of test sequences}}. \tag{8}$$

For calculating accuracies, we did not distinguish "Author", "Editor", "Translator", and "Other author" to treat them as authors, "Title" and "Book title" as titles, "Journal" and "Conference" as journals, "Volume", "Number", and "Page" as volumes, and "Location", "URL", and "Other" as others according to the classification of bibliographies used in our previous work [5]. The remaining "Publisher", "Day", "Month", and "Year" were distinguished separately. It is noteworthy that a CRF was only regarded as having succeeded in labeling when it assigned correct labels to all tokens for the bibliographies in a test token sequence. In other words, if a CRF assigned an incorrect label to one token but correctly labeled all the other tokens in the sequence, then it was regarded as having failed. However, we ignored confusion of a delimiter token with another kind of delimiter if it occurred.

We applied five-fold cross validation to each experimental dataset to calculate their respective labeling accuracies. When training CRFs, we set learning parameters such as balancing the degree of fit to default values given by CRF++.

4.2   Evaluation of Active Sampling

To evaluate the effectiveness of confidence measures used in active sampling, we observed the accuracy of CRFs for three journal datasets. For this experiment, we fixed the training sample size to 10 in both initial and update phases, i.e., $n_0 = n = 10$ in Eq. (6). The CRF accuracy was assessed using Eq. (8). For comparison, we measured the accuracy of the following sampling strategies.

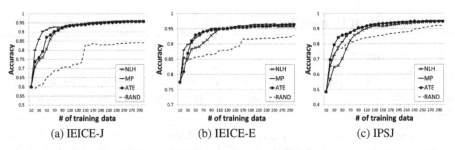

Fig. 2. CRF learning by active sampling

— *RAND*: Ten training samples are chosen randomly in both initial and update phases.
— *NLH*, *MP*, and *ATE*: Ten training samples are chosen randomly in the initial phase. Then 10 training samples are chosen according to the respective confidence measures defined by Eq. (3), (4), or (5) in each update phase.

RAND is regarded as a baseline.

Figs. 2(a), 2(b), and 2(c) respectively show the relation between the number of training samples up to 300 and the labeling accuracy in IEICE-J, IEICE-E, and IPSJ datasets. Each graph in the figures plots the accuracy of the CRF with respect to the size of training samples using the three confidence measures in addition to random sampling.

First, we observed that active sampling using any of the three confidence measures obtained much more accurate CRFs with fewer samples than random sampling RAND. This result indicates that the three confidence measures are extremely effective in reducing training costs in active sampling. For example, with 100 training samples, NLH, MP, and ATE respectively achieved accuracies of 0.929, 0.935, and 0.932 in the IEICE-J dataset whereas random sampling RAND achieved accuracy of only 0.709.

Second, when we compare the three confidence measures, MP obtains a better CRF with fewer training samples in the IEICE-J dataset as shown in Fig. 2(a), whereas ATE obtains a better CRF with fewer training samples in the IPSJ dataset as shown in Fig. 2(c).

4.3 Evaluation of Pseudo-training Data

We also evaluated the accuracy of CRFs for three journal datasets when using pseudo-training data. In this experiment, we also fixed the number of training samples to 10 in both initial and update phases. For comparison, however, $|P_t|$, the number of pseudo-training samples added at each iteration of active sampling is varied with the multiplication constant m in Eq. (7) among the values of 0, 1, 3, and 5. Actually, $m = 0$ signifies active learning itself with no pseudo-training sample although $m = 1$ signifies the addition of the same number of pseudo-training samples as those for the active sampling at each iteration because $|P_t| = m|S_t|$ holds. Furthermore, when we learned a CRF using the training sequences of one dataset, we used the other two datasets to create bibliographic element entity databases used for the generation of pseudo-training samples P_t by substituting the bibliographic entities in S_t.

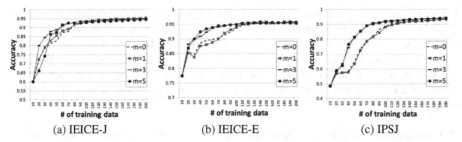

(a) IEICE-J   (b) IEICE-E   (c) IPSJ

Fig. 3. CRF learning by pseudo-training data in addition to active sampling (NLH)

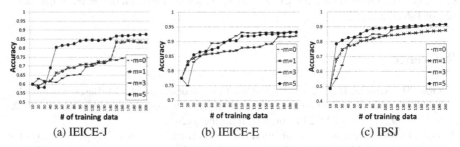

(a) IEICE-J   (b) IEICE-E   (c) IPSJ

Fig. 4. CRF learning by pseudo-training data in addition to random sampling (RAND)

Figs. 3(a), 3(b), and 3(c) respectively portray the relations between the number of training samples for active sampling and the labeling accuracy in IEICE-J, IEICE-E, and IPSJ datasets when using the confidence measure NLH. Figs. 4(a), 4(b), and 4(c) respectively show the relations between those in IEICE-J, IEICE-E, and IPSJ datasets when applying random sampling. In these figures, the horizontal axes stand for the number of training samples for active sampling. Therefore, the total training samples are almost $m + 1$ times as numerous as those for active sampling, depending on the multiplication constant m. Each graph of $m = 0$ in these figures is identical to that of NLH or RAND in Fig. 2. Therefore, they are regarded as baselines.

As presented in Fig. 3, adding three or five times as many pseudo-training samples as those used for active sampling is effective for learning accurate CRFs when selecting samples according to NLH. As Fig. 4 shows, adding pseudo-training samples is also effective for learning accurate CRFs when applying random sampling. However, we observed almost no significant difference when selecting samples according to the other two confidence measures: MP and ATE. Therefore, we present only the results for NLH and RAND here. Comparison of Fig. 2 and Fig. 3 clarifies that the resultant accuracies achieved by active sampling and pseudo-training data using NLH are competitive with those by active sampling using MP or ATE, although those obtained by active sampling alone using NLH are not.

5   Conclusion

We have examined three confidence measures obtained from a linear-chain CRF used for both active sampling and pseudo-training for extracting bibliographic information from reference strings of research papers. The experiment results revealed that every confidence measure is extremely effective in reducing training cost in an active sampling strategy and that the measures are also effective for selecting samples from which pseudo-training data are generated to improve the labeling accuracy. We plan to examine the availability of these confidence measures as metrics that indicate the fitness of a CRF for test samples for detecting changes in journals or formats of reference strings.

Acknowledgments. This work was supported by two JSPS Grants-in-Aid for Scientific Research (B) (23300040 and 24300097), a JSPS Grant-in-Aid for Scientific Research (C) (25330384), and the Collaborative Research Program of the National Institute of Informatics.

References

1. Ohta, M., Arauchi, D., Takasu, A., Adachi, J.: Error detection of CRF-Based bibliography extraction from reference strings. In: Chen, H.-H., Chowdhury, G. (eds.) ICADL 2012. LNCS, vol. 7634, pp. 229–238. Springer, Heidelberg (2012)
2. Peng, F., McCallum, A.: Accurate information extraction from research papers using conditional random fields. In: HLT-NAACL, pp. 329–336 (2004)
3. Councill, I.G., Giles, C.L., Kan, M.Y.: ParsCit: An open-source CRF reference string parsing package. In: Proc. of Language Resources and Evaluation Conference (LREC 20), pp. 661–667 (2008)
4. Takasu, A., Ohta, M.: Rule management for information extraction from title pages of academic papers. In: Proc. of ICPRAM 2014, pp. 438–444 (2014)
5. Ohta, M., Arauchi, D., Takasu, A., Adachi, J.: Empirical evaluation of CRF-based bibliography extraction from reference strings. In: Proc. of IAPR DAS 2014, pp. 287–292 (2014)
6. Kudo, T., Yamamoto, K., Matsumoto, Y.: Applying conditional random fields to Japanese morphological analysis. In: Proc. of EMNLP 2004, pp. 230–237 (2004)
7. Settles, B., Craven, M.: An analysis of active learning strategies for sequence labeling tasks. In: Proc. of EMNLP 2008, pp. 1070–1079 (2008)
8. Saar-Tsechansky, M., Provost, F.: Active sampling for class probability estimation and ranking. Machine Learning 54, 153–178 (2004)

An Automatic Library Data Classification
System Using Layer Structure
and Voting Strategy

June-Jei Kuo

Graduate Institute of Library and Information Science
National Chung Hsing University, Taichung, Taiwan
jjkuo@dragon.nchu.edu.tw

Abstract. This paper deals with issues of traditional one-layered book classification systems and employs the complementary attribute of various classifiers to propose a two layered book classification system using voting strategy. Moreover, the collection of dissertations from a university library and books from an electronic bookstore are used as the training and testing corpus. The classification codes of dissertations and books are employed as the gold standard as well. Each dissertation contains various components such as title, authors, table of contents, abstract or cited papers et al. To understand the classification effect of all the combinations of components, various combinations are studied as well and the best combination is recommended. The features extracted from abstracts and table of content are found to be most useful for document classification. On the other hand, to obtain the best classification performance, the combination of classifiers for a two-layered book classification system is studied and the best combination was also recommended as well.

1 Introduction

A library is an organized collection of sources of information and similar resources, made accessible to a defined community for reference or borrowing. Moreover, a bibliographic classification is a system of documents, library materials or any information organized by their subject and allocating a call number. The call number is arranged in a hierarchical tree structure, which makes it easier for library users to browse the shelves for materials on a specific topic. There are many bibliographic classification systems, such as the Dewey Decimal Classification (DDC); Library of Congress Classification (LC), and so on. The new classification scheme for Chinese language[1] is widely used for library classification throughout Taiwan, Hong Kong, and Malaysia. Whenever a new item is classified, the librarians employ both descriptive bibliography elements (titles, author names, publishers, dates of publication, etc.) and subject bibliography to manually assign a call number to that

---

[1] http://en.wikipedia.org/wiki/
New_Classification_Scheme_for_Chinese_Libraries

K. Tuamsuk et al. (Eds.): ICADL 2014, LNCS 8839, pp. 279–287, 2014.
© Springer International Publishing Switzerland 2014

item. Thus, in order to assign call numbers effectively and correctly, librarians need to thoroughly understand the domain knowledge.

Chen, Lo and Lin (2002) employed a subject framework to manually analyze 956 articles of Bulletin of The Library Association of China from No. 1 to No. 65. After preliminary analyses, they found that the average consistency of main categories was 82.46%, and that of subcategories was 69.82%. The consistencies for respective subcategories were from 59.20% to 74.09%. However, manual document classification is known to be a labor-intensive and time-consuming task. In contrast, Huang (2002) explored the feasibility of the automatic classification method applied to traditional library thesisclassification tasks. The author-defined keywords were collected as a content-representative corpus to extract meaningful keywords from titles and abstracts. The back-propagation neural classifier was adopted for feature processing and classification number identification. The average correct ratio of the first classification layer achieved 55% and improved when running deeper layers. Due to the low performance of using manual or automatic bibliographic classification, library users could not access all the needed items effectively and decreased their satisfaction towards the library. Thus, automatic classification has become an important researcharea due to the rapid increase of digital information today.The rest of this paper is organized as follows. In Section 2, the related works are presented and discussed. Then, a two layered automatic data classification System is proposed in Section 3. In Section 4, experiment setup, data set and results are provided and some interesting findings are described. Finally, Section 5 concludes the remarks and lays a foundation of future work.

2   Related Work

Document classification or document categorization is a problem in library science, information science and computer science. The task is to assign a document to one or more classes or categories. This may be done manually or automatically. Manual classification of documents (Tonta, 1991; Chen, 1999) has mainly resides in the province of library science, while the automatic classification of documents (Farbrizio, 2002; Tokkola, 2002) is used mainly in information science and computer science fields. The problems overlap and therefore, there is also interdisciplinary research on document classification. Although there is much research on automatic classification, very little focuses on library science. Larson (1992) and Yi (2006) focused on English document classification. On the other hand, Huang (2002), Huang (2008) and Chen et al. (2009) focused on Chinese document classification. Larson (1992) presented the results of his research of the automaticselection of Library of Congress Classificationnumbers based on the titles and subject headings inMARC records. The results indicated that if the best method for aparticular case could be determined, then up to 88% ofthe new records can be correctly classified. This singlemethod with the best accuracy was able to select thecorrect classification for about 46% of the new records. Yi (2006) gave an overview of previous projects and studied the related issues on text clustering using major library classification schemes, and summarized that text classification became a popular and attractive tool of organizing digital information. On the other hand, Huang (2008) put forward a strategy, which aimed to utilize both search engine expand document features and the author names as a record field to assist classifying. The experiment proved that this proposed strategy was helpful for promoting the effect of automatic bibliography classification effectively and efficiently. Its best accuracy was 0.6286. Chen et al. (2009) discussed how to apply text categorization to automatic book classification. Todistinguish books from general documents, data about books are divided into: (1) Description Data, including book title, introductions to book and author, and (2) Meta-Information, including author's name and publisher information. Based on the division of data about books, this paper employed support vector machines (SVM) to conduct the book classification. The proposed classification method was evaluated using a data set collected fromhttp://www.books.com.tw and was found to perform well. Under the principle of K-foldcross-validation, experimental results reached aclassification accuracy of 95%. In addition, Mandy and Darwish (2008) found that improving the performance of information retrieval indexing the headers and titles of books was nearly as effective as indexing the entire contents of books. Thus, searching for valuable book or document units for classification is an important issue.

With all the effort in this domain, there is still room for improvement and a great deal of attention is paid to developing highly accurate document classifiers. Recent studies have proposed the use of respective classification algorithm of data mining (Wu et al., 2008) in building effective classifiers for numerical data. However, most of them neglect the notions that classifier methods in library science can give information that is complementary to each other (Wang et al., 1996). In the following subsections, a detailed overview of the proposed research framework is described integrating the two domains, feature selection and classifier complementation. Moreover, the experimental results were presented to show its performance as well.

3   Two Layered Automatic Book Classification System

Traditional automatic document classification system employed one classifier, with a classification accuracy of 55%~95%. To further enhance the document classification accuracy, the layer structure, multiple classifiers and voting strategy were introduced. Figure 2 is the architecture of the proposed two layer document classification system.When the feature vectors of a classified document were inputted, classifier 1 and classifier 2 in the first layer classified it simultaneously. If the classification results were identical, they confirmed the classification category. In contrast, if the classification results were different, the inputted features were classified by classifier 3. Then, the voting strategy was used to decide the classification category. Thus, the classifiers in Layer 1 could introduce the quicker classifiers. On the other hand, as the comparison decreased, the high quality but slower classifier could be introduced in Layer 2. In other words, the proposed two layered document classification system could achieve high classification quality while spending less execution time.

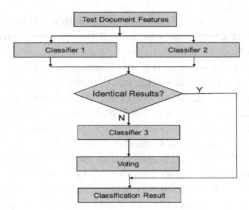

Fig. 1. Architecture of the proposed two layer document classification system

4   Experimental Results and Discussion

Figure 3 shows the experimental block diagram and the related database and its details are described in the following. There are four databases: dissertations (books), bibliographic record, stop words and document call number. Theses (books) are text collections which can be used as training or testing data. A bibliographic record is an entry in bibliographic database. Stop words are utilized to delete any low information Chinese words during document classification. Moreover, a document call number is a set of call number of theses (books) that are used as category answers for evaluation.

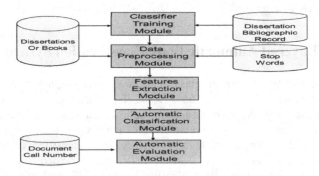

Fig. 2. Experimental block diagram and the related database

1. Classifier Training Module

    Feature selection with TFIDF was employed to extract feature words of training data. These feature data were used to train the various classifiers such as decision tree classifier and so on.

2. Data Preprocessing Module

    First, noisy information in the Chinese text, such as figures or tables, were deleted. Each text can be divided into six parts: (1) title, (2) abstract, (3) content, (4) references, (5) table of content and (6) keywords. Then, the Chinese segmentation system[2] was used to segment the content of the inputted text into Chinese words.

3. Feature Extraction Module

Words in selected parts of the inputted text, which have high term frequency and low inversed document frequency, were extracted as features for document classification.

4. Automatic Classification Module

Four state-of-art classifiers (Delveen et al., 2013) were employed in the proposed two layered classification system which are Naïve Bayes (NB), support vector machine (SVM), decision tree (C4.5) and K Nearest Neighborhood (KNN), respectively.

5. Automatic Evaluation Module

Precision was used to evaluate the document classification system by referring the document call number database. Moreover, the main class of the call number was used to evaluate the classification performance. And, 10-fold validation was adopted.

4.1 Data Sets

Master theses (2005~2010) from a large local library in Taichung were used to be the testing and training data. Five graduate schools were selected: Chinese Literature (20), Soil and Water Conservation (18), Animal Science (17), Entomology (12) and Horticulture (12). The number in parentheses is the number of dissertation. The total number of data sets is 79. As the thesis were PDF-form, it was first converted into word-form using character recognition software. After deleting some conversion errors, both record number and extracted feature number are shown in Table 1. Take "Title" as an example, only had 61 out of 79 theses with titles. Furthermore, after extracting the features and deleting the duplication words, there were 54 attribute words left. Moreover, due to the low TFIDF values, only 2 advisor names are remained.

Table 1. Data Description[3]

Content Names	Record Number	Attribute Number
(1) Title	61	54
(2) Abstract	76	734
(3) Content	73	784
(4) References	30	483
(5) Table of Content	74	971
(6) Keywords	48	213
(7) Advisor Names	79	2

---

[2] http://ckipsvr.iis.sinica.edu.tw/

[3] The advisor name feature can decide the category effectively. Thus, to understand the performance of other parts, the advisor name was not taken into consideration.

4.2   Data Preprocessing and Classifier Selection

To train the related classifiers in the proposed system, WEKA[4] (Waikato Environment for Knowledge Analysis) was employed. In general, a knowledge discovery process consists of the following steps: data cleaning, data integration, data selection, data transformation, data mining, pattern evaluation and knowledge presentation. Thus, data cleaning, data integration, data selection and data transformation were processed in this module.

Table 2. Precision of the first stage

Content Part	NB	SVM	C4.5	KNN(1)	MultiScheme[5]	Average
(1) Title	51.60	53.62	36.74	47.50	51.62	48.22
(2) Abstract	**97.91**	**95.96**	**51.21**	**63.46**	**97.79**	**79.33**
(3) Content	**89.77**	**90.80**	**76.75**	**75.18**	**88.57**	**81.75**
(4) References	**66.33**	**83.33**	**69.90**	**70.00**	**81.33**	**74.00**
(5) Table of Content	**90.89**	**84.11**	**73.64**	**31.11**	**90.89**	**74.13**
(6) Keywords	33.50	45.33	33.50	18.15	45.95	35.29

4.3   Experimental Results

4.3.1   The First Stage

The first stage was to understand the classification performance of single classifier and each component; the experimental results are shown as in Table2. We concluded that the useful components were the: abstract, content, references, and Table of contents, respectively. Additionally, the better classifiers were NB and SVM. Thus, these two classifiers could be recommended to be the classifiers of the first layer of the third stage experiment. On the other hand, C4.5 and KNN could be recommended to be the classifier in the second layer. Moreover, the best performance utilizing MultiScheme outperformed the performance of using single classifier (55%) as well.

Table 3. Data Set of Stage two

Data Set				Record Number	Attribute Number
(2) Abstract	(3) Content	(4) References	(5) Table of Content		
*	*			149	770
*		*		106	770
*			*	150	358
	*	*		103	471
	*		*	147	492
		*	*	104	424
*	*	*		179	666
*	*		*	223	650
	*	*	*	177	660
*	*	*	*	253	653

---

[4] http://www.cs.waikato.ac.nz/ml/weka/
[5] MultiScheme means the majority vote among four classifiers.

Table 4. Precision of Stage Two (unit: %)

Data Set				NB	SVM	MultiScheme
(2) Abstract	(3) Content	(4) References	(5) Table of Content			
*				97.91	95.96	97.79
	*			89.77	90.80	88.57
		*		66.33	83.33	82.33
			*	90.89	84.11	90.89
*	*			57.50	91.14	91.14
*		*		79.92	83.77	83.39
*			*	97.60	92.60	97.60
	*	*		82.15	85.78	85.12
	*		*	90.45	96.19	96.19
		*	*	83.28	83.07	83.49
*	*	*		89.95	95.10	94.99
*	*		*	93.36	97.81	97.81
	*	*	*	89.10	97.07	97.07
*	*	*	*	91.35	97.79	97.79

4.3.2   The Second Stage

In the second stage, the best dissertation components (abstract, content, references and table of content) and best classifiers (NB and SVM) from stage one were employed to understand the performance of using voting strategy. Table 3 shows both the record number and attribute number, which were used in the stage two experiment. Table 4 shows that the multiple classifiers using majority voting (MultiScheme) achieved higher classification performance than one classifier. This could be seen as an evidence of good performance of using voting strategy. Furthermore, as the precisions of those rows with grey color were over 85%, those same combinations of components could be thought of as useful features. Thus, the eight feature sets were used in the third experiment.

Table 5. Precision of the third stage (unit: %)

Data Set				NB/SVM Majority Voting	NB/SVM /C4.5 Majority Voting	NB/SVM → C4.5 two layer	NB/SVM → KNN Two layer
(2) Abstract	(3) Content	(4) References	(5) Table of Content				
*				97.79	97.79	100.00	100.00
	*			88.57	87.84	100.00	100.00
*			*	97.60	97.07	100.00	100.00
	*		*	96.19	96.61	98.64	98.64
*	*	*		94.99	97.49	98.88	98.88
*	*		*	97.81	97.62	100.00	100.00
	*	*	*	97.07	96.92	100.00	100.00
*	*	*	*	97.79	97.87	99.60	99.60
Average				95.97	96.16	99.64	99.64

4.3.3   The Third Stage

In the third stage, the performance of the proposed two layered classification system was compared to the one layered classifier with voting strategy. Table 5 shows two proposed two layered classification systems in grey. It was evident that the performances of two kinds of two layered classification systems were better than the one layered classification system with voting strategy. Moreover, the performances of either two layered system wereidentical. Additionally, as to the good performance of using voting strategy, it was generally unnecessary to execute the classifier in layer two. Thus, the execution time of either two layered classification system in Table 5 was under 10 minutes. Last but not least, by observing Table 5, both the abstract and table of content were discovered to be useful features that enhanced the classification performance. These two features were utilized in the next classification experiment using books.

Table 6. Precision of the classification experiment on books (unit:%)

Data Set		NB/SVM→ C4.5		NB/SVM→ KNN	
(2) Abstract	(5) Table of Content	After 1st Layer	After 2nd Layer	After 1st Layer	After 2nd Layer
*		97.6	100	97.6	98.8
	*	98.3	100	98.3	98.8
*	*	98.3	100	98.3	98.3

4.4   Experimental Results Using Book Data

Since the main resource in a library is books, it is necessary to evaluate the performance of the proposed two layered classification system on books. 250 books (separated into 5 categories: finance, decoration, medicine, computer, recipe; 50 books/category) and their related bibliographic data, such as call number, title, author name(s), abstract, table of contents and etc., were extracted from a web bookstore[6]. To understand the classification performance on books both the best features (Abstract and Table of Content) and the two classification systems (NB/SVM→ C4.5, NB/SVM→ KNN) from stage three were utilized in this experiment. The related classification performance is shown in Table 6. The classification performance on books was almost the same with the performance of the theses classification.

5   Concluding Remarks

The proposed library data classification system using layer structure and voting strategy was proven to be able to achieve better performance than traditional classification using a single classifier. On the one hand, in order to enhance the performance of the proposed system, the classifier SVM or NB should be employed in the first layer. On the other hand, the decision tree (C4.5) should be used in the second layer. The valuable components of documents for automatic classification were the abstract and table of contents, respectively. For future works, the scalability

---

[6] http://www.books.com.tw/

test using a large amount of testing and training data should be conducted. In addition, the effect of other portions of books, i.e. book headings, index pages, etc., recommended as future research.

Acknowledgements. Part of research results of this paper was supported by National Science Council, Taiwan, under the contracts NSC 101-2221-E-005-090. Moreover, I deeply appreciate her help and support of research assistant Miss. Huei-Jen Wu.

References

1. Chen, K.H., Lo, S.C., Lin, C.J.: The Investigation of the Consistency of Subject Cataloging for Academic Journal Articles of Library and Information Science. In: Proceedings of Information and Communication Conference, Taipei, pp. 125–142 (2002) (Chinese)
2. Chen, S.Y., Yeh, J.Y., Hwang, M.J., Lin, X.J., Ke, H.R., Yang, W.P.: Automatic Book Classification Method combined with Support Vector Machine and Metadata. International Journal of Advanced Information Technologies (IJAIT) 3(1), 2–21 (2009) (Chinese)
3. AL-Nabi, D.L.A., Ahmed, S.: Survey on Classification Algorithms for Data Mining(Comparison and Evaluation). Computer Engineering and Intelligent Systems 4(8), 18–24 (2013)
4. Farbrizio, S.: Machine Learning in Automated Text Categorization. ACM Computing Surveys 34(1), 1–47 (2002)
5. Huang, C.M.: A Neural Network Approach to Automatic Classification of Thesis Documents.,Report of National Science Council (NSC 89-2416-H-224-053), Taiwan (2002) (Chinese)
6. Huang, J.H.: A Study of Book Title Feature Extraction Based on the Automatic Classification -An Example of BibliographyAutomatically Classified System.Unpublished Master Thesis, Department of Library and Information Science of Fu-Jen Catholic University, Taipei (2008) (Chinese)
7. Larson, R.R.: Experiments in Automatic Library of Congress Classification. Journal of the American Society for Information Science 43(2), 130–148 (1992)
8. Magdy, W., Darwish, K.: Book Search: Indexing the Valuable Parts. In: Proceedings of the 2008 Workshop on Research Advances in Large Digital Book Repositories, pp. 53–56 (2008)
9. Tokkola, K.: Discriminative Features for Document Classification. In: Proceedings of the 16th International Conference on Pattern Recognition (ICPR 2002), vol. 1, pp. 472–475 (2002)
10. Wang, et al.: Complementary classification approaches for protein sequences. Protein Engineering 9(5), 381–386 (1996)
11. Wu, et al.: Top 10 algorithms in data mining. Knowledge and Information Systems 14(1), 1–37 (2008)
12. Yi, K.: Challenges in Automatic Classification using Library Classification Schemes. In: Proceedings of World Library and Information Congress: 72nd IFLA General Conference and Council, pp. 1–14 (2006)

Search Effectiveness and Efficiency of Facet-Based Online Catalog: A Crossover Study of Novice Users

Tanapan Tananta and Songphan Choemprayong[*]

Department of Library Science, Chulalongkorn University,
Bangkok, Thailand
{tanapan.ta,songphan.c}@chula.ac.th

Abstract. The effectiveness and efficiency of facet-based interface of an online catalog have yet explored much from a perspective of in experienced users. This crossover study compares search efficiency and effectiveness of novices using between facet-based and text-only interfaces of Koha OPAC. Twelve novice users in a secondary school were randomly recruited from November 12, 2013 to January 28, 2014. Participants were asked to perform 6 search tasks. Task completion and search accuracy, precision, recall, search time, and the number of search terms were observed and analyzed. The results from the comparisons of these measures indicate that the efficiency and effectiveness of novice users' search using faceted interfacetends to be poorer than ones of non-faceted interface in certain aspects. This study informs a design recommendation ofa library catalog search interface for novice users.

Keywords: Faceted navigation, integrated library system, library catalog, search efficiency, search effectiveness, novice users.

1 Introduction

As libraries have been improving their interactions with users, particularly helping users find relevant resources. Designing a usable search interface of a library catalog has become one of the key efforts in a community of library and information scientists. As Hearst [1] pointed out, designing a search interface is "highly dependent on and sensitive to the details of the design." (p.1) Faceted search (or faceted browsing) is one of the common search features integrated into the next-generation library catalog. [2] Although faceted search and structural representation of search results in library catalog have been reportedly useful and preferable for general users [3], the usability, particularly in terms of search efficiency and effectiveness, of such feature has yet explored from a perspective of inexperienced users.

While most comparative usability tests apply classical parallel experimental research design (i.e., one person is assigned to only one arm of intervention), this approach does not acknowledgement intra-subject variability. To overcome such

---

[*] Corresponding author.

K. Tuamsuk et al. (Eds.): ICADL 2014, LNCS 8839, pp. 288–299, 2014.

criticism, crossover design, where a participant is assigned to more than one arm of intervention, has been recommended. A number of usability studies, particularly evaluation of healthcare-related tools and technologies, have applied a crossover design. [4,5,6,7,8,9] However, none of them used such technique to evaluate usability of faceted search. Therefore, the objective of this study is to compare the search efficiency and effectiveness between using facet-based and traditional text-only online catalog from the view of first-time users. The study addresses the association between the use of faceted search by novice users and success in information retrieval in order to provide recommendations for the design and implementation of faceted search in online library catalogs.

2   Literature Review

Faceted search [10] (aka. faceted navigation or faceted browsing) is a grouping of attributes of entities (e.g.,documents, objects, persons, and places) that are relevant to a user's query, normally represented in a hierarchical structure. The key promises of faceted search are to provide an overview of the search results as well as to help users navigate the results. The attributes used to describe the characteristics of entities are so called facet. La Barre [11] defined facet as "the categories, properties, attributes, characteristics, relations, functions or concepts that are central to the set of documents or entities being organized and which are of particular interest to the user group." Hall [12] observed that the use of "facet" has been deviated from the facet theory, a classical classification framework proposed by Ranganathan, particularly regarding the practice of facet development and analysis.

The utilization of facet in categorizing and providing the context of search results has been evidenced in both commercial products (such as online shopping sites, website directory, and search engines) and academic projects (for example, Flamenco [1], Relation Browser [13] and mSpace [14]). Numerous details and techniques have been investigated to improve faceted navigation, for instance, multiple facet columns to display associated facets, dynamic facet display, facet highlighting technique [15], facet display orientation design, selection procedure, breadcrumb design, and the position of result viewer. [16]

Libraries have integrated faceted search into online catalog since 2006. [17] However, the integration of faceted interface in most library catalogs is rather simple, presenting in a single column of static facets. Common facets used in library catalogs are mostly bibliographic metadata elements including author, subject, format, subject heading, publication date, and language. [12]

Fagan [18] conducted a literature review of user studies of faceted search both inside and outside a library context. Overall, Fagan found numerous positive findings supporting the adoption of faceted search. For example, faceted search helps create navigation structures, facilitating efficient retrieval, avoiding dead ends, shortening search time, and so on. A number of usability studies of faceted search in library catalogs claim that facet-based search yields more relevant results and users are more satisfied with facet-based than text-only interface. [19,20]

In addition, a number of usability studies praised that faceted search empowers users to be in control and helps users not to feel lost. [21] Without facet, users may have to return to a search query page to revise their search terms and refine their search results. Faceted search allows library users to locate related items, as well as narrow, filter, and limit search results easily. Users may not need to plan their search strategies comprehensively in advance. [1], [11], [22]

In terms of precision and recall, English et al. [21] conducted a usability test with "motivated" participants and found that using a faceted interface yields higher precision and recall rates in exploratory search tasks than a non-faceted interface.

Nevertheless, based on the literature review, Fagan [18] observed that the majority of studies were either using an experimental interface outside of a library context or focusing on an overall interface rather than certain features. There was still skepticism on the benefits of facets in libraries.

The results from transaction log analysis studies in academic libraries show that faceted search were used less frequent than text-only interface. [17], [23], [24] Antelman, Lynema, and Pace [24] found that only 30 percent of users limit their searches in the search results screen. Furthermore, Lown [17] found that only 34 percent have chosen to restrict the results using faceted navigation at least once. This issue leads to a question whether or not faceted search is really usable in a real setting.

The first interaction with the interface perhaps plays an essential role in explaining this problem. Learning effect can be an important factor for the adoption and use of faceted search. Therefore, a study of novice user experience with faceted search may enhance our understanding of their perceptions, behavior, and experiences which may influence learning effect and task completion and success. In addition, Marchionini [25] argued that novice users' search experience is needed to be systematically observed in order to identify ways to develop features and instructional materials to enhance their search strategies.

Most usability studies of online catalogs draw samples from general users regardless of their prior exposure to the system. [3], [26], [27] There is a lack of understanding of the usability of faceted search in the view of novice users. Several studies indicate that during a usability testing process, inexperienced users tend to reveal and discover more issues and errors than users with experience. [28,29]

Efficiency and effectiveness are two major retrieval-related concepts used to evaluate usability of faceted-based interface. Rubin, Crisnell, and Spool [30] defined effectiveness as "the extent to which the product behaves in the way that users expect it to and the ease with which users can use it to do what they intend." (p.4) In a context of information retrieval, effectiveness concerns the ability to deliver relevant information to users. Precision and recall are the two major measures used to identify the effectiveness of search strategies. Efficiency takes costs to reach search completion into account. [30,31] The examples of costs in the context of information retrieval include time, computing resources, human labors and intellectual efforts, and money.

3   Methods

We observed novice users' search effectiveness and efficiency of facet-based online catalog comparing with traditional text-only online catalog in a randomized, controlled, two-arm crossover study. [32] As Nielsen pointed out, three to eight participants were able to demonstrate 80% of all problems. A higher number of participants recruited may not be worth the investment. [33] Therefore, we decided to recruit a small group of participants in order to feature a common practice in usability testing.

Twelve high-school students in the west region of Thailand who have not used an online library catalog were recruited from November 12, 2013 to January 28, 2014. As Whitmire [34] suggested, students from different disciplines have different information seeking behaviors, including using online library catalog. Therefore, we stratified the participants equally by track of study (i.e., science and mathematics, arts and mathematics, and arts and languages).

After providing consent, the participants were randomly divided into two groups equally (6 participants each). A sequence of the interface was designated to each group as shown in Figure 1. In each testing period, one interface at a time, students were asked to use a given interface to perform six search tasks. Each participant was given 20 minutes to complete each task. The first group performed six search tasks using the interface with faceted navigation and then another six tasks using the traditional text-only interface. Another group was asked to perform the tasks using the text-only interface first, followed by the faceted interface. Participants were given the same order of search tasks, as shown in Table 1, controlling for types of search question (known-item search, partially known item search, and exploratory search) and languages of items sought (Thai and English). All questions and the instructions are in Thai.

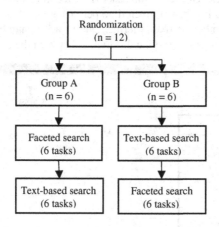

Fig. 1. Study design

Table 1. The order of search tasks

Task	Type of search task	Language of items sought
1	Known-item search	Thai
2	Partially known item search	Thai
3	Exploratory search	Thai
4	Known-item search	English
5	Partially known item search	English
6	Exploratory search	English

This study used the default OPAC module of Koha version 3.10 as a search platform. Five hundred bibliographic records, both in Thai and English, relevant to all search tasks were uploaded into the system. Koha is an open source integrated library system (ILS) which is, at the time of this study, the only open-source system that offers faceted navigation [2]. Koha has been implemented in many libraries around the world. [35] Therefore, the study may be replicated and compared elsewhere.

The only difference between the two interfaces is the appearance of faceted navigation column. The faceted navigation column is located on the left side of the search result screen, as shown in Figure 2. This feature is deactivated in the text-only search interface.

To obtain a reference set of relevant items for measuring recall, four professional librarians performed a relevance judgment on all exploratory search tasks. Participants' relevant items were compared with lists of items that were commonly identified relevant by all four librarians.

Three measures are used to evaluate search effectiveness, including task completion/search accuracy, precision rate, and recall rate. Search time and the number of search terms are used to evaluate search efficiency. Laplace's estimate of accuracy was used to evaluate task completion and search accuracy of known item searches and partially known item searches. Precision and recall rates were used to evaluate exploratory search performances. The analyses of search time and the number of search terms applied to all search types. Unsuccessful tasks (i.e., locating incorrect items for known item search or failing to finish in a given time period) are excluded from the analysis of search time and the number of search terms. Due to a low number of participants, we used non-parametric statistics to test the differences between the two groups.

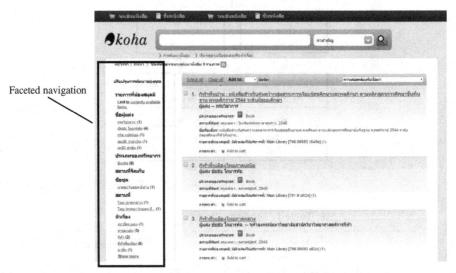

Faceted navigation

Fig. 2. Facet-based search result interface

Prior to the comparative analysis of measures, we conducted Mann-Whitney U test to detect the carryover effect by investigating the effect of the sequence of group assignment on four measures: precision rate, recall rate, search time, and the number of search terms, with 95% confidence level. We found a carryover effect on search time in task 1 (u=30.00; p=0.048) and task 4 (u=32.50; p=0.039). Both tasks represent known item search for Thai and English items respectively. Subsequently, only data from the first round of testing was analyzed for these two tasks.

After the investigation of carryover effect, Mann-Whitney U test was then performed in order to compare the differences of measures between facet-based and text-only search interfaces. All statistical analyses were performed using SPSS for Windows version 17.

4   Results

4.1   Participant Demographics

There was no dropout in this study. All participants took less than 60 minutes to complete six search tasks in one sequence. On a 4-point scale, the mode of the latest English grade is 3.5 which indicate a very good performance in English subject. On average, the participants used libraries about 6 times a month, use the Internet about 17 times a month, and spend about 2 hours using the Internet per day. On average, the Internet experience of the participants is about 7 years. It may also imply that these students, on average, spend time with the Internet for 7 years without visiting any online library catalog. It is interesting to note that these students seem to be familiar with using computers and the Internet. Table 2 compares the participants' characteristics and their experiences with libraries, computers, and the Internet between both groups. Although participants in Group B tend to have more experience using libraries, computers, and the Internet, the results from Mann-Whitney U test found no statistically significant differences of these characteristics between the two groups. Therefore, the comparisons of those measures that carryover effects were found, using only data from the first interface used, are not affected by participants' experience of using libraries, computers, and the Internet.

Table 2. Participants' characteristics

Participant characteristics	Group A (n=6)		Group B (n=6)		u-test	p-value
	Mean	Mean rank	Mean	Mean rank		
Study track (n)						
Science and mathematics		2		2		
Arts and mathematics		2		2		
Arts and languages		2		2		
English grade on 4-scale	3.5*	7	3*	6	15	0.614
Frequency of library use (times/month)	5.34	7.25	7.5	5.75	13.5	0.464
Frequency of the Internet use for searching (times/month)	15.67	6.25	19.17	6.75	16.5	0.806
Period of the Internet use for searching (hours/day)	1.5	6.08	2.1	6.92	15.5	0.686
Number of years using the Internet	8	7	9	6	15	0.604

* Mode

4.2   Task Completion and Search Accuracy

Instead of using an average percentage, Laplace's estimate [36,37] is applied to measure success in retrieving known and partially known items. By observing task completion and accuracy of chosen items, a task that a participant identified incorrect items for known item search or failed to finish in a given time frame is regarded as unsuccessful. As shown in Table 3, the ratio of task completion and search accuracy of partially known English item search using text-only interface is substantially higher than those using facet-based interface (92.86% and 42.86% respectively). For other search types, the ratios are somewhat in the same range, about 80-90%.

Table 3. Task completion and search accuracy rates between facet-based and text-only interfaces (N=12)

| Task | Task completion and search accuracy | | | |
| | Facet-based | | Text-only | |
	No. of participants with complete & correct responses	Laplace	No. of participants with complete & correct responses	Laplace
Thai language				
1. known item search	11	85.71	11	85.71
2. partially known item search	12	92.86	11	85.71
English language				
3. known item search	11	85.71	12	92.86
4. partially known item search	5	42.86	12	92.86

4.3   Precision

The analysis of precision is only relevant to exploratory search tasks. In general, the average precision rates in this study are relatively very high as seen in Table 4. This is perhaps due to the effect of a small number of testing collection, 500 bibliographic records. Nonetheless, for Thai language, performing facet-based search significantly yields lower precision rate (mean rank=8, $\bar{x}=0.86$) than one of text-only search (mean rank =17, $\bar{x}=1$; p<0.01). The precision rates of English item search using both interfaces are exactly the same.

Table 4. Precision rates between facet-based and text-only interfaces (N=12)

| Task | Precision | | | | | | | |
| | Facet-based | | | Text-only | | | | |
	n	Mean	Mean Rank	n	Mean	Mean Rank	u-test	p-value
Thai language								
1. exploratorysearch	12	0.86	8.00	12	1	17.0	8.00	0.00**
English language								
2. exploratorysearch	12	1	12.5	12	1	12.5	12.5	1.00

*p<0.05 **p<0.01

4.4   Recall

As shown in Table 5, the recall rates of faceted search are significantly lower than the recall rates of text based search in both exploratory tasks. For searching Thai items, the mean rank of recall rates of faceted search is 8.67 ($\bar{x}$=0.41), while the one of text-only search is 16.33 ($\bar{x}$=0.78; p<0.01). For English collection, although the average recall rate of both interfaces are exactly the same ($\bar{x}$=0.79), the mean ranks of recall rates of facet-based and text-only searches are 9 and 16 (p<0.05) respectively.

Table 5. Recall rates between facet-based and text-only interfaces (N=12)

| Task | Recall | | | | | | | |
| | Facet-based | | | Text-only | | | u-test | p-value |
	n	Mean	Mean Rank	n	Mean	Mean Rank		
Thai language								
3. exploratorysearch	12	0.41	8.67	12	0.78	16.33	26.00	0.007**
English language								
4. exploratorysearch	12	0.79	9.00	12	0.79	16.00	-1.23	0.012*

  *p<0.05 **p<0.01

4.5   Search Time

Illustrated in Table 6, the comparison of search time shows that participants spent significantly shorter time when conducting exploratory search in English language using faceted interface (mean rank=7.58, $\bar{x}_{\text{facet-based search}}$=4.91; mean rank=17.42, $\bar{x}_{\text{text-only search}}$=9.25; p<0.01). On the contrary, participants spent significantly more time searching partially known items when using the search interface with faceted navigation, compared to using the text-only interface (mean rank=14.20, $\bar{x}_{\text{facet-based search}}$=3.28; mean rank=6.83, $\bar{x}_{\text{text-only search}}$=1.28; p<0.01).The differences of search time between the two interfaces in other search types are not statistically significant and the differences are quite varied from task to task.

Table 6. Search time between facet-based and text-only interfaces (N=12)

| Task | Search time | | | | | | | |
| | Facet-based | | | Text-only | | | u-test | p-value |
	n	Mean	Mean Rank	n	Mean	Mean Rank		
Thai language								
1. known item search[+]	5	2.12	5.20	5	2.20	5.80	11.00	0.75
2. partially known item search	12	1.57	11.92	11	1.51	12.09	65.00	0.95
3. exploratory search	11	7.16	13.82	12	5.07	10.33	46.00	0.22
English language								
4. known item search[+]	6	2.31	7.67	6	1.75	5.33	11.00	2.62
5. partially known item search	5	3.28	14.20	12	1.28	6.83	82.00	0.006**
6. exploratory search	12	4.91	7.58	12	9.25	17.42	91.00	0.001**

*p<0.05 **p<0.01
[+]Due to crossover effect, only search time of the first sequence was analyzed.

4.6   Number of Search Terms

The number of search terms reflects participants' effort to complete search tasks. While the average number of search terms are not statistically significant in most search types as seen in Table 7, participants used significantly more search terms during facet-based search (mean rank=14.70, $\bar{x}$=2.40) than during text-only search (mean rank=6.63, $\bar{x}$=1.08) when conducting a partially known item search for English items (p<0.01).

Table 7. Number of search terms between facet-based and text-only interfaces (N=12)

Task	Number of search terms						u-test	p-value
	Facet-based			Text-only				
	n	Mean	Mean Rank	n	Mean	Mean Rank		
Thai language								
1. known item search[+]	12	1.33	11.67	11	1.27	12.36	62.00	0.73
2. partially known item search	12	1.50	12.83	11	1.18	11.09	56.00	0.35
3. exploratory search	11	1.82	13.00	12	1.58	11.08	55.00	0.43
English language								
4. known item search[+]	11	1.45	12.64	12	1.17	11.42	59.00	0.46
5. partially known item search	5	2.40	14.70	12	1.08	6.63	1.50	0.00**
6. exploratory search	12	1.67	11.50	12	2.00	13.50	60.00	0.44

*p<0.05 **p<0.01

5   Discussion and Conclusion

We conducted a crossover study comparing the search effectiveness and efficiency of novice users using between faceted-based and text-only online catalogs. The results show that faceted search seems to play a significant role for novice users when conducting certain partially known and exploratory search tasks, however, more likely in a negative direction. The results contradict to the results of many previously known usability studies among general users.[3], [17] Therefore, user's first exposure to or experience with the faceted navigation may be an important factor to take into consideration in a usability evaluation of faceted search. The learning effect seems to play an important role in explaining this phenomenon. Based on direct observation and follow-up interview, some participants were reluctant to use faceted navigation. Some participants did not even pay attention to the faceted navigation. They felt text-only function was sufficient to complete the tasks,

According to the results of this study, it can be implied that an introduction of faceted interface to a novice users on the first encounter to the online catalog may affect his/her search performance. Configuring a text-only interface as an alternative option or holding the introduction of faceted navigation until users are familiar with the system may improve the usability of the online catalog as a whole.

It is perhaps less surprising to find the impact of carryover effect on known-item search time. Apparently, participants completed the tasks faster in the second period. This may be because known item search seems to be less difficult than the other two search types. In addition, many participants finished the task within one single search session and had only a quick exposure to the result page as the answer can be identified easily.

There are certain limitations of this study which can be examined into four folds. Firstly, this study aims to replicate a usability testing where responses from a small group of participants can help explore usability issues. Although we found certain patterns of the effect of faceted search in online catalog using non-parametric statistics, a larger sample size would enhance the generalizability of this study. Secondly, the study was conducted in an experimental setting where only a limited number of bibliographic records were uploaded into the library catalog. An experiment study with a much larger dataset may resemble users' behavior in a more natural context where issues related to information overload are taken into consideration. Thirdly, even though we observed the task difficulty by controlling languages of items sought between a native and non-native language (i.e., Thai and English), the results from an ad-hoc follow-up interview indicated that perceived task difficulty seems to be one of the key factors of search effectiveness and efficiency. Task difficulty is not directly observed in this study. Therefore, this variable may need to be integrated in the future studies. Lastly, although search effectiveness and efficiency can be observed directly, the understanding of users' perceptions on searching experience can help researchers and designers address the importance of search effectiveness and efficiency in the context of usability and, perhaps, adoption of faceted interface. Qualitative data may help provide an extensive insight on users' experience using both search interfaces.

It is noted that search effectiveness and efficiency is one of the core components of usability according to Nielsen. [38] Thus, the results from this study provide a specific insight on the usability of faceted interface in novice users' perspective. Future studies may expand the scope of the investigation to a broader sense in order to provide more applicable and meaningful implications.

Acknowledgement. This study is supported by a grant from the Graduate School, Chulalongkorn University. The authors would like to thank Pongtawat Chippimolchai and Neelawat Intaraksa for advices on Koha installation and configuration, Teerawut Sripinit for his advice on statistical analysis, Paul Gasaway for editorial assistance, and three anonymous reviewers for their valuable comments.

References

1. Hearst, M.: Design Recommendations for Hierarchical Faceted Search Interfaces. In: ACM SIGIR Workshop on Faceted Search, pp. 1–5. ACM, New York (2006)
2. Yang, S.Q., Hofmann, M.A.: The Next Generation Library Catalog: A Comparative Study of the OPACs of Koha, Evergreen, and Voyager. Information Technology and Libraries 29, 141–150 (2013)
3. Ramdeen, S., Hemminger, B.M.: A Tale of Two Interfaces: How Facets Affect the Library Catalog Search. Journal of the American Society for Information Science and Technology 63, 702–715 (2012)
4. Ainsworth, J., Palmier-Claus, J.E., Machin, M., Barrowclough, C., Dunn, G., Rogers, A., Eysenbach, G.: A Comparison of Two Delivery Modalities of a Mobile Phone-based Assessment for Serious Mental Illness: Native Smartphone Application vs Text-Messaging Only Implementations. Journal of Medical Internet Research 15, e60 (2013)

5. Campos, C., Lajara, R., Deluzio, T.: Usability and Preference Assessment of a New Pre-filled Insulin Pen versus Vial and Syringe in People with Diabetes, Physicians and Nurses. Expert Opinion on Pharmacotherapy 13, 1837–1846 (2012)

6. Haak, T., Edelman, S., Walter, C., Lecointre, B., Spollett, G.: Comparison of Usability and Patient Preference for the New Disposable Insulin Device Solostar versus Flexpen, Lilly Disposable pen, and a Prototype Pen: An Open-label Study. Clinical Therapeutics 29, 650–660 (2007)

7. Haller, G.U.Y., Haller, D.M., Courvoisier, D.S., Lovis, C.: Handheld vs. Laptop Computers for Electronic Data Collection in Clinical Research: A Crossover Randomized Trial. Journal of the American Medical Informatics Association 16, 651–659 (2009)

8. Joseph, A.: Comparing the Usability of Apple and Palm Handheld Computing Devices among Physicians: A Randomized Crossover Study. Masters paper, University of North Carolina at Chapel Hill (2009)

9. Oyer, D., Narendran, P., Qvist, M., Niemeyer, M., Nadeau, D.A.: Ease of Use and Preference of a New versus Widely Available Prefilled Insulin Pen Assessed by People with Diabetes, Physicians and Nurses. Expert Opinion on Drug Delivery 8, 1259–1269 (2011)

10. Salaba, A., Zhang, Y.: User Perspectives on NextGen Catalog Features. In: Proceedings of the American Society for Information Science and Technology, pp. 1–4. Wiley, Hoboken (2009)

11. La Barre, K.: Faceted Navigation and Browsing Features in New OPACs: A More Robust Solution to Problems of Information Seekers? Knowledge Organization 34, 78–90 (2007)

12. Hall, C.E.: Facet-based Library Catalogs: A Survey of the Landscape. In: Proceedings of the American Society for Information Science and Technology, vol. 48, pp. 1–8. Wiley, Hoboken (2011)

13. Capra, R., Marchionini, G.: The Relation Browser Tool for Faceted Exploratory Search. In: Proceedings of the 2008 Conference on Digital Libraries, p. 420. ACM, New York (2008)

14. Schraefel, M.C., Wilson, M.L., Russell, A., Smith, D.A.: mSpace: Improving information access to multimedia domains with multimodal exploratory search. Communications of the ACM 49, 47–49 (2006)

15. Wilson, M.L., Andre, P., Schraefel, M.C.: Backward Highlighting: Enhancing Faceted Search. In: Proceedings of the 21st Symposium on User Interface Software and Technology, pp. 235–238. ACM, New York (2008)

16. Wilson, M.L., White, R.W.: Evaluating advanced search interfaces using established information-seeking models. Journal of the American Society for Information Science and Technology 60, 1407–1422 (2009)

17. Lown, C.: A Transaction Log Analysis of NCSU's Faceted Navigation OPAC. Master's paper, University of North Carolina at Chapel Hill (2008)

18. Fagan, J.C.: Usability Studies of Faceted Browsing: A Literature Review. Information Technology and Libraries 29, 58–66 (2010)

19. Wanda, P., Hearst, M.A., Fagan, L.M.: A Knowledge-Based Approach to Organizing Retrieved Documents. In: Proceedings of the Sixteenth National Conference on Artificial Intelligence, pp. 80–85. AAAI Press, Menlo Park (1999)

20. Uddin, M.N.: Implementing Faceted Classification within a Content Management System. Master's thesis, Asian Institute of Technology (2006)

21. English, J., Hearst, M., Sinha, R., Swearingen, K., Lee, K.P.: Flexible Search and Navigation using Faceted Metadata. Technical report, University of Berkeley (2002)

22. Novotny, E.: I Don't Think I Click: A Protocol Analysis Study of Use of a Library Online Catalog in the Internet Age. College and Research Libraries 65, 525–537 (2004)

23. Niu, X., Lown, C., Hemminger, B.M.: Log Based Analysis of How Faceted and Text Based Search Interact in a Library Catalog Interface. Technical report, University of North Carolina at Chapel Hill (2008),
http://www.ils.unc.edu/bmh/tmp/endeca/facetsearch-revised_repaired.pdf
24. Antelman, K., Lynema, E., Pace, A.K.: Toward a Twenty-First Century Library Catalog. Information Technology & Libraries 25, 128–139 (2006)
25. Marchionini, G.: Information-seeking Strategies of Novices Using a Full-text Electronic Encyclopedia. Journal of the American Society for Information Science 40, 54–66 (1989)
26. Craven, J., Johnson, F., Butters, G.: The Usability Online Catalogue. Aslib Proceedings 62, 70–84 (2010)
27. Denton, W., Coysh, S.J.: Usability Testing of VuFind at an Academic Library. Library Hi Tech 29, 301–319 (2011)
28. Gerardo, J.L.S.: The Efficiency of Novice Users in Usability Testing. Master's thesis, University of Oslo (2007),
https://www.duo.uio.no/bitstream/handle/123456789/9681/Gerardo.pdf?sequence=1
29. Nielsen, J.: Novice vs. Expert Users (2000),
http://www.nngroup.com/articles/novice-vs-expert-users
30. Rubin, J., Chisnell, D., Spool, J.: Handbook of Usability Testing: How to Plan, Design, and Conduct Effective Tests, 2nd edn. Wiley, Indianapolis (2008)
31. Croft, W.B., Metzler, D., Strohman, T.: Search Engines: Information Retrieval in Practice. Addison-Wiley, Boston (2010)
32. Campbell, N.: Discovering the User: A Practical Glance at Usability Testing. The Electronic Library 17, 307–311 (1999)
33. Nielsen, J.: Why You Only Need to Test with 5 Users (2000),
http://www.nngroup.com/articles/why-you-only-need-to-test-with-5-users
34. Whitmire, E.: Disciplinary Differences and Undergraduates' Information-seeking Behavior. Journal of the American Society for Information Science and Technology 53, 631–638 (2002)
35. Tajoli, Z., Carassiti, A., Marchitelli, A., Valenti, F.: OSS Diffusion in Italian Libraries; The Case of Koha by the Consorzio Interuniversitario Lombardo per l'Elaborazione Automatica(CILEA). OCLC Systems & Services 27, 45–50 (2011)
36. Laplace, P.S.: Theorie Analytique des Probabilities. Courcier, Paris (1812)
37. Lewis, J.R., Sauro, J.: When 100% Really isn't 100%: Improving the Accuracy of Small-Sample Estimates of Completion Rates. Journal of Usability Studie 1, 136–150 (2006)
38. Nielsen, J.: Usability 101: Introduction to Usability (2012),
http://www.nngroup.com/articles/usability-101-introduction-to-usability

Collapsing Duplicates at Data Entry: Design Issues in Building Taiwan Citations Index

Chia-Ning Chiang

National Central Library, Taiwan
cnchiang@ncl.edu.tw

Abstract. When building citation indexes, citation entries are found duplicated and variant by nature at the time of data entry. This paper's aim is to describe the design concept and functions supported by the Taiwan Citation Index – Humanities and Social Sciences system (TCI system) for collapsing duplicated entries while also improving the quality of citations.

Keywords: Taiwan Citations Index, Humanities, Social Sciences, Design Concept, Citation Indexes Construction, Citations Quality.

1   Introduction

Taiwan Citation Index - Humanities and Social Sciences (TCI-HSS) Initiative is a collaborative project of the National Central Library, the Department of Humanities and Social Sciences, Ministry of Science and Technology (DHSS, MOST), and the Science and Technology Policy Research and Information Center (STPI). This project takes on an initial response to the needs and expectations of humanities and social sciences scholars in Taiwan. The focus is on building a foundation of bibliographic data and citation indexes of the academic literature from 2000 to present. Citation indexes to scholarly works not only demonstrate the characteristics of literature use in the humanities and social sciences domain, but also establish perspectives rooted in Taiwan's local academic context and Chinese literature. The results of this project facilitate observation of long-term sustainable development of the academic literature and its profound impact on academia in Taiwan.

The TCI-HSS Initiative Phase 1 is intended to: (1) convert the data of Taiwan Social Sciences Citation Index (TSSCI) and Taiwan Humanities Citation Index (THCI) merged by the STPI into the TCI system; (2) develop the TCI database for online data entry; and (3) develop the TCI Website for searching and browsing, as well as providing an online citation analysis of major citation indicators known by academic researchers and the public.

The National Central Library has been building journal indexes, theses database, and library automation systems for a number of years. In the front-end of TCI Website, the source records are filtered to provide only those scholarly literature covering arts, humanities, and social sciences. However, in the back-end, the TCI database contains index records across all disciplines. Since authors may cite cross-disciplinary literature, citation records can be in any discipline. For this purpose, the National

K. Tuamsuk et al. (Eds.): ICADL 2014, LNCS 8839, pp. 300–311, 2014.

Central Library is offering its index records of periodicals and dissertations, a substantial body of scholarly bibliographic content, and converts them into the TCI database as the source records. After converting the merged citation records, immediately the TCI team faced a large amount of duplicated entries and on-the-fly repetitions from data entry. Finding an effective solution in data entry is essential. For accuracy purpose, the TCI team adopted the idea of checking references against the original sources to develop the Search-Apply-Merge module. Consequently, in the back-end, source records may be used as the benchmark record for citations. This method not only de-duplicates but also improves the accuracy of resulting citation entries. This paper's aim is to describe the design concept and functions supported by the Taiwan Citation Index – Humanities and Social Sciences system in collapsing the duplicated entries while also improving the quality of citations.

TCI Collections (see Table 1)

TCI database includes source and citation records. The sources are academic literature in humanities and social sciences, which includes scholarly journals published in Taiwan, Hong Kong, and Macau; major journals published in China; as well as doctoral dissertations and a number of selected scholarly books published in Taiwan. Source record types include:

1. Journals: The journal collection provides comprehensive coverage of scholarly articles in Humanities and Social Sciences of all domestic journals and the most important international journals published in the Chinese region relevant to meet the needs of Taiwanese researchers. In the journal selection process, it is essential to meet three basic criteria: "peer-reviewed", "timeliness of publication", and "at least three articles in each journal issue". The candidate list will be reviewed and approved by the TCI Committee, and then the journal records and reference lists will be scheduled for data entry.

2. Theses and Dissertations: Theses records of the NDLTD-Taiwan systems (as of June 2014 there are over 770,000 records) have been converted into the TCI database as source records and updated weekly, but only the doctoral dissertations in Humanities and Social Sciences are displayed and accessible in the TCI Website.

3. Books and book articles: The book collection covers "authored books" as well as "edited books" that present fully referenced articles. In the book selection process, the lists are generated from citation records of which the document type is book. Candidate book lists are selected according to a set of criteria by NCL staff. Then, after the lists are reviewed and approved by the TCI Committee, the books records and reference lists will be scheduled for data entry.

4. Name authority records: Considering the credit that citation counts can bring to academics, researchers and faculty would like to be able to identify each individual's scholarly work when accessing the TCI database. In the second year, the Name Authority metadata set has been developed for data entry, and 800 records are entered monthly since January 2014. To better distinguish authors who have the same name and citation counts, the advanced Name Authority module is currently under development to serve this purpose.

Citation records, on the other hand, consist of various document types and can be in any discipline. There are many document types, and to shorten the long list for data entry, we decided to limit them to 18 document types (see Table 2).

Table 1. TCI Collections -- by Document Type of Source Records (as of June 2014)

Document Type	Total Records (TCI Database)	Records in Humanities & Social Sciences (accessible in the TCI Website)
Journal Title	4,768	1,028
Journal Article	1,719,819	252,184
Thesis & Dissertation	771,351	(Doctoral Dissertations) 12,822
Authored Book	144	144
Book Article	313	310
Personal Name Authority	4,954	4,954
Corporate Name Authority	21	21

Table 2. TCI Collection – Citation Document Types in the TCI database (as of June 2014)

Document Type	No. of Citation Records	Document Type	No. of Citation Records
Journal Article	1,041,784	Archive	1,289
Authored Book	985,569	Manuscript	341
Thesis	135,397	Unpublished	158
Book Article	290,224	Patent	259
Proceedings	57,897	Standard	111
Conference Paper	9,733	Paper	497
Research Project	820	Database	678
Research Paper	38,088	Internet Resource	23,563
In Progress Paper	3	Non-book Material	357,290
Total			3,289,976

2   The Problem

Building the citation database, the database structure, and data entry functions is very different from building a conventional bibliographic information system. According to Galvez and Moya-Anegón [1], as cited by Hood and Wilson [2], most databases are primarily designed for the purpose of information retrieval, but not for secondary use, as in informetric research. While this phenomenon can appear within a single database, it is even greater if a number of databases are merged [3, 4], and this is exactly the situation the TCI database faced at the beginning of Phase 1.The linking relationship between the source and its citations needs to be maintained to avoid blind or false links, and citation entries are found duplicated and variant at the time of data entry and need to be standardized and collapsed.

In building citation databases, for those who plan to begin such an initiative the duplication issue continually needs to be addressed. During data entry, repetition is inevitably present in reference lists. Duplicate entries are the same bibliographic citation cited by different sources, and collapsing duplicates would result in the total number of citation counts. However, errors or variants in bibliographic citations would cause the same citation to result in different entries, and consequently duplicate entries could not be successfully collapsed.

Errors or variants found in major fields such as article titles, author names, journal/source titles, and publisher names could conceivably have the consequence of preventing important works from being retrieved, consulted, and recognized. Specifically, the accuracy of numerical data such as year of publication, volume, or page numbers is also considered important for citation databases to support informetric research. Previous studies have found error rates in reference list are high [5,6,7,8,9,10,11]. Most findings in their results showed that accuracy responsibility falls upon manuscript authors. Previous research [12] showed that authors, mostly educators, strongly revealed the need to instruct students on the accurate construction of reference lists. Others suggested possible solutions such as (1) to utilize the skills of the experienced LIS professionals in this area to ensure the references are cited in the manner specified by that particular journal, and conjectured that this may be the only method of improving the accuracy of the references in these journals [6]; (2) to check references against the original sources [13,14,15,16]; or (3) to utilize computer software to construct reference lists of scholarly papers as a strategy for reducing reference errors [16].

Inaccurate references hinder retrieval of documents, may prevent researchers from examining all of the work by an author and may result in authors not getting credit for their work [17]. Therefore, citations must be accurate so that the sources they point to may be located quickly. Solving this inevitable errors- or variants-correction problem is the major issue for anyone who plans to begin such an initiative in building citation databases.

Citation databases take error correction solutions to various degrees. For example, the Web of Science (or ISI citation indexes) database is mostly built manually, produced during the past 50 years by the Institute for Scientific Information. It is unclear whether they provide tools to automatically recognize citations [18]. Moed [19] explores in depth aspects of accuracy in the ISI citation indexes by conducting an analysis using 22 million cited references matched to about 18 million ISI source-article indexes. The findings indicated that advanced citation data handling procedures must take into account inaccurate, sloppy referencing, editorial characteristics of scientific journals, referencing conventions in scholarly subfields, language problems, author identification problems, unfamiliarity with foreign author names and data capturing procedures. CiteSeer, on the other hand, uses an Autonomous Citation Indexing (ACI) system that automatically locates articles, extracts citations, identifies identical citations that occur in different formats, and identifies the fields of citations. CiteSeer is built upon a set of rules (e.g., the format of any citation is uniform within one article) and external databases of author names and journal names [20, 21]. They reported a performance of 80.2% for Title, 82.1% for Authors, and 44.2% for Page Number. This accuracy rate for supporting bibliometric analyses still needs further improvements.

In the case of the Korean Citation Index, errors and typos are corrected manually when building the citation database. Further, an error correction system for references of papers is implemented. Park et al. [22] pointed out that to solve the style difference problem in journal titles, a journal indexing system is developed with a journal look up table. This table serves as an authority control of matching journal index from the various transformed forms and abbreviations of journal titles. In China, The Chinese Social Sciences Citation Index (CSSCI) project uses a dictionary of source journals and a dictionary of institution categories are used for correction of citations in the CSSCI. The errors are detected by the system and corrected manually23].

3   Data Quality Challenges the Building of TCI Database

3.1   The Legacy of Citation Data Merged from THCI, TSSCI, and STPI

At the end of the first year in TCI Phase 1, the STPI technical staff merged the records of THCI and TSSCI as well as those data entered on the STPI server in the first year into a Microsoft Access data set. The data quality problems, such as variations and errors, from the two data sets presented a great challenge to the conversion process.

After four months of trials-and-errors, the data conversion was successful in February 2013. The lesson learned was that there should have been more preparation steps in processing the conversion. More precise efforts were made to verify the content in the final merged dataset. Eventually, we used an Excel table aligning all the data fields, plus notes fields for conversion purposes, into 63 fields from the original merged dataset. T he table was delicate enough to selectively process the conversion in batches. In total, 96,000 source records and 2,210,000 citation records were converted into the TCI database. In addition to the STPI data set, source records imported from the NCL's systems include 1,673,474 journal article records and 755,847 theses and dissertation records (of which 12,579 were doctoral dissertations), but only those in humanities and social sciences were accessible through the TCI Website (front-end system).

Furthermore, over 238,000 groups of duplicated records resulted from converting the STPI dataset of merged records. A group may contain duplicated records ranging from 2 to over 1,000 identical entries. In the initial plan, the project team tried to find additional funding to clean up those groups of records; hence, those duplicated records were loaded into a different pool waiting to be cleaned up manually.

At that time, the TCI system was still under development, but the data entry module was up. Data entry was being carried out continuously, at an average of 2,000 source records and 57,000 citation records per month. With a vast amount of duplicated data in the database, while new errors and duplicates keep being added through data entry every day, it was difficult for the NCL project team to clean the pool and solve the new ones. Furthermore, in the Search Result page on the TCI Website, the citation counts resulted were shown as "Cited by 1" for each, not aggregated citation counts. Notified that there would be no further budget and resources, we must come up with an effective solution, and the decision must be made quickly because the TCI Website was scheduled to launch in September 2013.

3.2   Database Errors

Database errors were also introduced in the construction of the TCI database. The National Central Library received citation records from THCI, TSSCI, and STPI and converted them into the TCI database. Errors, variations (including semantic errors – some citations in full string while some others may be in an abbreviation; for example, American Library Association as abbreviated in ALA), and incomplete records were numerous. Most metadata elements were used to describe the same information, especially those major fields such as Author, Article Title, and Publication Year, etc., in all three databases. However, each system had its own additional metadata elements (e.g., Object Identifier or Document Identifier) or the same fields but defined differently, which would take extra effort in the mapping process. Oftentimes, authors' Chinese Name may be entered with one or more Romanization names, which are delimited with different punctuation marks. These punctuation marks may prevent that field to be converted correctly. In addition, the comprehensiveness of data in each field revealed differences of data entry rules. For example, in THCI the name after the equal sign may be the Chinese author's Romanization name or the Western author's Chinese name, which is additional information entered manually according to their cataloguing rules.

Coverage of journal data was intended to date back to the year 2000; however, the completeness of data entered varied by year, ranging from 25% to 75%. Another kind of database errors was called linking errors, which can be defined as the failure to establish an electronic link between the cited references and the corresponding database records. At the time of this article, these "orphaned records" remain unresolved and have not been converted into the database.

4   Citation Entries Are Found Duplicated and Variant by Nature

During data entry, many errors were found to be authors' errors. Authors make errors when creating the list of cited articles for their publications. According to Sweetland [14] citation errors, which can be traced back more than 100 years, "citation errors continued to appear, as did an increasing number of complaints about them" said Sweetland [14]. Previous studies have examined the bibliographic accuracy of citations in various disciplines, for example, LIS [6], medicine [24,25,26,16], nursing [27], psychology [28], and social work [29], etc. Most of these researchers have reported unacceptably high rates of errors from authors and editors.

The data set conversion at the initial phase of TCI project found errors from various stages of publishing and data entry processes. Errors could be defined as authors' and editors' errors, database errors, and certainly included data entry errors such as typographical errors, translation errors, OCR errors, misspelled citations, and complex author names, etc.

In the TCI, building citation entries also includes footnotes. In social sciences and humanities, citations can occur in footnotes instead of in the cited reference section at the end of the paper. Footnotes may be found at the bottom of the page or, in the case of endnotes, to the back of the volume. Past research [30] found that legal and historical journals typically have large numbers of footnotes. In addition, footnotes are printed in a variety of ways and publication manuals (e.g. APA, etc.) give different instructions on how to set to footnotes [31]. The recognized functions for footnoting include: (1) to give credit for borrowed material, (2) to provide the reader with access to research materials, (3) to provide an explanation in greater detail, and (4) to provide internal cross-referencing [32]. Depending on the author's arguments, footnotes can be discovered as substantive footnotes and/or bibliographic footnotes. Often times, abbreviations "Id." are used in footnote citations to state that the citation is found in the same work as the one previously cited. In the case of building the TCI, when entering data, the data-entry clerk would have to skim through the footnotes of each paper to identify the bibliographic citations, key-in only one citation of the same work, and check the "footnote" metadata field for noting that the source is from the footnote. According to our monthly data-entry statistics, on average, 15 percent of entries are footnotes. An interesting observation is that authors who cited more footnotes tended to cite more references.

Many duplicates were not identified and grouped because of errors such as mis-spelling, extra spaces, punctuation errors, etc., but we needed to deal with errors if we wanted to solve duplicate problems. It was by then acknowledged that citations entries were duplicated and variant by nature, and finding efficient and effective solutions to harness everlasting duplicates on a daily basis was the major challenge. One of the major functions of the second year in TCI Phase 1 was to develop the semi-automatic citation parsing algorithm for speeding up the data entry, the search-and-apply standard record, and the collapsing of duplicates functions.

5   Design Approach

Finding an approach to digest duplicates and obtain better quality on-the-fly for data entry is the ultimate goal. The NCL staff with the TCI software developer discussed possible design issues. We analyzed the data, database structure, data entry process, and batch processing functions. The analyses showed that the combination of manual editing and re-applying better quality records during the collapsing process, as well as an overnight batch process of merging all collapses is inevitable.

Decisions were made based on the answers of the following questions:

1. How to get correct citation counts? We need to aggregate duplicates, and the solution must be developed in the back-end system.
2. How to improve the data quality? Citation errors are numerous. On the other hand, the quality of source records imported from the NCL's systems is well-recognized, especially for journal articles. First of all, not only do source records contain more metadata elements, they have also gone through proofreading and editing at the time entered by the NCL staff in the PerioPath system. Second, they are readily available in the TCI database. Third, source records are later cited by others in

reference lists, and that is how they started to have errors and variants. Thus, source record is the best option to be the benchmark record to allow for the merging of citations when an article appears several times in the TCI database.

3. Does using computer algorithm for aggregating duplicate citations be an option? The answer is no. Taking the lessons from the STPI's merging process: (1) numerous errors can cause the successful rate to be low, (2) one solution can not fit all, and (3) the clean up process that follows may be even more laborious. However, using the Search function to find similar citations for later improvement is feasible. In addition, the search result will bring up all the matched similar citations in different source records, and selecting one standard and applying to all would also produce correct co-citation counts in the records of front-end Webpage.

4. Can on-the-fly manual correction be an option? Considering the skill set and limited amount of time data entry clerks have, the solution must be obvious and fast enough for them to accomplish the correction. Using the source records as the benchmark record is applicable, because we have large amount of source records already imported into the TCI database. Source record's RecordID is easily identified, and it can be top-ranked at the hit list from searching similar citations. An Apply-Standard function can be developed. Data entry clerk can easily applied the source record, which appears at the top of the hit list, to allow for the merging of duplicated citations without further need to manually correct errors. For those citations to which no source records can be applied, it may be possible to find a better quality one as the benchmark. Both the pros and cons are addressed that this approach may rely on people's knowledge and judgment. At least, it is agreed that this approach is effective and efficient to make local authors' literature appear in a better quality and citation counts more accurate.

5. How does one data entry clerk know that there are other duplicates created at the same time? The data entry clerk has no way of knowing the duplicates happening in parallel, and it would be impossible for the computer to process parallel collapsing at all time. The best option is using batch process to compare and merge all edited collapses in the night when no users are editing records online.

6. How should the Benchmark Record be designed and utilized? We select the source record or the better quality citation to be the benchmark record for a group of N citations. Then, the Apply-Standard function creates a new citation record by making a copy of the benchmark record, and points the original N records to this (N+1)th record (see Figure 1).

The discussions concluded that the system needed to support functions for collapsing citations and improving record quality on the fly. Five design issues of the Search Duplicates and Collapse module were identified. First, a working area is needed to support on-the-fly collapsing of identical citations found in both duplication sets and online data entry. In addition, a batch processing to merge all collapses performed at the end of day is required. Second, the identification of a standard record (e.g., the Periopath Index record) that has better quality than any other duplicates is required. Third, an Apply-Standard function needs to be devised for controlling variant citations. At the time of collapsing, the data entry clerk would search for variants, identify the standard record, select identical citations, and click the Apply-Standard to point the variants to the standard record. Fourth, the system would then put all the variant records pointed to the standard one and display them in the form and content of the standard thereafter. Fifth, for aggregating duplicates created on-the-fly in a day, using overnight batch process of merging all collapses is required.

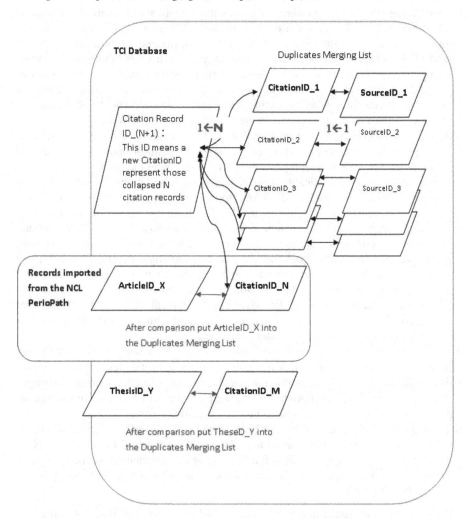

Fig. 1. The design concept of creating a new citation record for merging duplicates

After the Search Duplicates and Collapse module has been in service, the citation counts are given in the TCI records and aggregated to successfully show the total citation counts under "times cited." This module has been in service since July 2013. In July 2013, the module was under testing and not used in its full power. From August 2013 till June 2014, groups merged accounted for, on average, 16% of the total records in a month, which is speculated to be the percentage of duplicates in the citation records. In addition, only 66,779 groups remained in the pool. We believe this approach has proven to be effective and efficient.

6   Discussion

Previous researchers [33,34] discussed issues concerning the over-representation of English language journals in the overall coverage of ISI databases, especially in social science and the humanities [35]. Baneyx [36] pointed out that for humanities researchers who do not publish in English, ISI databases are not very useful. Hence, in order to improve the research on the analysis of domestic citation index and the level of the construction of domestic citation index resources, many non-English speaking counties and regions (such as China and Korea in Asia) have launched initiatives in building citation indexes of their own.

The major challenge is to process input data, clean data, correct errors, and merge data so that the data can be used for statistical analysis. Only a few articles we found made any mention of this issue. For example, Su [37] mentioned that the CSSCI system consists of data processing subsystem to serve this purpose. In the CSSCI system, an automatic fuzzy matching algorithm is devised in the CSSCI system for selecting records of authors, institutions, journals and article titles with high error possibility [23]. For the CSSCI system, dictionaries are applied in the algorithm for data quality control [23].

Building the TCI has proven to be a completely different experience from building a conventional database. We started out attempting to build it like any other bibliographic database, although deep in our minds we knew the one-source-to-N-citations relationship had to be a distinct characteristic of citation indexes. This became the major challenge we faced, and we needed to find a solution in order to build a successful system. Our innovative solution was the Search-Apply-Merge module.

This design approach of the TCI project accommodates not only the collapsing of records in two different areas in the TCI database, but also the adoption of better quality content by applying the standard record to lower quality duplicates. The mechanism must support on-the-fly online data entry as well as daily batch processing. In a nutshell, search, select, apply, collapse, and aggregate collapses are major functions needed in achieving the ultimate goal of efficiency and effectiveness.

7   Closing Remarks

Taiwan's scholarly literature has long been ignored or diluted in those citation data bases developed in China or other countries. The building of the TCI system brings attention to Taiwan's academic performance in humanities and social sciences. The citation data reveal the citing behavior and the characteristics of the use of Chinese literature. It is beneficial for Taiwan's academic community to understand the academic context and trend of the Chinese region and to have a channel to voice Taiwan's research. In particular, the results can highlight the academic literature and citations characteristics of Chinese humanities and social sciences research.

This paper shows that building a citation database like the Taiwan Citations Index is very different from conventional bibliographic databases. This paper describes an innovative design approach taken by the NCL's TCI project staff in finding an efficient way to digest the large amount duplicate into a day-to-day process, as well as an effective way to apply the standard record in place of variant citations for the betterment of citation quality.

The reliability of citation-based analyses strongly depends on the accuracy with which citation links are identified. The Search-Apply-Merge module is only the first step towards reaching the goal of trustworthy evaluation mechanisms. More work needs to be done to improve the citation data quality at the field level. Learning from the data entry experience, at the end of 2014, a dictionary of publication place and a dictionary of publisher names will be applied to improve the current citation parser. The future strategy will still focus on exploiting available sources and new technology that can accelerate the speed of data entry while obtain better quality.

References

1. Galvez, C., Moya-Anegón, F.: Standardizing Formats of Corporate Source Data. Sciento-metrics 70(1), 3–26 (2007)
2. Hood, W.W., Wilson, C.S.: Informetric Studies Using Databases: Opportunities and Challenges. Scientometrics 58(3), 587–608 (2003)
3. Braun, T., Brocken, M., Glaenzel, W., Rinia, E., Schubert, A.: Databases in Building Scientometric Indicators: Physics Briefs, SCI Based Indicators of 13 European Countries, 1980–1989. Scientometrics 33(2), 131–148 (1995)
4. French, J.C., Powell, A.L., Schulman, E.: Using Clustering Strategies for Creating Authority Files. J. Am. Soc. Inf. Sci. 51(8), 774–786 (2000)
5. Taylor, M.K.: The Practical Effects of Errors in Reference Lists in Nursing Research Journals. Nurs. Res. 47(5), 300–303 (1998)
6. Davies, K.: Reference Accuracy in Library and Information Science Journals. Aslib Proc. 64(4), 373–387 (2012)
7. Wyles, D.F.: Citation Errors in Two Journals of Psychiatry. Behavioral & Social Sciences Librarian 22(2), 27–51 (2004)
8. McLellan, M.F., Case, L.D., Barnett, M.C.: Trust but Verify: The Accuracy of References in Four Anesthesia Journals. Anesthesiology 77, 185–188 (1992)
9. Browne, R.F., Logan, P.M., Lee, M., Torreggiani, W.C.: The Accuracy of References in Manuscript Submitted for Publication. Can. Assoc. Radiol. J. 55(3), 170–173 (2004)
10. Holt, S., Siebers, R., Suder, A., Loan, R., Jeffery, O.: The Accuracy of References in Australian and New Zealand Medical Journals. N. Z. Med. J. 113, 416–417 (2000)
11. O'Connor, A.E.: A Review of the Accuracy of References in the Journal Emergency Medicine. Emerg. Med. 14, 139–141 (2002)
12. Wilks, S.E., Spivey, C.A.: Views of Reference List Accuracy from Social Work Journal Editors and Published Authors. Advances in Social Work 5(2), 172–181 (2004)
13. Foreman, M.D., Kirchhoff, K.T.: Accuracy of References in Nursing Journals. Res. Nurs. Health 10, 177–183 (1987)
14. Sweetland, J.H.: Errors in Bibliographic Citations: A Continuing Problem. Lib. Quarterly 59(4), 291–304 (1989)
15. Goldberg, R., Newton, E., Cameron, J., Jacobson, R., Chan, L., Bukata, W.R., Rakab, A.: Reference Accuracy in the Emergency Medicine Literature. Ann. Emerg. Med. 22(9), 1450–1454 (1993)
16. Fenton, J.E., Brazier, H., De Souza, A., Hughes, J.P., McShane, D.P.: The Accuracy of Citation and Quotation in Otolaryngology/Head and Neck Surgery Journals. Clin. Otolaryngol. 25, 40–44 (2000)

17. Oermann, M.H., Cummings, S.L., Wilmes, N.A.: Accuracy of References in Four Pedia-tric Nursing Journals. J. Pediatr. Nurs. 16(4), 263–268 (2001)
18. Zhang, Q., Cao, Y.G., Yu, H.: Parsing Citations in Biomedical Articles Using Conditional Random Fields. Comput. Biol. Med. 41(4), 190–194 (2011)
19. Moed, H.F.: Accuracy of Citation Counts. Citation Analysis in Research Evaluation, 173–179 (2005)
20. Giles, C., Bollacker, K., Lawrence, S.: CiteSeer: An Automatic Citation Index-ing System. In: Proceedings of the Third ACM Conference on Digital Libraries, pp. 89–98. ACM, New York (1998)
21. Lawrence, S., Giles, C.L., Bollacker, K.: Digital Libraries and Autonomous Cita-tion In-dexing. IEEE Computer 32(6), 67–71 (1999)
22. Park, J.H., Park, H.H., Kwon, Y.B.: Error Correction of Reference Indexing System In-cluding Multimedia Journals. Multimed Tools Appl. (2014),
    `http://dx.doi.org/10.1007/s11042-014-1971-9`
    (published online: April 6, 2014)
23. Su, X.N.: Quality Control of Data in Citation Indexes. Zhong Guo Tu Shu Guan Xue Bao (2), 76–78 (2001)
24. Aronsky, D., Ransom, J., Robinson, K.: Accuracy of References in Five Biomedical Informatics Journals. J. Am. Med. Inform. Assoc. 12, 225–228 (2005)
25. Lukić, I.K., Lukić, A., Glunčić, V., Katavić, V., Vučenik, V., Marušić, A.: Citation and Quotation Accuracy in Three Anatomy Journals. Clin. Ana. 17(7), 534–539 (2004)
26. Reddy, M.S., Srinivas, S., Sabanayagam, N., Balasubramanian, S.P.: Accuracy of Refer-ences in General Surgical Journals - An Old Problem Revised. The Surgeon 6(2), 71–75 (2008)
27. Lok, C.K., Chan, M.T., Martinson, I.M.: Risk Factors for Citation Errors in Peer-reviewed Nursing Journals. J. Adv. Nurs. 34(2), 223–229 (2001)
28. Faunce, G.J., Job, R.F.S.: The Accuracy of Reference Lists in Five Experimental Psychol-ogy Journals. Amer. Psychol. 56(10), 829–830 (2001)
29. Spivey, C.A., Wilks, S.E.: Reference List Accuracy in Social Work Journals. Res. Soc. Work Pract. 14(4), 281–286 (2004)
30. Legrand, P.: Sigla Law. Int. J. of Legal Inf. 23(2), 123–148 (1995)
31. Hartley, J.: What Do We Know About Footnotes? Opinions and Data. J. Inf. Sci. 25(3), 205–212 (1999)
32. Slomanson, W.R.: The Bottom Line: Footnote Logic in Law Review Writing. Legal Ref. Serv. Q. 7(1), 47–69 (1987)
33. MacRoberts, M., MacRoberts, B.: Problems of Citation Analysis. Scientometrics 36(3), 435–444 (1996)
34. MacRoberts, M., MacRoberts, B.: Problems of Citation Analysis: A Critical Review. J. Am. Soc. Inf. Sci. 40(5), 342–349 (1989)
35. Kousha, K., Thelwall, M.: Sources of Google Scholar Citations Outside the Science Citation Index. Scientometrics 74(2), 273–294 (2008)
36. Baneyx, A.: Publish or Perish as Citation Metrics Used to Analyze Scientific Output in the Humanities: International Case Studies in Economics, Geography, Social sciences, Philos-ophy, and History. Arch. Immunol. Ther. Exp. 56, 1–9 (2008)
37. Su, X.N., Deng, S.H., Shen, S.: The Design and Application Value of the Chinese Social Science Citation Index. Scientometrics 98, 1567–1582 (2014)

Simple Document-by-Document Search Tool "Fuwatto Search" Using Web API

Masao Takaku[1] and Yuka Egusa[2]

[1] University of Tsukuba
1-2 Kasuga, Tsukuba, Ibaraki, Japan
masao@slis.tsukuba.ac.jp
[2] National Institute for Educational Policy Research
3-2-2 Kasumigaseki, Chiyoda, Tokyo, Japan
yuka@nier.go.jp

Abstract. In this paper, we propose a new search method *Fuwatto Search* that allows users to retrieve documents in a document-by-document manner via a Web API. We present an implementation of the proposed method (i.e., Fuwatto CiNii Search), which targets the CiNii Article database, one of the largest academic article databases in Japan. The experimental evaluation of Fuwatto CiNii Search with newspaper articles demonstrates the retrieval effectiveness of 0.25 for precision at 10 and 0.17 for mean average precision.

Keywords: document retrieval, Web API, effectiveness, CiNii Articles.

1 Introduction

Digital libraries, domain-specific databases, and Web search engines are important for our daily lives. When we need certain information for health, fashion, travel, and many other areas, we typically use Web-based search services.

Most search services support keyword-based queries. In other words, we must specify keywords that are appropriate for our information needs. Keyword-based queries can cause a gap between users and search systems because users do not always have enough knowledge on how to express appropriate keywords that correspond to their information needs and database content.

One solution for this issue is to use another querying method, i.e., the document-as-a-query method. A search system that supports document-by-document queries accepts an existing document as a query and returns a list of similar documents. Currently, some news websites, electronic commerce websites, and digital library services support this function. On such websites, a user can obtain a list of other items that are similar to the current item on that page. Such content-based similarity search functions can be beneficial in certain situations. However, these functions are not always available for all databases.

In this paper, we propose a new content-based similarity search methodology, "Fuwatto Search." Fuwatto Search allows users to search any arbitrary search service with a document-by-document query via a simple keyword-based search Web API.

K. Tuamsuk et al. (Eds.): ICADL 2014, LNCS 8839, pp. 312–319, 2014.

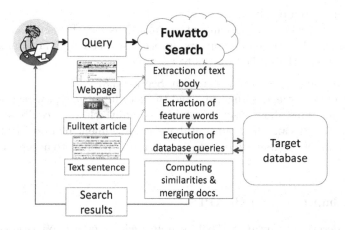

Fig. 1. Overview of Fuwatto Search

2 Proposed Methodology

An overview of the proposed *Fuwatto Search* methodology is shown in Figure 1.

Fuwatto Search is a document-by-document search method for remote databases. Fuwatto Search can search target databases that do not support document-by-document search functions. It iteratively accesses the keyword search functionality of a target database, and then analyzes and re-ranks the retrieved results. This process is described as follows.

1. Extraction of full text

   Fuwatto Search accepts PDF, HTML, and plain text data as a query. When a PDF or HTML page is given to Fuwatto Search as a query, the system first extracts the text content. For web pages written in HTML, the page header, footer and navigational elements are excluded. The system extracts the main body elements (i.e., the text) of an HTML page. We use the `extractcontent.rb` text extraction tool to extract main body elements from an HTML page [1].

2. Extraction of feature words with weights

   Extracted words are segmented using a Japanese morphological analyzer (i.e., MeCab). We simultaneously count the term frequency (TF) in the query document. TF is multiplied by the term occurrence cost, which is pre-defined in the MeCab dictionary.

3. Search execution

   We select the top n words from a vector of the feature words (computed by the previous process). Each of the top n words is sent as a query to the target database to determine if there is a match. If no hits are returned for a given word, we exclude that word from the set of feature words. We then tests the next feature word using the same process.

4. Merging search results
   The system merges all documents returned as search results into a single ranked list of retrieved documents in terms of specificity and similarity, and then presents the ranked results to the user.

Details of the process are described in Section 3.3.

This procedure was designed to avoid the zero hit problem, which returns no search results. This allows users to obtain as many relevant results as possible. This methodology can search any database in a document-by-document manner, even if the target database does not support any capability to accept documents as queries.

2.1 Mashup Using CiNii API

Here, we describe "Fuwatto CiNii Search," which uses CiNii Articles [2] as a target database for Fuwatto Search. Starting in January 2010, we developed Fuwatto CiNii Search as an implementation of the proposed methodology. Fuwatto CiNii Search is freely available at `http://fuwat.to/cinii`.

CiNii Articles is a Japanese academic article database service provided by the National Institute of Informatics. It contains bibliographic information for approximately 15 million articles. In addition, it supports a simple keyword-based search Web API using the OpenSearch protocol [3].

Fuwatto CiNii Search searches CiNii Articles database using the OpenSeach API. It uses a content extraction module for web pages, i.e., extractcontent.rb [1]. This content extraction module extracts body text from HTML web pages with block-based heuristics and simple rules for Japanese characters. The morphological analysis tool MeCab [4] is used to segment the query body text into the words, and to extract the feature words. To avoid the effects of noise, only Japanese nouns and adjectives are selected as feature words. For English, stop words [5] are also excluded from being used as feature words. The likeliness of feature words is computed from the MeCab (with the mecab-ipadic dictionary) morphological analysis results. The likeliness of a given word as a feature words is derived from the term occurrence cost score, which is pre-defined by the MeCab dictionary. The term occurrence cost is defined as a constant value that reflects the inverse term occurrence probabilities derived from the MeCab corpora.

Figure 2 shows screenshots of the Fuwatto CiNii Search top page. Fuwatto CiNii Search allows users to search a database using either a sentence query as input text or a webpage query to specify a query URL. It also provides links to national newspaper (i.e., Mainichi and Asahi) editorials as sample queries. Figure 3 shows the Fuwatto CiNii Search results page. The search results page lists the retrieved documents and shows links to corresponding CiNii Articles database items.

(a) Text query   (b) URL query

Fig. 2. Screenshots of Fuwatto CiNii Search

Fig. 3. Example search results

3   Experimental Evaluation

Here, we describe an experimental evaluation of our proposed methods. We evaluated retrieved results on the basis of effectiveness using content from newspaper articles on the web.

3.1   Topics

We used 34 newspaper articles for the evaluation. These articles were chosen from articles published by two major national newspapers, Sankei and Asahi newspapers). The newspaper articles were selected by random sampling from a population of articles published from March 19 to May 9, 2010.

For the evaluation, we used newspaper articles as the search topics. The articles were used as Fuwatto CiNii Search query documents, and the retrieved results were evaluated on the basis of their relevance to the original document. We also attempted several similarity scoring and search methods, and compared the obtained results according to topical relevance by manual assessment.

3.2   Relevance Assessments

We recruited one assessor for relevance assessment of the retrieved documents.

Relevance assessments were graded on three levels: A) relevant, B) partially relevant, and C) non relevant.

The documents pool for the assessment consisted of the top 50 search results retrieved from 34 newspaper article queries for several search methodologies described below. The assessor made relevance judgments on 22,005 documents, which on average, consisted of 647 documents per topic.

3.3   Experimental Runs

In the experimental evaluation, we implemented several versions of Fuwatto Search with modified feature words extraction and query execution methods, and then compared the results from these runs in terms of effectiveness. The following describe the methods used for feature word extraction and document ranking.

1. Feature word extraction and weighting
   - **TF**: Feature words are chosen on the basis of the term frequency.

$$weight(t) = TF(t)$$

   Here, t is a given word, $TF(t)$ is the term frequency for word t in the original document, and $weight(t)$ is the likeliness score for a feature word.
   - **LogCost**: Feature words are chosen on the basis of the total score value of logarithm of occurrence cost value computed by the MeCab morphological analyzer.

$$weight(t) = \sum_i log_2(Cost(t_i))$$

   Here, $Cost(t_i)$ is each term occurrence cost value.
   - **IDF**: The document frequency for each feature word is obtained by sending a given feature word as a keyword query to the target database. Feature words are chosen by multiplying the weighting score by the inverse document frequency in the target database.

$$weight'(t) = \frac{weight(t)}{log_2(DF(t))}$$

   Here, $DF(t)$ is the document frequency of term t in the target database.
2. Keyword querying
   - **AND**: The top n feature words are selected in order of score, and these feature words are joined (by the AND operator) to construct a new query. The joined query is sent to the target database. If less than m documents are retrieved from the target database, the query is modified to use fewer feature words (e.g., $n-1$, $n-2$, ...,) until the number of retrieved documents is greater than m.

- **Comb**: All combinations of three words from the top n feature words are extracted. These three words are then joined (AND operator) to generate query keywords. Then, all query keywords are sent to the target database.
3. Re-ranking
   - **Rerank**: The cosine similarity between a feature words vector and each retrieved document vector is computed, and all retrieved documents are re-ranked in the order of highest similarity.
   - **PRF(α)**: The top k ranked documents are retrieved and used to create a new words vector. This new vector is merged into the original feature words vector with a normalizing factor. All retrieved documents are re-ranked in the order of highest similarity with the modified words vector.

$$weight'(t) = (1 - \alpha)weight(t) + \alpha \cdot weight_d(t)$$

Here, $weight_d(t)$ is the new vector by pseudo relevance feedback (PRF), and α is a constant merging factor.

We used the number of feature words $n = 10$ and the number of search results $m = 100$ as evaluation parameters. In addition, we used the number of feedback documents $k = 20$ as the PRF weight parameter.

3.4   Evaluation Metrics

We used precision at 10 (Prec@10) and mean average precision (MAP) as evaluation metrics for the retrieved documents. In the evaluation, we considered relevance levels A and B as relevant.

4   Results and Discussions

4.1   Term Extraction, Weighting and Rankings

Table 1 shows the evaluation results for each method. The CiNii Articles is an academic database; therefore, we show evaluation results for newspaper articles on both the science section and other sections.

The querying and ranking methods based on Comb+Rerank demonstrated major improvements (0.11 over AND-based methods in terms of Prec@10). On an average, the Comb+Rerank method could retrieve at least one or extra relevant documents than the AND method. This seems to be due to the fact that the Comb method could obtain a greater number of relevant documents from the database, and Rerank could place relevant documents at higher rank using vector similarity. For the case of AND method, retrieval performance tends to rely heavily on the primary feature word vector. The Comb method seems to improve this drawback.

Among the methods used for weighting feature words, the IDF method demonstrated a slight performance improvement than over LogCost and TF; however, the differences among these methods were negligible.

On the other hand, the results for the PRF methods demonstrated weaker performance than the original Comb+Rerank methods.

Table 1. Evaluation results

Methods	Prec@10			MAP		
	Total	Science	Others	Total	Science	Others
AND+TF	0.079	0.111	0.040	0.064	0.056	0.074
AND+TF+IDF	0.094	0.079	0.113	0.058	0.020	0.110
AND+LogCost	0.106	0.116	0.093	0.060	0.050	0.081
AND+LogCost+IDF	0.077	0.074	0.080	0.058	0.020	0.105
AND+Rerank+TF	0.121	0.147	0.087	0.046	0.067	0.020
AND+Rerank+TF+IDF	0.138	0.142	0.133	0.046	0.043	0.050
AND+Rerank+LogCost	0.100	0.095	0.107	0.038	0.043	0.031
AND+Rerank+LogCost+IDF	0.132	0.158	0.100	0.044	0.046	0.041
Comb+Rerank+TF	0.218	0.258	0.167	0.167	0.207	0.117
Comb+Rerank+TF+IDF	0.232	0.274	0.180	0.167	0.215	0.106
Comb+Rerank+LogCost	0.232	0.253	0.207	0.168	0.201	0.126
Comb+Rerank+LogCost+IDF	0.250	0.279	0.213	0.170	0.214	0.114
PRF(.25)+Comb+Rerank+LogCost+IDF	0.235	0.263	0.200	0.032	0.041	0.090
PRF(.50)+Comb+Rerank+LogCost+IDF	0.197	0.226	0.160	0.103	0.132	0.067
PRF(.75)+Comb+Rerank+LogCost+IDF	0.106	0.126	0.080	0.053	0.071	0.030
PRF(1.0)+Comb+Rerank+LogCost+IDF	0.062	0.079	0.053	0.017	0.037	0.020
PRF(2.0)+Comb+Rerank+LogCost+IDF	0.006	0.011	0.000	0.005	0.008	0.001

4.2   Document Categories

Of the total 34 topic documents, 19 articles were from the science section, and 15 articles were from other sections. These target article categories can also affect retrieval performance. For nearly all Comb-based methods, retrieval performance for science articles was better than other articles because term usage in the source documents from the science section is similar to the target academic database, which seems to benefit document retrieval by feature words.

The varying categories of source documents may affect retrieval performance. This implies that it is possible to obtain better performance with adaptive approaches utilizing the similarity search methods that can switch according to the categories that the original document belongs.

4.3   Response Time

The proposed methodology is a mash-up that employs Web API protocols. For the implementing the Fuwatto Search, once a query (text or URL) is received, querying is performed over the Internet in real time. In this searching model, real time responses are also a key point. Depending on the querying methods, there are differences in the number of search queries issued and the extracted feature words. Notably, these differences may affect response time.

We counted the response time as the average from five trials per query topic. On average, the "AND+LogCost+IDF" method took 2.4 seconds for all topics, whereas the "Comb+Rerank+LogCost+IDF" method took 15.1 seconds. This difference in response time can be explained by the number of HTTP requests to the target database. The AND+X method sent 20 HTTP requests on average, whereas the Comb+X method sent 131 requests.

There is a tradeoff between response time and retrieval effectiveness. The Comb+X method outperformed the AND+X method in retrieval effectiveness, as is described in Section 4.1. However, the Comb method requires more HTTP accesses than the AND method. The Comb+X method took at most 30 seconds; therefore, it is inadequate when real-time response performance is important. Thus, the AND method is used when real-time responses are important, while the Comb method is used for indirect uses, such as for searching through the embedded content (e.g., Google AdSense).

5   Conclusion

This paper has proposed the Fuwatto Search method. We have demonstrated the effectiveness of the proposed method through experimental evaluation and implementation using CiNii Articles and its API. The evaluation results for Fuwatto CiNii Search with newspaper articles demonstrate performance of 0.25 for Prec@10, and 0.17 for MAP.

In future, we plan to improve our weighting and querying methods. In addition, we intend to evaluate the proposed method using other text categories, such as more general web content or other target databases.

Acknowledgment. This work was partially supported grants from the Japan Society for the Promotion of Science KAKENHI (No. 25730193 and No. 26330362).

References

1. Nakatani, S.: Body text extraction of web pages (in Japanese), http://labs.cybozu.co.jp/blog/nakatani/2007/09/web_1.html (updated September 12, 2007, accessed June 15, 2014)
2. National Institute of Informatics: CiNii Articles, http://ci.nii.ac.jp/en (accessed June 15, 2014)
3. National Institute of Informatics: Metadata and API: CiNii Articles OpenSearch for Articles, http://ci.nii.ac.jp/info/en/api/a_opensearch.html (accessed June 15, 2014)
4. Kudo, T.: MeCab: Yet another part-of-speech and morphological analyzer, https://code.google.com/p/mecab/ (accessed June 15, 2014)
5. Library of Congress: InQuery stopword list for THOMAS, http://thomas.loc.gov/home/stopwords.html (accessed February 10, 2010)

Concept-Based Cross Language Retrieval
for Thai Medicine Recipes

Jantima Polpinij

Intellect Laboratory, Faculty of Informatics, Mahasarakham University
Mahasarakham, Thailand
jantima.p@msu.ac.th

Abstract. This work aims to present a new methodology to retrieve the documents relating to the traditional Thai medicine recipe that is translated from the ancient palm leaf manuscripts. This methodology is developed based on three main concepts: sematic data, latent search indexing (LSI), and cross language information retrieval (CLIR). Our methodology consists of four main processing steps. They are document indexing, document representation based on LSI, user's query transformation, and document retrieval and ranking. After testing by the common performance measures for information retrieval system such as recall, precision, and F-measure, it would demonstrate that our methodology can achieve substantial improvements.

Keywords: Palm leaf Manuscript, Thai Medicine Recipe, Cross Language Information Retrieval, Latent Search indexing, Sematic Data.

1 Introduction

Palm leaf manuscript (PLM) is an ancient document form that comprises a significant documentary heritage of the Isan people of Northeastern Thailand [1][2]. PLMs contain a vast amount of knowledge, such as traditional Thai medicine recipe. Therefore, over the last few decades, the experts would access and read the ancient documents in order to translate the ancient characters to the present characters. Unfortunately, although the ancient characters are changed to the present characters, they are hard to understand because they still present in the form of ancient language or dialect (called '*Isanlanguage*').Then general people cannot understand. Thus, this may lead to poor performance in an information retrieval, where the language of the user's query is different from the language written in the documents.

As above, this work presents the solution to retrieve the documents relating to the traditional Thai medicine recipe that is translated from the ancient PLMs. The proposed methodology of retrieving traditional Thai medicine recipe is developed based on three main concepts:semantic data [4],latent search indexing (LSI)[4] and cross language information retrieval (CLIR) [5]. The proposed methodology is called *Concept-based Cross Language Retrieval*.

K. Tuamsuk et al. (Eds.): ICADL 2014, LNCS 8839, pp. 320–327, 2014.
© Springer International Publishing Switzerland 2014

2   Literature Reviews

Information retrieval systems mostly have been driven on the keyword search, which is insufficient option because of its low precision and recall [7]. This is because the keyword search may return inaccurate and incomplete results when different keywords are used to describe the same concept in the documents and in the queries [7-11]. The relationship between these related keywords may be semantic rather than syntactic, and capturing it thus requires access to comprehensive human world knowledge [8]. Thus, a concept-based information retrieval was proposed [9]. In the last decade, a concept-based information retrieval model is considered as a new and promising way of improving search space. Basically, concept-based information retrieval is search for information objects based on their meaning rather than on the presence of the keywords in the object. Some early works of concept-based information retrieval can be found in [10][11].Sowa [10] applied the conceptual graph to represent knowledge, where a conceptual graph is a bipartite graph that has two kinds of nodes, called concepts and conceptual relations. Riloff&Lehnert [11] presented the concepts by concept nodes. A concept node is a frame-like structure having slots that contain information about the concept such as its triggering words and patterns for extracting concept from text. Ozcan&Aslandogan[9]presented the concept-based information retrieval using ontologies and latent semantic analysis in order to address the ambiguity problem in natural language, where words can represent multiple concepts and different words may represent the same or very similar concepts.

3   The Dataset Description

Our dataset contains over 200 Thai medicine recipes. These recipes are translated from the Northeastern Thai palm-leaf manuscripts, done by the staffs of the Conservation Unit for the Northeastern Thai Palm Leaf Manuscript, Mahasarakham University. An example of the original palm leaf manuscript and its result of translation can be presented as Fig.1.

แบงนั้นให้ถากเอาเพียงปุ่มนั้นมาแช่น้ำให้กินดีแลฯ ผิว่ายาลองดูก ให้เอา นางขาม อัน ๑+ อ้อยดำ ๔ ท่อน มาผ่าแช่น้ำให้กิน ผิว่ายาแก้คันคาย ให้เอา โคยตาล มาฝนใส่ น้ำเหล้าเด็ด ผิวดีฯ ผิว่ายาลองแกว ให้เอา ดู่ทง

Fig. 1. An example of the original palm leaf manuscript and the result of translation

4   The Concept-Based Cross Language Retrieval Methodology

4.1   Preliminary: Isan-Thai Markup Language (ITML)

ITML is the controlled vocabulary thesaurus. It consists of sets of terms in a hierarchical structure that permits searching in the different languages. In this context, we concentrate on Isan language and Thai language. ITML is required in order to support the semantic analysis during text processing, where the inaccuracy of document retrieval can be due to the different languages between the user's query and the Thai medicine recipe documents. Therefore, ITML is a means to address this problem because it is utilized to provide the indexing for the Thai medicine recipe in the corpus.ITML is designed and developed in the modification format of XSD [6], where XSD is a standard of ontology language. In ITML, Each group of words having the similar meaning will have a concept presented as the surrogate of the class. An example of a concept stored in the ITML can be shown as Fig.2.

```xml
<?xml version="1.0" encoding="UTF-8" ?>
<xs:schema xmlns:xs="http://www.w3.org/2001/XMLSchema">

<xs:element name="เข้ามิ้น" language="Isan">
  <xs:language>
    <xs:dataType>
      <xs:synonyms>
        <xs:element name="ขมิ้น" langauge="Thai" type="xs:string"/>
        <xs:element name="ขี้มิ้น" langauge="Isan" type="xs:string"/>
        <xs:element name="ว่านเหลือง" langauge="Isan" type="xs:string"/>
        ......
      </xs:synonyms>
    </xs:dataType>
  </xs:language>
</xs:element>
.....
.....
</xs:schema>
```

Fig. 2. An example of the concept 'เข้ามิ้น' stored in the ITML

For an example of using ITML, if the user's query is 'ขมิ้น' (Ka-min), the query will be changed to the Isan word 'เข้ามิ้น' (Kao-min) by using ITML. This is because the Isan word 'เข้ามิ้น' is the main concept of the word 'ขมิ้น' (Ka-min), 'ขี้มิ้น' (Kee-min), 'ว่านเหลือง' (Wan-liang), and so on.

It is noted that all the concepts in the ITML are from the list of 650 Thai herbs, 320 symptomsof illness, and 500 of ancient Isan words. Finally, the total concepts contained in the current version of ITML contain about 998 concepts. The ITML can be updated manually.

4.2   The Proposed Methodology

Our methodology consists of four main processing steps. The overview of methodology is shown as Fig. 3.

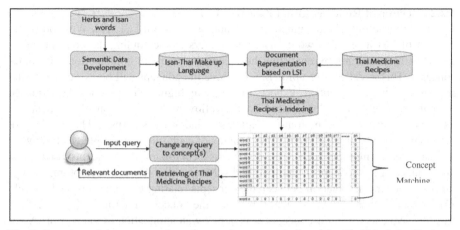

Fig. 3. Overview of the concept-based cross language retrieval for Thai Medicine Recipes

4.2.1   Document Indexing

Our indexing development is based on document-ITML matching. The approach consists of building the surrogate(s), called *conceptual indexing*, from a given document, which represents the document content. Our index is called *conceptual index*,because our system will find the words having the similar meaning, and then attempts to discover the concept of these through the use of ITML. As this, it can be considered that ITML is used as a dictionary to find the words in the corpus. The process of document indexing can be explained following. After a word is searched and detected by using ITML, the system will provide its concept and uses the concept as an index (surrogate) of a document. Simply speaking, we use the concepts as indexes of each document. It is noted that a document can have many surrogates. With the use of ITML, most indexes of each document are the concepts of herb and symptom. An example can be seen in Fig. 4.

It is noted that we also apply a numerical statistic, *term frequency* (*tf*), which is intended to reflect how important a word is to a document. However, *tf* is modified a bit in this work, where we concentrate on '*concept*', not '*term*' or '*word*'. Therefore, *tf* is changed to *concept frequency* (*cf*). Then, each *cf* value should be greater than or equal to 1. The number of indexes exists in may be equal to the number of unique words in that entire document.

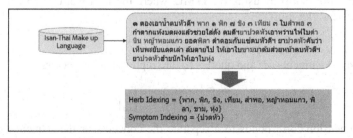

Fig. 4. An example of finding concepts in a Thai medicine recipe

4.2.2 Document Representation Based on LSI

This section presents the document representation based on LSI [12]. We modify the concept of LSI a bit. The word *'semantics'* refers to the finding the concepts associated with documents by analyzing how concepts work in combination with other concepts. This is called *concept network*, where the concept will be associated to the *sequence of multi-concepts*. It expects to reduce ambiguity. To produce the sequence of multi-concepts, it is done based on the following rules of concept association: <symptoms-herbs>, < symptoms–symptoms>, and <herbs-herbs>. These rules are provided by handcrafted analysis. The meaning of each rule is described as follows.

The rule <symptoms-herbs> means the association of the concepts relating to symptoms and the concepts relating to herbs. Meanwhile, the rule <symptoms- symptoms> means the association between the concepts relating to symptoms, and the rule <herbs-herbs> means the association between the concepts relating to herbs. To extract the sequence of multi-concepts, it is done by an application of the Apriori Association Rule algorithm [12].

An association rule (as a sequence of multi-concepts) is a pattern that states when *X* occurs, *Y* occurs with certain probability. To select interesting rules from the set of all possible rules, constraints on various measures of significance and interest can be used. The well-known constraints are minimum thresholds on support and confidence.

After obtaining the sequence of multi-concepts (including the single concepts), it is to convert each document in our index into a vector of concept occurrences. The number of dimensions our vector exists in may be equal to the number of unique words in the entire document set. The concepts (including the sequence of multi-concepts) are then weighted according to a kind of *tf-idf* that it is called *cf-idf*. Thus, global frequency of a concept c_i in a document d_i is:

$$Weight_{ij} = cf_{ij}\, idf_i \qquad (1)$$
$$= cf_{ij}\, \log_2 (N/df_i)$$

where N is the total number of documents and df(document frequency) is the number of documents a concept occurred in. Only the concepts and the sequence of multi-concepts with weight, that are greater than or equal to a threshold, are kept.

4.2.3 User's Query Transformation

User's query is also changed as the concept as well. It is done by using ITML. Suppose the user's query is 'ขมิ้น' (ka-min). This word will be changed to the Isan word 'เข้ามิ้น' (kao-min) by using the ITML, where the Isan word 'เข้ามิ้น' is the main concept of 'ขมิ้น' (ka-min).

4.2.4 Document Retrieval and Ranking

In this study, documents (d) and queries (q) are represented as vectors.

$$d_j = \{c_{1,j}, c_{2,j}, \ldots, c_{t,j}\}$$
$$q = \{c_{1,q}, c_{2,q}, \ldots, c_{t,q}\}$$

Each dimension corresponds to a separate the concepts or the sequence of multi-concepts. If a concepts or a sequence of multi-concepts occur in the document, its value in the vector is non-zero. Several different ways of computing these values, also known as (term) weights, have been developed. This work calculates the relevance ranking of documents in a concepts search, using the assumptions of document similarities theory (such as clustering analysis [13]), by comparing the deviation of angles between each document vector and the original query vector where the query is represented as the same kind of vector as the documents.

5   The Experimental Results

We evaluated the results of the experiments by using *precision* (*P*) [13, 14], *recall* (*R*) [13, 14], and *F-measure* (*F*) [13, 14]. Our collection includes 500 documents. We test with 50 queries of single concepts and 50 queries of sequence of multi-concepts. All queries are provided by domain experts.

Consider the experimental results shown in Table 1 and Table 2. It can be seen that the experimental results of keyword search show the unsatisfactory accuracy. This is because, if the language of user's query is different from the language written in documents, the efficiency of the information retrieval can be quite poor.

Table 1. The experimental results of keyword search

Query Types	Recall	Precision	F-measure
Single word	0.6	0.5	0.55
Multi-words	0.5	0.4	0.44

Table 2. The experimental results of the proposed methodology

Query Types	Recall	Precision	F-measure
Single concept	0.89	1.00	0.92
Sequence of multi-concepts	0.91	1.00	0.95

An example can be illustrated following. If the user's query is 'ขมิ้น' (ka-min), without the use of ITML, the system cannot understand for this word, and then the system cannot retreive the relevant document to the users. For another case, suppose a query is the word 'เข้ามิ้น' (kao-min), without the use of ITML, the documents containing the word 'ขมิ้น' (ka-min), 'ขี้มิ้น' (kee-min), and 'ว่านเหลือง' will be not retreived althouhg these words has the same meaning.All of these can lead to poor accuracy.In Table 2, it can be seen that the results of the proposed methodology are better than the result of keyword search shown in Table 1. This is because, when the concept is used as the surrogate of many words having the same meaning, it is to generate the semantics into these words. Therefore, if we need to retrieve the documents containing these words, the relevant documents will not be lost. As the results in Table 2 and 3, this would demonstrate that our proposed methodology can achieve substantial improvements.

6   Conclusion

This work proposes a solution to retrieve the documents relating to the traditional Thai medicine recipe, which is translated from the ancient PLMs. The proposed methodology is developed based on three main concepts: semantic data [4], latent search indexing (LSI) [4] and cross language information retrieval (CLIR) [5]. The semantic data is implemented and used as a semantic tool to interpret the meaning of words during computational text processing. Our sematic data will be stored in a modification format of XML Schema Definition (XSD) [6], called Isan-Thai Markup Language (ITML). Each group of words having the similar meaning will have a concept presented as the surrogate of the class. By using ITML, all words that appear in the corpus and the user's query will be transformed into the concepts, and then these concepts will be posed into a matrix for latent search analysis. Finally, CLIR is applied, where the concept of CLIR allows users to find documents written in different languages fromthat of their query. After testing by the IR measurement standard, it would demonstrate that our proposed methodology can achieve substantial improvements, when the experimental results of the proposed methodology are compared with the experimental results of the original technique that is called keyword search.

Acknowledgement. This work is a part of the research supported by the National Research Council of Thailand.

References

1. Iijima, A.: A Historical Approach to the Palm-Leaf Manuscripts Preserved in WatMahathat, Yasothon (Thailand), http://www.laomanuscripts.net/downloads/literaryheritageoflaos26_iijima_en.pdf
2. Manmart, L., Chamnongsri, N., Wuwongse, V.: Metadata Development for Palm Leaf Manuscripts in Thailand. In: Proc. International Conference on Dublin Core and Metadata Applications (2012)
3. Shi, Z., Setlur, S., Govindaraju, V.: Digital Enhancement of Palm Leaf Manuscript Images using Normalization Techniques. In: The 5th International Conference on Knowledge-based Computer Systems (2004)
4. Rosario, B.: Latent Semantic Indexing: An overview, http://people.ischool.berkeley.edu/~rosario/projects/LSI.pdf
5. Braschler, M., Peters, C., Schäuble, P.: Cross-Language Information Retrieval (CLIR) Track: Overview, http://trec.nist.gov/pubs/trec8/papers/trec8ov.pdf
6. van der Vlist, E.: XML Schema. O'Reilly (2002)
7. Haav, H.M., Lubi, T.L.: A Survey of Concept-based Information Retrieval Tools on the Web. The Fifth East-European Conference on Advances in Databases and Information Systems (ADBIS) (2001)
8. Egozi, O., Markovvitch, S., Gabrilovich, E.: Concept-based Information Retrieval Using Explicit Semantic Analysis. Journal of ACM Transactions on Information Systems (2011)

9. Guarino, N.: Formal Ontology and Information Systems. In: Guarino, N. (ed.) Proceedings of the 1st International Conference of Formal Ontology in Information Systems (1998)
10. Sowa, J.F.: Conceptual Structures: Information Processing in Minds and Machines. Addison-Wesley, Reading (1984)
11. Riloff, E., Lehnert, W.: Automated dictionary construction for information extraction from text. In: Proceedings of 9th IEEE Conference on Artificial Intelligence for Applications (1993); Baeza-Yates, R., Ribeiro-Neto, B.: Modern Information Retrieval. Addison Wesley (1999)
12. Tan, P.N., Steinbach, M., Kumar, V.: Association Analysis: Basic Concepts and Algorithms. In: Introduction to Data Mining. Addison-Wesley (2005)
13. Baeza-Yates, R., Ribeiro-Neto, B.: Modern Information Retrieval. Addison Wesley (1999)
14. Cormack, G.V., Lynam, T.R.: Statistical precision of information retrieval evaluation. In: Proceedings of the 29th Annual International ACM SIGIR (2006)

Computing Tag-Diversity
for Social Image Search

Eunggyo Kim, Takehiro Yamamoto, and Katsumi Tanaka

Graduate School of Informatics, Kyoto University
Yoshidahonmachi, Sakyo, Kyoto 606-8501, Japan
{kim,tyamamot,tanaka}@dl.kuis.kyoto-u.ac.jp

Abstract. "Image search" on the basis of social tags is now a popular tool provided by image-sharing services. Some images are annotated with similar tags, while others are annotated with dissimilar ones. In this study, a concept called "tag-diversity," which represents how diverse tags are annotated to an image, is proposed, and two methods to estimate it are proposed. We conducted the experiment to investigate how the two proposed methods accurately compute tag-diversity. The results of the experiment show that both methods outperformed the baseline method, which calculates tag-diversity on the basis of the number of annotated tags. We also show some images with low and high tag-diversity, and discuss how tag-diversity can improve the current image search.

Keywords: Image Retrieval, Social Tagging, Diversity.

1   Introduction

With the recent development of the Web, the number of images available for people to view has been drastically increasing. For example, the widespread usage of smartphones and tablets has made it surprisingly easier to take, upload, and share photos via image-sharing services. One of the most popular image sharing services is Flickr. Utilizing Flickr, users can annotate images uploaded by other users with *tags*, and they can search for images on the basis of these tags. Such a tagging system is called "social tagging" or "collaborative tagging," and many Web services, like del.icio.us and Last.fm, are employing this system.

While tags are useful to find desired images, the number of images returned to users is enormous, and the current ways to rank the images are still limited. For example, Flickr offers to rank images on the basis of upload time, view count, and relevance. If more ways to search for images were available, it would be easier to find the desired images.

In this study, a concept called *tag-diversity*, which represents the diversity of tags of an image, is proposed and used to enhance an image search provided by a social-tagging system. To explain the concept of tag-diversity, which considers the diversity of tags attached to an image, two images, namely, (a) and (b) in Figure 1, are shown as examples.

K. Tuamsuk et al. (Eds.): ICADL 2014, LNCS 8839, pp. 328–335, 2014.
© Springer International Publishing Switzerland 2014

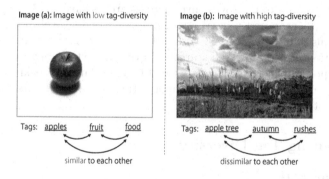

Fig. 1. The concept of tag-diversity. Images (a) and (b) have "apple" in their tags. In addition to "apple," image (a) has tags that are similar, while image (b) has tags that are dissimilar.

Tag-diversity can be used for enhancing a conventional image search provided by social tagging services. For example, image (a) is suitable for representing an apple since no other objects appear in it. Images with low tag-diversity would therefore be suitable for representing the query itself. On the other hand, images with high tag-diversity would represent some specific situations where users are difficult to find similar images relate to the query. Images with high tag-diversity would therefore be suitable for attracting people's interests because of their uniqueness. In this way, tag-diversity can offer additional image-ranking criterion to the conventional image-ranking criterion.

We propose two methods of computing tag-diversity for an image. The first method takes a "clustering" approach (namely, tags are clustered on the basis of their visual and annotation similarities) to calculate the diversity of tags. The second one takes a "hypernym relation" approach (namely, tags are grouped on the basis of hypernyms by utilizing an existing hypernym-hyponym dictionary) to calculate the diversity of tags. We conducted the experiment to investigate how the two proposed methods accurately compute tag-diversity. The results of the experiment show that both methods outperformed the baseline method, which calculates tag-diversity on the basis of the number of annotated tags.

To demonstrate how tag-diversity makes it possible to search for images that conventional ranking algorithms cannot retrieve, we also show several example images with low/high tag-diversity.

2 Related Work

Social tagging has been an area of active research. For example, Heymann *et al.* extensively analyzed the social-tagging data in del.icio.us (a social-bookmarking web service), which allows people to annotate Web documents with tags [4]. Shepitsen *et al.* [7] created a hierarchical concept by applying hierarchical clustering to the tags used in del.icio.us and applied it to improve document recommendation.

Ways to utilize tags to improve conventional searches have also been proposed. Yanbe *et al.* [10] proposed several algorithms for ranking Web documents by using del.icio.us data. Guo *et al.* [3] also utilized del.icio.us data and proposed a query suggestion method for Web searches. In the context of image search, Kato *et al.* [5] proposed a method of using social-tagging data in Flickr to improve conventional image searches, which cannot return accurate results for queries containing abstract terms.

3   Computing Tag-Diversity

3.1   Tag-Diversity

Some images are annotated with similar tags while others are annotated with dissimilar ones. These differences are thought to come from *the diversity of concepts to which an image belongs.*

Tag-diversity for an image is defined as follows:

Tag-Diversity: Diversity of the concepts to which the tags of an image belong.

Diversity has been studied from the viewpoints of not only information retrieval but also sociology, ecology, life science, economics, and so on. According to Stirling [8], diversity contains three properties: "variety," "balance," and "disparity." This idea of diversity can be applied to compute tag-diversity based on the following two criteria:

1. **Variety of Concepts**: If the number of concepts to which the tags of an image belong is large, the tag-diversity of the image will be high.
2. **Disparity of Concepts**: If the concepts to which the tags of an image belong are dissimilar, the tag-diversity of the image will be high.

Since computing the balance of concepts would be difficult, it is left as future work.

3.2   Overview of Computing Tag-Diversity

Images uploaded on Flickr are focused on hereafter. In Flickr, image p is annotated with a set of tags $T(p) = \{t_1, \ldots t_{n_p}\}$, where n_p is the number of tags annotated to p. Since tags are written in various languages in Flickr, Japanese tags are focused on hereafter. First, the tag-diversity-computation problem is defined. Given a set of images $P = \{p_1, p_2, \ldots, p_{|P|}\}$, the goal of the tag-diversity-computation is to calculate tag-diversity $\mathrm{TagDiv}(p)$ of image p for each image in P.

The proposed method consists of three steps: (1) collecting tags from a set of images P, (2) creating concepts from collected tags, and (3) computing tag-diversity $\mathrm{TagDiv}(p)$ on the basis of the concepts.

As for step (1), to compute the tag-diversity of an image, a set of all tags $T_P = \bigcup_{p_i \in P} T(p_i)$ is collected from a set of images, P. As for steps (2) and (3), two approaches are proposed. One employs a clustering approach to create the concepts on the basis of the visual and annotation similarities between tags. The other uses hypernym relations of words to obtain concepts of tags. Each approach is explained as follows.

3.3 Feature-Based Approach

To properly calculate the diversity of concepts, similar tags must be grouped according to concepts. There are several possible ways to create such concepts from tags. One way, namely, a feature-based approach, is proposed here. This approach calculates the similarity between tags on the basis of the visual features and annotation features of the tag. It then clusters tags on the basis of the similarity, and each cluster is viewed as a concept.

To calculate the similarity between two tags, t_i and t_j, two hypotheses are applied: (1) If the images that have t_i and those that have t_j are visually similar, t_i and t_j are similar (i.e., "visual" similarity); (2) if t_i and t_j are annotated with the same image, t_i and t_j are similar (i.e., "annotation" similarity).

As for visual similarity, let $\mathbf{v}_p$ be the visual feature vector of image p, and P_{t_i} ($P_{t_i} \subseteq P$) be a set of images that have tag t_i. The visual feature vector $\mathbf{f}_{t_i}^{\text{visual}}$ of t_i is defined as the mean vector of the visual feature vectors of images in P_{t_i} (i.e., $\mathbf{f}_{t_i}^{\text{visual}} = \frac{1}{|P_{t_i}|} \sum_{p \in P_{t_i}} \mathbf{v}_p$.) In this work, RGB histograms, HSV histograms [6], and "bag of visual words" (BoVW) [1] features constructed from the image collections in ILSVRC2010 [2] are used for extracting the visual features of an image. As for annotation similarity, let $\mathbf{f}_{t_i}^{\text{annot}}$ be the annotation feature vector of tag t_i. $\mathbf{f}_{t_i}^{\text{annot}}$ is defined as a $|P|$-dimensional vector, where $\mathbf{f}_{t_i}^{\text{annot}}[k] = 1$ if p_k has tag t_i; otherwise, $\mathbf{f}_{t_i}^{\text{annot}}[k] = 0$ ($1 \leq k \leq |P|$). Distance $d_{\text{tag}}(t_i, t_j)$ between two tags, t_i and t_j, is defined as:

$$d_{\text{tag}}(t_i, t_j) = \frac{(1 - \text{Sim}(f_{t_i}^{\text{visual}}, f_{t_j}^{\text{visual}})) + (1 - \text{Sim}(f_{t_i}^{\text{annot}}, f_{t_j}^{\text{annot}}))}{2} , \quad (1)$$

where $\text{Sim}(\cdot, \cdot)$ is a cosine similarity of two vectors.

To cluster tags into concepts, a hierarchical clustering with the complete-linkage method using the distance defined in Equation (1) is applied. A cutoff threshold θ is set to stop the clustering once the distance between clusters is above θ. From the hierarchical clustering, a set of clusters $\mathcal{C} = \{C^{(1)}, \ldots, C^{(m)}\}$ can be obtained. Here, m represents the number of obtained clusters, $C^{(i)} = \{t_1^{(i)} \ldots, t_{n_{C^{(i)}}}^{(i)}\}$ ($1 \leq i \leq m$), and $n_{C^{(i)}}$ represents the number of tags that are clustered in cluster C_i. Note that $\bigcup_{i=1}^{m} C^{(i)} = T_P$.

Once set of clusters $\mathcal{C}$ is obtained, tag-diversity $\text{TagDiv}(p)$ of image p is calculated on the basis of that set of clusters. Let $\mathcal{C}_p$ ($\mathcal{C}_p \subseteq \mathcal{C}$) be the set of clusters to which tags of image p belong. $\text{TagDiv}(p)$ is calculated by using the following equation:

$$\text{TagDiv}(p) = \frac{|\mathcal{C}_p|}{|\mathcal{C}|} + \frac{1}{\binom{|\mathcal{C}_p|}{2}} \sum_{C_i, C_j \in \mathcal{C}_p} d_{\text{cluster}}(C_i, C_j) , \quad (2)$$

where $d_{\text{cluster}}(C_i, C_j) = \max_{t_k^{(i)} \in C^{(i)}, t_l^{(j)} \in C^{(j)}} d_{\text{tag}}(t_k^{(i)}, t_l^{(j)})$. The left term calculates how many clusters the tags of image p belong to (variety of concepts proposed in Section 3.1). The right term calculates how these clusters are dissimilar (disparity of concepts proposed in Section 3.1). If the tags of image p belong to more and more dissimilar clusters, TagDiv(p) produces a higher score.

3.4   Hypernym-Relation-Based Approach

As another approach, which utilizes an existing concept hierarchy to compute tag-diversity, is proposed as follows. The proposed approach utilizes existing hypernym-hyponym relations to compute tag-diversity. The hypernym-relation data used was automatically created from noun phrases of headwords of articles or category names in Wikipedia, and it contains about six-million hypernym-hyponym relations [9]. This data can be used to find hypernyms or hyponyms of a given word.

This approach views each hypernym as a concept. Let $H_{t_i} = \{h_1, \ldots h_{n_{t_i}}\}$ be a set of hypernyms of tag t_i, where $n_{h_{t_i}}$ is the number of hypernyms of t_i found in the dictionary. The set of all hypernyms H_P of tags T_P can be obtained as $H_P = \bigcup_{t_i \in T_P} H_{t_i}$.

Once a set of hypernyms H_P is obtained, tag-diversity TagDiv(p) of image p is calculated on the basis of the hypernyms. To calculate the similarity between two hypernyms, the co-occurrence of hypernyms in Flickr is used. When a keyword query is sent to Flickr, the images that have the query in their tags are returned. It is hypothesized that if images returned by two hypernyms, h_i and h_j, are overlapped, h_i and h_j are similar. To calculate the overlap of images returned by two hypernyms, Dice's coefficient is used. Similarity $\text{Sim}_{\text{hyper}}(h_i, h_j)$ between hypernyms h_i and h_j is calculated by using the number of images returned by Flickr for keyword query h_i, and the number of images returned by Flickr for keyword query h_i AND h_j. The distance between hypernyms h_i and h_j, namely, $d_{\text{hyper}}(h_i, h_j)$, can then be calculated as:

$$d_{\text{hyper}}(h_i, h_j) = 1 - \text{Sim}_{\text{hyper}}(h_i, h_j) .$$

From the above equation, tag-diversity TagDiv(p) of image p is calculated. Let H_p be a set of hypernyms of tags of image p. H_p can be calculated as $\bigcup_{t_i \in T_p} H_{t_i}$. Tag-diversity TagDiv($p$) is calculated as follows:

$$\text{TagDiv}(p) = \frac{|H_p|}{|H_P|} + \frac{1}{\binom{|H_p|}{2}} \sum_{h_i, h_j \in H_p} d_{\text{hyper}}(h_i, h_j) . \tag{3}$$

In a similar manner to Equation (2), the left term calculates how many hypernyms the tags of image p belong to, and the right term calculates the extent to which these hypernyms are dissimilar.

4   Evaluation

To examine the effectiveness of the two methods proposed in the previous section, the following four methods are compared:

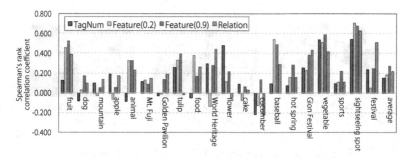

Fig. 2. Spearman's rank correlation coefficient between the ground-truth data and each method

- **TagNum:** The baseline method used in this work. It calculates the number of tags of an image as tag-diversity. It assumes that if an image has many tags, its tag-diversity is high.
- **Feature(0.2):** Tag-diversity of an image is calculated form Equation (2). Parameter θ for stopping the hierarchical clustering is set to 0.2.
- **Feature(0.9):** Tag-diversity of an image is calculated from Equation (2) with $\theta = 0.9$.
- **Relation:** Tag-diversity of an image is calculated from Equation (3).

The above four methods were implemented by using the APIs provided by Flickr, which return a set of images and their tags in response to a query.

To evaluate the extent to which the methods accurately calculate tag-diversity, ground-truth data of tag-diversity of images were created by asking the assessor to manually evaluate their tag-diversity. In the experiment, 20 queries, shown in Figure 2, were used. For each query, 1,000 images were first retrieved by using API, and their tag-diversity was calculated by using the above four methods. To create ground-truth data, for each of three methods, "TagNum," "Feature(0.2)," and "Relation," the top-five and bottom-five images ranked by tag-diversity were selected, and these selected images were used as the target images of our evaluation. (At most, 30 images for each query were therefore evaluated.)

To evaluate tag-diversity of each target image, two assessors were first asked to annotate the image with as many tags as possible. This is because some images in Flickr had few tags, so the ground-truth tags for each target image were thus created first. For each image, another assessor was then asked to evaluate its tag-diversity according to a five-point Likert scale ["1" (lowest tag-diversity) to "5" (highest tag-diversity)] by showing the ground-truth tags to the assessor. The data obtained from this process was used as the ground-truth tag-diversity.

To evaluate how the four methods accurately estimate tag-diversity of images, Spearman's rank correlation coefficients between the four methods and the ground-truth data described in the previous subsection were computed.

The correlation coefficients for the four methods are shown in Figure 2. If a method accurately estimates the tag-diversity, it scores 1.0. In the figure, "average" represents the average of the scores over 20 queries. According to the

Fig. 3. Example images with low/high tag-diversity

"average" results, the proposed methods (Feature(0.2), Feature(0.9), and Relation) outperformed the baseline method (TagNum). In other words, the proposed methods could compute tag-diversity more accurately compared with the baseline method.

Feature(0.9) achieved the highest score in terms of the average, while Feature (0.2) got worse scores than Feature(0.9) on most queries. The reason for this difference might be that the hierarchical clustering with parameter $\theta = 0.2$ tended to generate more clusters than that with $\theta = 0.9$; thus, the variety of concepts was not considered in the score with $\theta = 0.2$. As for Relation, it is clear that this method could not achieve high scores on the queries "tulip," "flower," and "cucumber." These queries are strongly associated with color, which Relation did not use.

5   Possibility of Using Tag-Diversity for Image Search

To show the possibilities of tag-diversity, in this section, several interesting images found from the experiment conducted in Section 4 were selected, and the relationships between them and their tag-diversities were investigated.

An image with low tag-diversity is focused on first. The left-hand side of Figure 3 shows an image that was evaluated as having low tag-diversity by the assessor. The image has tags which are related to vegetables; thus, the tag-diversity of this image is low. In this case, since the concept "vegetable" is represented as a set of instances of vegetable, this image would be useful to represent the concept of "vegetable." In this way, some images with low tag-diversity would be suitable to visually represent a certain concept.

The right-hand side of Figure 3 shows two images evaluated as having high tag-diversity by the assessor. Here, we hypothesize that some images with high tag-diversity would represent specific situations relate to the query; that is, there are few images similar to it in the search results. For example, since most images obtained from the query "dog" contained an actual dog (or dogs), it would be difficult for users to find images similar to the image in Figure 3 for the query "dog." Such images would attract people's interest because of their uniqueness.

We plan to develop a method for searching for the images described in this section. To this end, the combination of query relevance and tag-diversity is considered a key feature of this method.

6   Conclusion

In this study, we propose a concept called "tag-diversity," which represents the extent that diverse tags are annotated to an image. Moreover, two approaches to compute tag-diversity were also proposed. The results of the experiment show that our proposed methods based on these approaches outperformed the baseline method, which counts the number of tags as tag-diversity. Since their accuracies of the methods were not high, we plan to improve the methods of computing tag-diversity.

The proposed methods for calculating tag-diversity can be applied to not only Flickr but also other image-sharing services, such as Pinterest, which allows to group images with any themes to be created. We plan to apply tag-diversity to such a service to examine the usefulness of tag-diversity.

Acknowledgements.   This work was supported in part by KAKENHI (#24240013).

References

1. Csurka, G., Dance, C., Fan, L., Willamowski, J., Bray, C.: Visual categorization with bags of keypoints. In: Workshop on Statistical Learning in Computer Vision, ECCV (2004)
2. Deng, J., Dong, W., Socher, R., Li, L.-J., Li, K., Fei-Fei, L.: ImageNet: A Large-Scale Hierarchical Image Database. In: IEEE Computer Vision and Pattern Recognition (2009)
3. Guo, J., Cheng, X., Xu, G., Shen, H.: A Structured Approach to Query Recommendation with Social Annotation Data. In: Proc. of CIKM2010, pp. 619–628 (2010)
4. Heymann, P., Koutrika, G., Garcia-Molina, H.: Can social bookmarking improve web search? In: Proc. of WSDM 2008, pp. 195–206 (2008)
5. Kato, M., Ohshima, H., Oyama, S., Tanaka, K.: Can social tagging improve web image search? In: Bailey, J., Maier, D., Schewe, K.-D., Thalheim, B., Wang, X.S. (eds.) WISE 2008. LNCS, vol. 5175, pp. 235–249. Springer, Heidelberg (2008)
6. Makadia, A., Pavlovic, V., Kumar, S.: A new baseline for image annotation. In: Forsyth, D., Torr, P., Zisserman, A. (eds.) ECCV 2008, Part III. LNCS, vol. 5304, pp. 316–329. Springer, Heidelberg (2008)
7. Shepitsen, A., Gemmell, J., Mobasher, B., Burke, R.: Personalized recommendation in social tagging systems using hierarchical clustering. In: Proc. of RecSys 2008, pp. 259–266 (2008)
8. Stirling, A.: A general framework for analysing diversity in science, technology and society. Journal of the Royal Society Interface 4(15), 707–719 (2007)
9. Sumida, A., Yoshinaga, N., Torisawa, K.: Boosting precision and recall of hyponymy relation acquisition from hierarchical layouts in wikipedia. In: Proc. of International Language Resources and Evaluation, pp. 2462–2469 (2008)
10. Yanbe, Y., Jatowt, A., Nakamura, S., Tanaka, K.: Can social bookmarking enhance search in the web? In: Proc. of JCDL 2007, pp. 107–116 (2007)

Dynamic Web Application for Managing and Searching Antique and Art Object Information

Areerat Trongratsameethong[*] and Pongkwan Saejao

Department of Computer Science, Faculty of Science,
Chiang Mai University, Chiang Mai, Thailand
areerat.t@cmu.ac.th, saejao@gmail.com

Abstract. Antique and art object information plays more important role in ar-cheology, history, and culture. This valuable information continuously in-creased and accumulated every year. It requires effective system to transfer the available knowledge for people of the next generations. Therefore, this study aims to design a database to store the information; and to develop a dynamic web application to manage and search the information. The system consists of two main parts: 1) data manipulation and 2) advanced search. The first part is developed for museum staffs to store, update, and delete data. The second part is for general users to search the information efficiently by using a combination of keywords that are name, type, material, period, and art style; and two logical operators, "AND" and "OR". The application is useful as it provides convenient and effective manipulation and searching of antique and art object information via internet network.

Keywords: Dynamic Web Application, Antique and Art Object Information, Advanced Search, Museum Database.

1 Introduction

A museum is an organization collecting and managing antique and art object informa-tion. A very good data management is essential. Otherwise, this valuable information which is increased every year will not be efficiently transferred to the next genera-tions. Furthermore, the information querying and searching will be difficult. Most of the antique and art object information in Thailand is transferred among staffs and interested people through static web pages, museums' exhibitions, books, and so on. However, static web pages are no longer appropriate as the information may be changed frequently. Moreover, updating and creating tremendous amount of data on static webs are time consuming and inefficient. Releasing a new book for new and updated data takes times and costly. Visiting museum's exhibition also requires trans-portation times and costly for some people. Therefore, this study aims to design a database for storing antique and art object information; and to propose a dynamic web application for the information management and searching the information kept

---

[*] Corresponding author.

K. Tuamsuk et al. (Eds.): ICADL 2014, LNCS 8839, pp. 336–343, 2014.
© Springer International Publishing Switzerland 2014

in a database. The system consists of eight functions. Seven functions are designed for museum staffs to manipulate the following data through dynamic web pages: antique and art object, antique type, period, material, art style, display place, and museum. The last function is developed for general users to advance their search by combining keywords and logical operators. This function will help the users to enhance efficiency of search results. The system is an alternative solution for the museum staffs to manage data efficiently and the valuable knowledge is conveniently and sufficiently transferred to people at anytime and anywhere via internet network.

2   Related Work

2.1   Fine Arts Department of Thailand Web Page

The Fine Arts Department of Thailand web page [1] is an example of a static web used to present antique and art object information. The web page contains HyperText Markup Language (HTML) tags and contents that are unchanged or constant while they are loaded. Maintaining data on static pages must push much effort. The HTML file(s) related to changed information must be searched, modified, and republished. In addition, new HTML file(s) must be created for new information to be presented.

2.2   Chiang Mai National Museum Web Page

The Chiang Mai National Museum web page [2] is an example of a dynamic web page providing a keyword search for searching antique and art object information. A dynamic web page contains HTML tags and program code that can generate contents on-the-fly while they are loaded. As a result, only one dynamic web page can be developed to present any information based on user requests through a search interface.

2.3   Advanced Search

An example of a digital library providing an advanced search is referred in [3]. Users can specify multiple keywords including three logical operators, "AND", "OR", and "NOT". It will return more refined results than a single keyword search. The advanced search is very useful for users to enhance quality of search results.

2.4   British Museum Web Page

The British Museum web page referred in [4] provides online museum collection database. Data in the database are maintained every week. An advanced search containing combinations of keywords and two logical operators "AND" and "OR" are also provided to refine search results of the collections. All image collections of search results are shown first for guiding user to select an interesting collection to see more details but if many of search results are matched, several network traffic will be used to transfer these images.

3   System Analysis and Design

3.1   System Architecture

The system architecture is displayed in Fig. 1. User requests created by web browsers in form of Hyper Text Transfer Protocol (HTTP) requests are sent to the application run on a web server through Transmission Control Protocol/Internet Protocol (TCP/IP) network. The application was developed by Personal Home Page (PHP) and HTML5. PHP is an open source web programming language that can connect, query, and maintain data kept in a database through TPC/IP network. HTML5 is the latest standard for HTML used to present data on the web browser. The antique and art object database kept on a database server was created by an open source Database Management System (DBMS) named MySQL. For more details about HTML5, PHP, and MySQL are referred in [5,6,7], respectively. The data from the servers are sent back to clients in term of HTML tags that web browsers can interpret and display.

3.2   System Structure Chart

The system consists of eight functions as displayed in Fig. 2. Users are separated into two groups: 1) museums' staffs can manage and search data, and 2) general users can only search data. There are two groups of data in the system, master data and transaction data. Master data are data that are not change frequently which are type, material, display place, period, art style, and museum. Transaction data are data that change frequently which are antique and art objects.

3.3   Database Design

A database was created to store antique and art object information. It was designed systematically to reduce redundancy of data and avoid update anomalies by using normalization technique [8]. The database is normalized into third normal form [9]. Good database design is leaded to efficiency and convenience of data manipulation and data searching. The structure of antique and art object data and their relationship are represented in Entity Relationship (ER) diagram as displayed in Fig. 3. The ER diagram was generated by a visual database design system named DBDesigner [10].

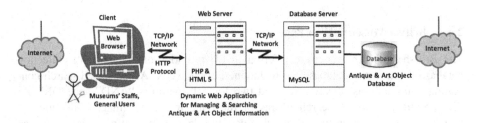

Fig. 1. System architecture

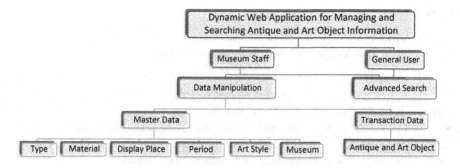

Fig. 2. System structure chart

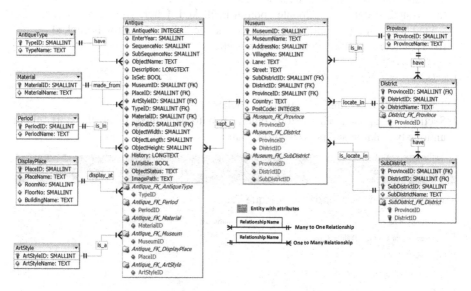

Fig. 3. ER diagram of antique and art object database

3.4   User Interface

User Interfaces (UIs) in the system are divided into three groups: 1) UIs for managing master data, 2) UIs for managing transaction data, and 3) UIs for searching data. Each UI contains many sections and each section referred by circle with section number inside. All data contents in the application are displayed in Thai language.

Managing Master Data. UIs in Fig. 4 are designed for museum staffs to manipulate antique type data. Other master data also use the same UI style and steps used for manipulating antique type data but only fields in each master table are different. Therefore, only UIs and steps for managing antique type are explained as the following steps.

Retrieve All.

1. The "+ Retrieve All" link in section 1 is pressed.
2. All records in antique type table are displayed in section 2.

Update/Delete Data.

1. The "+ Search for Update/Delete Data" link in section 1 is clicked.
2. Section 3 is opened for searching antique type data to be updated or deleted.
3. Records matching to specified search in section 3 are returned in section 4. Otherwise, the message "No data matching your search" is displayed.
4. The staff selects a record in section 4 and the selected record is displayed in section 5 for the staff to either update or delete:
   (a) To update data, the "Update" button is clicked. Later, section 6 is opened for the staff to modify antique type name and the "Update" button is clicked.
   (b) To delete data, the "Delete" button is clicked.

Add Data.

1. The "+ Add Data" link in section 1 is clicked.
2. Section 7 is opened. The antique type id is auto generated. Later, the staff fills in antique type name and presses "Add" button.

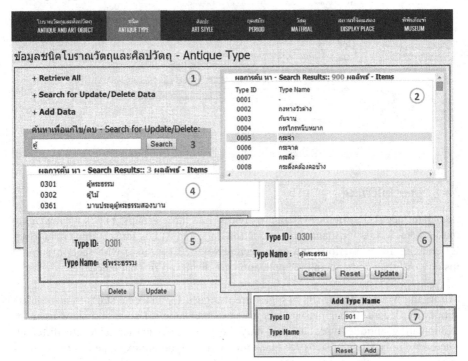

Fig. 4. UIs for manipulating antique type master data

Managing Transaction Data. UIs in Fig. 5 are designed for museum staffs to update, delete, and insert antique and art object data as the following steps.

Update/Delete Data.

1. The "+ Search for Update/Delete Data" link in section 1 is clicked.
2. Section 2 is opened. The museum staffs can search antique and art object data to update or delete by using either Antique ID or Advanced Search.
   (a) Search by Antique ID: antique id is specified in the "# Search by ID" section and "Search" button is clicked. The details of antique and art object information matching to the specified antique id are directly displayed in section 4. Otherwise, the message "No data matching your search" is displayed.
   (b) Advanced Search: keyword(s) and logical operator(s) are specified in the "# Advanced Search" section and "Search" button is clicked. The record(s) matching to search criteria are displayed in section 3 for a user to select the specific record to display more details in section 4. Otherwise, the message "No data matching your search" is displayed. The advanced search techniques used in the system are as follows:
      (i) The "LIKE" operator of Structure Query Language (SQL) is applied for each keyword search. That means all records matching to the contents specified in the keyword field are returned. This also used in section 3 of Fig. 4. For an example, if "ล้านนา", spelled as lan-na, is specified in a period field, the record(s) containing "ล้านนา" in the period field are returned. The records returned from other specified fields are merged based on logical operators and finally final results are returned.
      (ii) The "NOT" logical operator is not implemented in the system because if the specified keyword does not exist in the database the whole data in the database will be returned. This results in waste of communication resources.
3. Section 4 is opened.
   (a) To update data, fields are modified and then the "Update" button is pressed.
   (b) To delete data, the "Delete" button is clicked.

Add Data.

1. The "+ Add Data" link in section 1 is clicked.
2. The window that is similar to section 4 is opened but only "Cancel", "Reset", and "Save" buttons are displayed.
3. The staff fills in data and clicks "Save" button.

Searching Data. The advanced search displayed in section 2 of Fig. 5 is also provided for general users but the "# Search by ID" section is not provided. This is because general users are not familiar with antique id. In addition, all buttons in section 4 of Fig. 5 are disabled because general users cannot update and delete data.

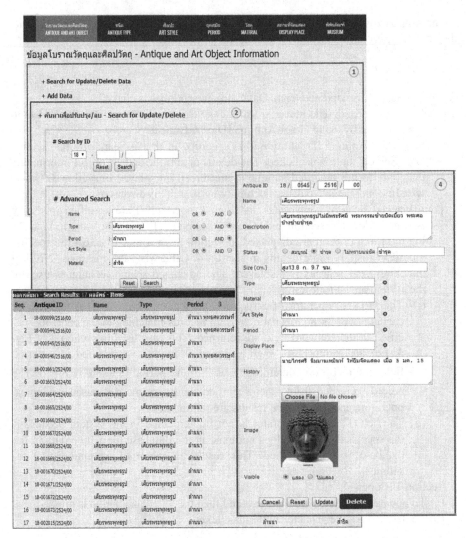

Fig. 5. UIs for manipulating antique and art object data

4   Conclusion

Dynamic web application is developed to store, maintain, and search antique and art object information. The database is designed systematically to store and manipulate data effectively. The advanced search of IEEE Xplore Digital Library is applied to refine search results. The system can be applied for other museums to manage and search antique and art object information. Furthermore, the system can be run anytime and anywhere via internet network and knowledge can be searched and transferred to people conveniently and efficiently.

5   Limitation

- The database and application are designed for only Thai data.
- The application is not displayed properly on mobile phone.
- A text box for specifying each keyword in advanced search is not appropriate for the users who have no ideas what contents should be specified in each keyword field.

6   Future Work

- The database and application can be designed to support Multilanguage.
- Responsive web design or mobile application can be developed to display information on mobile phone properly.
- A combo box can be designed for each keyword in advanced search to support users who have no ideas what contents should be specified in each keyword field.

Acknowledgement. We would like to thank the Chiang Mai National Museum for providing knowledge and information of antiques and art objects. We also would like to convey thanks to the Faculty of Science, Chiang Mai University for research funding. We also would like to thank Dr. Ouyporn Tonmukayakul for her proof reading.

References

1. Fine Arts Department of Thailand Website,
   http://www.finearts.go.th/parameters/ความรู้ทั่วไป/โบราณวัตถุ-ศิลปวัตถุ.html
2. Chiang Mai National Museum Website,
   http://museumthailand.com/chiangmainational/
3. IEEE Xplore Digital Library Advanced Search,
   http://ieeexplore.ieee.org/search/advsearch.jsp
4. British Museum Collection,
   http://www.britishmuseum.org/research/collec-tion_online/search.aspx
5. HTML5, http://www.w3schools.com/html/
6. PHP, http://www.w3schools.com/php/
7. MySQL Documentation, http://dev.mysql.com/doc/
8. Elmasri, R., Navathe, S.B.: Fundamentals of Database Systems, 6th edn., pp. 507–509. Addison-Wesley (2010)
9. Elmasri, R., Navathe, S.B.: Fundamentals of Database Systems, 6th edn., pp. 513–528. Addison-Wesley (2010)
10. DBDesigner, http://www.fabforce.net/dbdesigner4/

Information Retrieval Skills of Research Scholars of Social Sciences: A Study

M.R. Murali Prasad

Centre for Economic and Social Studies, Hyderabad, Andhra Pradesh, India
mrmp2k8@yahoo.com

Abstract. The main purpose of the study is to examine the information retrieval skills of social science scholars in Hyderabad, India. The data is collected through a questionnaire from 210 research scholars of social sciences to determine the preferred communication channels to search research information along with preferred search terms, concept understanding, key word searches, usage of Boolean operators for a given title, and identification of appropriate references.

Keywords: Information search, social sciences, information literacy, information seeking behavior.

1 Introduction

Social sciences are becoming indispensable to the functioning of society. Social policy has now-a-days to be 'evidence-based' and that evidence is the product of social science research. Social science research output provides information for the work and policies of governmental and non-governmental organizations. The policy and decision makers of different fields such as media, advertising and market researchers, etc. rely on the results of social science research. In all these areas, the contributions of social scientists are of dire need.

Obviously, it is very vital that all scientists develop high level information retrieval skills early on in the life of a research programme. Information search or Literature search is the backbone of a research. Effective information searches would highlight the gaps in the existing research, which will enable the scientists to construct an original research problem. Comprehensive and up-to-date retrieval of information will also add to the overall quality of research output.

Information retrieval/search skills are the stepping stones of all research projects. The importance of research students having an in-depth knowledge of Literature Search Techniques and associated skills is acknowledged by the Economic and Social Research Council (ESRC)[1]. In its guidelines on research training for PG students it stated that at a suitable early stage in the student's research career, departments will be expected to include training for all students in certain basic skills. These are likely to include the identification of library resources and how to use them; training in other bibliographic sources and methods; methods for keeping track of literature;

K. Tuamsuk et al. (Eds.): ICADL 2014, LNCS 8839, pp. 344–353, 2014.

the use of annuals, thesis, journals, conference proceedings and semi-publications; the maintenance of a personal research bibliography, etc. (ESRC Guidelines, 1989:13).[2]

The recent development in Information and Communication Technologies has resulted in the explosion of information both in print and digital forms. The focus on lifelong learning and the scarcity of skilled employees have highlighted the need for information-related competencies. The Social Scientists need to update their information retrieval skills to provide quality research output to the society. Information skills required by scientists in an e-age are of a different magnitude to those required in a traditional information age.

In this paper, the author studies the information retrieval skills of Social science scholars through a structured questionnaire to identify their understanding of concept [3, 4, 5] , search strategy to find resources and usage of the identified information resources [6].

2   Objectives of the Study

The main objectives of the present study are:

- To evaluate various bibliographic search strategies of social scientists
- To analyze the understanding of a research concept and its related search techniques of social scientists.

3   Limitations of the Study

This study is conducted in Centre for Economic and Social Studies (CESS), an Institute of Indian Council for Social Science Research (ICSSR) in Hyderabad, Telangana, India. Only the scholars of Doctor of Philosophy (Ph.D.) and Master of Philosophy (M.Phil.) pursuing their research programme in CESS from 2011 and visiting scholars (both Ph.D. and M.Phil.) of CESS Library were selected for the study, due to time and financial constraints.

4   About Centre for Economic and Social Studies (CESS)

The CESS was established as an autonomous body and registered under the Societies Act in the year 1980, by the State Government of Andhra Pradesh, India. Appreciating its role in the promotion of research and training, the Indian Council of Social Science Research (ICSSR) recognized it as a national institute in the year 1986 and included CESS in its network of institutions for annual grant. The Centre has been receiving maintenance grants from the State Government, the ICSSR, project – specific grants / fees from the state government, central government, Planning Commission, Reserve Bank of India, Asian Development Bank, World Bank, UNICEF, Jamshedji Tata Trust, Ford Foundation, European Union and other International Organisations for specific Project Studies.

The Centre's research revolves around the economic and social problems of Andhra Pradesh as well as the Indian economy and society. Over a period of years, the Centre's research has developed expertise in several areas, especially in Agriculture, Food Security, Poverty Alleviation & Unemployment, District Planning, Bovine & Dairy Development, Resettlement & Rehabilitation and State Finances.

The Centre has been recognised as a Centre for advanced research by the Dr. B.R. Ambedkar Open University and Osmania University of Hyderabad, India. It has also been recognised by the University of Hyderabad as Research Centre for external registration in Ph.D. programmes in Economics and Anthropology. The Centre has evolved a unique teaching-cum-research training programme leading to M.Phil and Ph.D in Development Studies. Both are part time programmes, undertaken in collaboration with the Dr. B.R. Ambedkar Open University.

Over the past two and a half decades, CESS has conducted exploratory research exercises on a wide range of issues concerning economics and other social sciences, the results of which have helped in formulation of policies and decision making for overall national development. These investigations have dealt with vital themes such as Budgeting, Work organization, Determinants of poverty, Reform process, Distribution of vital resources, Income convergence, Population migration, Trade structure vs. Economy, Health Insurance, Determinants of morbidity and mortality, Industrial pollution, etc.

In view of the wide practical implications of the findings of these researches, the centre has been periodically publishing comprehensive working papers, monographs, etc. on select important themes for the benefit of those who have academic and research interests in similar fields.

5   Methodology

A survey of research scholars of CESS and other visiting scholars of CESS Library was conducted to meet the objectives of the study. A structured questionnaire was designed to find out the information retrieval skills of research scholars of social sciences.

There are 128 M.Phil. and Ph.D. scholars that are pursuing research programmes in CESS since 2011. The researcher distributed 128 questionnaires to the scholars during the contact programme directly. 'Directly-administered' questionnaire has the advantage of high response rate, which usually reaches 100 percent and the presence of researcher himself to provide assistance to the queries is valuable. All the respondents (i.e. 128 research scholars) returned the filled in questionnaire of the researcher.

Out of 100 questionnaires distributed to the visiting scholars of CESS Library, the researcher received back 82 questionnaires through accidental sampling technique. This is because research scholars of various universities visited CESS Library at different times and days, thus the researcher collected the data whenever they visited the library.

All together the researcher received responses from 210 out of 228 respondents (92.10% of the sample) for this present study.

The questionnaire contains 11 questions with 7 aspects like channels of Information Communication, predominant information, preferred location, concept identification, different search strategies and tools, and the ability to find the citation of a given article by the scholars.

6   Analysis of Data and Discussions

After collecting responses from research a scholar, the data was analyzed according to the objectives stated above and is discussed below with tables.

6.1   Channels of Information Communication

The distribution of scholars according to their preferred ranking of channels to seek information [7,8] is shown in Table 1.

Table 1. Preferred channels by Scholars to seek information

Channel	Preferred rank					Total
	I	II	III	IV	V	
INFORMAL CHANNELS: Consulting a professional friend	149 (70.95%)	46 (21.91%)	8 (03.81%)	5 (2.38%)	2 (0.95%)	210 (100%)
Invisible college e.g. seminars, lectures, etc.	195 (92.86%)	9 (04.28%)	4 (1.91%)	2 (0.95%)	0	210 (100%)
Technological Gatekeepers	2 (0.95%)	6 (2.86%)	3 (1.43%)	14 (6.66%)	185 (88.09%)	210 (100%)
e- sources	201 (95.71%)	8 (3.80%)	1 (0.48%)	0	0	210 (100%)
FORMAL CHANNELS Primary sources e.g. periodicals	187 (89.05%)	14 (6.66%)	6 (2.86%)	2 (0.95%)	1 (0.48%)	210 (100%)
Secondary sources e.g. textbooks, etc.	196 (93.33%)	10 (04.76%)	2 (0.95%)	1 (0.48%)	1 (0.48%)	210 (100%)
Tertiary sources e.g. directories, encyclopedias, etc.	57 (27.14%)	8 (03.80%)	6 (02.86%)	13 (6.19%)	126 (60.00%)	210 (100%)

It is evident from Table 1 that majority of the scholars preferred e-sources to seek information (95.71 per cent) followed by invisible colleges e.g. seminars, lectures, etc. (92.86 per cent). Another observation that can be derived from the above table is that the researchers give least preference to Technological Gate keepers from the category of Informal Channels.

With regard to the category of Formal Channels, it is clear from the table above that most of the researchers (93.33 per cent) prefer secondary sources followed by primary sources (89.05 per cent) and according to them tertiary sources are the least preferred ones.

It is inferred from the above results that the researchers are very passionate to access e-sources as compared to printed material to gather information. It might be that the development of Information Communication Technologies is transforming the information scene.

6.2   Predominant Information Required by the Scholars

The distribution of scholars according to the information required by them is given in the table below.

Table 2. Predominant information required by the scholars

Required information	No. of students	Percentage
Health information	5	2.38
Information for their personal development	4	1.90
Academic and Research information	149	70.96
Employment information	42	20.00
Global information	10	04.76
Total	210	100

In Table 2 above, the results show that the predominant information required by scholars is academic and research information which is confirmed by 70.96 per cent scholars. Next to that is employment information (20%) followed by global information (04.76%). Other information required by the scholars which may not be as vital as academic and research information is: information for personal development and health information.

6.3   Preferred Location to Obtain Information

The following figure gives a view of the preferred place by scholars to obtain information

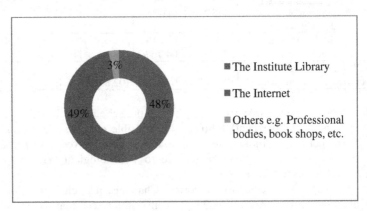

Fig. 1. The distribution of scholars according to their preferred location to obtain information

It is asserted by the above fig.1 that nearly half of the scholars prefer either their Institute's Library or the Internet as a source for obtaining information.

6.4   Concept Identification

A question has been asked to find out the understanding of concept of a given research problem by scholar. The following table gives the details.

Table 3. Distribution of scholars according to their responses regarding combination of words to find concept

Significant words of concept	Responses	Percentage
a)Family relations, academic results, colleges	90	42.86
b) Family relations, academic results	63	30
c) Effect, family relations, academic results	7	3.33
d) Effect, family relations, academic results, colleges	47	22.38
e) Others (please specify)	3	1.43
Total	210	100

It is evident from the table above that 42.86 percent of the research scholars chose the best answer. This answer includes the three concepts in the original question. Nearly o v e r one-quarter of the scholars (30%) chose answer (b) which does not include the "colleges" concept. 22.38 percent of the scholars do not appear to be able to distinguish between significant and non-significant terms when formulating a search statement, as they selected options which include the non-significant term "effect".

Table 4. Distribution of scholars according to their keyword search

Usage of keywords	Responses	Percentage
a) Impact, reduction, ozone layer, health	40	19.05
b)Ozone layer, health	135	64.29
c) Ozone layer	25	11.90
d) Skin cancer, ozone layer	6	02.86
e) Other(please, specify)	4	01.90
Total	210	100

Table 4 shows that the majority (64.29%) of the scholars were able to recognize significant words by selecting answer (b), however, 35.71% did not choose the most efficient strategy. Among these, those who opted for (c), "ozone layer", selected a strategy that is too broad; those who retained all the words in the statement and chose (a), which includes the non-significant term "impact", selected an overly restrictive search strategy. The same can be said of those who selected (d), since cancer is only one of the many effects of ozone layer depletion.

Table 5. Distribution of scholars according to their idea of concept for a given topic

Title choice	Responses	Percentage
a) Damage to the natural environment, India	25	11.90
b) Measures currently used, country	8	3.81
c) Damage, environment, measures currently used	37	17.62
d)Protective measures, environment, India	137	65.24
e) Other(please, specify)	3	1.43
Total	210	100

As per table 5, it can be concluded that 65.24 percent of the scholars did not hold to the wording of question and selected (d), retaining all the important concepts. More than 29.52 percent chose an answer in which one of the important concepts was missing.

To sum up, from the responses from the above three tables on concept identification, it can be observed that the scholars have difficulty in identifying significant words, even when their task is simplified by being presented with a choice of possible answers.

6.5   Search Strategy

It is apparent from the above table that, only 30.49 percent of the respondents chose the right answer (d) since for synonyms or related terms, the search operator to use is "OR". This operator tells the system to include in the search results all the documents that contain one or more of the query terms. M ajority of the scholars

Table 6. Distribution of scholars according to their usage of synonyms in search

Boolean operator	Responses	Percentage
a) AND	30	14.29
b) +	88	41.9
c) NOT	4	1.90
d) OR	64	30.49
e) Other	5	2.39
f) Don't know	19	9.07
Total	210	100

Table 7. Distribution of respondents according to their search strategy for a given concept

Search strategy	Responses	Percentage
a) By title	5	2.38
b) By publisher	2	0.95
c) By subject	63	30.00
d) By author	138	65.71
e) Other (pl. specify)	1	0.48
f) Don't know	1	0.48
Total	210	100

opted for "AND" and "+" operators (56.19%) which have the opposite effect to "OR" by limiting the search to documents containing all the terms. These results show that the Boolean operator "OR" is not properly understood by the scholars.

It is obvious from the table 7 that less than one-third (30%) of the research scholars chose the right answer (c), i.e. they would search the subject field to look for documents about an author. The answer (d), search by author, selected by 65.71 percent of the respondents would find texts written by Stephen Hackings but not documents about him. This question was not particularly difficult, but did not have a high success rate. Students must know how information is structured and indexed in a search tool, be it a catalogue, database or search engine.

Table 8. Distribution of respondents according to their search strategy to a given topic

Search strategy	Responses	Percentage
a) Depression and psychotherapy	14	6.67
b)Depression or psychotherapy or antidepressants	22	10.48
c)Depression and psychotherapy and antidepressants	129	61.43
d) Depression	34	16.18
e) Other(please, specify)	2	0.96
f) Don't know	9	4.28
Total	210	100

A large proportion of the scholars (61.43%) chose the correct answer, "depression and psychotherapy and antidepressants": This search strategy will retrieve the smallest number of documents. If we compare the results with those obtained for table 6, it is observed that the "AND" operator appears to be better understood than the "OR" operator.

6.6   Search Tools

The best answer is (b) because the search tool that enables one to search for journal articles is the database. Only 29.05 percent of the scholars chose this option. The library catalogue, (a), does not index journal articles, this answer is incorrect but was selected by 23.81 percent of the scholars.

Table 9. Distribution of respondents according to their responses regarding the information source used for a given key word

Information source	Response	Percentage
a) The library catalogue/OPAC	50	23.81
b)A database e.g. JSTOR	61	29.05
c) Search Engine e.g. Google, etc.	64	30.48
d) The journals in the library	18	8.57
e) Others (please, specify)	10	4.76
f) Don't know	7	3.33
Total	210	100

The search results show that very few scholars are familiar with databases despite the fact that they will have to use them to find periodical articles to complete their research works. To be successful in their research, scholars need not only to be familiar with databases, but also to understand the limitations of Internet search engines for finding journal articles.

6.7   Use of Results

A question has been asked to find out the journal citation from a given list of references by scholar. The following table and it's description gives the details.

Table 10. Distribution of respondents according to their responses regarding finding a journal article citation

Citation	Responses	Percentage
Miller, A.W. (1999). *Mobile communication technology*. Madison, CT, International University Press.	16	7.62
Anderson, K.H. (1999). "Ethical dilemmas and radioactive waste: A survey of the issues. *"Environmental Ethics*, 2(3):37-42.	97	46.19
Hartley, J.T. & D.A. Walsh. (2000). "Contemporary issues and new directions in internet security", in L.W. Poon (ed.), *Network security*, Washington, D.C., IEEE Press, pp.239-252.	32	15.23
Maccoby, E.E. & J. Martin. (1983). "Socialization in the context of the family: Parent-child interaction", in P.H. Mussen (ed.), *Child psychology: Socialization, personality, and social development*. New York, Wiley, vol.4, pp.1-101.	53	25.24
Don't know	12	5.72
Total	210	100

It is evident from the table above that, 46.19 percent of the scholars selected the correct answer, (b), and a large percentage (53.81%) was unable to identify the citation of a journal article. It can be deduced that if a research supervisor was to ask a scholar to locate documents using a bibliography, almost half of the scholars would have serious difficulties.

7   Conclusion

This study identifies the information search skills that social science research scholars need to improve upon. These include identifying the most efficient search strategy, evaluating Internet information and websites, as well as using information judiciously. Examination of the bibliographies shows that most scholars are not aware of the proper form of citation. It might be due to the lack of awareness among scholars on the importance of developing good information literacy skills. Scholars should be encouraged to use more scholarly resources in both print and electronic format. Another important implication of this study is that it is crucial to assess scholar's information literacy skills as a proactive action to evaluate and improve the effectiveness of an information literacy programme. Constant assessment and constructive efforts would lead to a more integrated curriculum and collaboration between academicians, researchers and librarians or information literacy specialists to produce well-designed information literates.

References

1. American Library Association. Presidential Committee on Information Literacy. Final Report (Chicago: American Library Association 1989),
   `http://www.ala.org/acrl/publications/whitepapers/presidential` (accessed)
2. Association of College & Research Libraries. Information Literacy Competency Standards for Higher Education,
   `http://www.ala.org/acrl/standards/informationliteracycompetency` (accessed)
3. Johnston, B., Webber, S.: Information Literacy in Higher Education: A review and case study. Studies in Higher Education 28(3), 321–324 (2003)
4. Margaret, C.W., Allison, S., Patrick, A.C.: Teaching information literacy skills: an evaluation. Nurse Education Today 20(6), 485–489 (2000)
5. Heather, M.: Information literacy skills: An exploratory focus group study of student perceptions. Research Strategies 15(1), 4–17 (1997)
6. Webber, S., Johnston, B.: Conceptions of information literacy: new perspectives and implications. Journal of Information Science 26, 381–397 (2000)
7. Murali Prasad, M.R.: Information gathering habits of engineering students: A study at Hyderabad, India. In: User Empowerment through Digital Technologies. International Conference Proceedings on the Convergence of Libraries, Archives and Museums, February 15-17, pp. 119–124. Pragun publications, New Delhi (2011)
8. Murali Prasad, M.: Information Literacy skills of Engineering Students: A study. In: Chandrasekhara Rao, V., Saroja, G. (eds.) Current Trends in Web Based Library Services. National Seminar Proceedings on Impact of World Wide Web on Library and Information Centers, February 3-4, pp. 69–79. Commonwealth Publishers, New Delhi (2014)
9. Chowdhury, G.G.: Introduction to Modern Information Retrieval, 3rd edn. Facet Publishing, London (2010)

The Design of an Information Literacy Game

Yan Ru Guo and Dion Hoe-Lian Goh

Wee Kim Wee School of Communication and Information,
Nanyang Technological University, Singapore
{W120030,ashlgoh}@ntu.edu.sg

Abstract. Information literacy (IL) has been of growing concern in education, at the workplace, and in daily life. The need for IL is also important for students, especially university students, as they routinely search for and synthesize information from multiple sources for various knowledge-intensive tasks such as writing a term paper. Given the infeasibility of face-to-face presentations to more than a fraction of students, digital technologies present an opportunity for librarians to reinvent the delivery of library services. Thus this study aims to design a digital IL game, by using participatory design approach. The data collected from the participatory designworkshop were analyzed based on GameFlow Model, and the result of one prototype is described. Implications of our work on game design are also discussed.

Keywords: Digital games, information literacy, information search process, low-fidelity prototype, participatory design, storyboard.

1   Introduction

The Internet has brought about the proliferation of and increased accessibility to information. As there is more information available now than ever before, the ability to seek, locate and navigate information effectively has become important, as is the ability to assess the accuracy and reliability of such information before usage. These are the very skills that information literacy (IL) provides – the skills that allow people to separate the wheat from the chaff in the quest to obtain high-quality content [1].

IL has been of growing concern in education, at the workplace, and in daily life. For example, IL forms the basis for lifelong learning and can improve the quality of one's education in formal and informal settings; increase his/her prospects of locating a satisfying job and moving up the career ladder [2].The need for IL is also important for students, especially university students, as they routinely search for and synthesize information from multiple sourcesfor various knowledge-intensive tasks. A student's academic performance is therefore closely related to his/her IL skills [3]. Further, because of the large collections found in digital libraries, it is important for students to understand how to make the best use of them.

However, students are increasingly unwilling to initiate interaction with librarians when they encounter difficulties searching for academic resources. Young students prefer to use information located through search engines instead, despite the uncertain

K. Tuamsuk et al. (Eds.): ICADL 2014, LNCS 8839, pp. 354–364, 2014.

quality and reliability of the sources[3]. This unwillingness to interact with humans does not relate exclusively to IL education, but to education in general. This poses an increasing challenge on how to educate young people in today's classrooms.

Digital technologies have substantially changed education in the last few decades[4]and redefined the role of libraries,Thispresents an opportunity for librarians to reinvent library services in support of the library's mission. Specifically, in digital game-based learning (DGBL), students' technological skills are fully utilized to support the learning process. Many of the pedagogical principles used in learning can also be found in digital games [5]. By infusing the elements of challenge, fantasy, control, feedback, social interaction, digitalgames could immerse players in an educational virtual environment.

However, apart from the growing body of literature on the use of DGBL to teach lower order thinking skills, facts, concepts, and procedures, there is limited literature on higher order thinking skills such as how to apply, analyze, or evaluate knowledge [6].Academic information searching involves higher order thinking skills as it teaches important procedural knowledge that synthesizes complex level of thinking and knowledge. Therefore, this study aims to fill this research gap by designing an IL game, using the participatory design (PD) approach, to glean insights into the perceptions of potential users of how such a game should be designed.

2   Background Literature

2.1   Digital Game-Based Learning in Information Literacy

There is today a growing consensus on the need for IL, and a sense of urgency about its implementation[7]. There are five tasks that an information literate person is able to do, namely, to determine the extent of information needed, to access the needed information effectively and efficiently; to evaluate information and its sources critically and incorporate selected information into one's knowledge base; to use information effectively to accomplish a specific purpose; and to understand the economic, legal, and social issues surrounding the use of information, and access and use information ethically and legally[8].

Interestingly,successful games meet most of the aboveIL Standards. For example, they teach students to *"determine the nature and extent of information needed"*, *"access needed information effectively and efficiently"*, and *"use information effectively to accomplish a specific purpose"* [5]. The authorcontended that libraries could harness elements of digital games to attract students' attention for IL programs. Academic libraries in the US were among the first to harness the power of DGBL in library instruction. For example, the University of Michigan implemented an IL game called *Defense of Hidgeon: the Plague Years*, and gathered positive feedback from students [9].While most students reported positive learning experiences during game play, some failed to recognize the general to specific rationales behind the game play. They also found that DGBLcouldnot stand on their own, but had to be combined with other game-related activities.

2.2   Participatory Design

While it is easy to engage designers and programmers in the design and development of the game, it is not easy nor obvious to engage the potential users who will use the game[10]. In the case of DGBL, the goal is to improve students' learning motivation and performance. Yet students are oftenneither enabled nor permitted to participate in the design ofthe new technology[10].PD makes it possible for potential users to communicate their ideas and concerns to educators, game designers and developers.

PD has been applied in educational system design projects. For example,it was used in the design of network-based software tools for middle and high school science education, where a group of teachers were invited to design the educational software [11].A recent example comes from the design of *Socialdrome*, an online educational game for enhancing children's social skills [12]. In the study, the PD approach was adopted to glean insights into the preference of children. Moreover, PD has also been employed in libraries, to renovate library layout, reprogram library services, and restructure library organization [10]. The University of Rochester Libraries used PD to improve the library course pages, where students were invited to interact with a poster-size version of the course page and contribute their ideas[13]. The current study will be one of the first attempts of using PD in designing an IL game.

3   Methodology

3.1   Participants Description and Data Collection

Seven tertiary students from a major local university were recruited to represent the potential users. The participants had diverse educational backgrounds in different stages of study, in order to maximize the exploration of different perspectives[14]. The sample consisted of three males and four females, aged between 21 and 27. There were three undergraduates (majoring in Sociology, Marketing, Communication respectively), one Master's student (majoring in Arts and Painting), and three doctoral students (majoring in Computer Science, Industrial Design and Graphic Design respectively). Participants reported being experienced gamers, playing computer games at least an hour per week, with two playing more than six hours per week.

The first author was involved as the facilitator in the PD workshop. The main task of the facilitator was to introduce the study objectives and to guide the discussion. Other than being proficient in playing games, the author had also attended training in interviewing techniques, and had experience conducting interviews prior to the study. The PD workshop was held in a focus group lab in a major university, lasting around two hours.All discussions were audio-recorded. At the beginning of theworkshop, participants were briefed on the research objective, which was to develop a game to teach IL skills to tertiary students, and specific steps necessary to develop an appropriate game design, including the overarching structure, affective EAs, and detailed content. During the workshop, participants were asked to jointly develop a game prototype. Storyboarding, a low-fidelity design approach was used, where blank paper and pencils were provided for participants to record their ideas [15].

3.2   Coding Frame and Coding Procedure

As in all qualitative content analysis, the data was analyzed for recurring "themes", and then organized into the eight criteria in the well-established GameFlow model [16]. This is to ensure thatthe coding was based on a sound theoretical foundation. Furthermore, the model provides game design heuristics, making it suitable for designing a game:

- **Concentration.** A game must be able to keep the players focused in order to be enjoyable. But in order to grab players' attention, the game must provide something worth attending to, such as detailed game worlds and brilliant stories.
- **Challenge.** An enjoyable game should provide appropriate challenges and have various levels of difficulty to meet individual player's needs, and there should also be an increase in level of difficulty for players to develop their skills.
- **Player skills.**Player skills must be matched with game challenges. Players should be taught how to play the game through interesting examples in the beginning.
- **Control.** Players must be allowed to exercise control over the game interface, characters and events. Games should hide the linear structure from players so that they can probe and experiment in the game world at their will.
- **Clear goals.** Games should provide players with clear and unambiguous overriding goals in the early stage of the game, which can be established through narratives or backstories.
- **Feedback**. It is important to send continuous feedback to players so that they understand what actions have been done and what have been accomplished, allowing the players to correct mistakes if any, and move on in the right direction.
- **Immersion.** Immersion refers to the experience of deep yet effortless involvement from players. To fully enjoy the game, players must immerse themselves through the pleasurable surrender of the mind to the game world.
- **Social interaction.** Options should be provided for players to interact, cooperate, or compete with each other, both inside and outside the game.

The audio recordings from the PD workshop were transcribed. To ensure anonymity, each participant was given a code from "P1" to "P7". The unit of analysis was taken to be a single comment. Other than the first author, one external coder was involved in the coding procedure and an intercoder reliability analysis using the Kappa statistic was performed to determine consistency between the two coders [17]. After discussing the coding scheme, the two coders independently coded the last 30 minutes of the PD workshop. The two coders reached almost perfect agreement, with intercoder reliability of 0.83 ($p< .001$).

4   Game Prototype

Participants decided to adapt from an existing genre of real-world game called "room escape". The "room escape" game requires players to escape from imprisonment by exploring their physical surroundings[18].In the participants' version of the IL game, called "Library Escape", players need to solve IL mysteries using various in-game clues within a one-hour time limit to escape from a deserted library building. The library building consists of multiple floors and rooms.Each room consists of a locked door, several objects to manipulate, and hidden clues or secret compartments. Soplayers must remember the directions that they have entered to save time. IL knowledge is acquired by exploring the objects and answering questions correctly.

4.1   Backstory and In-Game Rewards

The game begins with a short video clip that introduces the backstory to present the overriding goals of the game, as well as to grab the attention of players [16]. For the ease of discussion, this paper will refer to the protagonist as Tom (Fig. 1).

The final gradesof the previous semester were just released to students, and Tom only managed a "C" for his IL module. Disappointed with the poor grade, Tom consulted with the professor, Prof.Babbage, to find out the reason this. Prof. Babbagetoldhim that it was because the report was of low quality with reasons such as lack of citations, use of low quality sources of information, and arguments that did not make sense. To make things clearer, she searched for a "good" report for Tom to peruse.

Tom asked Prof. Babbagewhat he could do to improve his grade. The professor pondered for a while, led Tom to the front of a desertedlibrary building, and pushed him inside (Fig. 2), saying that this is the place where he could get appropriate training. Prof. Babbagesaid she would be back in one hour to check on his progress.

Fig.1. Tom (protagonist)   **Fig.2.** Library Escape

Though typically a reward is presented to players *after* they successfully complete a game, this issue was among the first to be discussed in the PD workshop, suggesting the importance of rewards to players. This is also confirmed by P4's remark that "*Ithink the reward is very important as it is what will keep the players going*". The participants thought virtual rewards would be effective, such as a virtual certificate with A+, or an IL completion certificate (Fig. 3). P7 commented, "*The final reward can be a gold A+ certificate*", and P6 added that "*Maybe if they need the printout, they need to go to the library*". This is to increase players' motivation to play, as well as their satisfaction toward the game.

Fig. 3. Virtual Certificate as Rewards

4.2   Game Missions

The Information Search Process (ISP) Model by [19] was utilized to structure the game. Themodel consists of six iterative stages: Task initiation, topic selection, prefocus exploration, focus formulation, information collection and search closure.What is unique about the ISP Model is that it takes into consideration the information seeker's affective states; and predicts situations during which information seekers are likely to experience positive affective states such as confidence and assurance, and also situations during which they are likely to experience negative affective states such as anxiety and frustration.Given the six stages, the participants created six corresponding missions through which Tom has to navigate in the game. Within each mission, Tom has to complete several tasks assigned to him in the forms of quests before he can proceed to the next mission (see Table 1).

Table 1. Missions and Quests in *Library Escape*

Missions: Venues ISP Stages	Topic	Quests (objects hidden in)
Mission 1: Closed Stacks Task initiation	General Introduction	1. Definitions of IL (book shelf) 2. The importance of IL to students (ceiling bulb) 3. Three modes of IL education delivery (whiteboard) 4. Five ACRL information tasks (stools)
Mission 2: Reference Desk Topic Selection	Affect in Information Behavior	1. Basis for topic selection (telephone) 2. Mellon (1986) library anxiety (clock pendulum) 3. Bates (1986) uncertainty (notebook) 4. Bostic (1992) five factors contributing to library anxiety (computer)
Mission 3: Open Shelves Prefocus Exploration	Information Seeking Behavior	1. What is information seeking (poster) 2. Wilson First Model(book) 3. Johnson Model (shelf) 4. Ellis Everyday Information seeking Model(magazines)
Mission 4: Virtual Library Focus Formulation	Kuhlthau's ISP Model	1. What is unique about ISP Model (ebooks) 2. Constructivist perspective (backward chaining) (ejournals) 3. Different stages of ISP, iterative process (databases) 4. Focus on students' feelings (searching bar)
Mission 5: Café Information Collection	Use of ISP Model	1. The development of the ISP model (coffee machine) 2. Other works on ISP model (forward chaining) (ice machine) 3. How the ISP model helps librarians (piano) 4. How the ISP model helps students (plants)
Mission 6: Exhibition Area Search Closure	Integrative session	1. When to stop looking for information? (screen) 2. Can information be "objective"? (sculpture) 3. Do people really "need" information? (painting) 4. "There is much more about IL than what is presented here!" as an exhortation to explore IL further (librarian)

Mission 1: Closed Stacks. Tom realizes that he is actually in a deserted library building. He only sees shelves of dusty books around. Mission 1 is designed to be easy for Tom to familiarize himself with the game rules. So here, he will only need to explore his surroundings to obtain some introductory IL knowledge such as the definitions of IL, the importance of IL, and some standards.

Mission 2: Reference Desk. Mission 2 takes place in the reference desk on Level 3 of the library. At the desk, Tom is presented with an overwhelmingly long list of IL topics, along with ambiguous instructions. He encounters a ghost librarian that could offer help and advice. So, Tom initiates a conversation with the librarian before selecting a topic. The ghost librarian recommends Tom to select information seeking behavior as the topic for his report. The reference desk has several objects, and quests are hidden in these objects and only reveal themselves when selected. Before leaving, the librarian whispers to Tom, *"Check out Z700 plus"*. Tom wonders whether what the code is about. He enters the lift, and it takes him to Level B1.

Mission 3: Open Shelves. Mission 3 takes Tom to the library's physical lending collections, and this mission requires Tom to investigate the information with the intent of finding a focus for the topic of information seeking behavior. The dusty books are neatly arranged in shelves. Tom browses the bookshelves aimlessly. Suddenly, he realizes that the code given to him in Mission 3 must refer to the code on the books. He rushes to the shelves with the Z700+ code, and starts to explore several books. Z700+ is where IL collections are located.

Mission 4: Virtual Library. Now, Tom enters a virtual world, which is the library's website. This is the place where books in the library's collection can be searched, and through which electronic books and electronic journals that the library subscribes to can be accessed. Tom has to formulate a focus from the information encountered. As with the open shelves, Tom realizes that the library has subscribed to thousands of ebooks and ejournals. Because of the sheer volume of the material he has to sift through, he is overcome by fear. Thankfully, the ghost librarian was helpful, and he reminds Tom to some searching techniques. Tom reveals the correct articles by clicking on the correct phrases to search.

Mission 5: Café. Mission 5 brings the search for information to a closure. It dawns upon Tom that the flurry of activity has caused him to be tired. He looks around, and notices that there is acafé on the corner. There is a counter, coffee machine, ice machine, oven, a fewsofas, a broken piano, and some withered plants. Tom starts to gather more information that defines, extends, and support the ISP Model, which are all hidden in the objects. He consolidates the information he has located, and feels much more confident of completing the report on time.

Mission 6: Exhibition Area. After getting to the exhibition area on Level 2, Tom notices a bigscreen there that displays the previous missions and quests he had completed. Tom clicks on the screen andis given an award, which is an A+certificate, showing that Tom has successfully completed all the tasks given. Prof.Babbage also comes in and is very happy to see his progress. Tom can choose to post his certificate on social networking sites (e.g., Facebook, Twitter). Tom feels that what he learnt is applicable to the rest of the modules he is taking at the university.

5   Findings and Analyses

This section will analyze how the game prototype reflected the game design heuristicsinthe GameFlow model.

Concentration. To help players concentrate, *Library Escape* is set in a three-dimensional world with multiple levels and rooms, so players must remember the directions that they have entered to save time. The one-hour time limit is an indication to players that they are to concentrate on the game, lest their time runs out.P2 came out with the idea of putting a time limit on the game, "*After one hour the professor will come back*", in order to create tension and excitement for the players.

Challenge. The level of challenge difficulty increases as the player progresses through each ISP stage, and each stage is built on previous stages. During the discussion, there was a split of opinions. P1 and P6 suggested making the challenge extremely difficult, as they reasoned "*We can borrow something from Flappy Bird because it is very frustrating and challenging. When you play, you keep on advancing your skills. You will actually achieve more this way*". But theiridea was opposed by others, as P3 and P4 argued "*that is a turnoff already to have it so difficult*", which indicated that a balance is required in the level of challenge in the game.

Player Skills. To achieve this end, Mission 0 is designed for players to familiarize themselves with the game first, so that players feel like playing the game. A leaderboard is available on social media for players to show their skills to friends. Additionally, players are given a virtual certificate for completing the game and learning the IL skills.P3 suggested"*You should give players a short demo at the beginning*". On the other hand, P6 said hedid not want to read a long text manual. Therefore, the help informationwas made concise.

Control. Players control their movements and actions in the game world. They also control the starting, stopping, saving functions of the game. Players are also free to invite others to collaborate with them in the same mission. This is supported by P5's comment that "*Give more control to the users. For example in this game, if I have troubles in one mission, and I can ask other players to join the game*".

Clear Goals. The overriding goal of *Library Escape* is clearly presented to the players at the beginning, which is to improve IL skills. Each mission is matched with one stage in the ISP Model, and players need to continue playing to find out the answers to each quest.There are multiple questsin each mission to keep players concentrated. The need for clear goals isconfirmed by P5's comment that "*Tell the story before we incorporate the educational parts, to interest the players first*".

Feedback. Feedback is given to players to verify theyhave completed the quests successfully. A status bar is provided during gameplay to track their progress in the game, and a leaderboard to compare their progress against others'. A map is available to guide players in the library. P4 suggested, "*You could put a leaderboard, showing their scoring, difficulty level, and where they are in the board*". P2 suggested using sound as auditory feedback, "*Maybe you could add some different effects, such as clapping of hands, after players answer the questions correctly*".

Immersion. *Library Escape* transports players into a virtual hauntedlibrary. To achieve this end, ituses a combination of stimuli (music, backstory, interface) to engage players, and the one-hour time limit can cause players to feel tension and excitement. For example, P7 said, "*I think it might be better to use the actual scene of the library. Just use photo images to make it real. If there are books there, you can really click on it and take it out and see what is inside*".

Social Interaction. To encourage social interaction, a multiplayer option is provided for players to interact with their friends to work on the same quest, which is done through social media. Players are encouraged topost their achievements on social media too. For example, P3 remarked that "*I prefer to play with another person, it will be more interesting*", and P4 added that "*I think it is nice to play in a team because when we don't know the answers, we could discuss it with teammates*".

6   Conclusion

This studywas one of the first attempts todesign an IL game using the PD approach. The ISP model was utilized to structure the game missions. The PD approach was adopted to glean insights into the perceptions of potential users of how such a game should be designed. This was achieved through storyboarding, a low-fidelityprototyping technique. The data collected from the PD workshopwas analyzed based on GameFlow model.

This study has both theoretical and practical implications. On the theoretical front, this study provides an example of how to infuse a theoretical model, the ISP Model, into an IL game design. Additionally, the use of the PD approach enabledpotential users to contribute to the design process. The fact that participants' discussions matched well with the GameFlow model demonstrated that PD was an effective approach in gathering user requirements from potential users. On the practical front, the prototype and design ideas fromthe PD workshop can be used by librarians as a starting point for exploration of DGBLin IL education. The outcomes of this study will be of interest to educators and researchers as the lessons learnt can inform and stimulate the further implementation of DGBL in libraries and schools.

The study also contributes to the body of knowledge on PD facilitation. First, despite the criticism that some potential users might not be able to articulate their thoughts, during this PD workshop, the participants showed surprising capabilities. Two participants took the initiative to set agenda for the discussion, for example they reminded the participants the priority of the discussion, when is enough for one topic and move to next. Second, building rapport with participants is a critical step before fruitful discussions can take place. Although PD places a strong focus on the knowledge from potential users and participants, and facilitators are regarded as the expert, PD is not against expert knowledge. In this PD workshop, the facilitator also joined the discussion at participants' request and participated in the discussion, and this turned out to be a good ice-breaking strategy.

In terms of limitations, the PD approach has been challenged in recent years, but controls have been put place to ensure maximal benefits could be harnessed.

For example, the actual stakeholders of the IL game will include students from all disciplines, librarians, and faculty members, whose population is much larger than the seven representative users in the PD workshop. Thus involving the representative users as participants would potentially bias the design towards the perceptions of only those who participated. However, this study attempted to mitigate this challenge by recruiting participants from a wide variety of disciplines and educational levels. Next, it should be noted that DGBL is not a panacea for the problems that arise in IL education, as it has its own limitations. DGBL is good in motivating students, but it is a supplemental education method that cannot be used alone, as the games are not designed to have answers to all potential doubts and questions from students. Despite the shortcomings, what is clear is that researchers should continue to develop the positive potential of integrating DGBL in IL education while remaining aware of the possible unintended negative effects and limitations.

References

1. Brockman, J.: Is the Internet Changing the Way You Think?: The Net's Impact on Our Minds and Future. HarperCollins, New York (2011)
2. Horton Jr., F.W.: Information literacy and information management: A 21st century paradigm partnership. International Journal of Information Management 26, 263–266 (2006)
3. Ng, J.Y.: Information Literacy needed for Singaporean students. MediaCorp. (2011)
4. Prensky, M.: "Engage Me or Enrage Me": What Today's Learners Demand. Educause Review 40, 60 (2005)
5. VanLeer, L.: Interactive gaming vs. library tutorials for information literacy: A resource guide. Indiana Libraries 25, 52–55 (2006)
6. Charsky, D.: From edutainment to serious games: A change in the use of game characteristics. Games and Culture 5, 177–198 (2010)
7. Zhang, X., Majid, S., Foo, S.: Environmental scanning: An application of information literacy skills at the workplace. Journal of Information Science 36, 719–732 (2010)
8. Association of College & Research Libraries Information literacy competency standards for higher education. Association of College & Research Libraries (2000)
9. Markey, K., Swanson, F., Jenkins, A., Jennings, B., St Jean, B., Rosenberg, V., Yao, X., Frost, R.: Will undergraduate students play games to learn how to conduct library research? The Journal of Academic Librarianship 35, 303–313 (2009)
10. Foster, N.F.: Introduction. Participatory Design in Academic Libraries: Methods, Findings, and Implementations. CLIR Publication (2012)
11. Carroll, J.M., Chin, G., Rosson, M.B., Neale, D.C.: The development of cooperation: Five years of participatory design in the virtual school. ACM (2000)
12. Tan, J.L., Goh, D.H.-L., Ang, R.P., Huan, V.S.: Child-centered interaction in the design of a game for social skills intervention. Computers in Entertainment 9, 2–17 (2011)
13. Lindahl, D.: Organizing the Library for User-Centered Design. CLIR Publication (2014)
14. Kitzinger, J.: Qualitative research: Introducing focus groups. British Medical Journal 311, 299–302 (1995)
15. Walsh, G., Foss, E., Yip, J., Druin, A.: FACIT PD: a framework for analysis and creation of intergenerational techniques for participatory design. ACM (2013)

16. Sweetser, P., Wyeth, P.: GameFlow: a model for evaluating player enjoyment in games. Computers in Entertainment 3, 3–8 (2005)
17. Cohen, J.: Weighted kappa: Nominal scale agreement provision for scaled disagreement or partial credit. Psychological Bulletin 70, 213–220 (1968)
18. Hou, H.-T., Chou, Y.-S.: Exploring the Technology Acceptance and Flow State of a Chamber Escape Game-Escape the Lab for Learning Electromagnet Concept (2012)
19. Kuhlthau, C.C.: Seeking meaning: A process approach to library and information services. Libraries Unlimited, Westport, CT (2004)

Dimensions of User Experience and Reaction Cards

Tanja Merčun and Maja Žumer

University of Ljubljana, Ljubljana, Slovenia
{tanja.mercun,maja.zumer}@ff.uni-lj.si

Abstract. A positive user experience is one of the deciding factors in the success of information systems such as digital libraries. But being a relatively new area of research, the concepts constituting a user experience do not have a strong framework and are also not easy to measure. The paper looks at the possibility of using results from reaction cards to identify meaningful concepts as well as suggests a new way of analysing the dimensions of user experience.

Keywords: user experience, evaluation, methodology, reaction cards.

1 Introduction

The concept of user experience has slowly established itself in the field of human-computer interaction, expanding the notion of usability and making an impact on user interface evaluation as well as design. Also within digital librariessome researchers believe that the qualities of fun, enjoyment, playfulness, and pleasure associated with user experience should be acknowledged [1]. However,as the definitions, frameworks, and elements of user experience are still evolving, the field lacks certain theoretical and empirical foundation [2]. Encompassing notions such as beauty, engagement,fun, pleasure, hedonic value, desirability, goodness, affect, and emotion, user experience is not only challenging to define, but also difficult to measure.

Clearly identifying the key dimensions that cover a significant area of variability in user experience would help considerably in setting up not only a more consistent basis for evaluation but also amore solid theoretical framework.Having sound conceptual frameworks that define user experience qualities wouldenable us to collect meaningful data and improve existing measures in terms of reliability, validity, and sensitivity [3]. However, to transform theoretical constructs into meaningful measures, we first need to have a clear idea and understanding of what constitutes user experience. This paperwill examine how reaction cards method could be applied to identify, test, and present the key dimensions of user experience.

2 Notions of User Experience

Literature provides a varied collection of views on user experience.O'Brien and Toms [5], for example, say that user experience examines the quality of information interactions from the perspective of the user, moving away from standard metrics of efficiency,

K. Tuamsuk et al. (Eds.): ICADL 2014, LNCS 8839, pp. 365–370, 2014.

effectiveness, and user satisfaction towards fulfilment, play, enjoyment, discovery, and engagement.Law [3] describes the notion of user experience as more complex than it appearsand mentions various user experience qualities, such as affect, emotion, fun, aesthetics, hedonic, flow, as well as more specific elements of emotion: pleasure, surprise, stimulation, frustration, delightfulness, immersion, challenge, excitement, boredom. In their review of papers from the field of user experience, Bargas-Avila &Hornbæk [4] notice the use of dimensions such as: affect/emotion, enjoyment/fun, aesthetics/appeal, hedonic quality, engagement/flow, motivation,enchantment, and frustration. Mahlke and Thüring [6], on the other hand, identified two types of qualities related to user experience: instrumental qualities connected to the usability and usefulness of a system, and non-instrumental qualities that are closely related to appeal and attractiveness.

With the variety of dimensions traced throughout the literature, the problem is that their relationships to established constructs are usually not made clear, which may lead to an endless number of concepts that describe a similar phenomenon[4]. Whether they really are all distinct dimensions or how they relate to one another are just some of the questions that appear with the numerous notions related to user experience.

3   Reaction Cards Method

Developed by Microsoft experts and first reported in 2002, the product reaction card method was described also as a desirability toolkit that "provides a way for users to tell the story of their experience, choosing the words that have meaning to them as triggers to express their feelings – negative or positive – about their experience" [7]. In its original form, the method was designed to use a set of 118 adjectives, positive and negative, but subsequent studies by other researchers reported on selecting only a smaller subset of the cards. Typically employed at the end of a testing session, participants in the study are asked to select the cards that best reflect their experience with the system and, in the next phase, use some of them as the basis for an interview discussion where they elaborate on the chosen aspects of the system.

Indicating how people perceive and experience an information system, reaction cards present a promising tool also for the evaluation of digital libraries. While in most cases still presented only qualitatively using word clouds,there are also other possibilities for analysing reaction cards. They can be used for comparing different systems or designs by analysing the number of selected adjectives, the ratio of positive and negative cards (example in Table 1), as well as the frequency of individual selected words (example in Figure 1).

Table 1. An example of system comparison using the frequency and the ratio of selected cards

	POSITIVE	NEGATIVE	TOTAL
SYSTEM 1	319 (76%)	103 (24%)	422
SYSTEM 2	418 (88%)	56 (12%)	474
SYSTEM 3	429 (91%)	27 (9%)	456

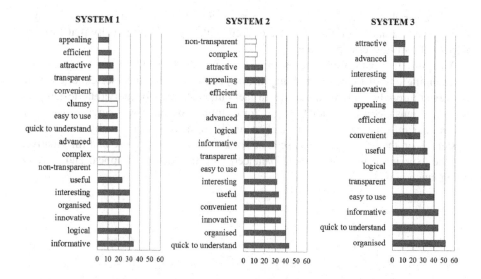

Fig. 1. Using the frequency of selected cards for system analysis and comparison

Either comparing several systems or evaluating a single one, our investigation suggests that reaction cards might also be used in a more advanced analysis of user experience. Grouping the adjectives based on their underlying semantics, the cards could reveal higher level concepts and allow us to examine and compare individual areas of user experience. Also Guzman and Schiller [8], for example, suggestedthat reaction cards could be processed using principal component analysis or other semantic analysis as that may provide more information than the techniques used in the existing body of work.

4   Experimenting with Reaction Card Analysis

Taking the results from our past usability study which compared several user interface prototype designs for representing and exploring results in a visual bibliographic information system, we examined if the adjectives could be logically grouped into meaningful categories using statistical methods. Although the study was not designed with this particular purpose in mind, we felt that even the small number of selected adjectives or reaction cards (15 positive and 14 negative) included in the test could provide an interesting starting point for exploration of this concept.With each prototype design being tested 72-times, the collection of data was also big enough to allow the application of statistics. Running a factor and principal component analysis on the 15 positive reaction cards in SPSS, a rotated component matrixtherefore revealed 4 main factors (primary component in bold):

1 – **easy to use, clear,** quick to understand, useful, organized, convenient
2 – **advanced,** fun, attractive, appealing
3 – **informative,** efficient,logical
4 – **interesting,** innovative

While variable 1 and 3 denote user's perceived usability and usefulness of the system, variable 2 and 4, on the other hand, convey the appeal and novelty that form an important part of user experience.

Mapping the data from our study on a radar plot with 4 axes (each axis representing one of the identified dimensions) illustrated that the user experience, as conveyed through reaction cards, was in fact quite different for individual tested prototype designs (see Fig. 2 - left). While, for example, System 3 was perceived as easy to use and informative, it clearly lacked on the dimensions of novelty and appeal. System 2, on the other hand, was seen as somewhat less easy to use and informative, but the experience was much more balanced with the factors of appeal and novelty being much higher.

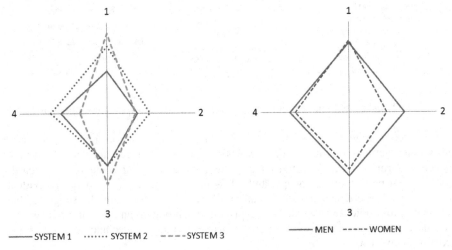

Fig. 2. A radar graph mapping reaction card results on 4 dimensions

Creating the four new factors in SPSS also allowed us to analyze the differences between systems by identifying statistical significance within each individual factor. Table 2, for example, shows that comparing our three systems, there were significant differences within all four factors. The pairwise comparison also confirmed the characteristics which were outlined in the graph, revealing significant differences between System 3 and System 2.

The same technique can also be used for comparing user experience of various user groups within a single system: Fig. 2 (right), for example, illustrates that in our study, one of the systems was perceived similarly by men and women on 3 dimensions, but was more appealing to men than women. Also here statistical analysis can then be used be used to identify which differences were significant. Table 3 presents an example of such an analysis, comparing how gender and the field of study influenced the perceptions of the tested systems.

Table 2. Possible use of factors for a statistical comparison of systems

		MEAN	ANOVA Sig.	PAIRWISE COMPARISON (p < 0,05)
FACTOR 1	SYSTEM 1	-,53	,000*	SYSTEM 3> 2 >1
	SYSTEM 2	,07		
	SYSTEM 3	,37		
FACTOR 2	SYSTEM 1	-,03	,019*	SYSTEM 2 >3
	SYSTEM 2	,15		
	SYSTEM 3	-,31		
FACTOR 3	SYSTEM 1	,05	,013*	SYSTEM 3 > 2
	SYSTEM 2	-,22		
	SYSTEM 3	,27		
FACTOR 4	SYSTEM 1	,10	,046*	SYSTEM 1,2 > 3
	SYSTEM 2	,06		
	SYSTEM 3	-,28		

Table 3. Factor comparison of designs by gender or field of study

		GENDER		FIELD OF STUDY	
		ANOVA Sig.	PAIRWISE COMP. (p < 0,05)	ANOVA Sig.	PAIRWISE COMP. (p < 0,05)
FACTOR 1	SYSTEM 1	-	-	-	science > education, humanities
	SYSTEM 2	-	-	-	-
	SYSTEM 3	-	-	-	-
FACTOR 2	SYSTEM 1	-	-	-	humanities > engineering
	SYSTEM 2	-	-	-	
	SYSTEM 3	-	-	-	-
FACTOR 3	SYSTEM 1	-	-	-	
	SYSTEM 2	-		-	science > humanities, social science
	SYSTEM 3	-	-	-	-
FACTOR 4	SYSTEM 1	-	-	,037*	humanities, engineering > social science
	SYSTEM 2	,049*	female > male	-	-
	SYSTEM 3	-	-	-	-

5   Conclusion and Future Work

So far, our initial investigations revealed a high correlation between the results collected using reaction cards and those measured with typical usability metrics. It was
the appeal and noveltyidentified using reaction cards (dimensions 2 and 4) that
showed important differences among individual designs.There are definite limitations

to our study that was not designed for this type of analysis and included only a small and random selection of adjectives. The initial investigation, however, suggests that such an analysis of user experience is feasible and should be tested more closely.

Nevertheless, an important feature that will need to be further investigated before such application can be more widely adopted is the grouping of reaction cards into dimensions, testing that the cards within each category really represent the same underlying concept. This will require a new study with a larger selection of reaction cards that will provide ample basis for the use of statistical methods and a more indepth investigation of user experience. We expect that such a study in combination with factor analysis should enable us to build a more solid framework that will clearly identify which cards constitute which concepts. While our current study with 15 cards revealed 4 dimensions, a broader assortment of cards is not only likely to identify more of them, but might alsorearrange the current distribution of adjectives. It will be interesting to observe how the concepts deriving from reaction cards and the concepts identified in literature compare to each other and how a more stable framework could provide a new basis for evaluating user experience also in digital libraries.

References

1. Toms, E.G., Dufour, C., Hesemeier, S.: Measuring the User's Experience with Digital Libraries. In: JCDL 2004 Proceedings of the Joint Conference on Digital Libraries, pp. 51–52. ACM (2004)
2. Law, E.L., Roto, V., Hassenzahl, M., Vermeeren, A., Kort, J.: Understanding, Scoping and defining user experience: a survey approach. In: CHI 2009 Proceedings of the SIGCHI Conference on Human Factors in Computing Systems, pp. 719–728. ACM (2009)
3. Law, E.L.: The measurability and predictability of user experience. In: EICS 2011 Proceedings SIGCHI Symposium on Engineering Interactive Computing Systems, pp. 1–10. ACM (2011)
4. Bargas-Avila, J.A.: Hornbæk. K.: Old Wine in New Bottles or Novel Challenges? A Critical Analysis of Empirical Studies of User Experience. In: CHI 2011 Proceedings of the SIGCHI Conference on Human Factors in Computing Systems, pp. 2689–2698. ACM (2011)
5. O'Brien, H.L., Toms, E.G.: Examining the generalizability of User Engagement Scale (UES) in exploratory search. Inf. Process. Manage. 49, 1092–1107 (2013)
6. Mahlke, S., Thüring, M.: Studying antecedents of emotional experiences in interactive contexts. In: Proceedings of the CHI Conference, pp. 915–918. ACM (2007)
7. Barnum, C.M., Palmer, L.A.: More than a feeling: understanding the desirability factor in user experience. In: CHI 2010 Extended Abstracts on Human Factors in Computing Systems, pp. 4703–4716. ACM (2010)
8. De Guzman, E.S., Schiller, J.: How Does This Look? Desirability Methods for Evaluating Visual Design. In: Stephanidis, C. (ed.) Posters, Part I, HCII 2011. CCIS, vol. 173, pp. 123–127. Springer, Heidelberg (2011)

A Multi-lingual and Multi-cultural Tool for Learning Herbal Medicine

Verayuth Lertnattee and Chanisara Lueviphan

Faculty of Pharmacy, Silpakorn University, Nakhon Pathom, Thailand
{verayuth,chanisara}@su.ac.th, verayuths@hotmail.com

Abstract. In Thailand, traditional medicine has been derived from several cultures, e.g., traditional Indian medicine (Ayurveda) and traditional Chinese medicine. Herbal medicine is an important part in Thai traditional medicine. Practitioners including pharmacists need knowledge of herbal medicine. However, it is hard for a student to familiar with several medicinal herbs with a limitation of time. To increase understanding in herbal medicine, a multi-lingual and multi-cultural learning tool for herbal medicine should be established. In this paper, KUIHerbRx2014, a Web-based supplement learning tool on herbal medicine, is introduced. The KUIHerbRx2014 supports a collaborative learning to improve knowledge and skills in multi-cultural herbal medicine with a scientific method. It also supports herb names in multi-lingual and multi-script. Activities of collecting, contributing new opinions, vote to existed opinions, and providing useful information to the system, were proposed to learn herbal medicine.

Keywords: collaborative learning, herbal medicine, traditional medicine, KUIHerb, collective intelligence.

1 Introduction

Traditional Thai medicine (TTM) has been influenced by several cultures, especially from China and India. Herbal medicine is a part of traditional medicine, which is set as important products on healthcare system. Pharmacists including other healthcare professionals now need basic knowledge of these topics for their professional practices [1, 2]. However, it is hard for a student to familiar with medicinal herbs with a limitation of time for study. Due to some special characteristics of herbal information, i.e., herb names and their medicinal usages which may be distinct according to their cultural background. These data should be contributed by contributors from different regions. With Web 2.0 system, it provides an opportunity for sharing information from a group of members on a topic of interest [3, 4]. The Knowledge Unifying Initiator for Herbal Information (KUIHerb), a system for collective intelligence on herbal medicine, is used as a platform for building a Web community for collecting the intercultural knowledge [5]. Information in the KUIHerb has been collected for a period of time. Therefore, at least three reasons that it is not suitable to use as a learning tool. Firstly, it has only a little room for a non or a little experienced student

K. Tuamsuk et al. (Eds.): ICADL 2014, LNCS 8839, pp. 371–378, 2014.

to share a new opinion. Secondly, information provided by members in KUIHerb may be from their experiences while pharmacy students should contribute herbal information related with scientific evidences. Herb names should be given in several languages, especially English and languages which are popular in the Southeast Asian countries. Finally, several errors in content may occur during the learning process. The consequent is that members and visitors of the KUIHerb, may receive incorrect information. In this paper, we present an idea for building a new and clean Website based on the KUIHerb and use it as a Web-based and social network learning tool on herbal medicine, which is called KUIHerbRx2014. Information of herbs in several regions can be distributed and exchanged among groups of students. Information about herb names are collected in Thai local names and multi-lingual names. Furthermore, opinions given to KUIHerbRx2014 should be evidence-based opinions, i.e., a set of reliable references should be suggested. In the rest of this paper, the concept of multi-lingual and multi-cultural herbal information is described in Section 2. Section 3 presents the design of a multi-lingual and multi-cultural herbal learning tool. Section 4 gives a detail of the experimental settings. The experimental results are described in Section 5. A conclusion and future work are made in Section 6.

2   Multi-lingual and Multi-cultural Herbal Information

In herbal medicine, the scientific name of an herb and its images are used for common understanding. However, common names are more popular than scientific names in communication between healthcare professionals and patients. Besides the TTM, Traditional Chinese Medicine (TCM) is also popular in Thailand. Although the standard dialect of Chinese languages, Mandarin, is increasing in popularity among the South East Asian countries [6], the names of crude drugs in Chinese drug store in Thailand are usually called in Teochew (Chaozhou) dialect [7]. This dialect is often used in the prefectures of eastern Guangdong [8], i.e., Chaozhou, Shantou, Jieyang and etc. Information of herbs and crude drugs can be found in the Chinese pharmacopoeia including English names, pharmaceutical names (in Latin), Chinese names by Chinese characters and Romanization (Pinyin) including scientific names. It is hard for a new generation of Thai pharmacist to recognize herbs or crude drugs with these dialects. However, several Chinese herbs and other natural products are not found in Thailand. There is no Thai name for these herbs and products. The name in Chaozhou and Mandarin dialects are still important to use for identifying a Chinese herb or a crude drug. For writing system, Chinese characters may be used and understand by a few persons. Thai characters are usually used to represent herbs' common names. If an herb name in Chaozhou dialect is commonly intelligible among Thai people, the name of the herb in Chaozhou pronunciation is written in Thai characters. Due to multi-cultural usages of an herb, searching herbal information is more efficient when applying terms in multiple languages, e.g., Chinese languages. In case of using Thai herb names to search information, applications of the herb, in Thailand, are found. However, when input herb names in Chinese languages, some different applications in China, may be found.

3   The Design of a Multi-lingual and Multi-cultural Herbal Learning Tool

In KUIHerb, a collaborative tool for herbal information creation, seven topics are taken into account, i.e., pictures, general characteristics, local name, indication or medicinal usages (i.e., part used with their indications and methods for preparation), precaution/toxicity, additional information (extra information) and references. Among these topics, a voting system is implemented on local names, medicinal usages and herb images. The topics of local names and medicinal usages are explicit voting system, i.e., the voting score is shown on each opinion. A student may initially post his/her opinions about those topics. In this version, scores from all members are given with equal weight. If other students agree with the opinion, a simple click on the button "Vote" will increase the score by one. The opinion with higher score will be moved up to upper part of the window. The topic of general characteristics is usually given by an administrator. The information of the other three topics, i.e., precaution/toxicity, additional information and references, are free text without majority voting. The modified version of KUIHerb, namely, KUIHerbRx2014, is used as a learning tool for pharmacy students to share multi-lingual and multi-cultural herbal information. Multi-lingual script can be applied on all topics. However, the topic of herb names, is modified to be able to input herb names in multiple languages with a systematic pattern. Four methods of inputting are defined with the example of an herb with the scientific name is *Datura metel*:

- *Characters*: this method presents the herb name (common names, local names) by its language with characters of that language, e.g., ลำโพง in Thai, Thorn Apple in English and 洋金花 in Chinese characters.
- *Romanization*: the Hanyu Pinyin has been used officially to Romanize Mandarin, which is often used to write the herb name in Mandarin dialect, e.g., Yang Jin Hua.
- *Transliteration*: this is a method for conversion of a text from one language to another. In Thailand, it is usually used for converting Chinese characters to Chaozhou dialect in Thai characters, e.g., 洋金花 (Chinese characters), is converted to เอี้ยงกิมฮวย (Chaozhou dialect in Thai characters).
- *Combination*: this method is the combination of the three methods, mostly, characters with transliteration to Thai or English in order to help users to pronounce the word correctly, e.g., 洋金花 (เอี้ยงกิมฮวย).

4   Experimental Settings

The KUIHerbRx2014 was constructed based on the structure of the KUIHerb. Some topics and conditions were modified for pharmacy students. For herb names, a list of languages and the countries where the language is used to call the herb, was introduced. Fifty four languages including dialects were provided. For Thai language, a student could input Thai local names with Thai characters and the location where the local name is recognized. For foreign languages, four methods were used to input herb names, i.e., characters, Romanization, transliteration as well as the combination of characters and transliteration. The third year pharmacy students in faculty of pharmacy, Silpakorn University who registered the course "health informatics" in the academic year of 2013 were assigned to share their opinions in the KUIHerbRx2014. The number of students was 166. The KUIHerbRx2014 was initialed with information of 844 herbs. The 200 herbs began with information on all topics to use as samples. The rest were initialed in topics of scientific names, English names and general characteristics. Three assignments were given to students: 1) each student was an initiator on two herbs in topics of herb names, indications, precaution/toxicity and additional information, as well as references to their opinions 2) each student had to vote some opinions on the other herbs and 3) the student should do the questionnaire about the KUIHerbRx2014. The students were encouraged to contribute local names in Thai and multi-lingual names especially, languages used in Southeast Asian countries. The period of two weeks was assigned for these assignments. Opinions provided to the KUIHerbRx2014 should be evidence-based information and avoid copyright violations. References could be added by a student and a list of references was shown in the topic of references. The citations were given in parentheses after opinions.

5   Experimental Results

5.1   The KUIHerbRx2014

Each student was assigned to contribute opinions in five topics, i.e., herb names, medicinal usages, precaution/toxicity, additional information and references. The contribution of herb images was optional. Figure 1 to Figure 3 present contributed opinions of the same herb. For local names (including multi-lingual names) and indications, a student who was assigned to be a creator for two herbs, had to contribute his/her opinions for these herbs. The other students could contribute their new opinions or vote for the existing opinions if they agree with the opinion. The Thai local names and herb names in several languages were shown in Figure 1. A popular Website for multi-lingual herb names is "MULTILINGUAL MULTISCRIPT PLANT NAME DATABASE" from the University of Melbourne, Australia. This Website was usually used as a source for finding multi-lingual herb names. Figure 2 presents the topic of indication for an herb. For each opinion, references about indications and methods for preparation are given in parenthesis. In this academic year, applications of an herb in multiple countries were considered. For precaution/toxicity and additional information, students should contribute their opinions with references to support their opinions. A list of references is shown in the topic of references (Figure 3).

From the results, the Figure 1 presents herb names in several languages. For Thai, the detail of locations from regions to district can be applied while only the level of country for the other languages. Due to relation between a language and a location is many-to-many, i.e, one location may have several languages and one language may used in several places, students should contribute opinions that they believe to be true. For example, a name is used in India but they do not distinguish between Tamil and Hindi.

For this case, the location is contributed while the language may be omitted. In the topic of indication (Figure 2), a part used, medicinal usages and method for preparation, were given. The citations were given in parentheses. The list of references for information of the herb in Figure 3 indicated that the student used references in Thai.

Thai Name	: ติ้วขาว
English Name	: -
Science Name	: *Cratoxylum formosum* (Jack) Dyer
Family Name	: GUTTIFERAE

Please contribute names of this herb in your local language. If possible, please contribute the location where the herb is called. Click VOTE for voting the names in a list OR Click +Contribute Other Names for the new name. **If the + does not appear, This indicates that you are not the member, please click** Go to Member Registration

Other Thai Name   Show all (18) | ◉ Previous 1 - 18 Next ◉

	Herb Name	Local Area Language and Method for Language	Vote Score
VOTE	ติ้วส้ม	นครราชสีมา (Thai, Character)	3
VOTE	แต้วหอม	พิษณุโลก (Thai, Character)	2
VOTE	ไม้ติ้ว	(Laos, Character)	2
VOTE	thành nganh đẹp	(Vietnamese, Romanization)	2
VOTE	越南黄牛木 yue nan huang niu mu	(Chinese, Mandarin, Character+Translit. to English)	2
VOTE	Kemutul	Indonesia (, Transliteration to English)	2
VOTE	Salinggogon	Philippines (, Transliteration to English)	2
VOTE	ติ้วขน	ภาคกลาง (Thai, Character)	1
VOTE	ติ้วขาว	กรุงเทพมหานคร (Thai, Character)	1
VOTE	เตา	เลย (Thai, Character)	1
VOTE	ขี้ติ้ว	(Thai, Character)	1
VOTE	ติ้วเหลือง	(Thai, Character)	1

Fig. 1. Sharing multi-lingual herb name in the KUIHerbRx2014

KUIHerb / Categories by Part-used / ยาง / **ติ้วขาว**

Herb Name : ติ้วขาว - *Cratoxylum formosum* (Jack) Dyer

| Herb Images | Characteristic | Herb Name | Indication | Precaution/Toxic | Extra |
| Information | References |

Please contribute your opinions about part used, indications on both folk and modern medicine and methods for preparation. Click VOTE for voting the opinions in a list OR Click +Contribute your opinions for the medicinal uses. **If the + does not appear, This indicates that you are not the member, please click** Go to Member Registration

Properties   Show all (9) | ◉ Previous 1 - 9 Next ◉

	Part-used	Indication	Method of Preparation	Vote Score
VOTE	ยาง	แก้สันเท้าแตก	ใช้ทารอยแตกของสันเท้า	2
VOTE	ใบ	แก้ปวดท้อง แก้โรคผิวหนัง เป็นยาระบาย		1
VOTE	เปลือกต้น	แก้โรคผิวหนัง		1
VOTE	ยอด	เป็นยาระบาย		1
VOTE	ยาง	รักษาแผล		1
VOTE	ยอด	Antioxidant [5]		1
VOTE	ราก	แก้ปัสสาวะขัด [3]	ผสมกับหัวแห้วหมูและรากปลาไหลเผือก ต้มน้ำดื่มวันละ 3 ครั้ง	1
VOTE	เปลือกต้น	แก้ธาตุพิการ [2]	ใช้ส่วนน้ำต้มเปลือกต้น	1
VOTE	ราก	แก้ปวดท้อง [2]		1

Fig. 2. Sharing a set of indications in the KUIHerbRx2014

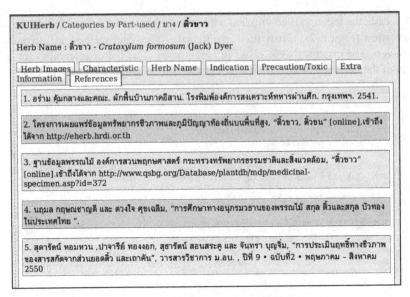

Fig. 3. Sharing a list of references in the KUIHerbRx2014

5.2   Statistics of Contributed Information from Students

Two patterns of statistics are shown in Table 1, i.e., the total opinions and the total herbs. The total opinion (Opinion) is the numbers of opinions contributed from the students for each topic. The total herb (Total Herb) is the numbers of herbs that students provide information for each topic. The result of top 10 herb names grouped by language, is shown in Table 2. Note that one language may be used by several countries. The several dialects of Chinese are combined. The Table 3 presents distributions of opinions by method of assigning languages to opinions.

From the results, some observations can be made. Students can collaborative work and contribute knowledge on all topics. From Table 1, the topic of herb name was the most contributed knowledge. In term of quantitative assessment, several opinions were not complete and/or not correct. Due to the fact that pharmacy students do not have strong background in linguistics, most pharmacy students did not distinguish between different Chinese dialects and transliterations. For indications, the number of contributions is satisfied. However, a few opinions are for applications of herbs in other countries. The contributions in topics of toxicity/precaution and additional information should be more given. Although contribution of images was optional, a set of images were also given. Several references in herbal medicine had been suggested. However, most references are written in Thai and drawn from the Internet. The references in journals which are written in English should be more suggested. Herb names in top 10 languages are listed in Table 2. Besides Thai and English, languages which are commonly used in the Southeast Asian countries, e.g., Chinese, Malay and Vietnamese are also reported. Furthermore, languages from India, origin of Ayurvedic medicine, e.g., Tamil and Hindi, are also important. From Table 3, the method of assigning languages is character. Although students cannot read and pronounce them correctly, these terms are valuable to use as keywords to find herbal information.

Table 1. Distributions of contributed information from students

Topic	Opinion	Total Herb
Local and Multi-lingual Name	3233	371
Medicinal Usage	2053	344
Precaution/Toxicity	175	118
Additional Information	371	219
Reference	1028	312
Image	172	95

Table 2. Distributions of herb names by language (top 10)

Language	Opinion
Thai	1301
English	329
Chinese	248
Malay	178
Vietnamese	108
Japanese	106
French	103
Tamil	75
German	71
Hindi	61

Table 3. Distributions of herb names by method of assigning languages

Method of Assigning Languages	Opinion
Character	2325
Transliteration to English	281
Romanization	256
Not Avaliable	180
Character + Transliteration to English	76
Transliteration to Thai	57
Character + Romanization	32
Character + Transliteration to Thai	24

6   Conclusion and Future Work

In this work, the KUIHerbRx2014, a modified version of the KUIHerb, was used as a Web-based supplement learning tool for multi-lingual and multi-cultural herbal medicine. Information of medicinal herbs in several regions can be distributed and exchanged among students. Several topics were assigned to students, e.g., local and multi-lingual herb names, indications, precaution/toxicity, additional information and references. In the topic of herb name, location, a set of languages and methods of assigning languages, were designed. Activities of collecting, contributing new evidence-based opinions or vote to exist opinions, and providing comments to the system, enhanced skill in herbal medicine. Skill in searching information using traditional method such as books or modern technology such as the Internet, was improved. With the assessment, the results show that the KUIHerb2014 is the useful collaborative learning tool for multi-lingual and multi-cultural herbal medicine. Some problems were found on method of assigning languages to herb names, especially on languages with several dialects (e.g., Chinese language). More time should be spent on teaching for these topics. These will be implemented for our future work.

Acknowledgments. This work was supported in part by the Research and Development Institute, Silpakorn University via research grant SURDI 53/01/12 as well as the National Electronics and Computer Technology Center (NECTEC) via research grant NT-B-22-MA-17-50-14.

References

1. Dvorkin, L., Gardiner, P., Whelan, J.S.: Herbal medicine course within pharmacy curriculum. Journal of Herbal Pharmacotherapy 4, 47–58 (2004)
2. Murtaza, G., Azhar, S., Noreen, S., Khan, S.A., Khan, A., Nasir, B., Mumtaz, A., Zaman, M., Rehman, M.S.U.: An evaluation of pakistani pharmacy students' knowledge of herbal medicines in pakistan. African Journal of Pharmacy and Pharmacology 6, 221–224 (2012)
3. Lin, K.J.: Building web 2.0. IEEE Computer 40, 101–102 (2007)
4. Gruber, T.: Collective knowledge systems: Where the solcial web meets the semantic web. Web Semantics: Science, Services and Agents on the World Wide Web 6, 4–13 (2007)
5. Lertnattee, V., Robkob, K., Sornlertlamvanich, V.: Collaborative platform for multicultural herbal information creation. In: Proceedings of the 2009 International Workshop on Intercultural Collaboration, IWIC 2009, pp. 13–22. ACM, New York (2009)
6. LaPolla, R.J.: Language contact and language change in the history of the sinitic languages. Procedia - Social and Behavioral Sciences 2, 34 (2010)
7. Trimethasil, W., Tiyaworanant, S., Suriyakai, S., Wattananamkul, V., Chawivat, C.: Database of traditional chinese crude drugs widely used in thailand. Journal of Thai Traditional and Alternative Medicine 7, 34 (2009)
8. Matthews, S., Xu, H., Yip, V.: Passive and unaccusative in the jieyang dialect of chaozhou. Journal of East Asian Linguistics 14, 267–298 (2005)

Calligraphy Character Synthesis from Small Sample Set

Kai Yu and Zhenming Yuan

School of Information Science and Engineering, Hangzhou Normal University, China
{yk,zmyuan}@hznu.edu.cn

Abstract.A novel approach to synthesize calligraphy characters is presented in this paper. Only a small set of calligraphy characters written by the specific calligrapher is needed. A robust polygon based radical and stroke extraction method is introduced, which can generate strokes and radicals preciselywith a few manually marked pixels. A new radical and stroke selection method called component selection algorithm is described, which can decide whether to use radicals or strokes and can find out the most suitable ones from the candidate radicals and strokes.After putting the radicals and strokes together and form the calligraphy character, the style difference among them must be minimized. In order to do this better, a new way to adjust the stroke widths is presented. A sample set containing only 30 selected calligraphy characters are used to synthesize new calligraphy characters. The results show that our approach works effectively.

Keywords: calligraphy character synthesis, component selection algorithm, small sample set.

1   Introduction

Chinese calligraphy is an important and inseparable part of human cultural heritages. Its delicate aesthetic effects are generally considered to be unique among all calligraphic arts.

The historical Chinese calligraphic works arevaluable parts of Chinese cultural heritage. In the China Academic Digital Associative Library (CADAL), lots of famous ancientcalligraphic works are digitized. However, for some ancient calligraphers, only tens of calligraphic characters are survived till now. Many characters which are needed in the tablet generation are missing. Therefore, a method to synthesize calligraphic characters in a specified style with a small set of sample calligraphic characters is a necessity in order to generate calligraphy tablets.

A novel approach is proposed in this paper to synthesize calligraphy characters in a specific style with only tens of sample calligraphy characters. The strokes and radicals are extracted with a new polygon based extraction method. A new radical and stroke comparison and selection method called component selection algorithm is presented to find out the most proper components. Finally, these components are adjusted and put together to form the new calligraphy character.

K. Tuamsuk et al. (Eds.): ICADL 2014, LNCS 8839, pp. 379–384, 2014.
© Springer International Publishing Switzerland 2014

2   Related Works

Lots of researches on Chinese calligraphy appeared in the last few years, including calligraphy character retrieval [1] and recognition [2], calligraphy synthesis[3-6], etc.

Xu [3] used a hairy brush model to synthesize calligraphy characters. A synthesis approach was proposed with a six-level hierarchical model, which could produce Chinese calligraphic characters in a variety of styles.Some years later, an intelligent system for Chinese calligraphy[6] was proposed which could derive parameters in an interactive way and judge the beauty of calligraphy.With these methods, calligraphy characters that seemed to be written by human beings could be produced, but the style cannot be decided.

A style consistency calligraphy synthesis system [4] was presented in 2009. It could synthesize calligraphy characters in a specific style. Xia [5] introduced an ontology based model to synthesize calligraphy characters. For these methods, a large number of sample calligraphy characters were needed. However, for many ancient famous calligraphers, only a few calligraphy characters preserved up to now. Thus, the existed method may not work effectively.

3   Calligraphy Character Synthesis from Small Sample Set

The whole system contains two parts. One is the preparation part and the other is the synthesis part.The first part is the preparation part. The strokes and radicals will be extracted from the sample characters and the style features will be collected, too. The second part is the synthesis part. The character to be synthesized will be extracted and the most suitable components, including radicals and strokes, will be selected. The components are then adjusted and the new character is formed.

3.1   Synthesis Preparation

In calligraphy characters, the structures are very complex. Traditional minimum bounding box can only find out separate radicals, as shown in the left of Figure 1, but cannot find out the radicals (the red part) shown in the right of Figure 1.

In most cases, the radicals are crossed over or even connected together. It is very difficult to extract automatically with a high precision. A polygon-based character extraction is introduced.

Fig. 1. Different radicals in calligraphy characters

Polygon Extraction

Polygon is composed by a certain number of connected lines, which can form a cycle. Thus, polygon can be represented as an ordered list of pixels.

When the turning pixels are pointed out, we only need to connect them one by one, and a polygon can be found. However, the user may click a pixel which is slice difference from the accurate point. It may cause a mistake in character extraction.

To make the polygon extraction more robust, the most proper pixel in the small neighborhood area of the specified pixel is found out.

If a small part of a line crosses a solid part of a stroke, one of the terminal points is probably in a wrong place. Thus, the terminal points need to be corrected. In most cases, only one terminal point must be moved.

Stroke or Radical Representation

The solid area in the polygon found above is just a component which can be a radical or a stroke. It is part of a calligraphy character. The positions and relative sizes of the components are very important in Chinese calligraphy characters. The same stroke in different part in a character will be very different, and what's more, the same stroke in the same part with different relative sizes may still be different in shape.

To represent the component, the position and relative size must be record. A simple way is finding the minimum bounding box of the component, and recording the left-top point and right-bottom point of the bounding box.

3.2   Calligraphy Character Synthesis

To synthesize a calligraphy character, the character in print style is used as the template. It is extracted into radicals and strokes firstly, and then the most proper radicals and strokes are selected for each component. Finally, they are put together and form the new calligraphy character.

The polygon based radical and stroke extraction method can also be used in component extraction for printed characters.

Components Selection

To synthesize a calligraphy character, choosing the proper components including strokes and radicals is one of the most important tasks.

To make the synthesis easier, we try to find out the proper radicals firstly. If the proper one cannot be found, we will find the strokes which form the radicals. The component selection algorithm is designed to touch the target. It contains three steps. The first is component comparison, which can find out the most similar component. The second is radical decision, which is deciding where to use radicals or strokes. The last is components global selection.

The most proper component is the component whose positions and relative sizes fit the character best. It is determined by many factors.

The calligraphy styles for different calligraphers are different, and for the same calligrapher, the style may change with increasing age. However, sometimes, different calligraphers may have similar styles because of the disciple.

Thus, a two-stage comparison is needed. In the first stage, the positions, relative sizes, calligraphers and the disciple is considered, and a candidate radical set is found out for each radical. In the second stage, the difference between radicals in the same character is considered, including the source of the radicals, the difference in stroke width, and the age when the calligrapher wrote the works.

When the most proper radical is found out, we must decide whether to use the found radical or extract the radical into strokes and found out the most proper strokes. When the first stage different $Diff_1$ is larger than a threshold, it is dropped and the extracted strokes are used.

In component comparison, the style difference among different radicals and strokes is not considered. When synthesizing a calligraphy character with different radicals and strokes, the style difference must be very small. An average style feature is calculated and considered as the style feature of the combined calligraphy character. Thus, we want to minimize $D = \Sigma\, Diff(x_i, y_i)$.

$Diff(x_i, y_j)$ is the difference between the style feature of component x and the average style feature of the combined calligraphy character. It is defined as follows:

$$Diff(x, y) = p \cdot DAuthor(x, y) + q \cdot DDisciple(x, y) + r \cdot DAge(x, y) + s \cdot DFeature(x, y) \tag{1}$$

where $DAuthor(x,y)$ is 0 when x and y are written by the same author, and it is 1 otherwise. $DDisciple(x,y)$ is between 0 and 1 which represent the relationship between the two authors. $DAge(x,y)$ is the age difference when the x and y are written by the same author, and its value is 100 if $DAuthor(x,y)$ is 1.

$DFeature(x,y)$ is the style features difference of the two calligraphy characters. It is a combination of the difference in many features, such as the real size of the characters, the average stroke widths of the radicals, the stroke densities of the characters and so on. Here the stroke density is one of the important factors. Usually, the character part with large stroke density will have thinner strokes. Thus, there's a negative relationship between the stroke widths and the stroke densities.

Component selection algorithm

The component selection algorithm is proposed with the above key steps. The input of the algorithm is the hierarchical components needed to synthesize a calligraphy character.The output is the selected components which can used to compose the calligraphy character directly. The steps are as follows:

1. For each component, find out the candidate ones with the components comparison method.
2. For each candidate components, the first stage comparison is operated and the different ones are removed.
3. For each component, if there's no candidate, extract it and redo step 1 for the extracted components.
4. Select most proper ones with the global component selection method.

Strokes and Radicals Combination and Character Generation

When the strokes and radicals are prepared, they are to be combined together and the calligraphy characters are formed.   Firstly, the strokes and radicals are put on the proper positions with the proper sizes. Then the stroke widths are adjusted. Thus, the new calligraphy character is generated.

The original positions and sizes of the strokes and radicals chosen are usually slightly different from the ones in the characters to be synthesized.The chosen strokes will be deformed to fit their areas in the characters to be synthesized.

The stroke widths of character components from different calligraphy characters may be very different. This may be worse when the components are scaled in different rates. It can be done with erosion and dilation operations in mathematical morphology. However, for some special strokes, such as long *Heng*(the horizontal curve) and *Shu*(the vertical curve), it may cause unscaled deformation on the ends of the strokes. To avoid this situation, an improved method will be used on such strokes.

Such stroke will be zoomed in or out to get a suitable stroke width. Then the zoomed stroke will be departed in to several parts, and the parts in the middle will be strengthened to get a new stroke. The whole process is shown in Figure 2. The first image shows the original stroke, whose stroke width need to be increased.The second one shows the segmentation result, and the last shows the stroke width adjust result.

Fig. 2. The whole process of the improved stroke width adjustment

4   Experiments and Discussion

A small set of 30 calligraphy characters from *Zhenqing Yan*, a famous calligrapher in *Tang* Dynasty (about 1300 years ago), were used as the learning sets. These calligraphy characters contained all the five basic strokes and some common used composed strokes. It is used to synthesize some calligraphy characters and compared them with the ones *Yan* really written. The result is shown in Figure 3.

Synthesized characters with small sample sets	程	位	工	吴
Synthesized characterswith large sample sets	程	位	工	吴
Characters written by *Yan Zhenqing*	程	位	工	吴

Fig. 3. Comparison of the synthesized calligraphy character and the original ones

The synthesis result is a little different from the original ones because that the strokes and radicals in the calligraphy characters were not in the sample set. Thus, some other components are used to form the calligraphy character.However, these calligraphy characters are all in *Zhenqing Yan*'s style.

Figure 4 shows some more synthesis samples. The last three characters are in simplified Chinese which are impossible to be written by *Yan*.

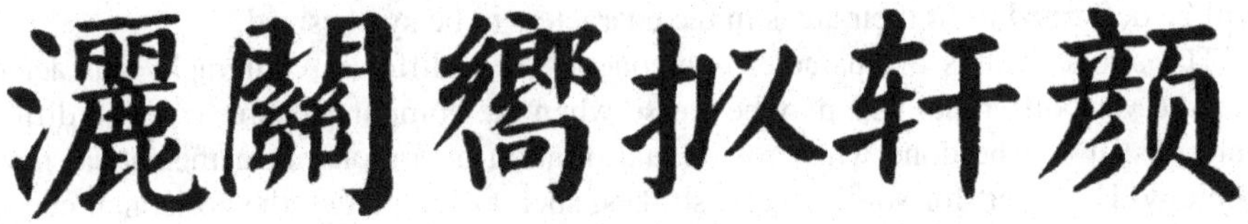

Fig. 4. Some more synthesis results

5   Conclusion

In this paper, a novel approach is proposed to synthesize calligraphy characters in a specific style. Compared with the methods presented before, only a small collection of sample characters are needed. Experiments show that the proposed approach can synthesize style-consistent calligraphy characters.

References

1. Lu, W., Wu, J., Wei, B., Zhuang, Y.: Efficient Shape Matching for Chinese Calligraphic Character Retrieval. Journal of Zhejiang University - Science C 12(11), 873–884 (2011)
2. Yu, K., Wu, J., Zhuang, Y.: Skeleton-Based Recognition of Chinese Calligraphic Character Image. In: Huang, Y.-M.R., Xu, C., Cheng, K.-S., Yang, J.-F.K., Swamy, M.N.S., Li, S., Ding, J.-W. (eds.) PCM 2008. LNCS, vol. 5353, pp. 228–237. Springer, Heidelberg (2008)
3. Xu, S., Lau, F.C., Cheung, W.K., Pan, Y.: Automatic Generation of Artistic Chinese Calligraphy. IEEE Intelligent Systems 20(3), 32–39 (2005)
4. Yu, K., Wu, J., Zhuang, Y.: Style-Consistency Calligraphy Synthesis Systemin Digital Library. In: 9th ACM/IEEE-CS Joint Conference on Digital Libraries, pp. 145–152. ACM Press, New York (2009)
5. Xia, Y., Wu, J., Gao, P., et al.: Ontology-based model for Chinese Calligraphy Synthesis. Computer Graphics Forum 32(7), 11–20 (2013)
6. Xu, S., Jiang, H., Lau, F.C., Pan, Y.: An Intelligent system for Chinese Calligraphy. In: The 22nd Conference on Association for the Advancement of Artificial Intelligence, pp. 1578–1583. AAAI, New York (2007)
7. Lu, W., Zhuang, Y., Wu, J.: Discovering Calligraphy Style Relationships by Supervised Learning Weighted Random Walk Model. Multimedia Syst. 15(4), 221–242 (2009)

Institutional Repositories in Thai Universities

Namtip Wipawin [1] and Aphaporn Wanna [2]

[1] Department of Information Science, School of Liberal Arts,
Sukhothai Thammathirat Open University, Thailand
namtip.wip@stou.ac.th, nwipawin@gmail.com
[2] Department of Information Science,
Phetchabun Rajabhat University.
Information Science, Department of Information Science,
School of Liberal Arts,
Sukhothai Thammathirat Open University, Thailand
aphaprn@gmail.com

Abstract. Institutional Repositories(IR) are infrastructures that ensure accessibility, stability and reliability of research data which requires policies, standards, and data management plan to deposit research data. The scholarly community needs reliable long-term access to research data. The data curation is important for the research community to develop a strategy for long term-use throughout its lifecycle, from creation, storage and dissemination to the time when it is archive. This paper describes an overview of the institutional repositories in Thai universities regarding the issues of the responsible units, the open access policy, the typology of repositories, the digital repositories structure, the catalog description, the format of research output, and the web portal. It also suggests the schemes for facilitating discovery and re-use of research data such as the national research data service and the registry of research data repositories.

Keywords: institutional repositories, research data, Thai universities.

1   Introduction

Many university libraries and research centers concern more about building Institutional Repositories (IR) to allow permanent access to research data. Institutional Repository (IR) or Research Data Repository (RDR) nowadays has become an infrastructure for research data sharing by connecting with the registry of research data repositories (re3data.org). The German Research Foundation (DFG) funded the re3data.org and it is a joint project of the Karlsruhe Institute of Technology (KIT), the German Research Centre for Geosciences (GFZ) and the Berlin School of Library and Information Science at the Humboldt Universität zu Berlin. In June 2014, there were more than 650 repositories registered at re3data.org. From the study of the European Commission in 2010 had a vision of how research data will be handled in 2030.They mentioned that the researchers would be able to find access and process the data they need by depositing their data in reliable

K. Tuamsuk et al. (Eds.): ICADL 2014, LNCS 8839, pp. 385–392, 2014.

repositories working based on international standards (High Level Expert Group on Scientific Data, 2010).

The IR or RDR needs the policy, metadata standards, quality and technical standards, general information, legal aspects and services. The report of "Science as an open enterprise" published in 2012 by the Royal Society, asked scientists to make their data accessible and usable in the sense of an "intelligent openness": "Where data justify it, scientists should make them available in an appropriate data repository." (The Royal Society, 2012). The European Commission demands from member states that they pass policies to ensure that "research data that result from publicly funded research become publicly accessible, usable and re-usable through digital e-infrastructures." (European Commission, 2012). Therefore, the research data management is an important issue in OECD member countries, the USA and cross-national initiatives to provide a national infrastructure to co-ordinate access to research output by IR. IRs in Thailand also need to be analyzed the missing components for future development.

Digital libraries (DL) are more popular than Institutional Repositories (IR) in Thai universities; even both are about collecting digital contents for archiving. IRs in the universities act as digital archives of the intellectual products or the storage of knowledge assets of the institutions as well as gateways to provide access to research data. The popular terms used for IR in Thailand are Intellectual Repository (IR) and Knowledge Bank (KB). Institutions such as the university or research organizations run most IRs. On university level, the scope of IR contents are multidisciplinary. An example of an institutional repository in Thailand is the Thai Library Integrated System or ThaiLIS. The IR consists of formally organized and managed collections of digital contents generated by faculty, staff, and students at an institution. It comprises use of pre-print and post-print of papers, thesis and dissertations, research reports, conference papers, teaching materials, and multimedia objects. The benefits of IRs are: it showcases research output of an institution, preserves and disseminates academic contents, provides access to unpublished research of faculty, staff, and students and ensures long term document availability through archiving.

Since 2005, Chulalongkorn University had implemented IRs by using the Thai version of DSpace was in cooperation with faculties in the Department of Computer Science. Yoowang (2012) noted 11 IRs were established in state and private universities (Wachiraporn Klungthanaboon 2013). The seminar on "Data Curation in Thai Institutional Repositories" in 22-23 May 2014 at Sukhothai Thammathirat University with 70 participants from libraries, research centers and computer centers who had agreed to deposit research data in IRs in Thai universities and identified the need to develop IR working group for cooperation. Since the development of IRs in Thailand, the research questions are how many IRs in Thai universities and what are the important issues to develop IRs.

The objectives of this study are to survey the IRs in Thailand and to analyze the IRs of Thai universities regarding the issues of the responsible units, the open access policy, the typology of repositories, the digital repositories structure, the catalog description, the format of research output, and the web portal.

2   Methodology

The study began with document research from university libraries websites, documentations and reports which mainly focused on institutional repositories in Thailand covering universities, academic institutions and research organizations by exploring 118 university libraries websites and 11 research databases in Thailand. The samples were 9 IRs in the directory of academic open access repositories (OpenDOAR), 23 IRs in the DSpace User Registry and 21 academic research databases in Thailand. Content analysis was used as a research methodology.

3   Findings

From 118 university libraries websites in Thailand, all of them provide access to bibliographic records of research data in the library databases. There are 43 online research databases available (which are 22 accessible IRs and 21 research databases providing abstracts and/or full-texts of research data). According to OpenDOAR (Directory of Open Access Repositories), there are only nine repositories in Thailand of different categories like government, disciplinary and institutional), 23 institutional repositories in the DSpace User Registry and 21 academic research databases in Thailand (comprise of 11 Thai research organizations, and 10 Thai universities). Most IR(s) were established for the purpose of electronic thesis so that the users can use the intellectual output of the institutions.

Table 1. Accessible IRs in Thailand according to OpenDOAR

No.	Name of IR	Software	Size	Policy	Protocol	URL
1	KKU IR	DSpace	4,122	-	OAI-PMH	http://kkuir.kku.ac.th/dspace/
2	PSU KB	DSpace	7,376	-	OAI-PMH	http://kb.psu.ac.th/psukb/
3	AGRIS	DSpace	3,373	-	OAI-PMH	http://anchan.lib.ku.ac.th/agnet/
4	SUT IR	DSpace	3,842	-	-	http://sutir.sut.ac.th:8080/sutir/
5	RMUTP IR	DSpace	877	-	-	http://repository.rmutp.ac.th/
6	RMUTS IR	DSpace	145	-	-	http://61.47.35.41:8181/ir_plus/
7	SSRU IR	DSpace	765	-	-	http://www.ssruir.ssru.ac.th/
8	KIDS-D	DSpace	2.115	-	-	http://kids-d.swu.ac.th/dspace/
9	NSTDA	DSpace	2,556	-	-	http://www.nstda.or.th/thairesearch/

(Source: http://www.opendoar.org/find.php)

From Table 1, there are 9 accessible IRs according to the directory of open access repositories(OpenDOAR), all of them are using DSpace software with no open access policy. Only 3 IRs in university libraries are using the OAI-PMH protocol (the Open Archives Initiative Protocol for Metadata Harvesting). The highest number of IR is PSU Knowledge Bank which is a digital repository created to allow Prince of Songkla University (PSU) members to self archive their works in full or partial text format.

All copyrights remain with the author and/or their publisher. All submitted works will be accessible via internet worldwide. The system is able to archive various types of files, as well as the bibliographic data. The highest number of IRs size is 7,376 records of Prince of Songkla university Knowledge Bank: PSU KB, followed by Intellectual Repository of KhonKaen University: KKU IR (4,122 records)

Table 2. Accessible IRs in Thailand according to DSpace User Registry

No.	Institutions	Typology	Type	Format	Meta data	URL
1	AIT	Project	VL	pdf	-	http://kids-d.swu.ac.th/dspace/
2	CU IR	Multidis.	Lib	pdf	DC	http://cuir.car.chula.ac.th/
3	KU CE	Multidis.	VL	pdf	-	http://naist.cpe.ku.ac.th/projectdoc/main.jsp
4	KKU IR	Multidis.	Lib	pdf	DC	http://kkuir.kku.ac.th/dspace/register
5	PSU KB	Multidis.	Lib	pdf	DC	http://kb.psu.ac.th/psukb/
6	SUT KB	Multidis.	Lib	pdf	DC	http://sutir.sut.ac.th:8080/sutir/
7	SPU KB	Multidis.	Lib	pdf	DC	http://dllibrary.spu.ac.th:8080/dspace/
8	SIU KB	Multidis.	Lib	pdf	DC	http://dspace.siu.ac.th/
9	SSRU KB	Multidis.	Lib	pdf	DC	http://www.ssruir.ssru.ac.th/
10	NIDA IR	Project	Lib	pdf	DC	http://repository.nida.ac.th/
11	TU DC	Multidis. Project	Lib	pdf	DC	http://beyond.library.tu.ac.th/cdm/h ttp://203.131.219.171/
12	TSU KB	Multidis.	Lib	pdf	DC	http://kb.tsu.ac.th/jspui/
13	RMUTP	Multidis.	Lib	pdf	DC	http://repository.rmutp.ac.th/
14	RMUTS	Multidis.	Lib	pdf	DC	http://61.47.35.41:8181/ir_plus/
15	RMUTT	Multidis.	Lib	pdf	DC	http://www.repository.rmutt.ac.th/
16	AGRIS	Discipl.	Lib	pdf	DC	http://anchan.lib.ku.ac.th/agnet/
17	QSNICH	Discipl.	VL	pdf	DC	http://dlibrary.childrenhospital.go.th/
18	HSRI	Discipl.	VL	pdf	DC	http://kb.hsri.or.th/dspace/handle/1 1228/1
19	MU ARMS	Project	Lib	pdf	DC	http://www.arms.mahidol.ac.th/
20	Breast feeding	Project	Lib	pdf	DC	http://breastfeedinglib.saiyairak.com/
21	Thai Airways	Discipl.	VL	-	-	N/A
22	Puparn	Project	VL	pdf	-	http://158.108.8.206:8080/pikmas
23	STKS	Multidis.	Lib	pdf	-	http://stks.or.th/nstdair

(Typology: Discipl.=Disciplinary, Multidis.= Multidisciplinary, Type: Lib= Library, RC= Research center,V=Virtual Library, DC= Dublin Core (Source: http://www.dspace.org/)

From Table 2, there are 23 IRs registered in DSpace User Registry but only 22 are accessible IRs, most of them are academic institutions with the typology of the multidisciplinary institutional repositories, followed by disciplinary IRs and projects, using Dublin Core(DC) metadata and linking to pdf file format. Chulalongkorn University Intellectual Repository (CUIR) is the first IR in Thailand, which most contents are theses (36,251 records).

Table 3. Research Databases in Thai Research Organizations (with abstract and/or full-text)

No.	Organization	Type	S/W	URL
1	TNRR	RC	MySQL	http://www.tnrr.in.th/2557/?page=search
2	TRF	RC	MySQL	http://elibrary.trf.or.th/search_basic.asp
3	TDRI	RC	PHP	http://tdri.or.th/research/
4	Labor	RC	PHP	http://research.mol.go.th/2013/
5	Health	RC	DSpace	http://kb.hsri.or.th/dspace/handle/11228/1
6	Education	RC	Dataface	http://www.thaiedresearch.org/thaied/
7	Southern Provinces	RC	PHP	http://soreda.oas.psu.ac.th/
8	Parliament	RC	HTML	http://library2.parliament.go.th/ebook/e_research.html
9	Moral	RC	PHP	http://www.moralcenter.or.th/research.php
10	Juvenile Protection	RC	PHP	http://www2.djop.moj.go.th/document/vijai
11	WHO	RC	DSpace	http://whothailand.healthrepository.org/

(Type: RC= Research Center)

From Table 3, there are 11 Research Databases in Thai Research Organizations (with abstract and/or full-text). All of them are databases in the research organizations; mostly use customized databases, only 2 organizations use DSpace software. TNRR or Thai National Research Repository , the research database of the National Research Council of Thailand was a member of Datacite in 2013 which can assign the Digital Object Identifier(DOI) for research data in Thailand.Thai National Research Repository (TNRR) is an initiative to provide access to research output and academic work created by scholars in government offices, universities, and research institutes. The awareness for IR policy and the management and dissemination of national research output should be aligned with national research master plans. The copyright policy needs to be discussed before registering DOI.

Table 4. Research Databases in Thai Universities (with abstract and/or full-text)

No.	Org.	Type	S/W	URL
1	ThaiLIS	Lib.	MySQL	http://dcms.thailis.or.th/tdc/
2	CMU	Lib.	PHP	http://library.cmu.ac.th/digital_collection/eresearch/
3	MSU	RC Lib.	ULIBM	http://www.research.msu.ac.th/rds/ http://www.library.msu.ac.th/web/index.php?forcehpmode=advsearch
4	MU	Lib	LIS	http://www.li.mahidol.ac.th/e-thesis/list-e-thesis.php
5	RU	Lib	eBridge	http://dcms.lib.ru.ac.th/main.nsp?view=DCMS
6	SU	Lib	MySQL	http://www.thapra.lib.su.ac.th/thesis/
7	UTCC	Lib	MySQL	http://library.utcc.ac.th/onlinethesis/default.asp
8	MCU	Lib	ULIBM	http://www.mcu.ac.th/site/thesiscontent.php
9	MJU	Lib	ULIBM	http://www.archives.mju.ac.th/mjuknowledgebank/
10	Nurse	Lib	PHP	http://www.lib.ns.mahidol.ac.th/nsr2e.html

(Type: Lib= Library, RC= Research Center)

From Table 4, there are 10 Research Databases in Thai Universities (with abstract and/or full-text), all of them use customized databases, ThaiLIS is Thai Library Integrated System Consortium of digital collection, 79 universities in Thailand participate in this consortium.

4   Conclusion and Discussion

Some issues associated with IR projects in Thai universities are discussed and recommended for future development of research data curation for the research community by using data management lifecycle. From this study, it was found that the missing components of IRs in Thai universities are policies, quality and technical standards, general information, and legal aspects. With the related findings of Wichada Sukantarat (2008) that the growing demand for digital content in Thailand requires long-range planning, financial support from the government, collaboration among libraries and consortia, and development of software utilities and programs. Only two components of metadata standards and services are available in all Thai IRs.

The well-known research database in Thai universities is TDC (Thai Digital Collection) in ThaiLIS (Thailand Library Integrated System) run by the Department of University's Affairs and Thai Library Integrated System Project. Most research data in Thai IRs are in the university libraries. The typology of repositories is a multidisciplinary institutional repositories. There are no open access policy as well as data management plan, therefore the digital repository structure depends on the software structure. DSpace is the most popular open source IR software in Thai universities. The catalog description is classified by Dublin Core (DC) metadata with links to abstract and full-text in pdf files. Most web portal of IRs in Thailand still use URL but not the permanent identifier such as Digital Object Identifier (DOI). The recommendations for this study are setting up the IR working group for the data sharing policy in the IR plan to develop research data services in the libraries or universities, and the need to register IR webs in the registry of research data repositories (re3data.org) for easy access. Also, OAI-PMH Protocol and standards in one stop service of Thai Research Data are recommended to help users access to information from one web portal.

To preserve and ensure long-term accessibility to digital research output in IRs, the supports from internal and external institutions are needed. Successful IRs will increase effectiveness and efficiency of scholarly communication and academic information sharing. Clear communication and policies from relevant administrative offices will enhance better understandings and increase IR contribution and usage. Therefore, academics and relevant institutions can optimize benefits from compliant, well-structured, and accessible research works in IRs. Apart from the depositing process and copyright issues, institutions should pay more attention to digital preservation issues. The cumulative digital materials in IRs raise concerns about digital preservation strategies across the higher educational sectors. (Wachiraporn Klungthanaboon and others 2012) The study of Wachiraporn Klungthanaboon (2013) also identified the IRs challenges in Thailand relate to content recruitment, low awareness, sustainable support, copyright clarification, lack of mandate policies, sustainable support from senior administrators, and contributors' reluctance to participate due to lack of clarification of what IRs implementation means. There should be more concern with the direction of Open Access (OA) policies and journal publishers' OA policies, which also influence IRs development in Thailand.

From the comparatively analyze the institutional repositories (IR) of Thai and foreign universities of Watcharee Petwong and Kulthida Tuamsuk (2010) found that most of the IR responsible units of Thai and foreign universities were the university's libraries. The recommendations for IR policies and users'guides can support long-term digital preservation plan. Data curation, which is the new term used in Thailand, is needed to be in the digital preservation plan of the university libraries expecially preserving and disseminating research data as an important asset of the university. The scholarly community needs reliable long-term access to research data. Therefore, IRs are infrastructures that ensure accessibility, stability and reliability of research data which requires policies, standards, and data management plan to deposit research data.

References

1. Data Curation in Thai Institutional Repositories, http://libarts.stou.ac.th/page/Showdata.aspx?PageId=77957&Datatype=2
2. Doctoral Theses Research Data, http://lib.hku.hk/etd2013/presentation/Maxi-ETD-20130925.pdf
3. DSpace User Registry, http://registry.duraspace.org/registry/dspace
4. European Commission, Commission Recommendation on access to and preservation of scientific information. C(2012) 4890 final, http://ec.europa.eu/research/sciencesociety/document_library/pdf_06/recommendation-access-and-preservation-scientificinformation_en.pdf
5. High Level Expert Group on Scientific Data. Riding the wave. How Europe can gain from the rising tide of scientific data, http://cordis.europa.eu/fp7/ict/einfrastructure/docs/hlg-sdi-report.pdf
6. Making Research Data Repositories Visible: The re3data.org Registry, https://peerj.com/preprints/21v1.pdf
7. OpenDOAR, http://www.opendoar.org/find.php
8. Organization for Economic Co-operation and Development. Principles and Guidelines for Access to Research Data from Public Funding (p. 24). Paris, Principles and Guidelines for Access to Research Data from Public Funding (2007).
9. Pryor, G.: Managing research data. Facet Publishing, London (2012)
10. Registry of Research Data Repository, http://www.re3data.org/tag/research-data-repositories/
11. Sukul, A., et al.: Complex legislative repository- Parliament of Thailand:development of mobile access, http://conference.ifla.org/past-wlic/2012/103-sukul-en.pdf
12. ThaiLIS: Thailand Library Integrated System, http://tdc.thailis.or.th/tdc/

13. The Royal Society, Science as an open enterprise. The Royal Society Science Policy Centre report 02/12,
    `http://royalsociety.org/uploadedFiles/Royal_Society_Content/policy/projects/sape/2012-06-20-SAOE.pdf`
14. Petwong, W., Tuamsuk, K.: The comparatively analyze the institutional repositories (IR) of Thai and foreign universities. Information Science Journal 29(3) (August-December) (in Thai)
15. Klungthanaboon, W., et al.: Institutional Repositories for Scholarly Communication in Thailand,
    `http://journal.it.kmitl.ac.th/getFile.php?articleId=4fc79346 1698b8562e000005`
16. Klungthanaboon, W.: University-Based Institutional Repositories and the Management of Research Output,
    `https://conferencepapers.shef.ac.uk/index.php/iFutures/if201 3/../11`
17. Sukantarat, W.: Digital initiatives and metadata use in Thailand. Program: Electronic Library and Systems 42(2), 150–162 (2008)
18. Yoowang, A.: Institutional repository management in university libraries. M.A. thesis, Chulalongkorn University (2012)

A Comparative Study of Key Phrase Extraction
for Cross-Domain Document Collections

Supaporn Tantanasiriwong[1,*], Choochart Haruechaiyasak[2], and Sumanta Guha[1]

[1] Computer Science and Information Management, School of Engineering and Technology,
Asian Institute of Technology, Thailand
{supaporn.tantanasiriwong,guha}@ait.ac.th
[2] Speech and Audio Technology Laboratory,National Electronics and Computer Technology
Center,National Science and Technology Development Agency, Thailand
choochart.haruechaiyasak@nstda.or.th

Abstract. An extraction tool, nowadays, has become useful for text mining researchers to find keywords and keyphrases from the documents. Performing keywords and keyphrases extraction for cross-domain information are more challenging since both domains of interest are different in word usage. In this paper, two popular keyphrases extraction tools, Maui and Carrot, are investigated, for extracting terms from cross-domain document databases. The characteristic of keywords or phrases matching among different domain collections is presented and used for determining the keyphrase extraction tool for patent documents and scientific publications. In our experiment, matching between a patent and its cited publication are the key point. For evaluation, the performance of cross-domain matching is measured by comparing the similarity measure among those extraction tool results. The experimental results show that Maui tool proves to be the appropriate keyphrases extraction tool with its best performance measured by Cosine similarity of 3.31% when compared with Carrot tool for cross-domain document collections matching.

Keywords: Keyphrase extraction tools, Cross-domain document collection, Patent, Publication, Similarity measures, Maui, Carrot.

1   Introduction

Today a digital library usually contains a large number of documents and most existing digital library databases are not linked to each other. Thus, finding relevant papers through one database at a time is a time-consuming process for researchers. Keyword extraction process becomes an important role to represent the main idea as keywords or phrases of that particular document. Therefore, we proposed keyphrases extraction for cross-domain document collections (CDDC) to enhance a digital library task where the patent document and the scientific publication are represented as two different domains. Our main goal is to find the most suitable extraction tool that can

---

* Corresponding author.

K. Tuamsuk et al. (Eds.): ICADL 2014, LNCS 8839, pp. 393–398, 2014.

suggest researchers or librarians for their relevant bibliographic papers from across database domains.

In this study, we investigate two popular keyphrase extraction tools which are Maui-indexer so-called Maui and Carrot2 technique. We focus on the comparison of the performance of cross-domain matching between Maui and Carrot where one is based on supervised learning approach, whereas the other are based on unsupervised learning approach. Maui has been applied in area of automatic text indexing and tagging [6] extended from classic KEA. In contrast, Carrot2 is mostly applied in search result clustering areas [8] and ontology-based semantic.Our work is based on the assumption that keyword or keyphrase extraction from patent documents should be similar to keyword or keyphrase obtained from scientific publications which are cited by their particular patent.

Table 1 shows the characteristic of words and phrases derived from a patent document and its cited publication obtained from the specific ACM scientific publication database where keywords and keyphrases have been extracted by Maui extraction tool.

Table 1. The characteristic of similar keyphrases between patent and its cited publication

Patent Title: Software-directed, energy-aware control of display.
Publication Title1: Energy-aware adaptation for mobile applications.
Publication Title2: Energy trade-offs in the IBM wristwatch computer.

| Patent No.6801811 | Scientific Publication (References) | |
	Publication 1	Publication 2
aware	adaptation	achieve
aware control	applications	battery
consumption	aware	battery life
control	aware adaptation	computer
directed	battery	device
display	battery life	dictates
display parameters	conserve	energy
energy	conserve energy	energy trade
energy aware	energy	ibm
energy consumption	energy aware	ibm wristwatch
energy model	mobile	life
parameters	mobile applications	offs
patterns	operating	power
portions	operating system	software
screen		trade offs
screen portions		
screen usage		
software		
software directed		

2   Related Works

The keyword section is the most important part in representing the main points of the research documents and they are listed by the author of that document. However, listing Keyword and keyphrases in the keyword section are sometimes ignored by many authors, or they are so sparing in words that they are unable to represent all the key points of the documents. In fact, assigning the relevant keywords requires both knowledge and comprehension toward fields of study in particular and it is a time-consuming process. Therefore, to overcome this difficulty, many extraction tools are utilized to help generate a list of keywords and keyphrases for a particular document.

Original existing methods in information retrieval papers usually use a standard technique such as vector space model (VSM) to extract terms usage from documents [7]. Previous work on query expansion area applies keyphrase extraction tools based on KEA supervise learning for assisting invalidity search in patent documents [9]. [3] proposed control vocabulary to construct KEA++ model and show the improvement over KEA by focusing on specific domain from the UN Food and Agriculture Organization (FAO) repository. This paper mainly focus on document keyphrase extraction from their own domain such as scientific publication domain [1,3] and patent domain [9]. In this paper, we explored two popular extraction tools Maui and Carrot2 in order to determine which extraction tool is well suited for cross-domain document collections.

3   Proposed Framework

We propose the framework of cross-domain document matching between patent and its reference that refer to scientific publication. This framework consists of four main process steps. The first step is data collection where we collect data from two different databases such as patent databases and databases of publication cited by that particular patent. The second step is term selection process using keywords or phrases extraction tools such as Maui and Carrot. The third step is similarity calculation where Cosine and Jaccard coefficient are computed to determine the similarity of term usage in the matching of two different domains. The fourth step is a score selection by choosing the highest score from such similarity computation.

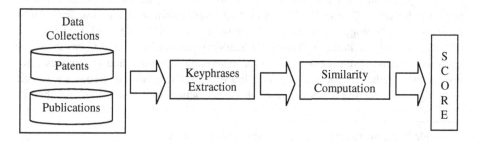

Fig. 1. Cross-domain document collections framework

3.1   Data Collections

Data collections on cross-domain document matching framework were selected from Google Patent Search[1] and Scientific Publication from ACM[2] or IEEE[3] that corresponds to its patent domain. Two categories, PHYSICS and OLED, in the International Patent Classification (IPC)[4] were selected for cross-domain document collections comparison.

3.2   Keyphrase Extraction Tools

Maui-Indexer. Maui [5] is the extension of a key phrase extraction (KEA) algorithm [10] and KEA++ [4] which adds on new feature of Wikipedia and also consider on document size for key phrase extraction. Maui also built in controlled vocabularies from Food and Agriculture Organization (FAO), Medical vocabulary (PubMed), Energy Physics thesaurus and also library of congress (LCSH). Maui work as a supervise learning by using a machine learning algorithm to generate key phrase candidate. Maui increases the significant feature of phrase length, node degree, Wikipedia link-age and semantic relatedness additional from first occurrence features by KEA. Maui have been proof to be outperforms existing popular KEA approach.

Carrot2. Carrot2 [8] has two algorithm usages. First is STC algorithm which is a kind of Suffix Tree. Second is lingo which works better than STC and apply using TF-IDF and LSA into this algorithm. Lingo can complete keyphrase search with some other constraints keyphrase. Carrot2 applies to use in search results clustering as it contains some components for bringing results from web search engines such as Google or Bing. In this paper, we apply Carrot2 to work as documents clustering and use their components for keyphrase extraction as its engine help to suggest the suitable keyphrase for documents clustering result.

4   Experiment and Results

4.1   Data Preparation

In our experiment, data collections were extracted from the patent domain and its related publication domain. They contain 500 patent-publication citations for each of innovation technology category. Two categories of PHYSICS and OLED were retrieved as group criteria to classify the category dataset. Maui and Carrot2 are applied to serve as a pre-processing step for generating keywords and keyphrases from documents. Then, we got a list of keyphrases along with weight frequency scored resulting from the implementation of those extraction tools. The total number of

---

[1]   Google Patent Search, http://patents.google.com
[2]   ACM Digital Library, http://dl.acm.org
[3]   IEEE Xplore Digital Library, http://www.ieee.org
[4]   IPC, http://www.wipo.int/classifications/ipc/en/

unique phrases generated from Maui and Carrot for two different categories are shown in Table 2. Maui found bigger numbers of unique phrases than Carrot2 found in both PHYSICS and OLED since Maui could yield a higher similarity. However, in PHYSICS subject there were smaller numbers of unique phrases found by Carrot2 while in OLED there were bigger numbers of unique phrases found by Maui. This might be because the generalization or specification of technical terms in these two different fields.

Table 2. Unique phrases generated from Maui and Carrot for PHYSICS and OLED categories

Patent - Publication	PHYSICS	OLED
Unique phrases by Maui	26,949	50,863
Unique phrases by Carrot2	444	285

4.2   Results and Discussion

To measure the performance of keyword and phrase extraction tools for cross-domain document collections, we assume that the patent with its cited publication tend to have a higher similarity score than one without cited publication. Then, we calculate the similarity between patent domain and scientific publication domain. The similarity result from each pair of patent and publication will be averaged out with the number of assigned patents of 500. The comparison of keyphrase extraction tools performance for CDDC using Cosine and Jaccard similarity are shown in Figure2.

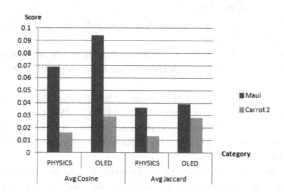

Fig. 2. Comparison the performance of extraction tools for CDDC using average Cosine and average Jaccard

According to the average of similarity measurement obtained from the implementation of Cosine and Jaccard method to those two different extraction tools, Maui and Carrot in CDDC, we found that Maui outperforms Carrot in terms of similarity score measured by Cosine and Jaccard in both categories, PHYSICS and OLED. This indicates that Maui proves to be more efficient than Carrot2 in extracting keyphrase for cross-domain document collection matching.

5   Conclusions and Future work

The purpose of this paper is to find the appropriate keyword and phrase extraction techniques for cross-domain document collections based on supervised and unsupervised learning approaches. To evaluate Maui and Carrot, we use standard similarity measurements such as Cosine and Jaccard. Experimental results indicate that Maui, a supervise extraction tool, outperforms Carrot, an unsupervised extraction tool, in cross-domain document collection matching. Therefore, it is recommended to use Maui as an automatic keyphrases extraction tool in order to achieve the cross-domain documents matching. In the future, we plan to apply Maui on a variety of datasets for cross-domain citation recommendation.

References

1. Nguyen, T.D., Kan, M.-Y.: Keyphrase Extraction in Scientific Publications. In: Goh, D.H.-L., Cao, T.H., Sølvberg, I.T., Rasmussen, E. (eds.) ICADL 2007. LNCS, vol. 4822, pp. 317–326. Springer, Heidelberg (2007)
2. Kaur, B. and Sidhu, B.: Methods for key phrase extraction from documents. In: Technological Research in Engineering (IJTRE) (2014)
3. Medelyan, O., Witten, I.H.: Thesaurus based automatic keyphrase indexing. In: JCDL 2006 (2006)
4. Medelyan, O., Witten, I.: Domain-independent automatic keyphrase indexing with small training sets. Journal of the American Society for Information Science and Technology (JASIST) 59, 1026–1040 (2008)
5. Medelyan, O.: Human-competitive automatic topic indexing. In: PhD thesis, University of Waikato, New Zealand (2009)
6. Medelyan, O., Frank, E., Witten, I.: Human-competitive tagging using automatic keyphrase extraction. In: Empirical Methods in Natural Language Processing, pp. 1318–1327 (2009)
7. Salton, G., Buckley, C.: Term-weighting approaches in automatic text retrieval. Journal of Information Processing and Management 24(5), 513–523 (1988)
8. Stefanowski, J., Weiss, D.: Carrot2 and language properties in Web search results clustering. In: 1st International Atlantic Web Intelligence Conference. Lecture Notes in Computer Science, pp. 240–249 (2003)
9. Verma, M., Varma, V.: Applying key phrase extraction to aid invalidity search. In: 13th International Conference on Artificial Intelligence and Law, pp. 249–255 (2011)
10. Witten, I., Paynter, G., Frank, E., Gutwin, C., Nevill-Manning, C.: Kea: Practical automatic keyphrase extraction. In: 4th ACM conference on Digital Libraries, pp. 254–255 (1999)

Development of a Book Recommendation System to Inspire "Infrequent Readers"

Shuntaro Yada

Graduate School of Education, University of Tokyo,
7–3–1 Hongo, Bunkyo-ku, Tokyo, 113-0033, Japan
shuntaroy@p.u-tokyo.ac.jp

Abstract. This research introduces *Serendy*, a book recommendation system available in Japanese language that presents book information referred to by friends within Twitter to those who have the desire to read but are not accustomed to reading (infrequent readers). *Serendy* relies not on the interests of users nor on the content of books, but on users' social capital within Social Networking Service (SNS). Through closed a beta test, *Serendy* has been enhancing its algorithm for accurately identifying book information mentioned in tweets.

Keywords: book recommendation system, social networks in Japan, bibliographic information extraction, Japanese morpheme analysis, regular expressions.

1   Introduction

While there are many social reading services which also include the function of book recommendation such as Goodreads[1] in the English-speaking world, and Booklog[2] in Japan, most of them target people who already have a habit of reading, not those who have the desire to read but are not accustomed to reading (henceforth they will be referred to as infrequent readers). This research developed a Web application named *Serendy* for supporting infrequent readers.

For infrequent readers (in Japan), the main reasons for their infrequent reading habits are one or both of the following two factors: limited time to read, and difficulty in determining which book to read next [1]. This research focuses on the latter, namely the group of infrequent readers who have (or are able to spare) enough time to read but are uncertain of which reading material to select. The problem of limited time to read seems to stem from some external factors such as social systematized or labor environmental ones.

Uncertainty of what material to read, for infrequent readers, comes from unawareness of their own interests within literature. They seem to, however, become aware of their interests when books are presented or suggested to them. Traditionally,

---

[1] https://www.goodreads.com/
[2] http://booklog.jp/

K. Tuamsuk et al. (Eds.): ICADL 2014, LNCS 8839, pp. 399–404, 2014.

infrequent readers have been thought to be directed to books partially through passive exposures to books (or book information), such as hearing a book title in informal chats with friends or other people. This research contends that it is important to address the needs of infrequent readers online as well. *Serendy*, therefore, inspire them to read by suggesting or recommending book information. It keeps up a stream which does not require users to make a conscious effort to obtain information [2].

2   Model

To recommend products or goods, including books, three recommender systems are used widely in the Web: *Collaborative filtering*, *Content-based recommender*, and *Knowledge-based recommender* [3]. Collaborative filtering is based on the idea that a user will be interested in the same item as other users who have similar interests to the user's. A content-based recommender takes into account that a user will like items similar to the ones the user liked in the past. A knowledge-based recommender suggests items matching a user's needs, based on specific domain knowledge about how certain item features meet particular needs.

These systems try to recommend items by matching between the items' content and users' interests, the latter of which are assumed by systems themselves or registered by users. As mentioned in section 1, however, infrequent readers are not aware of their interests. This research took an approach to them without meeting their interests and book contents, unlike those recommender methods.

Instead of relying on the degree of matching between the information content of books and a user's interests, this research defined three attributes to attract users' attention to books and make it more likely that they will move from the desire to read to actual reading (Fig. 1):

Daily-ness comes from the hypothesis that infrequent readers encounter book information primarily in the context of 'daily' activities, not in book-oriented environments such as bookstores, libraries, or book circles.

Proximity means that information has to be provided by a person or an organization who or which infrequent readers are related to or have interests in originally.

Considerateness means that book recommendations should not be too frequent or excessive for infrequent readers, as this may cause an infringement on their personal decision and may discourage them from reading the book.

Daily-ness and proximity guarantee that users do not need to make a conscious effort to obtain information about books. In other words, *Serendy* provides users with chances for 'Information Encountering' [4]. These three attributes can be postulated in a daily situation in which a person is inspired to read a book, for example:

A lunch-time chat with (a) frequent-reader *friend(s)* in which certain book titles *are naturally referred to* within the context of the conversation, attracting the attention of the infrequent reader.

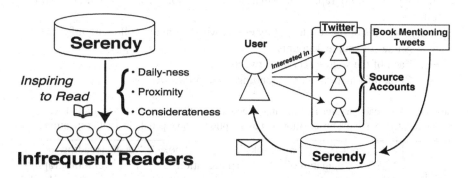

Fig. 1. The concept of inspiring infrequent readers to read

Fig. 2. The current model of *Serendy*'s recommendation

The situation of a lunch-time chat contains daily-ness, (a) friend(s) has proximity to the infrequent reader, and it has considerateness that the book information are naturally referred to. This situation can be considered as an instance of inspiring infrequent readers, and be restated in the following situation within the SNS sphere:

> Within SNS used by an infrequent reader, he/she sees friends' posts which contain book information within a context that may not be explicitly about books.

3   Implementation

Serendy was developed using Ruby on Rails. For the moment, the scope of SNS is Twitter[3], because its limited character counts satisfies the considerateness criteria. Users can sign up through the website and register source accounts in Twitter, from which users want to obtain book information, and receive notifying emails (Fig. 2). In the background process, *Serendy* materializes the model in section 2 by implementing the following functions:

1. Extracting tweets of source accounts containing the vocabulary about 'book' or 'reading' (Table 1) by the regular expressions in Japanese.
2. Building a search query from each of the extracted tweets, by connecting following bibliographic information with and.

Author. Any person's name in an extracted tweet is referred to as an author name, using online Japanese morpheme analysis engine provided by Yahoo! Japan API[4].

Title/Quote. Any type of parenthesized text in a extracted tweet is referred to as a book title or a quote of a book.

---

[3] https://twitter.com/
[4] http://developer.yahoo.co.jp/webapi/jlp/ma/v1/parse.html

3. Inferring the bibliographic information from a Google Books Search[5] using the built query.
4. Notifying users of the results list by email, which contains following information:
   — Names of source accounts
   — Each of the source accounts' tweets
   — Book information[6] corresponding each of the tweets

Table 1. The vocabulary set for filtering tweets mentioning 'book' or 'reading'. These words are enumerated by simple observation and assumption of how people in Twitter mention books.

Nouns	"本 (book)", "書籍 (book)", "図書 (book)", "読書 (reading book)", "雑誌 (magazine)", "刊 (publication)", "自伝 (autobiography)", "原作 (original work)", "著書 (one's book)", "冊 (counter suffix of book)", "一節 (a passage)", "読了 (finish reading)", "読破 (read through)"
Verbs	"読む (read)", "書く (write)"

4   Observations of Experimental Usage

4.1   Basic Statistics

Serendy is now in beta testing among 12 volunteer users, the main purpose of which is to evaluate whether the book identification process (step 1-3 in Section 3) can correctly find a book mentioned in a tweet. The total number of source accounts in Twitter is 35, while each of the users registered 1-13 acccount(s), the median of which was 2. *Serendy* executes the book identification process every 12 hours[7], and notifies users by email every 24 hours if any book information is identified. The mean frequency of the email notification to each of the users was 0.45 per day. However, the notification frequency of several users was over 0.7, which means *Serendy* notifies the users almost everyday. Because this number of notifications may be too frequent in regards to considerateness, users will be able to set the preference of notification frequency in a future implementation.

4.2   Diagnosis

Between May 30th and July 28th, 2014, *Serendy* recommended 1,586 records of book information in total. The accuracy of book identification in 742 records of the data set was manually analyzed. Through the analysis, the number of correct identifications was only 115 (15.6%), and error patterns were grouped by each corresponding to steps of the book identification process. Frequently-found cases and the numerical data are shown in Table 2.

---

[5] `http://books.google.co.jp/`
[6] This consists of title, author name, front cover image, description, and link URL for Google Books.
[7] In an early period of beta test, the process was executed every 1 hour.

Table 2. Failures' count grouped by reasons. The total number of the below summary is not equivalent to the total analized samples (742), because there are some samples applicable to multiple cases.

Step	Case	Count
1	**Extracting Not book mentioning tweets**	**397**
	Mentioning "図書館 (Library)"	133
	Mentioning Web and academic articles	127
2	**Building unsuitable queries**	**60**
	Extracting Not author name	37
	Extracting Not book title	21
3	**Google Books Search failure**	**83**
	Not collected	36
	Yet published	21
	System excluded pattern of book mentioning	**87**
	Not parenthesized book title	51
	Several books mentioned in a tweet	16
	A part of sequential tweets mentioning books	13
	Indirect mentioning books	6

The 53.5% of samples was the tweets not mentioning books, gathered by the vocabulary set (Table 1). One of the two main cases was to talk only about a "図書館 [*tosho-kan*]," or "library" in Japanese, which literally consists of "図書" and "館 (building)". The word "図書" can be excluded from the vocabulary set because it found to be rarely used in mentioning book among the informal text environment such as Twitter. The other case was referring to Web or academic articles. Though these articles were mentioned in very similar literal expressions to that of books, some of them were distinguishable by URL analysis.

Corresponding to step 2 of the book identification process, some failures of building queries were found. That is, even if step 1 of the process extracted book mentioning tweets, other regular person's name or not a title words were extracted in step 2. A possible way to deal with this problem is checking a pair of extracted a person's name and parenthesized words through a large bibliographic database. However, there are the tweets only containing either of the author's name or book title. As mentioned later, extracting not parenthesized book title has to be considered too.

"Google Books Search failure" in Table 2 means some books were not searchable even if a correct query was provided. The major reason of that is some kind of books are not contained in Google Books database. Newly-published books and even some already published books were not collected in the database. Part of the latter consists of magazines and ebooks provided only by other ebook stores. Yet published books were not contained too, while some books in a part of the case is now searchable. While most these books can be found in Amazon[8], searching multiple databases is a possible dealing.

---

[8] https://www.amazon.co.jp

Some cases which the book identification process is not intend to target but which is important as "book mentioning tweets" were accidentally gathered. These are listed in the bottom part of Table 2. Most frequent case was referring to book title in not a parenthesized way. Book title extraction will be difficult task because many title are named in daily expression. This problem may be included in "named-entity recognition" [5]. In Twitter, one book can be mentioned in several sequential tweets, while several books can be mentioned together in one tweet. There are some samples which only allude to a book, such as a expression of "his fresh publication" or of "her autobiography." Because these patterns of book mentioning tweets are likely to be excluded, basic research of how people in Twitter mention books is required.

5   Current Status and Outlook

Currently, in order to gather the tweets containing any book title or author name from a public timeline, a dictionary for Japanese morpheme analysis is being compiled, which consists of author names and book titles as exhaustively as possible. The tweet set will be statistically examined for word frequency, pre/post expression of book titles and author names, and relations of sequential tweets mentioning books.

As mentioned in Section 4, the book identification process of *Serendy* is rather inaccurate at this moment. Therefore, it is not yet possible to evaluate whether *Serendy* can inspire infrequent readers to read. However, when *Serendy* can execute reliable book identification, the evaluation of *Serendy*'s impact will be conducted through a follow-up survey.

Participants will be gathered widely from the Web through a public beta test of *Serendy* regardless of whether they are infrequent readers or not. Then *Serendy* will question reading infrequency of users by an instant Web form such as asking their interest to reading and reading frequency. Whether users read books recommended by *Serendy* or not will be questioned via email. Finally, the correlation of reading infrequency before and after using *Serendy* will be analyzed.

References

1. Japan Publishing Industry Foundation for Culture.: The Scope of Publishing World: The Survey of the Reading Habit of People Nowadays. Shuppan News, 25–27 (2009)
2. Rosenfeld, L., Morville, L.: Information Architecture for the World Wide Web, 2nd edn. O'Reilly Media, Massachusetts (2002)
3. Jannach, D., Zanker, M., Felfernig, A., Friedrich, G.: Recommender Systems: An Introduction. Cambridge University Press, Cambridge (2011)
4. Erdelez, S.: Information Encountering: It's More Than Just Bumping into Information. Bull. Am. Soc. Inf. Sci. Technol. 25, 26–29 (1999)
5. Etzioni, O., Cafarella, M., Downey, D., Popescu, A.-M., Shaked, T., Soderland, S., Weld, D.S., Yates, A.: Unsupervised named-entity extraction from the Web: An experimental study. Artif. Intell. 165, 91–134 (2005)

A Comparison of Dimensionality Reduction Algorithms for Improving Efficiency of PromoRank

Metawat Kavilkrue and Pruet Boonma

Faculty of Engineering, Chiang Mai University, Chiang Mai, Thailand
comengi49@gmail.com, pruet@eng.cmu.ac.th

Abstract. Promotion plays a crucial role in online marketing, which can be used in post-sale recommendation, developing brand, customer support, etc. It is often desirable to find markets or sale channels where an object, e.g., a product, person or service, can be promoted efficiently. For example, when a client borrows a book from a library, the library might want to suggest another related books to them based on their interest. However, since the object, e.g., book, may not be highly ranked in the global property space, PromoRank algorithm promotes a given object by discovering subspaces in which the target is top rank. Nevertheless, the computation complexity of PromoRank is exponential to the dimension of the space. This paper proposes to use dimensionality reduction algorithms, such as PCA or FA, in order to reduce the dimension size and, as a consequence, improve the performance of PromoRank. This paper evaluates multiple dimensionality reduction algorithms to obtain the understanding about the relationship between properties of data sets and algorithms such that an appropriate algorithm can be selected for a particular data set.

1   Introduction

Online marketing becomes an important tool for business and organization [1]. Big companies like Google (http://google.com) or Amazon (http://amazon.com) relies heavily on online marketing operations, such as, online advertising, recommendation or promotion. For instance, when a customer buys a book from Amazon, he/she will be provided with recommendation on similar books. These recommendation are automatically generated from customers buying/browsing history and also the target promotion from books publisher [2].

Ranking is a technique to carry out promotion. It is used widely, for instance, in many bookstores, where top selling books are shown on the front of the stores. This can accelerate those books selling because people are tend to believe that, because so many other customers already bought these books, they should be good. Because, the number of top ranking is limited, only those who are the best on every dimensions can be in the list. However, there are many cases that when consider only a subset of the dimensions, some interesting objects can be found.

Table 1 shows a concrete example of a multi-dimensional data set. From the table, there are one object dimension, *Object*, with three target objects, O_1, O_2, O_3. There are

K. Tuamsuk et al. (Eds.): ICADL 2014, LNCS 8839, pp. 405–410, 2014.
© Springer International Publishing Switzerland 2014

two subspace dimensions, *Genre and Year*, and a score dimension, *Score*. Consider O_1 as the target object to promote, Table 2 lists O_1 is 6 subspaces and the corresponding rank and object count in each subspace. The rank is derived from the sum-aggregate score of all objects in the subspace. For example, in {Science, 2012}, O_1 ranks 1st because the score of O_1:0.9 > O_2:0.5 > O_3:0.4. Object count is the number of objects in that subspace. Thus {Science, 2012} is a promotive subspace of O_1.

Table 1. Example of multidimensional data

Genre	Year	Object	Score
Science	2012	O_1	0.9
Fiction	2012	O_1	0.2
Fiction	2012	O_2	0.8
Fiction	2011	O_2	0.7
Science	2012	O_2	0.5
Science	2012	O_3	0.4
Fiction	2012	O_3	0.8

Table 2. Target object O_1's subspaces and its ranks

Subspace	Rank	Object Count
{*}	3	3
{Genre=Science}	1	3
{Genre=Fiction}	3	3
{Year=2012}	2	3
{Genre=Science, Year=2012}	1	2
{Genre=Fiction, Year=2012}	3	3

Thus, given a target object, the goal is to find subspace with large promotiveness, i.e., subspace where the target object is top-R. For example, observe that O_1, which is ranked third in all dimensions ({*}), should be promoted in {Science, 2012} because it is the first rank. In other words, {Science, 2012} is a promotive subspace of O_1.

PromoRank [3] proposes to use subspace ranking for promoting a target object by finding a subspace where the target object is in Top-R ranking. However, the computation complexity of PromoRank is exponential to the dimension size, this paper proposes to use dimensionality reduction algorithms to reduce the number of dimensions before performing PromoRank. This approach is explained in Section 2. Dimensionality reduction in recommendation system, in generally, has been studied for many years, e.g., in [4-6]; however, this work is the first attempt to apply dimensionality reduction technique to subspace ranking, in general, and PromoRank, in particular. The evaluation results, in Section 3, show that the dimensionality reduction can improve the performance of PromoRank with small impact on Top-R ranking result. The conclusion is given in Section 4.

2   Dimensionality Reduction for PromoRank

In order to further improve PromoRank, this paper proposes to reduce the number of dimensions (d) of the data set. From the computational complexity of PromoRank, reduce dimensions should impact the performance greatly [7, 8]. Moreover, this approach can be performed as a pre-processing for PromoRank; thus, it can be combined with the pruning approaches. However, not all reduction algorithms can be applied to all data set, this paper further investigate this approach by comparing multiple algorithms to find suitable algorithm for a data set with particular parameters.

Given a d-dimensional data set $\mathcal{D}$ with subspace dimension $\mathcal{A}$, a dimensionality reduction algorithm, such as PCA and FA, reduces the number of dimension to d^*, such that $d^*<d$, and a reduced data set $\mathcal{D}^*$ is produced with subspace dimension $\mathcal{A}^*$. Please note that, it does not necessary that $\mathcal{A}^* \subset \mathcal{A}$ because the dimensionality reduction algorithm might generate a new dimension for $\mathcal{A}^*$.

Thus, the top-R promotive subspace from PromoRank with original data set might differ from the top-R promotive subspace with reduced data set. As a consequence, they cannot be compared directly. In order to handle this, a simple mapping scheme is proposed based on the relationship between the original dimensions and reduced dimensions. Suppose that two original subspace dimensions, A_i and A_j, are reduced to a new subspace dimension A_k^*. Consequently, for a top-R promotive subspace contains $a_k^* \in A_k^*$, it will be compared with a subspace that has $a_i \in A_i$ and/or $a_j \in A_j$; together with the common other subspace dimensions. For example, let's assume that the original dimensions are {City, Country, Year}, then, after a dimensional reduction algorithm is performed on the data set, the new dimensions are {Location, Year} where *Location* is reduced from *City* and *Country*. Thus, if PromoRank considers a subspace {location=Lanna} where *Lanna* is reduced from *Chiang Mai* and *Thailand*, then, the subspace {location=Lanna} will be compared with the subspace {City=Chiang Mai}, {Country=Thailand} and {City=Chiang Mai, Country=Thailand}.

Performing dimensionality reduction algorithms incurs extra computational cost. However, dimensionality reduction algorithms such as PCA and FA have lower computational complexity than PromoRank. For instance, PCA that use Cyclic Jacobi's method has complexity of $O(d^3+d^2n)$ [9]. The polynomial complexity of PCA is much lower than the exponential complexity of PromoRank.

3   Experimental Evaluation

To investigate the impact of dimensionality reduction algorithm on data sets, an experimental evaluation with three data sets: Top US private collage (http://mathforum.org/~pdaley/datalibrary/), NBA (http://basketballreference.com) and Market analysis (http://stata.com), was carried out. A Java version of PromoRank was developed and tested on a computer with a 3GHz processor and 4GB RAM. The pruning optimization of PromoRank was disabled to remove the impact on the result.

This evaluation investigates three well-known dimensionality reduction algorithms, namely, principal component analysis (PCA), factor analysis (FA) and linear discriminant analysis (LDA). The evaluation compares the Top-R promotive subspace of dimensional-reduced data sets and original data sets with PromoRank to investigate the performance of each algorithms for reducing dimensions of the data set.

3.1   Top US Private College Data Set

This data set consists of 100 tuples with 8 subspace dimensions. The result of PCA shows that there are two new principle components, i.e., dimensions that represents four original dimensions, namely, *Grad Rate* and *Ratio*. *Grad Rate* strongly correlates, i.e., has low variance, with *4yrs Grad Rate* and *6yrs Grad Rate*. *Ratio* strongly correlates with *Admission Ratio* and *Admission Rate*. For FA, there is a strong collation between *4yrs Graduation Rate* and *6yrs Graduation Rate*, so the former one is removed. Finally, LDA reduces the number of dimensions from ten to six.

Table 3 compares ranks (marked as Ranks) of Top-5 promotive subspaces (marked as Subspaces) from the original US private college data set and reduced data sets of two target objects. With Rice University as the target object, when the Top-5 promotive subspace of original data are {6yrs Graduation Rate=90%}. In the PCA reduced data, the comparable subspace is {Graduation Rate=85%}. First of all, these two subspaces are compared because Graduation Rate is the principle component of 6yrs Graduation Rate. Then, to map these two subspaces, the subspace with the closest property to the original data set categories, i.e. 85, is assigned to the reduced data set category. As a consequence, it is possible that, when compared with the other object, the rank of the target object in the reduced subspace can be different from the original subspace. The differences are marked by a star symbol. However, this mismatch is infrequently happened. Therefore, the result shows that the ranking of Top-5 promotive subspace is mostly maintained even after the dimensionality reduction is performed on the data. The results also show that LDA, which can reduce the number of dimension (from ten to six) the most, maintains an acceptable ranking result compared with the original one. Thus, LDA is the most preferred for this data set.

Table 3. Subspace ranking of Top US private college data set

Target Object	Original Data Set Subspaces	Ranks	FA Subspaces	Ranks	PCA Subspaces	Ranks	LDA Subspaces	Ranks
	{*}	1	{*}	1	{*}	1	{*}	1
CalTech	{State=CA}	1	{State=CA}	1	{State=CA	1	{State=CA}	1
	{4yrs Grad .=70%}	1	{4yrs Grad R.=70%}	-	{Grad R.=85%}	1	{Grad R.=85%}	1
	{6yrs Grad .=90%}	1	{6yrs Grad R.=90%}	1	{Grad R.=85%}	1	{Grad R.=85%}	1
	{*}	2	{*}	2	{*}	2	{*}	2
Rice	{Enrollment=2}	1	{Enrollment=2}	1	{Enrollment=2}	1	{Enrollment=2}	1
Uni.	{Enrollment=2,	1	{Enrollment=2,	1	{Enrollment=2,	1	{Enrollment=2,	
	6yrs Grad R.=90%}		6yrs Grad R.=90%}		Grad R.=85%}		Grad R.=85%}	1
	{6yrs Grad .=90%}	2	{6yrs Grad R.=90%}	2	{Grad R.=85%}	2	{Grad R.=85%}	1*

3.2   NBA Data Set

This data set consists of 4,051 tuples with 12 subspace dimensions. The result from PCA and FA dictates that 6 dimensions, *Game, Minutes, Assists, Block, TurnOver* and *Coach* can be removed. Thus, after dimensional reduction, the reduced data set contains only six subspace dimensions, namely, *First Name, Last Name, Year, Career Stage, Position* and *Team*. On the other hand, LDA cannot be applied to this data set because the classification criterion cannot be met. In other words, LDA cannot distinguish between independent and dependent variables.

Table 4 shows results from NBA data set. The Top-5 promotive subspaces are hardly change in this data set. In particular, the result of FA and PCA does not change at all. This result show that, there are some data set that cannot be improved by LDA. So, FA and PCA are the only choices for such data set. The running time of Promo-Rank with reduced data set with FA and PCA are 16 and 15.2 minutes, respectively, compared with 20.5 minutes of the original data set.

Table 4. Subspace ranking of NBA data set

Target Object	Original Data Set Subspaces	Ranks	FA Subspaces	Ranks	PCA Subspaces	Ranks
	{*}	1	{*}	1	{*}	1
Kareem	{Pos.=Center}	1	{Pos.=Center}	1	{Pos.=Center}	1
Abdul-	{League=N}	1	{League=N}	1	{League=N}	1
Jabbar	{Team=LA Lakers,Yr=1978}	1	{Team=LA Lakers,Yr=1978}	1	{Team=LA Lakers,Yr=1978}	1
	{*}	2	{*}	2	{*}	2
Michael	{Pos.=Forward}	1	{Pos.=Forward}	1	{Pos.=Forward}	1
Jordan	{League=N}	2	{League=N}	2	{League=N}	2
	{Team=Utah Jazz}	1	{Team=Utah Jazz}	1	{Team=Utah Jazz}	1

3.3   Stock Market Data Set

This data set consists of 5,891 tuples with 23 dimensions. The result from PCA dictates that a subspace dimension, *Price/Piece* can be removed, and there are two new principle components, namely, *Price* and *Forward PE*. *Price* strongly correlates with *Stock Price* and *Market Price*. *Forward PE*, on the other hand, strongly correlates with *Current PE* and *Trailing PE*. FA can reduce only one dimension. *Stock Price* and *Market Price* are highly correlated, so the latter is removed. Similar to the previous data set, LDA cannot improve this data set.

Table 5 shows results from Stock market data set. From the table, there is no differences between original and reduced data set. Even though, PCA incurs more changes than FA but they are small and acceptable. On the contrarily, PCA can reduces three dimensions, compared with one of FA, so it should perform more efficient. As a conclusion, in some data set, FA can reduce only a few dimension, so, PCA performs better for such data set. The running time of PromoRank with reduced data set with FA and PCA are 108 and 99 minutes, respectively, compared with 124 minutes of the original data set.

Table 5. Subspace ranking of Stock market data set

Target Object	Original Data Set Subspaces	Ranks	FA Subspaces	Ranks	PCA Subspaces	Ranks
	{*}	1	{*}	1	{*}	1
Bank of America	{Stock Price=$6,Mkt. Price=$6}	1	{Stock Price=$6}	1	{Price=$6}	1
	{Size Class=10,FYE=31/12/2010}	1	{Size Class=10,FYE=31/12/2010}	1	{Size Class10,FYE=31/12/2010}	1
	{Current PE=20,Trailling PE=12}	1	{Current PE=20,Trailling PE=12}	1	{Current PE=20,Trailling PE=12}	1
	{*}	3	{*}	3	{*}	3
AppTech Corp	{Stock Price=$0,Mkt. Price=$0}	5	{Stock Price=$0}	1⋆	{Price=$0}	1⋆
	{Size Class=4}	1	{Size Class=4}	1	{Size Class=4}	1
	{Ind. Nm.=Softw.,Stock Price=$0}	1	{Ind. Nm.=Softw.,Stock Price=$0}	1	{Ind. Nm.=Softw.,Stock Price=$0}	2⋆

4 Conclusion

In this work, dimensionality reduction algorithms, e.g., PCA and FA, are utilized to reduce the size of data set in order to improve the performance, i.e., execution time, of PromoRank algorithm. The results confirm that the dimensionality reduction algorithm can reduce the execution time of PromoRank up to 25% while mostly maintains the ranking result. In particular, when a data set can met the classification criterion of LDA, then LDA is the best choices, in terms of the number of reduced dimensions, compared with the others. However, if LDA cannot be used, FA should be tested next to see the number of dimensions it can reduce. If it can reduce many, then it is the next best choices. Finally, if FA can reduce only one or two dimensions, PCA should be the best choice because, in general, PCA can reduce many dimensions.

References

1. Kotler, P., Keller, K.: Marketing Management. Prentice Hall (2008)
2. Wang, J., Zhang, Y.: Opportunity model for e-commerce recommendation: Right product; right time. In: Proceedings of the 36th International ACM SIGIR Conference on Research and Development in Information Retrieval, pp. 303–312. ACM, New York (2013)
3. Wu, T., Xin, D., Mei, Q., Han, J.: Promotion analysis in multi-dimensional space. In: International Conference on Very Large Databases, France. VLDB Endowment (2009)
4. Symeonidis, P., Nanopoulos, A., Manolopoulos, Y.: Tag recommendations based on tensor dimensionality reduction. In: ACM Conference on Recommender Systems, Lausanne, Switzerland. ACM (2008)
5. Kamishima, T., Akaho, S.: Dimension reduction for supervised ordering. In: International Conference on Data Mining, Hong Kong. IEEE Press (2006)
6. Ahn, H.J., Kim, J.W.: Feature reduction for product recommendation in internet shopping malls. International Journal of Electronic Business 4(5), 432–444 (2006)
7. Fodor, I.: A survey of dimension reduction techniques. Technical report, Center for Applied Scientific Computing, Lawrence Livermore National Research Laboratory (2002)
8. Ailon, N., Chazelle, B.: Faster dimension deduction. Commun. ACM 53(2), 97–104 (2010)
9. Forsythe, G.E., Henrici, P.: The cyclic Jacobi method for computing the principal values of a complex matrix. Transactions of the American Mathematical Society, 1–23 (1960)

Library Book Recommendations Based on Latent Topic Aggregation

Shun-Hong Sie[1] and Jian-Hua Yeh[2]

[1] Graduate Institute of Library & Information Studies, NTNU,
modify@ms37.hinet.net
[2] Department of Computer Science and Information Engineering,
Aletheia University
jhyeh@mail.au.edu.tw

Abstract. During recent years, how to provide personalized services has become an important research issue in library services. The libraries provide more and more personalized services such as customized web interface and reading suggestions. In the traditional approaches, the features of the books that a reader likes are used to construct the profile of the reader to support recommendation of books such as query keywords. But with the fact of the huge holdings in the libraries, the librarians need to effectively help the readers to find the books of interest. Collaborative filtering (CF) is a way to make it possible by use patron's circulation logs which contain their borrow history as favorite readings. In this paper, we first use Latent Dirichlet Allocation to find the latent topics existing in the circulation logs, then we combine patron reading histories with the generated latent topics to produce a suggestion list for the patron. With the elaborated experiments demonstrated in this paper, it showed good results from the volunteers' feedback.

Keywords: book suggestion, latent topic, library service, collaborative filtering.

1   Introduction

The librarians provide more and more personalize services in the recent years, for example, the personalized web and some reading suggestions. In traditional personal book suggestions, it is done by adopting the books' features compared with personal profiles or query keywords, trying to form suggestion lists for library readers. The librarians should provide more information to the patrons to fit their preferences by recommending suggestion book lists, and help the patrons to discover books which they may never seen but hold in the library.

According to the analysis of a patron's reading history or some query keywords given by the patron, the library is able to provide some new information or books about it. But sometimes the patron's query keywords or reading history might not be effective enough and may cause lot of time to identify the patron's need. Since the library contains a huge amount of holdings which can only be accessed or searched via on-line catalog or browsed stock by stock. So most people do not know the

K. Tuamsuk et al. (Eds.): ICADL 2014, LNCS 8839, pp. 411–416, 2014.

holding situation which may contain some information they need, and some of interesting books outside the hot topics will not be seen in library on-line catalog. On the other hand, basing on patron's search skill or behavior might cause some important resources or interest for patrons not found or unseen.

Base on use statistics on library circulation counting indicate that most books are utilized by very few patrons [1]. And these collaborative approaches might tend to recommend popular titles which might have high rating on it, perpetuating homogeneity in reading choices. It might impossible for a collaborative approach to recommend items that have no one rated on it or just purchased into the library.

Using data mining technologies on analyzing huge patrons' reading histories should be helpful to the librarians to recommend holdings for the patrons. In this research, we focus on building a model to render reading list suggestions for patrons through collaborative filtering. The Latent Dirichlet Allocation (LDA) model is adopted to find the latent topics in the library circulation logs, then the render suggestion list is produced by matching patron barrow history.

This paper aims at developing an personalized reading profile construction process to be used on personalized suggestion. Before developing the construction process, all the library's circulation logs should be fetched and processed. We use the National Taiwan Normal University library's circulation logs for our experiment, all the information with personal security concerns or private data was removed. We try to find a user's suggestion reading list which he/she may be interested in. Finally we use K-fold experiments with human questionnaire to evaluate our suggestion list. The experiment results shows that our system had good performance on users satisfaction.

2   Relate Works

In this section, we focus on the discussions about the relationships on catalog number and latent topic discovery which will be used to find the latent topics, and these topics are used to compare user profiles in order to make suggestion readings lists for them. The catalog number is used to represent knowledge organization in the library, not only for librarians but also for patron to search holdings in the library.

2.1   Catalog Number

Catalog number is a way of organizing library holdings. In most libraries, holdings are arranged according to subject-oriented classification schemes. The decimal system scheme which used in the National Taiwan Normal University library is named "Chinese Library Classification". It is based on Dewey Decimal System and is modified to fit the Chinese holding environment. It is a hierarchy classification system to represent knowledge from top level to bottom level, and group different holdings together which may contain different title or writer by different author.

2.2   Latent Topic Discovery

For the researches in latent topic discovery, most of the research focuses aim at topic detection in text data by using term distribution calculation among the documents. Several important algorithms were developed, including Latent Semantic Analysis (LSA)[3], Probabilistic Latent Semantic Analysis (pLSA)[2], and Latent Dirichlet Allocation (LDA)[4]. LSA is one of the semantic analysis algorithms which differs from traditional term frequency-inverse document frequency (TF-IDF) model. pLSA model is proposed to overcome the disadvantage found in by LSA model, trying to decrease the degree of computation by using probabilistic approach. pLSA and LSA try to represent the original document space with a lower dimension space called latent topic space. The algorithm of Latent Dirichlet Allocation (LDA) is more advantageous since LDA performs even better than previous research results in latent topic detection. In fact, LDA is a general form of pLSA, the difference between LDA and pLSA model is that LDA regards the document probabilities as a term mixture model of latent topics. Girolamin and Kaban [5] shows that pLSA model is just a special case of LDA when Dirichlet distributions are of the same.

The goal of our recommendation systems is to give personalized recommendation on items to users. Typically the recommendation is based on the former and current activity of the users, and the metadata about users and items if available.

3   Proposed Method

Call numbers are used to describe a book, it consists of a number, and is also used to indicates the location on the shelf where the item can be found. A call number is composed by catalog number, author number and volume number, sometimes it might add a special mark for labeling that it's a special collection. For example, the reference book will be labeled by adding an "R". This represents an item's subject matter and the different collection which have similar call number, that is, they should have similar subject. In this work, we use patron's circulation records for the suggestion of system data source.

For each patron, u, who's circulation records could be represented by $u = \{b_1, b_2, b_3, ..., b_n\}$, and for each book, b, which could be represented by call number c. Thus patron's circulation records could be formatted as $u = \{c_1, c, c_3, ..., c_n\}$. The patrons' circulation records could be treated as a sparse matrix. But the call number represents a subject, if we just use call number on the records, the recommendation list may not be correctly generated due to a narrow subject. In this work, the researchers decide to use the top subject, which means just fetch the first 4 number, by different weight of sum adjustment to represent the subject similarity. We define the PreMatch function to describe this situation. The number i,j represent two different call number, and PreMatch(i,j) return the a weight value w, see Eq. 1.

$$score\ w = \frac{PreMatch(i, j)}{|i|} \tag{1}$$

The researcher use LDA model to find the hidden subjects. Here we propose to use LDA to computed the circulation matrix and identify the latent topics which represent the subjects by call number. Finally, we use cosine similarity and adopt hierarchical agglomerative clustering (HAC)[6,7]   algorithm to classify the border subject. The output of a typical HAC algorithm is a classification with hierarchical structure, and there exists the need to merge the nearby nodes to generate subject groups. The result can be treated as a list profile with subjects represented by the composition of a lot of call numbers. By using the cosine similarity to compare the patron's historical circulation records and the list profile generated by the above steps, it is able to generate a possible subject list which a patron might be interested in.

4   Experiments and Evaluations

The following sections present empirical results obtained from evaluating our approach. We use the circulation log to test our method output, final we building a online evaluation web page to use human judge. The result show our system have made good suggestion holding list.

4.1   Data Sets

The data range is start from 2006 Aug. to 2007 Jun. The data set which contains 137400 records, all personal private information was removed.   For our evaluation, we divide entire data set   into 12 subset by month.

Table 1.show the catalog number distribution which show the catalog number 800 is most user barrow than the others, next one is 300. Its show maybe hidden a static information between the user and suggestion books, maybe most person like to read it. But the main catalog number 800 is a very big scope for user to read, it may contain lot of sub catalogs in it, which mean it could contain all kind of literature just like novels and poems. We hope the suggestion result should be extract match full catalog number as we can, in order to suggest the book in a limited scope that user will interest in.

Table 1. The user barrow count distribution in main catalog number

Catalog number	000	100	200	300	400
%	0.042	0.064	0.030	0.230	0.052
Catalog number	500	500	600	700	800
%	0.033	0.033	0.065	0.084	0.256

4.2   Experiment Setup and Result

In order to evaluate our framework, we conducted experiment real data provided by National Normal University Library circulation log. These data are contain patron id, book id and barrow date, but no catalog number in it. In order to perform our method, we have to enrich data by find the catalog number, title, and author information from the WEBPAC, using crawler to fetch. All the error data which might be miss catalog number or patron id were removed. These error data may be cause by the patron was leave school or the book was miss so the bibliography data was removed.

We conducted 12-fold cross-validations for the experiment. This means that we randomly divided sets of all examples into 12 sets of examples: 11 of these were used for learning and one was used for testing. Then the data set for testing was rotated for 12 times in order. For each time, we randomly selected 100 users from logs to eva-luate suggestion result compare with baseline trivial suggestion by using probability distribution. As a result, we can measure the performance for suggestion result by this experiment using recall and precision value. As can be seen from Table 4, our me-thod have 0.7 recall, 0.72 precision on average, and stable result among the different data sets, beside the moth Aug, Jun and Feb which are the vocation, less patron bar-row the books cause less information output

In order to examine our method in the real situation, we develop an on line ques-tionnaire system to collection user's feedback. This system will output twenty sugges-tion records mix from our method and base line, each record provider book jacket, summary, author and catalog number information. Twenty-five persons' feedback which total have 500 suggestion result were be collected as Table 2 show. Our sys-tem had got 60% user satisfy, it could renderer a good suggestion list to patron. In the other words, our suggestion method could satisfy user interest, user maybe barrow these book next time or read it.

Table 2. User on-line evaluation result

	N	Y
Our method	0.4	0.6
Base line	0.708333	0.291667

5   Conclusion and Future Work

In this paper, we discuss use Latent Dirichlet Allocation (LDA) to extract latent topics and renderer the suggestion book lists. Although it perform a good result, but still need to enhance. According to the patron response, we have summary follow issue:

1. Suggestion result should include the other topic which user might be interest. Not only to suggestion the top N in output suggestion list, but also need to choice some of book which might be sort at last.

2. Sometime the provider information which contain book jacket or book summary, might be effect user's interest. If we provider extra information about suggestion list, it might cause user change mind and barrow these book.

Because of limit by the system circulation log, each record does not have return date, so can not use barrow periods be a weight to measure patron's reading time. We can not trace the change of user interest, if he reading a book for long time, might be he interest in than other which reading time is shortly. If we can gather more information or user feedback, the suggestion result might become more exact by follow user interest change, it could suggest the new scope that user will interest but had not discovery.

We plan to further validate our findings on the National Taiwan Normal University library WEBPAC system. We will pursue this method by integrating a "book suggestion" functionality into library website. To enhance the personalize function and provider more customization service, just like new book suggestion or journal suggestion. On the more theoretical side, future work will consider when data is grown up, an on line system which many patron active log on it would be a big challenge and need to solve.

Acknowledgments. The authors acknowledge with National Taiwan Normal University library for making their data available. And books.com(http://www.books.com.tw) for providing their books summary and book jackets information. Thanks for volunteer help us to evaluation our suggestion results.

References

1. Kent, A., et al.: Use of library materials: the university of Pittsburgh study. Pittsburgh University, PA (1979)
2. Deerwester, S., Dumais, S.T., Furnas, G.W., Landauer, T.K., Harshman, R.: Indexing by latent semantic analysis. Journal of the American Society for Information Science 41(6), 391–407 (1990)
3. Hofmann, T.: Unsupervised learning by probabilistic latent semantic analysis. Machine Learning 42(1), 177–196 (2001)
4. Blei, D.M., Ng, A.Y., Jordan, M.I.: Latent Dirichlet allocation. Journal of Machine Learning Research 3(5), 993–1022 (2003)
5. Girolami, M., Kaban, A.: On an equivalence between PLSI and LDA. In: Proceedings of the 26th Annual International ACM SIGIR Conference on Research and Development in Information Retrieval, pp. 433–434 (2003)
6. Jain, A.K., Murty, M.N., Flynn, P.J.: Data Clustering: A Review. ACM Computing Surveys 31, 264–323 (1999)
7. Widyantoro, D., Ioerger, T.R., Yen, J.: An Incremental Approach to Building a Cluster Hierarchy. In: Proceedings of the 2002 IEEE International Conference on Data Mining, ICDM 2002 (2002)

Query Formulation for Action Search
by Bootstrapping

Yoshinori Kitaguchi, Hiroaki Ohshima, and Katsumi Tanaka

Department of Social Informatics, Graduate School of Informatics, Kyoto University
Yoshidahonmachi, Sakyo, Kyoto 606-8501, Japan
{kitaguchi,ohshima,tanaka}@dl.kuis.kyoto-u.ac.jp

Abstract. A method to formulate queries to search for concrete, practical, or detailed "actions" on the web is proposed. Sometimes, a user can only express a web search query as an abstract action. For example, if the user is a beginner golfer, they may use "to improve golf" as a web search query. The search results for this query are unlikely to contain many pages about concrete actions related to improving golf skills. To obtain more concrete information, more concrete actions must be used as web queries. The proposed method generates tuples of words such as (shanking, stop) and (distance, adjust), that consist of a noun and a verb. The proposed algorithm repeatedly searches for nouns from verbs and verbs from nouns in a bootstrapping manner. The proposed method verifies the usefulness of tuples. To reduce search costs, the proposed method also excludes useless tuples; i.e., tuples that cannot be used to obtain new useful tuples.

Keywords: bootstrap, action search, query formulation, search-result diversification.

1 Introduction

Web search can be used to obtain information about "actions." For example, a user wants to improve his golf skills; therefore, he searches for information about actions related to improving golf skills. If the user is a beginner golfer, the web search query used might be very abstract, such as "to improve golf." However, more useful actions may be related to more specific search terms, such as "to stop shanking" and "to adjust distance." However, such data are unlikely to be contained in the search result for the query "to improve golf." To solve this problem, we propose a method to generate queries that can be used to obtain information about concrete actions, when an abstract action is given by the user as an initial set of search terms. The generated query can be used to search the web for concrete, practical, or detailed information about specific actions.

Effective queries can effectively retrieve information about concrete actions. In this paper, effective queries are relevant to the initial query and appear frequently on the web. In addition, effective queries include a verb that is synonymous with that of the initial query.

K. Tuamsuk et al. (Eds.): ICADL 2014, LNCS 8839, pp. 417–422, 2014.

In the proposed method, extraction of nouns and verbs used to generate queries is conducted in a bootstrapping manner. Our bootstrapping method differs from general bootstrapping methods, which extracts intended words and patterns alternately. The proposed bootstrapping method extracts nouns using verbs and extracts verbs using nouns. These words are in turn used to extract other words. The proposed method continues to extract nouns and verbs until no new verbs can be obtained. Then, the proposed method generates queries that consist of a noun and a verb.

However, effective queries can include useless queries that cannot be used to obtain new information. If nouns obtained by searching with the query "to improve golf" are included in those that are obtained with the query "to master golf," then searching with the query "to improve golf" cannot obtain new nouns. Therefore, this search is unnecessary. To eliminate unnecessary searches, the proposed method excludes words that yield search results similar to another word by using diversity-based filtering.

Words that are not relevant to the initial query can be extracted by bootstrapping. Queries, such as "to buy golf irons" and "to purchase a golf driver" can be generated by the initial query "to improve golf." However, the generated queries are not related to improving golf skills. This problem is referred to as semantic drift[4]. To address semantic drift, the proposed method assigns drift scores to words and filters words on the basis of these scores. If a word can be used to extract several words that extracted the given word, then the drift score of that word is high.

Our contributions are as follows.

1. Extraction of effective nouns and verbs by bootstrapping
2. Reduction of unnecessary searches by filtering on the basis of diversity
3. Improvement of precision by filtering with drift scores

2   Related Work

Related work that we build upon includes actions, bootstrapping and pattern matching.

Actions

In previous studies, methods that discover actions from query logs have been proposed[7]. Lin et al.[6] introduce an entity-centric search experience, called Active Objects, in which entity-bearing queries are paired with actions that can be performed on the entities.

Bootstrapping

Bootstrapping is used to extract semantic lexicons. Kawai et al.[5] propose a cost-effective search strategy framework to extract keywords in the same semantic class from the Web. Other studies have proposed methods to reduce semantic drift[9,8]. Semantic drift is an important problem in bootstrapping.

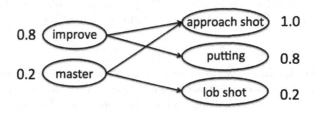

Fig. 1. The method for sending scores

Pattern Matching

Pattern matching methods have been explored by many studies[1,11,3]. There are pattern matching methods that use nouns or verbs[10]. For example, Torisawa et al.[12] have demonstrated that inference rules with temporal constraints can be acquired by using verb-verb co-occurrences and verb-noun co-occurrences in Japanese coordinated sentences.

3   Proposed Method

The input to the proposed method is a query that represents an abstract action. The input query consists of a topic word t and a query verb v_q. If the input query is "to improve golf," then (t,v_q) equals (golf, improve). The proposed method extracts nouns and verbs by bootstrapping using the input query. In bootstrapping, words are filtered on the basis of drift score to reduce semantic drift. Words are also filtered on the basis of diversity to reduce unnecessary searches. After extraction of nouns and verbs, tuples of a noun and a verb are generated. These tuples are used as effective queries to search for concrete actions.

Extraction of Nouns and Verbs by Bootstrapping

The method used to extract words assigns each noun a $Score(n)$. The method also assigns each verb a $Score(v)$. $Score(v_q)$ equals 1. Scores from the nouns are sent to the verbs. Figure 1 illustrates the sending of scores.

To extract nouns, the proposed method first obtains nouns that collocate with each verb v_i in the given verb set V. These nouns are extracted from the top k search results of the query formulated using the tuple (t, v_i). Each tuple of verb v_i and a noun that is an object of v_i such as (n_1, v_i), (n_2, v_i) is then extracted from the search results. In English, the next words of transitive verbs are objects. In our experiments, we extract the previous nouns and the next verbs of a Japanese particle "wo." If the extracted noun is included in a set of stop words, the noun is considered irrelevant to the topic word and is thus excluded. The proposed method counts the frequency of each tuple. The frequency of a tuple (n_1, v_i) is defined as $Freq(n_1, v_i)$. In this paper, the word used as a query is underlined. To exclude useless tuples, the proposed method adds tuples to the effective tuples set (ET) according to the following equation.

$$ET = ET \cup \{(n, v)|Freq(n, \underline{v}) > \theta_n\} \tag{1}$$

The threshold value θ_n is used to extract frequent nouns. In contrast, the threshold value θ_v is used to extract frequent verbs. After extracting nouns using each verb in V, the proposed method sends scores according to the following equation.

$$Score(n) = \sum_{v \in V_n} Score(v) \tag{2}$$

Here, V_n is the set of verbs that collocate with the noun n in tuples of ET. The extraction of verbs is performed in a similar manner.

Filtering Based on Diversity

Note that the naive method described above extracts nouns that cannot be used to extract new verbs. Such nouns only extract verbs that have already been extracted by other nouns. To exclude such nouns, the proposed method excludes nouns that are not selected by the Maximal Marginal Relevance (MMR[2]) algorithm. The MMR algorithm is used to obtain diverse search results. By using this algorithm, the proposed method can exclude nouns with low scores that cannot be used to extract new verbs.

To obtain effective nouns, the proposed method repeatedly shifts the noun MMR from the noun set N to the set S according to the following equation.

$$MMR = \arg \max_{n \in N \setminus S}[\lambda(Score(n)) - (1 - \lambda) \max_{n' \in S} \frac{Sim(n, n')}{|N|}] \tag{3}$$

Here, $Sim(n, n')$ is calculated according to the following equation.

$$Sim(n, n') = \frac{|V_n \cap V_{n'}|}{\sqrt{|V_n| \cdot |V_{n'}|}} \tag{4}$$

Nouns with a score (equation (3)) that is larger than 0 are shifted to the set S. Nouns in the set S are considered effective and can be used to extract verbs.

Filtering Based on Drift Scores

To reduce semantic drift, the proposed method excludes nouns with drift score that is less than the threshold value θ_{sd}. The drift score of a noun n is calculated according to the following equation.

$$NotDrift(n) = (\prod_{v \in V} log(Freq(\underline{n}, v) + 1) + 1)^{\frac{1}{|V|}} \tag{5}$$

If noun n extracts many verbs that collocate with the noun n many times, then $NotDrift(n)$ is high. Therefore this score can be used to exclude nouns that do not extract such verbs.

Table 1. Tuples of a topic word and a query verb

Initial queries

(FX, avoid), (iPhone, improve), (iPhone, prevent), (Mac, improve), (Mac, prevent), (camera, prevent), (golf, fix), (golf, prevent), (skiing, prevent), (climbing, prevent), (PC, resolve), (PC, improve), (PC, prevent), (headphone, prevent), (iPhone, practice), (Mac, master), (Mac, confirm), (guitar, master), (skiing, master), (PC, master), (cooking, master), (cooking, learn), (road bike, replace)

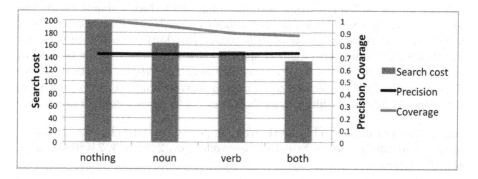

Fig. 2. Experimental results

Generating Queries

By using bootstrapping, we can obtain a noun set N and a verb set V, and queries are generated from these sets. Each noun n is attached to a verb v, which maximizes the product of $Freq(n, \underline{v})$ and $Score(v)$. The output of the proposed method is tuples of a noun and a verb.

4   Experiments

We search Japanese web pages to obtain actions using the Bing Search API [1]. To generate a list of stop words, we use SlothLib's stop word list[2]. Table 1 shows the 18 initial queries used in our experiments.

To examine the effectiveness of diversity-based filtering, we conducted experiments with the following conditions: filter nothing, filter noun, filter verb and filter both nouns and verbs. In each condition, we used the same method to reduce semantic drift. From the results of a preliminary experiment, we set the experimental parameters as follows: $(k, \lambda, \theta_n, \theta_v, \theta_{sd}) = (100, 0.5, 2, 4, 1.3)$.

In our experiments, we evaluated *search cost, precision, coverage*.

---

[1] https://datamarket.azure.com/dataset/bing/search

[2] http://svn.sourceforge.jp/svnroot/slothlib/CSharp/Version1/SlothLib/
NLP/Filter/StopWord/word/Japanese.txt

Figure 2 shows the experiment results. The noun and verb method filtering reduces search cost by more than 30%. In addition, the proposed method achieves coverage score that are greater than 0.8. That indicates that the proposed method can generate more than 80% correct queries. However, note that precision score is less than 0.8.

5 Conclusions

We have proposed a method to formulate queries to search for concrete, practical, or detailed "actions" on the Web. To generate queries, the proposed method extracts nouns and verbs using bootstrapping. To reduce semantic drift, the proposed method excludes words that cannot be used to extract correct words by filtering words on the basis of drift scores. In addition, to reduce unnecessary searches, the proposed method also excludes words that cannot be used to extract new words using diversity-based filtering. The proposed diversity-based filtering method reduces search cost and demonstrates high coverage. However, the proposed drift score filtering method does not demonstrate high precision.

Acknowledgements. This work was supported in part by the following projects: Grants-in-Aid for Scientific Research (Nos. 24240013, 24680008) from MEXT of Japan.

References

1. Bhagat, R., Hovy, E., Patwardhan, S.: Acquiring paraphrases from text corpora. In: Proc. of K-CAP 2009, pp. 161–168 (2009)
2. Carbonell, J., Goldstein, J.: The use of mmr, diversity-based reranking for reordering documents and producing summaries. In: Proc. of SIGIR1998, pp. 335–336 (1998)
3. Chang, C.-H., Lui, S.-C.: Iepad: Information extraction based on pattern discovery. In: Proc. of WWW 2001, pp. 681–688 (2001)
4. Curran, J.R., Murphy, T., Scholz, B.: Minimising semantic drift with Mutual Exclusion Bootstrapping. In: Proc. of PACLING 2007, pp. 172–180 (2007)
5. Kawai, H., Mizuguchi, H., Tsuchida, M.: Cost-effective web search in bootstrapping for named entity recognition. In: Haritsa, J.R., Kotagiri, R., Pudi, V. (eds.) DASFAA 2008. LNCS, vol. 4947, pp. 393–407. Springer, Heidelberg (2008)
6. Lin, T., Pantel, P., Gamon, M., Kannan, A., Fuxman, A.: Active objects: Actions for entity-centric search. In: Proc. of WWW 2012, pp. 589–598 (2012)
7. Lucchese, C., Orlando, S., Perego, R., Silvestri, F., Tolomei, G.: Discovering tasks from search engine query logs. ACM Trans. Inf. Syst., pp. 14:1–14:43 (2013)
8. McIntosh, T.: Unsupervised discovery of negative categories in lexicon bootstrapping. In: Proc. of EMNLP 2010, pp. 356–365 (2010)
9. McIntosh, T., Curran, J.R.: Reducing semantic drift with bagging and distributional similarity. In: Proc. of ACL 2009, pp. 396–404 (2009)
10. Pekar, V.: Acquisition of verb entailment from text. In: Proc. of HLT-NAACL 2006, pp. 49–56 (2006)
11. Sang, E.T.K., Hofmann, K.: Lexical patterns or dependency patterns: Which is better for hypernym extraction? In: Proc. of CoNLL 2009, pp. 174–182 (2009)
12. Torisawa, K.: Acquiring inference rules with temporal constraints by using japanese coordinated sentences and noun-verb co-occurrences. In: Proc. of HLT-NAACL 2006, pp. 57–64 (2006)

Transforming Publication List of LIS-TW in Author Identification Services to Open Linked Data for Mobile Application

Chao-Chen Chen, Hong-Shiu Liang[*], and Shun-Hong Sie

Graduate Institute of Library and Information Studies of National Taiwan Normal University,
Taipei, Taiwan
{joycechaochen,arshliang}@gmail.com, mayh@ntnu.edu.tw

Abstract. This paper presents an App prototype capturing Library Information Science in Taiwan (LIS-TW) for researchers' information from unique author identifiers such as Scopus Author Identifiers, ORCID and Google Scholar Citations. By using Linked Open Data technologies, this App can push not only the latest information of researchers but the links of publications to the Android platform devices. The study demonstrates a practical approach to personalize the researching information needs without any delay.

Keywords: Linked Open Data, Author Identification Services, Mobile Application.

1   Introduction

In the age of network, more and more research topics appear in a very short time and are focused by many researchers. Researchers usually want to know what issues are studied recently in their professions and find the papers as soon as possible. However, contemporary research is regarded as growingly complicated and difficult to gather all the works from different scholars. Data mining may be a way to solve the problem. Sun (2013) tried to detect ambiguous names at query time by mining digital library annotation data, and thereby decreasing noise in the bibliographic analysis and the proposed approach achieves with almost 80% of accuracy. It could be another solution to find the author's publication list by using unique identifiers for authors. There are several unique identifiers for author services on internet and it is hard to know which one is used by the researcher. This study is a new application which tries to complete the research about integrating three major author identifier systems (Google Scholar, ORCID and Scopus Author Identifier) and push the publication lists to the mobile devices need (Chen et al., 2013). By the mobile application in this study, researchers can instantly get the publication lists of particular scholar who they pay close attention in easy way.

---

[*] Corresponding author.

K. Tuamsuk et al. (Eds.): ICADL 2014, LNCS 8839, pp. 423–427, 2014.

2   Purpose of Research

Modeled on the Opened Linked Data experience and spirit (Chen et al., 2013), this study tries to build up a App prototype capturing LIS-TW researcher information, especially their publication lists from Scopus Author Identifiers, ORCID and Google Scholar Citations. We choose them for reasons. First, they all include rich data and international author identification services. Second, they have authority control by authors reviewing a list of all documents associated with their profiles in order to ensure that they indeed belong to him or her. We will move the duplicates, generalize the publication in RDF format, and then shift them to Open Linked Data to users. At last, we will make it a node of the global Linked Open Data cloud. On the other hand, we will design a mobile App and pushing information/publication lists automatically to mobile devices to make researchers keep sharp in their professional fields.

3   Implementation of the Prototype

The following preliminary system architecture diagram illustrates how to realize the purpose of research mentioned in the last section:

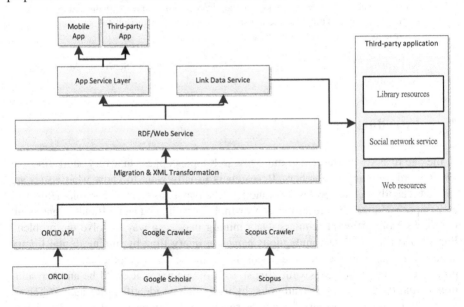

Fig. 1. System architecture overview

3.1   Data Collecting

We use crawler to collect the information in Google Scholar Citations and Scopus Author Identification and catch the publication list down to system. About ORCID, it has ORCID API as a bridge to communicate with, we can search email to find out the author's ORCID ID, and then obtain data in XML format. By using XSLT, we transform data from XML to RDF format. Figures 2 is an example.

```
        </orcid-history>
        <orcid-activities>
            <orcid-works>
                <orcid-work put-code="12194973">
                    <work-title>
                        <title>A Study on the relationship between organizational learning culture and organizational performance in Taiwan's university and college
libraries</title>
                    </work-title>
                    <work-citation>
                        <work-citation-type>bibtex</work-citation-type>
                        <citation>@article { chen2013,title = {A Study on the relationship between organizational learning culture and organizational performance in Taiwan's
university and college libraries},journal = {Journal of Educational Media and Library Science},year = {2013},volume = {50},number = {2},pages = {173-200},author = {Yu, T. and
Chen, C.-C.}}</citation>
                    </work-citation>
                    <work-type>journal-article</work-type>
                    <publication-date>
                        <year>2013</year>
                    </publication-date>
                    <work-external-identifiers>
                        <work-external-identifier>
                            <work-external-identifier-type>doi</work-external-identifier-type>
                            <work-external-identifier-id>10.6120/JoEMLS.2012.502/0516.RS.AM</work-external-identifier-id>
                        </work-external-identifier>
                        <work-external-identifier>
                            <work-external-identifier-type>issn</work-external-identifier-type>
                            <work-external-identifier-id>1013090X</work-external-identifier-id>
                        </work-external-identifier>
                        <work-external-identifier>
                            <work-external-identifier-type>eid</work-external-identifier-type>
                            <work-external-identifier-id>2-s2.0-84879429518</work-external-identifier-id>
                        </work-external-identifier>
                    </work-external-identifiers>
                    <url>http://www.scopus.com/inward/record.url?eid=2-s2.0-84879429518&amp;partnerID=MN8TOARS</url>
                    <work-contributors>
```


Fig. 2. Snap shot of one researcher's information send from ORCID

3.2 Data De-duplication

Because we catch data from three Author Identification Services, it will cause duplicate title of publication. Sometimes one paper has a different title because of typo, different positions due to punctuation, or additional spacebar pressing. We use dice similarity coefficient to recognize two similar titles as the same article (Dice, 1945). For offering Linked Data to other application, all data were transformed to RDF in ScholarlyArticle schema.

Table 1. Example of ScholarlyArticle format

Property	Reference element	Example
Author	Author	Chen, C.-C.
citation	citation	Chen, C. C., Yeh, J. H., & Sie, S. H. (2005). Government ontology and thesaurus construction: A taiwanese experience. In *Digital Libraries: Implementing Strategies and Sharing Experiences* (pp. 263-272). Springer Berlin Heidelberg.
contributor	Author 2, author 3, ...	Yeh, J. H., Sie, S. H.
Date published	Published date	2005
Publisher	Publisher	Springer Berlin Heidelberg
url	url*	

The result is present as in figure 3.

```
    <div vocab="http://schema.org/" typeof="ScholarlyArticle">
      <link property="audience" href="http://schema.org/ScholarlyArticle"/>
      <meta property="publicationType" content="twLIS"/>
      <span property="author">Chen, C.-C.</span>
      <span property="citation">Chen, C. C., Yeh, J. H., &amp Sie, S. H. (2005).
Government ontology and thesaurus construction: A taiwanese experience. In Digital
Libraries: Implementing Strategies and Sharing Experiences (pp. 263-272). Springer
Berlin Heidelberg.</span>
      <span property="contributor">Yeh, J. H.</span>
      <span property="contributor">Sie, S. H.</span>
      <span property="datePublished">2005</span>
      <span property="Publisher">Springer Berlin Heidelberg</span>
      <span
property="url">http://link.springer.com/chapter/10.1007/11599517_30</span>
    </div>
```

Fig. 3. Example of the result in RDF format

3.3   Results on App Interface

An app for Android was created. Readers can receive the newest publication list of researchers by this app. The result and interface are as follows:

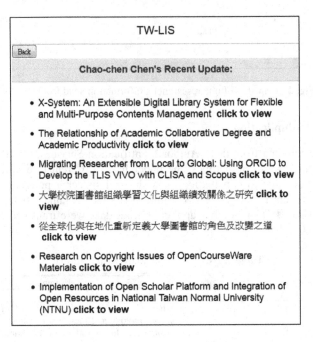

Fig. 4. Example of the app interface

4   Conclusion

Users usually have problems for query Chinese researchers' information because the same Chinese names, English names and Romanized names. Sun discovers that it is another solution to find the author's publication list by using unique identifiers for authors. However, there are several unique identifiers for author services on Internet and it is hard for users to know which one is used and updated by the researcher. In order to provide more complete and correct information of researchers in Taiwan, we integrate publication lists from ORCID, Google Scholar and Scopus and then transform them to open link data in RDF format. We also build an Android app for users to obtain the newest publication lists of researchers in Taiwan.

Reference

1. Albert, P.: Authoritative researcher metadata in one place via VIVO. Library Connect 11(1) (2013), http://libraryconnect.elsevier.com/
2. Bizer, C., Jentzsch, A., Cyganiak, R.: State of the LOD cloud (September 19, 2011), http://lod-cloud.net/state/
3. Bohyun, K.: The Present and Future of the Library Mobile Experience. Library Technology Reports 49(6), 15–28 (2013)
4. Chen, C.-C., Ko, M.W., Lee, V.T.-Y.: Migrating Researcher from Local to Global: Using ORCID to Develop the TLIS VIVO with CLISA and Scopus. In: Urs, S.R., Na, J.-C., Buchanan, G. (eds.) ICADL 2013. LNCS, vol. 8279, pp. 113–116. Springer, Heidelberg (2013)
5. Dice, L.R.: Measures of the amount of ecologic association between species. Ecology 26(3), 297–302 (1945)
6. Enserink, M.: Scientific publishing: are you ready to become a number? Science 323(5922), 1662–1664 (2009)
7. Fenner, M.: Author Identifier Overview. LIBREAS. Library Ideas 18 (2011), http://libreas.eu/ausgabe18/texte/03fenner.htm
8. Fenner, M.: ORCiD: connecting research and researchers. In: A Dialogue on Evaluation, Workshop, Bonn, Germany, December 6-7 (2012)
9. Garcia Gomez, C.: Launching the ORCID service for global author identification (2012), http://upcommons.upc.edu/e-prints/bitstream/2117/17103/1/orcidoviedo2012.pdf
10. Haak, L.L.: ORCID: connecting researchers and scholars with their works. Insights: The UKSG Journal 26(3), 239–243 (2013)
11. ISNI. ISNI for Researchers (2013), http://www.isni.org/resources
12. MIT Libraries. 2011 MIT Libraries Survey (2011), http://libguides.mit.edu/mitlibrarysurveys
13. Morgan, K., Reade, T.: Pioneering portals:MyLibrary@NCState. Information Technology and Libraries 19(4), 191–198 (2000)
14. Niu, J.: Evolving landscape in Name Authority Control. Cataloging & Classification Quarterly 51(4), 404–419 (2013), http://dx.doi.org/10.1080/01639374.756843
15. Notess, G.R.: Searching for Scholars. Online Searcher 37(1), 61–64 (2013)
16. Sun, X., Kaur, J., Possamai, L., Menczer, F.: Ambiguous author query detection using crowdsourced digital library annotations. Information Processing and Management 49, 454–464 (2013), doi:10.1016/j.ipm.2012.09.001
17. Wilson, B., Fenner, M.: Open Researcher & Contributor ID (ORCID): solving the name ambiguity problem. EDUCAUSE Review 47(3) (2012), http://www.educause.edu/ero/article/open-researcher-contributor-id-orcid-solving-name-ambiguity-problem
18. Wagner, A.B.: Author Identification Systems. Issues in Science & Technology Librarianship Archives 59(10) (2009)

Documentation and Dissemination of Kotagede's *Local Wisdom* by Kotagede Heritage Library: The Best Practice

Nur Cahyati Wahyuni[1], Lista Rantika[2], and Imam Zakaria[2]

[1] Gadjah Mada University, Librarian and Graduate Student of Higher Education Management, Special Province of Yogyakarta, Indonesia
cahyati_w@yahoo.com
[2] Kotagede Heritage Library, Management Team, Special Province of Yogyakarta, Indonesia
{rantikalista,imamzet}@gmail.com

Abstract. In 2007, The World Monuments Fund (WMF) declared Kotagede as one of the 100 world's cultural sites threatened to extinction. Therefore, any efforts to preserve the heritage of the remains of Mataram Kingdom between 1582-1640 must be done. The efforts should involve all parties that concern with tangible and intangible aspects of Kotagede's cultural heritage.

Located in Kotagede, Kotagede Heritage Library (KHL) plays an important role in preserving Kotagede as an area of cultural heritage through its digital library (Kotagedelib.com). The digital library is aimed at providing public as well as researchers and students who are in need of references about Kotagede. The library collects data and information about Kotagede, by employing printed, audio, and multimedia data collection methods to get tacit knowledge documentation from senior citizens and common people of Kotagede. At the same time, the Kotagedelib.com disseminates the knowledge to the public and encourages our awareness of Kotagede Heritage Preservation.

Keywords: Digital Humanities, data curation, digital heritage collection development, Kotagede.

1 Introduction

Located about 6 km to the Southeast of Yogyakarta, Kotagede Cultural Heritage was declared as one of the 100 world cultural sites' most threatened to extinction by the World Monuments Fund (WMF) in 2007. It requires all parties' efforts to preserve the remains of the heritage area of Mataram Kingdom that dated back to 1582 - 1640 AD, both in terms of its tangible and intangible aspects [1]. A tangible aspect of physical relics are arranged in an area with a certain city plan named Catur Gatra Tunggal, four elements of a single entity meaning separated but connected [2]. The Four elements which a city must have consist of a palace (Keraton) as a power center, a market (pasar) as an economic center, a mosque (Masjid) as a worship center, and a square (Alun-Alun) as a cultural center. Those indicate the presence of a strong bond among the government and economy, religion, and community.

K. Tuamsuk et al. (Eds.): ICADL 2014, LNCS 8839, pp. 428–433, 2014.

Meanwhile, the intangible heritage in the forms of local wisdom of Kotagede such as that in the religious practice, economy, arts (macapat, srandul, keroncong, and kethoprak), and life cycle rites, as well as recipes, are important parts that need to be preserved, documented, and disseminated for public information or research alike. Aside from being a relic of the ancient Mataram kingdom area rich of Javanese culture, the Islamic "Muhammadiyah" social organization makes Kotagede as one of the bases of Islam movement together with Kampung Kauman [3]. The majority of the Islamic Religious Community of Kotagede practice Islam with the influence of Javanese culture. Meanwhile, Kotagede contributes to the local economy with the development of silver, copper, and textiles products [4].

After the earthquake disaster in 2006, Kotagede experienced physical and psychological changes due to the partial or complete collapses of "Joglo" traditional houses; silversmiths were losing their working tools; and trauma experiencing by the residents. This heritage area needs unique revitalization and empowerment programs (human resources, economics, and environment) from governments, agencies, and international institutions to reconstruct the area [5][6]. This program contributed to the improvement of Joglo Kotagede hall (Pendopo), the formation of Joglo Forum (a forum which strengthens the heritage area) and establishment of Kotagede Heritage Library (for documentation and publications of Kotagede Heritage programs).

Documentation and publications in Kotagede community started in 1963 with the publication of "Brosur Lebaran", a local annual periodical issued by young people of Muhammadiyah (AMM-Angkatan Muda Muhammadiyah). The periodical captures the national impacts to Kotagede culturally, politically, and economically and the local issues within the community. It also proves that literacy awareness has been present in Kotagede, but lack of physical documentation activities, in the form of information center or a library.

Kotagede Heritage Library was designed as both physical and digital library in order to develop written knowledge about Kotagede by documenting any forms of information in both printed and digital formats. So far, the library users are academicians, researchers, tourists, and Kotagede community. The website is also expected to attract more people to visit Kotagede to visit and learn the physical and real life of Kotagede and interact directly with the community. People's visit to Kotagede is believed to contribute to public interest, economic development, and sustainability of this heritage area.

2   Kotagede Heritage Library

Kotagede Heritage Library (KHL) was established in Kotagede in 2010 with a vision to be a source of fun, information, research, and knowledge concerning with the heritage of Kotagede in particular and Yogyakarta in general. The missions are to facilitate information about Kotagede heritage in particular and Yogyakarta heritage in general; to cultivate public interest in Kotagede and Yogyakarta heritage; to create a dynamic sphere for the library; and to increase participation and contribution, especially from the community for Kotagede heritage conservation. The project is not without any challenges.

KHL's first challenge is lack of written document on Kotagede as some resources are available in the hands of researchers, very few records of the historical events, limited number of people who understand the region's history, the absence of a specialised information system for Kotagede collection, and poor awareness of the importance of this region.

The second challenge for KHL is how to increase the number of users physically as information about Kotagede is now available online via newspapers, and YouTube. At the same time KHL needs to keep the community's interest in the heritage by presenting a website "Kotagedelib.com" with a special collection. This also opens the opportunity to learn the knowledge-based preservation. Another challenge is voluntary work in the library. KHL invites the young generation from Kotagede who has skills to support the program voluntarily. KHL needs volunteers to collect and disseminate its printed and digital information obtained from researchers and writers in Indonesia and abroad, while documenting Kotagede's community events and looking for information from the the elderly people in Kotagede about Kotagede in the past.

2.1   Development of www.kotagedelib.com

The website about Kotagede Cultural Heritage (www.kotagedelib.com) provides open access information [7]. This website is integrated with library information systems and social media to increase its information dissemination [8].

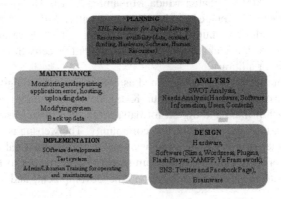

Fig. 1. Kotagedelib.com: Website Development

KHL uses free and simple software and applications for the library resources management, such as WordPress, flash player which supports FLV to play the audiovisual and audio format, PDF reader to read documents, JPEG Format for Photographs [7], YouTube link to collect Kotagede's documentation in social media, twitter and facebook page to engage with users.

This WordPress-based website functions as an easy Content Management System (CMS) to operate and update [9], providing online public access catalogue (OPAC) using "Meranti Slims 5" OS software [10] and Yii Framework (Fig.1). It has links to websites and blogs of communities of and events in Kotagede.

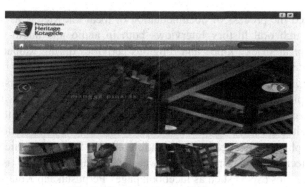

Fig. 2. Homepage kotagedelib.com

In the homepage, the menu options are Profile, Catalogue, Events, Kotagede on Media, Stories of Kotagede and Contacts. Profile and Contacts are static pages, accommodating the event updates. The Menu page is a link that leads to information about Kotagede [Fig.2]. The logo is put in the upper left to show the status of the website ownership (KHL). The menu displays right underneath. There is a slide below the image of traditional doors and roofs. In the Javanese philosophy, it symbolizes the welcome greeting and aesthetic openness. The roof of the hall has a reception function for others while the door is the boundary between the living room and the public, adapted to the purpose of the library, open and close with the community. Below the images, there are several examples of library activities.

The website containing free information accessible by visitors and has links to YouTube, Posters, Photos, and Cataloque. The Digital Library contains information intended for members by logging-in and may access special collection "Stories of Kotagede.".

2.2 Digital Collection Development and Dissemination

KHL decided to develop its digital collection to minimise the physical space, disseminate better, and gain more community's awareness. The collection includes magazine articles, scholarly journal articles, books, audio-visual resources prioritising topics related to Kotagede, ranging subjects from history, fiction, architecture, and travelling to art.

Digital Collection Development. KHL develops its collection in 3 steps. First, clipping activities written in mass media and other scientific publications. KHL found that the community in Kotagede actively contribute ideas to Kotagede's development in various ways, such as through events, promotional articles, and research projects. Second, initiation of documenting Kotagede's historical information through visual media [11] and oral historical approach. This documentation represents the knowledge and experience of the history of the various classes of community instead of the authority or the elite [12]. The documentation through oral history interviews emphasises reflection and in-depth experience of the individuals at certain time and place around the world [13][14], so did the dissemination and preservation [15] and collection development [16].

KHL initiated the process of documentation of local knowledge as a pilot project conducted through oral history interviews both in audio and audio-visual formats [11][17]. A typical snack "kipo" and religious activities during Ramadhan have not been documented and will be another pilot project. This activity is intended as an initiation of heritage area documentation movement with village youngsters.

Asking people to donate their writings, photos, and publications is the third step. Some donated documents are put in a selected category entitled "Stories of Kotagede." The digital documents consist of short film, audio record, Periodical "Brosur Lebaran", Pamphlets of Kotagede, Preservation manual, Scientific Articles, and so on.

Digital Collection Dissemination. The website "Kotagedelib.com" is linked to social networking sites (SNS) such as facebook page "Perpustakaan Kotagede Heritage" and twitter @kotagedelib. The use of SNS plays an active role in interaction in the virtual world and shows a good impact as it reached over 1000 peoples of Kotagede and about 300 visitors per month for the website. Meanwhile, the former facebook group "KotagedeYogya" was launched in 2012 as a media for nostalgia and discussion about Kotagede. It has about 3,116 members consisting of Kotagede's community and those interested in Kotagede, 49 files and 684 photos. This SNS is a good place to promote events and invite active participation, and to disseminate information.

KHL also creates events "Weekends Talks" with various themes and speakers to attract young generation and public. The program consists of movies and a film workshop involving young people from Kotagede as speakers and participants. KHL explores further information and disseminates it for the community for better heritage awareness. The activities showing cultural values obtained from the community are disseminated to community for their understanding and preservation.

3   Conclusion

Kotagede Heritage pilot project of oral history will lead KHL as a special library that supports preservation of Kotagede's tangible and intangible cultural heritage. It will also generate the enthusiasm of documenting community's knowledge values in the format appropriate for the younger generation.

The digital library plays an important role to develop reading awareness among young people and other potential users. Attracting them through a variety of interesting programmes in Kotagede Heritage Library by ways of (a) heritage trail to trace the civilization of the ancient Islamic Mataram, (b) other events, held in Kotagede regularly.

KHL and the websites and blogs of Kotagede will be important references for research and recreational needs of general public, students, faculty, researchers, as well as domestic and foreigners who are interested in learning further about Kotagede Kotagede Heritage Library collaborates with other websites and blogs of Kotagede will be an important reference of research and recreational information for general public, students, faculty, researchers, as well as domestic and foreigners who are interested in learning further about Kotagede.

References

1. Park, H.Y.: Heritage Tourism Emotional Journeys into Nationhood. Annals of Tourism Research 37(1), 116–135 (2010)
2. Wibowo, R.B.: Toponim Kotagede:Asal Muasal Nama Tempat. Rekompak, Jogjakarta (2011)
3. Nakamura, M.: The Crescent arises Over the Banyan Tree. Gadjah Mada University Press, Special Province of Yogyakarta (1993)
4. Purwanto, B.: Conflict and Coexistence: Multicultural Images of Urban Yogyakarta in the First Hal of Twentieth Century. Coexistence 2 (2005), http://urp.fib.ugm.ac.id/images/download/Bambang-Coexistence.pdf
5. Khudori, D.: Rebuilding Kotagede. Brosur Lebaran No.1427 pp. 73–79 1427H/2006. Muhammadiyah Kotagede for Youth, Yogyakarta (2006)
6. Adhisakti, L.T.: Community Empowerment Program on the Revitalization of Kotagede Heritage District. In: Kidokoro, T., Okata, J., Matsumura, S., Shima, N. (eds.) Indonesia Post Earthquake. Vulnerable Cities: Realities, Innovations and Strategies, vol. 8, pp. 241–256. Springer, Osaka (2009)
7. Lesk, M.: Understanding Digital Libraries. Elseiver, New York (2005)
8. Rantika, L., et al.: Making Kotagede close to The Community: a Report. Special Province of Yogyakarta (2014)
9. Jones, M., et al.: Storybank: An Indian village to Digital Library. In: Proceeding of 7th ACM/IEEE-CS Joint Conference on Digital Library, pp. 257–258 (2007)
10. Slims Developer.:Slims Documentations, http://slims.web.id/
11. Leary, S.: About WordPres. In: Beginning Wordpress 3. Apress, http://nitinmauryalko.files.wordpress.com/2010/07/apress-beginning-wordpress-3-jun-2010.pdf
12. Mazikana, P., Moss, W.: Introduction: oral tradition and oral history in Audiovisual archives: A practical reader, General Information Programme and UNISIST United Nations Educational, Scientific and Cultural Organization, Paris, UNESCO (1997), http://www.unesco.org/webworld/ramp/html/r9704e/r9704e0k.htm
13. Oral History Association: Principles and Best Practices: Principles for Oral History and Best Practices for Oral History, Adopted (October 2009), http://www.oralhistory.org/about/principles-and-practices/
14. Stevens, K.W., Latham, B.: Giving Voice to the Past: Digitizing Oral History. International Digital Library Perspectives 25(3), 212–220 (2009)
15. Swain, E.D.: Oral History in the Archives: Its Documentary Role in the Twenty-first Century. The American Archivist 66, 139–158 (2003)
16. Songhui, Z.: Developing Oral History in Chinese Libraries. The Journal of Academic Librarianship 34(1), 74–78 (2008)
17. Buttler, R.P.: Oral History as Educational Technology Research. Tech Trends 52(4), 34–41 (2008)

Author Index